SINCE PREDATOR CAME

SINCE PREDATOR CAME

Notes from the Struggle for American Indian Liberation

by
Ward Churchill

preface by
Haunani-Kay Trask

*a*igis *p*ublications
Littleton, Colorado

Printed on recycled acid-free paper with soy-based inks. Manufactured in the United States.

Cover illustration by Katherine Berney
Cover design by Mark Ivins and Pavlos Stavropoulos
Book design and typesetting by Debbie McLeod and Pavlos Stavropoulos

Library of Congress Cataloging-in-Publication Data
Churchill, Ward.
Since predator came: notes from the struggle for American Indian liberation / by Ward Churchill; preface by Haunani-Kay Trask.
        p.   cm.
Includes bibliographical references and index.
ISBN 1-883930-04-9 (hc: alk. paper). — ISBN 1-883930-03-0 (pbk.: alk. paper)
1. Indians of North America — Government relations. 2. Indians of North America — Government policy. 3. Indians of North America — Politics and government. I. Title.
E91.C48   1995
323.1' 197—dc20   95–32397
                                CIP

*a*igis books are available at special discounts for bulk purchases by organizations, study groups, or for educational use. For more information contact:

*a*igis *p*ublications
1449 West Littleton Boulevard, Suite 200
Littleton, Colorado 80120-2127 USA
303.730.6232 tel.,   303.798.6568 fax
books@aigis.com

Other Books by Ward Churchill

Authored: *Fantasies of the Master Race*:
Literature, Cinema and the Colonization of American
Indians, 1992

Struggle for the Land:
Indigenous Resistance to Genocide, Ecocide and
Expropriation in Contemporary North America, 1993

Indians Are Us?
Culture and Genocide in Native North America, 1994

Co–authored: *Culture Versus Economism:*
Essays on Marxism in the Multicultural Arena
with Elisabeth R. Lloyd, 1984

Agents of Repression:
The FBI's Secret Wars Against the Black Panther Party
and the American Indian Movement
with Jim Vander Wall, 1988

The COINTELPRO Papers:
Documents from the FBI's Secret Wars Against Dissent
in the United States
with Jim Vander Wall, 1990

Edited: *Marxism and Native Americans*, 1983

Critical Issues in Native North America, 1989

Critical Issues in Native North America, Vol. II, 1990

Co–edited: *Cages of Steel*:
The Politics of Imprisonment in the United States
with Jim Vander Wall, 1992

Acknowledgments

A number of people have contributed in various ways to the content of this book. Among the more influential have been Mike Albert, Dennis Brutus, Noam Chomsky, Chrystos, Vine Deloria, Jr., Bill Dunne, Jimmie Durham, Richard Falk, Larry Giddings, Don Grinde, Lennox Hinds, bell hooks, Moana Jackson, Lilikala Kame'eleihiwa, Winona LaDuke, Dian Million, John Mohawk, Glenn T. Morris, Susan Rosenberg, Mike Ryan, Kirkpatrick Sale, David Stannard, George Tinker, Haunani–Kay and Mililani Trask, Jim and Jennie Vander Wall, Sharon Venne, Robert A. Williams, and Howard Zinn. To them I owe a real intellectual debt, although none bear responsibility for, nor even necessarily share, the particular formulations and conclusions I've arrived at. Thanks are also due to the people at Aigis Publications, especially Pavlos Stavropoulos, Riki Matthews, David Crawford, and Lisa Wigutoff, for the thought and effort which they put into making the final product both attractive and coherent. I also want to thank Alexandria Lord for her excellent maps.

Several of the essays which follow were initially published in various journals in one or another form. A much different version of "White Studies" made its debut in *Integrateducation*, Vol. XIX, Nos. 1–2 (Winter–Spring 1982); "Genocide: Toward a Functional Definition," first appeared in *Alternatives*, Vol. XI, No. 3 (July 1986); "Between a Rock and a Hard Place" was published in *Cultural Survival Quarterly*, Vol. 11, No. 3 (Fall 1988); "False Promises" appeared initially in *Society and Nature*, Vol. 1, No. 2 (1992); "Deconstructing the Columbus Myth" appeared in *Indigenous Thought*, Vol. 1, Nos. 2–3 (March–June 1991); a truncated version of "Since Predator Came" was put forth in *Covert Action Quarterly*, No. 40 (Spring 1992). "The Bloody Wake of Alcatraz" has been published in the *American Indian Culture and Research Journal* and the current version of "White Studies" is forthcoming in the same journal.

Finally, special appreciation is due to a number of groups and individuals who have seen me through some especially trying times these past few months, as the book went through the final stages of completion. Heading the list of the former are my Keetoowah people, the membership of Colorado AIM, the Region IV Peltier Support Network and my colleagues in the Center for Study of Ethnicity and Race in America. Without their active support, things might well have turned out differently. The same can be said with regard to my aunt and uncle, Joe and Vivian Locust, and more than a few of my friends, notably Faith Townsend Attiguile, Angie Burnham, Annie Coelho, Shelly Davis, Dan Debo, Jim Kimball, Heike Kleffner, Russ Means, Dian Million, Teresa Mullins, Hilary Old, Jim Page, Bob and Richard Robideau, Paul Shultz, Bob Sipe, Troy Lynne Yellow Wood, and Phyllis Young. My deepest thanks to one and all. One day perhaps I will be able to repay your kindness.

To Leah,
my one true love,
mother of my as yet unborn

Table of Contents

Table of Maps

Chapter 6: The Earth Is Our Mother

Chapter 10: About That Bering Strait Land Bridge....

Chapter 13: Between a Rock and a Hard Place

Fasting Day: Thanksgiving Day

by Dennis Brutus

Let us be grateful
Let us gather to give thanks
and as we celebrate earth's bounty
let us give thanks for all good things

Let us remember those who labored
and those who sacrificed for us
but let us remember especially
those deprived and those we deprived
and resolve to make amends:

to those who were robbed or slaughtered
Let us make reparations
Let us be giving to those
from whom much was taken away
Let us, in this, truly give thanks.

for Ward Churchill
November 25, 1993

Since Genocide Began

Ward Churchill—indigenist activist, spokesperson, professor, and internationally recognized scholar of the American Indian—has achieved a reputation for publishing and speaking on Native issues unparalleled in North America. His well-deserved public stature grows partly out of his large and varied publishing record: ten books on subjects ranging from Marxism and Native Americans to FBI wars against the Black Panthers and the American Indian Movement to cultural criticism on American literature and film. All this in 15 years.

But Ward Churchill's reputation also stems from his tireless travels on behalf of Native peoples to testify before international tribunals, to teach young Native people about their history and contemporary rights, to support Native nations engaged in land and resource disputes, even to aid besieged Native colleagues in their various conflicts with Western institutions.

By combining research and engagement, teaching and activism, Churchill has achieved what few authors ever achieve: analysis that predicts as well as describes. Thus, in the fast–changing world of indigenous issues, Ward Churchill demonstrated, in 1983, how conflicts between indigenous peoples and Marxists are the result of vastly different cultural views rather than opposing analytic interpretations. In *Marxism and Native Americans*, he concluded that Native people as land–based people would always be at odds with Marxists, for whom land is a resource, not the mother of all beings. Later, in his 1992 best–seller, *Fantasies of the Master Race: Literature, Cinema and the Colonization of American Indians*, Churchill interpreted the cultural neuroses that drive Westerners to adopt a false identity as Natives. Having taken nearly everything by murder and theft from American Indians, Westerners are now stealing Native spirituality. These "spirit vultures" include American poets, like Robert Bly, and German "fake" Indians who appear at the United Nations

Working Group on Indigenous Populations demanding recognition as Native people.

A year following his book on cultural criticism, Churchill published in 1993 what some believed, at that point, to be his finest work: *Struggle for the Land: Indian Resistance to Genocide, Ecocide and Expropriation in Contemporary North America*, a compendium of Native American land thefts from the Iroquois in New York to the Navajo–Hopi peoples in Arizona.

Now, Ward Churchill has once again surprised and pleased his indigenous as well as scholarly public with yet another amazing effort, appropriately titled in this post–Columbus era, *Since Predator Came*.

Although this new work spans enormous historical ground—from the arrival of Columbus to the insurrection in Chiapas, Mexico—contemporary politics, literature, and intellectual issues are covered in detail. In what has come to be characteristic Churchill style, cavalier humor is blended with unrelenting analysis to render a fresh perspective on subjects ranging from "White Studies" to Nicaraguan Indian resistance to North American Indian poetry.

But for those of us familiar with the increasing international attention now being given to indigenous human rights, it is the incisive discussion of genocide in legal as well as cultural terms that makes this a truly peerless work. As a Native scholar and nationalist myself, I salute Churchill's clarity in his detailed rendering of the issue of genocide, particularly since the denial of the Indian holocaust in the Americas continues unabated.

Those who flinch from the application of the terms "holocaust" and "genocide" to any but the Nazi holocaust and to any but its Jewish victims will be stunned by Churchill's marshaling of evidence—juridical, historical, sociological—in support of his argument that "genocide" is precisely what has been occurring against Indians of the Americas since the arrival of Columbus.

Finally, Churchill's section on a "Typology of Genocide" is the finest distillation of legal and political thinking on the problem of the definition of genocide. Churchill's solution—to identify genocide by degrees following the gradient statutory code pertaining to individual murder—is not only brilliant but workable at the international, national, and local levels.

All of us in the indigenous world who have been following Churchill's career as activist and academic rejoice yet again. Another superb work has been given to us from the best in the field.

Haunani–Kay Trask

Only Indians Help Indians

If necessary, I will fight alone.

Geronimo, 1881

During a conversation in the early 1980s about the relationship of AIM to a variety of other oppositional groups and tendencies, American Indian Movement leader Russell Means said to me, "Indians just don't fit in anywhere. We aren't part of anybody's agenda except our own." A few years later, in 1985, he demonstrated the pervasiveness of this viewpoint among those who struggle for indigenous rights, this time in a talk delivered at the University of Colorado on the resistance of the Miskito, Sumu, and Rama peoples of the Nicaraguan Atlantic Coast region to being subordinated to that country's leftist Sandinista régime. Quoting a slogan carved into the stock of an AK–47 assault rifle carried by a Miskito fighter, Means announced his belief that "only Indians help Indians."

This book is about the situation underlying such sentiments, endeavoring as it does not only to explain in some part what has happened to Native America since commencement of the hemispheric invasion inaugurated by the Columbian landfall of October 12, 1492, but how and why such realities have been masked or hidden by the increasingly smug and triumphalist descendants of those original waves of invaders. The resulting panorama is exceedingly ugly. It will prove, or at least it should, to be disquieting to anyone who encounters it. This, to be sure, is the hoped–for outcome of any reading, because, as C. Wright Mills once observed, it is precisely and perhaps only in such disquietude—or "cognitive dissonance," as he termed it—that the potential for positive change may be said to rest.

The approach to assembling the collection of essays which follows may be less than readily apparent. They begin with a brief homage to the late Cherokee anthropologist Robert K. Thomas, not only as a much deserved tribute to his memory, but as a way of offering a preliminary glimpse of the analytical principles which will be deployed throughout the remainder of the volume. From there, I move, in a piece entitled "Deconstructing the Columbus Myth," to an examination of the Spanish devastation of the native population of the Caribbean Basin at the outset of Europe's process of transatlantic conquest and colonization, and the manner in which subsequent eurocentric academics have sought to suppress the facts of the onslaught, at time even inverting the historical record with the goal of thus "naturalizing" eurosupremacist domination in the Americas.

The hegemony at issue is then explored with respect to what followed in the wake of the Columbian adventure, both in North America ("Since Predator Came") and in South/Central portions of the hemisphere ("Genocide in the Americas"). With this laid out, it seems appropriate that conventional utilization of the concept of genocide itself be explored with an eye towards discovering why it is not usually applied to either the historical or contemporary experiences of American Indians and other indigenous peoples, and why it should be. This is done in an essay entitled "Genocide: Toward a Functional Definition."

It is important to understand that the physically and culturally debilitating impact upon Native America ushered in by the invasion of 1492 are an ongoing phenomena, not mere historical curiosities. Although it is intended that this point will already have been made in several of the preceding essays, it is amplified and expanded through examinations of contemporary conditions suffered by the indigenous peoples of the United States in "The Earth Is Our Mother" and "Like Sand in the Wind." Relatedly, "The Bloody Wake of Alcatraz" discusses the kinds of treatment to which native people within the United States are subjected whenever they organize themselves to alter the abysmal conditions under which they are presently forced to live.

From these empirical investigations of current circumstance, the focus shifts to a greater emphasis upon the scholarly subterfuge through which such things have not only been hidden, but often converted into an illusion of being the opposite of what they are. "White Studies: The Intellectual Imperialism of U.S. Higher Education" begins with an overview of the entire edifice of eurosupremacism in American academia. This is followed, as a more specific illustration of how the "Other" is negated by America's modern eurocentric orthodoxy, with a piece entitled "About That Bering Strait Land Bridge...."

It is of course necessary to discuss how such rarefied deformities of reality as are perfected among the intelligentsia of the status quo come to be translated into something more practical and meaningful: the policy pronouncements of American political leaders, for example, articulations which directly shape our everyday lives at the level of life and death. Selected for this purpose, in an essay entitled "On Gaining 'Moral High Ground'," are certain postulations advanced by former President George Bush during the 1990–91 Gulf War. These are dissected under the light of U.S. posturing concerning the indigenous nations it holds internal to itself and revealed in all their stunning hypocrisy.

While such a squalid stance might simply be anticipated from those, such as Bush, representing the interests of America's imperial élite, better—or at least radically different—might be equally expected of those ostensibly most committed to imperialism's utter and complete eradication: the purveyors of marxian ideology. "False Promises," however, shows that many of marxism's most central tenets bind it squarely to the same sort of attitudes and behaviors concerning indigenous peoples as capitalism. More explicitly, in a piece entitled "Between a Rock and a Hard Place," co-authored with Glenn T. Morris, the records of the Vietnamese Communist Party concerning the h'Mong of Laos during the 1960s, and that of the aforementioned Nicaraguan Sandinistas vis-á-vis the Miskito, Sumu, and Rama during the 1980s, are inspected and found to be no better than that of the capitalist order both marxian entities propose to oppose.

This leads almost unerringly to the conclusion announced by Means toward the end of his University of Colorado lecture:

> Capitalism and communism are simply the opposite signs of the same eurocentric coin. Both are part and parcel of the European tradition. Both are intellectually and materially imperialist, leading inevitably and by design to the subordination of anything and everything non–European to their own white supremacist order. What we need—what the world needs—is not a choice between capitalism and communism, between one aspect of eurocentrism, or eurosupremacism, and another. What we need is a genuine revolutionary alternative, an alternative to the European tradition as a whole. I believe the struggle of the Sumu, Rama, and Miskito Indians in Nicaragua represents that kind of alternative. That's why I support not only the Indian resistance in Nicaragua, but the liberation struggles of indigenous peoples everywhere on this planet.

I concurred then, and I concur now. Hence, the inclusion of my brief 1986 statement of position and principle entitled "On Support of the Indian Resistance in Nicaragua." Hence also the volume's next essay, "The Meaning of Chiapas," a piece which seeks to show what I take to be the validity of the alternative to eurosupremacist colonialism's business as usual extended by the much more recent revolt of the indigenous Mayan populace in that Mexican province. It seems worth noting before closing that the Mayas of Chiapas, as do I and others, refer to the alternative they pose as being "indigenist." In the simplest terms, this means the taking of the rights, interests, and insights of native people as the essential premise for viable and sustainable social, economic, and political transformation of the existing order whenever and wherever it is to be confronted.

To contextualize the conflicts in South Dakota, Nicaragua, Chiapas, and elsewhere, and to conclude on a note of what I consider to be the profound promise these phenomena imply, I end with a sequence of three short essays—"Generations of Resistance," "From a Warrior Woman," and "Another Vision of America"—concerning the embodiment of contemporary native thought and sensibility in poetic form. Herein, I believe, lies the most essential articulation of indigenist sensibility, and readers would do well to understand and appreciate it.

Since Predator Came is not meant to serve, by any definition, as a guidebook to the thought and action of indigenism. Nonetheless, it does contain at least some of the informational ingredients and analytical tools needed for readers to begin to develop an indigenist apprehension of the world around them. It follows, in my view, that to the extent that this is true, the book contributes to the prospect that Indians, instead of fitting into no one else's agenda, will necessarily begin to be central to everyone's agenda in the years ahead; that Indians, instead of being constrained to finding help only among themselves—to "fight alone," as Geronimo put it—will find assistance increasingly accruing from all quarters; that, rather than interacting in ways which serve only to perpetually reproduce the legacy of Columbus, Indians and non–Indians will at last be able to begin collaborating in such fashion as to begin undoing the damage done since 1492.

Put another way, what is desired is that we, all of us, native and non–native alike, are eventually imbued with the consciousness to initiate the project of restoring the relational balance and harmony required to make the coming five centuries a thoroughgoing reversal of the past five centuries of global genocide, settler state colonialism, and imperialism, both economic and intellectual. If this book proves itself in any way successful in inculcating such sensibilities among even a small fraction of those who acquire it, it will have accomplished its author's objectives quite admirably.

Ward Churchill
Boulder, Colorado
January 1995

Remembering Bob Thomas

His Influence on the American Indian Liberation Struggle*

> The Indian picture isn't any blacker than it always was. It is just that American Indians are trying to do something about their problems and injustices. They are speaking out more and making their wishes known. Maybe a new day is dawning for the Indian.
>
> *Robert K. Thomas, Indian Voices, 1966*

Although Robert K. Thomas was known primarily as an ethnographer and cultural anthropologist of considerable stature, his interests and activities transcended all boundaries conventionally associated with those fields. Stan Steiner, for one, went to some lengths in recording Bob's involvement with organizations like the National Indian Youth Council during the 1960s,[1] and careful students will discover not a few explicitly political treatises published under his by-line, mostly appearing in the American Indian activist pulp venues of the day, papers like *Indian Voices* and *ABC: Americans Before Columbus*. On the scholarly side of things, too, he was known to make such excursions into what has today come to be known as "applied" anthropology. His essay "Powerless Politics," for example, published in the Winter 1966-67 edition of *New University Thought*, a small-circulation academic journal produced at the University of Chicago, is known to have had a significant impact upon the

---

*This essay originally appeared in *Dark Night,* Vol. 1, No. 2 (Fall 1994).

leadership of the fish-in protests of the Pacific Northwest in 1967, the occupation of Alcatraz Island in 1969, and the 1972 Trail of Broken Treaties.

It is one of the latter cluster of writings, also published in the 1966-67
issue of *New University Thought*, that I believe may turn out in the end to have
been the most influential of all his many endeavors. The essay, entitled
"Colonialism: Internal and Classic," was short, more a tentative probing of
ideas than a finished piece of scholarship. Yet for me, and for many of those
with whom I've worked over the past two decades, it has assumed a decisive
conceptual importance in terms of our understandings of ourselves and what it
is we are about. Perhaps predictably, perhaps ironically, many of those most
affected by it at this point have forgotten—or were never really aware of—the
article itself. By the same token, it is certain that Bob himself was, by the end
of his life, both amazed and to a large extent perplexed by the directions in
which some of us have taken his seminal perspective on the nature of the
American Indian relationship to the United States. Most likely, he was also a
bit frightened by certain of our prescriptions as to what should be done about it.

The Concept

What Bob Thomas accomplished in this one brief excursus was to redeem
an entire classification of socioeconomic and political relations seemingly
denied to analyses of the Indian condition in the United States, one which
appeared to have been permanently foreclosed by passage of the United
Nations' General Assembly Resolution 1541 (XV)—or "Blue Water Thesis,"
as it is often called—in 1960. According to the U.N. definition, a situation of
colonialism can be properly (and legally) said to exist if, and only if, one nation
directly and as a matter of policy dominates the social, economic, and political
life of another from which it is physically separated by at least 30 miles of open
water. In such instances, the dominated nations are construed as being absolutely entitled to relief from their circumstances under international law, and,
whenever their colonizers prove reluctant to comply with legal requirements in
this regard, the colonized are accorded the right of pursuing decolonization and
self-determination by any and all means available to them. Conversely, nations
dominated by others to which they are contiguous, or within which they are
encapsulated, are cast by Resolution 1541 not as colonies per se, but as
"minorities" domestic to the dominating power. While such minorities are
guaranteed (or conceded) a certain range of rights under international law, both
the type and extent of these rights, and the means by which they may be lawfully
pursued, are very much constricted when compared to those acknowledged as
being inherent to colonies.[2]

Indirectly, and in the somewhat homey style which was his trademark,
Bob pointed to the obvious. In effect, he argued that while the definition of

colonialism at issue might be adequate to describe the traditional form marked by historical empires such as those of France, Spain, and Great Britain—most of which had passed into oblivion by the late 1960s—it plainly failed to address the realities underlying a number of other readily observable phenomena. Following the reasoning imbedded in Resolution 1541 would, for instance, force one to conclude that the Poles and the French had been somehow transformed into "German minority groups" by virtue of the World War II nazi conquest and occupation of Poland and France, both of which were/are contiguous to Germany. Clearly, any such conclusion would be absurd, and is universally recognized as such; no one questions that France remained France, and Poland Poland, after the German invasion of each country; hence, no one questions the rights of the Poles and the French to liberate themselves from German rule. Why then, Thomas asked by implication, should the situation be perceived as different for a host of other nations—those of American Indians, for example—which can be readily shown to have suffered entirely similar processes of conquest and occupation of *their* homelands at the hands of contiguous aggressors?

"If it walks like a duck, and talks like a duck," goes the old adage, "it's probably a duck." All evidence, Blue Water notwithstanding, combining to suggest that American Indians suffer exactly the same kinds of domination and exploitation as, say, the Algerians under French rule, or the Congolese under the Belgians, and for most of the same reasons, Bob concluded that the concept of colonization is as appropriate to describing the circumstances of indigenous nations within the United States as it is to describing those of the country's more easily recognizable colonies abroad (for example, Hawai'i, Guam, the Philippines, Puerto Rico, the "U.S." Virgin Islands, "American" Samoa, and the Marshall Islands, among others). To make his concept immediately comprehensible, he offered a formulation in which colonialism might be viewed as a system divided into two overarching types or categories: "classic" would be the descriptor used to designate those colonies separated from their colonizer by open water; and "internal," the term used to define colonies appended to or incorporated directly into the territory claimed by the colonizing power as constituting its own home turf.

Bob's notion of internal colonialism, applied as it was to the specific context of American Indians in the late twentieth century, has yielded a powerful analytical utility to those of us seeking to decipher the peculiarly convoluted relationship of the federal government to North America's native peoples, and how this relationship has caused Indians in "the land of the free"—despite our nominal retention of land and resources sufficient to make us the wealthiest single racial/ethnic population aggregate on the continent—to experience literal Third World levels of impoverishment.[3] By the mid-1970s, the idea of Indians as colonies had taken firm hold among a number of scholars exploring questions of Indian rights. Even elements within the government itself had to some extent admitted the validity of the premise, with the U.S. Civil Rights Commission publishing a major study of conditions among the Navajos entitled *The Navajo Nation: An American Colony*.[4] A whole new understanding of the Native North American context was beginning to evolve.

Applications

A perhaps even more significant effect could be found within the milieu of Indian political activism, of which Bob was himself a part, that had emerged in the wake of Afroamerican initiatives in the Deep South during the 1950s and 1960s. Jolted by the implication of his arguments, many turned away from their tendency to struggle only for civil rights within the federal system, which inadvertently reinforced U.S. contentions that Indians and Indian Affairs should be properly understood as integral parts of the U.S. itself.[5] By 1971, there was an increasingly militant trend—manifested mainly but not exclusively through the American Indian Movement (AIM)—to concentrate on rights obtained under the proliferation of treaties with indigenous peoples by which the United States had acquired possession of the bulk of its continental land base between 1778 and 1871. Through their de-emphasizing of civil rights in favor of treaty rights—which by both U.S. constitutional and international legal definition pertain *only* to nations, *never* to minority groups—AIM and like-minded activist organizations, in common with many reservation traditionals, adopted a vision of Indian prerogatives falling well within the rubric of decolonization (or "national liberation" as it is often called) inherent to Bob's position.[6]

In substance, AIM, sometimes called "the shock troops of Indian sovereignty," demanded that the United States respect the treaty–implied rights of American Indian peoples as having the status of nations completely separate and distinct from the United States. This status, in turn, legally entitles native nations to reassert full control over their lands and other resources, determining for themselves the forms of their own political organization as well as the nature of their relationships with other nations, in a manner free from restriction or coercion by the United States. To the extent that exercise of these prerogatives by Indians was/is hampered or denied, AIM insists, the United States stands in violation of international laws requiring decolonization as a universal norm, and provides native people with a legal footing upon which to pursue extraordinary methods of compelling U.S. compliance.[7]

AIM's stance, punctuated during the early to mid-seventies by instances of armed resistance to federal authority, quickly linked American Indian rights issues to the well-recognized decolonization struggles of other peoples around the world. Consequently, 1974 saw the founding of the International Indian Treaty Council (IITC), often referred to as AIM's "international diplomatic arm," created to handle liaisons with other national liberation movements and supportive governments on a global basis, and to take the matter of Indian treaties before the United Nations.[8] The latter objective was attained in 1977, when IITC was able to bring about a conference on native rights attended by representatives of some 98 indigenous nations throughout the Americas and conducted at U.N. facilities in Geneva, Switzerland. By 1981, the results of this initial hearing had been translated into the establishment of a formal U.N. Working Group on Indigenous Populations, lodged under the U.N. Economic and Social Council (ECOSOC), charged with conducting annual hearings and a comprehensive study of the conditions in which native peoples exist. The Working Group's ultimate mandate was from the outset to collect the information necessary to predicate a "Universal Declaration of the Rights of Indigenous Peoples" to be incorporated for the first time as a principle of "black letter" international law by the General Assembly in 1993.[9]

In turn, all of this practical political ferment stimulated, rather naturally, a rapid expansion of the theoretical beachhead Bob had achieved by being the first to openly and coherently apply the concept of colonization to American Indians. In short order, other radical Indian scholars—people like John Mohawk, Roxanne Dunbar Ortiz, Russel Barsh, and Jimmie Durham[10]—began to explore ways of adapting the work of such major anti-colonialist thinkers as Frantz Fanon and Albert Memmi to the Native American setting.[11] The door was thereby opened to utilization of related concepts like the dependency theory articulated by Eduardo Galeano, and theories of underdevelopment deployed by André Gunder Frank, Immanual Wallerstein, and others.[12] One particularly fruitful avenue of investigation turned out to be that of the internally colonizing process—analyzed particularly well by Michael Hector in his 1975 book, *Internal Colonialism*—by which modern Europe had originally created itself.[13]

This last has led to the forging of an understanding that the notion of internal colonialism must itself be subcategorized into two discrete domains or spheres if it is to adequately reflect the realities experienced by Indians and other indigenous peoples. One domain involves the subordination of many of the smaller nations within Europe itself—the Euskadis (Basques), Scots, Welsh, Freislanders, Magyars, and others—as part of a process of consolidating statist structures desired by the European subcontinent's dominant peoples. The other sphere consists of a "settler state" variety of colonialism in which populations exported from Europe first subordinate native nations elsewhere, occupying the natives' land on behalf of one or another European state, then wrest their own national independence from that state (decolonizing themselves), a matter anchored in the continuing colonization of the native people whose land they occupy.[14]

It is, of course, the latter type of colonialism which afflicts Indians and other indigenous peoples such as the Inuits and native Hawaiians in the United States and Canada, as well as in much of Latin America. Literal settler state colonization is, moreover, the presiding form of domination suffered by numerous indigenous peoples elsewhere, notably in Northern Ireland, South Africa, Australia, New Zealand, and Israel.[15] Alternatively—as in China and Vietnam—the substance of settler state colonialism is visited upon smaller indigenous nations by large and thoroughly Europeanized local peoples striving to replicate the forms of Western-style statist consolidation (usually in the name of "socialism"), after the departure of the European colonists themselves.[16]

Apprehension of this typology of colonialism, one which seems peculiar to the ongoing rather than historical exploitation and oppression of non-Western indigenous nations, has done much to foster a worldwide sense of commonality and incipient unity among native peoples. Simultaneously, it has done quite a lot to erode potential reliance among indigenous rights activists upon traditional Eurocentric "solutions," embodied mainly in the tenets of marxism–leninism, to the colonialist order.[17] Rather, as was demonstrated during the 1980s by the struggle of the Miskito, Sumu, and Rama Indians of eastern Nicaragua against forcible subordination to the dictates of that country's leftist Sandinista regime, marxism has come to be seen as constituting as great a threat to native sovereignty and self-determination as capitalism.[18] Increasingly, the national liberation movements pursuing native interests, both in North America and elsewhere, have taken to defining themselves as representing a "third way," aligned with neither capitalism nor socialism, but rather with the explicitly non-Western heritage from which they spring. This outlook has come to be referred to most frequently as "indigenism" or "Fourth Worldism."[19]

A Legacy

Altogether, it could seem a bit much to suggest, as I may appear to have done, that alterations in thought and action as profound as those sketched above should have accrued from a single abbreviated essay published in an obscure journal in the United States. Indeed, any such "explanation" of what is described herein would be grotesquely simplistic. My point, then, is not that everything that has happened since is somehow directly attributable to a few pages of text produced by Robert K. Thomas. Instead, my thinking is that "Colonialism: Classic and Internal" represents what Herbert Marcuse once described as a "breach of false consciousness," an insight, the appropriateness and explanatory power of which "can provide the Archimedian point for a more comprehensive emancipation" of thought and action. Such breaches typically occur "on an infinitely small space," Marcuse concluded, "but the chance for change depends upon the widening of such small spaces."[20]

It is self-evident that, before Bob wrote his little essay, Indians were by and large groping about for ways to make sense of what it was that had been happening to us throughout the twentieth century. After *New University*

Thought published his piece, enough of us could put a name to it to find our voices, and thereby to begin moving together in a constructive direction. A dynamic was unleashed which undoubtedly surpassed anything he might in his wildest imaginings have envisioned when he sat down to write what was on his mind in 1966. The small Archimedian space he crafted has, by this point, been expanded beyond all recognition. Change has certainly occurred because of it, for better or worse, and it will inevitably continue to occur for some time. Quite possibly, things have gone in a direction very different from whatever it was he originally desired to see come of his work. That is often the fate of those who give birth to a new and different approach to understanding.

Indication that Thomas may not have been entirely comfortable with the conclusions reached by some of his politico-intellectual progeny was brought home to me one night in the mid-eighties when we sat together in a San Diego bar during a lull in the annual Western Social Science Association conference. Ever the senior scholar, he promptly broke the ice by inquiring into the nature of my research. My response, and mention of the fact that his essay on colonialism had had an especially deep influence on me, provoked an outright interrogation. As I summed up, as succinctly as I could, what I had been thinking and why, and what it was I was doing to try and put the ideas into practice, he fixed me with a somewhat baleful eye. "You'd have to dismantle the entire goddamn United States of America to make that work," he grumbled. I conceded that this was true. "Well then," he said, glaring ferociously, "you're just about the most dismal son-of-a-bitch I ever met." Startled, I inquired as to why that might be. "Because," he replied, "if *that's* what it takes to win this thing, then we're beat before we start, aren't we? You'd better think about what you're saying." With that, he abruptly left me alone to do just that.

Still, as I was leaving for the airport the next morning, I saw him making a beeline for me across the hotel lobby. "I just wanted to say good-bye," he informed me, eyes now twinkling, "Take care of yourself. And, whatever else you do, give 'em hell for me." I told him he could count on it, and he laughed. "That's the spirit," he said, moving off to finish his breakfast. Whatever the depth of his tension with his conceptual offspring, it is thus plain that he was ultimately unprepared to disavow them entirely. More likely, with the sharpness to which his rank as elder statesman entitled him, he remained committed to the end to pushing us all to ponder our propositions, to clarify and hone our postulations to the point that they might see service in the way he knew we meant them. He could see that we were engaged in what he would call "serious business," an involvement appropriate only if we took it seriously. And, figurative father of us all, he bothered himself whenever possible to see that we did.

So much has happened since Bob died that bears on his ideas, or at least what it is that has been done with them. One can only wonder how the recent disintegration of the world's other great super-state, the Soviet Union, and the re–emergence of a host of long-suppressed nationalities as self-determining entities within its former territoriality, might have affected his skepticism that the United States, too, might be ultimately dismembered, replaced in part by an archipelago of decolonized American Indian nations. Similarly, one would like to know his views on the ethnic strife which has broken out amidst the rubble of what was once Yugoslavia. Would he see hope for the actualization of an independent Kurdistan? Nagaland? A Karin Free State in what used to be Burma? What would he think of the home rule arrangement achieved by the Inuits of Greenland vis-à-vis Denmark, or the prospect of a self-governing territory to be carved out of northern Canada by those same circumpolar people? Would he see potential in the creation of an autonomous zone for the Maoris in New Zealand? The Kooris and other "aboriginals" of Australia? There are scores of such queries one would wish to pose.

One can wish, but the man is gone. We must answer such questions for ourselves, now. That he was instrumental, whatever his personal hesitancies or ultimate misgivings about where it was all going to end up, in providing us the analytical tools with which to do so is no small legacy. In the end, it is fair to say that Bob Thomas achieved a genuine breakthrough for American Indian people, setting out a much-needed conceptual beacon in the depths of a very dark night of ignorance and confusion. That is quite a lot for any one person to accomplish. It is now up to each of us to honor his accomplishment, using his beacon as a guide with which to steer our liberatory project home, keeping in mind that only when we find ourselves in a Native America freed from every vestige of the plague of colonization, internal and otherwise, will we be able to say truthfully that we've at last arrived. Let *that* be *our* legacy to those who come after *us*.

Notes

1. Stan Steiner, *The New Indians* (New York: Delta Books, 1968).

2. On Resolution 1541 and its context, *see* Gordon Bennett, *Aboriginal Rights in International Law* (London: Royal Anthropological Society of Great Britain and Ireland/Survival International, 1978).

3. Dividing the 50 million acres of remaining reservation land by the census count of Indians in the United States reveals Indians as the population with the most acreage on a per capita basis in North America. This acreage is the most mineral-rich on the continent, holding as much as two-thirds of U.S. uranium reserves, about a quarter of the low-sulfur coal, a fifth of the oil and natural gas, and an abundance of copper, zeolites and other ores, all of it heavily mined over the past half–century. On paper, this computes to Indians being the wealthiest population aggregate in North America, on a per capita basis. Instead, according to the federal government's own data, we are the very poorest, experiencing, by a decisive margin, the lowest annual and lifetime incomes of any overall group. Correlated with this are all the statistical indices of dire poverty: highest infant mortality rate, highest rates of death by

malnutrition, exposure, and plague, and shortest life expectancy. The factor reconciling this potential wealth on the one hand to the practical poverty evidenced on the other is the manner in which U.S. colonial domination of Indian Country has diverted profit from the development of indigenous resources to American corporations. For a detailed examination of this process, *see* Ward Churchill, *Struggle for the Land: Indigenous Resistance to Genocide, Ecocide and Expropriation in North America* (Monroe, Maine: Common Courage Press, 1993).

4. U.S. Commission on Civil Rights, *The Navajo Nation: An American Colony* (Washington, D.C.: U.S. Government Printing Office, 1975).

5. A selection of essays and primary documents articulating the agenda of the civil rights phase of Indian activism may be found in Alvin Josephy, *Red Power: The American Indians' Fight for Freedom* (New York: American Heritage Press, 1971).

6. The transition is discussed in Vine Deloria, Jr., *Behind the Trail of Broken Treaties: An Indian Declaration of Independence* (New York: Delta Books, 1974).

7. For AIM's perspective on these matters, *see* Bruce Johansen and Roberto Maestas, *Wasi'chu: The Continuing Indian Wars* (New York: Monthly Review Press, 1979).

8. The founding of IITC is well covered in Rex Weyler, *Blood of the Land: The U.S. Government and Corporate War Against the American Indian Movement* (New York: Everest House Publishers, 1982).

9. *See* Gudmundur Alfredsson, "International Law, International Organizations, and Indigenous Peoples," *Journal of International Affairs*, Vol. 36, No. 1 (1982), pp. 113-25.

10. *See*, for example, Roxanne Dunbar Ortiz, *Indians of the America: Human Rights and Self-Determination* (London: Zed Press, 1984); Russel Barsh and James Youngblood Henderson, *The Road: Indian Tribes and Political Liberty* (Berkeley: University of California Press, 1980); and Jimmie Durham, *Columbus Day* (Minneapolis: West End Press, 1983).

11. The most relevant works here are Frantz Fanon, *The Wretched of the Earth* (New York: Grove Press, 1965), and *Black Skin, White Masks* (New York: Grove Press, 1967); and Albert Memmi, *The Colonizer and the Colonized* (Boston: Beacon Press, 1965).

12. Eduardo Galeano, *The Open Veins of Latin America: Five Centuries of the Pillage of a Continent* (New York: Monthly Review Press, 1975); André Gunder Frank, *Capitalism and Underdevelopment in Latin America: Historical Studies of Chile and Brazil* (New York: Monthly Review Press, 1967); Immanual Wallerstein, *The Modern World System* (New York: The Academic Press, 1974).

13. Michael Hector, *Internal Colonialism: The Celtic Fringe in British National Development, 1536-1966* (Berkeley: University of California Press, 1975).

14. Independent Commission on International Humanitarian Issues, *Indigenous Peoples: A Global Quest for Justice* (London: Zed Press, 1987).

15. *See* J. Sakai, *Settlers: The Mythology of the White Proletariat* (Chicago: Morningstar Press, 1983). *See* also Ronald Weitzer, *Transforming Settler States: Communal Conflict and Internal Security in Northern Ireland and Zimbabwe* (Berkeley: University of California Press, 1992).

16. On the record of China, Vietnam, and other socialist states, *see* Walker Connor, *The National Question in Marxist-Leninist Theory and Strategy* (Princeton, New Jersey: Princeton University Press, 1984).

17. For elaboration, *see* Ward Churchill, ed., *Marxism and Native Americans* (Boston: South End Press, 1983).

18. On the Indian/Sandinista conflict, *see* Glenn T. Morris and Ward Churchill, "Between a Rock and a Hard Place: Left-Wing Revolution, Right-Wing Reaction, and the Destruction of Indigenous Peoples," *Cultural Survival Quarterly*, Vol. 11, No. 3 (1987), pp. 17-24. Reprinted in this volume of essays.

19. On the terminology involved, *see* George Manuel and Michael Posluns, *The Fourth World: An Indian Reality* (New York: The Free Press, 1974).

20. Herbert Marcuse, "Repressive Tolerance," in *A Critique of Pure Tolerance*, Robert Paul Wolf, Barrington Moore, Jr., and Herbert Marcuse, eds. (Boston: Beacon Press, 1965), p. 111.

Deconstructing the Columbus Myth

Was the "Great Discoverer" Italian or Spanish, Nazi or Jew?*

> Christopher Columbus was a genuine titan, a hero of history and of the human spirit.... To denigrate Columbus is to denigrate what is worthy in human history and in us all.
>
> *Jeffrey Hart,* National Review, *October 15, 1990*

It is perhaps fair to say that our story opens at Alfred University, where, during the fall of 1990, I served as distinguished scholar of American Indian Studies for a program funded by the National Endowment for the Humanities. Insofar as I was something of a curiosity in that primarily Euroamerican staffed and attended institution, situated as it is within an area populated primarily by white folk, it followed naturally that I quickly became a magnet for local journalists seeking to inject a bit of color into their otherwise uniformly blanched columns and commentaries. Given our temporal proximity to the much–heralded quin-centennial celebration of Christopher Columbus' late fifteenth–century "discovery" of a "New World" and its inhabitants, and that I am construed as being in some part a direct descendant of those inhabitants, they were wont to query me as to my sentiments concerning the accomplishments of the Admiral of the Ocean Sea.

---

*This essay originally appeared in *Indigenous Thought*, Vol. 1, Nos. 2–3 (March–June 1991).

My response, at least in its short version, was (and remains) that celebrating Columbus and the European conquest of the Western Hemisphere that he set off is greatly analogous to celebrating the glories of nazism and Heinrich Himmler. Publication of this remark in local newspapers around Rochester, New York, caused me to receive, among other things, a deluge of lengthy and vociferously framed letters of protest, two of which I found worthy of remark.

The first of these was sent by a colleague at the university, an exchange faculty member from Germany, who informed me that while the human costs begat by Columbus' navigational experiment were "tragic and quite regrettable," comparisons between him and the Reichsführer SS were nonetheless unfounded. The distinction between Himmler and Columbus, his argument went, resided not only in differences in "the magnitude of the genocidal events in which each was involved," but the *ways* in which they were involved. Himmler, he said, was enmeshed as "a high–ranking and responsible official in the liquidation of entire human groups" as "a matter of formal state policy" guided by an explicitly "racialist" ideology. Furthermore, he said, the enterprise Himmler created as the instrument of his genocidal ambitions incorporated, deliberately and intentionally, considerable economic benefit to the state in whose service he acted. None of this pertained to Columbus, the good professor concluded, because the "Great Discoverer" was ultimately "little more than a gifted seaman," an individual who unwittingly set in motion processes over which he had little or no control, in which he played no direct part, and which might well have been beyond his imagination. My juxtaposition of the two men, he contended, therefore tended to "diminish understanding of the unique degree of evil" which should be associated with Himmler, and ultimately precluded "proper historical understandings of the Nazi phenomenon."

The second letter came from a member of the Jewish Defense League in Rochester. His argument ran that, unlike Columbus (whom he described as "little more than a bit player, without genuine authority or even much of a role, in the actual process of European civilization in the New World which his discovery made possible"), Himmler was a "responsible official in a formal state policy of exterminating an entire human group for both racial and economic reasons," and on a scale "unparalleled in all history." My analogy between the two, he said, served to "diminish public respect for the singular nature of the Jewish experience at the hands of the Nazis," as well as popular understanding of "the unique historical significance of the Holocaust." Finally, he added, undoubtedly as a crushing capstone to his position, "It is a measure of your anti–semitism that you compare Himmler to Columbus" because "Columbus was, of course, himself a Jew."

I must confess the last assertion struck me first, and only partly because I'd never before heard claims that Christopher Columbus was of Jewish ethnicity. "What possible difference could this make?" I asked in my letter of reply. "If Himmler himself were shown to have been of Jewish extraction, would it then suddenly become anti–semitic to condemn him for the genocide he perpetrated against Jews, Gypsies, Slavs, and others? Would his historical crimes then suddenly be unmentionable or even 'okay'?" To put it another way, I continued, "Simply because Meyer Lansky, Dutch Schultz, Bugsey Siegel and Lepke were all Jewish 'by blood', is it a gesture of anti–semitism to refer to them as gangsters? Is it your contention that an individual's Jewish ethnicity somehow confers exemption from negative classification or criticism of his/her conduct? What *are* you saying?" The question of Columbus' possible Jewish-ness nonetheless remained intriguing, not because I held it to be especially important in its own right, but because I was (and am still) mystified as to why any ethnic group, especially one which has suffered genocide, might be avid to lay claim either to the man or to his legacy. I promised myself to investigate the matter further.

A Mythic Symbiosis

Meanwhile, I was captivated by certain commonalities of argument inherent to the positions advanced by my correspondents. Both men exhibited a near–total ignorance of the actualities of Columbus' career. Nor did they demonstrate any particular desire to correct the situation. Indeed, in their mutual need to separate the topic of their preoccupation from rational scrutiny, they appeared to have conceptually joined hands in a function composed more of faith than fact. The whole notion of the "uniqueness of the Holocaust" serves both psychic and political purposes for Jew and German alike, or so it seems. The two groups are bound to one another in a truly symbiotic relationship grounded in the mythic exclusivity of their experience: one half of the equation simply completes the other in a perverse sort of collaboration, with the result that each enjoys a tangible benefit.

For Jews, at least those who have adopted the zionist perspective, a "unique historical suffering" under nazism translates into fulfillment of a biblical prophecy that they are "the chosen," entitled by virtue of the destiny of a special persecution to assume a rarified status among—and to consequently enjoy preferential treatment from—the remainder of humanity. In essence, this translates into a demand that the Jewish segment of the Holocaust's victims must now be allowed to participate equally in the very system which once victimized them, and to receive an equitable share of the spoils accruing therefrom. To this end, zionist scholars such as Irving Louis Horowitz and Elie Wiesel have labored long and mightily, defining genocide in terms exclusively related to the forms it assumed under nazism. In their version of "truth," one must literally see smoke pouring from the chimneys of Auschwitz in order to apprehend that a genocide, per se, is occurring.[1] Conversely, they have coined terms such as "ethnocide" to encompass the fates inflicted upon other peoples throughout history.[2] Such semantics have served, not as tools of understanding, but as an expedient means of arbitrarily differentiating the experience of their people—both qualitatively and quantitatively—from that of any other. To approach things in any other fashion would, it must be admitted, tend to undercut ideas like the "moral right" of the Israeli settler state to impose itself directly atop the Palestinian Arab homeland.

For Germans to embrace a corresponding "unique historical guilt" because of what was done to the Jews during the 1940s is to permanently absolve themselves of guilt concerning what they may be doing *now*. No matter how ugly things may become in contemporary German society, or so the reasoning goes, it can *always* be (and is) argued that there has been a marked improvement over the "singular evil which was nazism." Anything other than outright nazification is, by definition, "different," "better," and therefore "acceptable" ("Bad as they are, things could always be worse."). Business as usual—which is to say assertions of racial supremacy, domination, and exploitation of "inferior" groups, and most of the rest of the nazi agenda—is thereby free to continue in a manner essentially unhampered by serious stirrings of guilt among the German public *so long as it does not adopt the literal trappings of nazism.* Participating for profit and with gusto in the deliberate starvation of much of the Third World is no particular problem if one is careful not to goose step while doing it.

By extension, insofar as Germany is often seen (and usually sees itself) as exemplifying the crowning achievements of "Western Civilization," the same principle covers all European and Euro–derived societies. No matter what they do, it is never "really" what it seems unless it was done in precisely the fashion the nazis did it. Consequently, the nazi master plan of displacing or reducing by extermination the population of the western USSR and replacing it with settlers of "biologically superior German breeding stock" is roundly (and rightly) condemned as ghastly and inhuman. Meanwhile, people holding this view of nazi ambitions tend overwhelmingly to see consolidation and maintenance of Euro–dominated settler states in places like Australia, New Zealand, South Africa, Argentina, the United States, and Canada as "basically okay," or even as "progress." The "distinction" allowing this psychological phenomenon is that each of these states went about the intentional displacement and extermination of native populations, and their replacement, in a manner slightly different in its particulars from that employed by nazis attempting to accomplish exactly the same thing. Such technical differentiation is then magnified and used as a sort of all–purpose veil, behind which almost anything can be hidden, so long as it is not openly adorned with a swastika.

Given the psychological, socio–cultural, and political imperatives involved, neither correspondent, whether German or Jew, felt constrained to examine the factual basis of my analogy between Himmler and Columbus before denying the plausibility or appropriateness of the comparison. To the contrary, since the paradigm of their mutual understanding embodies the a priori presumption that there *must be no such analogy*, factual investigation is precluded from their posturing. It follows that any dissent on the "methods" involved in their arriving at their conclusions, never mind introduction of countervailing evidence, must be denied out of hand with accusations of "overstatement," "shoddy scholarship," "stridency" and/or "anti–semitism." To this litany have lately been added such new variations as "white bashing," "ethnic McCarthyism," "purveyor of political correctitude," and any other epithet deemed helpful in keeping a "canon of knowledge" fraught with distortion, deception, and outright fraud from being "diluted."[3]

Columbus as Proto-Nazi

It is time to delve into the substance of my remark that Columbus and Himmler, nazi *lebensraumpolitik*, along with the "settlement of the New World" bear more than casual resemblance to one another. It is not, as my two correspondents wished to believe, because of his "discovery." This does not mean that if this were "all" he had done he would be somehow innocent of what resulted from his find, no more than is the scientist who makes a career of accepting military funding to develop weapons in any way "blameless" when they are subsequently used against human targets. Columbus did not sally forth upon the Atlantic for reasons of "neutral science" or altruism. He went, as his own diaries, reports, and letters make clear, fully expecting to encounter wealth belonging to others. It was his stated purpose to seize this wealth, by whatever means necessary and available, in order to enrich both his sponsors and himself.[4] Plainly, he prefigured, both in design and by intent, what came next. To this extent, he not only symbolizes the process of conquest and genocide which eventually consumed the indigenous peoples of America, but bears the personal responsibility of having participated in it. Still, if this were all there was to it, I might be inclined to dismiss him as a mere thug rather than branding him a counterpart to Himmler.

The 1492 "voyage of discovery" is, however, hardly all that is at issue. In 1493 Columbus returned with an invasion force of 17 ships, appointed at his own request by the Spanish Crown to install himself as "viceroy and governor of [the Caribbean islands] and the mainland" of America, a position he held until 1500.[5] Setting up shop on the large island he called Española (today Haiti and the Dominican Republic), he promptly instituted policies of slavery (*encomiendo*) and systematic extermination of the native Taino population.[6] Columbus' programs reduced Taino numbers from as many as 8 million at the outset of his regime to about 3 million in 1496.[7] Perhaps 100,000 were left by the time the governor departed. His policies, however, remained, with the result that by 1514 the Spanish census of the island showed barely 22,000 Indians remaining alive. In 1542, only 200 were recorded.[8] Thereafter, they were considered extinct, as were Indians throughout the Caribbean Basin, an aggregate population which totaled more than 15 million at the point of first contact with the Admiral of the Ocean Sea, as Columbus was known.[9]

This, to be sure, constitutes an attrition of population *in real numbers* every bit as great as the toll of 12 to 15 million—about half of them Jewish—most commonly attributed to Himmler's slaughter mills. Moreover, the proportion of indigenous Caribbean population destroyed by the Spanish in a single generation is, no matter how the figures are twisted, far greater than the 75 percent of European Jews usually said to have been exterminated by the nazis.[10] Worst of all, these data apply *only* to the Caribbean Basin; the process of genocide in the Americas was only just beginning at the point such statistics become operant, not ending, as they did upon the fall of the Third Reich. All told, it is probable that more than 100 million native people were "eliminated" in the course of Europe's ongoing "civilization" of the Western Hemisphere.[11]

It has long been asserted by "responsible scholars" that this decimation of American Indians which accompanied the European invasion resulted primarily from disease rather than direct killing or conscious policy.[12] There is a certain truth to this, although starvation may have proven just as lethal in the end. It must be borne in mind when considering such facts that a considerable portion of those who perished in the nazi death camps died, not as the victims of bullets and gas, but from starvation, as well as epidemics of typhus, dysentery and the like. Their keepers, who could not be said to have killed these people directly, were nonetheless found to have been culpable in their deaths by way of deliberately imposing the conditions which led to the proliferation of starvation and disease among them.[13] Certainly, the same can be said of Columbus' regime, under which the original residents were, as a first order of business, permanently dispossessed of their abundant cultivated fields while being converted into chattel, ultimately to be worked to death for the wealth and "glory" of Spain.[14]

Nor should more direct means of extermination be relegated to incidental status. As the matter is framed by Kirkpatrick Sale in his book, *The Conquest of Paradise*:

> The tribute system, instituted by the Governor sometime in 1495, was a simple and brutal way of fulfilling the Spanish lust for gold while acknowledging the Spanish distaste for labor. Every Taino over the age of fourteen had to supply the rulers with a hawk's bell of gold every three months (or, in gold–deficient areas, twenty–five pounds of spun cotton); those who did were given a token to wear around their necks as proof that they had made their payment; those who did not were, as [Columbus' brother, Fernando] says discreetly, "punished"—by having their hands cut off, as [the priest, Bartolomé de] Las Casas says less discreetly, and left to bleed to death.[15]

It is entirely likely that more than 10,000 Indians were killed in this fashion, on Española alone, as a matter of policy, during Columbus' tenure as governor. Las Casas' *Brevísima relación*, among other contemporaneous sources, is also replete with accounts of Spanish colonists (*hidalgos*) hanging Tainos *en mass*, roasting them on spits or burning them at the stake (often a dozen or more at a time), hacking their children into pieces to be used as dog feed and so forth, all of it to instill in the natives a "proper attitude of respect" toward their Spanish "superiors."

> [The Spaniards] made bets as to who would slit a man in two, or cut off his head at one blow; or they opened up his bowels. They tore the babes from their mother's breast by their feet and dashed their heads against the rocks.... They spitted the bodies of other babes, together with their mothers and all who were before them, on their swords.[16]

No SS trooper could be expected to comport himself with a more unrelenting viciousness. And there is more. All of this was coupled to wholesale and persistent massacres:

> A Spaniard ... suddenly drew his sword. Then the whole hundred drew theirs and began to rip open the bellies, to cut and kill [a group of Tainos assembled for this purpose]—men, women, children and old folk, all of whom were seated, off guard and frightened.... And within two credos, not a man of them there remain[ed] alive. The Spaniards enter[ed] the large house nearby, for this was happening at its door, and in the same way, with cuts and stabs, began to kill as many as were found there, so that a stream of blood was running, as if a great number of cows had perished.[17]

Elsewhere, Las Casas went on to recount:

> In this time, the greatest outrages and slaughterings of people were perpetrated, whole villages being depopulated.... The Indians saw that without any offense on their part they were despoiled of their kingdoms, their lands and liberties and of their lives, their wives, and homes. As they saw themselves each day perishing by the cruel and inhuman treatment of the Spaniards, crushed to earth by the horses, cut in pieces by swords, eaten and torn by dogs, many buried alive and suffering all kinds of exquisite tortures ... [many surrendered to their fate, while the survivors] fled to the mountains [to starve].[18]

The butchery continued until there were no Tainos left to butcher. One might well ask how a group of human beings, even those like the Spaniards of Columbus' day, maddened in a collective lust for wealth and prestige, might come to treat another with such unrestrained ferocity over a sustained period.

The answer, or some substantial portion of it, must lie in the fact that the Indians were considered by the Spanish to be *untermenschen*, subhumans. That this was the conventional view is borne out beyond all question in the recorded debates between Las Casas and the nobleman, Francisco de Sepulveda, who argued for the majority of Spaniards that American Indians, like African blacks and other "lower animals," lacked "souls." The Spaniards, consequently, bore in Sepulveda's estimation a holy obligation to enslave and destroy them wherever they might be encountered.[19] The eugenics theories of nazi "philosopher" Alfred Rosenberg, to which Heinrich Himmler more or less subscribed, elaborated the mission of the SS in very much the same terms.[20] It was upon such profoundly racist ideas that Christopher Columbus grounded his policies as initial governor of the new Spanish empire in America.[21]

In the end, all practical distinctions between Columbus and Himmler—at least those not accounted for by differences in available technology and extent of socio–military organization—evaporate upon close inspection. They are cut of the same cloth, fulfilling precisely the same function and for exactly the same reasons, each in his own time and place. If there is one differentiation which may be valid, it is that while the specific enterprise Himmler represented ultimately failed and is now universally condemned, that represented by Columbus did not and is not. Instead, as Sale has observed, the model for colonialism and concomitant genocide Columbus pioneered during his reign as governor of Española was to prove his "most enduring legacy," carried as it was "by the conquistadors on their invasions of Mexico, Peru, and La Florida."[22] The Columbian process is ongoing, as is witnessed by the fact that, today, his legacy is celebrated far and wide.

The Emblematic European

This leaves open the question as to whom, exactly, the horror which was Columbus rightly "belongs." There are, as it turns out, no shortage of contenders for the mantle of the man and his "accomplishments." It would be well to examine the nature of at least the major claims in order to appreciate the extent of the mad scramble which has been undertaken by various peoples to associate themselves with what was delineated in the preceding section. One cannot avoid the suspicion that the spectacle bespeaks much of the Eurocentric character.

Was Columbus Italian?

The popular wisdom has always maintained that Christopher Columbus was born in Genoa, a city–state which is incorporated into what is now called Italy. Were this simply an historical truth, it might be accepted as just one more uncomfortable fact of life for the Italian people, who are—or should be—still trying to live down what their country did to the Libyans and Ethiopians during the prelude to World War II. However, there is much evidence that draws Columbus' supposed Genoese origin into question. For instance, although such records were kept at the time, there is no record of his birth in that locale. Nor is there reference to his having been born or raised there in any of his own written work, including his personal correspondence. For that matter, there is no indication that he either wrote or spoke any dialect which might be associated with Genoa, nor even the Tuscan language which forms the basis of modern Italian. His own writings—not excluding letters penned to Genoese friends and the Banco di San Grigorio, one of his financiers in that city—were uniformly articulated in Castilian, with a bit of Portuguese and Latin mixed in.[23] Moreover, while several variations of his name were popularly applied to him during his lifetime, none of them was drawn from a dialect which might be considered Italian. He himself, in the only known instance in which he rendered his own full name, utilized the Greek *Xpõual de Colón*.[24] Still, Genoa, Italy, and those of Italian descent elsewhere in the world (Italo–Americans, most loudly of all) have mounted an unceasing clamor during the twentieth century, insisting he *must* be theirs. Genoa itself invested considerable resources into "resolving" the question during the 1920s, ultimately printing a 288–page book assembling an array of depositions and other documents—all of them authenticated—attesting that Columbus was indeed Genoese. Published in 1931, the volume, entitled *Christopher Columbus: Documents and Proofs of His Genoese Origin*, presents what is still the best circumstantial case as to Columbus' ethnic identity.[25]

Spanish?

Counterclaims concerning Columbus' supposed Iberian origin are also long–standing and have at times been pressed rather vociferously. These center primarily on the established facts that he spent the bulk of his adult life in service to Spain, was fluent in both written and spoken Castilian, and that his mistress, Beatriz Enríquez de Arana, was Spanish.[26] During the 1920s, these elements of the case were bolstered by an assortment of "archival documents" allegedly proving conclusively that Columbus was a Spaniard from cradle to grave. In 1928, however, the Spanish Academy determined that these documents had been forged by parties overly eager to establish Spain's exclusive claim to the Columbian legacy. Since then, Spanish chauvinists have had to content themselves with arguments that The Discoverer is theirs by virtue of employment and nationality, if not by birth. An excellent summary of the various Spanish contentions may be found in Enrique de Gandia's *Historia de Cristóbal Colón: analisis crítico*, first published in 1942.[27]

Portuguese?

Portuguese participation in the fray has been less pronounced, but follows basically the same course—*sans* forged documents—as that of the Spanish. Columbus, the argument goes, was plainly conversant in the language and his wife, Felipa Moniz Perestrello, is known to have been Portuguese. Further, the first point at which his whereabouts can be accurately determined was in service to Portugal, plying that country's slave trade along Africa's west coast for a period of four years. Reputedly, he was also co–proprietor of a book and map shop in Lisbon and/or Madiera for a time, and once sailed to Iceland on a voyage commissioned by the Portuguese Crown. Portugal's desire to extend a serious claim to Spain's Admiral of the Ocean Sea seems to be gathering at least some momentum, as is witnessed in Manuel Luciano de Silva's 1989 book, *Columbus Was 100% Portuguese.*[28]

Jewish?

The idea that Columbus might have been a Spanish Jew is perhaps best known for having appeared in Simon Weisenthal's *Sails of Hope* in 1973.[29] Therein, Weisenthal contends that the future governor of Española hid his ethnicity because of the mass expulsion of Jews from Spain ordered by King Ferdinand of Aragon on March 30, 1492 (the decree was executed on August 2 of the same year). The logic goes that because of this rampant anti–semitism, the Great Navigator's true identity has remained shrouded in mystery, lost to the historical record. Interestingly, given the tenacity with which at least some sectors of the Jewish community have latched on to it, this notion is not at all Jewish in origin. Rather, it was initially developed as a speculation in a 1913 article, "Columbus a Spaniard and a Jew?", published by Henry Vignaud in the *American History Review.*[30] It was then advanced by Salvador de Madariaga in his unsympathetic 1939 biography, *Christopher Columbus.* Madariaga's most persuasive argument, at least to himself, seems to have been that Columbus' "great love of gold" proved his "Jewishness."[31] This theme was resuscitated in Brother Nectario Maria's *Juan Colón Was a Spanish Jew* in 1971.[32] Next, we will probably be told that *The Merchant of Venice* was an accurate depiction of medieval Jewish life, after all. And, from there, that the International Jewish Bolshevik Banking Conspiracy really exists, and has since the days of the Illuminati takeover of the Masonic Orders. One hopes the Jewish Defense League doesn't rally to defend these "interpretations" of history as readily as it jumped aboard the "Columbus as Jew" bandwagon.[33]

Other Contenders

By conservative count, there are presently 253 books and articles devoted specifically to the question of Columbus' origin and national/ethnic identity. Another 300–odd essays or full volumes address the same questions to some extent while pursuing other matters.[34] Claims to his character, and some imagined luster therefrom, have been extended not only by the four peoples already discussed, but by Corsica, Greece, Chios, Majorca, Aragon, Galicia, France, and Poland.[35] One can only wait with baited breath to see whether or not the English might not weigh in with a quincentennial assertion that he was actually a Britain born and bred, sent to spy on behalf of Their Royal British Majesties. Perhaps the Swedes, Danes, and Norwegians will advance the case that Columbus was actually the descendant of a refugee Viking king, or the Irish that he was a pure Gaelic adherent to the teachings of Saint Brendan. And then there are, of course, the Germans...

In the final analysis, it is patently clear that we really have no idea who Columbus was, where he came from, or where he spent his formative years. It may be that he was indeed born in Genoa, perhaps of some "degree of Jewish blood," brought up in Portugal, and ultimately nationalized as a citizen of Spain, Province of Aragon. Perhaps he also spent portions of his childhood being educated in Greek and Latin while residing in Corsica, Majorca, Chios, or all three. Maybe he had grandparents who had immigrated from what is now Poland and France. It *is* possible that each of the parties now vying for a "piece of the action" in his regard are to some extent correct in their claims. And, to the same extent, it is true that he was actually *of* none of them in the sense that they mean it. He stands, by this definition, not as an Italian, Spaniard, Portuguese, or Jew, but as the quintessential European of his age, the emblematic personality of all that Europe was, had been, and would become in the course of its subsequent expansion across the face of the earth.

As a symbol, then, Christopher Columbus vastly transcends himself. He stands before the bar of history and humanity, culpable not only for his literal deeds on Española, but, in spirit at least, for the carnage and cultural obliteration which attended the conquests of Mexico and Peru during the 1500s. He stands as exemplar of the massacre of Pequots at Mystic in 1637, and of Lord Jeffrey Amherst's calculated distribution of smallpox–laden blankets to the members of Pontiac's confederacy a century and a half later. His spirit informed the policies of John Evans and John Chivington as they set out to exterminate the Cheyennes in Colorado during 1864, and it road with the 7th U.S. Cavalry to Wounded Knee in December of 1890. It guided Alfredo Stroessner's machete–wielding butchers as they strove to eradicate the Aché people of Paraguay during the 1970s, and applauds the policies of Brazil toward the Jivaro, Yanomami, and other Amazon Basin peoples at the present moment.

Too, the ghost of Columbus stood with the British in their wars against the Zulus and various Arab nations, with the United States against the "Moros" of the Philippines, the French against the peoples of Algeria and Indochina, the Belgians in the Congo, the Dutch in Indonesia. He was there for the Opium Wars and the "secret" bombing of Cambodia, for the systematic slaughter of the indigenous peoples of California during the nineteenth century and of the

Mayans in Guatemala during the 1980s. And, yes, he was very much present in the corridors of nazi power, present among the guards and commandants at Sobibor and Treblinka, and within the ranks of the *einsatzgruppen* on the Eastern Front. The Third Reich was, after all, never so much a deviation from as it was a crystallization of the dominant themes—racial supremacism, conquest, and genocide—of the European culture Columbus so ably exemplifies. Nazism was never unique: it was instead only one of an endless succession of "New World Orders" set in motion by "The Discovery." It was neither more nor less detestable than the order imposed by Christopher Columbus upon Española; 1493 or 1943, they are part of the same irreducible whole.

The Specter of Hannibal Lecter

At this juncture, the entire planet is locked, figuratively, in a room with the socio–cultural equivalent of Hannibal Lecter. An individual of consummate taste and refinement, imbued with indelible grace and charm, he distracts his victims with the brilliance of his intellect, even while honing his blade. He is thus able to dine alone upon their livers, his feast invariably candlelit, accompanied by lofty music and a fine wine. Over and over the ritual is repeated, always hidden, always denied in order that it may be continued. So perfect is Lecter's pathology that, from the depths of his scorn for the inferiors upon whom he feeds, he advances himself as their sage and therapist, he who is incomparably endowed with the ability to explain their innermost meanings, he professes to be their savior. His success depends upon being embraced and exalted by those upon whom he preys. Ultimately, so long as Lecter is able to retain his mask of omnipotent gentility, he can never be stopped. The socio–cultural equivalent of Hannibal Lecter is the core of an expansionist European "civilization" which has reached out to engulf the planet.

In coming to grips with Lecter, it is of no useful purpose to engage in sympathetic biography, to chronicle the nuances of his childhood, and catalogue his many and varied achievements, whether real or imagined. The recounting of such information is at best diversionary, allowing him to remain at large just that much longer. More often, it inadvertently serves to perfect his mask, enabling him not only to maintain his enterprise, but to pursue it with ever more arrogance and efficiency. At worst, the biographer is aware of the intrinsic evil lurking beneath the subject's veneer of civility, but—because of morbid fascination and a desire to participate vicariously—deliberately obfuscates the truth in order that his homicidal activities may continue unchecked. The biographer thus reveals not only a willing complicity in the subject's crimes, but a virulent pathology of his or her own. Such is and has always been the relationship of "responsible scholarship" to expansionist Europe and its derivative societies.

The sole legitimate function of information compiled about Lecter is that which will serve to unmask him and thereby lead to his apprehension. The purpose of apprehension is not to visit retribution upon the psychopath—he is, after all, by definition mentally ill and consequently not in control of his more lethal impulses—but to put an end to his activities. It is even theoretically possible that, once he is disempowered, he can be cured. The point, however, is to understand what he is and what he does well enough to stop him from doing it. This is the role which must be assumed by scholarship vis-à-vis Eurosupremacy, if scholarship itself is to have any positive and constructive meaning. Scholarship is *never* "neutral" or "objective"; it *always* works either for the psychopath or against him, to mystify socio-cultural reality or to decode it, to make corrective action possible or to prevent it.

It may well be that there are better points of departure for intellectual endeavors to capture the real form and meaning of Eurocentrism than the life, times, and legacy of Christopher Columbus. Still, since Eurocentrists the world over have so evidently clasped hands in utilizing him as a (perhaps *the*) preeminent signifier of their collective heritage, and are doing so with such an apparent sense of collective jubilation, the point has been rendered effectively moot. Those who seek to devote their scholarship to apprehending the psychopath who sits in our room thus have no alternative but to use him as a primary vehicle of articulation. In order to do so, we must approach him through deployment of the analytical tools which allow him to be utilized as a medium of explanation, a lens by which to shed light upon phenomena such as the mass psychologies of fascism and racism, a means by which to shear Eurocentrism of its camouflage, exposing its true contours, revealing the enduring coherence of the dynamics which forged its evolution.

Perhaps through such efforts we can begin to genuinely comprehend the seemingly incomprehensible fact that so many groups are presently queuing up to associate themselves with a man from whose very memory wafts the cloying stench of tyranny and genocide. From there, it may be possible to at last crack the real codes of meaning underlying the sentiments of the Nuremberg rallies, those spectacles on the plazas of Rome during which fealty was pledged to Mussolini, and that amazing red-white-and-blue, tie-a-yellow-ribbon frenzy gripping the U.S. public much more lately. If we force ourselves to see things clearly, we can understand. If we can understand, we can apprehend. If we can apprehend, perhaps we can stop the psychopath before he kills again. We are obligated to try, from a sense of sheer self-preservation, if nothing else. Who knows, we may even succeed. But first we must stop lying to ourselves, or allowing others to do the lying for us, about who it is with whom we now share our room.

Notes

1. *See*, for example, Irving Louis Horowitz, *Genocide: State Power and Mass Murder* (New Brunswick, New Jersey: Transaction Books, 1976); and Elie Weisel, *Legends of Our Time* (New York: Holt, Rinehart and Winston Publishers, 1968). The theme is crystallized in Roger Manvell and Fraenkel Heinrich, *Incomparable Crime; Mass Extermination in the 20th Century: The Legacy of Guilt* (London: Hinemann Publishers, 1967).

2. *See*, for example, Richard Falk, "Ethnocide, Genocide, and the Nuremberg Tradition of Moral Responsibility," in *Philosophy, Morality, and International Affairs*, Virginia Held, Sidney Morganbesser and Thomas Nagel, eds. (New York: Oxford University Press, 1974), pp. 123–37; Monroe C. Beardsley, "Reflections on Genocide and Ethnocide," in *Genocide in Paraguay*, Richard Arens, ed. (Philadelphia: Temple University Press, 1976), pp. 85–101; and Robert Jaulin, *L'Ethnocide à travers Les Amériques* (Paris: Gallimard Publishers, 1972), and *La décivilisation, politique et pratique de l'ethnocide* (Brussels: Presses Universitaires de France, 1974).

3. Assaults upon thinking deviating from Eurocentric mythology have been published with increasing frequency in U.S. mass circulation publications such as *Time, Newsweek, U.S. News and World Report, Forbes, Commentary, Scientific American*, and the *Wall Street Journal* throughout 1990–91. A perfect illustration for our purposes here is Jeffrey Hart, "Discovering Columbus," *National Review* (15 Oct. 1990), pp. 56–57.

4. *See* Samuel Eliot Morison, ed. and trans., *Journals and Other Documents on the Life and Voyages of Christopher Columbus* (New York: Heritage Publishers, 1963).

5. The letter of appointment to these positions, signed by Ferdinand and Isabella, and dated May 28, 1493, is quoted in full in Benjamin Keen, trans., *The Life of the Admiral Christopher Columbus by His Son Ferdinand* (New Brunswick, New Jersey: Rutgers University Press, 1959), pp. 105–06.

6. The best sources on Columbus' policies are Troy Floyd, *The Columbus Dynasty in the Caribbean, 1492–1526* (Albuquerque: University of New Mexico Press, 1973); and Stuart B. Schwartz, *The Iberian Mediterranean and Atlantic Traditions in the Formation of Columbus as a Colonizer* (Minneapolis: University of Minnesota Press, 1986).

7. Regarding the 8–million figure, *see* Sherburn F. Cook and Borah Woodrow, *Essays in Population History*, Vol. I (Berkeley: University of California Press, 1971), esp. Chap. VI. The 3–million figure pertaining to the year 1496 derives from a survey conducted by Bartolomé de Las Casas in that year, covered in J. B. Thatcher, *Christopher Columbus*, Vol. 2 (New York: Putnam's Sons Publishers, 1903–1904), p. 348ff.

8. For summaries of the Spanish census records, *see* Lewis Hanke, *The Spanish Struggle for Justice in the Conquest of America* (Philadelphia: University of Pennsylvania Press, 1947), p. 200ff. *See* also Salvador de Madariaga, *The Rise of the Spanish American Empire* (London: Hollis and Carter Publishers, 1947).

9. For aggregate estimates of the pre–contact indigenous population of the Caribbean Basin, *see* William Denevan, ed., *The Native Population of the Americas in 1492* (Madison: University of Wisconsin Press, 1976); Henry Dobyns, *Their Numbers Become Thinned: Native American Population Dynamics in Eastern North America* (Knoxville: University of Tennessee Press, 1983); and Russell Thornton, *American Indian Holocaust and Survival: A Population History Since 1492* (Norman: University of Oklahoma Press, 1987). For additional information, *see* Henry Dobyns' bibliographic *Native American Historical Demography* (Bloomington: University of Indiana Press, 1976).

10. These figures are utilized in numerous studies. One of the more immediately accessible is Leo Kuper, *Genocide: Its Political Use in the Twentieth Century* (New Haven, Connecticut: Yale University Press, 1981).

11. *See* Henry F. Dobyns, "Estimating American Aboriginal Population: An Appraisal of Techniques with a New Hemispheric Estimate," *Current Anthropology*, No. 7, pp. 395–416.

12. An overall pursuit of this theme will be found in P. M. Ashburn, *The Ranks of Death* (New York: Coward Publishers, 1947). *See* also John Duffy, *Epidemics in Colonial America* (Baton Rouge: Louisiana State University Press, 1953). Broader and more sophisticated articulations of the same idea are embodied in Alfred W. Crosby, Jr., *The Columbia Exchange: Biological and Cultural Consequences of 1492* (Westport, Connecticut: Greenwood Press, 1972), and *Ecological Imperialism: The Biological Expansion of Europe, 900–1900* (Melbourne, Australia: Cambridge University Press, 1986).

13. One of the more thoughtful elaborations on this theme may be found in Bradley F. Smith, *Reaching Judgement at Nuremberg* (New York: Basic Books, 1977).

14. *See* Tzvetan Todorov, *The Conquest of America* (New York: Harper and Row Publishers, 1984).

15. Kirkpatrick Sale, *The Conquest of Paradise: Christopher Columbus and the Columbian Legacy* (New York: Alfred A. Knopf Publishers, 1990), p. 155.

16. Bartolomé de las Casas, *The Spanish Colonie (Brevísima revación)* University Microfilms reprint, 1966).

17. Bartolomé de Las Casas, *Historia de las Indias*, Vol. 3, Augustin Millares Carlo and Lewis Hanke, eds. (Mexico City: Fondo de Cultura Económica, 1951), esp. Chap. 29.

18. Bartolomé de Las Casas, quoted in J. B. Thatcher, op. cit., p. 348ff.

19. *See* Lewis Hanke, *Aristotle and the American Indians: A Study in Race Prejudice in the Modern World* (Chicago: Henry Regnery Company, 1959). *See* also Rob Williams, *The American Indian in Western Legal Thought* (London: Oxford University Press, 1989).

20. The most succinctly competent overview of this subject matter is probably Robert Cecil, *The Myth of the Master Race: Alfred Rosenberg and Nazi Ideology* (New York: Dodd and Mead Company, 1972).

21. The polemics of Columbus' strongest supporters among his contemporaries amplify this point. *See*, for example, Oviedo, *Historia general y natural de las Indias* (Seville, 1535; Salamanca, 1547, 1549) (Valladoid, 1557) (Madrid: Academia Historica, 1851–55), esp. Chaps. 29, 30, 37.

22. Kirkpatrick Sale, op. cit., p. 156.

23. On Columbus' written expression, *see* V. I. Milani, "The Written Language of Christopher Columbus," *Forum italicum* (1973). *See* also Cecil Jane, "The question of Literacy of Christopher Columbus," *Hispanic American Historical Review*, Vol. 10 (1930).

24. On Columbus' signature, *see* J. B. Thatcher, op. cit., p. 454.

25. City of Genoa, *Christopher Columbus: Documents and Proofs of His Genoese Origin* (Genoa: Instituto d'Arti Grafiche, 1931) (English language edition, 1932).

26. José de la Torre, *Beatriz Enríquez de Harana* (Madrid: Iberoamericana Publishers, 1933).

27. Enrique de Gandia, *Historia de Cristóbal Colón: analisis crítico* (Buenos Aires, 1942).

28. Manuel Luciano de Silva, *Columbus Was 100% Portuguese* (Bristol, Rhode Island: self–published, 1989).

29. Simon Weisenthal, *Sails of Hope* (New York: Macmillan Publishers, 1973).

30. Henry Vignaud, "Columbus a Spaniard and a Jew?" *American History Review*, Vol. 18 (1913). This initial excursion into the idea was followed in more depth by Francisco Martínez in his *El descubrimiento de América y las joyas de doña Isabel* (Seville, 1916); and Jacob Wasserman in *Christoph Columbus* (Berlin: S. Fisher Publishers, 1929).

31. Salvador de Madariaga, *Christopher Columbus* (London: Oxford University Press, 1939). His lead was followed by Armando Alvarez Pedroso in an essay, "Cristóbal Colón no fue hebero" (*Revista de Historica de América*, 1942) and Antonio Ballesteros y Beretta in *Cristóbal Colón y el descubrimiento de América* (Barcelona/Buenos Aires: Savat Publishers, 1945).

32. Brother Nectario Maria, *Juan Colón Was A Spanish Jew* (New York: Cedney Publishers, 1971).

33. A much sounder handling of the probabilities of early Jewish migration to the Americas may be found in Meyer Keyserling, *Christopher Columbus and the Participation of the Jews in the Spanish and Portuguese Discoveries* (Longmans, Green Publishers, 1893) (reprinted 1963).

34. For a complete count, *see* Simonetta Conti, *Un secolo di bibliografia colombiana 1880–1985* (Genoa: Cassa di Risparmio di Genova e Imperia, 1986).

35. These claims are delineated and debunked in Jacques Heers, *Christophe Columb* (Paris: Hachette Publishers, 1981).

Since Predator Came

A Survey of Native North America Since 1492*

> History, history! We fools, what do we know or care? History begins for
> us with murder and enslavement, not with discovery. No, we are not
> Indians, but we are men of their world. The blood means nothing; the
> spirit, the ghost of the land moves in the blood, moves the blood. It is we
> who ran to the shore naked, we who cried "Heavenly Man!" These are
> the inhabitants of our souls, our murdered souls that lie ... agh.
>
> *William Carlos Williams*

Before October 12, 1492, the day Christopher Columbus first washed up on
a Caribbean beach, North America had been long endowed with an abundant
and exceedingly complex cluster of civilizations. Having continuously occupied the continent for at least 50,000 years, the native inhabitants evidenced a
total population of perhaps 15 million, cities as large as the 40,000–resident
urban center at Cahokia (in present–day Illinois), highly advanced conceptions
of architecture and engineering, spiritual traditions embodying equivalents to
modern eco–science, refined knowledge of pharmacology and holistic medicine, and highly sophisticated systems of governance, trade, and diplomacy.[1]
The traditional economies of the continent were primarily agricultural, based
in environmentally sound farming procedures which originated well over half
the vegetal foodstuffs now consumed by peoples the world over.[2] By and large,
the indigenous societies demonstrating such attainments were organized along
extremely egalitarian lines, with real property held collectively, and matrifo-
cality a normative standard.[3] War, at least in the Euro–derived sense the term
has today, was virtually unknown.[4]

---

*An earlier version of this essay first appeared in the *Covert Action Information Bulletin*,
No. 40 (Spring 1992).

The "Columbian Encounter," of course, unleashed a predatory, five–century–long cycle of European conquest, genocide, and colonization in the "New World," a process which changed the face of Native America beyond all recognition. Indeed, over the first decade of Spanish presence in the Caribbean, the period in which Columbus himself served as governor, the mold was set for all that would follow. By 1496, the policies of slavery (*encomiendo*) and wanton slaughter implemented by the "Great Discoverer" had, in combination with the introduction of Old World pathogens to which they had no immunity, reduced the native Taino population of just one island, Española (presently the Dominican Republic and Haiti), from as many as 8 million to less than 3 million. Six years later, the Tainos had been diminished to fewer than 100,000, and, in 1542, only 200 could be found by Spanish census–takers.[5] Thereafter, the "Indians" of Española were declared extinct, along with the remainder of the indigenous peoples of the Caribbean Basin, an overall body which had numbered upwards of 14 million only a generation before.[6]

In North America, a similar dynamic was set in motion by the 1513 expedition of Ponce de Léon into Florida. The resulting smallpox pandemic spanned the continent, and before it had run its course in 1524, it had destroyed about three–quarters of all indigenous people north of the Río Grande. This was only the beginning. Between 1520 and 1890, no fewer than 41 smallpox epidemics and pandemics were induced among North American Indians. To this must be added dozens of lethal outbreaks of measles, whooping cough, tuberculosis, bubonic plague, typhus, cholera, typhoid, diphtheria, scarlet fever, pleurisy, mumps, venereal disease, and the common cold.[7] The corresponding attrition of native population by disease has usually been treated as a tragic but wholly inadvertent and unintended by–product of contact between Indians and Europeans. Such was certainly not the case in all instances, however, as is attested by the fact that the so–called King Philip's War of 1675–76, fought between the Wampanoag and Narragansett nations and English colonists, resulted largely from the Indians' belief that the latter had deliberately inculcated smallpox among them.[8]

That such perceptions of British tactics and intentions were hardly far–fetched is amply borne out by written orders issuing from Lord Jeffrey Amherst in 1763, instructing a subordinate named Bouquet to infect the members of Pontiac's Algonquin confederacy "by means of [smallpox contaminated] blankets as well as ... every other means to extirpate this execrable race." A few days later, it was reported to Amherst that "[W]e gave them two blankets and a handkerchief out of the smallpox hospital. I hope it will have the desired effect." It did. At a minimum, 100,000 Indians died in the epidemic brought on by Amherst's resort to biological warfare.[9] In a similar instance, occurring in 1836, the U.S. Army knowingly distributed smallpox–laden blankets among the Missouri River Mandans; the resulting pandemic claimed as many as a quarter–million native lives.[10]

Beginning in the early seventeenth century, with the establishment of England's Plymouth and Virginia colonies, and the Dutch toehold at New Amsterdam, the eradication of North America's indigenous population assumed much cruder forms. A classic example occurred on the night of May 26, 1637, when the British surrounded the Pequot town of Mystic (Pennsylvania), set it ablaze, and then slaughtered some 800 fleeing men, women, and children, hacking them to pieces with axes and swords.[11] Such "incidents" occurred with ever greater frequency throughout most of the eighteenth century, a period which found Britain and France engaged in the "French and Indian Wars," a protracted series of struggles in North America to determine which country would wield ultimate hegemony over the continent. While the outcome of these contests eventually proved all but irrelevant to the European colonial powers, given the subsequent revolt and decolonization of the initial 13 U.S. states, the nature of the fighting created a context in which indigenous nations were increasingly compelled to battle one another to the death. The reduction of the indigenous population was thereby accelerated dramatically.[12]

Enter the United States

For its part, the fledgling United States embarked almost immediately upon a course of territorial acquisition far more ambitious than any exhibited by its Euro–colonial precursors. Although it renounced rights of conquest and pledged to conduct its affairs with Indians in "utmost good faith" via the 1789 Northwest Ordinance, the United States comported itself otherwise from the outset.[13] From 1810 to 1814, a succession of extremely brutal military campaigns were conducted against the followers of the Shawnee leader, Tecumseh, in the Ohio River Valley, and against the Creek Confederacy farther south.[14] With native military capacity east of the Mississippi thus eliminated, the government launched, during the 1820s and 1830s, a policy of forced relocation of entire indigenous nations to points west of that river, "clearing" the eastern United States more or less *en toto* for repopulation by white "settlers."[15] Attrition among the affected populations was quite severe; more than half of all Cherokees, for example, died along the 1,500–mile "Trail of Tears," over which they were marched at bayonet–point.[16] This federal "removal policy" was to find echoes, of course, in the articulation of *"lebensraumpolitik"* by Adolf Hitler a century later.[17]

To cast a veneer of legality over his government's conduct, Chief Justice John Marshall penned a series of high court opinions during the 1820s and 1830s, based in large part upon the medieval Doctrine of Discovery. He remained on firm juridical ground long enough to contend that the doctrine imparted a right to the United States to acquire Indian territory by treaty, a matter which led to ratification of at least 371 such nation–to–nation agreements over the next four decades. In a bizarre departure from established principles of international law, however, Marshall also argued that the United States possessed an inherently "higher" sovereignty than the nations with which it was treating: Indians held no right *not* to sell their land to the United States, in his view, at whatever price the United States cared to offer. Within this formulation, *any* resistance by "the savages" to the taking of their territories could thus be cast as an "act of war" theoretically "justifying" a U.S. "response" predicated in armed force.[18] By 1903 the "Marshall Doctrine" had evolved—and the indigenous ability to offer physical resistance had been sufficiently crushed—to the point that the Supreme Court was confident in asserting an "intrinsic" federal "plenary" (full) power over all Indians within its borders, releasing the United States from any treaty obligations it found inconvenient while leaving the land title it purported to have gained through the various treaty instruments intact. In conjunction with this novel notion of international jurisprudence, the high court simultaneously expressed the view that the government enjoyed "natural" and permanent "trust" prerogatives over all residual native property.[19]

Meanwhile, having consolidated its grip on the eastern portion of its claimed territoriality during the 1840s—and having militarily seized "rights" to the northern half of Mexico as well—the United States proclaimed itself to be imbued with a "Manifest Destiny" to expand westward to the Pacific.[20] There being essentially no land available within this conception for Indian use and occupancy, a rhetoric of outright extermination was quickly adopted both by federal policy makers and by a sizable segment of the public at large.[21] These sentiments led unerringly to a lengthy chain of large–scale massacres of Indians in the Great Plains and Basin regions by U.S. troops. Among the worst were the slaughters perpetrated at the Blue River (Nebraska, 1854), Bear River (Idaho, 1863), Sand Creek (Colorado, 1864), Washita River (Oklahoma, 1868), Sappa Creek (Kansas, 1875), Camp Robinson (Nebraska, 1878), and Wounded Knee (South Dakota, 1890).[22] In 1894, the U.S. Census Bureau observed that the United States had waged "more than 40" separate wars against native people in barely a century, inflicting some number of fatalities "very much greater" than its minimum estimate of 30,000 in the process.[23]

The indigenous death toll generated by "private actions" during U.S. continental expansion was also, the Census Bureau admitted, "quite substantial." In all probability, it was far higher than that stemming from formal military involvement, given that the native population of the State of California alone was reduced from approximately 300,000 in 1800 to less than 20,000 in 1890, "chiefly [because of] the cruelties and wholesale massacres perpetrated by ... miners and the early settlers."[24] In Texas, to take another prominent example, a bounty was paid for the scalp of any Indian brought to a government office, no questions asked: "The facts of history are plain. Most Texas Indians [once the most diverse population in North America] were exterminated or brought to the brink of extinction by [Euroamerican civilians] who often had no more regard for the life of an Indian than they had for that of a dog, sometimes less."[25] The story in other sectors of the western United States, while sometimes less spectacular, reveals very much the same pattern. As the indigenous population was liquidated—along with the buffalo and other animal species consciously exterminated in order to deny Indians a "commissary" once their agricultural economies had been obliterated by the invaders—white settlers replaced them on the vast bulk of their land.[26]

By 1890, fewer than 250,000 Indians remained alive within the United States, a degree of decimation extending into the upper 90th percentile.[27] The survivors were lodged on a patchwork of "reservations" even then being dismantled through application of what was called the "General Allotment Act."[28] Under provision of this statute, effected in 1887, a formal eugenics code was utilized to define who was (and who was not) "Indian" by U.S. "standards."[29] Those who could, and were willing to, prove to federal satisfaction that they were "of one–half or more degree of Indian blood," and to accept U.S. citizenship into the bargain, received a deed to an individual land parcel, typically of 160 acres or less.[30] Once each person with sufficient "blood quantum" had received his or her allotment of land, the remaining reservation land was declared "surplus" and opened up to non–Indian homesteading, corporate acquisition, or conversion into national parks and forests. Through this mechanism, the best 100 million acres of the reserved native land base was stripped away by 1930, the Indians ever more concentrated within the 50 million arid or semi–arid acres—about 2.5 percent of their original holdings— left to them.[31] The model was later borrowed by the apartheid government of South Africa in developing its "racial homeland" system of territorial apportionment.[32]

The Contemporary Era

Culmination of this trajectory in U.S. colonial administration of Indian Country occurred during the mid–1950s, with the enactment of a series of "termination" statutes by which the federal government unilaterally dissolved more than 100 indigenous nations and their reservation areas.[33] Concomitantly, legislation was effected to "encourage" the relocation of large numbers of Indians from the remaining reservations to selected urban centers, a strategy designed to preclude reemergence of social cohesion within most land–based native communities.[34] Although it was suspended in the late 1970s, the federal relocation program had by 1990 fostered a native diaspora which found more than half of all indigenous people in the United States, a total of about 880,000 persons, scattered in the ghettoes of cities.[35]

The government's termination and relocation policies coupled quite well with other techniques employed by the Bureau of Indian Affairs (BIA) to undermine the socio–cultural integrity of native existence. Salient in this regard is a generations–long program of "blind adoptions" in which Indian babies are placed for adoption with non–Indian families, their birth records permanently sealed so they can never know their true heritage.[36] Similarly, beginning in the 1870s and continuing into the present moment, the BIA administered a system of boarding schools to which indigenous children were sent, often for a decade or more, without being allowed to return home, speak their native languages, practice their religions, or otherwise manifest their identity as Indians.[37] Encompassed under the benign–sounding rubric of "assimilation," both of these youth–oriented undertakings were and are blatant violations of the provision of the 1948 Convention on Punishment and Prevention of the Crime of Genocide, which makes it a crime against humanity for a government to engage in the systematic forced transfer of the children of a targeted racial or ethnic group to another group.[38] Contemporary violation of another provision of the Genocide Convention may be found in a program of involuntary sterilization imposed by the BIA's "Indian Health Service" upon approximately 40 percent of the female population of childbearing age during the 1970s.[39]

Ironically, the final and complete dissolution of Native North America seems to have been averted mainly by the fact that the barren areas left to native habitation after allotment turned out to be inordinately rich in mineral resources. Current estimates suggest that about two–thirds of all U.S. domestic uranium deposits, a quarter of the readily accessible low sulphur coal, a fifth of the oil and natural gas, and substantial deposits of copper and other ores lie within reservation boundaries.[40] Government planners discovered by 1920 that certain advantages could be maintained in terms of their ability to control the pace and nature of resource extraction, royalty rates, and the like, through exercise of federal "trust responsibilities" over indigenous assets.[41] The same principle was seen to pertain to manipulations of water policy throughout the arid West.[42] Such options being unavailable to them should Indian Country as a whole be converted into private property under state and local jurisdiction, it was found to be in the U.S. interest to maintain the majority of reservations as discrete internal colonies.

To this end, the Indian Reorganization Act (IRA) was passed in 1934 to create a federally designed regulatory or "governing" body on most reservations.[43] Although the IRA boards were and are composed exclusively of native people, their authority stems from—and thus their primary allegiance adheres to—the United States rather than their ostensible indigenous constituents; their major function during the half–century of their existence has been to sow confusion, providing an illusion of Indian consent to the systematic Euroamerican expropriation of native resources, and to vociferously denounce any Indian audacious enough to object to the theft. They serve, in effect, as American Indian Movement (AIM) leader Russell Means once put it, as "Vichy Indians."[44] For this reason, their position in Indian Country has been steadily reinforced over the years by passage of additional federal statutes, among them the Indian Civil Rights Act of 1968 and the Indian "Self–Determination" and Educational Assistance Act of 1975.[45]

The results have embodied themselves in situations like the "Hopi–Navajo Land Dispute" in northeastern Arizona, a scenario in which the United States has been able to utilize the carefully tailored pronouncements of two of its puppet governments to create the impression of an inter–Indian conflict requiring federal intervention/resolution as a means of "avoiding bloodshed." Behind this humanitarian facade resides a U.S. governmental/corporate desire to bring about the compulsory relocation of more than 10,000 traditional Navajos from the contested area, a matter which will serve to clear the way for the real objective: the strip mining of more than 20 billion tons of high–quality coal.[46] Comparable circumstances have prevailed with regard to the conversion of the Western Shoshone homeland (Newe Segobia) in Nevada into a U.S. nuclear weapons testing area, removal of more than 90 percent of the 1868 Fort Laramie Treaty Territory from Lakota control, upcoming implementation of the "Alaska Native Claims Settlement Act," and other examples.[47]

Coherent efforts by native people to oppose such manipulations—AIM's resistance during the mid–70s to IRA government collaboration in a plan to transfer title over one–eighth of the Pine Ridge Reservation to the National Forest Service, for example—have been put down by the use of outright counterinsurgency warfare techniques (such as death squads) similar in many respects to the methods employed by U.S. agencies in Asia, Africa, and Latin America.[48] During the Pine Ridge "reign of terror" alone, the body count came to about 70 fatalities and nearly 350 serious physical assaults on AIM members and supporters over a bare three–year period.[49] This was correlated with an outright military–style occupation of the reservation by federal forces, a comprehensive government propaganda campaign directed against the "insurgents," and an extensive series of show trials such as those of the so–called Wounded Knee Leadership during 1974–75, and of the "RESMURS Defendants" (including AIM security leader Leonard Peltier) in 1976–77.[50]

For grassroots Indian people, the broader human costs of ongoing U.S. domination are abundantly clear. The 1.6 million American Indians within the United States remain, nominally at least, the largest per capita land owners in North America.[51] Given the extent of the resources within their land base, Indians should by logical extension comprise the wealthiest "ethnic group" in North American society. Instead, according to the federal government's own statistics, they are the poorest, demonstrating far and away the lowest annual and lifetime incomes, the highest rate of unemployment, lowest rate of pay when employed, and lowest level of educational attainment of any North American population aggregate. Correspondingly, they suffer, by decisive margins, the greatest incidence of malnutrition and diabetes, death by exposure, tuberculosis, infant mortality, plague, and similar maladies.[52] These conditions, in combination with the general disempowerment which spawns them, breed an unremitting sense of rage, frustration, and despair which is reflected in the spiraling rates of domestic and other forms of intragroup violence, alcoholism and resulting death by accident or fetal alcohol syndrome.[53] Consequently, the average life expectancy of a reservation–based Native American male in 1980 was a mere 44.6 years, that of his female counterpart less than three years longer.[54] Such a statistical portrait is obviously more indicative of a Third World environment than that expected of people living within one of the world's most advanced industrial states.

Moving Forward

Plainly, all official polemics to the contrary notwithstanding, the agony induced by 500 years of European/Euroamerican predation in North America has done anything but diminish at this juncture. For the indigenous people of the continent it has become obvious there are no real alternatives except either to renew their commitment to struggle for survival or to finally pass into the realm of extinction which has been relentlessly projected for them since the predator's arrival on their shores. For everyone else, the situation is rapidly becoming—or in some cases has already become—much the same. The time has arrived when a choice *must* be made: Non–Indians, in both the New World and the Old, must decide whether they wish to be a willing part of the final gnawing on the bones of their native victims, or whether they are at last prepared to join hands with Native North America, ending the wanton consumption of indigenous lands and lives which has marked the nature of our relationship to date.

The sort of alliance at issue no longer represents, as it did in the past, an exercise in altruism for non–Indians. Anti–imperialism and opposition to racism, colonialism, and genocide, while worthy enough stances in and of themselves, are no longer the fundamental issues at hand. Ultimately, the same system of predatory goals and values which has so busily and mercilessly consumed the people of the land these past five centuries has increasingly set about consuming the land itself. Not only indigenous peoples, but the lands to which they are irrevocably linked, are now dying. When the land itself dies, it is a certainty that *no* humans can survive. The struggle which confronts us—*all* of us—is thus a struggle to save our collective habitat, to maintain it as a "survivable" environment, not only for ourselves, but for the generations to come. Self–evidently, this cannot be approached either from the posture of the predator, or any other position which allows the predator to continue with business as usual. At long last, we have arrived at the point where there is a tangible, even overriding, confluence of interest between natives and non–natives.

The crux of the matter rests, not merely in resistance to the predatory nature of the present Eurocentric status quo, but in conceiving viable socio–cultural alternatives. Here, the bodies of indigenous knowledge evidenced in the context of Native America at the point of the European invasion—large–scale societies which had perfected ways of organizing themselves into psychologically fulfilling wholes, experiencing very high standards of material life, and *still* maintaining environmental harmony—shine like a beacon in the night. The information required to recreate this reality is still in place in many indigenous cultures. The liberation of significant sectors of Native America stands to allow this knowledge to once again be actualized in the "real world," not to recreate indigenous societies as they once were, but to recreate themselves as they *can be* in the future. Therein lies the model—the laboratory, if you will—from which a genuinely liberatory and sustainable alternative can be cast for all humanity. In a very real sense, then, the fate of Native America signifies the fate of the planet. It follows that it is incumbent upon every conscious human—red, white, black, brown, or yellow, old or young, male or female—to do whatever is within their power to ensure the next half–millennium heralds an antithesis to the last.

Notes

1. For a good survey of the data indicating native occupancy in North America for 50 millennia or more, *see* Jeffrey Goodman, *American Genesis: The American Indian and the Origins of Modern Man* (New York: Summit Books, 1981). On population size, *see* Henry F. Dobyns, *Their Numbers Become Thinned: Native American Population Dynamics in Eastern North America* (Knoxville: University of Tennessee Press, 1983). On Cahokia, *see* Melin T. Fowler, "A Pre–Columbian Urban Center on the Mississippi," *Scientific American*, No. 233 (1975), pp. 92–101. On architecture and engineering, *see* Peter Nabokov and Robert Easton, *Native American Architecture* (London/New York: Oxford University Press, 1988). On medicine and pharmacology, *see* Virgil Vogel, *American Indian Medicine* (Norman: University of Oklahoma Press, 1975). On governance and diplomacy, *see*, for example, William Brandon, *Old Worlds for New: Reports from the New World and Their Effect on the Development of Social Thought in Europe, 1500–1800* (Athens: Ohio University Press, 1986).

2. According to even a hostile source like R. Douglas Hurt, in his *Indian Agriculture in America: Prehistory to the Present* (Lawrence: University Press of Kansas, 1987), about two–thirds of the dietary requirements of Native North America were met by "horticultural" rather than "hunting and gathering" means. As to the variety of vegetal foodstuffs developed by pre–contact indigenous people in this hemisphere and then adopted elsewhere, *see* Jack Weatherford, *Indian Givers: How the Indians of the Americas Transformed the World* (New York: Crown Publishers, 1988).

3. A good, if somewhat overstated, examination of Native North American sexuality and gender relations may be found in Paula Gunn Allen, *The Sacred Hoop: Recovering the Feminine in American Indian Traditions* (Boston: Beacon Press, 1986).

4. *See* Tom Holm, "Patriots and Pawns: State Use of American Indians in the Military and the Process of Nativization in the United States," in *The State of Native America: Colonization, Genocide and Resistance*, M. Annette Jaimes, ed. (Boston: South End Press, 1992).

5. *See* Kirkpatrick Sale, *The Conquest of Paradise: Christopher Columbus and the Columbian Legacy* (New York: Alfred A. Knopf Publishers, 1990).

6. Ibid., citing Woodrow W. Borah and Sherburn F. Cook.

7. Henry F. Dobyns, op. cit., pp. 15–23.

8. *See* Douglas Edward Leach, *Flintlocks and Tomahawks: New England in King Philip's War* (New York: W. W. Norton, 1958).

9. E. Wagner Stearn and Allen E. Stearn, *The Effects of Smallpox on the Destiny of the Amerindian* (Boston: Bruce Humphries, 1945), pp. 44–45; P. M. Ashburn, *The Ranks of Death* (New York: Coward, 1947).

10. The dispensing of smallpox–infected blankets at Fort Clark is covered in Russell Thornton, *American Indian Holocaust and Survival: A Population History Since 1492* (Norman: University of Oklahoma Press, 1987), pp. 94–96.

11. The estimate of Pequot casualties derives from an extremely conservative source. *See* Robert M. Utley and Wilcomb E. Washburn, *Indian Wars* (Boston: Houghton–Mifflin, 1977), p. 42.

12. An excellent analysis of these dynamics can be found in Francis Jennings, *The Invasion of America: Indians, Colonialism, and the Cant of Conquest* (New York: W. W. Norton, 1976).

13. 1 *Stat.* 50; for background, *see* Thomas Perkins Abernathy, *Western Lands and the American Revolution* (New York: Russell and Russell, 1959).

14. On Tecumseh, *see* John Sugden, *Tecumseh's Last Stand* (Norman: University of Oklahoma Press, 1985). On the Redsticks, *see* Joel W. Martin, *Sacred Revolt: The Muskogees' Struggle for a New World* (Boston: Beacon Press, 1991).

15. The policy was implemented under provision of the Indian Removal Act (Ch. 148, 4 *Stat.* 411), passed on May 28, 1830. For details, *see* Grant Foreman, *Indian Removal: The Immigration of the Five Civilized Tribes* (Norman: University of Oklahoma Press, 1953).

16. *See* Russell Thornton, "Cherokee Population Losses During the Trail of Tears: A New Perspective and a New Estimate," *Ethnohistory*, No. 31 (1984), pp. 289–300.

17. The *lebensraum* concept is laid out in Adolf Hitler's *Mein Kampf* (Verlag FRZ, Eher Nachf, G.M.B.H., 1925). *See* also Robert Cecil, *The Myth of the Master Race: Alfred Rosenberg and Nazi Ideology* (New York: Dodd, Mead & Co., 1972).

18. The sequences of cases consists of *Johnson v. McIntosh* (21 U.S. 98 [Wheat.] 543 [1823]); *Cherokee Nation v. Georgia* (30 U.S. [5 Pet.] 1 [1831]); and *Worcester v. Georgia* (31 U.S. [6 Pet.] 551 [1832]).

19. *Lonewolf v. Hitchcock* (187 U.S. 553 [1903]). A prelude to articulation of this juridical absurdity may be found in *U.S. v. Kagama* (118 U.S. 375 [1886]).

20. For a brilliant elaboration of this theme, *see* Reginald Horsman, *Race and Manifest Destiny: The Origins of Racial Anglo–Saxonism* (Cambridge: Harvard University Press, 1981).

21. *See*, for example, David Svaldi, *Sand Creek and the Rhetoric of Extermination: A Case–Study in Indian–White Relations* (Washington, DC: University Press of America, 1989).

22. On Bear River, *see* Brigham D. Madsen, *The Shoshone Frontier and the Bear River Massacre* (Salt Lake City: University of Utah Press, 1985). On Sand Creek and the Washita, *see* Stan Hoig, *The Sand Creek Massacre* (Norman: University of Oklahoma Press, 1961), and *The Battle of the Washita: The Sheridan–Custer Indian Campaign of 1867–69* (Lincoln: University of Nebraska Press, 1976). On Blue River, *see* Mari Sandoz, *Crazy Horse: The Strange Man of the Oglalas* (Lincoln: University of Nebraska Press, 1961), pp. 63–85; on Sappa Creek and Camp Robinson, *see* her *Cheyenne Autumn* (New York: Avon Books, 1964). For an excellent overview of the sort of warfare waged against the indigenous people of the plains region, *see* Ralph Andrist, *The Long Death: The Last Days of the Plains Indians* (New York: Collier Books, 1964).

23. U.S. Bureau of the Census, *Report on Indians Taxed and Indians Not Taxed in the United States (except Alaska) at the Eleventh U.S. Census: 1890* (Washington, DC: U.S. Government Printing Office, 1894), pp. 637–38.

24. James M. Mooney, "Population," in *Handbook of the Indians North of Mexico,* Frederick W. Dodge, ed. (Washington, DC: Vol. 2, Bureau of American Ethnology, Bulletin No. 30, Smithsonian Institution, 1910), pp. 286–87.

25. W. W. Newcome, Jr., *The Indians of Texas* (Austin: University of Texas Press, 1961), p. 334.

26. On "eradication" of the North American Bison, *see* Francis Haines, *The Buffalo* (New York: Thomas Y. Crowell, 1970).

27. U.S. Bureau of the Census, *Abstract of the Eleventh Census: 1890* (Washington, DC: U.S. Government Printing Office, 1896).

28. Ch. 119, 24 Stat. 388, now codified as amended at 25 U.S.C. 331 *et seq.* The General Allotment Act is also known as the "Dawes Act" or "Dawes Severalty Act" after its sponsor, Massachusetts Senator Henry M. Dawes.

29. On this aspect, *see* Ward Churchill, "Nobody's Pet Poodle: Jimmie Durham, an Artist for Native America," in Ward Churchill, *Indians Are Us? Genocide and Colonization in Native North America* (Monroe, Maine: Common Courage Press, 1994).

30. As of 1924, all Native Americans who had not been made U.S. citizens through the allotment process were unilaterally declared to be such *en mass*, and whether they wanted to be or not—through provision of the Indian Citizenship Act (Ch. 233, 43 Stat. 25).

31. *See* Janet A McDonnell, *The Dispossession of the American Indian, 1887–1934* (Bloomington/Indianapolis: Indiana University Press, 1991).

32. On these linkages, *see* George M. Fredrickson, *White Supremacy: A Comparative Study in American and South African History* (London/New York: Oxford University Press, 1981).

33. The "Act" is actually House Concurrent Resolution 108, pronounced on August 1, 1953, which articulated a federal policy of unilaterally dissolving specific native nations. What followed was the "termination"—suspension of federal services to and recognition of the existence of—the Menominee on June 17, 1954 (Ch. 303, 68 *Stat.* 250); the Klamath on August 13, 1954 (Ch. 732, 68 *Stat.* 718, codified as 25 U.S.C. 564 *et seq.*); the "Tribes of Western Oregon" on August 13, 1954 (Ch. 733, 68 *Stat.* 724, codified at 25 U.S.C. 691 *et seq.*); and so on. In all, 109 native nations, or elements of native nations, were terminated by congressional action during the late 1950s. A handful were "restored" to federal recognition during the 1970s.

34. The "Relocation Act" (P.L. 959) was passed in 1956 to provide funding to establish "job training centers" for American Indians in various urban centers, and to finance the relocation of individual Indians and Indian families to these locales. It was coupled with a denial of

funds for similar programs and economic development on the reservations themselves. Those who availed themselves of the "opportunity" for jobs, etc., represented by the federal relocation programs were usually required to sign agreements that they would not return to their respective reservations to live. For further information, *see* Donald L. Fixico, *Termination and Relocation: Federal Indian Policy, 1945–1960* (Albuquerque: University of New Mexico Press, 1986).

35. U.S. Bureau of the Census, *1990 Census of the Population, Preliminary Report* (Washington, DC: U.S. Government Printing Office, 1991).

36. *See* Tillie Blackbear Walker, "American Indian Children: Foster Care and Adoptions," in *Conference on Educational and Occupational Needs of American Indian Women, October 1976*, the U.S. Department of Education, Office of Educational Research and Development, National Institute of Education, (Washington, DC: U.S. Government Printing Office, 1980), pp. 185–210.

37. For a comprehensive overview of this process, *see* Jorgé Noriega, "American Indian Education in the U.S.: Indoctrination for Subordination to Colonialism," in *The State of Native America*, op. cit.

38. For the complete text of the 1948 Genocide Convention, *see* Ian Brownlie, ed., *Basic Documents on Human Rights* (London/New York: Oxford University Press, 1971).

39. *See* Brint Dillingham, "Indian Women and IHS Sterilization Practices," *American Indian Journal*, Vol. 3, No. 1 (Jan. 1977), pp. 27–28. *See* also Janet Larson, "And Then There Were None: IHS Sterilization Practice," *Christian Century*, No. 94 (26 Jan. 1976). *See* also Bill Wagner, "Lo, the Poor and Sterilized Indian," *America*, No. 136 (29 Jan. 1977).

40. On resource distribution, *see* generally, Michael Garrity, "The U.S. Colonial Empire Is as Close as the Nearest Reservation," in *Trilateralism: The Trilateral Commission and Elite Planning for World Government*, Holly Sklar, ed. (Boston: South End Press, 1980), pp. 238–68. *See* also Joseph Jorgenson, ed., *Native Americans and Energy Development II* (Cambridge: Anthropology Resource Center/Seventh Generation Fund, 1984).

41. The prototype for this policy emerged with the BIA's formation of the "Navajo Grand Council" to approve drilling leases at the behest of Standard Oil in 1923. *See* Laurence C. Kelly, *The Navajo Indians and Federal Indian Policy, 1900–1935* (Tucson: University of Arizona Press, 1968).

42. *See* Marianna Guerrero, "American Indian Water Rights: The Blood of Life in Native North America," in *The State of Native America*, op. cit. *See* also Daniel McCool, *Command of the Waters: Iron Triangles, Federal Water Development, and Indian Water* (Berkeley: University of California Press, 1987).

43. The IRA (Ch. 576, 48 *Stat.* 948, now codified at 25 U.S.C. 461–279) is also known as the "Wheeler–Howard Act" after its Senate and House sponsors.

44. Quoted in Rebecca Robbins, "Self–Determination and Subordination: The Past, Present and Future of American Indian Governance," in *The State of Native America*, op. cit. On propaganda functions, *see* Ward Churchill, "'Renegades, Terrorists and Revolutionaries': The U.S. Government's Propaganda War Against the American Indian Movement," *Propaganda Review*, No. 4 (Spring 1989).

45. The Indian Civil Rights Act, P.L. 90–284 (82 *Stat.* 77, codified in part at 25 U.S.C. 1301 *et seq.*) locked indigenous governments—as a "third level" of the *federal* government—into U.S. constitutional requirements. The "self–determination" aspect of the 1975 Act (P.L. 93–638; 88 *Stat.* 2203, codified at 25 U.S.C. 450a and elsewhere in titles 25, 42, and 50, U.S.C.A.)—dubbed the "Self-*Administration* Act" by Russell Means—provides for a

greater degree of Indian employment within the various federal programs used to subordinate native people.

46. On the supposed dispute between the Hopis and Navajos, and the federal–corporate role in fostering it, *see* Jerry Kammer, *The Second Long Walk: The Navajo–Hopi Land Dispute* (Albuquerque: University of New Mexico Press, 1980). *See* also Anita Parlow, *Cry, Sacred Ground: Big Mountain, USA* (Washington, DC: Christic Institute, 1988).

47. On the Western Shoshone, *see* Glenn T. Morris, "The Battle for Newe Segobia: The Western Shoshone Land Rights Struggle," in *Critical Issues in Native North America, Vol. II*, Ward Churchill, ed. (Copenhagen: IWGIA Document 68, 1991), pp. 86–98. On the Black Hills, *see* the special issue of *Wicazo Sa Review*, Vol. IV, No. 1 (Spring 1988). On Alaska, *see* M. C. Berry, *The Alaska Pipeline: The Politics of Oil and Native Land Claims* (Bloomington/Indianapolis: Indiana University Press, 1975).

48. The best overview—including the uranium connection—may be found in Peter Matthiessen, *In the Spirit of Crazy Horse* (New York: Viking Press [2d ed.], 1991). *See* also Rex Weyler, *Blood of the Land: The U.S. Government and Corporate War Against the American Indian Movement* (Philadelphia: New Society [2d ed.], 1992).

49. The term "reign of terror" accrues from an official finding by the U.S. Commission on Civil Rights (*Report of an Investigation: Oglala Sioux Tribe, General Election, 1974*, Rocky Mountain Regional Office, Denver, 1974). For statistical comparison to Third World contexts, *see* Bruce Johansen and Roberto Maestas, *Wasi'chu: The Continuing Indian Wars* (New York: Monthly Review Press, 1978).

50. For detailed analysis, *see* Ward Churchill and Jim Vander Wall, *Agents of Repression: The FBI's Secret Wars Against the Black Panther Party and the American Indian Movement* (Boston: South End Press, 1988). Official use of the term "insurgents"—as opposed to "extremists," or even "terrorists"—vis-à-vis AIM is documented via FBI memoranda in Ward Churchill and Jim Vander Wall, *The COINTELPRO Papers: Documents from the FBI's Secret Wars Against Dissent in the United States* (Boston: South End Press, 1990). On the RESMURS (Reservation Murders) trials, *see* Jim Messerschmidt, *The Trial of Leonard Peltier* (Boston: South End Press, 1983). For a brief overview, *see* "The Bloody Wake of Alcatraz" in this book.

51. This is based on the approximately 50 million acres still designated as reservation land. It should be noted that the United States never acquired even a pretense of legal title via treaties and other "instruments of cession" to fully one-third of the area (about 750 million acres) encompassed by the 48 contiguous states. The larger acreage should be balanced against the fact that, while federal census data recognizes only about one and a half million Indians residing within the U.S., the actual number may well be ten times that; *see* Jack D. Forbes, "Undercounting Native Americans: The 1980 Census and the Manipulation of Racial Identity in the United States," *Wicazo Sa Review*, Vol. VI, No. 1 (Spring 1990).

52. U.S. Department of Health and Human Services, *Chart Series Book* (Washington, DC: Public Health Service, 1988 [HE20.9409.988]).

53. *See* Rosemary Wood, "Health Problems Facing American Indian Women," in U.S. Department of Education, *Conference on Educational and Occupational Needs of American Indian Women*, op. cit. *See* also Charon Asetoyer, "Fetal Alcohol Syndrome—'Chemical Genocide'," in *Indigenous Women on the Move* (Copenhagen: IWGIA Document 66, 1990), pp. 87–92.

54. U.S. Department of Health and Human Services, *Chart Series Book*, op. cit.

Genocide
in the Americas
Landmarks from "Latin" America Since 1492

I become death, the scatterer of worlds.

Bhagavad–Gita

On October 12, 1492, the day Christopher Columbus first set foot in what came to be called the "New World," the Western Hemisphere was inhabited by a population of well over 100 million people.[1] Two centuries later, it is estimated that the indigenous population of the Americas had been diminished by some 90 percent and was continuing to fall steadily.[2] In the United States, the native population bottomed out during the 1890s at slightly over 237,000—a 98 percent reduction from its original size.[3] Such an extreme demographic catastrophe as that evidenced in the United States—indicative of a population "collapse" or "obliteration" rather than of a mere "decline"—is not atypical.[4]

In fact, the average nadir population for surviving indigenous peoples everywhere in the Americas is about 5 percent (meaning we experienced a reduction of 97–98 percent during the years of invasion, conquest, and colonization which have afflicted us all).[5] Moreover, the processes at issue cannot be relegated to some "tragic and regrettable"—but unalterable—past. Instead, they are very much *ongoing* as this is written, imbedded in the policies of the various settler–states of North, South, and Central America, and in the attitudes of the immigrant citizenry of these states.[6]

As I have noted often in my writing and public lectures, the genocide inflicted upon American Indians over the past five centuries is unparalleled in human history, both in terms of its sheer magnitude and in terms of its duration. For the most part, with the exception of occasional forays into describing the real nature of the Columbian endeavor in the Caribbean,[7] I have focused my attention, and that of my readers/listeners, on the genocide perpetrated on my own home ground of North America, mostly by Angloamericans. In this essay, I would like to break with that tradition to some extent, laying out what I take to be a few of the landmarks of the post–Columbian record of genocide perpetrated to the south, in what is presumptuously termed "Latin" America, mostly by those of Iberian origin or descent.

Invasion and Conquest

> Into this sheepfold ... there came some Spaniards who immediately behaved like ravening beasts.... And Spaniards have behaved in no other way during the past 40 years down to the present time, for they are still acting like ravening beasts, killing, terrorizing, afflicting, torturing and destroying the native peoples, doing all this with the strangest and most varied new methods of cruelty, never seen or heard of before.
>
> *Bartolomé de Las Casas, 1550*

In 1519, when the Spanish conquistador Hernan Cortés captured the Mexica (Aztec) capital of Tenochtitlán—a huge metropolis constructed in the midst of a volcanic lake—he first laid siege and allowed a smallpox epidemic to run its course, weakening the city's defenses.[8] Then, after a series of assaults which resulted in the Indians being reduced to the point of almost complete defenselessness— as his letters recount, "They no longer had nor could find any arrows, javelins or stones" with which to respond—he initiated the wholesale slaughter of those who surrendered, were captured, or who were simply trapped by his troops. Twelve thousand people, many of them noncombatants, were butchered in a single afternoon, another 40,000 the following day, before Cortés withdrew because he and his men "could no longer endure the stench of the dead bodies" that lay in the streets.[9]

When the Spaniards returned the next day, their commander surveyed his "starving, dehydrated, and disease–wracked" opponents, already decimated during the previous assaults, and announced his intent to "attack and slay them all."[10] By the time it was over, perhaps two–thirds of Tenochtitlán's population of about 350,000 was dead.[11]

> The people of the city had to walk upon their dead while others swam or drowned in the waters of that wide lake where they had their canoes; indeed, so great was their suffering that it was beyond our understanding how they came to endure it. Countless numbers of men, women and children came out towards us, and in their eager-ness to escape many were pushed into the water where they drowned amidst that multitude of corpses; and it seemed that more than fifty thousand of them had perished from the salt water they had drunk,

their hunger and the vile stench.... And so in the streets where they were we came across such piles of the dead that we were forced to walk on them.[12]

By 1525, with the conquest of the Mexicas complete, one of Cortés' lieutenants, Pedro de Alvardo, mounted a campaign to the south, against the Mayas and other peoples of what are now the far southern portion of Mexico, as well as Guatemala, Belize, western Honduras and Nicaragua, and Panama. As Las Casas described it at the time, they "advanced killing, ravaging, burning, robbing and destroying all the country" as they went.[13]

> By massacres and murders ... they have destroyed and devastated a kingdom more than a hundred leagues square, one of the happiest in the way of fertility and population in the world. This same tyrant [Alvardo] wrote that it was more populous than the kingdom of Mexico; and he told the truth. He and his brothers, together with the others, have killed more than four or five million people in fifteen or sixteen years, from the year 1525 until 1540, and they continue to kill and destroy those who are still left; and so they will kill the remainder.[14]

North of the former Mexica empire, things were much the same, or perhaps worse, during the period of conquest.

> Nuño Beltrán de Guzmán was one of those who led armies to the north, torturing or burning at the stake native leaders, such as the Tarascan king, while seizing or destroying enormous native stores of food. Guzmán later was followed by Alvar Nuñez Cabazza de Baca, by Francisco Vásquez de Coronado, by Francisco de Ibarra, and countless other conquerors and murderers. As elsewhere, disease, depredation, enslavement, and outright massacres combined to extinguish entire Indian cultures in Mexico's northwest.[15]

Meanwhile, Francisco Pizarro's "Conquest of the Incas" in what are now called Peru and Chilé evidenced far less direct killing.[16] In no small part, this was because the conquistadors in this region managed to capture much of the Incan leadership very early on in their campaign, and developed certain methods of "convincing" them to betray their people.

> One ingenious European technique of getting what they wanted involved burying Indian leaders in earth up to their waists.... In that helpless position, they were beaten with whips and [given instructions].... When they did not comply ... more earth was piled about them and the whippings continued. Then more earth. And more beating. At last, says the Spanish informant on this particular matter, "they covered them to the shoulders and finally to the mouths." He

then adds as an afterthought, "I even believe that a great number of natives were burned to death."[17]

By March of 1549, the Portuguese had joined in, with Pedro Alvars Cabral's establishment of his first base of operations at the Bay of Bahia, on the coast of what is now Brazil. For the next decade, Cabral and his colleagues waged a brand of attritional warfare "which destroyed [the natives] little by little," the survivors fleeing into the Amazonian interior.[18] As an unnamed priest explained in a subsequent report to the Church, it was a complete mismatch, the Portuguese, armed with swords and muskets, riding down thousands of unmounted Tupi and Tapuya warriors equipped only with bows and spears. Then "they razed and burned entire villages," the priest said, "which are generally made of dry palm leaves, roasting alive in them those that refused to surrender as slaves."[19] And so it went, area by area, region by region, until the preferred portions of America's southern hemisphere had been "subdued."[20]

Colonization

Some of the *indias* even as late as the 1580s were being broken physically, their insides literally bursting under the heavy loads they had to carry. Unable to endure more, some of them committed suicide by hanging, starving themselves, or eating poisonous herbs. Encomenderos forced them to work in open fields where they tried to care for their children.... Mothers occasionally killed their offspring at birth to spare them future agonies.... [Others returned] home after weeks or months of separation from their children only to find that they had died or had been taken away.

William L. Sherman, Native Forced Labor

Horrific as the processes of invasion and conquest must have been to those who suffered them, what came after was far more so, and vastly more consequential in terms of its impact on indigenous populations. In central Mexico, Cortés followed up his "triumph" at Tenochtitlán by establishing a colony dubbed "New Spain" that was based on the most brutal use of Indians as slave labor.[21] The methods of pacification and conscription are instructive. As contemporary historian David Stannard explains:

Numerous reports, from numerous reporters, tell of Indians being led to the mines in columns, chained together at the neck, and decapitated if they faltered. Of children trapped and burned alive in their houses, or stabbed to death because they walked too slowly. Of the routine cutting off of women's breasts, and the tying of heavy gourds to their feet before tossing them to drown in lakes and lagoons. Of babies taken from their mothers' breasts, killed, and left as roadside markers. Of "stray" Indians dismembered and sent back to their villages with their chopped off hands and noses strung around their necks. Of "pregnant and confined women, children, old men, as many as they could capture," thrown into pits in which stakes had been imbedded and "left stuck on the stakes, until the pits were filled." And much, much more.[22]

Within the area of the former Mexica kingdom, the people, who numbered more than 25,000,000 at the time of the conquistadors' arrival, were literally worked to death, mainly in mining and plantation enterprises.[23] According to the Spanish census of that year, barely 1.3 million Indios remained alive in the entire region by 1595.[24] To the north, where Beltrán de Guzmán and his ilk had ventured, it was no better.

> Among the region's Serrano culture groups, in barely more than a century the Tepehuán people were reduced in number by 90 percent; the Irritilla people by 93 percent; the Acaxee people by 95 percent. It took a little longer for the various Yaqui peoples to reach this level of devastation, but they too saw nearly 90 percent of their number perish, while for the varied Maya peoples the collapse was 94 percent. Scores of other examples from this enormous area followed the same deadly pattern.[25]

To the south, the handiwork of Alvarado and his cohorts was equally evident. Overall, the population of southern Mexico, numbering about 1.7 million at the point of the invasion, dropped to less than a quarter-million over the next century and a half.[26] In Córdoba, on the Gulf of Mexico, the population fell by 97 percent during the century after Tenochtitlán was sacked. Off the coast, on the island of Cozumel, 96 percent of the population was eradicated. Inland, in the province of Jalapa, the decimation reached 97 percent.[27] In the Yucatán, "the Spaniards pacified [the Indians of Cochua and Chetumal] in such a way that these provinces, which were formerly the thickest settled and most populous, remained the most desolate in the country," recounted Bishop Diego de Landa.[28] Another observer, Alonso de Zorita, added that there were "certain birds that, when an Indian falls, pick out his eyes and kill and eat him; it is well known that these birds appear whenever the Spaniards make an incursion or discover a mine."[29] The litany goes on in Central America.

> By 1542 Nicaragua alone had seen the export of as many as half a million of its people for slave labor (in effect, a death sentence) in distant areas whose populations had been destroyed. In Panama, it is said, between the years 1514 and 1530 up to 2,000,000 Indians were killed.... In the Cuchumatan Highlands of Guatemala the

population fell by 82 percent within the first half–century following European contact, and by 94 percent—from 260,000 to 16,000—in less than a century and a half. In western Nicaragua, 99 percent of the people were dead (falling in number from more than 1,000,000 to less than 10,000) before sixty years had passed from the time of the Spaniards' initial appearance. In western and central Honduras 95 percent of the people were exterminated in little more than a century.[30]

Still farther south, in the Andes, where Pizarro's minions wielded the whips and swords, the population dropped from as many as 14,000,000 before the invasion to barely a million by the end of the sixteenth century.[31] The manner of their dying was essentially the same as that of their cousins in Mexico and Central America. As one Spanish observer in Peru put it as early as 1539:

> The Indians are being totally destroyed and lost.... They [plead] with a cross to be given food for the love of God. [But the soldiers are] killing all the llamas they want for no greater need than to make tallow candles.... The Indians are left with nothing to plant, and since they have no cattle and can never obtain any, they cannot fail to die of hunger.[32]

Simultaneously, massive numbers of the sick and starving people were impressed into slave labor on Spanish cocoa plantations, and in silver mines like that at Potosí, in Peru.[33] As Spanish officials estimated, "between a third and a half of the annual quota of cocoa workers died as a result of their five month service."[34] Those who survived were simply subjected to another stint, the cycle repeated again and again, until, as Spain's King Philip remarked in 1551, "an infinite number of Indians perish[ed]."[35] Both the scale and rate of death were in some ways as bound up in the attitudes of the colonizers towards native people as it was in the physical conditions they imposed upon them. Consider the following assessment by conquistador Pedro de Ciez de León:

> I would not condemn the employment of Indian [slaves] ... but if a [Spaniard] had need of one pig, he killed twenty; if four Indians were wanted, he took a dozen ... and there were many who made the poor Indians carry their whores on hammocks borne upon their shoulders. Were one ordered to enumerate the great evils, injuries, robberies, oppression, and ill treatment inflicted upon the natives during these operations ... there would be no end of it ... for they thought no more of killing Indians than if they were useless beasts.[36]

The silver mines were even worse—the very "mouth of hell," to quote Spanish chronicler Domingo de Santo Tomás.[37] "If twenty healthy Indians enter [a mine] on Monday," wrote Rodrigo de Loaisa in another firsthand account, "half may emerge crippled on Saturday."[38] More often, they did not emerge at all.

> Dropped down a shaft bored as far as 750 feet into the earth, taking with them only "some bags of roasted maize for their sustenance," observed [Loaisa], the miners remained below ground for a week at a time. There, in addition to the dangers of falling rocks, poor ventilation, and the violence of brutal overseers, as the Indian laborers chipped away at the rock faces of the mines they released and inhaled the poisonous vapors of cinnabar, arsenic, arsenic anhydride, and mercury.... For as long as there appeared to be an unending supply of brute labor it was cheaper to work an Indian to death, and replace him or her with another native, than it was to feed and care for either of them properly. It is probable, in fact, that the life expectancy of an Indian engaged in forced labor in a mine or on a plantation during these early years of Spanish terror in Peru was not much more than three or four months—about the same as that of someone working at slave labor in the synthetic rubber manufacturing plant at Auschwitz in the 1940s.[39]

The Portuguese, for their part, were proceeding apace in Brazil, primarily through the development of the vast plantations which, by 1600, supplied the great bulk of Europe's sugar.[40] Such endeavors entailed equally vast applications of forced labor—over a third of a million Indians were held in bondage at the peak—obtained by slaving expeditions up the Amazon.[41]

> For the Indians brought to the slave markets of the coast, life was frightful. Families were broken up during the raids, and a large proportion of the men were killed. The women and children were taken down river in chains and sold. On the sugar plantations, they were forced to work seven days a week. The work was punishing. It required clearing and irrigating huge tracts of land, building mills, houses and roads, and cutting and pressing cane. Like the Indians who were subjected to the Spanish, the Indians of Brazil, by virtue of enforced labor and the onslaught of disease, suffered greatly. Not many survived.[42]

In fact, less than 10 percent of Brazil's preinvasion indigenous population of approximately 2.5 million lived into the seventeenth century.[43] "In the end," says one account, "things grew so bad that there was no one to make graves and some were buried in dunghills and around huts, but so badly that the pigs routed them."[44] By then, however, the Portuguese had begun the importation of the more than 3.5 million African slaves with which they not only expanded the plantation system, but diversified into timbering and large–scale cattle ranching.[45]

Notes on Genocide as Art and Recreation

So that their flowers should live, they maimed and destroyed the flower of others.... Marauders by day, offenders by night, murderers of the world.

Chilam Balam

It would be inaccurate and unfair to suggest that life revolved exclusively around matters of commerce and industry for the Iberian colonists. They were, after all, resourceful people, capable of devising forms of entertainment for themselves, even in the midst of the wilderness they'd so recently invaded and conquered. One of the favorites, as was the case with Columbus' *hidalgos* on Española a bit earlier, had to do with wagering on the amount of damage which might be inflicted upon an unarmed Indian, often a child, with a single sword stroke.[46] Another similar entertainment between the earliest Spanish colonists in the Caribbean and their later mainland counterparts was that of massacring entire villages, apparently for the sheer "sport" of it.[47]

In Central America, a new innovation, "dogging," shortly made its appearance. This had to do with setting vicious mastiffs and wolfhounds—raised on a diet of human flesh, trained to disembowel upon command, and often equipped with special armor—loose on hapless natives. This was sometimes done to captives in a betting situation, sometimes as a form of "hunting," sometimes in conjunction with pacification efforts, or usually in some combination of the three.[48]

A properly fleshed dog could pursue a 'savage' as zealously and effectively as a deer or a boar.... To many of the conquerors, the Indian was merely another savage animal, and the dogs were trained to rip apart their human quarry with the same zest as they felt when hunting wild beasts.[49]

In one account, the favorite dog of the noted conquistador Vasco Nuñez de Balboa ripped the head completely off the body of a Cuna leader in Panama, much to the glee of the entourage accompanying the owner of the "pet."[50] At another point, Balboa is recorded as having ordered the bodies of 40 of his victims fed to his dogs.[51] In Peru, this practice was so common that Cieza de León found it not particularly remarkable that "a Portuguese named Roque Martin [regularly] had quarters of Indians hanging on his porch to feed his dogs with."[52]

Then there was the matter of sex. For all their supposedly devout Catholicism, the Iberians, Spanish, and Portuguese alike, excelled at rape, forced concubinage, and compulsory prostitution. In part, this seems to have been a grotesque psychological stratagem to effect the final degradation and disempowerment of indigenous men as well as women; as a group of Dominican friars reported rather early on, when an enslaved native man emerged from the mines of Mexico at the end of a day, "not only was he beaten or whipped because he had not brought up enough gold, but further, most often, he was bound hand and foot and flung under the bed like a dog, before [a Spanish overseer] lay down, directly over him, with his wife."[53]

> These were just [adjuncts, however,] to the open trade in enslaved women that the Spanish delighted in as the decades wore on. Native women—or indias—were gambled away in card games and traded for objects of small value, while stables of them were rented out to sailors who desired sexual accompaniment during their travels up and down the coast. If an *india* attempted to resist, she was whipped or tortured or burned alive. Even when laws were passed to curb the more extreme of such atrocities, the penalties were a joke. When, for example, an uncooperative Nicaraguan Indian woman was burned to death in her hut by a Spaniard who tried to rape her, he was prosecuted by the governor—and fined five pesos.[54]

Nor was travel neglected, especially of the adventurous and potentially profitable sort. For a long while, expeditions set with a certain regularity from Peru in search of a fabled *El Dorado* (City of Gold) believed by the Spanish to lie somewhere along the upper Amazon. "Some two or three hundred Spaniards go on these expeditions," Santo Tomás recorded, "[taking] two or three thousand Indians to serve them and carry their food and fodder.... Few or no Indians survive, because of lack of food, the immense hardships of the long journeys through wastelands, and from the loads themselves."[55] Francisco Pizzaro himself was more direct in such matters: "When the Indians grew exhausted, they cut off their heads without untying them from their chains, leaving the roads full of bodies."[56]

In sum, Iberian colonization on the American mainland equated to a complete dehumanization and devaluation of indigenous people in the minds of their conquerors. From that sprang the processes by which the native population was consumed, for reasons both systematically calculated and utterly sadistic, in numbers which are truly stupefying. All told, it is reasonably estimated that, from the Río Grande southward into Chilé, as many as 80,000,000 human beings were killed in the Spanish/Portuguese drive for wealth and imperial grandeur by the year 1700.[57]

Artistically, the holocaust attending the first two centuries of Iberian rule is still celebrated as a source of tremendous national/cultural pride throughout the "Hispanic" portion of America; paintings, murals, sculpture, and public statuary, much of it officially commissioned, continue to abound in commemoration of the immense "achievement" this "rich Spanish heritage" of rape, pillage, and slaughter invoked. Perhaps exemplary in this regard is the Montejo House in the city of Mérida, on the Yucatán peninsula, near the ancient Mayan centers at Uxmal and Chichén Itzá, the locale of some of the worst atrocities of the mid–sixteenth century. There, one may stare in awe and admiration at a facade depicting in lavishly bold relief a pair of noble conquistadors, each of them casually resting a foot atop the severed head of a fallen Indian.[58]

The Maintenance and Expansion of Empire

This man born in degradation, this stranger brought by slavery into our midst, is hardly recognized as sharing the common features of humanity. His face appears to us hideous, his intelligence limited, and his tastes low; we almost take him to be some intermediary between man and beast.

Alexis de Tocqueville

As the native populations under Iberian sway eroded like snow beneath an August sun, the intensity of killing necessarily abated. By and large, colonial regimes throughout South and Central America, as well as Mexico and the southwestern portion of the present–day United States, settled in to consolidating the New Order within their domains in accordance with rigid and often elaborate racial codes.

Every mixture possible, starting from the three pure original racial types [ostensibly Caucasian, Black African, and Indian], received its individual name. The terms *mestizo, mulato*, and *zambo* were of long standing, and need no further clarification. *Tercerón, cuarterón* (quadroon), and *quinterón* (quintroon) are self–explanatory. Peruvian Spanish still retains the terms *cholo* and *chino*. But who nowadays remembers the significance of such names as *castizo, morisco, lobo, jíbaro, albarazado, cambujo, barcino, puchel, coyote, chamiso, gálfarro, genizaro, grifo, jarocho*, and *sambiago*, or the more picturesque *salta atrás, tente en aire, no te entiendo, ahí estés*, and so forth?[59]

The point is amplified by a portion of one such code, effective in eighteenth–century New Spain, which is illustrative of all such lists compiled in Iberian–occupied America:

1. Spaniard and Indian beget mestizo
2. Mestizo and Spanish woman beget castizo
3. Castizo woman and Spaniard beget Spaniard
4. Spanish woman and Negro beget mulatto.
5. Spaniard and mulatto woman beget morisco
6. Morisco woman and Spaniard beget albino
7. Spaniard and albino woman beget torna atrás
8. Indian and torna atrás woman beget lobo

9. Lobo and Indian woman beget zambiago
10. Zambiago and Indian woman beget cambujo
11. Cambujo and mulatto woman beget albarazado
12. Albarazdo and mulatto woman beget barcino
13. Barcino and mulatto beget coyote
14. Coyote woman and Indian beget chamiso
15. Chamiso woman and mestizo beget coyote mestizo
16. Coyote mestiso and mulatto woman beget ahí te estás[60]

Indians were placed on the very bottom rung of these hierarchies, and were in many cases defined virtually out of existence.[61] Hence, the race codes were coupled directly to an ongoing process of dispossessing native people of their residual land base, a matter more often accomplished throughout the eighteenth century by legalistic sleight of hand than by armed assault and physical eradication.[62] The two were never mutually exclusive propositions, however.

A prime example is that of the *reduccione* program inaugurated by the Chilean government in 1866, designed to constrict the Mapuche people of that country's southern region to certain specified tracts while opening up the remainder of their holdings to acquisition by members of the ruling Latino oligarchy. This led to the hard–fought Mapuche Revolt of 1880–1882, quelled by Chilean troops with such extreme violence that rebellion has never again been attempted.[63]

> After the final defeat of the Mapuches, the *reducciones indigena* ... were further reduced in size, the expropriated land being used to expand the haciendas. The Mapuches ... retained less than 500,000 hectares of the 10 million hectares they had held before.... Unable to support themselves on their now diminished lands, the Mapuches became a migrant labour force on the haciendas; the reservations became a reservoir of land and labour for the great landowners.[64]

There were, of course, occasional requirements to put down other native insurrections—for instance, the Mayas in Guatemala during the 1630s and 1640s, the 1680 Pueblo Revolt in New Mexico, the insurgency led by the Manau leader Ajuricaba in Brazil during the mid–1700s, another headed by Túpac Amaru II in Peru in 1780, and several others—but these were mostly transient phenomena, quickly and bloodily suppressed.[65] Mexico also continued right into the twentieth century with its harsh campaigns to subdue the Yaquis and, to a somewhat lesser extent, the Apaches, but these concerned areas considered to be of such marginal value by ruling élites that, while ferocious in their own right, they were not pursued with the vigor marking the Conquest proper.[66]

Sometimes, however, it was deemed important to expand the reach of empire into localities which had been previously ignored altogether. Then, the genocidal fury that had marked the performances of conquistadors like Cortés and Alvardo was again unleashed in full force, albeit on a smaller scale. Such was the case in Argentina when, in 1879, General Julio Roca set out to seize the sprawling pampas south of Buenos Aires, and eventually all of Patagonia below the Río Negro.[67] The idea was to incorporate territory, much of it ideal for ranching, into the country's dominant *estanchieros* system, controlled by a handful of *caudillos* to whom Roca owed his position. The only obstacle was the existence of the Araucaño Indians, perhaps one–half million of them, who occupied the coveted terrain.[68]

> Roca's campaign, he said, was a civilizing mission, intended to bring scientists and engineers to the frontier. Indeed, Roca's army of 6,000 troops was to have the most modern technology available, including four pieces of heavy artillery. In addition, Roca ordered the construction of the first telegraph lines into the countryside, so that his orders could be carried immediately to the front.... [Then he directed] lightening raids against unsuspecting villages, killing or imprisoning the inhabitants, seeking to sow terror through the tribes of the pampas. The battles were bloody. Often the Indians realized that their lances were no match for the soldiers' rifles and "they threw their lances to the ground and began to fight with us hand–to–hand, to grab the rifles out of our grasp." Many of the hand–to–hand battles ended with soldiers on horseback trampling fleeing Indians.... Roca systematically exterminated the Indians. Vast *estancias* were established on what novelist V. S. Naipal has called the "stolen, bloody land." Many of the *estancias* were allotted to the victorious generals. Roca himself was rewarded with the presidency.[69]

In the aftermath, surviving Araucaños were interned in concentration camps where many thousands more died of a measles epidemic. What remained were then placed on tiny *colonias* where starvation and disease continued to take a huge toll. In less than a generation these tiny reserves of Indian land were also dissolved, the pitifully small numbers by the Araucaños—fewer than 25,000 by some estimates—dispersed as subsistence labor in urban sweatshops or on the *estancias*.[70] As Naipal has observed, although Argentines tend to be pompous in their pride over an imagined martial prowess, theirs is really only "a simple history of Indian genocide and European takeover."[71] Thus, the Iberian tradition of inflicting the utmost lethal savagery upon the indigenous peoples of America has been maintained up until the present era.

Contemporary Latino Savagery

I didn't know. But is it only an excuse? I can't think of any other. I didn't know that this evil was going on—was still going on. I didn't know that thirty years after the collapse of the Nazi regime, men and women were still living under its inhuman spell in a so–called free country.... I am compelled to make this comparison, even though reluctantly. It is because, until now, I always forbade myself to compare the Holocaust of European Judaism to events which are foreign to it.... There are here indications, facts which cannot be denied: it is indeed a matter of a Final Solution.

Elie Wiesel, 1976

These words were written by one of the best–known philosophers of the nazi–induced holocaust during World War II, a long–time proponent of the "uniqueness of the Jewish experience" of genocide, after he finally consented to review documents concerning the ongoing extermination of the Aché Indians in Paraguay during the 1960s and 1970s. After reviewing irrefutable evidence that perhaps 85 percent of the estimated 25,000 Achés still alive in 1959 had been systematically hunted down and killed by teams of executioners operating under the sanction of Paraguayan President Alfredo Stroessner—often dispatched with machetes to "save the expense of bullets"—Wiesel was moved to write that he "read and reread these documents, these testimonies, with a mixed feeling of horror, disgust, and shame."[72]

These men, hunted, humiliated, murdered for the sake of pleasure; these young girls, raped and sold; these children, killed in front of their parents reduced to silence by pain.... [The killers] aim at exterminating this tribe. Morally and physically. So that nothing will remain, not even a cry or a tear. Efficient technique, tested elsewhere. The individual is dragged away from his tribe, from his family, from his past. He is deprived of his strength, his dignity. And of his memory, too. He is diminished He is forced to look at himself through the eyes of his enemy in order to become his own enemy, and thus wish his own death.... Deculturation, ghettos, collective murders, and agonies: that in a country so near ours humans can still be locked with impunity inside stifling camps, can still be tracked down like wild beasts before being reduced to slavery, that husbands can be separated from their wives, children from their mothers, individuals from their language, their religion, their rituals, their songs and litanies, their tales, and their speech, that such torments can be inflicted on a free [people] which thirsts for poetry, torments which, in the past, were inflicted upon another people, this ought to baffle anyone who still believes in Man, in his conscience, and his possibility of survival.[73]

Unfortunately, the commentator, for all his eloquence of outrage, understated the reality almost entirely. Not only did he overlook the entire genocidal sweep of history in Ibero–America—a process of which the Aché slaughter is only the tiniest of recent parts—he managed to miss many contemporaneous examples as well. In 1979, the Fourth International Russell Tribunal was convened in Rotterdam to consider State crimes committed against the indigenous peoples of the Western Hemisphere. It concluded that in Columbia, for example, genocide was proceeding inexorably as the government, representing the perceived interests of 23 million Spanish–speaking citizens, sought to clear the country's remaining 179,000 Indians from what was left of their territory in the area of the Amazon headwaters.[74]

> The Russell Tribunal found the Columbian government guilty of violating international and [its] own laws in the expropriation of Purace land, and they found the multinational mining company Ceanese and its subsidiary Industrias Purace guilty of violating trade union, pollution, and safety agreements which they had signed in their occupation and exploitation of Purace land. The Tribunal collected evidence of forty–five resistance leaders murdered since 1971 in the Purace area alone. These crimes, however, were only indicative of a much larger government program to "deindianize" Colombia.[75]

The residue of Columbia's native population was being "virtually exterminated," as evidenced in the actions of both the public and private sectors of the dominant Latino society. The former is implicated by repeated reports of "Columbian navy riverboats [which] cruise the rivers, machine–gunning Indians on the bank."[76] As concerns the private sector, one illustration is that of Anselmo Aguirre and Marcelino Jiminez, a pair of white ranchers, who, in concert with a local policeman named Luis Enrique Morín, invited a group of Cuibas Indians to a "Christmas Feast" in 1967. They then used guns, machetes, clubs, and hatchets to slaughter 16 of the 19 Indians present, including an infant and five small children. In this case, there was actually a trial, at which it was admitted that the mass murder had occurred because the perpetrators desired their victims' land. The judge then ordered charges dismissed against the accused because "they did not know it was wrong to kill Indians" in Columbia.[77]

> The systematic extermination of indigenous populations in Columbia has [also] paralleled, predictably, the development plans of energy corporations and other corporate interests in the area. In 1960, a Texaco–Gulf oil consortium began exploration in southern Columbia; by 1968 they operated forty–seven productive wells and a 193–mile pipeline from the region to an oil terminal on the Pacific Coast. In 1970 the World Bank began a loan program to Columbia for development of the remote Amazon region. In March of 1979 the Columbian government under Julio Cesar Tabay signed a $500 million contract with the National Uranium Company of Spain for

the exploration of uranium in the southeastern province of Vaupes where the Guahibo Indians had been continuously hunted and slaughtered. In the southern province of Cauca, home of the Purace Indians ... 51,000 acres of the Indians subsistence bean crop was reduced to 7,200 acres in the 1960s. During that same time, the multi–billion–dollar international farm feeding company, Ralston Purina, had gained control of some 200,000 acres in the province for the production of chicken feed.[78]

In Brazil's Amazon Basin—where a 1972 *U.S. News and World Report* outline of development opportunities listed "soil deficiencies, tropical diseases, insects, and hostile Indian tribes" as being the major barriers to "progress"—the Russell Tribunal found solid evidence of ongoing genocide.[79] Spurred on by the profit incentives embodied in the region's deposits of uranium, bauxite, oil, gold, zinc, copper, nickel, titanium, coal, tin, and other minerals, as well as lush timber potentials, the government had entered into "development" relationships with a host of transnational corporations, including Bethlehem Steel, Georgia Pacific, Royal Dutch Shell, Texaco, Gulf Oil, Cominco, Litton Industries, U.S. Steel, Komatsu, Caterpillar, Alcan, Rio Tinto Zinc, Westinghouse, Gulf & Western, and the W. R. Grace Company. The upshot was the beginning of a serious onslaught against the vast Amazon rainforest, vital to planetary ecology, and systematic eradication of the area's 100,000 remaining Indians.[80]

> The most isolated of the Amazon indigenous nations had been the Yanomami Indians until gold, diamonds, and uranium were discovered in their land in 1974. The Yanomami had already been pushed north by early [Portuguese] settlement and the rubber industry, and had established their home in the Branco River Valley, a remote Amazon tributary in the northernmost Brazilian province of Roriama. After the discovery of uranium in the area, the Brazilian government began cutting a road through 225 kilometers of Yanomami land. Fourteen of the southern villages were soon decimated by highway workers, vigilante raids, and disease. Population in the villages was reduced from 400 to 79 by 1975. In 1975 Fernando Ramos Periera, governor of Roraima Province, told the press that the area "is not able to afford the luxury of conserving a half–a–dozen Indian tribes who are holding back development." A 1972 report from the Reuter news service detailed the existence of hunting parties in the Amazon jungles which "murdered and raided the peaceful Indian tribes".... "On other occasions," reported Reuter, "planes bombarded the Indian villages with dynamite or dropped poisoned food into the villages."[81]

Even as the Yanomami, Jivaro, and other Amazonian peoples were being butchered or shunted into tiny reservations, or "parks" as they are called in

Brazil, Chilean military dictator Augusto Pinochet was completing the *reduccione* process imposed upon the Mapuches by his predecessors. On September 12, 1978, he announced "the promulgation in the near future of an act relating to indigenous property. This act ... will enable those descendants [of the Mapuche "race"] voluntarily and freely to opt for private land ownership in those cases where they prefer this formula to the present system of community ownership."[82]

> In 1979 Pinochet's government introduced a law designed to divide the Mapuches' communally–held lands and turn them into small holdings. The law facilitated the breakup by providing that any one member of an Indian community could require that the land be divided.... The draft version of the 1979 law provided that once the land was divided among the Indians, the Indian landholders would no longer be considered to be Indians.... Today, only twenty Mapuche reservations remain intact. The new civilian government has agreed to enact a law to stop further division, but given the drastic loss of land already incurred, this is more symbolism than anything else.[83]

In 1977, Antonio Millape, a Mapuche, testified before the United Nations on the methods by which the regime's objectives were already being achieved: "Go to any Mapuche home today, and you will find the dog outside will not bark, because it is too weak. If you go inside you will find one or more children lying sick, dying of starvation. There may be more children outside, and they will tell you their parents are not at home. Do not believe them. If you go inside you will find them, too, dying of starvation and extreme malnutrition. This is the form of extermination today, under Pinochet."[84] Millape also spoke of "torture, murder and the terror of ... military death squads. Juan Condori Urichi, a Minkaía Indian from Bolivia, spoke of similar atrocities against his people."[85] Delegates representing various indigenous peoples of South America have been testifying to the same effect—and usually providing extensive documentation to substantiate their statements—before the UN's Working Group on Indigenous Populations every year since.[86]

> The stories of other Latin American Indian populations are similar, with local variations. Argentina, like Paraguay, has been ruled by the military, and has systematically exterminated most of the indigenous population; 200,000 survive in a population of 23 million. Uruguay has virtually eliminated all Indians within its borders.... In Peru, Quechua–Aymara Andean Indians make up about half of the 11 million population; their land has been continually eroded by forest, oil, and mining industries. Development pressures in Ecuador, Venezuela, Guyana, and Surinam have, likewise, driven the

indigenous populations from their traditional lands. The same is true in Central America, from Panama to Mexico.[87]

Actually, in Central America, things may be even worse. It has been reliably estimated that, since the overthrow of democratic President Jacobo Arbenz in a CIA–backed coup in 1954, a succession of military governments headed by men like Fernando Lucas García, Efraín Rios Mott, and Mejia Victores have slaughtered somewhere between 100,000 and 150,000 highland Mayas in the country's northern provinces. Another quarter–million have been driven into exile in southern Mexico and Belize.[88] Although the slaughter began in the wake of the coup—about 8,000 Indians being killed over a two–year period—and was sustained during much of the 1960s, the process began in earnest in 1976, when "the Guatemalan army occupied El Quiche province; a wave of terror followed. Indians were kidnapped, tortured, assassinated, raped and burned out of their homes and fields."[89]

> In northern Guatemala, a development corridor, the Franja Transversal del Norte, was carved out of an isolated territory that is the homeland of the Kekchi and Ixil Indians. Many of the agribusinesses along the corridor are owned by senior members of the armed forces; these estates together are known as the "Zone of the Generals." In May 1978, the Indians who were displaced by the generals staged a march on the city of Panzos.... As they reached the town square, government forces and local vigilantes positioned on the roofs of buildings around the square fired into the throng. More than a hundred Indians were killed within minutes, and more died trying to escape the massacre. Their bodies were buried in mass graves that had been prepared by bulldozers the day before.[90]

From there, the military essentially went berserk, butchering Indians with a bestial fury reminiscent of the worst the conquistadors—or the SS—had to offer: "The [soldiers] searched the houses and pulled people out and took us to a churchyard. The Lieutenant walked up and down, pointing at people, saying, 'These will go to hell, these will go to heaven'. The ones he said would go to hell he took ... to the cemetery with their hands tied behind their backs. They dug a big ditch and lined them up at the edge. We all had to come and watch.... They shot each one with a bullet in the face from about a meter away."[91]

> The people were surrounded and could not leave the church. Then the soldiers called out people's names, including children, and took them to the clinic nearby. All the names were of people who had learned to read and write.... The women were raped before the eyes of the men and the children in the clinic. The men and the boys had their testicles cut off. Everybody's tongues were cut out. Their eyes were gouged out with nails. Their arms were twisted off. Their legs

were cut off. The little girls were raped and tortured. The women had their breasts cut off.[92]

In nearby El Salvador, dispossession of indigenous people by the ruling Latino élite—the so-called Fourteen Families (actually, about 200)—has followed a comparable trajectory.[93] In 1961, the number of landless Indians in the country came to 12 percent of the native population. By 1971, the figure had risen to 30 percent; by 1975, 41 percent; in 1980 it was estimated that two–thirds of El Salvador's Indians had been rendered landless as the oligarchy consolidated its *latifundia* system.[94] Those who were evicted were thrown into total destitution and increasingly constricted upon tiny infertile plots.

Predictably, these expropriations were accomplished through the wholesale application of violence from both the Salvadoran army and "private civic organizations" like ORDEN.[95] The following account of a November 29, 1974, massacre in the hamlet of La Cayetana in San Vicente Province, carried out jointly by ORDEN and the army, is indicative:

> I saw the plaza covered with people's hair. The National Guard had cut off their hair with machetes, taking part of the skin with it.... The National Guard arrived in Cayetana with 60 machine guns, tear gas, a cannon.... When the [Indians] came, they grabbed their machine guns and sprayed them with gunfire.... Those they killed, they cut their faces in pieces and chopped up the bodies with machetes. If you like, I will show you where they buried the brains.[96]

Specially trained and equipped "counterinsurgency units," such as the Atlacatl Battalion, were also raised during the late 1970s to work in conjunction with the Salvadoran air force in driving Indians from preferred areas. White phosphorous, napalm, and fragmentation ordnance were specifically aimed at native villages during air strikes, driving into the open those who were not killed outright.[97] Concomitantly, the Atlacatl, ORDEN, and cooperation forces would comb targeted areas on foot, often killing whomever they encountered, driving the population before them.

> In the Guazapa area ... regular air attacks against civilian targets continued [into the mid–80s]. The scattered remnants of the population hid from ground sweeps following the shelling and bombardment by helicopters and jet aircraft, watching their children die of starvation and thirst.... "If they find somebody, they kill, they even kill the poor dogs and other animals," [a] refugee testified, reporting night bombing and ambushing of people fleeing in October 1984. The soldiers also destroyed crops and houses, "even pans one uses to cook in ... in order to leave one without anything." Fleeing women and children were killed by bullets and grenades, or sliced to pieces and decapitated with machetes.[98]

By 1980, at least 30,000 Indians had been exterminated, another 600,000—13 percent of El Salvador's total population—made refugees.[99] Thousands of people, many of them defined as "opposition leaders," were being killed more "surgically" by ORDEN death squads, their bodies dumped at night at locations such as El Playón.[100] Large–scale massacres were also occurring at places like Los Llanitos, the Río Gualsinga, Las Vueltas, and El Mozote.[101]

> The first major massacre was at the Rio Sampul on May 14 [1980], when thousands of peasants fled to Honduras to escape a military operation. As they were crossing the river, they were attacked by helicopters, members of ORDEN and troops. According to eyewitness testimony reported by Amnesty International and the Honduran clergy, women were tortured, nursing babies were thrown into the air for target practice, children were drowned by soldiers or decapitated or slashed to death with machetes, pieces of their bodies were thrown to dogs.... At least 600 unburied corpses were prey for dogs and buzzards while others were lost in the waters of the river, which was contaminated by their dead bodies.[102]

In all of Central America today, only Costa Rica is reputedly free of such treatment of indigenous people. Like Uruguay on the southern continent, however, Costa Rica also claims at this point to have no surviving native population to exterminate.[103] This perhaps is the key to an understanding of the entire phenomenon of genocide in Ibero–America: left to run its course, the process of liquidating American Indians, begun the moment the first Spaniard set foot in this hemisphere, will end only when there are no more Indians left to kill. The question thus becomes how to prevent it from running its course.

Denying the Holocaust

> The truth is a weapon more potent than any rifle or bomb.
> *John Trudell, National Chair, American Indian Movement, 1979*

For constructive alteration of any process to occur, it is plainly essential that it be recognized for what it is. As concerns the continuing genocide of the indigenous people of South and Central America, denial rather than recognition has been the norm almost from the moment of inception. As early as the sixteenth century, the Spanish began an endless series of attempts to pass off accounts of their anti–Indian atrocities submitted by their own officials and historians as no more than a "Black Legend," a smear campaign mounted by their Protestant European enemies to discredit them. Despite its patent falsity— comparable to assertions by a certain school of "historical revisionism" that depicts the nazi extermination of the Jews as merely "Zionist propaganda"—the

Black Legend theme persists through the present day, especially among self–described "Hispanic" polemicists, and is afforded much currency in the mass media.[104]

Closely tied to such outright denial has been the efforts of "minimizers," usually "responsible scholars," who have sought to diminish the magnitude of genocide in America by making it appear that the native population at the outset of the invasion was vastly smaller than it actually was. Preeminent in this regard was the "Dean of American Anthropology" Alfred L. Kroeber, who in 1939 established as canonical "truth" the proposition that the hemispheric total of American Indians in 1492—which may have been as high as 125 million—was actually only 8.4 million.[105] Instructively, the technique is identical to that deployed by those who would rehabilitate the reputation of nazism; it would appear they learned the method from "reputable" types like Kroeber rather than the other way around.[106]

In any event, having scaled the American genocide down to more or less manageable proportions, deniers have consistently moved to dismiss its significance altogether, conceding that the conquistadors were "perhaps not saints" before arguing that their victims were "as bad or worse," therefore "deserved what they got," and that the "world is a better place" for their demise.[107] A salient theme in this respect, first advanced by Cortés himself in 1522, and established as another modern academic Truth despite a complete absence of tangible evidence to support it, is the myth that the Mexicas—described in every standard text as having been a "warlike" and "bloodthirsty" people—were given to ritually sacrificing as many as 20,000 human beings each year.[108] The fact is, as Peter Hassler has explained:

> Bernal Díaz del Castillo is the classic source of information about mass sacrifice by the Aztecs. A literate soldier in Cortés' company, Díaz claimed to have witnessed such a ritual.... The observers, however, were watching from their camp ... three or four miles away. From that point, Díaz could neither have seen nor heard anything.... The only concrete evidence comes to us not from the Aztecs but from the Mayan civilization of the Yucatán. These depictions are found in the records of trials conducted during the Inquisition, between 1561 and 1565. These supposed testimonies about human sacrifice, however, were coerced from the Indians under torture and have been judged worthless as ethnographic evidence.... After careful and systematic study of the sources, I find no evidence of institutionalized mass human sacrifice among the Aztecs.[109]

Although one might well be reminded of certain Germanic fables about "Jewish ritual murder" offered as justification of the nazis' treatment of semitic *untermensch* during the 1930s and 1940s,[110] such tales of "Aztec sacrifice" are seldom treated with skepticism by the scholarly community, much less classified as being among the rationalizations of mass murderers. To the contrary, such contrived denigration of American Indians—and there are a multitude of variations on the theme[111]—are typically embraced in such a way as to culminate in a note of hearty self–congratulations among the heirs of those who came along to end such savagery once and for all: "[Euroamericans] might as well celebrate the mammoth achievement of the past five centuries.... Let's hear it for Columbus."[112]

On balance, eurocentrism and its counterpart, eurosupremacism—the racist fundaments which have always fueled the genocidal process in America—have proven themselves ideologically transcendent among Euroamericans. The preceding mythologies are as rampant in radical dissident circles as they are among conservatives: the Revolutionary Communist Party, USA, has been just as prone to accept Kroeber's low–counting of precolumbian indigenous populations as the Smithsonian Institution ever was;[113] a leftist like Roxanne Dunbar Ortiz has been as quick to repeat the conquistadors' propaganda about human sacrifice in Mesoamerica as any court historian;[114] self–proclaimed "eco–anarchists" such as George Weurthner can hold their own with the most arcane and reactionary anthropologist in decrying imagined "ravages" inflicted by native people upon the environment long before Columbus;[115] Christopher Hitchens has shown himself as apt to applaud the Columbian legacy in the pages of *The Nation* as Jeffrey Hart has been in the pages of *National Review*.[116]

In Peru, the Quechua leader Hugo Blanco, once a hero of the Left, learned such lessons well: "When he turned his support towards Quechua land rights, the Communist Party of Peru dropped him. The rightist government already had a price on his head, so he became a hunted, isolated [indigenist] roaming the hills with three hundred Quechua guerrillas."[117] Today in Peru, a far more extreme leftist formation, the *Sendero Luminoso* ("Shining Path"), conducts a new *requerimiento*, methodically murdering Andean Quechuas in a grotesque effort to compel them to adopt its peculiar "principles of revolutionary Marxism."[118] In the revolutionary Nicaragua of the 1980s, the marxian Sandinista regime employed somewhat gentler methods to the same end, selectively imprisoning and imposing mass relocation upon the Sumu, Miskito, and Rama Indians of the country's Atlantic Coast region to facilitate incorporation of these reluctant people into its Latino–oriented statist structure.[119] In Mexico and other Latin American countries, "indigenista" is a term surpassing even "capitalist" as an expression of revulsion and contempt among marxists.[120]

Even among intellectuals who have devoted themselves explicitly to the task of apprehending the implications of the nazi extermination of the Jews—and of rejoining neo–nazi attempts to deny, minimize, or negate the meaning of that holocaust—there has been a thundering silence with regard to the genocide, both historical and contemporary, of American Indians. Not only Elie Wiesel, but figures as prominent as Hannah Arendt and Irving Louis Horowitz have consistently turned a blind eye, refusing to address the matter when it has been laid squarely before them.[121] Most recently, holocaust scholars like Deborah Lipstadt and Pierre Vidal–Naquet have come forth with entire books dissecting and refuting in great detail the arguments of "the Holocaust didn't happen school of historical revision"; Lipstadt closes with a survey of other genocidal processes—apparently offered only as "proof" that her own people had it worse than any people ever had it—without so much as mentioning the fate of the indigenous people in the Western Hemisphere.[122]

The place of figures like Lipstadt and Vidal–Naquet among the ranks of those denying the historical genocide of American Indians, and its contemporary implication of ongoing holocaust, demonstrates as perhaps nothing else can the degree to which the denial in which they participate is more entrenched, insidious, and effective than the peculiar and virulent form of neonazi apologetics they've elected to confront.[123] Indeed, it appears that there is so pervasive a confluence of interest, both real and perceived, underlying denial of the American Holocaust that it has assumed the posture of Truth, transcending all ideological boundaries defining Left and Right within the presently dominant society.

On balance, the performance of those American institutions devoted to conditioning public consciousness with regard to American Indians—these extend from academia through the mass media to popular literature and the entertainment industry—is about the same as might have been expected of their German counterparts with regard to Jews, Gypsies, Slavs, and others in the aftermath of a nazi victory in World War II. The overall intent of this establishmentarian endeavor is plainly to put a lid on the possibility of any genuinely popular consideration of the genocidal dimensions of the post–1492 "American Experience," thus precluding the emergence of the sort of broad cognitive dissonance which might serve eventually to undermine the smooth functioning of business as usual.

Out of the Maze

> Our sense of history works this way: everything is connected. In order to understand where you're going and how to get there, you must know where you are now; in order to understand that, you must know where it is that you've been.
>
> *Matthew King, Oglala Lakota elder, 1981*

Certainly, there have been Euroamerican scholars, intellectuals, and activists who have deviated from the mainstream in these respects. Some, like Woodrow Borah, Sherburn Cook, Henry Dobyns, and Carl O. Sauer, seem to have been motivated by the more or less "pure" academic desire to see the record at last set straight on questions such as the size of precolumbian native populations in America and the manner in which it was reduced.[124] Others, such as David Stannard, Kirkpatrick Sale, and Eduardo Galeano, have evidenced a more consciously political agenda, seeking to use honest depictions of the extermination of American Indians as a lever with which to uncover in its entirety the eurosupremacist hegemony necessary to sustain the ordained order of things in "the modern world."[125]

In this, they have at least figuratively joined hands with a growing number of indigenous scholars, like Vine Deloria, Jr., Don Grinde, and Robert A. Williams, Jr.,[126] who have begun the laborious task of reinterpreting the record of interaction between natives and invaders in such a way as to conform to reality rather than the ideological prescriptions of domination.[127] In the case of the indigenous scholars, the motivation is one undoubtedly born of an emic knowledge (i.e., knowledge from within a group's cultural context) of their people's victimization and marginalization. For the Euroamericans, the process is, to borrow from Edward Said, more one of achieving a hermeneutic understanding of the circumstances experienced by the indigenous, and then acting in ways which at once reveal an unqualified commitment to the pursuit of truth and a bona fide solidarity with the oppressed embodied in that truth.[128] This, in turn, and taken in combination with similar undertakings in related spheres,[129] creates the basis for what may ultimately prove to be a general supplanting of the prevailing hegemony in favor of a new and liberatory one.[130]

This places us at something of a socio–political and cultural/intellectual crossroads. As material offering a more accurate and insightful appreciation of the actual process by which the Americas were taken from the conditions which prevailed before the Columbian landfall to the point at which we find ourselves today becomes increasingly available, those purporting to desire fundamental change in the way in which our lives have been orchestrated confront, many for the first time, the alternative of opting out of eurosupremacist orthodoxy altogether. Therein lie the intellectual tools for creating not only a whole new vision of our collective past, present, and future, but a practical means of implementing it.

The status quo has been quick to recognize the subversive nature of this project, particularly as regards individuals like Stannard and Sale.[131] Efforts by the champions of orthodoxy to "debunk" their work—mainly by way of personal attacks designed to discredit them as being no more than "academically irresponsible purveyors of political correctitude"—have been widespread.[132] Meanwhile, hack historians like James Axtell, whose self–assigned task appears primarily to be a repackaging of the usual mythology in somewhat more sophisticated wrapping advanced as being the new luminaries of "responsible" scholarship.[133]

The choice, ultimately, is ours. If we elect, sheep–like, to accept the definitions of entities like Harvard University, the Smithsonian Institution, and

Newsweek as to what comprises "proper" or "appropriate" recountings of historical fact and meaning, we will merely have consigned ourselves to more of what has already transpired. If, on the other hand, we move to embrace, absorb, and extend the kind of work pioneered by Deloria, Grinde, Williams, Stannard, and Sale, we equip ourselves to change it in a profoundly positive fashion.

It is of course true that nothing can undo what has been done. Coming to grips with the significance of the relentless butchery marking the European conquest of America no more changes its nature than does recognition of the horror that was embodied in Auschwitz and the operations of the *einsatzgruppen* in the western USSR serve to alter what transpired during the nazi perpetration of genocide. The point in either case, however, is not to try and make the past go away—that undertaking may be left to the Axtells of the world—but to utilize the insights gained from it in such a way as to intervene constructively in its outcomes, to put an end to the ongoing slaughter of indigenous people in Guatemala, for example, or the obliteration of native environments in Amazonia.

In the end it is a matter of redefining our understandings in such a way as to rearrange our values and priorities. This allows for a thoroughgoing and vitally necessary reconstitution of the relationship between ourselves as individuals, as peoples, and, in the aggregate, as human beings. In its turn, any such reconstitution sets the stage for the forging of a future which is radically different from our past and present. Together, we have the self–evident capacity to accomplish this. And we have the obligation to do so, not only for ourselves and one another, but for our children, our children's children, and their children on through the coming generations.

Notes

1. Henry F. Dobyns, "Estimating Aboriginal American Population: An Appraisal of Techniques with a New Hemispheric Estimate," *Current Anthropology*, No. 7 (1966); Russell Thornton, *American Indian Holocaust and Survival: A Population History Since 1492* (Norman: University of Oklahoma Press, 1987).

2. Woodrow W. Borah, "Conquest and Population: A Demographic Approach to Mexican History," *Proceedings of the American Philosophical Society*, No. 113 (1968), pp. 177–83; Ann F. Ramenofsky, *Vectors of Death: The Archaeology of European Contact* (Albuquerque: University of New Mexico Press, 1987).

3. U.S. Bureau of the Census, "Indian Population by Divisions and States, 1890–1930," *Fifteenth Census of the United States, 1930: The Indian Population of the United States and Alaska* (Washington, D.C.: U.S. Government Printing Office, 1937), p. 3.

4. I first encountered the useful concept of "population collapse" through historian David E. Stannard, in his fine study of the destruction of Hawai'i's indigenous population, *Before the Horror: The Population of Hawai'i on the Eve of Western Contact* (Honolulu: Social

Science Research Institute of Hawai'i Press, 1989). Stannard informs me that he himself adopted the idea from David Nobel Cook's *Demographic Collapse: Indian Peru, 1520–1620* (Cambridge, MA: Cambridge University Press, 1981).

5. Henry F. Dobyns, "More Methodological Perspectives on Historical Demography," *Ethnohistory*, No. 36 (1989).

6. For a survey of such matters, *see* Ward Churchill, *Struggle for the Land: Indigenous Resistance to Genocide, Ecocide and Expropriation in North America* (Monroe, Maine: Common Courage Press, 1993).

7. Ward Churchill, "Deconstructing the Columbus Myth: Was the 'Great Discoverer' Italian or Spanish, Nazi or Jew?" in *Confronting Columbus: An Anthology*, John Ewell and Chris Dodge, eds. (Charlotte, North Carolina: McFarland Publishers, 1992), and included in this collection of essays.

8. Bernal Díaz Portillo, *The Discovery and Conquest of Mexico, 1517–1521* (London: George Routledge & Sons, 1926); Miguel Leon–Portilla, ed., *The Broken Spears: The Aztec Account of the Conquest of Mexico* (Boston: Beacon Press, 1962).

9. Hernan Cortés, *Letters from Mexico* (New York: Grossman, 1971), pp. 257–62.

10. The first quote is from David E. Stannard, *American Holocaust: Columbus and the Conquest of the New World* (New York: Oxford University Press, 1992), p. 79; for the second, *see* Hernan Cortés, op. cit., p. 263.

11. Tenochtitlán, an architectural marvel, was, with a population of about 350,000, about five times the size of London or Seville. On respective populations, *see* Rudolph van Zantwijk, *The Aztec Arrangement: The Social History of Pre–Spanish Mexico* (Norman: University of New Mexico, 1985), p. 281; Lawrence Stone, *The Family, Sex and Marriage in England, 1500–1800* (London: Weidenfeld & Nicolson, 1977), p. 147; J. H. Elliot, *Imperial Spain, 1469–1716* (New York: St. Martin's Press, 1964), p. 177.

12. Hernan Cortés, op. cit., p. 263.

13. Quoted in Pedro de Alvarado, *An Account of the Conquest of Guatemala in 1524* (Boston: Milford House, 1972), p. 126.

14. Ibid., pp. 131–32.

15. David E. Stannard, *American Holocaust*, op. cit., p. 81; he is relying primarily on Donald E. Chipman, *Nuño de Guzmán and the Province of Panuco in New Spain, 1518–1610* (Glendale, California: Arthur C. Clark, 1967).

16. *See* Nathan Wachtel, *The Vision of the Vanquished: The Spanish Conquest of Peru Through Indian Eyes, 1530–1570* (Sussex: Harvester Press, 1977).

17. David E. Stannard, *American Holocaust*, op. cit., p. 87; the quotes are taken from John Hemming, *The Conquest of the Incas* (New York: Harcourt Brace Jovanovich, 1970), p. 359.

18. John Hemming, *Red Gold: The Conquest of the Brazilian Indians, 1500–1760* (Cambridge, Massachusetts: Harvard University Press, 1978), pp. 139–41.

19. Quoted in Thomas Berger, *The Long and Terrible Shadow: White Values and Native Rights in America, 1492–1992* (Seattle: University of Washington Press, 1991), p. 44.

20. Lyle N. McAlister, *Spain and Portugal in the New World, 1492–1700* (Minneapolis: University of Minnesota Press, 1984).

21. Bernardino de Sahagún, *The Conquest of New Spain* (Salt Lake City: University of Utah Press, 1989 [publication of a translation of the original 1585 Spanish language edition]).

22. David E. Stannard, *American Holocaust,* op. cit., pp. 82–83; he is relying heavily on William L. Sherman, *Native Forced Labor in Sixteenth Century Central America* (Lincoln: University of Nebraska Press, 1979).

23. On demography, *see* Woodrow Borah and Sherburn F. Cook, *The Aboriginal Population of Central Mexico on the Eve of the Spanish Conquest* (Berkeley: University of California Press, *Ibero–Americana* No. 45, 1963). On Cortés' colonial enterprises, *see* France V. Scholes, "The Spanish Conqueror as Business Man: A Chapter in the History of Fernando Cortés," *New Mexico Quarterly,* No. 28 (1958); and Francisco López de Gómera, *Cortés: The Life of the Conqueror by His Secretary* (Berkeley: University of California Press, 1965).

24. Sherburn F. Cook and Woodrow Borah, *The Indian Population of Central Mexico, 1531–1610* (Berkeley: University of California Press, *Ibero–Americana* No. 44, 1960).

25. David E. Stannard, *American Holocaust,* op. cit., pp. 81–83; he is relying on Daniel T. Reff, *Disease, Depopulation, and Culture Change in Northern New Spain, 1518–1764* (Salt Lake City: University of Utah Press, 1991), pp. 194–242. *See* also Peter Gerhard, *The Northern Frontier of New Spain* (Princeton, New Jersey: Princeton University Press, 1982), pp. 23–25.

26. Peter Gerhard, *The Southwest Frontier of New Spain* (Princeton, New Jersey: Princeton University Press, 1979), p. 25.

27. Peter Gerhard, *A Guide to the Historical Geography of New Spain* (Princeton, New Jersey: Princeton University Press, 1972), pp. 22–25.

28. Quoted in Grant D. Jones, *Maya Resistance to Spanish Rule: Time and History on a Colonial Frontier* (Albuquerque: University of New Mexico Press, 1989), p. 42.

29. Alonzo de Zorita, *Life and Labor in Ancient Mexico: The Brief and Summary Relation of the Lords of New Spain* (New Brunswick, New Jersey: Rutgers University Press, 1963), p. 210.

30. David E. Stannard, *American Holocaust,* op. cit., pp. 82, 86; he is relying on W. George Lovell, *Conquest and Survival in Colonial Guatemala: A Historical Geography of the Chuchumatan Highlands, 1500–1821* (Montréal: McGill–Queen's University Press, 1985), p. 145; David R. Randall, "The Indian Slave Trade and Population of Nicaragua During the Sixteenth Century," in *The Native Population of the Americas in 1492,* William M. Denevan, ed. (Madison: University of Wisconsin Press, 1976), pp. 67–76; Linda Newson, *The Cost of Conquest: Indian Decline in Honduras Under Spanish Rule* (Boulder, Colorado: Westview Press, 1986), pp. 107–08.

31. Sherburn F. Cook, op. cit., p. 114.

32. Quoted in John Hemming, *Conquest of the Incas,* op. cit., p. 351.

33. On Potosí and its significance to funding Europe's "industrial revolution," *see* Eduardo Galeano, *The Open Veins of Latin America: Three Centuries of the Pillage of a Continent* (New York: Monthly Review Press, 1975).

34. Quoted in John Hemming, *Conquest of the Incas,* op. cit., p. 368.

35. Ibid.

36. Pedro de Cieza de León, *The Incas* (Norman: University of Oklahoma Press, needs the date of publication), p. 62.

37. Quoted in John Hemming, *Conquest of the Incas,* op. cit., p. 369.

38. Ibid.

39. David E. Stannard, *American Holocaust*, op. cit., p. 89; on the life expectancy of Buna workers at Auschwitz, he references Raul Hillberg, *The Destruction of the European Jews* (Chicago: Quadrangle Books, 1961), p. 596.

40. John Hemming, *Red Gold*, op. cit., pp. 143–44; *Amazon Frontier: The Defeat of the Brazilian Indians* (Cambridge, Massachusetts: Harvard University Press, 1987).

41. Stuart B. Schwartz, "Indian Labor and New World Plantations: European Demands and Indian Responses in Northeast Brazil," *American Historical Review*, No. 83 (1978).

42. Thomas Berger, op. cit., pp. 44–45.

43. David E. Stannard, *American Holocaust*, op. cit., p. 94.

44. Quoted in John Hemming, *Red Gold*, op. cit., p. 142.

45. Thomas Berger, op. cit. pp. 44–45.

46. For descriptions of this "sport" as practiced by Columbus' men and those on the mainland, *see*, e.g., Tzvetan Todorov, *The Conquest of America: The Question of the Other* (New York: Harper & Row, 1984), pp. 139–41.

47. For accounts of this sort of activity on Española, *see*, e.g., Bartolomé de Las Casas, *The Devastation of the Indies: A Brief Account* (New York: Seabury Press, 1974); on the mainland, *see*, e.g., Alonzo de Zorita, op. cit.

48. John Grier Varner and Jeanette Johnson Varner, *Dogs of Conquest* (Norman: University of Oklahoma Press, 1983).

49. Ibid., pp. 192–93.

50. Ibid., pp. 36–37.

51. Ibid., pp. 38–39.

52. Pedro de Ciez de León, op. cit., p. Lix.

53. Quoted in Tzvetan Todorov, op. cit., p. 139.

54. David E. Stannard, *American Holocaust*, op. cit., p. 85; he draws his example from William L. Sherman, op. cit., p. 311.

55. Quoted in John Hemming, *Conquest of the Incas*, op. cit., p. 363.

56. Diego de Almagro, quoted in ibid., p. 364.

57. The figure derives from Spanish and Portuguese census data showing an aggregate native population of about 10,000,000 for the areas discussed in 1700. This is juxtaposed with Henry F. Dobyns' figure of approximately 90,000,000 indigenous people in the same regions prior to the invasion; Henry F. Dobyns, "Estimating Aboriginal American Population," op. cit.

58. A photograph of this macabre work is included in Robert S. Weddle, *Spanish Sea: The Gulf of Mexico in North American Discovery, 1500–1685* (College Station: Texas A&M Press, 1985), insert between pp. 158–59.

59. Nicolás Sánchez–Alboronoz, *The Population of Latin America: A History* (Berkeley: University of California Press, 1974), pp. 129–30. I say "ostensibly" in connection with the three "pure" racial classifications because many of the supposed Caucasians from Iberia actually weren't. Of the 200,000–odd "Spaniards" arriving in Mexico by 1570, for example, it has been estimated that about a third were actually of Moorish descent, another third Sefardic Jews who had converted to Catholicism ("*conversos*"); Peter Boyd–Bowman, *Patterns of Spanish Immigration to the New World, 1493–1580* (Buffalo: State University of New York Council on the Humanities, 1973).

60. Magnus Mörner, *Race Mixture in the History of Latin America* (Boston: Little, Brown & Co., 1967), p. 58.

61. Again, the process is comparable to that later implemented in the United States for the same purpose; *see* Ward Churchill, "Nobody's Pet Poodle: Jimmie Durham, an Artist for Native America," in Ward Churchill, *Indians Are Us? Genocide and Colonization in Native North America* (Monroe, Maine: Common Courage Press, 1994).

62. Interestingly, although it was a U.S. jurist, John Marshall, who originally articulated the legal doctrine through which such maneuverings transpired, many South American governments seem to have implemented it in wholesale fashion well before the United States; on Marshall, *see*, e.g., Ward Churchill, "Perversions of Justice: Examining the Doctrine of U.S. Rights to Occupancy in North America," in *Struggle for the Land*, op. cit., pp. 33–83; on Latino precursors to U.S. implementation in 1887, *see* Thomas Berger, op. cit., pp. 106–07; on U.S. implementation, *see*, e.g., Janet A. McDowell, *The Dispossession of the American Indian, 1887–1934* (Bloomington: University Press of Indiana, 1991).

63. Bernardo Berdichewsky, *The Araucanian Indian in Chile* (Copenhagen: IWGIA Doc. No. 20, 1975).

64. Thomas Berger, op. cit., p. 107.

65. On the Mayas, *see* Grant D. Jones, *Maya Resistance*, op. cit.; on the Pueblo Revolt, *see* Oakah L. Jones, Jr., *Pueblo Warriors and the Spanish Conquest* (Norman: University of Oklahoma Press, 1966); on the Manaus, *see* John Hemming, *Red Gold*, op. cit.; and *Amazon Frontier*, op. cit.; on Peru, *see* the collected volume, editors, *Túpac Amaru II* (Lima: n. p., 1976).

66. On the Yaquis, *see* Evelyn Hu–DeHart, *Yaqui Resistance and Survival* (Madison: University of Wisconsin Press, 1984); on the Apaches, *see* Frank C. Lockwood, *The Apache Indians* (Lincoln: University of Nebraska Press, 1938).

67. An earlier campaign to clear the Araucaños from the pampas, undertaken by President Juan Manuel Rosas in 1833, was unsuccessful; David Rock, *Argentina, 1516–1987* (Berkeley: University of California Press, 1987).

68. Juan Carlos Walther, *La Conquista del Desierto* (Buenos Aires: Editorial Universitorio Buenos Aires, 1971).

69. Thomas Berger, op. cit., pp. 96–97; his first quote is of Julio Roca, in David Rock, op. cit.; his second is from V. S. Naipal, *The Return of Eva Perón* (New York: Alfred A. Knopf, 1980).

70. David Rock, op. cit.

71. V. S. Naipal, op. cit., p. 149.

72. On the Aché extermination, *see* Richard Arens, ed., *Genocide in Paraguay* (Philadelphia: Temple University Press, 1976); Elie Wiesel is quoted from the first page of his epilogue to this volume, "Now We Know," pp. 165–67.

73. Elie Wiesel, op. cit., pp. 167–68.

74. *Report of the Fourth Russell Tribunal on the Rights of the Indians of the Americas* (Nottingham, United Kingdom: Bertrand Russell Foundation, 1980), p. 25.

75. Rex Weyler, *Blood of the Land: The U.S. Government and Corporate War Against the American Indian Movement* (New York: Everest House, 1982), p. 221.

76. *New York Times* News Service, 6 Jan. 1973.

77. Rex Weyler, op. cit., p. 221.

78. Ibid., p. 222; the author is relying on Robert L. Ledogar, *Hungry for Profits* (New York: International Documentation, 1975).

79. Reported in *Akwesasne Notes*, Spring (1972), p. 29.

80. *Report of the Fourth Russell Tribunal*, op. cit., p. 97; on the ecological issues involved, *see* Susanna Hecht and Alexander Cockburn, *The Fate of the Forest: Developers, Destroyers and Defenders of the Amazon* (London: Verso Books, 1989).

81. Rex Weyler, op. cit., p. 224; he is relying on *Brazilian Information Bulletin* (Berkeley: American Friends of Brazil, 1973) and *The Yanomami Indian Park* (Boston: Anthropology Resource Center, 1981).

82. Quoted in Thomas Berger, op. cit., p. 107.

83. Ibid., pp. 107–08.

84. Quoted in Rex Weyler, op. cit., p. 229.

85. Ibid., p. 215.

86. For an overview of the Working Group process, *see* S. James Anaya, "The Rights of Indigenous People and International Law in Historical and Contemporary Perspective," in *American Indian Law: Cases and Material*, Robert N. Clinton, Nell Jessup Newton, and Monroe E. Price, eds. (Charlottesville, Virginia: Michie Co., Law Publishers, 1991), pp. 1257–276.

87. Rex Weyler, op. cit., p. 229.

88. Noam Chomsky, "Introduction," in *Bridge of Courage: Life Storie of the Guatemalan Compañeros and Compañeras*, Jennifer Harbury, ed. (Monroe, Maine: Common Courage Press, 1994), p. 17. For background on the 1954 coup, *see* Bryce Wood, *The Dismantling of the Good Neighbor Policy* (Austin: University of Texas Press, 1985); Robert M. Carmack, ed., *Harvest of Violence: The Maya Indians and the Guatemala Crisis* (Norman: University of Oklahoma Press, 1988); Piero Gleijeses, *Shattered Hope: The Guatemalan Revolution and the United States, 1944–1954* (Princeton, New Jersey: Princeton University Press, 1991).

89. Rex Weyler, op. cit., p. 219. For further background, *see* Julie Hodson, *Witness to Political Violence in Guatemala* (New York: Oxfam America, 1982); Rigoberta Menchú, *I, Rigoberta Menchú* (London: Verso Press, 1983); James Painter, *Guatemala: False Hope, False Freedom* (London: Catholic Institute for International Relations, 1987); Jean–Marie Simon, *Guatemala: Eternal Spring, Eternal Tyranny* (New York: W. W. Norton, 1987); Edward R. F. Sheehan, *Agony in the Garden: A Stranger in Guatemala* (New York: Houghton–Mifflin, 1989).

90. Thomas Berger, op. cit., p. 119.

91. Anonymous Indian, quoted in ibid., p. 114.

92. Anonymous Indian, quoted in Ronald Wright, *Time Among the Maya: Travels in Belize, Guatemala and Mexico* (New York: Viking Press, 1989), p. 220.

93. The families had come to power in 1932, following the "*Matanza*," a series of massacres resulting in the deaths of about 30,000 Indians; Thomas P. Anderson, *Matanza: El Salvador's Communist Revolt of 1932* (Lincoln: University of Nebraska Press, 1971); Philip Russell, *El Salvador in Crisis* (Denver: Colorado River Press, 1984).

94. Jenny Pearce, *Under the Eagle: U.S. Intervention in Central America and the Caribbean* (Boston: South End Press, 1981), p. 209.

95. "From 1963 to 1970 General 'Chele' Medrano was the closest collaborator of the U.S. military agencies in El Salvador and the main liaison with the CIA. He had a record of extreme brutality and had been responsible for torturing political prisoners and common criminals. In 1967 he became head of the National Guard. It was Medrano, with CIA help, who founded ORDEN in 1968. A US Office of Public Safety (OPS) programme was started in El Salvador in 1967 and an OPS adviser was involved in working with Medrano to establish a special intelligence unit in the National Guard and, to work with it, what was described as a 30,000 man informant network—this was to become known as "ORDEN"; ibid., p. 214. On OPS overall, *see* A. J. Langguth, *Hidden Terrors: The Truth About U.S. Police Operations in Latin America* (New York: Pantheon Books, 1978).

96. Anonymous Salvadoran priest, quoted in *El Salvador—A Revolution Brews* (New York: NACLA, 1980).

97. *El Salvador's Other Victims: The War on the Displaced* (New York: Americas Watch/Lawyers Committee for International Human Rights, Aug. 1984).

98. Noam Chomsky, *Turning the Tide: U.S. Intervention in Central America and the Struggle for Peace* (Boston: South End Press, 1985), p. 25; he is relying on two reports by Americas Watch: *Free Fire* (Aug. 1984) and *Draining the Sea...* (March 1985).

99. Cynthia Arnson, *El Salvador: A Revolution Confronts the United States* (Washington, D.C.: Institute for Policy Studies, 1982), pp. 84–85.

100. Ray Bonner, *Weakness and Deceit* (New York: *Times* Books, 1984), pp. 325–26.

101. On the Los Llanitos massacre, perpetrated by the Atlacatl Battalion in July 1984 (68 dead), as well as the Río Gualsinga Massacre committed by the same unit the same month, *see* James LeMoyne's article in the *New York Times*, 9 Sept. 1984; on the Las Vueltas Massacre, perpetrated by the Atlacatl Battalion on August 30, 1984 ("several dozen" dead), *see Washington Report on the Hemisphere*, 30 Oct. 1984.

102. Noam Chomsky, *Turning the Tide*, op. cit., p. 105; he is relying on testimony by U.S. State Department officials before the Senate Select Committee on Foreign Affairs, Report on Human Rights in El Salvador (Washington, D.C.: U.S. Government Printing Office, 1983), pp. 57, 168–69.

103. The claim, however, is not entirely true, as it is not in other supposedly "Indian Free Zones" like Cuba and Puerto Rico. In 1986, Colorado AIM leader Glenn Morris and others had occasion to visit a native village in Costa Rica, located in a remote area near the Panamanian border. There are others.

104. *See*, e.g., Gregory Cerio, "The Black Legend: Were the Spaniards That Cruel?" *Newsweek: Columbus Special Issue*, Fall/Winter (1992); for a good survey of the related brand of "revisionism," *see* Deborah E. Lipstadt, *Denying the Holocaust: The Growing Assault on Truth and Memory* (New York: Free Press, 1993).

105. For analysis, *see* Russell Thornton, op. cit., pp. 20–25; a particularly useful overview of how Kroeber and others "cooked the books" on estimates of precolumbian native population may be found in Francis Jennings, *The Invasion of America: Indians, Colonialism and the Cant of Conquest* (New York: W. W. Norton, 1976), esp. the chapter entitled "The Widowed Land."

106. The classic articulation among nazi apologists is Paul Rassinier's *Debunking the Genocide Myth: A Study of the Nazi Concentration Camps and the Alleged Extermination of European Jewry* (Torrance, California: Institute for Historical Review, 1978).

107. For recent samples of this sort of argument, *see*, e.g., Jeffrey Hart, "Discovering Columbus," *National Review*, 15 Oct. 1990; Raymond Sokolov, "Stop Hating Columbus," *Newsweek: Columbus Special Issue*, Fall/Winter (1992).

108. For a good survey, *see* Elizabeth H. Boone, ed., *Ritual Human Sacrifice in Mesoamerica* (Washington, D.C.: Dumbarton Oaks Research Library, 1984).

109. Peter Hassler, "The Lies of the Conquistadors: Cutting Through the Myth of Human Sacrifice," *World Press Review*, Dec. 1992; he is referencing Bernal Díaz del Castillo's *Historia Verdadera de la Conquista de la Nueva España*, published posthumously in 1632, but acknowledges that "Cortes fathered the lie in 1522, when he wrote a shorter version of the tale to Emperor Charles V."

110. R. Po–Chia Hsia, *The Myth of Ritual Murder: Jews and Magic in Reformation Germany* (New Haven: Yale University Press, 1988); Norman Cohn, *Warrant for Genocide: The Myth of the Jewish World–Conspiracy and the Protocols of the Elders of Zion* (New York: Harper & Row, 1967).

111. For instance, the claim that Indians precipitated some sort of never–quite–defined–or–documented environmental devastation of America before the arrival of Europeans; *see*, e.g., Paul Valentine, "Dancing with Myths," *Washington Post*, 7 Apr. 1991.

112. Raymond Sokolov, op. cit.

113. Revolutionary Communist Party, USA, "Searching for the Second Harvest," in *Marxism and Native Americans*, Ward Churchill, ed. (Boston: South End Press, 1983), pp. 35–58; the source of the title is the quaint notion—sometimes described as the "Indians Eat Shit Thesis"—that American Indians traditionally ate fecal material as an integral part of their diet.

114. Roxanne Dunbar Ortiz, *Indians of the Americas: Human Rights and Self–Determination* (London: Zed Books, 1984), pp. 5–6: "A religious cult came to dominate which required the daily ritual human sacrifice of thousands of people to the Sun God."

115. George Weurthner, "An Ecological View of the Indian," *Earth First!*, Vol. 7, No. 1 (Aug. 1987); for the earlier elaboration of precisely the same view by two of the most inept and reactionary anthropologists in recent memory, *see* Paul S. Martin and H. E. Wright, *Pleistocene Extinctions: The Search for a Cause* (New Haven: Yale University Press, 1967).

116. Christopher Hitchens, "Minority Report;" *The Nation*, 19 Oct. 1992; Jeffrey Hart, op. cit.

117. Rex Weyler, op. cit., p. 230; *see* also Hugo Blanco, *Land or Death* (New York: Pathfinder Press, 1977).

118. Simon Strong, *Shining Path: Terror and Revolution in Peru* (New York: *Times* Books, 1992); on the *requerimiento*, the Spanish law requiring Indians to convert to Catholicism on pain of death, *see* Charles Gibson, *The Spanish Tradition in Mexico* (Columbia: University of South Carolina Press, 1968), pp. 53–60.

119. Glenn T. Morris and Ward Churchill, "Between a Rock and a Hard Place: Left–Wing Revolution, Right–Wing Reaction and the Destruction of Indigenous Peoples," *Cultural Survival Quarterly*, Vol. 11, No. 3 (Fall 1988), and included in this collection of essays.

120. For an especially strong articulation, *see* Héctor Diaz–Polanco, "Indigenismo, Populism, and Marxism," *Latin American Perspectives*, Vol. 9, No. 2 (Spring 1982).

121. *See*, e.g., Hannah Arendt, *The Origins of Totalitarianism* (New York: Harcourt Brace Jovanovich, 1951) or *Eichmann in Jerusalem: A Report on the Banality of Evil* (New York: Penguin Books, 1965); and Irving Louis Horowitz, *Genocide: State Power and Mass Murder*

(New Brunswick, New Jersey: Transaction Books, 1976) or *Taking Lives: Genocide and State Power* (New Brunswick, New Jersey: Transaction Books, 1982).

122. Deborah E. Lipstadt, op. cit.; Pierre Vidal–Naquet, *Assassins of Memory: Essays on Denial of the Holocaust* (New York: Columbia University Press, 1992).

123. A good example of the "reasoning" Lipstadt and Vidal–Naquet incite may be found in Arthur D. Butz, *The Hoax of the Twentieth Century: The Case Against the Presumed Extermination of European Jewry* (Torrance, California: Institute for Historical Review, 1977).

124. Sherburn F. Cook and Woodrow Borah, op. cit.; Woodrow Borah and Sherburn F. Cook, op. cit.; Henry F. Dobyns, op. cit.; Carl O. Sauer, *Selected Essays, 1963–1975* (Berkeley: Turtle Island Foundation, 1981).

125. David E. Stannard, op. cit.; Kirkpatrick Sale, *The Conquest of Paradise: Christopher Columbus and the Columbian Legacy* (New York: Alfred A. Knopf, 1990); Eduardo Galeano, *The Open Veins of Latin America: Five Centuries of the Pillage of a Continent* (New York: Monthly Review Press, 1973), and *Memory of Fire: Genesis* (New York: Pantheon Books, 1985).

126. *See,* e.g., Vine Deloria, Jr., *God Is Red* (Golden, Colorado: Fulcrum Press [2d ed.], 1992); Donald A. Grinde, Jr., and Bruce Johansen, *Exemplar of Liberty* (Los Angeles: UCLA American Indian Studies Center, 1991); and Robert A. Williams, Jr., *The American Indian in Western Legal Thought: The Discourses of Conquest* (London/New York: Oxford University Press, 1990).

127. Aside from the recent work of various American Indians of both continents, illustrations should include that of indigenous Hawaiians. *See,* e.g., Lilikala Kame'eleihiwa, *Native Lands and Foreign Desires* (Honolulu: Bishop Museum Press, 1992); Haunani–Kay Trask, *From a Native Daughter: Colonialism and Sovereignty in Hawai'i* (Monroe, Maine: Common Courage Press, 1993).

128. Edward Said, *The Pen and the Sword: Conversations with David Barsamian* (Monroe, Maine: Common Courage Press, 1994). *See* also John D. Caputo, *Radical Hermeneutics: Repetition, Deconstruction, and the Hermeneutic Project* (Bloomington: Indiana University Press, 1987).

129. *See,* e.g., Edward Said, *Orientalism* (New York: Random House, 1978). *See* also Martin Bernal, *Black Athena: The Afroasiatic Roots of Classical Civilization, Vol. 1: The Fabrication of Ancient Greece, 1785–1985* (New Brunswick, New Jersey: Rutgers University Press, 1987).

130. This is intended in the Gramscian sense. For elaboration, *see* Walter L. Adamson, *Hegemony and Revolution: A Study of Antonio Gramsci's Political and Cultural Theory* (Berkeley: University of California Press, 1980).

131. The demographers, to be sure, have come in for their fair share of criticism; *see,* e.g., David Henige, "Their Number Become Thick: Native American Historical Demography as Expiation," in *The Invented Indian: Cultural Fictions and Government Policies,* James Clifford, ed. (New Brunswick, New Jersey: Transaction Books, 1990).

132. *See,* e.g., the review of David E. Stannard by J. H. Elliott in the *New York Review of Books,* 24 June 1993; *see* also Stannard's reply, published in the *New York Review* on October 21. The nature of the contended issues is revealed more broadly in Paul Berman, ed., *Debating P.C.: The Controversy Over Political Correctness on College Campuses* (New York: Laurel Books, 1992). The ideological framework employed by Elliot and others of his persuasion is articulated succinctly in an essay by Wilcomb E. Washburn, alleged "Dean"

of American Indianist historians, entitled "Distinguishing History for Moral Philosophy and Public Advocacy"; *see* Calvin Martin, ed., *The American Indian and the Problem of History* (New York: Oxford University Press, 1987), pp. 91–97.

133. James Axtell, *The European and the Indian: Essays in the Ethnohistory of North America* (New York: Oxford University Press, 1981), and *Beyond 1492: Encounters in Colonial North America* (New York: Oxford University Press, 1992).

Genocide

Toward a Functional Definition*

Genocide is always and everywhere an essentially political decision.

Irving Louis Horowitz

One of the more perplexing problems confronting contemporary socio–political theorists concerns the persistence of genocide, both as an overt instrument of state policy and as an almost incidental by–product of the functioning of advanced industrial society. While it can be said with virtual certainty that genocide today exists on a widespread and possibly growing basis, it cannot be correspondingly contended that the phenomenon is understood.

At the most fundamental level, it may be asserted that we presently lack even a coherent and viable description of the processes and circumstances implied by the term "genocide." A host of theses attempt to offer sociological definitions, variously holding that the essence of the genocidal process may be discerned in the physical liquidation of individual members of targeted groups, and that meaning should be associated with the scale of annihilation or the specific nature of the state apparatus established to effect the lethal process. Among the more juridically minded, definitional questions seem to center upon the literal intent of the perpetrators of specific mass murders and the locus of conceptual lines differentiating genocide from the related crimes of war and crimes against humanity. The aggregate result, however, provides not so much for clarity and understanding of the subject discussed, but for a confusing and highly volatile welter of definitional contradictions.

---

*This essay originally appeared in *Alternatives*, Vol. XI, No. 3 (July 1986).

In such a context, it is clear that effective analytical endeavors and resultant bodies of law and policy cannot emerge. To be sure, without the latter we cannot hope to stop the cancer of genocide, a disease that everyone seems to agree must be expunged. Indeed, as things now stand, we cannot even rationally hope to bring its consumptive proliferation under control.

The purpose of this essay, then, is to make some small contribution to a better understanding of genocidal occurrences, at least to the extent that it may be readily understood and agreed when a genocide is taking place. To this end, a number of the prevailing notions of the phenomenon, both legal and sociological, will be discussed in passing as a means to arrive at a single typology. Such a synthesis should yield a greater utility for judicial, political, and scholarly work on genocide than is currently possible. The reader is cautioned that no single study of this sort can lay claim to being either an exhaustive or definitive examination of the subject matter. Rather, it is intended to spark further consideration of the topic at hand and, hopefully, to bring about a refocusing of research.

An Elemental Confusion

All too often, otherwise sensitive and thoughtful individuals are reduced to defensive simplisms and mechanistic formulations when the word "genocide" is discussed. Many, of whom Likud–oriented zionists are perhaps the most pronounced example, are wont to restrict the definition to the narrow (and perhaps marginal) arena of the Hitlerian slaughter mills. While the political reasons for this zionist posture may be somewhat nebulous, the emotional reasons are not. As Robert Davis and Mark Zannis, Canadian researchers into the question of genocide, have noted: "The argument is sometimes made that to define genocide in terms other than mass homicide is to cheapen its currency and make a mockery of the memory of the millions who died in Hitler's holocaust."[1] However, as the authors go on to observe, the situation is really rather more complex.

> No one would deny the unspeakable horror of the Nazi mass murder. [But] the quality that made these deeds truly monstrous is the realization that ... man has attained the capacity to systematically wipe out an entire race.... *To destroy a people and their shared life is the crime*, and it can be accomplished as efficiently by means other than mass homicide.[2] (emphasis added)

Such a view is in accord with the expressed opinions of Adolph Hitler himself, as when he stated that "[t]here are many ways, systematical and comparatively painless, or at any rate bloodless, of causing undesirable races to die out."[3] Elsewhere, in discussing the planned destruction of Europe's Jews,

Gypsies, Slavs, and Poles, he explained that "I don't necessarily mean destroy; I will simply take systematic measures to dam their great fertility."[4] Of course, actual circumstances forced the compression of Hitler's agenda for the elimination of "undesirables," with results that are far too well known to bear recounting here. What is important to recall is that until the so–called Wannsee Conference of January 20, 1942, nazi policy was formally committed to relocation/deportation as the "solution of the race question," and that this earlier phase held precisely the same goal as "the final solution" (that is, eradication of the targeted groups in Europe).[5]

Among the most common ideologically motivated misinterpretations of the meaning (real or potential) of genocide are those evident in the posturings of subscribers on one side or the other of the Cold War. Among orthodox marxists it is commonly held that the phenomenon is specifically linked to machinations of "late capitalism," a matter to be overcome through appropriate application of socialist principles. While there is undoubtedly a certain merit to the marxian analysis, it is an obviously skewed perspective, opting as it does to ignore numerous situations—and their causes—within the socialist world itself.

Instances which bring up the question of genocide abound in China, Vietnam, and other socialist states. However, the example of the USSR, as the first and ostensibly most developed socialist country, seems particularly instructive. Here, Nikolai K. Deker and Andrei Lebed have compiled a survey of what they believe would be traditionally posited as cases of Soviet genocide. The list includes the complete destruction of such peoples as the Crimean Turks, Kalmyks, various nationalities of the north Caucasus, and the Volga Germans. Also at issue for Deker and Lebed is the partial destruction of other peoples such as the Armenians, Azerbaidzhanis, Byelorussians, Georgians, Jews, (Great) Russians, Turkestanis, and Ukrainians, as well as the complete or partial destruction of religious groups, including Moslems, Buddhists, Catholics, and Autocephelics.[6]

For what may be politically obvious reasons, marxist polemicists on the subject of genocide tend to remain silent on such matters, regardless of the clear theoretical significance involved. The marxian analysis of genocide (either as to its meaning or its causes) cannot therefore be said to be particularly more helpful than that of zionism in contributing substantially to the evolution of a coherent definition or causal theory of the phenomenon.[7]

Similarly, proponents of anti–communist "Free World" ideology, whether in its corporate–liberal or conservative variants, tend to focus exclusively on examples drawn from the socialist bloc, ignoring even the most obvious circumstances and practices of countries comprising their "sphere of influence." A salient example of this is represented by a *Time* magazine article by David Aikman, published on July 31, 1978, and entitled "Cambodia: An Experiment in Genocide." According to Aikman, the Khmer Rouge regime in

Kampuchea (revolutionary Cambodia) had by the time of his writing exterminated more than a million people from its total population of 7 million. He went on to note that "somehow the enormity of the Cambodian tragedy—even leaving aside the grim question of how many or how few actually died in the [Khmer Rouge] experiment in genocide—has failed to evoke an appropriate response of outrage in the West." Yet as Noam Chomsky and Edward S. Herman observed, "Figures apart, what is striking about this claim is that nowhere in the article is there reference to any US responsibility, no indication that deaths from starvation or disease may be something other than a 'bloodbath' by the Khmer Rouge."[8] After all, the extent and effects of long–term U.S. saturation bombing of Kampuchea's major food producing areas—a factor which could hardly have avoided engendering massive starvation and accompanying disease—was well known.[9]

With the postulations on genocide extended by anti–communists as tainted in those of their marxist opponents, and for quite identical reasons (albeit, in mirror image), it follows that so–called free world analyses will yield no more utility in arriving at adequate definitions of either the fact or function of genocide than do marxist or zionist models. No matter in which direction we turn for guidance at present, conventional perceptions of genocide are so politicized and circumscribed as to be useless or worse. Rather than fostering clarity and understanding of the phenomenon so as to lead to an effective means of combating it, they induce an elemental confusion that forestalls remedy. To unravel and move beyond this current impasse, it is necessary to trace the historical contours of the evolution of genocide.

The Evolution of a Concept

The period following World War I saw a good deal of concern and debate in the international circles about the level of casualties inflicted through the application of Karl von Clausewitz's famous formulation that "war is politics pursued by other means." Perhaps the major impetus leading to such considerations was the scale and sheer barbarity evident in the conduct of the First World War itself. Nonetheless, special attention was focused on the policies of the Turkish Ottoman Empire toward its Armenian minority population from 1915 onward. As Vakahn N. Dadrian summarized the situation:

> In 1915, the leaders of the Turkish Empire put into action a plan to remove and exterminate its Armenian population of approximately 1,800,000 persons. The Turks were not particular about the methods they employed to this end: of at least a million and a half Armenians forced to leave their homes, supposedly to be deported, from 600,000 to 800,000 were murdered before ever reaching their destinations.

Descriptions of this massacre clearly indicate an attempt to deliberately, systematically exterminate all or most of this group.[10]

Attempts to come to grips with the ramifications of the Turkish horror fell somewhat naturally upon the League of Nations. The League, not unlike the academic organizations from which it drew expertise and guidance, lacked any sort of formal conceptualization that could accommodate what had transpired. Casting about for a basis in extant law from which to develop a legalistic proscription of conduct such as that visited on the Armenians, the League's scholars were forced to make do with Article 22 of the 1907 (Fourth) Hague Convention: "The right of belligerents to adopt means of injuring the enemy is not unlimited...." Consequently, intellectualization of the destruction of the Armenians was made to run in channels describing the Turks as being on one side of the war (aligned with Germany), while the Armenians, being of "Russian" descent, were consigned to being on the other (allied) side.

If the description thus tendered failed to match the circumstances that occurred, neither did the corrective legislation produced at the 1929 Geneva Convention on the Rules of War. Although an entire battery of international law was created to protect civilians in time of war, its provisions were designed essentially to accommodate the civilian population of one country when invaded by another, or the civilians of one nation trapped by a sudden declaration of war within the territory of another (hostile) power. Not much was said concerning the possibility that a given country might unleash its armed power upon its *own* citizenry, or that civilians might well be liquidated en masse by military or other means during periods not typically understood as constituting "times of war."

The Geneva Convention was, of course, following an honorable tradition dating back at least to the third century AD, with the famous pronouncement of St. Augustine of Hippo that war might be divided into two types: just and unjust. While it was the duty of moral men to pursue just warfare, it was equally their duty to refuse participation in unjust wars, and to punish those who nonetheless chose to pursue them. The intent of the Convention, at least in part, was to define actions such as those undertaken by the Turks as clearly constituting "unjust war," and therefore to be illegal. Nevertheless, it was apparent almost from the outset that the supposed remedy was a failure.

The rise and consolidation of Hitlerian Germany ultimately crystallized what was bothersome and lacking in the League's appreciation of what had occurred in Turkey. By 1944, Professor Raphael Lemkin had coined a new word to describe the phenomenon and had provided a remarkably lucid and sensitive definition (for a first effort):

> Generally speaking, genocide does not necessarily mean the immediate destruction of a nation, except when accomplished by mass killings of all members of a nation. It is rather intended to signify a

coordinated plan of different actions aimed at the essential foundations of the life of national groups, with the aim of annihilating the
groups themselves. The objectives of such a plan would be the
disintegration of the political and social institutions of culture,
language, national groups, and the destruction of the personal security, liberty, health, dignity and even the lives of the individuals
belonging to such groups. Genocide is directed against individuals,
not in their individual capacity, but as members of the national
group.[11]

Elsewhere in his seminal treatise, Lemkin noted that "Genocide has two
phases: one, destruction of the national pattern of the oppressed group; the
other, the imposition of the national pattern of the oppressor."[12] He also called
for the establishment of "[p]rocedural machinery for the extradition of [war]
criminals ... [and] an adequate machinery for the international protection of
national and ethnic groups."[13]

In light of the dimensions of the Holocaust accompanying the Second
World War, Lemkin's pioneering analysis and suggestions began to bear fruit
within two years. On December 11, 1946, the newly founded United Nations
General Assembly passed Resolution 96(I), which stated in part:

Genocide is a denial of the right of existence of entire human groups
as homicide is the denial of the right to life of individual human
beings; such a denial of the right of existence shocks the conscience
of mankind, results in great losses to humanity in the form of cultural
and other contributions represented by these human groups, and is
contrary to moral law and to the spirit and aim of the United Nations.

And lest anyone misunderstand that the General Assembly was concerned only with the particular form(s) of genocide visited upon Europe's
"untermenschen" by the nazis, the Resolution continued:

Many instances of such crimes of genocide have occurred when
racial, religious, political and other groups have been destroyed,
entirely or in part. (emphasis added)

Finally, the Resolution concluded that "[t]he punishment of genocide is
a matter of international concern." This language was endorsed by every nation
participating in the formation of the United Nations, and no exception has been
entered by any nation joining since.

To be sure, the preoccupation of the international community during this
period was with the punishment of the perpetrators of genocidal criminality
inside the vanquished Third Reich. Accordingly, the first—and, to date, only—
precedent of the desired international punishment for the crime of genocide was
a series of trials, executions, and imprisonments of the nazi hierarchy at
Nuremberg, Germany.

Ultimately, the "Nuremberg Doctrine" under which nazi and other World War II defendants were prosecuted encompassed three discrete areas of criminality:

* *Crimes Against the Peace* encompassed a range of acts broadly construed as indicating the planning or otherwise preparing for an unprovoked war (such as a war of conquest; generally termed "aggressive war").

* *War Crimes* included the actual waging of an aggressive war as well as violation of specific tenets of codified international law such as focusing military attacks upon civilian targets, utilizing proscribed weapons, mistreating prisoners of war, and so forth.

* *Crimes Against Humanity* was taken to include actions directed against noncombatant populations for other than strictly military reasons. These included imposing conditions of slave labor, massive forced relocation, deprivation of fundamental human rights, and the like.

As Telford Taylor, U.S. Chief Counsel at Nuremberg tells us, the third category was created specifically "to get at" the notion of genocide.[14]

Twenty–three nations adhered to the formal treaty instrument under which the Nuremberg trials were conducted, a process which opened with Justice Robert H. Jackson stating that "if it is to serve any useful purpose it must condemn aggression by any other nations, including those who now sit here in judgement." Upon completion of the trials, the U.N. General Assembly affirmed "the principles of international law" embodied in their administration.[15] When the Nuremberg criminal proceedings ended in 1950, Taylor estimated conservatively that some 10,000 persons, two–thirds of them in Europe, had been tried.[16]

Even as the Nuremberg trials proceeded, the United Nations was energetically considering measures to provide a fuller and more precise codification of the crime of genocide under international law than that provided by the aforementioned Crimes Against Humanity category which was felt to overlap too much with war crimes and to deal inadequately with group *destruction* rather than group abuse as a crime. On March 28, 1947, the U.N. Economic and Social Council passed Resolution 47 (IV), calling upon the Secretary General to draw up a draft convention on genocide. The secretariat's draft document (U.N. Document A/362) was duly generated, pushed through the organization's various review and revision processes, and, in 1948, became the *United Nations Convention for the Prevention and Punishment of the Crime of Genocide.*

Although the Convention was severely weakened in its passage from draft to final form by the political necessity of accommodating an array of objections to various provisions from a number of actions (most notably from the United States),[17] it still offered sufficient latitude for thoughtful interpreters to begin to systematically recognize genocide when it occurred, at least in particular major contours. Genocide was specified to be those actions that affect an identifiable racial, ethnic, or religious group, whether in whole or in part, in the following ways:

A) Killing members of the group.

B) Causing serious bodily and mental harm to members of the group.

C) Deliberately inflicting on the group conditions of life calculated to bring about its physical destruction in whole or in part.

D) Imposing measures intended to prevent births within the group.

E) Forcibly transferring children of the group to another group.

In addition, not only was the actual execution of these actions considered criminal within the meaning of the Convention, conspiracy to commit such acts and incitement of others to commit such acts were also held to be crimes.

The Convention provides that "[a]ny contracting party may call upon the competent organs of the United Nations to take such action under the Charter of the United Nations as they consider appropriate for the prevention and suppression of acts of genocide." It also binds the contracting parties to "pledge themselves in such cases to grant extradition in accordance with their laws and treaties in force." Further:

> Persons charged with genocide or any other acts enumerated [in the Convention] shall be tried by competent tribunal of the State in the territory of which the act was committed, or by such international tribunal as may have jurisdiction with respect to those Contracting Parties which shall have accepted its jurisdiction.

With overwhelming international ratification of the Convention essentially committing most of the world to abide by its content on pain of criminal prosecution, and with the precedent of a full–fledged international tribunal similar to that posited in the Convention having just convened in Nuremberg,[18] the United Nations then proceeded *not* to follow up with hammering out the precise jurisdictional mechanism(s) through which all this might be facilitated. Perhaps the most compelling reason for this sudden loss of momentum was the flat refusal of the United States to ratify the Convention (the only major nation to refuse) on the grounds that it would "interfere with exercise of its national sovereignty."[19] The Convention has since languished, an ineffectual and rhetorical gesture, little more. The U.N. forum, a vehicle which should have yielded a significant broadening, deepening, and maturing of the general understanding of genocide over the past four decades, has proved itself barren. To date, there has been no further formal development of the conceptualization of genocide within the United Nations; needless to say, there has been no genocide–related sanction applied, never mind indictment or prosecution of perpetrators of genocide, under U.N. auspices since the Convention went into effect.

In retrospect, the minimal progress in dealing with genocide is perhaps not surprising. The same United States that had played a major role in emasculating the secretariat's draft convention before scuttling it altogether was soon busily obtaining the early release from prison of many nazi criminals that the international tribunal it had been so instrumental in forming had convicted and sentenced.[20] As Ladislas Farago summed up the situation:

> In the early fifties, the Allies magnanimously amnestied thousands of Nazi criminals, the exact circumstances of which represent a festering but carefully concealed scandal. As the Cold War was heating up, in a process begun in 1946 by Secretary of State James F. Byrnes and inspired by Dean Acheson, the United States shifted its traditional alignment in Europe from Britain and France to the renascent Germany of Konrad Adenauer. The great pied piper of Bonn (whose own chief aide was a former Nazi official who had drafted the lethal anti–Jewish laws) promoted the idea, at first subtly, then vigorously, that the wholesale prosecution of Nazis was putting "a heavy psychological burden on the rearmament problem" in the course of West Germany's rehabilitation for its role in the "defense of Western Europe."[21]

Theoretical Forays

With legalistic channels at least temporarily denuded of potential, consideration of genocide in any meaningful sense became the domain of academics. Much of this work was sterile, consisting of a seemingly endless recapitulation of the horrors of Auschwitz and Babi Yar, perpetual dissections of this and that aspect of the nazi death–delivery mechanisms, and a constant righteous belaboring of the obvious: the form of genocide peculiar to nazi Germany could never be allowed to happen again.

Of course, there were flashes of brilliance within the gloom, as when Hannah Arendt remarked upon "the banality of evil" in her study of Adolf Eichmann, a major player in the nazi genocide. Her point was that, rather than being some sort of "outlaw aberration," nazidom and the individuals who by and large composed it were dull, ordinary, and well within a conventional "business as usual" status quo:

> [We] are forced to conclude that Eichmann acted fully within the kind of judgement required of him: he acted in accordance with the rule, examined the order given to him for its "manifest" legality, namely regularity; he did not fall back upon his "conscience," since he was not one of those who was unfamiliar with the laws of his country.[22]

From this, it might be argued that the primary basis for the popular perception of the nazis' unique culpability lay, not with their patent deviation from the norms of civilized behavior, but with their advancement of certain forms of it "to excess." To this extent, genocide would be a much more widely practiced activity than most people (or governments) would be comfortable in admitting. Such an analysis would conform well to Adolf Hitler's own impression that he was basing his racial policies upon earlier models, notably those of Britain in handling the Boers and the United States' treatment of American Indians during the nineteenth century.[23]

Having opened the intellectual door slightly toward examining genocide as a phenomenon possessing at least a potentially broad range of forms and permutations that extend across a wide array of societies, and having been rather thoroughly chastised by a number of scholars within her own Jewish community for her efforts, Arendt abruptly abandoned the field. Scarcely a year after her Eichmann foray, she was at work negating the import of her own glimpse at the face of genocidal reality and reinforcing the conventional wisdom that insisted on the link between genocide and "totalitarianism" being absolute:

> At this point the fundamental difference between the totalitarian and all other concepts of law comes to light. Totalitarian policy does not replace one set of laws with another, does not establish its own *consensus juris*, does not create, by one revolution, a new form of legality. Its defiance of all, even its own positive laws implies that it believes it can do without any *consensus juris* whatever.... It can do without the *consensus juris* because it promises to release the fulfillment of law from all action and will of man.[24]

In other words, Arendt's final explanation of Eichmann and genocide lay precisely in the very "outlaw" social characteristics she herself had so clearly and firmly rejected by previously describing him as being so commonplace as to be banal. Perhaps such a gross contradiction in Arendt's otherwise acute perceptions can be accounted for in what must have been the utterly terrifying realization that, if Eichmann could truly be said to symbolize "everyman," then genocide must be an integral aspect even of the society in which she found herself. Unable to countenance the possibility of genocide as a norm rather than an aberration, she beat a hasty if not altogether tenable intellectual retreat.

Others, however, did pick up Arendt's initial theme. Irving Louis Horowitz, for example, announced in the introduction to his monograph on the subject (dedicated to Arendt) that "Genocide is not simply a sporadic or random event such as the Katyn Forest Massacre in which 15,000 Polish troops were presumed to have been destroyed by the Red Army during World War II. In addition to its systematic character, genocide must be conducted with the approval of, if not direct intervention by, the state apparatus."[25] Having thus allowed for a possible proliferation of genocidal activities well beyond the definitional constraints typically applied, Horowitz proceeded to utilize illustrative examples of what he held to be genocides as diverse as the *violencia* in Colombia, the United States' handling of its "Indian question," and Idi Amin's performance in Uganda, in addition to such standard fare as the 1915 Turkish slaughter of Armenians, the Holocaust, and the Stalinist policy of reducing nationalities.

Horowitz also attempted to go beyond the definitional characteristics of the U.N. Convention, rendering a description of genocide which would be more functional in terms of perceiving and understanding when genocide occurred, if not to prevent or punish it:

> In addition to the legal definition of genocide, it is necessary to add a sociological dimension. Two points must be subsumed under such a heading: first, genocide represents a systematic effort over time to liquidate a national population, usually a minority; second, it functions as fundamental political policy to assure participation by the citizenry.[26]

He goes on to note, "There are exceptions to each point. Sometimes, as it is in the apartheid policy of South Africa, it is the minority that practices forms of genocide on the majority. Also, there are many cases in which overt statements of a government only vaguely reflect its covert actions, for instance, the case of Soviet policy toward its national minorities."[27] Additionally, "A formal distinction between genocide and assassination is also required. Genocide is ... *a structural and systematic destruction of innocent people by a state bureaucratic apparatus*" (emphasis in the original).[28]

In the third, expanded, edition of his book, Horowitz added much that was of a purely polemical nature—that is, subscribing to the "Free World" posture inherent to the cold warrior, thereby ignoring much and elsewhere insisting upon driving round pegs into square holes—hence diluting the sharpness of its initial impact upon the mythology of genocide.[29] Nonetheless, he did include another essay that represented a significant contribution toward clarifying the meaning of the term. Entitled "Genocide and Holocaust: On the Exclusivity of Collective Death," this short piece virtually demolished the major tenets advanced by Emil Fackenheim, perhaps *the* leading proponent of the zionist "exclusivity of the Jewish experience" idea.[30] Again, the door to a broader understanding of genocide has been wedged open, if only slightly.

Horowitz had called for the incorporation of genocide as a central issue of the social sciences and pointed to "the possibility of defining the state not in terms of communism, liberalism, or conservatism, but to what degree it permits the official and arbitrary termination of the lives of its citizens."[31] But it may be safely asserted that precious few scholars have followed this lead, including Horowitz himself (it is instructive that he deleted this phrase from later versions of his own material).[32] Consequently, the prevailing definition(s) of genocide remain lacking.

Definitional Problems

A central difficulty inherent to present conceptualizations of genocide goes to a contradiction embedded in the juridical logic applied to the initial formulation(s) of the term. Having likened genocide to murder (albeit of a group rather than of an individual) in its description, the United Nations promptly dropped this illuminating parallel, stating that, "In the present Convention, genocide means any of the following acts committed *with intent* to destroy, in whole or in part, a national, ethnical, racial, or religious group" (emphasis added).

Following the original analogy with the crime of murder, what was ultimately described in the Convention as constituting the crime of genocide parallels *only* murder in the first degree (that is, murder committed with intent and premeditation, the worst and most severely punished type). The question that must be posed now is whether the United Nations was attempting to proscribe and penalize the actual destruction of groups, or the intentions of the perpetrators. Since all accounts (and U.N. records) bear out that the United Nations desired to achieve the former rather than the latter result, using the word "intent" becomes extremely problematic.

In developed statutory codes such as that of the United States, it is clearly acknowledged that murder can be and is often accomplished in a range of degrees. Only first degree murder requires intent, a subjective and exceedingly difficult factor to prove in most cases. Thus, there is a second degree of murder covering actions where the death of the victim is not necessarily sought or desired by the perpetrator, but where death occurs while the perpetrator is engaged in some other form of suspect or illegal behavior. There is also a third degree of murder, often called "negligent homicide," where the death of the victim is not directly intended but results from the irresponsible or insensitive conduct of the perpetrator.[33]

Finally, there is a non–murder category covering inflicted deaths, usually called "manslaughter," in which it is held that the perpetrator definitely does *not* seek or desire the death of the victim, but that the victim is killed through the poor judgment of the perpetrator. In general, all actions resulting in the death of another are construed as culpable (and punishable) in common law unless there is clear evidence that the killer acts in self–defense, forestalling a potentially lethal threat forthcoming from the victim. "Justifiable homicide" is then held to pertain.

This formulation of the criminal code is quite consistent with the eleventh–century strictures on universal mayhem advanced by St. Thomas Aquinas in his *Summa Theologiae*: "It is to them that it belongs to bear the sword in combats for the defense of the State against external enemies ... those attacked must, to a fault, deserve to be attacked ... [and] those who wage wars justly have peace as the object of their intention." It also accords with slightly less archaic principles such as Francisco Suarez's observation that defensive war is always just because "the right of self–defense is a natural and necessary one."[34]

Further, the multifaceted structure of the code concerning homicide allows for the cognitive apprehension of victimization in a variety of forms rather than locking the analyst/observer into entirely subjective—or even conjectural—estimations of the intentions of the victimizer(s). That this more sensitive and rational approach to defining genocide was avoided by the United Nations is in many ways inexplicable. The confusion and arcane debate (How many angels *can* dance on the head of a pin?) engendered by its flawed formulation, on the other hand, seems beyond any doubt.[35]

In pursuit of the proof of intent to establish genocide as required by the United Nations, quite serious analysts of the question have become obsessed with locating systemic instruments designed to directly and efficiently obtain genocidal results. Horowitz, to name a prime example, uses the word "systematic" no less than 54 times in one 31–page effort to explain what is required to make "genocidal society."[36] All of this leads, sometimes inadvertently or even reluctantly, back to the flimsy premise that genocide must be identified by its structural correspondence to the forms exhibited in the Third Reich. It omits altogether the possibility (indeed, probability) that such specifically focused evidence may *may not* be present in a given instance of genocide.

No less, it evades the fact that governments, the same as murderers, are quite capable of masking and/or lying about both the nature of their actions and the intentions underpinning them. One can hardly expect that every incidence of genocide will be accompanied by the clear record of intentions offered by nazi Germany. Even in that case, as Davis and Zannis have pointed out:

> If the genocide convention had been in force in Hitler's time, he almost certainly could be expected to have replied to charges of genocide in the following manner: "Quite the contrary, I abhor genocide and worked in a singular effort to punish and prevent dangerous elements in the Jewish community who were engaged in a sinister plot to wipe out the entire Aryan race. No one has worked harder than I to uphold the genocide convention and I wholeheartedly subscribe to it."[37]

Such a contentious and restrictive environment concerning what can and cannot rightly be viewed as truly genocidal activity has engendered considerable trepidation on the part of many individuals concerned with the issue. Lord Bertrand Russell, who was well aware of the semantic and definitional pitfalls involved in deploying genocide as a charge under international law, to give but one prominent example, chose to impanel his 1967 tribunal investigating U.S. conduct in Vietnam as a body to inquire into possible war crimes rather than genocide per se. This led to a lengthy examination of American bombing patterns, deployment of certain types of ordnances, and the like, as well as to an attempt to assemble a battery of charges on the waging of aggressive war and crimes against the peace, similar in their particulars to those brought at Nuremberg.[38]

Insofar as the Russell Tribunal was taken seriously—and it was, as is evidenced by the side range of U.S. intellectual debate it sparked (or which at least cited it extensively), a matter that became of more than passing interest to the U.S. government—it was immediately drawn into a quagmire of protocol and stipulations within the relatively highly evolved Laws of War. This led Telford Taylor, an expert on the subject and rather sympathetic to the tribunal's aims, to conclude on a point–by–point basis that the legal logic imbedded in the charges was faulty or impossible under existing treaties and conventions. Although he never quite brought himself to employ the word genocide, Taylor did observe that Crimes Against Humanity seemed a more fruitful avenue of pursuit, and that the Russell Tribunal was missing the mark in hammering at the notion of war crimes.[39]

It was left to Jean–Paul Sartre, the tribunal's executive president, to essentially concur with Taylor's assessment and to go beyond it. Altering the apparent thrust of the tribunal's findings, Sartre branded the nature of the U.S. actions in Southeast Asia as genocide, without equivocation or mitigation. In its essence, Sartre's thesis was as radical as it was simple. The proof of genocide, he asserted, lies in the results of policy, not in the intentions by which it may be undertaken. The fact of Vietnamese decimation in itself established that genocide was occurring in Indochina, regardless of the U.S. government's oft–stated rationale that its intent was to liberate the Vietnamese and safeguard their freedom. Negative intentions need not be proven, Sartre held, in order to observe that negative results attended given policies; and it is the results—not the intentions—which are at issue.[40]

Moreover, he continued, intent itself seemed sufficiently established by the fact that the United States was determined to fight a counter–insurgency war in Vietnam. It is axiomatic within military doctrine that suppression of a bona fide popular insurgency entails eliminating "the sea" in which the insurgents swim, that is, the conduct of warfare on the populations rather than military formations per se. This, Sartre points out, is an *inherently* genocidal proposition accepted willingly by the Americans from the moment General William Westmoreland undertook his "strategy of massive attrition." The United States was clearly perpetrating genocide in Southeast Asia; whether this was/is a crime prosecutable under existing international law was/is another question.[41]

Following Sartre's breakthrough, reference to American genocidal practices in Indochina became quite common,[42] as did reference to related categories (some of them virtually coined for the occasion), such as "ecocide."[43] At the level of international law, not much was done other than the entering of a pair of resolutions, one on November 29, 1972, and the other on December 9, 1974, that might be viewed as attempts to curtail under the Laws of War certain military practices upon which the United States relied heavily in Indochina. The first of these, Resolution 2932 A (XXVII), deplores the use of napalm and other incendiary weapons in all conflicts. The second, Resolution 3255 B (XXIX), condemns the use of these weapons in circumstances which affect human beings or may cause damage to the environment and/or natural resources; all states are urged to refrain from production, stockpiling, proliferation, and use of such weapons.[44]

In essence, the definitional problems associated with the concept of genocide that led to such intellectual convolutions as sketched above could be reasonably and easily resolved by simply following the prescriptions established through the statutory codes on murder, the crime to which genocide has been compared all along. We will then be able to confront the specter of group destruction without becoming inevitably mired in considerations of government intentions, whether they matter (other than to establish the degree of criminality involved), whether given actions would be more appropriately or fruitfully termed war crimes than genocide, and so forth.

A Typology of Genocide

With certain modifications, the existing U.N. Convention could be utilized for purposes of offering a more adequate definition. Perhaps the easiest in this connection would be the elimination of the emphasis on demonstrating intent. More difficult (though possibly not, as the United States—apparently the major obstruction in this regard—only ratified the Convention in February 1986, and may therefore be in less of a position to object than was the case in 1947) would be the reinsertion of the two major deletions from the original secretariat's draft convention:

1) The two aspects of cultural genocide originally broken out in their own right would become points *f* and *g* of the acts of genocide enumerated under Article III of the Convention; and

2) Article III would conclude with the observation that genocidal processes might be considered in a twofold light rather than being restricted to overt destruction only.[45]

Finally, it seems likely that an entirely new article will need to be written and inserted into the Convention before it can assume true functional utility, either definitionally or juridically. This would be designed to articulate the varying types or degrees of genocide possible, and should probably echo the gradient statutory code pertaining to individuated murder:

Genocide in the First Degree would encompass instances where clear intent to commit genocide was evident, could be docu-mented/proven, and where the systematic/efficient focus of policy and resources toward accomplishment of genocide has occurred. Historical examples of this degree of genocide, which may serve to orient us to it, might be that undertaken by nazi Germany, the USSR under Stalin, and much of U.S. conduct towards its aboriginal population during the nineteenth century.

Genocide in the Second Degree would encompass instances where intent to commit genocide per se is unclear, but where genocide occurred while its perpetrator was engaged in otherwise criminal activities such as the waging of aggressive war, territorial expropria-tion, etc. Historical examples of this degree of genocide would include the U.S. "effort" in Southeast Asia, the Turkish reduction of Armenians, the military strategy directed toward its Algerian colony by France during the late 1950s, and Japanese policies in occupied China before and during the Second World War.[46]

Genocide in the Third Degree would encompass instances where genocidally specific intent is probably lacking, and where the per-petrator is not otherwise engaging in activities judged to be illegal, but—through recklessness, insensitivity, or some combination—the perpetrator allows genocide to occur as an "inevitable by–product" of its national activities (water diversion, mineral extraction, and other forms of majority group "development" come immediately to mind as the possible generative processes in this regard). Historical examples of this sort of genocide are aspects of forced collectiviza-tion in China, some elements of the Khmer Rouge "autogenocide" in Kampuchea, much of twentieth–century U.S. and Canadian policy towards their Indian populations, twentieth–century Australian and New Zealand policies towards their aboriginal populations, and Vietnamese practice regarding the so–called Montagnard population of the Annamese Cordillera.

Genocide in the Fourth Degree, which should be viewed as corre-sponding to manslaughter rather than murder, would accommodate instances where intent, other forms of criminality, and reckless insensitivity are all unclear or lacking, but where genocide nonethe-less occurs. Such cases, where poor (or arrogant) judgement is at issue rather than overt maliciousness, might seem fewer than in the other three categories, but include U.S. assimilation and termination programs directed at American Indians ("for their own good") in the twentieth century, certain Arab "development" efforts extended at the South Sahara Bedouins, aspects of the Soviet collectivization experience, and so on.[47]

While such a multilayered gradient of criminality would do much to release the concept of genocide from its present straightjacket of definition, it would in itself do little to resolve the jurisdictional problems associated with enforcement of the convention, as with other elements of international law. This seems all the more true in a period when the president of the United States, for example, has suggested that World Court authority extends no further than the arbitration of trade matters between nation–states,[48] and that ratification of the Genocide Convention itself may now be undertaken without fear of its ultimate enforcement.

It is all well and good to argue, as Richard Falk has, that "[t]he President is bound to act in accordance with governing law, including international law. The customary and treaty norms of international law enjoy the status of 'the laws of the land' and the President has no discretion to violate these norms in the course of pursuing objectives of foreign policy."[49] The suggestion that violations of international standards are, or should be, accommodated within the domestic laws of each nation is of course accurate, and would go far toward solving the dilemma of jurisdiction. If accepted on its merits, it would also lead undoubtedly toward the consolidation of a viable World Court system in the future.

We are, however, confronted with the sad fact that Nuremberg remains the sole instance of the effective prosecution of national *policymakers* (as opposed to occasional enlisted marines or low–ranking officers) for engaging in the sort of illegality really at issue. It is also self–evident that we cannot rely on the absolute military defeat of any government guilty of genocide as an expedient to seeing justice done and the crime deterred. In a formal sense, then, the jurisdictional question may be so problematic as to seem to thwart the purpose of improving upon present understanding of genocide (or crimes against humanity, war crimes, etc.).

A possible way out of this apparent impasse is pointed out by Falk when he notes that a strictly formal application of legalism, which he terms "the indictment model," is hardly the only means of bringing the law to bear. To the contrary, he rightly contends that "a conception of crime based on a community's obligation to repudiate certain forms of governmental behavior and the consequent responsibility of individuals and groups to resist policies involving this behavior" is often more effective, especially as regards application of international law.[50]

Indeed, while the formal prosecution of government, military, and corporate leaders for all manner of violations of international law has languished since 1950, Falk's "responsibility model" has seen considerable active service.

One need only examine the outcome of the political careers of Lyndon B. Johnson and Richard M. Nixon in the United States to acquire a glimpse of the potential afforded by Falk's thesis. More sharply, the assignment of individual responsibility to Indira Gandhi for her policies vis–à–vis India's Sikh religious community is also instructive.

Viewed in this light, an improved codification of genocide, allowing for a more sensitive and flexible interpretation of the phenomenon as well as a far broader range of culpability than is presently the case in international law, would be an extremely hopeful sign. Augmented as it surely would be by elaboration from disciplines such as sociology and political science, a typological recodification of the Genocide Convention would go far toward providing an adequate conceptual basis for an effective global *consensus juris* vis–à–vis genocide in all its ugly manifestations. Surely such a development cannot be other than a positive step towards the humane world order system called for so eloquently by Falk and others.[51]

Additional Difficulties

Establishment of the sort of flexible and graduated schema of culpability in the perpetration of genocide proposed in the preceding section can achieve something of its full utility only when two further conceptual barriers are overcome. These can be viewed as associated with ideas of genocide being an act or process of some specific magnitude (vast numbers of bodies must be generated by a genocide) and employing a specific methodology (killing people outright). Each assumption will be examined in turn so that it may be responded to and be useful to those who would challenge the "appropriateness" of certain of the illustrations accompanying the typology. Although there is nothing in present legal language or in serious theoretical studies concerning genocide that posits scale of destruction as a criterion, popular conception seems to hold that without vast numbers of bodies whatever has occurred cannot appropriately be considered as constituting that particular crime. No doubt this situation derives from an understandable (and perhaps subconscious) association of the term itself specifically with the Holocaust. Nonetheless, as was noted earlier, however understandable such associations may be, they tend to muddle rather than clarify the issue.

If an effective model of community responsibility is ever to emerge, the circumstances involved in the genocidal context must be understood as that an identifiable *group* of people *as such* is being or has been destroyed, regardless of the size of that group. The literal number of individual people slaughtered in a given process is not in itself indicative of genocide; there is no magical "body count" below which genocide cannot rightly be said to exist. While the scale of destruction will necessarily run into millions when a large group such as the Khmers or Jews is targeted, the numbers of victims involved in the genocide of smaller peoples such as culturally distinct indigenous tribal peoples around the world may amount to only a few thousand or, in some cases, even a few hundred.

Thus it does not make sense to argue that the destruction of approximately one–third of the total Jewish population in the 1940s is somehow a "greater crime" or "worse" than the destruction of perhaps 80 percent of the total Cheyenne population during the 1860s and 1870s. Granted, in the former case, upwards of 6 million individuals were killed while in the latter instance the figure may well be less than 3,000. But in terms of *group* destruction, the subsequent ability of the Jewish people to recover and sustain itself as a *group* was obviously much greater than that of the Cheyennes. This is not a calculation to be taken lightly if genocide is to be comprehended in its rightful sense as group destruction, rather than as merely a fancy–labeled version of the rather clearer–cut crime of mass murder.

From this perspective, historical examples of genocide begin to proliferate. Horowitz mentions the British destruction of the Zulus during the nineteenth century, as well as Belgian policies toward the tribal people of present–day Zaire which were implemented during the same period.[52] The holocaust perpetrated by the Spanish in the Caribbean, in which the Tainos, for example, were obliterated, also comes to mind. Similarly, there is the utter and complete Spanish destruction of Aztec and other tribal societies flourishing in sixteenth–century Mexico, as well as the British demolition of native Hawaiian culture, the "conquest" of the Maoris of New Zealand, and the "settlement" of Australia's aboriginal interior. U.S. history is also replete with instances other than the example of the Cheyenne: the "removal" of the so–called Five Civilized Tribes from the southeast during the 1830s is a salient example, as are the Round Valley Wars in California and the Kit Carson Campaign against the Navajo later in the century. Clearly, the list could go on and on.[53]

It is important to bear in mind when engaging in such considerations that we are by no means restricted to the arena of historical inquiry. Entirely similar processes are at work in the contemporary setting. Norman Lewis has this example of Brazil during the 1970s:

> The huge losses sustained by the Indian tribes in this tragic decade were catalogued. Of 19,000 Munducurus believed to have existed in the thirties, only 1,200 were left. The strength of the Guaranis had been reduced from 5,000 to 300. There were 400 Carajas left out of 4,000. Of the Cintas Largas, who had been attacked from the air and driven into the mountains, possibly 500 survived out of 10,000. The proud and noble nation of the Kadiweus—the Indian Cavaliers—had shrunk to a pitiful scrounging band of about 200. A few hundred only remained of the formidable Chavantes, who prowled in the background of Peter Fleming's Brazilian journey, but they had been

reduced to mission fodder—the same melancholy fate which had overtaken the Bororos, who had helped change Levi Strauss's views on the nature of human evolution. Many tribes were now represented by a single family, a few by one or two individuals. Some, like the Tapiunas—in this case from a gift of sugar laced with arsenic—had disappeared altogether. It is estimated that between 50,000 and 100,000 Indians survive today. Brazil's leading social historian believes that not a single one will be alive by 1980.[54]

The Brazilian social historian referred to by Lewis was somewhat off on his timetable, though not in the spirit of his projection, as is evidenced by the fact that the Brazilian government is still quite busy killing Indians today.[55] Nor is Brazil alone in its lethal policies towards Indians—*as* Indians—in the topical context. Richard Arens has compiled a volume detailing the slaughter of the Aché people of Paraguay in which a contributor notes that:

I can state that at least 343 persons have been killed outright or enslaved and induced to die between September 1968 and June 1973.... Turning from these minimum figures ... one must note that at least three Northern Ache tribes have disappeared between 1968 and 1972, either through killing or kidnapping, by private or official hunts.... In my judgment, it is reasonable to say that approximately 50 percent of Northern Ache men, women and children have been wiped out by disease, despair and murder between 1962 and 1972. All these figures refer exclusively to the Northern Ache. I have no exact data about the Ache living further to the south. It seems highly probable, however, that they too have been the victims of massacre and enslavement.[56]

Elsewhere in the same volume, Elie Wiesel, one of the great students of the Holocaust, having first acknowledged that he had always resisted any sort of comparison to the genocide of European Jewry, professed that the record in Paraguay was sufficient to alter his assessment and that "our society prefers not to know anything about all that. Silence everywhere. Hardly a few words in the press. Nothing is discussed at the United Nations, or among the politicized intellectuals or the moralists. The great conscience kept quiet."[57] Well intentioned though he undoubtedly was, Wiesel dramatically underestimated the legacy of confusion concerning the meaning of genocide created by 30–odd years of insistence upon "the uniqueness of the Jewish experience" he himself had done so much to create. "The great consciences," by–and–large, preferred to debate whether the Aché example was significant enough, or monumental enough even to warrant "proper" identification as a genocide.

The situation is hardly unique. Noam Chomsky, to name but one example, has consistently encountered such semantic polemics, beginning with his efforts to expose the decimation of h'Mong tribesmen in Laos during the mid–1960s.[58] This has continued up through his attempts to alert people to the impact of the Indonesian invasion and occupation of East Timor during the late 1970s.[59] Even the Public Broadcasting System has been accused of "terminological overkill" when, in a 1984 documentary film, it described the wanton destruction of Guatemalan Indians as being "a hidden holocaust."

The Americas, of course, are not the only—or even necessarily the primary—locale in which "small scale" exterminations have occurred, are occurring, or will occur in the future. There is every indication that similarly horrible events occur in virtually every corner of the planet. This is all the more reason why it should be unequivocally asserted that, simply because a group may be small and "marginal," its physical eradication is no less genocidal than on the rare occasions when larger groups are targeted for extinction.

Cultural Genocide

Not only must juridical appreciations of genocide be steered clear of confinement to the concept of specific intent, popular conceptions of the phenomenon itself must also be guided away from butchery per se, regardless of scale. Here, a formulation offered by Richard Arens seems especially helpful:

> Genocide can take the form of what anthropologists have called deculturation, and it can involve the disintegration of some or all of the following: political and social institutions, culture, language, national feelings, religion, economic stability, personal security, liberty, health and dignity. It does not take much imagination to see death in the destruction of a population's health or economic stability. We need not, however, depend on imagination and empathy alone. Deculturation has been studied for decades, and its lethal effects have been demonstrated beyond reasonable doubt.[60]

What Arens is describing is sometimes disparagingly referred to as "cultural genocide" by those who insist on seeing extermination factories and crematoria as "proof" that genocide is actually taking place. As Davis and Zannis have observed in this regard:

> One should not speak lightly of "cultural genocide" as if it were a fanciful invention.... The cultural mode of extermination is genocide, a crime. Nor should "cultural genocide" be used in the game: "Which is more horrible, to kill and torture; or, to remove the reason and will to live?" Both are horrible.[61]

Actually, this case was well presented in 1948 by the Lebanese representative to the ad hoc committee revising the U.N. draft instrument on genocide. Commenting on the "actual and intentional destruction of a human group as such," he concluded that it was necessary to acknowledge that each human group, definable as such, has a right to be considered as "an absolute entity which it would be criminal to attack." He also noted that world conscience was revolted by—or *should* be revolted by—"the thought of the destruction of a group, *even though the individual members survived*"[62] (emphasis added).

The key to the problem lies in the use of the term "destruction." All too often this has been interpreted in the narrowest possible sense (that is, in the more or less immediate physical death of group members) although this is quite illogical even under existing descriptive language. The first point of the 1948 Convention that enumerated genocidal activities concerns the killing of group members; it would of course be redundant to proscribe it a second time, never mind five times over. Yet something other than sheer physical death has always been implied within the notion of group destruction. Davis and Zannis pose these questions:

> What constitutes the "death" of a group, which may disintegrate while the lives of its individual members may proceed more or less intact? Under what conditions may a group be "killed" or "destroyed"? Is there a "group existence," separate from the lives of its members, which may follow a separate course unparalleled by the rights of its members? If so, can a "group" be defined is such a way as to spell out the conditions under which it can be "killed" or "destroyed"?[63]

The authors answer each question in the affirmative, citing the original U.N. Secretariat's draft convention which covered such "slow death measures," now termed "cultural genocide," as forced transfer of children to another human group, forced and systematic exile of individuals representing the culture targeted, the prohibition on the use of a national language, systematic destruction of books printed in a national language, systematic destruction of historical or religious monuments (or their diversion to alien uses), suppression of new publications concerning a definable group, destruction or dispersion of documents or objects pertaining to the historical, artistic, and religious heritage of a targeted group, and the like. They then conclude that:

> A culture's destruction is not a trifling matter.... If people suddenly lose their "prime symbol," the basis of their culture, their lives lose meaning.... A social disorganization often follows such loss, they are often unable to insure their own survival.... The loss and human suffering of those whose culture has been healthy and is suddenly attacked and disintegrated is incalculable.[64]

Since it was the United States, followed closely by Canada, which led the effort to delete such considerations from the Genocide Convention during the 1947–48 draft revision process, we would do well to pay particular attention to possible motives for such obstructionism. Upon even superficial examination, it is readily observable that both nations consistently engaged in what has been openly termed as "assimilationist policies" directed at indigenous populations within their borders. Aspects of these policies have and in many instances still include the legal suppression of indigenous religions and languages, the unilateral supplanting of indigenous governmental forms, the compulsory "education" of indigenous youth (often entailing their forced transfer to "boarding schools") in accordance with cultural and religious mores antithetical to their own, the unilateral imposition of definitions of group membership based upon "blood quantum" (eugenics) formulas rather than nationality, and the unilateral extension of "trust responsibility" (under the transparently neocolonial concept of plenary power) over the entire range of their affairs. Such policies make perfect sense when it is understood that the stated objective of forced assimilation is to bring about the complete dissolution of the targeted groups *as such*, causing their disappearance ("death") as individual members are absorbed into "mainstream society"; they are but clinical descriptions of the process of cultural genocide.[65]

Occasionally, such policies jell into a more blatantly physical form, as when the Canadian government drowns the homeland of the James Bay Cree in the world's largest hydroelectric project, the U.S. government announces plans to forcibly relocate and disperse some 13,500 traditional Navajos from their homeland in Arizona in order to mine coal there, or when either government announces the "termination" (the ending of legal existence) of an identified indigenous people.[66] Again, cultural if not physical genocide is implicit in the Untied States having done 80 percent of its uranium production on Indian land since 1960, thereby rendering the land base itself uninhabitable in many areas and ultimately forcing the dispersal of tribal groups.[67]

More often, however, procedures of cultural genocide pioneered in North America seem to have become an item of export to countries sympathetic to such ideas of organization and development, bearing out Arendt's thesis on the commonality, even banality, of genocidal evil to a degree and in ways she never envisioned. This is certainly the case in South Africa, as George M. Fredrickson has demonstrated compellingly.[68] And virtually all of the Americas south of the Río Grande have, to one extent or another, adopted North American assimilationist postures as a means of furthering the "development" of their indigenous populations, a situation clearly echoed in Australia, New Zealand, portions of Indonesia, and at various other points in the Pacific Basin.[69]

Throughout the continent of Africa even the most progressive governments seem to have determined that "tribalism" is the greatest problem confronting the consolidation of the new nation–states. Often their boundaries were, ironically enough, demarcated across "problematic" tribal territories not by progressive Africans, but by their European colonizers in years gone by. Hence, "detribalization" (another word for assimilation) that was initially introduced by Europeans during the sixteenth century seems to have become something of a continental priority, completing at an accelerated pace the process of emulsifying traditional African societies *as such*.[70]

As Richard Sklar put it, "tribalism is widely supposed to be the most formidable barrier to national unity in Africa ... [and] nearly every African state has at least one serious problem of ethnic or regional separation."[71] One need only look to the writings of Ghana's Kwame Nkrumah, in expositions intended not only to explain the policies of his own government but to chart a course for all of progressive Africa, to find Sklar's perception validated.[72] More concretely, there is Julius Nyerere's plan of village collectivization advanced under the Arusha Declaration. Initiated in Tanzania in 1967 as a means of "unifying and developing" tribal economies, *ujamaa* in 1974–75 became a mass forced relocation program designed to eradicate "recalcitrant" tribal societies.[73]

The basic thrust of the Tanzanian process of group destruction should be understood in the context of Nyerere's outspoken admiration for the marxist–leninist Mengista regime in Ethiopia at the onset of its virulent policy of forcibly incorporating Eritrean tribal peoples "into the revolution."[74] And it should not be divorced from the rather less doctrinaire and dramatic example of Kenya, summed up by Colin Leys:

> Analytically speaking, the peasantry [tribal peoples] in Africa may be best seen as a transitional class, in between the period of primitive cultivators living in independent communities and that of capitalist development in which peasants are restratified into capitalists and proletarians; but under the conditions of growth of neocolonialism it seems clear that in Kenya at least the stage during which the peasantry itself goes through the process of development [is occurring].[75]

In a single collection of essays concerning revolutionary Africa, John S. Saul identifies similar thinking and processes of compulsory tribal group dissolution as occurring in Mozambique, Zimbabwe, Angola, Uganda, and elsewhere.[76]

In South and Southeast Asia, the same principles apply as the virulence of India's policies suppressing ethnic and religious minorities are rivaled only by those of Bangladesh and Thailand. Likewise, the Burmese attempt to force incorporation of the Karin into their "developing state," the Vietnamese pursue the same course with respect to the Rhade and other Montagnard peoples of the highlands region, and the Manila government proceeds in the same direction against the Moros of the southern Philippines. Nor, on their part, do the Kurds of Persia, the Sammis of northern Scandinavia, or the Inuits of the Arctic circumpolar region fare better.[77]

As was previously noted, the compulsory homogenization of various "national minorities" within the so–called socialist bloc of nations has been endemic since the 1920s. Left or right, regardless of geographical location or variations of practice and intent, the problem—which is so pervasive as to have entered social science terminology as the principle of "cultural leveling"—remains essentially the same. This is true whether it assumes the form of Israeli treatment of Palestinian Arabs or the present Sandanista effort to compel the effective absorption of Miskito, Sumu, and Rama Indians into the overall structure of Nicaragua's "revolutionary state."

The point at issue is that whole cultures, whole peoples, are being forced to cease to exist *as such*. The result is genocide, whether such elimination is accomplished in the name of racial/cultural superiority on the one hand, or on the basis of technological/economic development on the other. Until the principle is accepted that the essence of genocide is to be discovered in the coercive elimination of human groups per se, by *whatever* means and under *any* rubric, the term will likely not only remain ill–defined, but largely devoid of any practical meaning at all.

Conclusion

If this essay has accomplished anything, it is hoped that it has compellingly demonstrated the inadequacy of current definitional criteria describing genocide, and pointed out that viable conceptual alternatives to the present muddle exist. This is in conformity with the objective, stated in the introduction, of (re)opening fundamental questions rather than sealing them off.

The process of tracing the evolution of the concept of genocide as a criminal phenomenon distinct from any other, a process which contained clearly critical elements of analysis, was not intended to condemn the groups and individuals cited. Rather, it was utilized as a way of clarifying the kinds of ideological, political, and emotional factors which have served to theoretically constrain understanding of the phenomenon itself. Criticism is thus offered in the spirit that only in the cognizance of the nature of conceptual inadequacy can it be transcended, offset, or corrected, and more appropriate or functional understanding allowed to emerge.

In arguing toward a broadening of the definition of genocide to include not only large and small group annihilation, but externally imposed group destruction per se, I have sought to come to grips with the central element of genocide as a contemporary and historical fact, accurately detected by Raphael Lemkin and others but somehow lost within the polemics of codification and application. Hopefully, this "return to basics" will prove useful in establishing a more generalized understanding of when and where genocide has occurred and is occurring, in fact if not codified in law.

The posited "typology of genocide," on the other hand, represents a suggestion as to how law might seek to follow sound appreciations of genocide as a socio–political reality, rather than attempting to restrict understanding to some narrower theoretical paradigm. In extending the analogy of genocide to murder in what I take to be its logical dimensions, the typology should be viewed not as a "plan," but as a model through which—if it were appropriately developed—juridical apprehensions of genocide might be made to conform more closely to the nature of the phenomenon. Such a development in law could hardly help but benefit the emergence of a more just and humane world order.

While attempting to articulate the basis for a more functional definition of genocide, one which takes into account the full range of gradients and nuances marking the phenomenon, I have sought to avoid the pitfalls of ideological posturing, drawing examples from both communist and non–communist nations, as well as from both contemporary and historical events. I will, however, confess to the exercise of a certain "bias"—no doubt already noticed by the discerning reader—believing as I do that traditional indigenous cultures and societies possess every right to their continued existence as do their industrialized, "developing" or at any rate "modern" counterparts.

This "indigenist" notion that genocide permeates trans–ideological scientism's obliteration of indigenous peoples in the name of technology and order is one that I hope to see considered and discussed in many quarters. And I will readily admit a firm desire to see "progress" tempered, both socially and legally, by formal acknowledgment of the *absolute* right of *all* peoples to the conditions necessary to the perpetuation of themselves *as peoples*.

Notes

1. Robert Davis and Mark Zannis, *The Genocide Machine in Canada: The Pacification of the North* (Montréal: Black Rose Books, 1973), p. 179.

2. Ibid.

3. Quoted in Herman Raushning, *The Voice of Destruction* (New York: Putnam and Sons, 1940), p. 138.

4. Ibid.

5. Concerning the Wannsee Conference, *see* William L. Shirer, *The Rise and Fall of the Third Reich: A History of Nazi Germany* (New York: Simon & Schuster, 1960), p. 965. On nazi policy concerning the Jewish question in the period prior to the conference, *see* Hienze Hohne, *The Order of the Death's Head: The Story of Hitler's SS,* Richard Barry, trans. (New York: Coward–McCann, Inc., 1969), pp. 196–258.

6. Nikolai K. Deker and Andrei Lebed, *Genocide in the USSR: Studies in Group Destruction* (New York: The Scarecrow Press, 1958).

7. An excellent example of the marxist deployment of the term "genocide" is to be found on pp. 440–41 of *The Large Soviet Encyclopedia (Bolshaya sovetskaya enstisklopedia)* (Moscow: State Publishing House, 1952); therein, genocide is defined as "an offshoot of decaying imperialism."

8. Noam Chomsky and Edward S. Herman, "After the Cataclysm: Postwar Indochina and the Reconstruction of Imperial Ideology," in *The Political Economy of Human Rights, Vol. II* (Boston: South End Press, 1979), p. 164.

9. A comprehensive analysis of the U.S. impact upon Kampuchea (Cambodia), including detailed maps of the "overlapping box" method of U.S. saturation bombing before 1975, is found in William Shawcross, *Sideshow: Nixon, Kissinger and the Bombing of Cambodia* (New York: Simon & Schuster, 1979). Of particular interest is Shawcross's citation, on p. 375, of an April 1975 U.S. Aid report which noted that, "Slave labor and starvation rations for half [of Kampuchea's] people ... will be a cruel necessity for this year, and general deprivation and suffering will stretch over the next two or three years [as a result of the American bombing]." Such information became increasingly and conveniently "lost" in the Western examination of Pol Pot's "autogenocide."

10. Vakahn N. Dadrian, "Factors of Anger and Aggression in Genocide," *The Journal of Human Relations*, Vol. 19, No. 3 (1971), p. 384.

11. Dr. Raphael Lemkin, *Axis Rule in Occupied Europe* (Concord, New Hampshire: Rumford Press/Carnegie Endowment for International Peace, 1944), p. 79. It is noteworthy that Lemkin's book was acquired by the McGill Law Library in 1945, but despite its obvious importance as a groundbreaking text in an important aspect of international law, it was checked out only twice in the subsequent 28 years.

12. Ibid.

13. Ibid.

14. Telford Taylor, *Nuremberg and Vietnam: An American Tragedy* (New York: Quadrangle Books, 1970), p. 96.

15. Ibid, p. 14.

16. Ibid, p. 28.

17. Among the more important provisions of the secretariat's draft convention scrapped largely at the insistence of the United States was the inclusion of two categories of genocidal activity: (1) planned disintegration of the political, social, or economic structure of a group or nation, and (2) systematic moral debasement of a group, people, or nation. Additionally, the draft convention contained an important nuance deleted from the final version, again largely at the insistence of the United States. This concerned defining genocidal acts in a two–fold way: (1) the destruction of a group (in whole or in part), and (2) preventing the preservation and development of the group. Ultimately, only the first of these two was retained.

18. An interesting point in reference to the International Military Tribunal which tried many of the Nuremberg defendants is made by Ladislas Farago in his *Aftermath: Martin Bormann and the Fourth Reich* (New York: Simon & Schuster, 1974). This is that there was nothing in the Charter, subscribed to by the participating nations, which set a concluding date for the tribunal's activities. Hence, its mandate might be correctly viewed as still being in effect and the tribunal might be properly and legally reconvened at any time. It could serve not only to continue to try nazi criminals (as Farago suggests), but, at least in principle, could serve as the instrument of justice for those guilty of comparable crimes in subsequent years; the covenants employed at Nuremberg, after all, covered categories of criminality rather than membership in given nationalities or political parties per se. A legitimate means to solve at least a portion of the jurisdictional problems/questions associated with the 1948 Genocide Convention therefore exists in a technical sense. But there has never been an effort to use this means in any way.

19. Robert Davis and Mark Zannis, op. cit., p. 21. Since their analysis, the U.S. Senate has finally ratified the Convention; it was signed into law by Ronald Reagan in February 1986.

20. Perhaps the most notorious example of this sort of thing was the release of Alfred Krupp von Bohlen und Hallbach on February 3, 1951. Krupp had served barely three years of a prison sentence passed on him for crimes including the massive use of slave labor in keeping his sprawling armaments empire humming on behalf of the Third Reich. Krupp's release was effected by John J. McCloy, acting on behalf of the U.S. government, which felt Krupp's managerial genius would be a significant tool in bolstering a revived German industry in following an anti–communist Cold War course. This is well detailed in William Manchester's, *The Arms of Krupp, 1857–1968* (New York: Bantam Books, 1968), pp. 754–70.

21. Ladislas Farago, op. cit., p. 19. Throughout his book, Farago illustrates his point with a number of case studies, including, for example, that of Alfred Franz Six (recounted on pp. 326–27). Six (NSDAP No. 245,670/1930; SS No. 107,840/1935) was a Brigadeführer (major general) in the SS by the end of the war. Apparently a former university professor, he had attained his high rank via his expedient, excellent performance with the *Einsatzgruppen* (murder squads) butchering Jews in the USSR. He was sentenced on April 10, 1949, by the American military tribunal to serve 20 years imprisonment for his crimes. By early 1951, U.S. General Thomas Handy had reduced his sentence by half. Shortly thereafter, he was amnestied and released on orders from U.S. High Commissioner in Germany, John J. McCloy. He immediately entered an executive position with Porsche–Diesel, within which he rose to become publicity and advertising manager by 1965. All the while he served as a "consultant" with the Gehlen Organization—a reconstitution of the nazi Abwehr intelligence apparatus—assisting U.S. intelligence in conducting propaganda operations against the Soviet Bloc.

22. Hannah Arendt, *Eichmann in Jerusalem: A Report on the Banality of Evil* (revised and enlarged edition) (New York: Penguin Books, 1965). Arendt has the good grace to note, on p. 294, that Israeli troops were being subjected to similar sorts of pressures, as was Eichmann, in Israel's prosecution of its war against the Palestinian population (but she chooses not to develop the implications of this). She also observes on p. 40 that Eichmann believed, with apparent sincerity, that he himself was an ardent zionist (again, she fails to speculate upon the implications of this).

23. Hitler's candid views on such matters are brought out in the memoirs of his confidant, Heinrich Hoffmann, *Hitler Was My Friend* (London: Burke Publishers, 1955) and elsewhere. They are noted by John Toland in his definitive two volume biography of the nazi dictator, *Adolf Hitler* (New York: Doubleday, 1976).

24. Hannah Arendt, *The Origins of Totalitarianism* (New York: Harcourt, Brace & World, 1976).

25. Irving Louis Horowitz, *Taking Lives: Genocide and State Power* (New Brunswick, New Jersey: Transaction Books, 1976), pp. 1–6.

26. Ibid., p. 18.

27. Ibid.

28. Ibid.

29. Irving Louis Horowitz, *Taking Lives: Genocide and State Power* (New Brunswick, New Jersey: Transaction Books [3d ed.], 1982).

30. Ibid., pp. 193–212.

31. Irving Louis Horowitz, *Taking Lives*, 1976 ed., p. 31.

32. Irving Louis Horowitz, *Taking Lives*, 1982 ed., p. 23.

33. An interesting argument is offered by Hugo Adam Bedau, in an essay entitled "Genocide in Vietnam?" in *Philosophy, Morality, and International Affairs,* Virginia Held et al., eds. (London: Oxford University Press, 1974), pp. 5–46, that yet another category of murder might be used to parallel genocide. Commonly termed "felony murder," this category is one in which death is not inflicted directly by the perpetrator in any way at all, but in which death nonetheless ensues for the victim as a by–product of the perpetrator's commission of other criminal (felonious) acts. It is probable that any comprehensive typology of genocide will ultimately include a clear analogy to this category.

34. Francisco Suarez (1548–1617), as quoted in Telford Taylor, op. cit., p. 63.

35. Adam Bedau, op. cit., provides an excellent illustration of the sorts of convoluted reasoning which occurs under the rigid application of the intent criteria as the only possible definition under which conceptions of genocide may be lodged.

36. Irving Louis Horowitz, *Taking Lives,* 1976 ed.

37. Robert Davis and Mark Zannis, op. cit., p. 18.

38. John Duffett, ed., *Against the Crime of Silence: Proceedings of the Russell War Crimes Tribunal* (New York/London: O'Hare Books/Bertrand Russell Peace Foundation, 1968).

39. Telford Taylor, op. cit. Taylor actually went further than suggesting another focus, stating in his conclusion on p. 207 that, "Somehow we failed ourselves to learn the lessons we undertook to teach at Nuremberg and that failure is today's American tragedy." (One assumes it was also something of a tragedy for the Vietnamese, Kampucheans, and the Laotians victimized by America's failure to learn its own lessons.) By my conservative count, Taylor's is one of not less than 40 widely read volumes referenced closely to the Russell Tribunal proceedings which emerged in the United States during the period. Government participants such as Robert McNamara and Clark Clifford have acknowledged that the growing degree and quality of accusations of U.S. criminality made them increasingly uncomfortable in pursuing Johnson's policies in Southeast Asia.

40. Jean–Paul Sartre, *On Genocide* (Boston: Beacon Press, 1968), pp. 57–85.

41. All this was, of course, before Daniel Ellsberg "leaked" the so–called "Pentagon Papers" in which "confidential" U.S. goals, objectives, and assessments of methodologies were spelled out. This thoroughly eliminated the contrived murk surrounding the question of American intentions in Southeast Asia, but nonetheless resulted in no charges being brought. *See The Pentagon Papers: The Defense Department History of the United States Decision-making on Vietnam* (Gravel Edition) 4 vols. (Boston: Beacon Press, 1971).

42. *See,* for example, *The Dellums Committee Hearings on War Crimes in Vietnam* (New York: Vintage Books, 1972); Noam Chomsky, *For Reasons of State* (New York: Vintage Books, 1973); and all the testimony collected in the Winter Soldier Archive in Berkeley, California (very little of which has been published).

43. Barry Weisberg, *Ecocide in Indochina: The Ecology of War* (San Francisco: Canfield Press, 1970).

44. While the United States was a signatory to both of these Resolutions, it by no means has refrained from the production (including the development of new forms, such as pyophoric incendiaries based on depleted uranium), stockpiling, or proliferation. *See* Frank Barnaby, ed., *Incendiary Weapons* (Cambridge, Massachusetts: MIT Press, 1975), pp. 101–09. In terms of the use of incendiaries, this has only been indirect: a notable example was the Israeli army's massive use of American–supplied white phosphorous ordnance, with full U.S. diplomatic support, against Beirut in 1982. *See* Noam Chomsky, *The Fateful Triangle: The United States, Israel and the Palestinians* (Boston: South End Press, 1983).

45. Even without the latter pair of insertions, the elimination of words such as "knowingly" and "with intent" from the Convention, coupled to the latitude of interpretation arguably possible under Article III (d), should provide flexibility of analysis and response heretofore impossible under the Convention, a situation which might well cover the ground implied by the insertions themselves.

46. For purposes of this paper, Bedau's analogy to Felony Murder should be considered as encompassed under Genocide in the Second Degree.

47. In the event that this last category seems unfair, it should be noted that under common law, "good intentions" do not necessarily mitigate results. U.S. courts have, for example, undertaken the successful manslaughter prosecution of "holy roller" parents who, with the best intentions (the salvation of their children's immortal souls, in their view), have denied medical treatment to their offspring. When the children die, the parents are held accountable; why should governments be less so, in principle?

48. The Reagan administration's response was sparked by the Sandinista government of Nicaragua bringing a dispute before the World Court in The Hague, Netherlands, during 1984. The Sandinistas argued that the U.S. action of mining its harbors was a violation of international law. The Court agreed and called for removal of the mines. Interestingly, the mines were removed even while the United States was preparing a response challenging the Court's authority to reach a finding in the matter.

49. Richard Falk, "International Law and the United States' Role in the Vietnam War," in *From Nuremberg to My Lai*, Jay W. Baird, ed. (Toronto: D.C. Heath & Co., 1972), p. 189. All Professor Falk had to do in order to discern the practical fallacy of this argument was to review the history of relations extant between the U.S. government and American Indians; of 371 formal treaty agreements entered into by the United States with various Indian sovereignties since 1789, *all* were systematically violated, and remain so to this day. It seems likely that the process of treaty violation was designed as an integral aspect of American expansion in precisely the same fashion as became evident in Hitlerian *realpolitik*.

50. Richard Falk, "Ecocide, Genocide, and the Nuremberg Tradition of Individual Responsibility," in *Philosophy, Morality, and International Affairs*, op. cit., p. 126.

51. *See*, for example, Richard Falk, *The End of World Order: Essays on Normative International Relations* (New York: Holmes & Meier, 1983), especially "Part Five: Normative Horizons," pp. 277–336.

52. Irving Louis Horowitz, *Taking Lives*, 1976 ed., op. cit., pp. 56–57.

53. A sample of literature addressing the examples provided includes Lynwood Carranco and Estele Bear, *Genocide and Vendetta: The Round Valley Wars of California* (Norman: University of Oklahoma Press, 1983); Maurice Collins, *Cortez and Montezuma* (New York: Avon Books, 1944); Jennings C. Wise, *The Red Man in the New World Drama* (New York: Macmillan Publishing Co., 1971); and Gloria Jahoda, *The Trail of Tears: The Story of the American Indian Removals, 1813–1855* (New York: Holt, Reinhart & Winston, 1975).

54. Norman Lewis, "Genocide," in *A Documentary Report on the Conditions of the Indian People of Brazil* (Berkeley, California: American Friends of Brazil/*Indigena*, 1974), pp. 9–10.

55. *The Yanomami Indian Park: A Call For Action* (Boston, Massachusetts: Anthropology Resource Center, 1981).

56. Mark Munzel, "Manhunt," in *Genocide in Paraguay*, Richard Arens, ed. (Philadelphia, Pennsylvania: Temple University Press, 1976), pp. 37–38.

57. Elie Weisel, "Now We Know," in *Genocide in Paraguay*, Richard Arens, ed., op. cit., p. 167.

58. Noam Chomsky, *American Power and the New Mandarins* (New York: Pantheon Books, 1967), pp. 168–90.

59. Noam Chomsky and Edward S. Herman, "The Washington Connection and the Third World Fascism," in *The Political Economy of Human Rights, Vol. I* (Boston, Massachusetts: South End Press, 1979), pp. 129–204.

60. Richard Arens, ed., *Genocide in Paraguay*, op. cit., p. 137.

61. Robert Davis and Mark Zannis, op. cit., p. 18.

62. *U.N. Doc. E/A.C. 25/S.R. 1–28.*

63. Robert Davis and Mark Zannis, op. cit., p. 18.

64. Ibid., p. 20.

65. A sampling of available literature taking up this theme includes, of course Robert Davis and Mark Zannis, op. cit. *See* also Estelle Fuchs and Robert H. Havighurst, *To Live on This Earth: American Indian Education* (New York: Anchor Books, 1973); Vine Deloria Jr. and Clifford M. Lytle, *The Nations Within: The Past and Future of American Indian Sovereignty* (New York: Pantheon Books, 1984); and Vine Deloria Jr. and Clifford M. Lytle, *American Indians, American Justice* (Austin: University of Texas Press, 1983).

66. Concerning James Bay, *see* Robert Davis and Mark Zannis, op. cit. On the planned forced relocation of Navajos from the Big Mountain area of Arizona, *see* Jerry Kammer, *The Second Long Walk: The Navajo–Hopi Land Dispute* (Albuquerque: University of New Mexico Press, 1978); or Ward Churchill, "Navajos: No Home on the Range," *The Other Side*, Vol. 21, No. 1 (Jan.–Feb. 1985), pp. 22–27. Concerning termination, *see* Sarah M. Sneed, "Termination: The Indian Trust Responsibility During the Eisenhower Administration," unpublished honors paper submitted to Professor George Pilcher, University of Colorado/Boulder, 5 Apr. 1982.

67. For an overview of the uranium contamination problem in the United States, *see* Ward Churchill and Winona LaDuke, "Radioactive Colonization and the American Indian," *Socialist Review*, Vol. 15, No. 3 (May–June 1985). This particular problem also applies to Namibia and Australia.

68. On this possibly odd-sounding point, *see* George Fredrickson, *White Supremacy: A Comparative Study in American and South African History* (New York: Oxford University Press, 1981).

69. Although it is an imperfect document, the most comprehensive recounting of the conditions referred to here are to be found in Jose R. Martinez Cobo, *Study of the Problem of Discrimination Against Indigenous Populations*, U.N. Document E/CN.4/Sub.2/1983/Add.8., 30 Sept. 1983.

70. As Kenneth L. Adelman describes in his *African Realities* (New York: Crane, Russak & Co., 1980), p. 5, "Meeting in Berlin in 1884, the European Powers carved up Africa without taking into account geographic and demographic conditions in that distant continent. Their legacy—borders making little if any political, ethnic, economic or strategic sense—set the stage for decades of squabbles, if not all out wars, by the fiercely nationalistic new states.... Since ethnic groups straddle borders, conditions are ripe for irredentism.... Even Africa's sacrosanct principle of 'territorial integrity' does not help much with states that never, in fact, accepted the old boundaries (such as Somalia) or with those plagued with secessionist movements (such as Eritrea and Biafra). After all, Biafra was recognized as 'independent' by Tanzania, Zambia, Gabon and the Ivory Coast."

71. Richard Sklar, "Political Science and National Integration—A Radical Approach," *The Journal of Modern African Studies*, Vol. 9, No. 2 (1971), pp. 137–38.

72. Kwame Nkrumah, *I Speak for Freedom: A Statement of African Ideology* (New York: Praeger Paperbacks, 1961), e.g., p. 167, "...[we] are opposed to imperialism, colonialism, racial, tribal and religious chauvinism." Again, on the following page, he states: "...until we purge from our minds this tribal chauvinism and prejudice of one against the other, we shall not be able to cultivate the wider spirit of brotherhood which our objective Pan Africanism calls for. We are all Africans and peoples of African descent...." In other words, the distinct identities and continuing existence of tribal peoples *as such* is something to be eliminated from the progressive scenario.

73. Kenneth L. Adelman, op. cit., pp. 126–27.

74. Ibid., pp. 130–31.

75. Colin Leys, "Politics in Kenya: The Development of Peasant Society," *The British Journal of Political Science*, No. 1 (1970), p. 326.

76. John S. Saul, *The State and Revolution in Eastern Africa* (New York: Monthly Review Press, 1979). It should be noted that Saul does not offer his recounting of group emulsification as a criticism of the states in question.

77. Jose R. Martinez Cobo, op. cit.

The Earth
Is Our Mother

Struggles for American Indian Land and
Liberation in the Contemporary United States*

The inhabitants of your country districts regard—wrongfully, it is
true—Indians and forests as natural enemies which must be
exterminated by fire and sword and brandy, in order that they may seize
their territory. They regard themselves, and their posterity, as collateral
heirs to all the magnificent portion of land which God has created from
Cumberland and Ohio to the Pacific Ocean.

Pierre Samuel Du Pont de Nemours, letter to
Thomas Jefferson, December 17, 1801

Of course our whole national history has been one of expansion.... That
the barbarians recede or are conquered, with the attendant fact that
peace follows their retrogression or conquest, is due solely to the power
of the mighty civilized races which have not lost their fighting instinct,
and which by their expansion are gradually bringing peace into the red
wastes where the barbarian peoples of the world hold sway.

Theodore Roosevelt, The Strenuous Life, 1901

Since the inception of the U.S. republic, and before, control of land and the
resources within it has been the essential source of conflict between the
Euroamerican settler population and indigenous nations. In effect, contentions

---

*This essay originally appeared in *The State of Native America*, M. Annette Jaimes, ed.
(Boston: South End Press, 1992).

over land usage and ownership have served to define the totality of U.S.–Indian relationships from the first moment onward to the present day, shaping not only the historical flow of interactions between invader and invaded, but the nature of ongoing domination of native people in areas such as governance and jurisdiction, identification, recognition, and education. The issue of a proprietary interest of non–Indians in the American Indian land base has also been and remains the fundamental principle of popular (mis)conceptions of who and what Indians were and are, whether they continue to exist, and even whether they ever "really" existed. All indications are that these circumstances will continue to prevail over the foreseeable future.

The situation has been prefigured from the period of planning which went into Columbus' first voyage, which—according to the "Great Discoverer's" own journals—was never about discovery or scientific inquisitiveness as such, but rather about seizing wealth belonging to others for his sponsors and himself.[1] But this is not to imply that Columbus enjoyed an entirely free hand. Contrary to contemporary orthodoxy, there were even then laws concerning how such wealth, especially land, might be legitimately acquired by mercenary adventurers like Columbus, and the various European Crowns which fielded them. Primary among these were the so–called Doctrine of Discovery and pursuant Rights of Conquest. Such elements of the "Laws of Nations" are much misunderstood in North America today, largely as a result of their systematic misinterpretation over the past century by Eurocentric academics and the U.S. Supreme Court. In its actual formulation, however, the Discovery Doctrine never conveyed title to discoverers over any lands already occupied at the time of the discovery.[2]

> [The doctrine's] basic tenet—that the European nation which first "discovered" and settled lands previously unknown to Europeans thereby gained the right to acquire those lands from their inhabitants—became part of the early body of international law dealing with aboriginal peoples.... [B]y the time Europeans settled in North America, it was well–established international law that natives had property rights which could not be lawfully denied by the discovering European nation.... The right of discovery served mainly to regulate the relations between European nations. It did not limit the powers or rights of Indian nations in their homelands; its major limitation was to prohibit Indians from diplomatic dealings with all but the "discovering" European nation.... Moreover, the right of discovery gave a European nation the right to extinguish Indian land title only when the Indians consented to it by treaty.[3]

Conquest rights were also quite restrictive, pertaining only to the results of "Just Wars," conflicts fought as the result of unprovoked Indian aggression against their supposed discoverers.[4] Hence, although the Laws of Nations were—as was certainly the case with Columbus—plainly broken from time to time:[5]

> As a matter of both legal principle and practicality, European nations dealt with Indian nations as they did other nations in the world. In general, Indian lands were acquired by agreement, through the use of international diplomacy—specifically, through formal treaties of cession. Indian lands were seldom acquired by military conquest or fiat, and the practices of Spain, France [England, Portugal] and the Netherlands did not differ in this regard.[6]

The reality of colonial North America was that indigenous nations tended to be militarily superior to their would–be colonizers, or at least held the balance of military power between European states such as England and France.[7] The matter was of such concern in London that, in 1763, King George III—specifically to retain the allegiance of the powerful Haudenosaunee (Iroquois) and Muscogee (Creek) Confederacies vis–à–vis England's French rivals—issued a proclamation prohibiting acquisition of lands west of a line drawn along the Allegheny and Appalachian mountain chains.[8] This, probably more than "taxation without representation," was a major contributing factor in sparking the extended decolonization struggle which resulted in the independence of the original 13 U.S. states.[9] George Washington, Thomas Jefferson, John Adams, James Madison, Anthony Wayne, and numerous others among the "Founding Fathers" all had considerable speculative investments in westerly Indian lands at the time the 1763 edict was handed down. The rank and file soldiers who fought in their "revolutionary" army arguably did so not for abstract ideals of "freedom" and "equality," but because of promises made by their leaders that their services would be rewarded with grants of Indian land "in the West" after victory had been secured.[10]

U.S. Theory and Practice

As Vine Deloria, Jr., has observed, the United States emerged from its successful war against the British Crown (perhaps the most serious offense imaginable under prevailing law) as a pariah, an outlaw state which was considered utterly illegitimate by almost all other countries and therefore shunned by them, both politically and economically. Survival of the new nation was entirely dependent upon the ability of its initial government to change such perceptions and thereby end its isolation. Desperate to establish itself as a respectable entity, and lacking other alternatives with which to demonstrate its sense of international legality, the government was virtually compelled to present the appearance of adhering to the strictest of protocols in its dealings with Indians.[11] Indeed, what the Continental Congress needed more than anything at the time was for indigenous nations—many of whose formal national integrity and legitimacy had already been recognized by the European powers through treaties—to convey a comparable recognition upon the fledgling United States by entering into treaty relationships with *it*.

Consequently, both the Articles of Confederation and the Constitution of the United States contain clauses reserving interactions with Indian peoples, as recognized "foreign powers," to the federal government. The United States also officially renounced, in the 1789 Northwest Ordinance and elsewhere, any aggressive intent vis–à–vis these nations, especially with regard to their land base. As it was put in the Ordinance:

> The utmost good faith shall always be observed towards the Indian; their land property shall never be taken from them without their consent; and in their property, rights, and liberty, they shall never be invaded or disturbed ... but laws founded in justice and humanity shall from time to time be made, for wrongs being done to them, and for preserving peace and friendship with them.[12]

Such lofty–sounding (and legally correct) rhetoric was, of course, belied by the actualities of U.S. performance. As the first Chief Justice of the Supreme Court, John Marshall, pointed out rather early on, almost every white–held land title in "our whole country"—New England, New York, New Jersey, Pennsylvania, Maryland, and parts of the Carolinas—would have been clouded had the standards of international law truly been applied.[13] More, title to the pre–revolutionary acquisitions made west of the 1763 demarcation line made by the new North American politico–economic élite would have been negated, along with all the thousands of grants of land in that region bestowed by Congress upon those who'd fought against the Crown. Not coincidental to Marshall's concern in the matter was the fact that he and his father had each received 10,000–acre grants of such land in what is now West Virginia.[14] Obviously, a country which had been founded largely on the basis of a lust to possess native lands was not about to relinquish its pretensions to "ownership" of them, no matter what the law said. Moreover, the balance of military power between Indians and whites east of the Mississippi River began to change rapidly in favor of the latter during the post–revolutionary period. It was becoming technically possible for the United States to simply seize native lands at will.[15]

Still, the requirements of international diplomacy dictated that things *seem* otherwise. Marshall's singular task, then, was to forge a juridical doctrine which preserved the image of enlightened U.S. furtherance of accepted international legality in its relations with Indians on the one hand, while accommodating a pattern of illegally aggressive federal expropriations of Indian land on the other. This he did in opinions rendered in a series of cases beginning with *Fletcher v. Peck* (1810) and extending through *Johnson v. McIntosh* (1822) to *Cherokee Nation v. Georgia* (1831) and *Worcester v.*

Georgia (1832).[16] By the end of this sequence of decisions, Marshall had completely inverted international law, custom, and convention, finding that the Doctrine of Discovery imparted "preeminent title" over North America to Europeans, the mantle of which implicitly passed to the United States when England quitclaimed its 13 dissident Atlantic colonies, mainly because Indian–held lands were effectively "vacant" when Europeans "found" them. The Chief Justice was forced to coin a whole new politico–legal expression—that of "domestic, dependent nations"—to encompass the unprecedented status, neither fish nor fowl, he needed native people to occupy.[17]

Within this convoluted and falsely premised reasoning, Indian nations were entitled to keep their land, but only so long as the intrinsically superior U.S. sovereignty agreed to their doing so. Given this, Indians could be legally construed as committing "aggression" whenever they resisted invasion by the United States, a matter which literally rendered any military action the United States chose to pursue against native people, no matter how unprovoked, a "Just War." With all this worked out, Marshall argued that the United States should nonetheless follow accepted European practice wherever possible, obtaining by formal treaty negotiations involving purchase and other considerations, native "consent" to land cessions. This, he felt, would complete the veneer of "reason and moderation" attending international perceptions of federal expropriations of Indian land. Ultimately, Marshall's position reduces to the notion that indigenous nations inherently possess sufficient sovereign rights "for purposes of treating" to hand over legal title to their territories, but never enough to retain any tract of land the United States wants as its own.

The carefully balanced logical contradictions imbedded in the "Marshall Doctrine," which allowed the United States to pursue one course of action with regard to Indian land while purporting to do the exact opposite, formed the theoretical basis for the entire 5,000–plus statute body of what is now called "Indian Law" in this country. Through a lengthy series of subsequent "interpretive" decisions—especially *Ex Parte Crow Dog* (1883), *U.S. v. Kagama* (1886), *Lonewolf v. Hitchcock* (1903), *Tee–Hit–Ton v. United States* (1955), and *Dann v. United States* (1985)—the Supreme Court extended Marshall's unfounded concept of native nations occupying a status of subordinate or "limited" sovereignty to include the idea that the United States enjoyed an inherent "plenary" (full and absolute) power over them in such crucial domains as governance and jurisdiction.[18] An aspect of this self–assigned power, articulated most clearly in *Lonewolf*, is that Congress has the prerogative to unilaterally abrogate aspects of U.S. treaties with Indian nations which it found inconvenient or burdensome while continuing to hold the Indians to those provisions of the treaties by which they agreed to cede land.[19]

In these decisions, the high court also extended Marshall's baseless notion that self–sufficient indigenous nations were somehow "dependent" upon the United States to include the idea that the federal government thereby inherited a "trust responsibility" to Indians—actually *control* over their remaining property—in the "management of their affairs." While the "Trust Doctrine" has been used as a device to offset and soften the impressions created by exercise of the "Rights of Plenary Power" over indigenous people, it has in reality served as an instrument through which that power is administered:

> [U]nder United States law, the government has no legal trusteeship duties toward Indians except those it imposes upon itself. Stripped of its legal trappings, the Indian trust relationship becomes simply an assertion of unrestrained political power over Indians, power that may be exercised without Indian consent and without substantial legal restraint. An early twentieth century critic of the European colonial "trusteeship for civilization" [in Africa and Asia], which is closely related to the American model, summed it up as "an impudent act of self assertion."[20]

While the U.S. judiciary was thus busily collaborating with the federal legislature in creating a body of "settled law" to serve as "the perfect instrument of empire," the federal government was also consistently engaged in creating the physical fact of that empire, all the while declaring itself in the most vociferous terms possible to be devoutly *anti*–imperial.[21] This was done by the waging of at least 40 "Indian Wars"[22]—each of which was packaged as a campaign to defend U.S. citizens from the "depredations" of "savage natives" resisting the invasion of their homelands or comparable abuse—and negotiation of several hundred treaties and agreements with native nations.[23] Together with an assortment of unilateral executive and congressional actions, these wars and negotiated arrangements resulted in Native America being constricted to about 2.5 percent of its original 2 billion–acre land base within the 48 contiguous states of the union by the early twentieth century (*see* Map I).[24] And federal control over even this remnant was virtually complete. Under such circumstances, it is not difficult to see why Indians were viewed, often hopefully, as a "vanishing race" during this period.[25]

The Indian Claims Commission

At the turn of the century, Indian efforts to maintain what little real property was left to them, or to receive compensation for lands which were still being arbitrarily seized by the government, were ridiculed and largely dismissed out of hand.[26] Although native people were supposedly entitled to due process through U.S. law after a District Court in Nebraska recognized them as "persons" during the 1879 *Standing Bear v. Crook* case, the significance was largely meaningless.[27] From 1881 to 1918, only 31 claims involving the illegal taking of native land were accepted by federal courts; 14 resulted in recoveries

Map I

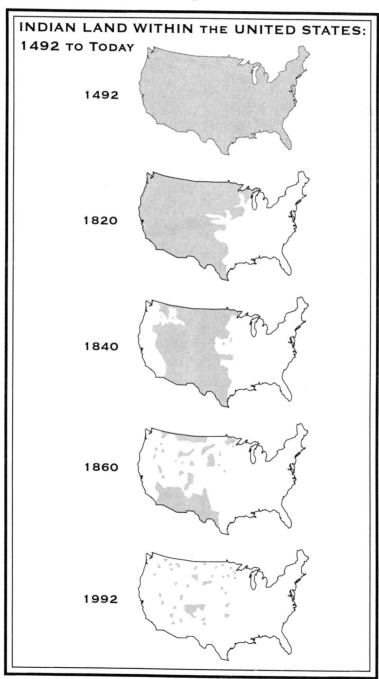

INDIAN LAND WITHIN THE UNITED STATES:
1492 TO TODAY

1492

1820

1840

1860

1992

of land adding up to less than 10,000 acres.[28] In 1928, a government commission termed even this degree of judicial recourse to be "burdensome and unfair" to non–Indians.[29] Meanwhile, some 100 million acres—about two–thirds of all land native people had left at the conclusion of the period of their military resistance—was stripped away under provision of the 1887 General Allotment Act.[30] Power and possession, the rule of thugs as it were, constituted all of the law in North America where Indian land rights were concerned.

Throughout most of the first half of the twentieth century, the United States devoted itself to perfecting the mechanisms through which it would administer the tiny residual fragments of Indian Country for its own purposes. Nothing beyond the most *pro forma* gesture was made to address the fact that a considerable proportion of the land which was said to have passed from native ownership during the previous 150 years had been transferred in direct contravention of every known form of legality, including even the patently self–serving theories of U.S./Indian property relations developed by the United States itself. In 1924, federal courts accepted a mere five native land claims cases; in 1925, there were seven; in 1926, there were 10; in 1927, the total was 15. Most of these were dismissed in the early stages; none resulted in land recovery or payment of significant compensation.[31] Things might have remained locked firmly in this mode were it not for geopolitical considerations emerging in the context of World War II.

As part of an overall strategy to advance U.S. interests in its planned post–war role as a hegemonic global power, the United States set out to project an enhanced image of itself as a "white knight" to the world's oppressed peoples. At least temporarily, until its own preferred style of neocolonialism could become entrenched as the dominant force in international affairs, the United States needed to be widely perceived as a beneficent and staunchly democratic alternative, not only to the "totalitarian impulse" represented by fascism and communism, but to the classic colonial orders maintained in Third World locales by France, Great Britain, and other American allies. A part of this ploy resided within President Franklin D. Roosevelt's wartime opposition to reconstitution of the old European empires of the French and Dutch in Africa and Asia after the conclusion of hostilities (this trend was shortly reversed by Roosevelt's successor, Harry Truman, as part of his Cold War policy of prioritizing "containment of communism" above all else).[32]

The centerpiece of the entire international public relations gambit, however, rested in the U.S. assumption of the decisive role in formulating and implementing the "Nuremberg Doctrine" under which the surviving leadership of nazi Germany was accused, tried, convicted, and in most cases executed or imprisoned, for having engaged in "Crimes Against the Peace," "Aggressive War," and "Crimes Against Humanity."[33] The primary messages intended for popular consumption in the U.S. performance against the nazi defendants were that behavior such as that displayed by the nazis was considered criminal and intolerable by all "civilized peoples," and that the United States—first and foremost—would stand as the guarantor that all governments would be held accountable to the standards of comportment established at Nuremberg. The nazi leaders were to stand forever as the symbol of the principle that international aggression would be punished, not rewarded (this is, of course, precisely the same line trotted out by George Bush in explaining the rather interesting U.S. behavior against Iraq during 1990–91).[34]

A primary flaw in this otherwise noble–seeming U.S. posture on international human rights law was (and is) that no less prominent a nazi than Adolf Hitler had long since made it quite clear that he had based many of his more repugnant policies directly on earlier U.S. conduct against Native America. Hitler's conception of *lebensraumpolitik*—the idea that Germans were innately entitled by virtue of their racial and cultural superiority to land belonging to others, and that they were thus morally free to take it by aggressive military action—obviously had much in common with the nineteenth–century American sense of "Manifest Destiny."[35] Further, his notion of how to attain this "living room"—the "clearing of inferior racial stock" from its land base in order that vacated areas might be "settled by ethnic Germans"—followed closely from such U.S. precedents as the 1830 Indian Removal Act and subsequent military campaigns against the indigenous nations of the Great Plains, Great Basin, and Senora Desert Regions. Even the nazi tactic of concentrating "undesirables" prior to their forced "relocation or reduction" was drawn from actual U.S. examples, including internment of the Cherokees and other "Civilized Tribes" during the 1830s, before the devastatingly lethal Trail of Tears was forced upon them, and the comparable experience of the Navajo people at the Bosque Redondo from 1864 to 1868.[36]

This potential embarrassment to U.S. pretensions abroad precipitated something of a sea change in the country's approach to indigenous issues. Seeking to distance its own history from comparison to that of the Germans it was even then prosecuting—and thus to stand accused of conducting an exercise in mere "victor's justice" at Nuremberg—the federal government was for the first time prepared to admit openly that "unfortunate and sometimes tragic errors" had been made in the process of its continental expansion. Unlike nazi Germany, federal spokespersons intoned, the United States had never held aggressive territorial intentions against Indians or anyone else; the Indian Wars notwithstanding, the United States had always bought, rather than conquered, the land it occupied. As proof of this thesis, it was announced that a formal mechanism was being created for purposes of "resolving any lingering issues" among Native Americans concerning the legitimacy of U.S. title to its territory.[37] The book, which had been closed on Indian land claims for a full generation and more, was suddenly opened again.

What was ultimately established, on August 13, 1946, was a quasi–judicial entity, dubbed the "Indian Claims Commission," of the sort long desired by those who had followed the wisdom of Chief Justice Marshall's enjoinder that appearances demanded a veneer of legality, even one applied *post hoc*, be affixed to all U.S. expropriations of native territory. As early as 1910, Indian Commissioner Francis E. Leupp had suggested "a special court, or the addition of a branch to the present United States Court of Claims, to be charged with the adjudication of Indian claims exclusively."[38] He was followed by Assistant Commissioner Edgar B. Merritt, who recommended in 1913 that a special commission be impaneled to investigate the extent to which native land had been taken without legal justification/rationalization, and what would be necessary to attain retroactive legitimation in such instances.[39] In 1928, the Meriam Commission had recommended a similar expedient.[40] Congress had persistently balked at the ideas of acknowledging that the United States had effectively stolen much of its territoriality, and/or of belatedly making even token payments for what had been taken.[41]

The new commission was charged with investigating *all* native claims contesting U.S. title, to define precisely the territory involved in each case, and to determine whether legal procedures not devolving from outright conquest had ever been applied to its transfer out of Indian hands. In instances where it was concluded that there was no existing legal basis for non–Indian ownership of contested lands, or where the price originally paid for such lands was deemed "unconscionably low," the commission was responsible for fixing what might have been a "fair market price" (according to the buyers, not the sellers) *at the time the land was taken.* Corresponding sums were then paid by Congress— $29.1 million (about 47¢ per acre) for the entire state of California in the 1964 "Pit River Land Claim Settlement," for example—as "just compensation" to indigenous nations for their loss of property.[42] At the point such payment was accepted by an Indian people, the title at issue in its land claim was said to be "quieted" and "justice served."

In reality, as Jack Forbes and others have pointed out, non–Indian titles were being *created* where none had existed before.[43] As even the Chair of the Senate Subcommittee on Indian Affairs, Henry M. Jackson, put it at the time: "[Any other course of action would] perpetuate clouds upon white men's title that interfere with development of our public domain."[44] The stated presumptions underlying the commission's mandate were simply a continuation of the Marshall Doctrine that preeminent rights over Indian Country were inherently vested in the United States, and that native nations had in any event always wished to sell their land to the federal government. The unstated premise, of course, was that Indians had no choice in the matter anyway. Even if they *had* desired to convert their property into cash by the late 1940s, the commission was not authorized other than in a very narrow range of circumstances to award payment interest in retroactive land "sales," although the "bills" owed by the government were in many instances more than a century overdue.[45] In *no* event was the commission authorized to return land to native claimants, no matter *how* it had been taken from them.[46] Hence, during the 1950s, the commission served as a perfect "liberal" counterpart to the more extremist ("conservative") federal termination policies.

Nonetheless, the existence of the Claims Commission afforded native people a forum in which they might clarify the factual nature of their grievances for the first time. Consequently, by the end of 1951, more than 600 cases (only 26 of which were adjudicated at that point) had been docketed.[47] Things continued to move grudgingly, a matter which caused the process to be extended.[48] During the first 15 years of its operations, the commission completed only 80 cases, dismissing 30 outright, and finding "validity" in only 15. Its awards of monetary compensation totaled only $17.1 million by 1959. The "civil rights era" of the early '60s saw something of a surge in performance, with 250 cases completed (another $111 million in awards) and 347 pending (of which 42 had still seen no action at all).[49] During the early '70s, Indians began increasingly to appeal the commission's rulings to federal courts; of 206 such appeals filed by 1975, the commission was affirmed in 96 instances, partially affirmed in 31, and overruled in 79.[50] At the end of its life on September 30, 1978, the Claims Commission still had 68 docketed cases (plus an indeterminate number of emerging appeals) still pending. These were turned over to the U.S. Court of Claims.[51]

Cracks in the Empire

While it is clear that the Indian Claims Commission functioned mainly as a subterfuge designed and intended to cast an undeserved mantle of humanitarianism and legitimacy over U.S. internal territorial integrity,[52] it inadvertently served indigenous interests as well. As a result of its lengthy exploration of the factual record, necessary to its mission of nailing down federal land title in every area of the country, the commission revealed the full extent to which the United States had occupied areas to which it had no lawful title (even under its own rules of the game). Indeed, one cumulative result of the commission's endeavor was to catalogue the fact that, according to the last known U.S. judicial rulings and legislative actions in each respective instance, legal title to more than 35 percent of the continental United States remained in the hands of native nations (*see* Map II).

> The fact is that about half the land area of the country was purchased by treaty or agreement at an average price of less than a dollar an acre; another third of a [billion] acres, mainly in the West, were confiscated without compensation; another two–thirds of a [billion] acres were claimed by the United States without pretense of a unilateral action extinguishing native title.[53]

Map II

Map by Jeff Holland and Ward Churchill redrawn by Alexandria Lord

INDIAN LANDS JUDICIALLY RECOGNIZED AS UNCEDED

HAUDENOSAUNEE

SEMINOLE

CHEROKEE

CREEK

OTTOWA

WINNE-
BAGO

KICKAPOO

SAC and
FOX

IOWA

OSAGE

ANISHINABE

DAKOTA

PONCA

OMAHA

PAWNEE

LIPAN
APACHE

NAKOTA

CHEYENNE
and
ARAPAHO

KIOWA

COMANCHE
and
KIOWA

APACHE

ARIKARA

MANDAN

HIDATSA

LAKOTA

JICARILLA
APACHE

ASSINBOINE

MESCALERO
APACHE

BLACKFEET and
GROS
VENTRE

CROW

NAVAJO

CHIRICAHUA
APACHE

KOOTENAI

SALISH

LEMHI

SHOSHONE

UINTAH
UTE

HOPI

HAVASUPAI

YAVAPAI

O'ODAM

NEZ
PERCE

GOSHUTE

SOUTHERN
PAIUTE

SALISH

YAKIMA

KLAMATH

NORTHERN
PAIUTE

WESTERN
SHOSHONE

NORTHERN
PAIUTE

INDIANS of CALIFORNIA

Ceded Lands

Contested Lands

Judicially Established

Indians were quick to seize upon the implications of this, arguing that the commission process had no bearing at all on land title other than to resolve questions concerning who held title to precisely which parts of the United States, and providing a means by which the government could provide native owners with "back rent" on lands which had been "borrowed" by the United States for generations. The "underbrush of confusion as to who owns what" having been finally cleared away, it is appropriate in this view for Indians inside the United States to begin reasserting their national property rights over the approximately 750 million acres of North America which remain theirs by accepted legal definition.[54] Such knowledge has fueled a resurgent indigenous national "militancy" which, beginning in the early 1970s with the emergence of the American Indian Movement (AIM), has led to a series of spectacular extralegal confrontations over land and liberty (several of which are covered in "The Bloody Wake of Alcatraz" in this volume) with federal authorities. These, in turn, have commanded the very sort of international attention to U.S. territorial claims, and Indian policy more generally, that the Claims Commission was supposed to avert.

Beginning in the late '70s, the Native North Americans—spearheaded by AIM's "diplomatic arm," the International Indian Treaty Council—were able to escalate this trend by establishing a place for themselves within the United Nations structure, and entering annual reports concerning the conduct of both the U.S. and Canadian governments vis-à-vis native peoples and their lands. In this changing context, the federal government has once again begun to engage in "damage control," allowing a calculated range of concessions in order to preserve what it seeks to project as its image abroad. Notably, in 1974, the U.S. Supreme Court announced for the first time that Indians had a right to pursue actual recovery of stolen land through the federal judiciary.[55] Although resort to the courts of the conqueror is hardly an ideal solution to the issues raised by Indian nations, it does place another tool in the inventory of means by which they can now pursue their rights. And it has resulted in measurable gains for some of them over the past 15 years.

Probably the best example of this is that of the suit, first entered in 1972 under auspices of a sponsoring organization, of the basically landless Passamaquoddy and Pennobscot Nations in present–day Maine to some 12 million acres acknowledged as being theirs in a series of letters dating from the 1790s and signed by George Washington.[56] Since it was demonstrated that no ratified treaty existed by which the Indians had ceded their land, U.S. District Judge Edward T. Gignoux ordered a settlement acceptable to the majority of the native people involved.[57] This resulted in the recovery, in 1980, of some 300,000 acres of land, and payment of $27 million in compensatory damages by the federal government.[58] In a similarly argued case, the Narragansetts of Rhode Island— who were not previously recognized by the government as still existing—were in 1978 able to win not only recognition of themselves, but to recover 1,800 acres of the remaining 3,200 stripped from it in 1880 by unilateral action of the state.[59] In another example, the Mashantucket Pequot people of Connecticut filed suit in 1976 to recover 800 of the 2,000 acres comprising their original reservation, created by the Connecticut Colony in 1686 but reduced to 184 acres by the State of Connecticut after the American Revolution.[60] Pursuant to a settlement agreement arrived at with the state in 1982, Congress passed an act providing funds to acquire the desired acreage. It was promptly vetoed by Ronald Reagan on April 11, 1983.[61] The Senate Select Committee on Indian Affairs then convened hearings on the matter, which gave Reagan an excuse to give in to the pressure, so after agreeing to a slight revision of the statute, he finally affixed his signature on October 18 the same year.[62]

Other nations, however, have not fared as well, even in an atmosphere in which the United States has sometimes proven more than usually willing to compromise as a means to contain questions of native land rights. The Wampanoags of the Mashpee area of Cape Cod, for instance, filed suit in 1974 in an attempt to recover about 17,000—later reduced to 11,000—of the 23,000 acres which were historically acknowledged as being theirs (the Commonwealth of Massachusetts having unilaterally declared their reservation a "township" in 1870). At trial, the all–white jury, all of whom had property interests in the Mashpee area, were asked to determine whether the Wampanoag plaintiffs were "a tribe within the meaning of the law." After deliberating for 21 hours, the jury returned with the absurd finding that they were *not* such an entity in 1790, 1869, and 1870 (the years which were key to the Indians' case), but that they *were* in 1832 and 1834 (years which it was important they have been "a tribe" for purposes of alienating land to the U.S. government. Their claim was then denied by District Judge Walter J. Skinner.[63] An appeal to the U.S. First Circuit Court failed, and the U.S. Supreme Court refused to review the case.[64]

Still pending land claims cases include those of the presently landless Schaghticoke and Mohegan peoples of Connecticut, each of which is attempting to recover approximately 1,000 acres lost to unilateral state actions during the nineteenth century.[65] Another is that of the Catawbas of South Carolina, who filed suit in 1980 for recovery of their original 144,000–acre reservation, created by George III in 1760 and 1763, and acknowledged by the fledgling United States before being dissolved in a fraudulent treaty negotiated by the state and ratified by the Senate.[66] In 1981, the state, arguing that federal termination of the Catawbas in 1959 invalidated their right to sue, asked for and received a dismissal of the case. On appeal in 1983, however, the Fourth Circuit reinstated the case.[67]

Given such mixed results, it is plain that justice in native land claims cases in the United States cannot really be expected to accrue through the federal court system. Eventual resolution must inevitably reside within bodies such as the U. N. Working Group on Indigenous Populations (a subpart of the Commission on Human Rights), which is even now engaged in drafting a new element of international law entitled "The Universal Declaration of the Rights of Indigenous Peoples," and the World Court, which must interpret and render opinions based on such law.[68] From there, it can be expected that international scrutiny and pressure, as well as changed sentiments in a growing portion of the U.S. body politic, will serve to force the United States to edge ever closer to a fair and equitable handling of indigenous rights.

In the meantime, nearly every litigation of land claims within the federal system adds to the weight of evidence supporting the international case presented by native people: when they win, it proves they were entitled to the land all along; when they lose, it proves that the "due process rights" the United States insists protect their interests are, at most, inconsistently available to them. Either way, these legalistic endeavors force cracks in the ideological matrix of the American empire. In combination with extralegal efforts such as refusal to leave their homes by Indian traditionals and physical occupations of contested areas by groups such as AIM, as well as the increasing extent of international work by indigenous delegations, these legal endeavors comprise the core of the ongoing land struggles which represent the future survival of Native North America.

Current Land Struggles

Aside from those already mentioned, there is no shortage of ongoing struggles for their land rights undertaken by native people within the United States today, any or all of which are admirably suited to illustrate various aspects of the phenomenon. In Florida, the descendants of a group of Seminole (Miccosukee) "recalcitrants," who had managed to avoid forced relocation to Oklahoma during the 1830s by taking refuge in the Everglades, simply "squatted" in their homeland for more than 130 years, never agreeing to a "peace accord" with the United States until the mid–60s. Because of their unswerving resistance to moving, the state finally agreed to create a small reservation for these people in 1982, and the Congress concurred by statute in 1982.[69] In Minnesota, there is the struggle of the Anishinabe Akeeng (People's Land Organization) to reassert indigenous control over the remaining 20 percent—250,000 acres—of the White Earth Chippewa Reservation, and to recover some portion of the additional 1 million acres reserved as part of White Earth under an 1854 treaty with the United States but that was declared "surplus" through the General Allotment Act in 1906.[70]

In southern Arizona, the Tohono O'Odham (Papago) Nation continues its efforts to secure the entirety of its sacred Baboquivari Mountain Range, acknowledged by the government to be part of the Papago Reservation in 1916, but opened to non–Indian "mineral development interests—especially those concerned with mining copper—both before and since."[71] In the northern

portion of the same state, there are ongoing struggles by both the Hopis and
Diné (Navajos) to block the U.S. Forest Service's scheme to convert San
Francisco Peaks, a site sacred to both peoples, into a ski resort complex.[72] And,
of course, there is the grueling and government–instigated land struggle occurring between the tribal councils of these same two peoples within what was
called the "Navajo–Hopi Joint Use Area." The matter is bound up in energy
development issues—primarily the strip mining of an estimated 24 billion tons
of readily accessible low sulfur coal—and entails a program to forcibly relocate
as many as 13,500 traditional Diné who have refused to leave their land.[73]

In Massachusetts, the Gayhead Wampanoags, proceeding slowly and
carefully so as to avoid the pitfalls encountered by their cousins at Mashpee,
are preparing litigation to regain control over ancestral lands.[74] In Alaska,
struggles to preserve some measure of sovereign indigenous (Indian, Aleut, and
Inuit) control over some 40 million oil–rich acres corporatized by the 1971
Alaska Native Claims Settlement Act are intensifying steadily.[75] In Hawai'i,
the native owners of the islands, having rejected a proffered cash settlement for
relinquishment of their historic land rights in 1974,[76] are pursuing a legislative
remedy which would both pay monetary compensation for loss of use of their
territory while restoring a portion of it.[77] The fact of the matter is that, wherever
there are indigenous people within the United States, land claims struggles are
occurring with increasing frequency and intensity.

In order to convey a sense of the texture of these ongoing battles over
land, it will be useful to consider a small selection of examples in a depth not
possible, given constraints upon essay length, in every case which has been
cited. For this purpose, the claims of the Iroquois Confederacy in upstate New
York, the Lakota Black Hills Land Claim in South Dakota, and the Western
Shoshone claims, primarily in Nevada, should serve quite well. Although they
are hardly unique in many of their characteristics—and are thus able to
represent the generalities of a broad range of comparable struggles—they are
among the most sustained and intensively pursued of such efforts.

The Iroquois Land Claims

One of the longest fought and more complicated land claims struggles in
the United States is that of the Haudenosaunee, or Iroquois Six Nations
Confederacy. While the 1782 Treaty of Paris ended hostilities between the
British Crown and its secessionist subjects in the 13 colonies, it had no direct
effect upon the state of war existing between those subjects and indigenous
nations allied with the Crown. Similarly, while by the treaty George III
quitclaimed his property rights under the Doctrine of Discovery to the affected
portion of North America, it was the opinion of Thomas Jefferson and others
that this had done nothing to vest title to these lands in the newly born United
States.[78] On both counts, the Continental Congress found it imperative to enter
into treaty arrangements with Indian nations as expeditiously as possible. A

very high priority in this regard was accorded the Iroquois Confederacy, four members of which—the Mohawks, Senecas, Cayugas, and Onondagas—had fought with the British (the remaining two, the Oneidas and Tuscaroras, having remained largely neutral but occasionally providing assistance to the colonists).[79]

During October 1784, the government conducted extensive negotiations with representatives of the Six Nations at Fort Stanwix, the result being a treaty by which the Indians relinquished claim to all lands lying west of a north–south line running from Niagara to the border of Pennsylvania—territory within the Ohio Valley (this was a provision reinforced in the 1789 Treaty of Fort Harmar) —and the land on which Fort Oswego had been built. In exchange, the United States guaranteed three of the four hostile nations the bulk of their traditional homelands. The Oneida and Tuscarora were also "secured in the possession of the lands on which they are now settled." Altogether, the area in question came to about 6 million acres, or half of the present state of New York (*see* Map III). The agreement, while meeting most of the Indians' needs, was quite useful to the U.S. central government:

> First ... in order to sell [land in the Ohio River area] and settle it, the Continental Congress needed to extinguish Indian title, including any claims by the Iroquois [nations] of New York. Second, the

Map III

IROQUOIS TREATY LANDS IN 1794

MOHAWKS

ONEIDAS

SENECAS

CAYUGAS

ONONDAGAS

Fort Stanwix Treaty 1768

NEW YORK

Map by Ward Churchill & Jeff Holland, redrawn by Alexandria Lord.

commissioners wanted to punish the ... Senecas. Thus they forced the Senecas to surrender most of their land in New York [and Pennsylvania] to the United States.... Third, the United States ... wanted to secure peace by confirming to the [nations] their remaining lands. Fourth, the United States was anxious to protect its frontier from the British in Canada by securing land for forts and roads along lakes Erie and Ontario.[80]

New York state, needless to say, was rather less enthusiastic about the terms of the treaty, and had already attempted, unsuccessfully, to obtain additional land cessions from the Iroquois during meetings conducted prior to arrival of the federal delegation at Fort Stanwix.[81] Further such efforts by the state were barred by Article IX of the Articles of Confederation—and subsequently by Article I (Section 10) and the commerce clause of the Constitution—all of which combined to render treaty–making and outright purchases of Indian land by states illegal. New York then resorted to subterfuge, securing a series of 26 "leases," many of them for 999 years, on almost all native territory within its boundaries. The Haudenosaunee initially agreed to these transactions because of Governor Clinton's duplicitous assurances that leases represented a way for them to *keep* their land, and for his government to "extend its protection over their property against the dealings of unscrupulous white land speculators" in the private sector. The first such arrangement was forged with the Oneidas. In a meeting begun at Fort Schuyler on August 28, 1788:

> The New York commissioners ... led them to believe that they had [already] lost all their land to the New York Genesee Company, and that the commissioners were there to restore title. The Oneidas expressed confusion over this since they had never signed any instruments to that effect, but Governor Clinton just waved that aside.... Thus the Oneidas agreed to the lease arrangement with the state because it seemed the only way they could get back their land. The state received some five million acres for $2,000 in cash, $2,000 in clothing, $1,000 in provisions, and $600 in annual rental. So complete was the deception that Good Peter [an Oneida leader] thanked the governor for his efforts.[82]

Leasing of the Tuscaroras' land occurred the same day, by a parallel instrument.[83] On September 12, the Onondagas leased almost all their land to New York under virtually identical conditions.[84] The Cayugas followed suit on February 25, 1789, in exchange for "payment of $500 in silver, plus an additional $1,625 the next June and a $500 annuity."[85] New York's flagrant circumvention of constitutional restrictions on non–federal acquisitions of Indian land was a major factor in congressional tightening of its mechanisms of control over such activities in the first so–called Indian Trade and Intercourse Act of 1790 (1 *Stat.* 37).[86] Clinton, however, simply shifted to a different ruse, back–dating his maneuvers by announcing in 1791 that the state would honor a 999 year lease negotiated in 1787 by a private speculator named John Livingston. The lease covered 800,000 acres of mainly Mohawk land, but had been declared null and void by the state legislature in 1788.[87]

Concerned that such dealings by New York might push the Iroquois, the largely landless Senecas in particular, into joining the Shawnee leader Tecumseh's alliance resisting further U.S. expansion into the Ohio Valley, the federal government sent a new commission to meet with the Haudenosaunee leadership at the principle Seneca town of Canandaigua in 1794. In exchange for the Indians' pledge not to bear arms against the United States, their ownership of the lands guaranteed them at Fort Stanwix was reaffirmed, the state's leases notwithstanding, and the bulk of the Seneca territory in Pennsylvania was restored.[88] Nonetheless, New York began parceling out sections of the leased lands in subleases to the very "unscrupulous whites" it had pledged to guard against. On September 15, 1797, the Holland Land Company—in which many members of the state government had invested—assumed control over all but 10 tracts of land, totaling 397 square miles, of the Fort Stanwix Treaty area. The leasing instrument purportedly "extinguished" native title to the land[89] (*see* Map IV).

Map IV

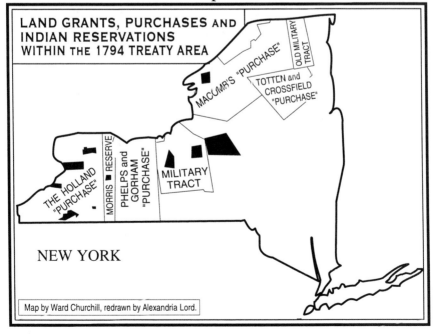

LAND GRANTS, PURCHASES AND INDIAN RESERVATIONS WITHIN THE 1794 TREATY AREA

OLD MILITARY TRACT

MACOMB'S "PURCHASE"

TOTTEN and CROSSFIELD "PURCHASE"

MORRIS ■ RESERVE

PHELPS and GORHAM "PURCHASE"

THE HOLLAND "PURCHASE"

MILITARY TRACT

NEW YORK

Map by Ward Churchill, redrawn by Alexandria Lord.

Given the diminishing military importance of the Six Nations after Tecumseh's 1794 defeat at Fallen Timbers, Washington did nothing to correct the situation despite Iroquois protests. New York was thus emboldened to proceed with its appropriations of native land. In 1810, the Holland Company sold some 200,000 acres of its holdings in Seneca and Tuscarora land to its accountant, David A. Ogden, at a price of 50¢ per acre. Ogden then issued shares against development of this land, many of them to Albany politicians. Thus capitalized, he was able to push through a deal in 1826 to buy a further 81,000 acres of previously unleased reservation land at 53¢ per acre. A federal investigation into the affair was quashed by Secretary of War Peter B. Porter, himself a major stockholder in the Ogden Land Company, in 1828.[90] Under such circumstances, most of the Oneidas requested in 1831 that what was left of their New York holdings, which they were sure they would lose anyway, be exchanged for a 500,000–acre parcel purchased from the Menominees in Wisconsin. President Andrew Jackson, at the time pursuing his policy of general Indian removal to points west of the Mississippi, readily agreed.[91]

In the climate of removal, Washington officials actively colluded with the speculators. On January 15, 1838, federal commissioners oversaw the signing of the Treaty of Buffalo Creek, wherein 102,069 acres of Seneca land was "ceded" directly to the Ogden Company. The $202,000 purchase price was divided almost evenly between the government (to be held "in trust" for the Indians), and individual non–Indians seeking to buy and "improve" plots in the former reservation area. At the same time, what was left of the Cayuga, Oneida, Onondaga, and Tuscarora holdings were wiped out, at an aggregate cost of $400,000 to the Ogden Company.[92] The Iroquois were told they should relocate *en masse* to Missouri. Although the Six Nations never consented to the treaty, and it was never properly ratified by the Senate, President Martin Van Buren proclaimed it to be the law of the land on April 4, 1840.[93]

By 1841, Iroquois complaints about the Buffalo Creek Treaty were being reinforced by increasing numbers of non–Indians outraged not so much by the loss of Indian land as by the obvious corruption involved in its terms.[94] Consequently, in 1842, a second Treaty of Buffalo Creek was negotiated. Under its provisions, the United States again acknowledged the Haudenosaunee right to reside in New York and restored small areas as the Allegany and Cattaraugus Seneca reservations. The Onondaga Reservation was also reconstituted on a 7,300 acre land base, the Tuscarora Reservation on about 2,500 acres. The Ogden Company was allowed to keep the rest.[95] The Tonawanda Seneca Band immediately filed a formal protest of these terms with the Senate,[96] and, in 1857, received a $256,000 "award" of their own money with which to "buy back" a minor portion of its former territory from Ogden.[97]

Beginning in 1855, the Erie Railway Company entered the picture, setting out to lease significant portions of both Cattaraugus and Allegany. Sensing the depth of the then–prevailing federal support for railroad construction, the state judiciary seized the opportunity to cast an aura of legitimacy upon all of New York's other illicit leasing arrangements:

> Though the leases were ratified by New York, the state's supreme court in 1875 invalidated them. In recognition of this action, the New York legislature passed a concurrent resolution [a century after the fact] that state action was not sufficient to ratify leases because "Congress alone possesses the power to deal with and for the Indians." Instead of setting aside the leases, Congress in 1875 passed an act authorizing [them]. The state now made leases renewable for twelve years, and by an amendment in 1890 the years were extended to ninety–nine. Later the Supreme Court of New York deemed them perpetual.[98]

As a result, by 1889, 80 percent of all Iroquois reservation land in New York was under lease to non–Indian interests and individuals. The same year, a commission was appointed by Albany to examine the state's "Indian Problem." Rather than "suggesting that the leasing of four–fifths of their land had deterred Indian welfare, the commission criticized the Indians for not growing enough to feed themselves," thereby placing an "undue burden" on those profiting from their land. Chancellor C. N. Sims of Syracuse University, a commission member, argued strongly that only "obliteration of the tribes, conferral of citizenship, and allotment of lands" would set things right.[99] Washington duly set out to undertake allotment, but was stunned to discover it was stymied by the "underlying title" to much of the reserved Iroquois land it had allowed the Ogden Company to obtain over the years. In 1895, Congress passed a bill authorizing a buy–out of the Ogden interest (again at taxpayer expense), but the company upped its asking price for the desired acreage from $50,000 to $270,000. Negotiations thereupon collapsed, and the Six Nations were spared the trauma (and further land loss) of the allotment process.[100]

Not that the state didn't keep trying. In 1900, Governor Theodore Roosevelt created a commission to reexamine the matter. This led to the introduction of another bill (HR 12270) in 1902 aimed at allotting the Seneca reservations (with 50,000 in all, they were by far the largest remaining Iroquois land areas) by paying the Ogden Company $200,000 of the *Indians'* "trust funds" to abandon its claims on Allegany and Cattaraugus.[101] The Senecas retained attorney John VanVoorhis to argue that the Ogden claim was invalid because, for more than 100 years, the company had not been compelled to pay so much as a nickel of tax on the acreage it professed to "own." By this, VanVoorhis contended, both the Ogden Company and the government had all along admitted—for purposes of federal law—that the land was really still the property of "Indians not taxed." The new bill was withdrawn in some confusion at this point, and allotment was again averted.[102] In 1905, the Senecas carried the tax issue into court in an attempt to clear their land title, but the case was dismissed under the premise that they had "no legal standing to sue" non–Indians.[103]

A third attempt to allot the Six Nations reservations (HR 18735) foundered in 1914, as did a New York state constitutional amendment, proposed in 1915, to effectively abolish the reservations. Even worse, from New York's viewpoint, in 1919 the U.S. Justice Department for the first time acted on behalf of the Iroquois, filing a suit which (re)established a 32–acre "reservation" in the state for the Oneidas.[104] The state legislature responded by creating yet another commission, this one headed by attorney Edward A. Everett, to conduct a comprehensive study of land title questions in New York and to make recommendations as to how they might be cleared up across–the–board, once and for all.[105] After more than two years of hearings and intensive research, Everett handed in a totally unanticipated conclusion: The Six Nations still possessed legal title to all 6 million acres of the Fort Stanwix treaty area.

> He cited international law to the effect that there are only two ways to take a country away from a people possessing it—purchase or conquest. The Europeans who came here did recognize that the Indians were in possession and so, in his opinion, thus recognized their status as nations.... If then, the Indians did hold fee to the land, how did they lose it?... [T]he Indians were [again] recognized by George Washington as a nation at the Treaty of 1784. Hence, they were as of 1922 owners of all the land [reserved by] them in that treaty unless they had ceded it by a treaty equally valid and binding.[106]

Everett reinforced his basic finding with reference to the Treaties of Fort Harmar and Canandaigua, discounted both Buffalo Creek Treaties as fraudulent, and rejected both the leases of the state and those taken by entities such as the Holland and Ogden Companies as having no legal validity at all.[107] The Albany government quickly shelved the report rather than publishing it, but it couldn't prevent the implications from being discussed throughout the Six Nations. On August 21, 1922, a council meeting was held at Onondaga for purposes of retaining Mrs. Lulu G. Stillman, Everett's secretary, to do research on the exact boundaries of the Fort Stanwix treaty area.[108] The Iroquois land claim struggle had shifted from dogged resistance to dispossession to the offensive strategy of land recovery, and the first test case, *James Deere v. St. Lawrence River Power Company* (32 F.2d 550), was filed on June 26, 1925 in an attempt to regain a portion of the St. Regis Mohawk Reservation taken by New York. The federal government declined to intervene on the Mohawks' behalf—as it was its "trust responsibility" to do—and the suit was dismissed by a district court judge on October 10, 1927. The dismissal was upheld on appeal in April 1929.[109]

Things remained quiet on the land claims front during the 1930s, as the Haudenosaunee were mainly preoccupied with preventing the supplanting of their traditional Longhouse form of government by "tribal councils" sponsored by the Bureau of Indian Affairs via the Indian Reorganization Act of 1934. Probably as a means of coaxing them into a more favorable view of federal intentions under the Indian Reorganization Act (IRA), Indian Commissioner John Collier agreed towards the end of the decade that his agency would finally provide at least limited support to Iroquois claims litigation. This resulted, in 1941, in the Justice Department's filing of *U.S. v. Forness* (125 F.2d 928) on behalf of the Allegany Senecas. The suit—ostensibly aimed at eviction of an individual who had refused to pay his $4–per–year rent to the Indians for eight years—actually sought to enforce a resolution of the Seneca Nation canceling hundreds of low–cost 99–year leases taken in the City of Salamanca, on the reservation, in 1892. Intervening for the defendants was the Salamanca Trust Corporation, a mortgage institution holding much of the paper at issue. Although the case was ultimately unsuccessful in its primary objective, it did clarify that New York law had no bearing on Indian leasing arrangements.[110]

This was partly "corrected," in the state view, on July 2, 1948, and September 13, 1950, when Congress passed bills placing the Six Nations under New York jurisdiction in first criminal and then civil matters.[111] Federal responsibility to assist Indians in pursuing treaty–based land claims was nonetheless explicitly preserved.[112] Washington, of course, elected to treat this obligation in its usual cavalier fashion, plunging ahead during the 1950s—while the Indians were mired in efforts to prevent termination of their federal recognition altogether—with the flooding of 130 acres of the St. Regis Reservation near Messena (and about 1,300 acres of the Caughnawaga Mohawk Reserve in Canada) as part of the St. Lawrence Seaway Project.[113] The government also proceeded with plans to flood more than 9,000 acres of the Allegany Reservation as a by–product of constructing the Kinzua Dam. Although studies revealed an alternative siting of the dam would not only spare the Seneca land from flooding but better serve "the greater public good" for which it was supposedly intended, Congress pushed ahead.[114] The Senecas protested the project as a clear violation of the Fort Stanwix guarantees, a position with which lower federal courts agreed, but the Supreme Court declined to review the question, and the Army Corps of Engineers completed the dam in 1967.[115]

Meanwhile, the New York State Power Authority was attempting to seize more than half (1,383 acres) of the Tuscarora Reservation, near Buffalo, as a reservoir for the Niagara Power Project. In April 1958, the Tuscaroras physically blocked access by construction workers to the site, and several were arrested (charges were later dropped). A federal district judge entered a temporary restraining order against the state, but the appellate court ruled that the congressional issuance of a license to the Federal Power Commission constituted sufficient grounds for the state to "exercise eminent domain" over native property.[116] The Supreme Court again refused to hear the resulting Haudenosaunee appeal. A "compromise" was then implemented in which the state flooded "only" 560 acres, or about one–fifth of the remaining Tuscarora land.[117]

By the early '60s, it had become apparent that the Iroquois, because their territory fell "within the boundaries of one of the original thirteen states," would be disallowed from seeking redress through the Indian Claims Commission.[118] The decade was largely devoted to a protracted series of discussions between state officials and various sectors of the Iroquois leadership. Agreements were reached in areas related to education, housing, and revenue sharing, but on the issues of land claims and jurisdiction, the position of Longhouse traditionals was unflinching. In their view, the state holds *no* rights over the Iroquois in either sphere.[119] Their point was punctuated on May 13, 1974, when Mohawks from St. Regis and Caughnawaga occupied an area at Ganiekeh (Moss Lake), in the Adirondack Mountains. They proclaimed the site to be sovereign Mohawk territory under the Fort Stanwix Treaty—"[We] represent a cloud of title not only to [this] 612.7 acres in Herkimer County but to all of northeastern N.Y."—and set out to defend it (and themselves) by force of arms.[120]

After a pair of local vigilantes engaged in harassing the Indians were wounded by return gunfire in October, the state filed for eviction in federal court. The matter was bounced back on the premise that it was not a federal issue, and the New York attorney general—undoubtedly discomfited at the publicity prospects entailed in an armed confrontation on the scale of the 1973 Wounded Knee siege—let the case die.[121] Alternatively, the state dispatched a negotiating team headed by future governor Mario Cuomo. In May 1977, the "Moss Lake Agreement" was reached, and the Mohawks assumed permanent possession of a land parcel at Miner Lake, in the town of Altona, and another in the McComb Reforestation Area.[122] Mohawk possession of the sites remains ongoing in 1995, a circumstance which has prompted others among the Six Nations to pursue land recovery through a broader range of tactics and, perhaps, with greater vigor than they might otherwise (e.g., Mohawk actions taken in Canada, concerning a land dispute at the Oka Reserve, near Montréal, during 1990).

As all this was going on, the Oneidas had, in 1970, filed the first of the really significant Iroquois land claims suits. The case, *Oneida Indian Nation of New York v. County of Oneida* (70–CV–35 [N.D.N.Y.]), charged that the transfer of 100,000 acres of Oneida land to New York via a 1795 lease engineered by Governor Clinton was fraudulent and invalid on both constitutional grounds and because the government violated the 1790 Trade and Intercourse Act. It was dismissed because of the usual "Indians lack legal standing" argument, but reinstated by the Supreme Court in 1974.[123] Compelled to actually examine the merits of the case for the first time, the U.S.

District Court agreed with the Indians (and the Everett Report) that title still rested with the Oneidas.

> The plaintiffs have established a claim for the violation of the Nonintercourse Act. Unless the Act is to be considered nugatory, it must be concluded that the plaintiff's right of occupancy and possession of the land in question was not alienated. By the deed of 1795, the State acquired no rights against the plaintiffs; consequently, its successors, the defendant counties, are in no better position.[124]

Terming the Oneidas a "legal fiction," and the lower courts' rulings "racist," attorney Allan Van Gestel appealed to the Supreme Court.[125] On October 1, 1984, the high court ruled against Van Gestel and ordered his clients to work out an accommodation, indemnified by the state, including land restoration, compensation, and rent on unrecovered areas.[126] Van Gestel continued to howl that "the common people" of Oneida and Madison Counties were being "held hostage," but as the Oneidas' attorney, Arlinda Locklear, put it in 1986:

> One final word about responsibility for the Oneida claims. It is true that the original sin here was committed by the United States and the state of New York. It is also no doubt true that there are a number of innocent landowners in the area, i.e., individuals who acquired their land with no knowledge of the Oneida claim to it. But those facts alone do not end the inquiry respecting ultimate responsibility. Whatever the knowledge of the claims before then, the landowners have certainly been aware of the Oneida claims since 1970 when the first suit was filed. Since that time, the landowners have done nothing to seek a speedy and just resolution of the claims. Instead, they have as a point of principle denied the validity of the claims and pursued the litigation, determined to prove the claims to be frivolous. Now that the landowners have failed in that effort, they loudly protest their innocence in the entire matter. The Oneidas, on the other hand, have since 1970 repeatedly expressed their preference for an out–of–court resolution of their claims. Had the landowners joined with the Oneidas sixteen years ago in seeking a just resolution, the claims would no doubt be resolved today. For that reason, the landowners share in the responsibility for the situation in which they find themselves today.[127]

Others would do well to heed these words because, as Locklear pointed out, the Oneida case "paved the legal way for other Indian land claims."[128] Not least of these are other suits by the Oneidas themselves. In 1978, the New York Oneidas filed for adjudication of title to the entirety of their Fort Stanwix claim—about 4.5 million acres—a case affecting not only Oneida and Madison Counties, but Broome, Chenango, Cortland, Herkimer, Jefferson, Lewis, Onondaga, Oswego, St. Lawrence, and Tiago Counties as well (this matter was shelved, pending final resolution of the first Oneida claims litigation).[129] In December 1979, the Oneida Nation of Wisconsin and the Thames Band of Southgold, Ontario, joined in an action pursuing rights in the same claim area, but naming the state rather than individual counties as defendant.[130] The Cayuga Nation, landless throughout the twentieth century, has also filed suit against Cayuga and Seneca Counties for recovery of 64,015 acres taken during Clinton's leasing foray of 1789 (the Cayuga claim may develop into an action overlapping with those of the Oneida; *see* Map V).[131]

The latter case, filed on November 19, 1980, resulted from attempts by the Cayugas to negotiate some sort of land base and compensation for themselves with federal, state, and county officials from the mid–70s onward. By August 1979, they had worked out a tentative agreement that would have provided them with the 1,852–acre Sampson Park area in southern Seneca County, the 3,629–acre Hector Land Use Area in the same county, and an $8 million trust account established by the Secretary of the Interior (up to $2.5 million of which would be used to buy additional land).[132] Although not one square inch of their holdings was threatened by the arrangement, the response

Map V

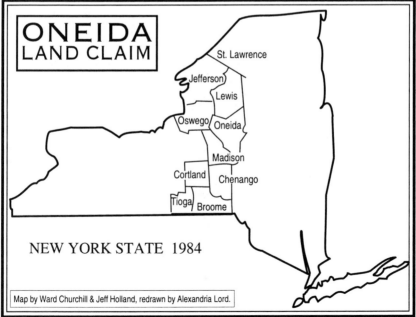

ONEIDA
LAND CLAIM

St. Lawrence

Jefferson

Lewis

Oswego Oneida

Madison

Cortland   Chenango

Tioga Broome

NEW YORK STATE 1984

Map by Ward Churchill & Jeff Holland, redrawn by Alexandria Lord.

of the local non–Indian population was rabid. To quote Paul D. Moonan, Sr., president of the local Monroe Title and Abstract Company: "The Cayugas have no moral or legal justification for their claim." Wisner Kinne, a farmer near the town of Ovid, immediately founded the Seneca County Liberation Organization, premised on a virulent anti–Indianism. SCLO attracted several hundred highly vocal members from the sparsely populated county.

A bill to authorize the settlement subsequently failed due to this "white backlash," and so the Cayugas went to court to obtain a much larger area, eviction of 7,000 county residents, and $350 million in trespass damages. Attempts by attorneys for SCLO to have the suit dismissed failed in 1982, as did a 1984 compromise offer initiated by Representative Frank Horton. The latter, which might have well been accepted by the Cayugas, would have provided them the 3,200–acre Howland Game Management Reserve along the Seneca River, a 2,850–acre parcel on Lake Ontario (owned by the Rochester Gas and Electric Company), and a 2,000–acre parcel adjoining Sampson State Park. Additionally, the Cayugas would have received "well in excess" of the $8 million they'd originally sought. While SCLO appears to have decided acquiescence was by this point the better part of valor, the proposal came under heavy attack from non–Indian environmentalists "concerned about the animals in the Howland Reserve." Ultimately, it was nixed by Ronald Reagan in 1987, not because he was concerned with area fauna, but because he was angry with Horton for voting against contra–aid. The suit is therefore ongoing.[133]

At the town of Salamanca, to which the leases expired at the end of 1991, the Allegany Senecas also undertook decisive action during the second half of the '80s. Beginning as early as 1986, they stipulated the intent not to renew, and to begin eviction proceedings against non–Indian lease and mortgage holders in the area, unless the terms of a new arrangement were considerably recast in their favor (i.e., clarification of Seneca title, shorter leasing period, fair rates for property rental, and "preeminent jurisdiction" over both the land and cash income derived from it).[134] A further precondition to lease renewal was that compensation be made for all non–payment and under–payment of fair rental values of Seneca property accruing from the last lease. Although these demands unleashed a storm of protest from local whites—who, as usual, argued vociferously that the Indian owners of the land held no rights to it—they were unsuccessful in both court and Congress.[135] At this juncture, all essential Seneca terms have been met, and Congress has passed the Seneca Nation Settlement Act of 1990, including a settlement award of $60 million (the cost of which is to be shared by federal, state, and local non–Indian governments) for rental monies they should have received over the past 99 years, but didn't.[136]

The Black Hills Land Claim

A much more harshly fought struggle, at least in terms of physical combat, has been the battle waged by the Lakota Nation ("Western Sioux") to

Map VI

LAKOTA NATIONS, RESERVATIONS, AND CEDED LANDS

MONTANA

Yellowstone R.

UNCEDED INDIAN TERRITORY

NORTH DAKOTA

SOUTH DAKOTA

Missouri River.

WYOMING

HUNTING RESERVE

COLORADO

North Platte River

NEBRASKA

Map prepared by Ward Churchill & Jeff Holland. Redrawn by Alexandria Lord.

☐ 20th Century Takings
▨ 1868 Great Sioux Res.
▨ 1877 Black Hills Taking
■ Current Reservations
✦ 1868 Unceded Territory
◹ Additional Territory Under 1851 Treaty

retain their spiritual heartland, the Black Hills. In 1851, in exchange for right of way to California and Oregon along what was called the Platte River Road, the government entered into the first Fort Laramie Treaty with the Lakota. The treaty recognized Lakota ownership of and sovereignty within a vast area amounting to approximately 5 percent of the continental United States (*see* Map VI).[137] By 1864, however, silver had been discovered in Montana, and the United States, seeking the shortest route to the mines, violated the treaty by attempting to establish the "Bozeman Trail" directly through Lakota territory. This led to the so–called Red Cloud War of 1866–68, in which the Lakota formed a politico–military alliance with the Cheyenne and Arapaho Nations, laid siege to U.S. military posts along the trail, and defeated the Army several times in the field. For the first time in its history, the government sued for peace. All Lakota terms were agreed to in a second Fort Laramie Treaty, signed during the spring of 1868, in exchange for the United States being allowed to withdraw its remaining soldiers without further damage.[138]

The provisions of the 1868 Fort Laramie Treaty were clear and unequivocal. All land from the east bank of the Missouri River westward within the present boundaries of the State of South Dakota was recognized by the United States as a "Great Sioux Reservation," exclusively for Indian use and occupancy. Contiguous portions of North Dakota and Montana, and about a third of Wyoming were also recognized as being "Unceded Indian Territory" belonging to the "Greater Sioux Nation," and all of Nebraska north of the North Platte River was perpetually reserved as hunting territory. A stipulation in the 1868 treaty acknowledged that its terms would not impair any Lakota land rights reserved under any earlier treaties, and the United States pledged to use its military to prevent its citizens from trespassing again in Lakota territory.[139] Finally, the way in which any future transfer of Lakota title might occur was spelled out:

> No [subsequent] treaty for cession of any portion of the reservation herein described which may be held in common shall be of any validity or force as against said Indians, unless executed and signed by at least three–fourths of all adult male Indians, occupying or interested in the same.[140]

In 1863, a Catholic priest named Jean de Smet, after sojourning illegally in the Black Hills, reported the presence of gold there. In short order, this incentive proved sufficient to cause Washington to violate the new treaty, sending Lt. Colonel George Armstrong Custer and his élite 7th Cavalry Regiment (heavily reinforced) to explore the Hills. When Custer, during the summer of 1874, reported that he too had found gold, the government dispatched a commission to purchase the region from the Lakotas while developing contingency plans for a military seizure in the event negotiations were unsuccessful.[141] During the fall of 1875, the commission reported failure, and "Sioux Affairs" were shifted to the War Department.[142] The latter announced that all Lakotas who failed to congregate by mid–January at Army posts—where they could be taken under military command—would be henceforth considered "hostile" and subject to "punishment" the following summer. In Washington, the refusal of most Lakotas to comply with this presumption was publicized as an "Act of War" against the United States.[143]

Seeking to compensate for its earlier humiliation at the hands of these same Indians, the Army launched a huge three–pronged invasion, involving several thousand troops, of the Powder River sector of Unceded Indian Territory during the spring of 1876. The idea was to catch all the "Sioux recalcitrants" in a giant vise, overwhelm them, and then—with the Lakota military capacity destroyed—simply take whatever land area the United States desired. Things did not work out so quickly or so easily. First, on June 17, the southern command (a force of about 1,500 under General George Crook) was met and decisively defeated along the Rosebud Creek by several hundred warriors led by the Oglala Lakota, Crazy Horse.[144] Then, on June 25, Custer and a portion of his 7th Cavalry (part of the eastern command) were annihilated in the valley of the Little Big Horn River by a combined force of perhaps 1,000 led by Crazy Horse and Gall, a Hunkpapa Lakota.[145] The balance of the U.S. troops spent the rest of the summer and fall chasing Indians they could never quite catch.[146]

In the end, the Army was forced to resort to "total war" expedients, pursuing a winter campaign of the type developed on the southern plains with the 1864 Sand Creek Massacre and Custer's massacre at the Washita River in 1868. An expert in such operations, Colonel Ranald McKenzie, was imported for this purpose and spent the snowy months of 1876–77 tracking down one village after another, killing women, children, and ponies as he went.[147] By the spring of 1877, all Lakota groups other than a portion of the Hunkpapas led by Sitting Bull and Gall, and a segment of the Oglalas led by Crazy Horse, had surrendered. The Hunkpapas sought asylum in Canada, while U.S. negotiators tricked Crazy Horse into standing down in May.[148] The great Oglala leader was assassinated on September 5, 1877.[149]

With the Lakotas increasingly disarmed, dismounted, and under guard, Congress felt confident in taking possession of the western–most portion of the Great Sioux Reservation, in which the Black Hills were located. On August 15, 1876, it had passed an act (Ch. 289, 19 *Stat.* 176, 192) announcing the Lakota Nation had given up its claim to the desired geography. Concerned that this appear to be a legitimate transfer of title rather than outright conquest, however, it was written so as not to take effect until such time as Lakota "consent" was obtained. Another commission, this one headed by George Manypenny, was dispatched for this purpose. When even noncombatant Lakota men refused to cooperate, rations for the captive people as a whole were suspended. Ultimately, some 10 percent of all "adult Lakota males" signed the cession instrument in order to feed their families. Although this was a far cry from the 75 percent express written consent required by the 1868 treaty to make the matter legal, Congress decided the gesture was sufficient. Meanwhile, on February 28, 1877, the legislators followed up with another law (19 *Stat.* 254), stripping away the Unceded Indian Territory. Since the 1851 treaty boundaries were simply ignored, the Great Sioux Nation had shrunk, almost overnight, from approximately 134 million acres to less than 15 million.[150]

Beginning in 1882, the United States began to impose an "Assimilation Policy" upon the Lakota Nation, outlawing key spiritual practices such as the Sun Dance, extending its jurisdiction over Lakota territory through the 1885 Major Crimes Act, and systematically removing children to remote boarding schools at which their language and cultural practices were not only prohibited, but replaced with those of their conquerors.[151] As part of this concerted drive to destroy the socio–cultural integrity of the Lakotas, allotment of the Great Sioux Reservation was undertaken, starting in 1889, with the consequence that some 80 percent of the remaining Lakota land base was declared surplus by unilateral action of the federal government over the next 20 years. Resulting land losses—about 7 million acres—caused separation of the various Lakota bands from one another for the first time, through emergence of a "complex" of much smaller reservations (i.e., Pine Ridge for the Oglala, Rosebud for the Sicangu ["Brûlé"], Standing Rock for the Hunkpapa and Minneconju, and Cheyenne River for the Itazipco ["Sans Arcs"], Sihasapa ["Blackfeet"] and Oohinunpa ["Two Kettles"]. (*See* Map VI, p. 134).[152]

By 1890, despair at such circumstances among the Indians was so high that there was widespread adoption of the Ghost Dance religion, a phenomenon entailing belief among its adherents that performance of specified rituals would cause a return of the buffalo and people killed by the Army, as well as disappearance of the invaders themselves. Deliberately misconstruing the Ghost Dance as evidence of "an incipient uprising," local Indian agents seized the opportunity to rid themselves of those most resistant to the new order they were seeking to install. A special police unit was used to murder Sitting Bull—who had returned from Canada in 1881—at his home on December 15. On December 28, four companies of the reconstituted 7th Cavalry were used to massacre some 350 followers of Big Foot, a Minneconjou leader, along Wounded Knee Creek. In Washington, it was generally believed "the recalcitrant Sioux" and other "Indian troublemakers" had finally "gotten the message" concerning the permanent and unconditional nature of their subordination.[153] The government felt free to consolidate its grip over even the last residue of land left nominally in native hands:

> In 1891 an amendment was made to the General Allotment Act (26 *Stat.* 794) that allowed the secretary of interior to lease the lands of any allottee who, in the secretary's opinion, "by reason of age or other disability," could not "personally and with benefit to himself occupy or improve his allotment or any part thereof." In effect this amendment gave almost dictatorial powers over the use of allotments since, if the local agent disagreed with the use to which lands were being put, he could intervene and lease the land to whomsoever he pleased.[154]

During the early part of the twentieth century, virtually every useful parcel of land on the Lakota lands had been let in this fashion on long–term and at extremely low–costs ($1 per acre, per year for 99 years being the typical arrangement).[155] At the same time, however, Sioux resistance surfaced in another form. A young Santee Dakota named Charles Eastman began to publish books, including, among other things, accounts of the means by which the Black Hills had been expropriated and of his own experiences as part of a burial detail at Wounded Knee. These were widely read in Europe.[156] Hence, questions on such topics were posed to U.S. observers at the Geneva convention of the newly founded League of Nations in 1919 (there is a school of thought holding that Congress refused to allow formal U.S. participation in the League because, at least in part, it was aware that federal Indian policy would never stand up to international scrutiny). Always inclined to paste a patina of fairness and legality over even its most murderous misdeeds, the United States responded to this embarrassment with an act (41 *Stat.* 738) authorizing the Lakota to file suit in federal court if they felt they'd been dealt with "less than honorably." The thinking was apparently that an "equitable settlement"—consisting of a relatively minor amount of cash—would end the matter.

No consideration at all seems to have been given to the possibility that the Lakotas might have other ideas as to what "equity" might look like. In 1923 they pitched a curve, entering the first Black Hills case with the U.S. Court of Claims, premised on land restoration rather than monetary compensation. Bewildered by this unexpected turn of events, the claims court simply stalled for 19 years, endlessly entertaining motions and counter–motions while professing to "study" the matter. Finally, in 1942, when it became absolutely clear the Lakota Nation would not accept cash in lieu of land, the court simply dismissed the case, asserting the situation was a "moral issue" rather than a constitutional question over which it held jurisdiction.[157] In 1943, the U.S. Supreme Court refused to review the claims court decision.[158]

Although the litigational route appeared stalemated at this point, passage of the Indian Claims Commission Act in 1946 revived the Lakotas' judicial strategy. A case was filed with the commission in 1950, but was deemed by the commissioners to have been "retired" by the earlier claims court dismissal and Supreme Court denial of *certiorari*. Thus, the commission also dismissed the case in 1954.[159] Undeterred, the Lakota entered an appeal which was denied and refiled. In 1958, the Black Hills claim was reinstated on the basis of a ruling that they had been represented by "inadequate counsel" during the 1920s and 1930s. The Justice Department then attempted to have the whole issue simply set aside, submitting a *writ of mandamus* in 1961 which requested "extraordinary relief" from continued Lakota litigation. The government's argument was rejected by the court of claims later in the same year.[160] Hence, the claims commission was compelled to actually consider the case.[161]

After another long hiatus, the commission entered an opinion in 1974 that Congress had been merely exercising its "power of eminent domain" in taking the Lakota land, and that such action was therefore "justified." On the other hand, the commission held, it was constitutionally required that the Indians be "justly compensated" for their loss.[162] The Justice Department responded immediately by filing an appeal to minimize any cash award. This resulted, in 1975, in the government's securing of a *res judicata* prohibition against payment of public funds "in excess of the value of said property at the time it was taken."[163] By official estimation, this came to exactly $17.1 million, against which the Department of the Interior levied an "offset" of $3,484 for rations issued to its captives in 1877.[164] The Lakota attempted an appeal to the Supreme Court, but once again the justices declined to review the matter.[165]

As all this was going on, the frustrations of grassroots Lakotas finally boiled over in such a way as to radically alter the extralegal context in which their Black Hills claim was situated. Early in 1973, traditionals on the Pine Ridge Reservation requested assistance from AIM in confronting the corrupt (and federally–installed) tribal government, in part to block another illegal land transfer. At issue was the uranium–rich northwestern one–eighth of Pine Ridge—known as the Sheep Mountain Gunnery Range—which the Department of the Interior wished to incorporate into the adjoining Badlands National Monument. AIM's physical intervention resulted in its being besieged for 71 days in the symbolic hamlet of Wounded Knee by massive federal forces. By the time the spectacular armed confrontation had ended, international attention was riveted on U.S. Indian affairs as never before. In an attempt to contain the situation, the government fought a veritable counterinsurgency war against AIM and the traditional Oglalas of Pine Ridge during the three years following Pine Ridge.[166]

By the time the gunnery range was finally transferred in 1976, the Oglalas—who had sustained at least 69 fatalities and nearly 350 serious physical assaults on their reservation during the period of federal repression—were in no mood to accept further abuse.[167] They not only mounted a storm of protest which caused a partial reversal of the transfer instrument, but also rallied the rest of their nation to demand that the three–fourths express consent clause of the 1868 treaty (now including adult women as well as men) be applied to the claims commission award. Organizing a referendum on the matter under the slogan "The Black Hills Are *Not* For Sale," the United Sioux Tribes of South Dakota voted overwhelmingly in 1977 to refuse the settlement.[168] Meanwhile, AIM had created the International Indian Treaty Council (IITC) and managed to have Lakota treaty issues (as well as other indigenous rights questions) docketed with the United Nations Commission on Human Rights.[169]

Under these circumstances, Congress once again backpedaled, passing an act in 1978 which set aside all judicial decisions leading up to the 1977 award amount, and ordering *pro novo* review by the claims court on the question of how much the Lakota compensation package should add up to.[170] The following year, the court determined that 5 percent simple annual interest should pertain to the claims commission's award of principal, a factor which upped the amount offered the Lakota to $122.5 million.[171] The Justice Department appealed this outcome to the Supreme Court, a circumstance which prompted the high court—after denying Indian requests to do the same thing for nearly 40 years—to finally examine the Black Hills case:

In 1980, the Supreme Court, on *writ of certiorari* from the Court of Claims, held that the 1877 act did not effect a "mere change of form in investment in Indian tribal property," but, rather, effected a taking of tribal property which had been set aside by the treaty of Fort Laramie for the Sioux's exclusive occupation, which taking implied an obligation on the government's part to make just compensation, including an award of interest, to the Sioux. Justice Rehnquist filed a blistering dissenting opinion in which he charged the majority had been led astray by "revisionist historians."[172]

The Lakota remained entirely unsatisfied. Opponents to monetary settlement pointed out that Homestake Corporation alone had removed about $18 *billion* in gold from one site near the Black Hills towns of Lead and Deadwood since 1877. They also noted that a 1979 poll of the reservations showed that the great bulk of residents, although being among the most impoverished people in North America, were no more willing to accept the new offer than they were the old one.[173] In July 1980—while a week–long "Survival Gathering" attended by 10,000 people was occurring just across the fence from the Strategic Air Command's Ellsworth Air Force Base, ten miles from the Hills—the Oglalas filed a new suit demanding the return of significant acreage and $11 billion in damages.[174] Although the case was dismissed by a federal district judge in September of the same year on the premise that "the matter has already been resolved," and subsequently denied on appeal, the point had been made.[175]

It was reinforced in April 1981 when AIM leader Russell Means led a group to an 880–acre site in the Black Hills about 13 miles outside Rapid City, named it "Yellow Thunder Camp," and announced it was the first step in the physical reoccupation of "Paha Sapa," as the Hills are known in the Lakota language. The U.S. Forest Service, which claimed the land on which Yellow Thunder Camp was situated, filed suit for eviction and requested the federal marshal's service to carry it out. When it became apparent that AIM was prepared to offer physical resistance à la Wounded Knee, a federal judge in the state capitol of Pierre issued a restraining order on federal authorities.[176] During the following summer, several other occupation camps sprang up, some of them sponsored by usually more timid tribal council governments.[177] Although they were mostly short–lived, the AIM occupation was continuous for nearly five years.

While it was going on, the Forest Service eviction suit was litigated before U.S. District Judge Robert O'Brien, with AIM countersuing on the basis that the federal government was in violation of the 1868 treaty, the 1978 American Indian Religious Freedom Act (AIRFA), and several of its own anti–discrimination statutes. In 1985, the government was stunned when O'Brien upheld AIM's contentions, entering a potential landmark opinion that whole geographical areas rather than specific locations might be considered "sacred lands" within the meaning of AIRFA, and enjoining the Forest Service from further harassing Yellow Thunder occupants.[178] The decision was reversed by the Eighth Circuit Court in 1988, however, in the wake of the Supreme Court's decision in the *Lyng* case.[179] By that time, the government had deposited the Lakota settlement monies in an escrow account at an Albuquerque bank, where it continues to draw interest (reportedly, it now totals slightly more than $200 million, no Lakota having accepted a disbursement check).[180]

Throughout the first half of the '80s, IITC reported developments in the Black Hills struggle annually to the U.N. Working Group on Indigenous Populations, formed by the Human Rights Commission in 1982.[181] The U.S. United Nations delegation was forced to file formal responses to information provided through this medium, a circumstance causing greater international exposure of the inner workings of federal Indian policy than ever before. This, in combination with the persistence of Lakota litigation efforts and physical confrontations, precipitated an unprecedented governmental initiative to re-solve the Black Hills issue during the late '80s. It took the form of a bill, S.1453, first introduced by New Jersey Senator Bill Bradley in 1987, to "reconvey title"—including water and mineral rights—over 750,000 acres of forest land within the Paha Sapa to the Lakota Nation. Additionally, specified sacred sites adding up to several thousand acres, and a 50,000 acre "Sioux Park," would be retitled without mineral rights. A "Sioux National Council," drawn from all Lakota reservations, would share jurisdictional and policy–making preroga-tives—as well as revenues from leasing, royalties, etc.—over the balance of the original Great Sioux Reservation with federal and state authorities. Finally, the 1980 claims court award, plus subsequently accrued interest, would be con-verted into compensation for damages rather than payment for land per se,[182]

Although the Bradley Bill hardly afforded a full measure of Lakota rights to land and sovereignty, it was the sort of substantive compromise arrangement which the bulk of Lakotas might have accepted as workable. Certainly, Lakota support for the bill had become pronounced by 1988, even as a local white backlash—whipped up in part by South Dakota Senator Larry Pressler and former governor William Janklow—mounted steadily. If enacted in some form, it might have created a viable model for eventual indigenous land rights resolutions throughout North America. Unfortunately, the bill was withdrawn by its sponsor in 1990, after a two–year period of highly publicized anti–Bradley agitation by an individual named Phil Stevens, previously unknown to the Indians but purporting to be "Great Chief of all the Sioux." (At present, Lakota land–claim efforts are primarily devoted to resuscitating the bill, or developing a reasonable variant of it.)[183]

The Western Shoshone Land Claims

A differently waged, and lesser known, struggle for land has been undertaken by the Western Shoshone, mainly in the Nevada desert region. In 1863, the United States entered into the Treaty of Ruby Valley (13 *Stat.* 663)

Map VII

TRADITIONAL SHOSHONE TERRITORY

IDAHO

WYOMING

Wind River

Duck Valley

Fort Hall

NEVADA

UTAH

COLORADO

ARIZONA

☐ Newe Segobia
▦ Other Traditional Territory
■ Contemporary Reservations

CALIFORNIA

Map by Ward Churchill & Glenn Morris, prepared by Jell Holland, redrawn by Alexandria Lord.

with the Newe (Western Shoshone) Nation, agreeing—in exchange for Indian commitments of peace and friendship, willingness to provide right–of–way through their lands, and the granting of assorted trade licenses—to recognize the boundaries encompassing the approximately 24.5 million acres of the traditional Western Shoshone homeland, known in their language as Newe Segobia (*see* Map VII).[184] The United States also agreed to pay the Newe $100,000 in restitution for environmental disruptions anticipated as a result of Euroamerican "commerce" in the area. As researcher Rudolph C. Ryser has observed:

> Nothing in the Treaty of Ruby Valley ever sold, traded or gave away any part of the Newe Country to the United States of America. Nothing in this treaty said that the United States could establish counties or smaller states within Newe Country. Nothing in this

treaty said the United States could establish settlements of U.S. citizens who would be engaged in any activity other than mining, agriculture, milling and ranching.[185]

From the signing of the treaty until the mid–twentieth century, no action was taken by either Congress or federal courts to extinguish native title to Newe Segobia.[186] Essentially, the land was an area in which the United States was not much interested. Still, relatively small but steadily growing numbers of non–Indians did move into Newe territory, a situation which was generally accommodated by the Indians so long as the newcomers did not become overly presumptuous. By the late 1920s, however, conflicts over land use had begun to sharpen. Things worsened after 1934, when the federal government installed a tribal council form of government—desired by Washington but rejected by traditional Newes—under provision of the IRA.[187] It was to the IRA council heading one of the Western Shoshone bands, the Temoak, that attorney Ernest Wilkinson went with a proposal in early 1946.

Wilkinson was a senior partner in the Washington–based law firm Wilkinson, Cragun, and Barker, commissioned by Congress toward the end of World War II to draft legislation creating the Indian Claims Commission. The idea he presented to the Temoak council was that his firm be retained to "represent their interests" before the claims commission.[188] Ostensibly, his objective was to secure the band's title to its portion of the 1863 treaty area. Much more likely, given subsequent events, his purpose was to secure title for non–Indian interests in Nevada, and to collect the 10–percent attorney's fee he and his colleagues had written into the Claims Commission Act as pertaining to any compensation awarded to native clients.[189] In any event, the Temoaks agreed, and a contract between Wilkinson and the council was approved by the Bureau of Indian Affairs in 1947.[190] Wilkinson followed up, in 1951, with a petition to the claims commission that his representation of the Temoaks be construed as representing the interests of the entire Newe Nation. The commission concurred, despite protests from the bulk of the people involved.[191]

From the outset, Wilkinson's pleadings led directly away from Newe rights over the Ruby Valley Treaty Territory. As Morris has framed the matter in what is probably the best article on the Western Shoshone land struggle to date:

> In 1962, the commission conceded that it "was unable to discover any formal extinguishment" of Western Shoshone to lands in Nevada, and could not establish a date of taking, but nonetheless ruled that the lands were taken at some point in the past. It did rule that approximately two million acres of Newe land in California was taken on March 3, 1853 [contrary to the Treaty of Ruby Valley, which would have supplanted any such taking], but without documenting what specific Act of Congress extinguished the title. With-

out the consent of the Western Shoshone Nation, on February 11, 1966, Wilkinson and the U.S. lawyers arbitrarily stipulated that the date of valuation for government extinguishment of Western Shoshone title to over 22 million acres of land in Nevada occurred on July 1, 1872. This lawyers' agreement, entered without the knowledge or consent of the Shoshone people, served as the ultimate loophole through which the United States would allege that the Newe had lost their land.[192]

By 1872 prices, the award of compensation to the Newe for the "historic loss" of their territory was calculated, in 1972, at $21,350,000, an amount revised upwards to $26,154,600 (against which the government levied an offset of $9,410.11 for "goods" delivered in the 1870s) and certified on December 19, 1979.[193] In the interim, by 1976, even the Temoaks had joined the other Newe bands in maintaining that Wilkinson did not represent their interests; they fired him, but the BIA (Bureau of Indian Affairs) continued to renew his contract "in their behalf" until the claims commission itself was concluded in 1980.[194] Meanwhile, the Newe had retained other counsel and filed a motion to suspend commission proceedings with regard to their case. This was denied on August 15, 1977, appealed, but upheld by the U.S. Court of Claims on the basis that if the Newe desired "to avert extinguishment of their land claims, they should go to Congress" rather than the courts for redress. The amount of $26,145,189.89 was then placed in a trust account with the U.S. Treasury Department in order to absolve the United States of further responsibility in the matter.[195]

> One analyst of the case suggests that if the United States were honest in its valuation date of the taking of Newe land, the date would be December 19, 1979—the date of the ICC award—since the [commission] could point to no other extinguishment date. The United States should thus compensate the Shoshone in 1979 land values and not those of 1872. Consequently, the value of the land "that would be more realistic, assuming the Western Shoshone were prepared to ignore violations of the Ruby Valley Treaty, would be in the neighborhood of $40 billion. On a per capita basis of distribution, the United States would be paying each Shoshone roughly $20 million.... The [U.S.] has already received billions of dollars in resources and use from Newe territory in the past 125 years. Despite this obvious benefit, the U.S. government is only prepared to pay the Shoshone less than a penny of actual value for each acre of Newe territory.[196]

The Newe as a whole have refused to accept payment for their land, under the premise articulated by Raymond Yowell, Chair of the Western Shoshoni Sacred Lands Association, that: "We entered into the Treaty of Ruby Valley as co–equal sovereign nations... The land to the traditional Shoshone is sacred. It is the basis of our lives. To take away the land is to take away the lives of the people."[197] Giving form to this sentiment, two sisters—Mary and Carrie Dann, refused eviction from their homes by the U.S. Bureau of Land Management, which claimed by that point to own the property that had been in their family for generations—and challenged *all* U.S. title contentions within the Newe treaty area when the Bureau attempted to enforce its position in court. The litigation has caused federal courts to flounder about in disarray ever since.

In 1977, the federal district court for Nevada ruled that they were "trespassers" because the claims commission had resolved all title questions. This decision was reversed on appeal to the Ninth Circuit Court in 1978 because, in its view, the question of land title "had not been litigated, and has not been decided."[198] On remand, the district court waited until the claims commission award had been paid into the Treasury, and then ruled against the Danns in 1980. The court, however, in attempting to rationalize both its present decision and its past reversal, observed that, "Western Shoshone Indians retained unextinguished title to their aboriginal lands *until December of 1979*, when the Indian Claims Commission judgment became final" (emphasis added).[199] This, of course, demolished the basis for the commission's award amount. It also pointed to the fact that the commission had comported itself illegally in the Western Shoshone case insofar as the Indian Claims Commission Act explicitly disallowed the commissioners (never mind attorneys representing the Indians) from extinguishing previously unextinguished land titles. Thus armed, the Danns went back to the Ninth Circuit and obtained another reversal.[200]

The government appealed the circuit court's ruling to the Supreme Court and, entering yet *another* official (and exceedingly ambiguous) estimation of when Newe title was supposed to have been extinguished, the justices reversed the circuit court's reversal of the district court's last ruling. Having thus served the government's interest on appeal, the high court declined in 1990 to hear an appeal from the Danns concerning the question of whether they might retain individual aboriginal property rights based on continuous occupancy even if the collective rights of the Newe were denied.[201] As of 1995, despite their adverse experiences with the federal judiciary, the Dann sisters remain on their land in defiance of federal authority. Their physical resistance, directly supported by most Newes, forms the core of whatever will come next.

One route to them—and undoubtedly the locus of much of the intensity with which the government has rejected their land claims—rests in the fact that U.S. nuclear weapons testing facilities lie squarely in the heart of Newe territory. According to geographer Bernard Nietschmann, the U.S. detonation of 651 atomic weapons there since 1963 makes Newe Segobia "the most bombed country in the world."[202] The Newe portion of Nevada was also the area specified for siting of the MX missile system, and, currently, the government is planning to store a variety of nuclear wastes in repositories bored into

Yucca Mountain, in the southwestern sector of Newe treaty land. For obvious reasons, the Newe oppose both testing and the dumping of such wastes in their homeland. Given this, it may be possible that their land rights can be fruitfully pursued through emergence of a broad coalition with non–Indian environmental, anti–war and anti–nuclear organizations. That such a potential is not furthest from the minds of Newe strategists is witnessed by the wording of a permit issued to all protesters arriving to oppose nuclear experiments at military bases in the area: "The Western Shoshone Nation is calling upon citizens of the United States, as well as the world community of nations, to demand that the United States terminate its invasion of our lands for the evil purpose of testing nuclear bombs and other weapons of war."[203]

Where Do We Go from Here?

The question which inevitably arises with regard to indigenous land claims, especially in the United States, is whether they are "realistic." The answer, of course, is "no they aren't." Further, *no* form of decolonization has *ever* been realistic when viewed within the construct of a colonialist paradigm. It wasn't realistic at the time to expect George Washington's rag–tag militia to defeat the British military during the American Revolution. Just ask the British. It wasn't realistic, as the French could tell you, that the Vietnamese should be able to defeat U.S.–backed France in 1954, or that the Algerians would shortly be able to follow in their footsteps. Surely, it wasn't reasonable to predict that Fidel Castro's pitiful handful of guerrillas would overcome Batista's regime in Cuba, another U.S. client, after only a few years in the mountains. And the Sandinistas, to be sure, had no prayer of attaining victory over Somoza 20 years later. Henry Kissinger, among others, knew that for a fact.

The point is that in each case, in order to begin their struggles at all, anti–colonial fighters around the world have had to abandon orthodox realism in favor of what they knew (and their opponents knew) to be right. To paraphrase Daniel Cohn–Bendit, they accepted as their agenda—the goals, objectives and demands which guided them—a redefinition of reality in terms deemed quite impossible within the conventional wisdom of their oppressors. And, in each case, they succeeded in their immediate quest for liberation.[204] The fact that all but one (Cuba) of the examples used subsequently turned out to hold colonizing pretensions of its own does not alter the truth of this—or alter the appropriateness of their efforts to decolonize themselves—in the least. It simply means that decolonization has yet to run its course, that much remains to be done.

The battles waged by native nations in North America to free themselves, and the lands upon which they depend for ongoing existence as discernible peoples, from the grip of U.S. (and Canadian) internal colonialism is plainly part of this process of liberation. Given that their very survival depends upon their perseverance in the face of all apparent odds, American Indians have no real alternative but to carry on. They must struggle, and where there is struggle there is always hope. Moreover, the unrealistic or "romantic" dimensions of our aspiration to quite literally dismantle the territorial corpus of the U.S. state begins to erode when one considers that federal domination of Native America is utterly contingent upon maintenance of a perceived confluence of interest between prevailing governmental/corporate élites and common non–Indian citizens. Herein lies the prospect of long–term success. It is entirely possible that the consensus of opinion concerning non–Indian "rights" to exploit the land and resources of indigenous nations can be eroded, and that large numbers of non–Indians will join in the struggle to decolonize Native North America.

Few non–Indians wish to identify with or defend the naziesque characteristics of U.S. history. To the contrary, most seek to deny it in a rather vociferous fashion. All things being equal, they are uncomfortable with many of the resulting attributes of federal posture and—in substantial numbers—actively oppose one or more of these, so long as such politics do not intrude into a certain range of closely guarded self–interest. This is where the crunch comes in the realm of Indian rights issues. Most non–Indians (of all races and ethnicities, and both genders) have been indoctrinated to believe the officially contrived notion that, in the event "the Indians get their land back," or even if the extent of present federal domination is relaxed, native people will do unto their occupiers exactly as has been done to them; mass dispossession and eviction of non–Indians, especially Euroamericans, is expected to ensue.

Hence, even those progressives who are most eloquently inclined to condemn U.S. imperialism abroad and/or the functions of racism and sexism at home tend to deliver a blank stare or profess open "disinterest" when indigenous land rights are mentioned. Instead of attempting to come to grips with this most fundamental of all issues on the continent upon which they reside, the more sophisticated among them seek to divert discussion into "higher priority" or "more important" topics like "issues of class and gender equity" in which "justice" becomes synonymous with a redistribution of power and loot deriving from the occupation of Native North America even while the occupation continues (presumably permanently). Sometimes, Indians are even slated to receive "their fair share" in the division of spoils accruing from expropriation of their resources. Always, such things are couched—and typically seen—in terms of some "greater good" than decolonizing the .6 percent of the U.S. population which is indigenous.[205] Some marxist and environmentalist groups have taken the argument so far as to deny that Indians possess *any* rights distinguishable from those of their conquerors.[206] AIM leader Russell Means snapped the picture into sharp focus when he observed in 1987 that:

> So–called progressives in the United States claiming that Indians are
> obligated to give up their rights because a much larger group of

non–Indians "need" their resources is exactly the same as Ronald Reagan and Elliot Abrams asserting that the rights of 250 million North Americans outweighs the rights of a couple million Nicaraguans. Colonialist attitudes are colonialist attitudes, and it doesn't make one damn bit of difference whether they come from the left or the right.[207]

Leaving aside the pronounced and pervasive hypocrisy permeating their positions, which add up to a phenomenon elsewhere described as "settler state colonialism,"[208] the fact is that the specter driving even the most radical non–Indians into lockstep with the federal government on questions of native land rights is largely illusory. The alternative *reality* posed by native liberation struggles is actually much different:

- While government propagandists are wont to trumpet—as they did during the Maine and Black Hills land disputes of the '70s—that an Indian win would mean individual non–Indian property owners losing everything, the native position has always been the exact opposite. Overwhelmingly, the lands sought for actual recovery have been governmentally and corporately held. Eviction of small land owners has been pursued only in instances where they have banded together—as they have during certain of the Iroquois claims cases—to prevent Indians from recovering any land at all, and to otherwise deny native rights.

- Official sources contend this is inconsistent with the fact that all non–Indian title to any portion of North America *could* be called into question. Once "the dike is breached," they argue, it's just a matter of time until "everybody has to start swimming back to Europe, or Africa, or wherever."[209] Although there is considerable technical accuracy to admissions that all non–Indian title to North America is illegitimate, Indians have by and large indicated they would be content to honor the cession agreements entered into by their ancestors even though the United States has long since defaulted. This would leave somewhere around two–thirds of the continental United States in non–Indian hands, with the real rather than pretended consent of native people. The remaining one–third, the areas delineated in Map II to which the United States never acquired title at all, would be recovered by its rightful owners.

- The government holds that, even at that, there is no longer sufficient land available for unceded lands, or their equivalent, to be returned. In fact, the government itself still directly controls more than one–third of the total U.S. land area, about 770 million acres. Each of the states also "owns" large tracts, totaling about 78 million acres. It is thus quite possible—and always has been—for *all* native claims to be met in full without the loss to non–Indians of a single acre of privately held land.

When it is considered that 250 million–odd acres of the total land "privately" held are now in the hands of major corporate entities, the *real* dimension of the "threat" to small landholders (or, more accurately, lack of it) stands revealed.[210]

- Government spokespersons have pointed out that the disposition of public lands does not always conform to treaty areas. While this is true, it in no way precludes some process of negotiated land exchange wherein the boundaries of indigenous nations are redrawn by mutual consent to an exact, or at least a much closer, conformity. All that is needed is an honest, open, and binding forum—such as a new bilateral treaty process—with which to proceed. In fact, numerous native peoples have, for a long time, repeatedly and in a variety of ways, expressed a desire to do just that.[211]

- Nonetheless, it is argued, there will still be at least some non–Indians "trapped" within such restored areas. Actually, they would not be trapped at all. The federally imposed genetic criteria of "Indian–ness" discussed elsewhere in this book not withstanding, indigenous nations have the same rights as any other to define citizenry by allegiance (naturalization) rather than by race. Non–Indians could apply for citizenship, or for some form of landed alien status which would allow them to retain their property until they die. In the event they could not reconcile themselves to living under any jurisdiction other than that of the United States, they would obviously have the right to leave, and they *should* have the right to compensation from their own government (which got them into the mess in the first place).[212]

- Finally, and one suspects this is the real crux of things from the government/corporate perspective, any such restoration of land and attendant sovereign prerogatives to native nations would result in a truly massive loss of "domestic" resources to the United States, thereby impairing the country's economic and military capacities.[213] For everyone who queued up to wave flags and tie yellow ribbons during America's recent imperial adventure in the Persian Gulf, this prospect may induce a certain psychic trauma. But, for progressives at least, it should be precisely the point.

When you think about it like this, the great mass of non–Indians in North America *really* have much to gain, and almost nothing to lose, from native people succeeding in struggles to reclaim the land which is rightfully ours. The tangible diminishment of U.S. material power which is integral to our victories in this sphere stands to pave the way for the realization of most other agendas— from anti–imperialism to environmentalism, from Afroamerican liberation to feminism, from gay rights to the ending of class privilege—pursued by progressives on this continent. Conversely, succeeding with any or even *all* these other agendas would still represent an inherently oppressive situation if their realization is contingent upon an ongoing occupation of Native North America without the consent of Indian people. Any North American revolution which failed to free indigenous territory from non–Indian domination would be simply a continuation of colonialism in another form.

Regardless of the angle from which you view the matter, the liberation of Native North America, liberation of the land first and foremost, is *the* key to fundamental and positive social changes of many other sorts. One thing, as they say, leads to another. The question has always been, of course, which "thing" is to be first in the sequence. A preliminary formulation for those serious about achieving (rather than merely theorizing and endlessly debating) radical change in the United States might be "First Priority to First Americans." Put another way, this would mean, "U.S. Out of Indian Country." Inevitably, the logic leads to what we've all been so desperately seeking: The United States—at least as we've come to know it—out of North America altogether. From there, it can be permanently banished from the planet. In its stead, surely we can join hands to create something new and infinitely better. That's *our* vision of "impossible realism." Isn't it time we *all* went to work on attaining it?

Notes

1. *See* Samuel Eliot Morison, ed. and trans., *Journals and Other Documents on the Life and Voyages of Christopher Columbus* (New York: Heritage Publishers, 1963). For context, *see* John Horace Parry, *The Establishment of European Hegemony, 1415–1713* (New York: Harper and Row [revised ed.], 1966).

2. *See* M. D. Vattel, *The Laws of Nations* (Philadelphia: T. & J. W. Johnson Publishers, 1855), pp. 160–61. Vattel is drawing on the mid–sixteenth century discourses of Spanish legal theorist Franciscus de Victoria, published as *De Indis et De Jure Belli Reflectiones* by the Carnegie Institution in 1917. *See* also James Brown Scott, *The Spanish Origin of International Law* (Oxford: Clarendon Press, 1934); and Alfred Nussbaum, *A Concise History of the Laws of Nations* (New York: Macmillan Publishing Co. [revised ed.], 1954).

3. Robert T. Coulter and Steven M. Tullberg, "Indian Land Rights," in *The Aggressions of Civilization: Federal Indian Policy Since the 1880s*, Sandra L. Cadwalader and Vine Deloria, Jr., eds. (Philadelphia: Temple University Press, 1984), pp. 185–213, quote at pp. 190–91. Additional information may be obtained from John Horace Parry, *The Spanish Theory of Empire in the Sixteenth Century* (Cambridge, Massachusetts: Cambridge University Press, 1940).

4. Victoria, following Saint Augustine, framed the conditions for "Just Wars" by Europeans against Indians in 1577. For articulation and analysis, *see* Robert A. Williams, Jr., *The American Indian in Western Legal Thought: The Discourses of Conquest* (New York: Oxford University Press, 1990), pp. 96–108. With regard to England per se, *see* K. Knorr, *British Colonial Theories, 1570–1850* (Toronto: University of Toronto Press, 1944). On the Augustinian formulation, *see* Herbert Andrew Deane, *The Political and Social Ideas of St. Augustine* (New York: Columbia University Press, 1963).

5. On Columbus' violation of prevailing laws, both international and Spanish, *see* Floyd Trof, *The Columbus Dynasty in the Caribbean, 1492–1526* (Albuquerque: University of New Mexico Press, 1973). *See* also Kirkpatrick Sale, *The Conquest of Paradise: Christopher Columbus and the Columbian Legacy* (New York: Alfred A. Knopf, 1990).

6. Robert T. Coulter and Steven M. Tullberg, op. cit., p. 191. The authors are drawing on L. Oppenheim, *International Law*, Vol. I (London: Longmans, Green and Co., 1955), pp. 588–89. For a comprehensive overview, *see* Howard Peckman and Charles Gibson, eds., *Attitudes of the Colonial Powers Towards American Indians* (Salt Lake City: University of Utah Press, 1969). On evolution of the British tradition in this respect, *see* David Beers Quinn, *England and the Discovery of America, 1481–1620* (New York: Alfred A. Knopf, 1974). Excellent collections of the actual treaty texts at issue may be found in Francis Gardiner Davenport, ed., *European Treaties Bearing on the History of the United States and Its Dependencies*, 2 Vols. (Washington, DC: Carnegie Institution of Washington, 1917); and Alden T. Vaughan, *Early American Indian Documents: Treaties and Laws, 1607–1789* (Washington, DC: University Publications of America, 1979).

7. For an examination of the military balance, *see* Howard Henry Peckman, *Pontiac and the Indian Uprising* (New York: Russell and Russell Publishers, 1970). For deeper background, *see* Harry Culverwell Porter, *The Inconstant Savage: England and the American Indian, 1500–1600* (London: Duckworth Publishers, 1979).

8. On the British military alliance with the Iroquois Confederacy, *see* James Thomas Flexner, *Lord of the Mohawks: A Biography of Sir William Johnson* (Boston: Little, Brown & Co., Inc., 1979). On the Muscogee, *see* Walter Stilt Robinson, *The Southern Colonial Frontier, 1607–1763* (Albuquerque: University of New Mexico Press, 1979). Overall, *see* Wilbur Jacobs, *Dispossessing the American Indian: Indians and Whites on the Colonial Frontier* (New York: Charles Scribner, 1972).

9. This thesis is brought forward quite forcefully in Merrill Jensen, *Founding of a Nation: A History of the American Revolution, 1763–1776* (London/New York: Oxford University Press, 1968), pp. 3–35. *See* also Thomas Perkins Abernathy, *Western Lands and the American Revolution* (New York: Russell and Russell, 1959); and Bernard Bailyn, *The Ideological Origins of the American Revolution* (Cambridge, Massachusetts: Harvard University Press, 1967).

10. In general, *see* Merrill Jensen, *The Articles of Confederation: An Interpretation of the Socio–Constitutional History of the American Revolution, 1774–1778* (Madison: University of Wisconsin Press, 1940), esp. pp. 154–62, 190–232. *See* also Gordon Wood, *The Creation of the American Republic, 1776–1787* (Chapel Hill: University of North Carolina Press, 1969); and Gordon Lewis, *The Indiana Company, 1763–1798* (Glendale, California: Clark Publishers, 1941).

11. Vine Deloria, Jr., "Sovereignty," in *Economic Development in American Indian Reservations*, Roxanne Dunbar Ortiz and Larry Emerson, eds. (Albuquerque: Native American Studies Center, University of New Mexico, 1979). For context, *see* Walter Harrison Mohr, *Federal Indian Relations, 1774–1788* (Philadelphia: University of Pennsylvania Press, 1933).

12. The Northwest Ordinance, 1789.

13. The case at issue is *Johnson v. McIntosh* (1822).

14. L. Baker, *John Marshall: A Life in Law* (New York: Macmillan Publishing Co., 1963), p. 80.

15. *See* Reginald Horsman, *Expansion and American Indian Policy, 1783–1812* (East Lansing: Michigan State University Press, 1967).

16. For further discussion of Marshall's and others' thinking during this period, *see* Howard R. Berman, "The Concept of Aboriginal Rights in the Early Legal History of the United States," *Buffalo Law Review*, No. 28 (1978), pp. 637–67. *See* also Felix S. Cohen, "Original Indian Title," *Minnesota Law Review*, No. 32 (1947), pp. 28–59.

17. An interesting analysis of Marshall's emerging doctrine may be found in Russel Barsh and James Youngblood Henderson, *The Road: Indian Tribes and Political Liberty* (Berkeley: University of California Press, 1980).

18. *See* C. Harvey, "Constitutional Law: Congressional Plenary Power Over Indian Affairs—A Doctrine Rooted in Prejudice," *American Indian Law Review*, No. 10 (1982), pp. 117–50.

19. *See* Ann Laquer Estin, "*Lonewolf v. Hitchcock*: The Long Shadow," in *The Aggressions of Civilization*, op. cit., pp. 215–45. *See* also Charles F. Wilkinson and John M. Volkman, "Judicial Review of Treaty Abrogation: 'As Long as the Water Flows, or Grass Grows upon the Earth'—How Long a Time Is That?" *California Law Review*, No. 63 (May 1975), pp. 601–61.

20. Robert T. Coulter and Steven M. Tullberg, op. cit., p. 203. The authors are quoting from J. A. Hobson, *Imperialism: A Study* (Ann Arbor: University of Michigan Press, 1965), p. 240. *See* also Robert T. Coulter, "The Denial of Legal Remedies to Indian Nations Under U.S. Law," *American Indian Law Journal*, Vol. 9, No. 3 (1977), pp. 5–9.

21. Professions of formal U.S. anti–imperialism began to be put forward in a serious fashion by government propagandists in 1823, the year in which the Monroe Doctrine was articulated (that is, within one year of the *Johnson v. McIntosh* opinion in which John Marshall began his project of legitimating wholesale conquest and colonization of Native America). It was always used as a cover for North American economic and political domination. *See* Jenny Pearce, *Under the Eagle: U.S. Intervention in Central America and the Caribbean* (Boston: South End Press, 1982).

22. The count of 40 Indian Wars is the conservative official view. *See* U.S. Bureau of the Census, *Report on Indians Taxed and Indians Not Taxed in the United States* [except Alaska] *at the Eleventh Census: 1890* (Washington, DC: U.S. Government Printing Office, 1894), p. 637.

23. The standard count has been that the U.S. Senate ratified 371 treaties with various indigenous nations between 1778 and 1868. The texts of these are reproduced verbatim in Charles J. Kappler, *Indian Treaties, 1778–1883* (New York: Interland Publishing Co., 1973). In addition, the Sioux scholar Vine Deloria, Jr., has collected the texts of an additional nine ratified treaty texts not contained in Kappler, as well as the texts of some 300 additional treaty instruments negotiated by the federal executive, and upon which the United States now professes to anchor title to assorted chunks of territory, although they were never ratified. For further background, *see* Dorothy V. Jones, *License for Empire: Colonialism by Treaty in Early America* (Chicago: University of Chicago Press, 1982). *See* also Donald Worcester, ed., *Forked Tongues and Broken Treaties* (Caldwell, Idaho: Caxton Publishers, 1975).

24. The official record of the cumulative reductions in the native land base leading to this result may be found in Charles C. Royce, *Indian Land Cessions in the United States: 18th Annual Report, 1896–97*, 2 Vols. (Washington, DC: Smithsonian Institution, Bureau of American Ethnography, 1899). The 2.5 percent figure derives from computing 50 million acres against the total acreage.

25. For use of this term during the period at issue, *see* Rodman Wanamaker, *The Vanishing Race: A Record in Picture and Story of the Last Great Indian Council, Including the Indians' Story of the Custer Fight* (New York: Crown Publishers, MCMXIII).

26. In 1903, the U.S. Supreme Court opined in the *Lonewolf v. Hitchcock* case that Indians had no right either to block the wholesale transfer of their reserved and treaty–guaranteed lands to non–Indians under the 1887 General Allotment Act, or to receive compensation for the loss of such lands. The high court held that federal plenary power over native property was absolute, and that Indians had no right to sue the government for breach of its concomitant trust responsibility in such matters. *See* Felix S. Cohen, *Handbook on Federal Indian Law* (Albuquerque: University of New Mexico Press [reprint of 1942 U.S. Government Printing Office Edition], n.d.), p. 96.

27. *See* Helen Hunt Jackson, *A Century of Dishonor* (New York: Harper Torchbooks [reprint of the 1881 ed. by A. F. Rolfe], 1965), p. 204.

28. U.S. House of Representatives, Committee on Interior and Insular Affairs, *Indirect Services and Expenditures by the Federal Government for the American Indian*, 86th Cong., 1st Sess. (Washington, DC: U.S. Government Printing Office, 1959), pp. 11–14.

29. Lewis Meriam et al., *Problems of Indian Administration* (Baltimore, Maryland: Johns Hopkins University Press, 1928), pp. 805–11.

30. On the effects of the General Allotment Act, or the "Dawes Act" as it is often known, *see* Janet A. McDonnell, *The Dispossession of the American Indian, 1887–1934* (Bloomington/Indianapolis: Indiana University Press, 1991). *See* also D. S. Otis, *The Dawes Act and the Allotment of Indian Land* (Norman: University of Oklahoma Press, 1973).

31. Alice Ehrenfeld and Robert W. Barker, comps., *Legislative Material on the Indian Claims Commission Act of 1946* (Washington, DC: unpublished study, n.d.).

32. An interesting handling of the geopolitical dynamics involved during the Roosevelt era may be found in Paul A. Varg, *America: From Client State to World Power* (Norman: University of Oklahoma Press, 1990), esp. pp. 167–207. *See* also Walter Isaacson and Evan Thomas, *The Wise Men: Six Friends and the World They Made* (New York: Simon & Schuster, 1986). On Truman's shift, *see* Noam Chomsky, *Towards a New Cold War: Essays on the Current Crisis and How We Got There* (New York: Pantheon Books, 1982).

33. On the formulation of the Nuremberg Doctrine, and the primacy of the U.S. role in that regard, *see* Bradley F. Smith, *The Road to Nuremberg* (New York: Basic Books, 1981).

34. On the handling of the Nuremberg Trials, and the messages embodied in it, *see* Bradley F. Smith, *Reaching Judgement at Nuremberg: The Untold Story of How the Nazi War Criminals Were Judged* (New York: Basic Books, 1977). *See* also Eugene Davidson, *The Trial of the Germans: Nuremberg, 1945–1946* (New York: Macmillan Publishing Co., 1966). Concerning George Bush's recent use of Nuremberg rhetoric, *see* George Cheney, "'Talking War': Symbols, Strategies, and Images," *New Studies on the Left*, Vol. XIV, No. 3 (Winter 1990–91), pp. 8–16.

35. For a detailed analysis of the American concept, *see* Frederick Merk, *Manifest Destiny and Mission in American Life* (New York: Vintage Books, 1966); and Reginald Horsman, *Race and Manifest Destiny* (Cambridge, Massachusetts: Harvard University Press, 1981). To sample the philosophy at issue from the proverbial horse's mouth, *see* John Fiske, "Manifest Destiny," in *American Political Ideas Viewed from the Standpoint of Universal History* (New York: Houghton–Mifflin Publishers, 1885). For purposes of comparison to nazi ideology, *see* Robert L. Koehl, *German Resettlement and Population Policy, 1939–1945* (Cambridge, Massachusetts: Harvard University Press, 1957).

36. *See* Adolf Hitler, *Hitler's Secret Conversations* (New York: Signet Books, 1961), and *Hitler's Secret Book* (New York: Grove Press, 1961). The nazi leader's attributions to U.S. policy are also noted in Heinrich Hoffman, *Hitler Was My Friend* (London: Burke, 1955); John Toland, *Adolf Hitler*, 2 Vols. (Garden City, New York: Doubleday, 1976), and elsewhere. For details on nazi policy applications, *see* Alexander Dallin, *German Rule in Russia, 1941–1944* (London: Macmillan Publishing Co., 1957).

37. Discussion of such measures began in Congress in the fall of 1944, at the same time that planning for Nuremberg was entering its final stages. *See* Bradley F. Smith, *The American Road to Nuremberg: The Documentary Record* (Palo Alto, California: Stanford University Press, 1981). For summative discussion of the mechanism to be used in retiring Indian claims and motives for creating it, *see* U.S. House of Representatives, Committee on Indian Affairs, *Hearings on H.R. 1198 and H.R. 1341*, 79th Cong., 1st Sess. (Washington, DC: U.S. Government Printing Office, 1945).

38. Francis E. Leupp, *The Indian and His Problem* (New York: Charles Scribner's Sons, 1910), pp. 194–96. For an overview of such sentiments, *see* John T. Vance, "The Congressional Mandate and the Indian Claims Commission," *North Dakota Law Review*, No. 45 (1969), pp. 325–36.

39. U.S. House of Representatives, Committee on Indian Affairs, *Hearing on the Appropriation Bill of 1914*, 64th Cong., 2d Sess. (Washington, DC: U.S. Government Printing Office, 1913), p. 99.

40. Lewis Meriam et al., op. cit., pp. 805–11.

41. *See*, as examples, U.S. Senate, Committee on Interior and Insular Affairs, Subcommittee on Indian Affairs, *Hearings on S. 2731*, 74th Cong., 1st Sess. (Washington, DC: U.S. Government Printing Office, 1935); and U.S. House of Representatives, Committee on Indian Affairs, *Hearings on H.R. 7837*, 74th Cong., 1st Sess. (Washington, DC: U.S. Government Printing Office, 1935).

42. The case involved was *Thompson v. United States*, 13 Ind. Cl. Comm. 369 (1964).

43. Jack Forbes, "The 'Public Domain' of Nevada and Its Relationship to Indian Property Rights," *Nevada State Bar Journal*, No. 30 (1965), pp. 16–47.

44. *Congressional Record*, 20 May 1946, p. 5312.

45. The exception here involved claims entered under provision of the Fifth Amendment, of which there were almost none. Interest was denied as a matter of course in other types of claim, based on the outcome of the *Loyal Creek Case*, 1 Ind. Cl. Comm. 22. *See* Thomas LaDuc, "The Work of the Indian Claims Commission Under the Act of 1946," *Pacific Historical Review*, No. 26 (1957), pp. 1–16.

46. Actually, there is one exception. In 1965, the Claims Commission recommended (15 Ind. Cl. Comm. 666) restoration of 130,000 acres of the Blue Lake area to the Taos Pueblo (*see* R. C. Gordon–McCutchan, *The Taos Indians and the Battle for Blue Lake* (Santa Fe, New Mexico: Red Crane Books, 1991). In 1970, Congress followed up by restoring a total of 48,000 acres (85 *Stat.* 1437). For further information, *see* Richard A. Nielson, "American Indian Land Claims: Land Versus Money as a Remedy," *University of Florida Law Review*, Vol. 19, No. 3 (1973), pp. 308–26.

47. U.S. House of Representatives, Committee on Indian Affairs, *Providing a One–Year Extension of the Five–Year Limitation on the Time for Presenting Indian Claims to the Indian Claims Commission*, H. Rep. 692, 82d Cong., 1st Sess. (Washington, DC: U.S. Government Printing Office, 1951), pp. 593–601.

48. The Claims Commission was initially authorized for a length of 10 years. In 1956, it was extended for a further five years. The process was repeated in 1961, 1967, 1972, and 1976. *See* U.S. House and Senate, Joint Committee on Appropriations, *Hearings on Appropriations for the Department of Interior*, 94th Cong., 1st Sess. (Washington, DC: U.S. Government Printing Office, 1976).

49. U.S. Senate, Committee on the Interior and Insular Affairs, Subcommmmittee on Indian Affairs, *Hearings on S. 307*, 90th Cong., 1st Sess. (Washington, DC: U.S. Government Printing Office, 1967).

50. U.S. Senate, Committee on the Interior and Insular Affairs, Subcommittee on Indian Affairs, *Hearings on S. 876*, 94th Cong., 1st Sess. (Washington, DC: U.S. Government Printing Office, 1975).

51. Indian Claims Commission, *Final Report* (Washington, DC: U.S. Government Printing Office, 1978).

52. For a prime example of the sort of academic apologetics for U.S. conduct engendered by the Claims Commission process, *see* Imre Sutton, ed., *Irredeemable America: The Indians' Estate and Land Tenure* (Albuquerque: University of New Mexico Press, 1985).

53. Russel Barsh, "Indian Land Claims Policy in the United States," *North Dakota Law Review*, No. 58 (1982), pp. 1–82.

54. *See*, for instance, Vine Deloria, Jr., *A Better Day for Indians* (New York: Field Foundation, 1977). For official quantification of the acreage involved, *see* Public Land Law Review Commission, *One Third of the Nation's Land* (Washington, DC: U.S. Department of the Interior, 1970).

55. *Oneida Indian Nation v. County of Oneida*, 414 U.S. 661 (1974). For background on the strategy involved in such litigation, *see* Mark Kellogg, "Indian Rights: Fighting Back with White Man's Weapons," *Saturday Review* (Nov. 1978), pp. 24–30.

56. The letters were found in an old trunk by an elderly Passamaquoddy woman in 1957, and turned over to township governor John Stevens. It took the Indians 15 years to bring the matter to court, largely because it was denied they had "legal standing" to do so. *See* Paul Brodeur, *Restitution: The Land Claims of the Mashpee, Passamaquoddy, and Penobscot Indians of New England* (Boston: Northeastern University Press, 1985).

57. *Passamaquoddy Tribe v. Morton*, 528 F.2d, 370 (1975). For additional background, *see* Francis J. O'Toole and Thomas N. Tureen, "State Power and the Passamaquoddy Tribe: A Gross National Hypocrisy?" *Maine Law Review*, Vol. 23, No. 1 (1971), pp. 1–39.

58. Maine Indian Land Claims Settlement Act of 1980, 94 *Stat.* 1785.

59. The case is *Narragansett Tribe of Indians v. S.R.I. Land Development Corporation*, 418 F. Supp. 803 (1978). The decision was followed by the Rhode Island Indian Claims Settlement Act of 1978, 94 *Stat.* 3498.

60. *Western Pequot Tribe of Indians v. Holdridge Enterprises, Inc.*, Civ. No. 76–193 (1976).

61. The Mashantucket Pequot Indian Claims Settlement Act (S.366) was passed by Congress in December 1982. Reagan's veto is covered in the *Congressional Quarterly*, Vol. 41, No. 14, pp. 710–11.

62. The revised version of the Mashantucket Pequot Indian Claims Settlement Act (S.1499) was signed on 18 Oct. 1983.

63. *Mashpee Tribe v. Town of Mashpee*, 447 F. Supp. 940 (1978).

64. *Mashpee Tribe v. New Seabury Corporation*, 592 F.2d (1st Cir.) 575 (1979), *cert. denied* (1980). For further information, *see* Harry B. Wallace, "Indian Sovereignty and the Eastern Indian Land Claims," *New York University Law School Law Review*, No. 27 (1982), pp. 921–50. See also Paul Brodeur, op. cit.

65. *Mohegan Tribe v. Connecticut*, 483 F. Supp. 597 (D. Conn. 1980) and *Schaghticoke Tribe v. Kent School Corporation*, 423 F. Supp. 780 (D. Conn. 1983).

66. By the 1840 Treaty of Nation Ford, the Catawbas agreed to relinquish the reservation in exchange for a $5,000 acquisition of replacement lands. The state defaulted on the agreement, and the Catawbas were left entirely homeless for two years. Finally, in 1842, South Carolina spent $2,000 to buy 630 acres (apparently from itself) *of the former reservation* for "Catawba use and occupancy." *See* Charles M. Hudson, "The Catawba Indians of South Carolina: A Question of Ethnic Survival," in L. William Walter, ed., *Southeastern Indians Since the Removal Era* (Athens: University of Georgia Press, 1979), pp. 110–20.

67. *Catawba Indian Tribe of South Carolina v. State of South Carolina* (11 Oct. 1983).

68. For an assessment of the progress made in this arena, *see* S. James Anaya, "The Rights of Indigenous Peoples and International Law in Historical and Contemporary Perspective," in *American Indian Law: Cases and Materials*, Robert N. Clinton, Nell Jessup Newton, and Monroe E. Price, eds. (Charlottesville, Virginia: The Michie Co., Law Publishers, 1991), pp. 1257–276. For the principles involved in resolving issues of this sort through such means, *see* Richard B. Lillich, *International Claims: Their Adjudication by National Commission* (New York: Syracuse University Press, 1962).

69. Florida Indian Land Claim Settlement Act, 96 *Stat.* 2012 (1982). For background, *see* Robert T. Coulter et al., "Seminole Land Rights in Florida and the Award of the Indian Claims Commission," *American Indian Journal*, Vol. 4, No. 3 (Aug. 1978), pp. 2–27.

70. *See* Winona LaDuke, "The White Earth Land Struggle," in *Critical Issues in Native North America*, Ward Churchill, ed. (Doc. 63, International Work Group on Indigenous Affairs, Copenhagen, 1989), pp. 55–71, and "White Earth: The Struggle Continues," in *Critical Issues in Native North America, Vol. II*, Ward Churchill, ed. (Doc. 68, International Work Group on Indigenous Affairs, Copenhagen, 1991), pp. 99–103. *See* also E. M. Peterson, Jr., "The So-Called Warranty Deed: Clouded Land Titles on the White Earth Reservation in Minnesota," *North Dakota Law Review*, No. 59 (1983), pp. 159–81.

71. *See* Daniel McCool, "Federal Indian Policy and the Sacred Mountains of the Papago Indians," *Journal of Ethnic Studies*, Vol. 9, No. 3 (1981), pp. 57–69.

72. *See* Richard A. Lovett, "The Role of the Forest Service in Ski Resort Development: An Economic Approach to Public Lands Management," *Ecology Law Review*, No. 10 (1983), pp. 507–78. *See* also George Lubick, "Sacred Mountains, Kachinas, and Skiers: The Controversy Over the San Francisco Peaks," in *The American West: Essays in Honor of W. Eugene Hollan*, R. Lora, ed. (Ohio: University of Toledo Press, 1980), pp. 133–53.

73. *See* Ward Churchill, "Genocide in Arizona? The Navajo–Hopi Land Dispute in Perspective," in *Critical Issues in Native North America, Vol. II*, op. cit., pp. 104–46.

74. *See* Jack Campisi, "The Trade and Intercourse Acts: Indian Land Claims on the Eastern Seaboard," in Imre Sutton, ed., *Irredeemable America*, op. cit., pp. 337–62.

75. For the basis of this struggle, *see* M. C. Berry, *The Alaska Pipeline: The Politics of Oil and Native Land Claims* (Bloomington/Indianapolis: Indiana University Press, 1975). *See* also John Berger, *Report from the Frontier: The State of the World's Indigenous Peoples* (London: Zed Press, 1987).

76. On the rejection, *see* U.S. House of Representatives, *House Report 15066*, 94th Cong., 1st Sess. (Washington, DC: U.S. Government Printing Office, 1974). In 1980, Congress passed an act (94 *Stat.* 3321) mandating formation of a Native Hawaiians Study Commission (six federal officials and three Hawaiians) to find out "what the natives really want." The answer, predictably, was *land*.

77. For the basis of the native argument here, *see* L. Cannelora, *The Origin of Hawaiian Land Titles and the Rights of Native Tenants* (Honolulu: Security Title Corporation, 1974).

78. Jefferson and other "radicals" held U.S. sovereignty accrued from the country itself and did not "devolve" from the British Crown. Hence, U.S. land title could not devolve from the Crown. Put another way, Jefferson—in contrast to John Marshall—held that Britain's asserted discovery rights in North America had *no* bearing on U.S. rights to occupancy on the continent. *See* Gordon Wood, op. cit., pp. 162–96.

79. *See* generally, Barbara Graymont, *The Iroquois in the American Revolution* (Syracuse, New York: Syracuse University Press, 1975). The concern felt by Congress with regard to the Iroquois as a military threat, and the consequent need to reach an accommodation with them, is expressed often in early official correspondence. *See* Washington C. Ford et al., eds. and comps., *Journals of the Continental Congress, 1774–1789*, 34 Vols. (Washington, DC: U.S. Government Printing Office, 1904–1937).

80. Jack Campisi, "From Fort Stanwix to Canandaigua: National Policy, States' Rights and Indian Land," in *Iroquois Land Claims*, Christopher Vescey and William A. Starna, eds. (New York: Syracuse University Press, 1988), pp. 49–65; quote from p. 55. *See* also Henry M. Manley, *The Treaty of Fort Stanwix, 1784* (Rome/New York: Rome Sentinel Publications, 1932).

81. For an account of these meetings, conducted by New York's Governor Clinton during August and September 1784, *see* Franklin B. Hough, ed., *Proceedings of the Commissioners of Indian Affairs, Appointed by Law for Extinguishment of Indian Titles in the State of New York*, 2 Vols. (Albany, New York: John Munsell Publishers, 1861), pp. 41–63.

82. Jack Campisi, op. cit., p. 59. Clinton lied, bald–faced. New York's references to the Genesee Company concerned a bid by that group of land speculators to lease Oneida land which the Indians had not only rejected, but which the state legislature had refused to approve. In effect, the Oneidas had lost *no* land, were unlikely to, and the governor knew it.

83. *See* George Clinton, *Public Papers of George Clinton: First Governor of New York*, Vol. 8 (Albany: State of New York, 1904).

84. The price paid by New York for the Onondaga lease was "1,000 French Crowns, 200 pounds in clothing, plus a $500 annuity." *See* Helen M. Upton, *The Everett Report in Historical Perspective: The Indians of New York* (Albany: New York State Bicentennial Commission, 1980), p. 35.

85. Ibid., p. 38.

86. The relevant portion of the statute's text reads: [N]o sale of lands made by any Indians, or any nation or tribe of Indians within the United States, shall be valid to any person or persons, or to any state, whether having the right of pre–emption to such lands or not, unless the same shall be made and duly executed at some public treaty, held under the authority of the United States.

87. Helen M. Upton, op. cit., p. 40.

88. For ratification discussion on the meaning of the Treaty of Canandaigua, see *American State Papers: Documents, Legislative and Executive of the Congress of the United States, from the First Session to the Third Session of the Thirteenth Congress, Inclusive*, Vol. 4

(Washington, DC: Gales and Seaton Publishers, 1832), pp. 545–70. On Tecumseh's alliance, *see* R. David Edmunds, *Tecumseh and the Quest for Indian Leadership* (Boston: Little, Brown & Co., Inc., 1984).

89. *See* Paul D. Edwards, *The Holland Company* (Buffalo, New York: Buffalo Historical Society, 1924).

90. *See* Georgiana C. Nammack, *Fraud, Politics, and the Dispossession of the Indians: The Iroquois Frontier and the Colonial Period* (Norman: University of Oklahoma Press, 1969). *See* also Henry S. Manley, "Red Jacket's Last Campaign," *New York History*, No. 21 (Apr. 1950).

91. *See* Henry S. Manley, "Buying Buffalo from the Indians," *New York History*, No. 28 (July 1947).

92. Charles J. Kappler, op. cit., pp. 374–78. *See* also Society of Friend (Hicksite), *The Case of the Seneca Indians in the State of New York* (Stanfordville, New York: Earl E. Coleman Publisher [reprint of 1840 ed.], 1979).

93. Most principle leaders of the Six Nations never signed the Buffalo Creek Treaty. Each of the three consecutive votes taken in the Senate on ratification (requiring two–thirds affirmation to be lawful) resulted in a tie, broken only by the "aye" vote of Vice President Richard Johnson. *See* Henry S. Manley, "Buying Buffalo from the Indians," op. cit.

94. U.S. House of Representatives, H. Doc. 66, 26th Cong., 2d Sess., 6 Jan. 1841.

95. Charles J. Kappler, op. cit., p. 397.

96. The Tonawanda protest appears as U.S. Senate, S. Doc. 273, 29th Cong., 2d Sess., 2 Apr. 1842.

97. On the award, made on 5 Nov. 1857, *see Documents of the Assembly of the State of New York*, 112th Sess., Doc. 51, Albany (1889), pp. 167–70.

98. Helen M. Upton, op. cit., p. 53. The New York Supreme Court's invalidation of the leases is covered in *U.S. v. Forness*, 125 F.2d 928 (1942). On the court's deeming of the leases to be perpetual, *see* U.S. House of Representatives, Committee on Indian Affairs, *Hearings in Favor of House Bill No. 12270*, 57th Cong., 2d Sess. (Washington, DC: U.S. Government Printing Office, 1902).

99. Assembly Doc. 51, op. cit., pp. 43, 408.

100. 28 *Stat.* 887, 2 Mar. 1895.

101. *Hearings in Favor of House Bill No. 12270*, op. cit. p. 23.

102. Ibid., p. 66.

103. The original case is *Seneca Nation v. Appleby*, 127 AD 770 (1905). It was appealed as *Seneca Nation v. Appleby*, 196 NY 318 (1906).

104. The case, *United States v. Boylan*, 265 Fed. 165 (2d Cir. 1920), is important not because of the paltry quantity of land restored, but because it was the first time the federal judiciary formally acknowledged New York had never acquired legal title to Iroquois land. It was also one of the very few times in American history when non–Indians were actually evicted in order that Indians might recover illegally taken property.

105. New York State Indian Commission Act, Chapter 590, Laws of New York, 12 May 1919.

106. Helen M. Upton, op. cit., p. 99.

107. The document is Edward A. Everett, *Report of the New York State Indian Commission* (Albany, NY: unpublished, 17 Mar. 1922), pp. 308–09, 322–30.

108. Stenographic record of 21 Aug. 1922 meeting, Stillman files.

109. Helen M. Upton, op. cit., pp. 124–29.

110. The total amount to be paid the Senecas for rental of their Salamanca property was $6,000 per year, much of which had gone unpaid since the mid–30s. The judges found the federal government to have defaulted on its obligation to regulate state and private leases of Seneca land, and instructed it to take an active role in the future. *See* Laurence M. Hauptman, "The Historical Background to the Present–Day Seneca Nation–Salamanca Lease Controversy," in *Iroquois Land Claims*, op. cit., pp. 101–22. *See* also Arch Merrill, "The Salamanca Lease Settlement," *American Indian*, No. 1 (1944).

111. These laws, which were replicated in Kansas and Iowa during 1952, predate the more general application of state jurisdiction to Indians embodied in Public Law 280, passed in August 1953. U.S. Congress, Joint Legislative Committee, *Report* (Leg. Doc. 74), 83rd Cong., 1st Sess. (Washington, DC: U.S. Government Printing Office, 1953).

112. This was based on a finding in *United States v. Minnesota* (270 U.S. 181 [1926], s.c. 271 U.S. 648) that state statutes of limitations do not apply to federal action in Indian rights cases.

113. *See* Jack Campisi, "National Policy, States' Rights, and Indian Sovereignty: The Case of the New York Iroquois," in *Extending the Rafters: Interdisciplinary Approaches to Iroquoian Studies*, Michael K. Foster, Jack Campisi, and Marianne Mithun, eds. (Albany: State University of New York Press, 1984).

114. For the congressional position, and commentary on the independent study of alternative sites undertaken by Dr. Arthur Morgan, *see* U.S. Senate, Committee on the Interior and Insular Affairs, *Hearings Before the Committee on Interior and Insular Affairs: Kinzua Dam Project, Pennsylvania*, 88th Cong., 1st Sess. (Washington, DC: U.S. Government Printing Office, May–Dec. 1963).

115. For further detail on the struggle around Kinzua Dam, *see* Lawrence M. Hauptman, *The Iroquois Struggle for Survival: World War II to Red Power* (Syracuse, New York: Syracuse University Press, 1986).

116. *Tuscarora Indians v. New York State Power Authority*, 257 F.2d 885 (1958).

117. On the compromise acreage, *see* Laurence M. Hauptman, "Iroquois Land Claims Issues: At Odds with the 'Family of New York'," in *Iroquois Land Claims*, op. cit., pp. 67–86.

118. It took another 10 years for this to be spelled out definitively; *Oneida Indian Nation v. United States*, 37 Ind. Cl. Comm. 522 (1971).

119. For a detailed account of the discussions, agreements, and various factions within the process, see Helen M. Upton, op. cit., pp. 139–61.

120. *See* Margaret Treur, "Ganiekeh: An Alternative to the Reservation System and Public Trust," *American Indian Journal*, Vol. 5, No. 5 (1979), pp. 22–26.

121. *State of New York v. Danny White* et al., Civ. No. 74–CV–370 (N.D.N.Y.) (Apr. 1976); *State of New York v. Danny White* et al., Civ. No. 74–CV–370, Memorandum Decision and Order, 23 (Mar. 1977).

122. On the Moss Lake Agreement, *see* Richard Kwartler, "'This Is Our Land': *Mohawk Indians v. The State of New York*," in *Roundtable Justice: Case Studies in Conflict Resolution*, Robert B. Goldman, ed. (Boulder, Colorado: Westview Press, 1980).

123. *Oneida Indian Nation of New York v. County of Oneida*, 14 U.S. 661 (1974).

124. *Oneida Indian Nation of New York v. County of Oneida*, 434 F. Supp. 527, 548 (N.D.N.Y.) (1979).

125. Allan Van Gestel, "New York Indian Land Claims: The Modern Landowner as Hostage," in *Iroquois Land Claims*, op. cit., pp. 123–39. *See* also the revision published as "When Fictions Take Hostages," in *The Invented Indian: Cultural Fictions and Government Policies*, James E. Clifton, ed. (New Brunswick, New Jersey: Transaction Books, 1990), pp. 291–312, and "The New York Indian Land Claims: An Overview and a Warning," *New York State Bar Journal* (Apr. 1981).

126. *County of Oneida v. Oneida Indian Nation of New York*, 84 L.Ed.2d 169, 191 (1984).

127. Arlinda Locklear, "The Oneida Land Claims: A Legal Overview," in *Iroquois Land Claims*, op. cit., pp. 141–53.

128. Ibid., p. 148.

129. This suit was later recast to name the state rather than the counties as the primary defendant, and enlarged to encompass 6 million acres. It was challenged but upheld on appeal; *Oneida Indian Nation of New York v. State of New York*, 691 F.2d 1070 (1982). Dismissed by a district judge four years later (Claire Brennan, "Oneida Claim to 6 Million Acres Voided," *Syracuse Post–Standard*, 22 Nov. 1986), it was reinstated by the Second Circuit Court in 1988 (*Oneida Indian Nation of New York v. State of New York*, 860 F.2d 1145), and is ongoing as of this writing.

130. *Oneida Nation of Indians of Wisconsin v. State of New York*, 85 F.D.R. 701, 703 (N.Y.D.C.) (1980).

131. New York has attempted various arguments to obtain dismissal of the Cayuga suit. In 1990, the state's contention that it had obtained bona fide land title to the disputed area in leases obtained in 1795 and 1801 was overruled at the district court level (*Cayuga Indian Nation of New York v. Cuomo*, 730 F. Supp. 485). In 1991, an "interpretation" by the state attorney general that reservation of land by the Six Nations in the Fort Stanwix Treaty "did not really" invest recognizable title in them was similarly overruled (*Cayuga Indian Nation of New York v. Cuomo*, 758 F. Supp. 107). Finally, in 1991, a state contention that only a special railroad reorganization would have jurisdiction to litigate claims involving areas leased to railroads was overruled (*Cayuga Indian Nation of New York v. Cuomo*, 762 F. Supp. 30). The suit is ongoing.

132. The terms of the agreement were published in *Finger Lakes Times*, 18 Aug. 1979.

133. For further details, *see* Chris Lavin, "The Cayuga Land Claims," in *Iroquois Land Claims*, op. cit., pp. 87–100.

134. The one jurisdictional exception is that the Second Circuit ruled in 1988 that a federal statute passed in 1875 empowers the City of Salamanca, rather than the Senecas, to regulate zoning within the leased area so long as the leases exist (*John v. City of Salamanca*, 845 F.2d 37).

135. The non–Indian city government of Salamanca, a sub–part of which is the Salamanca Lease Authority, filed suit in 1990 to block settlement of the Seneca claim as "unconstitutional," and to compel a new 99–year lease on its own terms (*Salamanca Indian Lease Authority v. Seneca Indian Nation*, Civ. No. 1300, Docket 91–7086). They lost and appealed. The lower court decision was affirmed by the Second Circuit Court on March 15, 1991, on the basis that the Senecas enjoy "sovereign immunity" from any further such suits.

136. Public Law 101–503, 104 *Stat.* 1179.

137. For the treaty text, *see* Charles J. Kappler, op. cit., pp. 594–96. For background, *see* Remi Nadeau, *Fort Laramie and the Sioux* (Lincoln: University of Nebraska Press, 1967); and LeRoy R. Hafen and Francis Marion Young, *Fort Laramie and the Pageant of the West, 1834–1890* (Lincoln: University of Nebraska Press, 1938).

138. *See* Dee Brown, *Fort Phil Kearny: An American Saga* (Lincoln: University of Nebraska Press, 1971). *See* also Grace Hebard and E. A. Brindenstool, *The Bozeman Trail*, 2 vols. (Cleveland: Arthur H. Clark Publishers, 1922).

139. The treaty text will be found in Charles J. Kappler, op. cit. Lakota territoriality is spelled out in Articles 2 and 16, non–abrogation of 1851 treaty land provisions in Article 17.

140. Ibid., Article 12. The gender provision is of U.S. rather than Lakota origin.

141. *See* Donald Jackson, *Custer's Gold: The United States Cavalry Expedition of 1874* (Lincoln: University of Nebraska Press, 1966). *See* also U.S. Department of the Interior (William Ludlow), *Report of a Reconnaissance of the Black Hills of Dakota* (Washington, DC: U.S. Government Printing Office, 1875). It should also be noted that, prior to the outbreak of hostilities in 1876, a second U.S. invasion of Lakota territory—the 1875 "Jenny Expedition"—was sent into the Black Hills to corroborate Custer's findings (*see* U.S. Department of the Interior (Walter P. Jenny), *Report to Congress on the Mineral Wealth, Climate and Rainfall, and Natural Resources of the Black Hills of South Dakota* (Exec. Doc. 51), 44th Cong., 1st Sess. (Washington, DC: U.S. Government Printing Office, 1876). The Lakota responded militarily to neither violation of the treaty.

142. U.S. Department of the Interior, Bureau of Indian Affairs, *Annual Report of the Commissioner of Indian Affairs, 1875* (Washington, DC: U.S. Government Printing Office, 1875).

143. U.S. Department of War, *Annual Report of the Secretary of War*, 43rd Cong., 2d Sess. (Washington, DC: U.S. Government Printing Office, 1876), p. 441. *See* also James C. Olsen, *Red Cloud and the Sioux Problem* (Lincoln: University of Nebraska Press, 1965).

144. J. W. Vaughn, *With Crook at the Rosebud* (Lincoln: University of Nebraska Press, 1956).

145. On the Custer fight, *see* Mari Sandoz, *The Battle of the Little Big Horn* (New York: Curtis Books, 1966). For further contextualization, see John E. Gray, *Centennial Campaign: The Sioux War of 1876* (Norman: University of Oklahoma Press, 1988). Another excellent reading is Stephen E. Ambrose, *Crazy Horse and Custer: The Parallel Lives of Two American Warriors* (Garden City, New York: Doubleday Publishers, 1975).

146. *See* John E. Gray, *Centennial Campaign: The Sioux Wars of 1876* (Norman: University of Oklahoma Press, 1988).

147. For a detailed account of one of these slaughters, *see* Jerome Greene, *Slim Buttes, 1877: An Episode in the Great Sioux War* (Norman: University of Oklahoma Press, 1982). For more on Colonel McKenzie, who had made his reputation in a winter attack upon a Comanche village in Palo Duro Canyon (Texas) in 1874, *see* T. R. Fehrenbach, *Comanches: The Destruction of a People* (New York: Alfred A. Knopf Publishers, 1975), pp. 516–21.

148. On the Hunkpapa evasion to Canada, *see* Stanley Vestal, *Sitting Bull: Champion of the Sioux* (Norman: University of Oklahoma Press, 1932). On the false promises made to Crazy Horse (through Red Cloud), *see* Dee Brown, *Bury My Heart at Wounded Knee: An Indian History of the American West* (New York: Holt, Rinehart & Winston, Inc., 1970), pp. 308–10.

149. For first–hand accounts, *see* Robert A. Clark, ed., *The Killing of Chief Crazy Horse* (Lincoln: University of Nebraska Press, 1976).

150. This legislative history is covered quite well in a contribution entitled "1986 Black Hills Hearing on S.1453, Introduction," prepared by the staff of Senator Daniel Inouye, Chair of the Senate Select Committee on Indian Affairs, for *Wicazo Sa Review*, Vol. IV, No. 1 (Spring 1988). Total "Sioux" treaty territory—including that of the Nakota ("Prairie Sioux") and Dakota ("Woodland Sioux") east of the Missouri River—added up to 160 to 175 million acres according to the Indian Claims Commission *Final Report*, op. cit.

151. See Henry E. Fritz, *The Movement for Indian Assimilation, 1860–1890* (Philadelphia: University of Pennsylvania Press, 1963).

152. See *Sioux Tribe v. United States* (2 Ind. Cl. Comm. 671) for computation of acreage.

153. For a good dose of the propaganda prevailing at the time, *see* Herbert Welsh, "The Meaning of the Dakota Outbreak," *Scribner's Magazine* (Apr. 1891), pp. 439–52. A more comprehensive and considered topical view, albeit one generally conforming to ideological requirements, is James M. Mooney, *The Ghost–Dance Religion and the Sioux Outbreak of 1890* (Washington, DC: Smithsonian Institution, Bureau of American Ethnology, U.S. Government Printing Office, 1896). The most balanced and accurate account may probably be found in Dee Brown, *Bury My Heart at Wounded Knee*, op. cit.

154. Vine Deloria, Jr., and Clifford M. Lytle, *American Indians, American Justice* (Austin: University of Texas Press, 1983), p. 10.

155. For an official assessment of this situation, *see* the memorandum of Indian Commissioner John Collier; U.S. House of Representatives, Committee on Indian Affairs, *Hearings on HR 7902 Before the House Committee on Indian Affairs*, 73rd Cong., 2d Sess. (Washington, DC: U.S. Government Printing Office, 1934), pp. 16–18.

156. Eastman's books include *Old Indian Days* (New York: McClure Publishers, 1907), *The Soul of the Indian: An Interpretation* (New York: Johnson Reprint Corp., 1971), originally published in 1911, *From Deep Woods to Civilization: Chapters in an Autobiography of an Indian* (Boston: Little, Brown & Co., Inc., 1916), and *Indian Heroes and Great Chieftains* (Boston: Little, Brown & Co., Inc., 1918).

157. *Sioux Tribe v. United States*, 97 Ct. Cl. 613 (1942).

158. *Sioux Tribe v. United States*, 318 U.S. 789, *cert. denied* (1943).

159. *Sioux Tribe v. United States*, 2 Ind. Cl. Comm. (1956).

160. *Wicazo Sa Review*, Vol. IV, No. 1, op. cit., pp. 10–11.

161. *United States v. Sioux Nation of Indians*, 448 U.S. 371, 385 (1968). The grounds, however, were exceedingly narrow. The commission was charged only with discovering 1) What, if any, land rights vis-à-vis the Black Hills had been acquired in 1877; 2) What consideration had been given by the United States in exchange for these lands; and 3) If no consideration had been given, had the United States made *any* payments which might offset its obligation to provide consideration.

162. *Sioux Nation v. United States*, 33 Ind. Cl. Comm. 151 (1974); the decision was of course legally absurd. The United States holds "eminent domain" powers over the property of *no* foreign nation, such as the Lakota *had* to be in order for the 1868 treaty to be consummated. Fifth Amendment compensation hardly provides redress to an invaded country. *See* Nick Meinhart and Diane Payne, "Reviewing U.S. Commitments to the Lakota Nation," *American Indian Journal*, No. 13 (Nov.–Dec. 1975), pp. 15–17.

163. *United States v. Sioux Nation of Indians*, 207 Ct. Cl. 234, 518 F.2d 1293 (1975).

164. *Wicazo Sa Review*, Vol. IV, No. 1, op. cit., p. 12. On the concept of government "offsets," *see* John R. White, "Barmecide Revisited: The Gratuitous Offset in Indian Claims Cases," *Ethnohistory*, No. 25 (1978), pp. 179–92.

165. *Sioux Nation of Indians v. United States*, 423 U.S. 1016, *cert. denied* (1975).

166. For additional information, *see* Peter Matthiessen, *In the Spirit of Crazy Horse* (New York: Viking Press [2d ed.], 1991). *See* also Ward Churchill and Jim Vander Wall, *Agents of Repression: The FBI's Secret Wars Against the Black Panther Party and the American Indian Movement* (Boston: South End Press, 1988).

167. The transfer instrument, entitled *Memorandum of Agreement Between the Oglala Sioux Tribe of South Dakota and the National Park Service of the Department of Interior to Facilitate Establishment, Development, Administration and Public Use of the Oglala Sioux Tribal Lands, Badlands National Monument*, was signed secretly by Tribal President Richard Wilson on January 2, 1976. Although the arrangement hardly conformed to the provisions for Lakota land cessions in the still–binding 1868 treaty, Congress acted as it had in 1877, quickly passing Public Law 90–468 to take possession of the property. When Lakota protest became too great, the act was amended to provide that the Indians could recover the *surface* rights at any time they elected to do so by referendum (thus inverting the treaty requirements), but not the *mineral* rights (thus removing any question as to whether the whole thing hadn't been about taking the Lakota uranium rather than enlarging a national park). *See* Jacqueline Huber et al., *The Gunnery Range Report* (Pine Ridge, South Dakota: Oglala Sioux Tribe, Office of the Tribal President, 1981).

168. "The Black Hills Are *Not* For Sale," *Native American Support Committee (NASC) Newsletter*, Vol. V, No. 10 (Oct. 1977).

169. On the building of IITC, *see* Rex Weyler, *Blood of the Land: The U.S. Government and Corporate War Against the American Indian Movement* (New York: Everest House Publishers, 1982), pp. 213–16.

170. Public Law 95–243, 25 U.S.C. #70s (Supp. II, 1978).

171. *Sioux Nation of Indians v. United States*, 220 Ct. Cl. 442, 601 F.2d 1157 (1979).

172. Wilcomb E. Washburn, "Land Claims in the Mainstream, in *Irredeemable America*, Imre Sutton, ed., op. cit., pp. 21–33; quote from p. 26. The opinion is *Sioux Nation of Indians v. United States*, 448 U.S. 371 (1980). For a sample of Rehnquist's own extremely inaccurate and highly politicized historical revisionism, *see* his opinion in the 1978 *Oliphant* case.

173. Russell Means, "The Black Hills: They're Still Not For Sale!" *Oyate Wicaho* (May 1980). *See* also Steven C. Hanson, "*United States v. Sioux Nation*: Political Questions, Moral Imperative and National Honor," *American Indian Law Review*, Vol. 8, No. 2 (1980), pp. 459–84.

174. On the 1980 Black Hills Survival Gathering, *see* Anonymous, *Keystone for Survival* (Rapid City, South Dakota: Black Hills Alliance, 1981). *See* also Bill Tabb, "Marx Versus Marxism," in *Marxism and Native Americans*, Ward Churchill, ed. (Boston: South End Press, 1983), pp. 159–74.

175. *Oglala Sioux Tribe v. United States*, Cir. No. 85–062, W.D.N.D. 1980; 448 U.S. 371, *cert. denied* (1980).

176. For analysis of the AIM strategy in the Yellow Thunder occupation, *see* Ward Churchill, "Yellow Thunder *Tiyospaye*: Misadventure or Watershed Action?" *Policy Perspectives*, Vol. 2, No. 2 (Spring 1982). *See* also Rex Weyler, op. cit.; esp. Chapter 8, "Yellow Thunder," pp. 251–64.

177. The Oglala Sioux Tribal Council, for example, sponsored what was called Crazy Horse Camp, in Wind Cave State Park, from July through September 1981. The Cheyenne River Sioux established a camp at Craven Canyon, deep in the Black Hills, during the same period.

178. *United States v. Means* et al., Civ. No. 81–5131, D.S.D., 9 Dec. 1985.

179. *See* Vine Deloria, Jr., "Trouble in High Places: Erosion of American Indian Rights to Religious Freedom in the United States," *The State of Native America*, op. cit.

180. The deposit was made pursuant to a claims court ruling; *Sioux Tribe v. United States*, 7 Cl. Ct. 80 (1985).

181. On establishment of the Working Group and its mandate, *see* S. James Anaya, op. cit.

182. For further delineation of the Bradley Bill, and a comprehensive analysis of its implications, *see Wicazo Sa Review*, Vol. IV, No. 1, op. cit.

183. Stevens, a successful Defense Department contractor in the Los Angeles area, retired and sold off his company at a reputed $60 million profit during the early '80s. He then allegedly discovered he was in some part Lakota, traveled to South Dakota, and announced "his people" were entitled to much more than was being offered in the Bradley Bill (which, of course, was true). He then stipulated that, if he were named "Great Chief of all the Sioux" (a position which has never existed), he would be able—based on his executive expertise—to negotiate a multi–billion dollar settlement and recover the whole 1868 reservation area. Some Lakotas endorsed this strategy. Tellingly, once S.1453 was withdrawn, Stevens also withdrew, and has not been heard from since. It is widely suspected he was an operate for anti–Indian interests. For details, see *Lakota Times*, 1988–89, inclusive.

184. The full treaty text may be found in Charles J. Kappler, op. cit.

185. Rudolph C. Ryser, *Newe Segobia and the United States of America*, Occasional Paper (Kenmore, Washington: Center for World Indigenous Studies, 1985). *See* also Peter Matthiessen, *Indian Country* (New York: Viking Press, 1984), pp. 261–89.

186. Actually, under U.S. law, a specific Act of Congress is required to extinguish aboriginal title; *United States ex rel. Hualapi Indians v. Santa Fe Railroad*, 314, U.S. 339, 354 (1941). On Newe use of the land during this period, *see* Richard O. Clemmer, "Land Use Patterns and Aboriginal Rights: Northern and Eastern Nevada, 1858–1971," *The Indian Historian*, Vol. 7, No. 1 (1974), pp. 24–41, 47–49.

187. Rudolph C. Ryser, op. cit., pp. 15–16.

188. Wilkinson had already entered into negotiations to represent the Temoak before the Claims Commission Act was passed; ibid., p. 13, n. 1.

189. The Temoaks have said consistently that Wilkinson always represented the claim to them as being for land rather than money. The firm is known to have run the same scam on other Indian clients; ibid., pp. 16–17.

190. Ibid., p. 16. *See* also Robert T. Coulter, op. cit., and Robert T. Coulter and Steven M. Tullberg, op. cit.

191. *See* Glenn T. Morris, "The Battle for Newe Segobia: The Western Shoshone Land Rights Struggle," in *Critical Issues in Native North America, Vol. II*, op. cit., pp. 86–98.

192. Ibid., p. 90. The case is *Western Shoshone Identifiable Group v. United States*, 11 Ind. Cl. Comm. 387, 416 (1962). The whole issue is well covered in Jack D. Forbes, "The 'Public Domain' in Nevada and Its Relationship to Indian Property Rights," *Nevada State Bar Journal*, No. 30 (1965), pp. 16–47.

193. The first award amount appears in *Western Shoshone Identifiable Group v. United States*, 29 Ind. Cl. Comm. 5 (1972), p. 124. The second award appears in *Western Shoshone Identifiable Group v. United States*, 40 Ind. Cl. Comm. 305 (1977).

194. This is the final Court of Claims order for Wilkinson's retention in *Western Shoshone Identifiable Group v. United States,* 593 F.2d 994 (1979). *See* also "Excerpts from a Memorandum from the Duckwater Shoshone Tribe, Battle Mountain Indian Community, and the Western Shoshone Sacred Lands Association in Opposition to the Motion and Petition for Attorney Fees and Expenses, July 15, 1980," in *Rethinking Indian Law*, op. cit., pp. 68–69.

195. *Western Shoshone Identifiable Group v. United States,* 40 Ind. Cl. Comm. 311 (1977).

196. Glenn T. Morris, quoting Rudolph C. Ryser, op. cit., p. 8, n. 4.

197. Quoted in Rudolph C. Ryser, op. cit., p. 20.

198. *United States v. Dann,* 572 F.2d 222 (1978). For background, *see* Kristine L. Foot, "*United States v. Dann*: What It Portends for Ownership of Millions of Acres in the Western United States," *Public Land Law Review*, No. 5 (1984), pp. 183–91.

199. *United States v. Dann,* Civ. No. R–74–60, 25 Apr. 1980.

200. *United States v. Dann,* 706 F.2d 919, 926 (1983).

201. Glenn T. Morris, op. cit., p. 94.

202. Bernard Nietschmann and William Le Bon, "Nuclear States and Fourth World Nations," *Cultural Survival Quarterly*, Vol. 11, No. 4 (1988), pp. 4–7. *See* also Martha C. Knack, "MX Issues for Native American Communities," in *MX in Nevada: A Humanistic Perspective*, Francis Hartigan, ed. (Reno: Nevada Humanities Press, 1980), pp. 59–66.

203. Bernard Nietschmann and William Le Bon, op. cit., p. 7.

204. The actual quote, used as a slogan during the French student rebellion of 1968, is "Be realistic, demand the impossible." For details, *see* Daniel Cohn–Bendit, *Obsolete Communism: The Left–Wing Alternative* (New York: McGraw–Hill Books, 1968).

205. *See,* for example, Imre Sutton, "Indian Land Rights and the Sagebrush Rebellion," *Geographical Review*, No. 72 (1982), pp. 357–59. *See* also David Lyons, "The New Indian Claims and Original Rights to Land," *Social Theory and Practice*, No. 4 (1977), pp. 249–72; and Richard D. Clayton, "The Sagebrush Rebellion: Who Would Control Public Lands?" *Utah Law Review*, No 68 (1980), pp. 505–33.

206. For a sample of environmentalist arguments, *see* T. H. Watkins, "Ancient Wrongs and Public Rights" *Sierra Club Bulletin*, Vol. 59, No. 8 (1974), pp. 15–16, 37–39; M. C. Blumm, "Fulfilling the Parity Promise: A Perspective on Scientific Proof, Economic Cost and Indian Treaty Rights in the Approval of the Columbia Fish and Wildlife Program," *Environmental Law*, Vol. 13, No. 1 (1982), pp. 103–59; and every issue of *Earth First!* 1986–89. For exemplary marxist articulations, see Revolutionary Communist Party, U.S.A., "Searching for the Second Harvest," in *Marxism and Native Americans*, op. cit., pp. 35–58; and David Muga, "Native Americans and the Nationalities Question: Premises for a Marxist Approach to Ethnicity and Self–Determination," *Nature, Society, Thought,* Vol. 1, No. 1 (1987).

207. Russell Means, speech at the University of Colorado at Denver, Apr. 1986 (tape on file).

208. For use of the term, and explanation, *see* David Stock, "The Settler State and the U.S. Left," *Forward Motion*, Vol. 9, No. 4 (Jan. 1991), pp. 53–61.

209. The quote can be attributed to paleo–conservative pundit Patrick J. Buchanan, delivered on the CNN talk show *Crossfire*, 1987.

210. *See* Laurie Ensworth, "Native American Free Exercise Rights to the Use of Public Lands," *Boston University Law Review*, No. 63 (1983), pp. 141–79. *See* also Barbara Hooker, "Surplus Lands for Indians: One Road to Self–Determination," *Vital Issues*, Vol. 22, No. 1 (1972); and R. A. Hodge, "Getting Back the Land: How Native Americans Can Acquire Excess and Surplus Federal Property," *North Dakota Law Review*, Vol. 49, No. 2 (1973), pp. 333–42.

211. *See* Rebecca L. Robbins, "Self–Determination and Subordination: The Past, Present, and Future of American Indian Governance," in *The State of Native America*, op. cit.

212. This is taken up in some detail in Russell Means and Ward Churchill, *TREATY: A Program for the Liberation of Native North America* (Porcupine, South Dakota: Tabloid Circular, 1983).

213. *See* Ward Churchill, "Radioactive Colonization: Hidden Holocaust in Native North America," in *Struggle for the Land* (Monroe, Maine: Common Courage Press, 1993).

Like Sand in the Wind

The Making of an American Indian Diaspora
in the United States

They are going away! With a visible reluctance which nothing has overcome but the stern necessity they feel impelling them, they have looked their last upon the graves of their sires—the scenes of their youth, and have taken up the slow toilsome march with their household goods among them to their new homes in a strange land. They leave names to many of our rivers, towns, and counties, and so long as our State remains the Choctaws who once owned most of her soil will be remembered.

Vicksburg Daily Sentinel, *February 25, 1832*

We told them that we would rather die than leave our lands; but we could not help ourselves. They took us down. Many died on the road. Two of my children died. After we reached the new land, all my horses died. The water was very bad. All our cattle died; not one was left. I stayed till one hundred and fifty–eight of my people had died. Then I ran away....

Standing Bear, *January 1876*

Within the arena of Diaspora Studies, the question of whether the field's analytical techniques might be usefully applied to the indigenous population of the United States is seldom raised. In large part, this appears to be due to an unstated presumption on the part of diaspora scholars that because the vast bulk of the native people of the United States remain inside the borders of that nation–state, no population dispersal comparable to that experienced by Afroamericans, Asian Americans, Latinos—or, for that matter, Euroamericans—is at issue. Upon even minimal reflection, however, the fallacy imbedded at the core of any such premise is quickly revealed.

To say that a Cherokee remains essentially "at home" so long as s/he resides within the continental territoriality claimed by the United States is equivalent to arguing that a Swede displaced to Italy or a Vietnamese refugee in Korea would be at home simply because they remain in Europe or Asia. Native Americans, no less than other peoples, can and should be understood as identified with the specific geographical settings by which they came to identify themselves as peoples. Mohawks are native to the upstate New York/southern Québec region, not Florida or California. Chiricahua Apaches are indigenous to southern Arizona and northern Sonora, not Oklahoma or Oregon. The matter is not only cultural, although the dimension of culture is crucially important, but political and economic as well.

Struggles by native peoples to retain use and occupancy rights over their traditional territories, and Euroamerican efforts to supplant them, comprise the virtual entirety of U.S./Indian relations since the inception of the republic. All 40 of the so–called Indian Wars recorded by the federal government were fought over land.[1] On more than 370 separate occasions between 1778 and 1871, the Senate of the United States ratified treaties with one or more indigenous peoples by which the latter ceded portions of its land base to the United States. In every instance, a fundamental *quid pro quo* was arrived at: Each indigenous nation formally recognized as such through a treaty ratification was simultaneously acknowledged as retaining a clearly demarcated national homeland within which it might maintain its socio–political cohesion and from which it could draw perpetual sustenance, both spiritually and materially.[2]

At least five succeeding generations of American Indians fought, suffered, and died to preserve their peoples' residency in the portions of North America which had been theirs since "time immemorial." In this sense, the fundamental importance they attached to continuing their linkages to these areas seems unquestionable. By the same token, the extent to which their descendants have been dislocated from these defined, or definable, land bases is the extent to which it can be observed that the conditions of diaspora have been imposed upon the population of Native North America. In this respect, the situation is so unequivocal that a mere sample of statistics deriving from recent census data will be sufficient to tell the tale:

- By 1980, nearly half of all federally recognized American Indians lived in off–reservation locales, mostly cities. The largest concentration of indigenous people in the country—90,689—was in the Los Angeles Metro Area.[3] By 1990, the proportion of urban–based Indians was estimated to have swelled to approximately 55 percent.[4]

- All federally unrecognized Indians—a figure which may run several times the approximately 1.6 million that the United States officially admits still exist within its borders—are effectively landless and scattered everywhere across the country.[5]

- Texas, the coast of which was once one of the more populated locales for indigenous people, reported a reservation–based Native American population of 859 in 1980.[6] The total Indian population of Texas was reported as being 39,740.[7] Even if this number included only members of peoples native to the area (which it does not), it would still represent a reduction of about 1.5 million from the point of first contact with Europeans.[8]

- A veritable vacuum in terms of American Indian reservations and population is now evidenced in most of the area east of the Mississippi River, another region once densely populated by indigenous people. Delaware, Illinois, Indiana, Kentucky, Maryland, New Hampshire, New Jersey, Ohio, Pennsylvania, Rhode Island, Tennessee, Vermont, Virginia, and West Virginia show no reservations at all.[9] The total Indian population reported in Vermont in 1980 was 968. In New Hampshire, the figure was 1,297. In Delaware, it was 1,307; in West Virginia, 1,555. The reality is that a greater number of persons indigenous to the North American mainland now live in Hawai'i, far out in the Pacific Ocean, than in any of these easterly states.[10]

The ways in which such deformities in the distribution of indigenous population in the United States have come to pass have been anything but natural. To the contrary, the major causative factors have consistently derived from a series of official policies implemented over more than two centuries by the federal government of the United States. These have ranged from forced removal during the 1830s, to concentration and compulsory assimilation during the 1880s, to coerced relocation beginning in the late 1940s. Interspersed through it all have been periods of outright liquidation and dissolution, continuing to the present time. The purpose of this essay is to explore these policies and their effects on the peoples targeted for such exercises in "social engineering."

The Post–Revolutionary Period

During the period immediately following the American Revolution, the newly formed United States was in a "desperate financial plight ... [and] saw its salvation in the sale to settlers and land companies of western lands" lying outside the original 13 colonies.[11] Indeed, the revolution had been fought in significant part in order to negate George III's Proclamation of 1763, an edict restricting land acquisition by British subjects to the area east of the Appalachian Mountains and thereby voiding certain speculative real estate interests held by the U.S. Founding Fathers. During the war, loyalty of rank and file soldiers, as well as major creditors, was maintained through warrants advanced by the Continental Congress with the promise that rebel debts would be retired through issuance of deeds to parcels of Indian land once the revolution had succeeded.[12] A substantial problem for the fledgling republic was that in the immediate aftermath, it possessed neither the legal nor the physical means to act on such commitments.

In the Treaty of Paris, signed on September 3, 1783, England quitclaimed its rights to all present U.S. territory east of the Mississippi. Contrary to subsequent Americana, this action conveyed no bona fide title to any of the Indian lands lying within the area.[13] Rather, it opened the way for the United States to replace Great Britain as the sole entity entitled under prevailing international law to *acquire* Indian land in the region through negotiation and purchase.[14] The United States—already an outlaw state by virtue of its armed rejection of lawful Crown authority—appears to have been emotionally prepared to seize native property mainly through force, thereby continuing its initial posture of gross illegality.[15] Confronted by the incipient indigenous alliance espoused by Tecumseh in the Ohio River Valley (known at the time as the "Northwest Territory") and to the south by the powerful Creek and Cherokee confederations, however, the United States found itself militarily stalemated all along its western frontier.[16]

The Indian position was considerably reinforced when England went back on certain provisions of the Treaty of Paris, refusing to abandon a line of military installations along the Ohio until the United States showed itself willing to comply with minimum standards of international legalism, "acknowledging the Indian right in the soil" long since recognized under the Doctrine of Discovery.[17] To the south, Spanish Florida also aligned itself with native nations as a means of holding the rapacious settler population of neighboring Georgia in check.[18] Frustrated, federal authorities had to content themselves with the final dispossession and banishment of such peoples as the Huron (Wyandotte) and Delaware (Lenni Lanape)—whose homelands fell within the original colonies, and who had been much weakened by more than a century of warfare—to points beyond the 1763 demarcation line. There, these early victims of a U.S.–precipitated indigenous diaspora were taken in by stronger nations such as the Ottawa and Shawnee.[19]

Meanwhile, George Washington's initial vision of a rapid and wholesale expulsion of all Indians east of the Mississippi, expressed in June 1783,[20] was tempered to reflect a more sophisticated process of gradual encroachment explained by General Philip Schuyler of New York in a letter to Congress the following month:

As our settlements approach their country, [the Indians] must, from the scarcity of game, which that approach will induce, retire farther back, and dispose of their lands, unless they dwindle to nothing, as all savages have done ... when compelled to live in the vicinity of civilized people, and thus leave us the country without the expense of purchase, trifling as that will probably be.[21]

As Washington himself was to put it a short time later:

[P]olicy and economy point very strongly to the expediency of being on good terms with the Indians, and the propriety of purchasing their Lands in preference to attempting to drive them by force of arms out of their Country.... The gradual extension of our Settlements will certainly cause the Savage as the Wolf to retire.... In a word there is nothing to be gained by an Indian War but the Soil they live on and this can be had by purchase at less expense.[22]

By 1787, the strategy had become so well accepted that the United States was prepared to enact the Northwest Ordinance, codifying a formal renunciation of what it had been calling its "Rights of Conquest" with respect to native peoples: "The utmost good faith shall always be observed towards the Indian; their land shall never be taken from them without their consent; and in their property, rights, and liberty, they shall never be invaded or disturbed—but laws founded in justice and humanity shall from time to time be made, for wrongs done to them, and for preserving peace and friendship with them."[23]

The Era of Removal

By the early years of the nineteenth century, the balance of power in North America had begun to shift. To a certain extent, this was due to a burgeoning of the Angloamerican population, a circumstance actively fostered by government policy. In other respects, it was because of an increasing consolidation of the U.S. state and a generation–long erosion of indigenous strength resulting from the factors delineated in Schuyler's policy of gradual expansion.[24] By 1810, the government was ready to resume what Congress described as the "speedy provision of the extension of the territories of the United States" through means of outright force.[25] Already, in 1803, provision had been made through the Louisiana Purchase for the massive displacement of all eastern Indian nations into what was perceived as the "vast wasteland" west of the Mississippi.[26] The juridical groundwork was laid by the Supreme Court with Chief Justice John Marshall's opinion in *Fletcher v. Peck*, a decision holding that the title of U.S. citizens to parcels of Indian property might be considered valid even though no Indian consent to cede the land had been obtained.[27]

With the defeat of Great Britain in the War of 1812, the subsequent defeat of Tecumseh's confederation in 1813, and General Andrew Jackson's defeat of the Creek Redsticks in 1814, the "clearing" of the East began in earnest.[28] By 1819, the United States had wrested eastern Florida from Spain, consummating a process begun in 1810 with assaults upon the western ("panhandle") portion of the territory.[29] Simultaneously, the first of a pair of "Seminole Wars" was begun on the Florida peninsula to subdue an amalgamation of resident Miccosukees, "recalcitrant" Creek refugees, and runaway chattel slaves naturalized as free citizens of the indigenous nations.[30] In 1823, Chief Justice John Marshall reinforced the embryonic position articulated in *Peck* with *Johnson v. McIntosh*, an opinion inverting conventional understandings of indigenous status in international law by holding that U.S. sovereignty superseded that of native nations, even within their own territories. During the same year, President James Monroe promulgated his doctrine professing a unilateral U.S. "right" to circumscribe the sovereignty of all other nations in the hemisphere.[31]

In this environment, a tentative policy of Indian "removal" was already underway by 1824, although not codified as law until the Indian Removal Act was passed in 1830. This was followed by Marshall's opinions, rendered in *Cherokee v. Georgia* and *Worcester v. Georgia*, that Indians comprised "domestic dependent nations," the sovereignty of which was subject to the "higher authority" of the federal government.[32] At that point, the federal program of physically relocating entire nations of people from their eastern homelands to what was then called the "Permanent Indian Territory of Oklahoma" west of the Mississippi became full–fledged and forcible.[33] The primary targets were the prosperous "Five Civilized Tribes" of the Southeast: the Cherokee, Creek, Chickasaw, Choctaw, and Seminole Nations. They were rounded up and interned by troops, concentrated in camps until their numbers were sufficient to make efficient their being force–marched at bayonet–point, typically without adequate food, shelter, or medical attention, often in the dead of winter, as much as 1,500 miles to their new "homelands."[34]

There were, of course, still those who attempted to mount a military resistance to what was happening. Some, like the Sauk and Fox nations of Illinois, who fought what has come to be known as the "Black Hawk War" against those dispossessing them in 1832, were simply slaughtered *en masse.*[35] Others, such as the "hard core" of Seminoles who mounted the second war bearing their name in 1835, were forced from the terrain associated with their normal way of life. Once ensconced in forbidding locales like the Everglades, they became for all practical intents and purposes invincible—one group refused to make peace with the United States until the early 1960s—but progressively smaller and more diffuse in their demography.[36] In any event, by 1840 removal had been mostly accomplished (although it lingered as a policy until 1855), with only "the smallest, least offensive, and most thoroughly integrated tribes escaping the pressure to clear the eastern half of the continent from its original inhabitants."[37] The results of the policy were always catastrophic for the victims. For instance, of the approximately 17,000 Cherokees subjected to the removal process, about 8,000 died of disease, exposure, and malnutrition along what they called the "Trail of Tears."[38] In addition:

> The Choctaws are said to have lost fifteen percent of their population, 6,000 out of 40,000; and the Chickasaw ... surely suffered severe losses as well. By contrast the Creeks and Seminoles are said to have suffered about 50 percent mortality. For the Creeks, this came primarily in the period immediately after removal: for example, "of the 10,000 or more who were resettled in 1836–37 ... an incredible 3,500 died of 'bilious fevers'."[39]

Nor was this the only cost. Like the Seminoles, portions of each of the targeted peoples managed through various means to avoid removal, remaining in their original territories until their existence was once again recognized by the United States during the twentieth century. One consequence was a permanent socio–cultural and geographic fragmentation of formerly cohesive groups; while the bulk of the identified populations of these nations now live in and around Oklahoma, smaller segments reside on the tiny "Eastern Cherokee" Reservation in North Carolina (1980 population 4,844); "Mississippi Choctaw" Reservation in Mississippi (pop. 2,756); the Miccosukee and "Big Cypress," "Hollywood," and "Brighton" Seminole Reservations in Florida (pops. 213, 351, 416, and 323, respectively).[40]

An unknown but significant number of Cherokees also went beyond Oklahoma, following their leader, Sequoia, into Mexico in order to escape the reach of the United States altogether.[41] This established something of a precedent for other peoples such as the Kickapoos, a small Mexican "colony" that persists to this day.[42] Such dispersal was compounded by the fact that throughout the removal process varying numbers of Indians escaped at various points along the route of the march, blending into the surrounding territory and later intermarrying with the incoming settler population. By and large, these people have simply slipped from the historical record, their descendants today inhabiting a long arc of mixed–blood communities extending from northern Georgia and Alabama, through Tennessee and Kentucky, and into the southernmost areas of Illinois and Missouri.[43]

Worse was yet to come. At the outset of the removal era proper, Andrew Jackson—a leading proponent of the policy who had ridden into the White House on the public acclaim deriving from his role as commander of the 1814 massacre of the Redsticks at Horseshoe Bend and a subsequent slaughter of noncombatants during the First Seminole War—offered a carrot as well as a stick to compel tribal "cooperation."[44] In 1829, he promised the Creeks that:

> Your father has provided a country large enough for all of you, and
> he advises you to remove to it. There your white brothers will not
> trouble you; they will have no claim to the land, and you can live
> upon it, you and all your children, as long as the grass grows or the
> water runs, in peace and plenty. It will be yours forever.[45]

Jackson was, to put it bluntly, lying through his teeth. Even as he spoke, Jackson was aware that the Mississippi, that ostensible border between the United States and Permanent Indian Territory proclaimed by Thomas Jefferson and others, had already been breached by the rapidly consolidating states of Louisiana, Arkansas, and Missouri in the south, and Iowa, Wisconsin, and Minnesota in the north.[46] Nor could Jackson have been unknowing that his close friend, Senator Thomas Hart Benton of Missouri, had stipulated as early as 1825 that the Rocky Mountains rather than the Mississippi should serve as an "everlasting boundary" of the United States.[47] By the time the bulk of removal was completed a decade later, Angloamerican settlements were reaching well into Kansas. Their cousins who had infiltrated the Mexican province of Texas had revolted, proclaimed themselves an independent republic, and were negotiating for statehood. The eyes of empire had also settled on all of Mexico north of the Río Grande, and the British portion of Oregon as well.[48]

Peoples such as the Shawnee and Potawatomi, Lenni Lanape and Wyandotte, Peoria, Sac, Fox, and Kickapoo, already removed from their eastern homelands, were again compulsorily relocated as the western Indian Territory was steadily reduced in size.[49] This time, they were mostly shifted southward into an area eventually conforming to the boundaries of the present state of Oklahoma. Ultimately, 67 separate nations (or parts of nations), only six of them truly indigenous to the land at issue, were forced into this relatively small dumping ground.[50] When Oklahoma, too, became a state in 1907, most of the territorial compartments reserved for the various Indian groups were simply dissolved. Today, although Oklahoma continues to report the second largest native population of any state, only the Osage retain a reserved land base which is nominally their own.[51]

Subjugation in the West

The United States' "Winning of the West," which began around 1850—that is, immediately after the northern half of Mexico was taken in a brief war of conquest—was, if anything, more brutal than the clearing of the East.[52] Most of the U.S. wars against native people were waged during the following 35 years under what has been termed an official "rhetoric of extermination."[53] The means employed in militarily subjugating the indigenous nations of California and southern Oregon, the Great Plains, Great Basin, and northern region of the

Sonora Desert devolved from a lengthy series of wholesale massacres. Representative of these are the slaughter of about 150 Lakotas at Blue River (Nebraska) in 1854, some 500 Shoshones at Bear River (Idaho) in 1863, as many as 250 Cheyennes and Arapahos at Sand Creek (Colorado) in 1864, perhaps 300 Cheyennes on the Washita River (Oklahoma) in 1868, 175 Piegan noncombatants at the Marias River (Montana) in 1870, and at least 100 Cheyennes at Camp Robinson (Nebraska) in 1878. The parade of official atrocities was capped off by the butchery of another 300 unarmed Lakotas at Wounded Knee (South Dakota) in 1890.[54]

Other means employed by the government to reduce its native opponents to a state of what it hoped would be abject subordination included the four–year internment of the entire Navajo (Diné) Nation in a concentration camp at the Bosque Redondo, outside Fort Sumner, New Mexico, beginning in 1864. The Diné, after having been force–marched in what they called the "Long Walk," a 400–mile trek from their Arizona homeland, were then held under abysmal conditions, with neither adequate food nor shelter, and died like flies. Approximately half had perished before their release in 1868.[55] Similarly, if less dramatically, food supplies were cut off to the Lakota Nation in 1877—militarily defeated the year before, the Lakotas were being held under army guard at the time—until starvation compelled its leaders to "cede" the Black Hills area to the United States.[56] The assassination of resistance leaders, such as the Lakotas' Crazy Horse (1877) and Sitting Bull (1890), was also a commonly used technique.[57] Other recalcitrant figures like Geronimo (Chiricahua) and Satanta (Kiowa) were separated from their people by being imprisoned in remote facilities like Fort Marion, Florida.[58]

In addition to these official actions, which the U.S. Census Bureau acknowledged in an 1894 summary as having caused a minimum of 45,000 native deaths, there was an even greater attrition resulting from what were described as "individual affairs."[59] These took the form of at large Angloamerican citizens killing Indians, often systematically, under a variety of quasi–official circumstances. In Dakota Territory, for example, a $200 bounty for Indian scalps was paid in the territorial capitol of Yankton during the 1860s; the local military commander, General Alfred Sully, is known to have privately contracted for a pair of Lakota skulls with which to adorn the city.[60] In Texas, first as a republic and then as a state, authorities also "placed a bounty upon the scalp of any Indian brought in to a government office—man, woman, or child, no matter what 'tribe'—no questions asked."[61] In California and Oregon, "the enormous decrease [in the native population of 1800] from about a quarter–million to less than 20,000 [in 1870 was] due chiefly to the cruelties and wholesale massacres perpetrated by the miners and early settlers."[62]

> Much of the killing in California and southern Oregon Territory resulted, directly and indirectly, from the discovery of gold in 1848 and the subsequent influx of miners and settlers. Newspaper ac-

counts document the atrocities, as do oral histories of the California Indians today. It was not uncommon for small groups or villages to be attacked by immigrants ... and virtually wiped out overnight.[63]

It has been estimated that Indian deaths resulting from this sort of direct violence may have run as high as one–half million by 1890.[64] All told, the indigenous population of the continental United States, which may still have been as great as 2 million when the country was founded, had been reduced to well under 250,000 by 1900.[65] As the noted demographer Sherburn F. Cook has observed, "The record speaks for itself. No further commentary is necessary."[66]

Under these conditions, the United States was able to shuffle native peoples around at will. The Northern Cheyennes and those Arapahos who were closely allied with them, for instance, were shipped from their traditional territory in Montana's Powder River watershed to the reservation of their southern cousins in Oklahoma in 1877. After the Cheyenne remnants, more than one–third of whom had died in barely a year of malaria and other diseases endemic to this alien environment, made a desperate attempt to return home in 1878, they were granted a reservation in the north country. But not before the bulk of them had been killed by army troops. Moreover, they were permanently separated from the Arapahos, who were "temporarily" assigned to the Wind River Reservation of their hereditary enemies, the Shoshone, in Wyoming.[67]

A faction of the Chiricahua Apaches who showed signs of continued "hostility" to U.S. domination into the 1880s were yanked from their habitat in southern Arizona and "resettled" around Fort Sill, Oklahoma.[68] Hinmaton Yalatkit (Chief Joseph) of the Nez Percé and other leaders of that people's legendary attempt to escape the army and flee to Canada were also deposited in Oklahoma, far from the Idaho valley they'd fought to retain.[69] Most of the Santee Dakotas of Minnesota's woodlands ended up on the windswept plains of Nebraska, while a handful of their relatives remained behind on tiny plots which are now called the "Upper Sioux" and "Lower Sioux" reservations.[70] A portion of the Oneidas, who had fought on the side of the rebels during the revolution, were moved to a small reservation near Green Bay, Wisconsin.[71] An even smaller reserve was provided in the same area for residual elements of Connecticut's Mahegans, Mohegans, and other peoples, all of them lumped together under the heading "Stockbridge–Munsee Indians."[72] On and on, it went.

Allotment and Assimilation

With the native ability to militarily resist U.S. territorial ambitions finally quelled, the government moved first to structurally negate any meaningful residue of national status on the part of indigenous peoples, and then to dissolve them altogether. The opening round of this drive came in 1871, with the attachment of a rider to the annual congressional appropriations act suspending any further treaty making with Indians. This was followed, in 1885, with passage of the Major Crimes Act, extending U.S. jurisdiction directly over reserved Indian territories for the first time. Beginning with seven felonies delineated in the initial statutory language, and combined with the Supreme Court's opinion in *U.S. v. Kagama* that Congress possessed a unilateral and "incontrovertible right" to exercise its authority over Indians as it saw fit, the 1885 act opened the door for the subsequent enactment of more than 5,000 federal laws that presently regulate every aspect of reservation life and affairs.[73]

In 1887, Congress passed the General Allotment Act, a measure designed expressly to destroy what was left of the basic indigenous socio–economic cohesion by eradicating traditional systems of collective landholding. Under provision of the statute, each Indian identified as such by demonstrating "one–half or more degree of Indian blood" was to be issued an individual deed to a specific parcel of land—160 acres per family head, 80 acres per orphan or single person over 18 years of age, and 40 acres per dependent child—within existing reservation boundaries. Each Indian was required to accept U.S. citizenship in order to receive his or her allotment. Those who refused, such as a substantial segment of the Cherokee "full–blood" population, were left landless.[74]

Generally speaking, those of mixed ancestry whose "blood quantum" fell below the required level were summarily excluded from receiving allotments. In many cases, the requirement was construed by officials as meaning that an applicant's "blood" had to have accrued from a single people; persons whose cumulative blood quantum derived from intermarriage between several native peoples were thus often excluded as well. In other instances, arbitrary geographic criteria were also employed; all Cherokees, Creeks, and Choctaws living in Arkansas, for example, were not only excluded from allotment, but permanently denied recognition as members of their respective nations as well.[75] Once all eligible Indians had been assigned their allotments within a given reservation—all of them from the worst land available therein—the remainder of the reserved territory was declared "surplus" and opened to non–Indian homesteaders, corporate acquisition, and conversion into federal or state parks and forests.[76]

> Under the various allotment programs, the most valuable land was the first to go. Settlers went after the rich grasslands of Kansas, Nebraska, and the Dakotas; the dense black–soil forests of Minnesota and Wisconsin; and the wealthy oil and gas lands of Oklahoma. In 1887, for example, the Sisseton Sioux of South Dakota owned 918,000 acres of rich virgin land on their reservation. But since there were only two thousand of them, allotment left more than 600,000

acres for European American settlers.... The Chippewas of Minnesota lost their rich timber lands; once each member had claimed [their] land, the government leased the rest to timber corporations. The Colvilles of northeastern Washington lost their lands to cattlemen, who fraudulently claimed mineral rights there. In Montana and Wyoming the Crows lost more than two million acres, and the Nez Percés had to cede communal grazing ranges in Idaho. All sixty-seven of the tribes in Indian Territory underwent allotment.... On the Flathead Reservation [in Montana]—which included Flatheads, Pend Oreilles, Kutenais, and Spokanes ... the federal government opened 1.1 million acres to settlers. A similar story prevailed throughout the country.[77]

By the time the allotment process had run its course in 1930, the residue of native landholdings in the United States had been reduced from approximately 150 million acres to less than 50 million.[78] Of this, more than two–thirds consisted of arid or semiarid terrain deemed useless for agriculture, grazing, or other productive purposes. The remaining one–third had been leased at extraordinarily low rates to non–Indian farmers and ranchers by local Indian agents exercising "almost dictatorial powers" over remaining reservation property.[79]

Indians across the country were left in a state of extreme destitution as a result of allotment and attendant leasing practices. Worse, the situation was guaranteed to be exacerbated over succeeding generations insofar as what was left of the reservation land base, already insufficient to support its occupants at a level of mere subsistence, could be foreseen to become steadily more so as the native population recovered from the genocide perpetrated against it during the nineteenth century.[80] A concomitant of allotment was thus an absolute certainty that ever–increasing numbers of Indians would be forced from what remained nominally their own land during the twentieth century and dispersed into the vastly more numerous American society at large. There, it was predictable (and often predicted) that they would be "digested," disappearing once and for all as anything distinctly Indian in terms of socio–cultural, political, or even racial identity. The record shows that such outcomes were anything but unintentional.

The purpose of all this was "assimilation," as federal policymakers described their purpose, or—to put the matter more unabashedly—to bring about the destruction and disappearance of American Indian peoples as such. In the words of Francis E. Leupp, Commissioner of Indian Affairs from 1905 through 1909, the Allotment Act in particular should be viewed as a "mighty pulverizing engine for breaking up the tribal mass" which stood in the way of complete Euroamerican hegemony in North America. Or, to quote Indian Commissioner Charles Burke a decade later, "[I]t is not desirable or consistent with the general welfare to promote tribal characteristics and organization."[81]

The official stance was consecrated in the Supreme Court's determination in the 1903 *Lonewolf v. Hitchcock* decision—extended from Marshall's "domestic dependent nation" thesis of the early 1830s—that the United States possessed "plenary" (full) power over all matters involving Indian affairs. In part, this meant the federal government was unilaterally assigning itself perpetual "trust" prerogatives to administer or dispose of native assets, whether these were vested in land, minerals, cash, or any other medium, regardless of Indian needs or desires.[82] Congress then consolidated its position with passage of the 1906 Burke Act, designating the Secretary of the Interior as permanent trustee over Indian Country. In 1924, a number of loose ends were cleaned up with passage of the Indian Citizenship Act imposing U.S. citizenship upon all native people who had not otherwise been naturalized. The law was applied across the board to all Indians, whether they desired citizenship or not, and thus included those who had forgone allotments rather than accept it.[83]

Meanwhile, the more physical dimensions of assimilationist policy were coupled to a process of ideological conditioning designed to render native children susceptible to dislocation and absorption by the dominant society. In the main, this assumed the form of a compulsory boarding school system administered by the Interior Department's Bureau of Indian Affairs (BIA) wherein large numbers of indigenous children were taken, often forcibly, to facilities remote from their families and communities. Once there, the youngsters were prevented from speaking their languages, practicing their religions, wearing their customary clothing or wearing their hair in traditional fashion, or in any other way overtly associating themselves with their own cultures and traditions. Instead, they were indoctrinated—typically for a decade or more—in Christian doctrine and European values such as the "work ethic." During the summers, they were frequently "farmed out" to Euroamerican "foster homes" where they were further steeped in the dominant society's views of their peoples and themselves.[84]

> Attendance was made compulsory [for all native children, aged five to eighteen] and the agent was made responsible for keeping the schools filled, by persuasion if possible, by withholding rations and annuities from the parents, and by other means if necessary.... [Students] who were guilty of misbehavior might either receive corporal punishment or be imprisoned in the guardhouse [a special "reform school" was established to handle "incorrigible" students who clung to their traditions].... A sincere effort was made to develop the type of school that would destroy tribal ways.[85]

The intention of this was, according to federal policy makers and many of its victims alike, to create generations of American Indian youth who functioned intellectually as "little white people," facilitating the rapid dissolution of traditional native cultures desired by federal policy makers.[86] In combination with a program in which native children were put out for wholesale adoption by Euroamerican families, the effect upon indigenous peoples was devastating.[87] This systematic transfer of children not only served to accelerate the outflow of Indians from reservation and reservation–adjacent settings, but the return of individuals mentally conditioned to conduct themselves as non–Indians escalated the rate at which many native societies unraveled within the reservation contexts themselves.[88]

The effects of the government's allotment and assimilation programs are reflected in the demographic shifts evidenced throughout Indian Country from 1910 through 1950. In the former year, only 0.4 percent of all identified Indians lived in urban locales. By 1930, the total had grown to 9.9 percent. As of 1950, the total had grown to 13.4 percent. Simultaneously, the displacement of native people from reservations to off–reservation rural areas was continuing apace.[89] In 1900, this involved only about 3.5 percent of all Indians. By 1930, the total had swelled to around 12.5 percent, and, by 1950, it had reached nearly 18 percent.[90] Hence, in the latter year, nearly one–third of the federally recognized Indians in the United States had been dispersed to locales other than those the government had defined as being "theirs."

Reorganization and Colonization

It is likely, all things being equal, that the Indian policies with which the United States ushered in the twentieth century would have led inexorably to a complete eradication of the reservation system and corresponding disappearance of American Indians as distinct peoples by some point around 1950. There can be no question but that such a final consolidation of its internal land base would have complemented the phase of transoceanic expansionism into which the United States entered quite unabashedly during the 1890s.[91] That things did not follow this course seems mainly due to a pair of ironies, one geological and the other unwittingly imbedded in the bizarre status of "quasi–sovereignty" increasingly imposed upon native nations by federal jurists and policy makers over the next hundred years.

As regards the first of these twin twists of fate, authorities were becoming increasingly aware by the late 1920s that the "worthless" residue of territory to which indigenous people were consigned was turning out to be extraordinarily endowed with mineral wealth. Already, in 1921, an exploratory team from Standard Oil had come upon what it took to be substantial fossil fuel deposits on the Navajo Reservation.[92] During the next three decades, it would be discovered just how great a proportion of U.S. "domestic" resources lay within American Indian reservations. For example:

Western reservations in particular ... possess vast amounts of coal, oil, shale oil, natural gas, timber, and uranium. More than 40 percent of the national reserves of low sulfur, strippable coal, 80 percent of the nation's uranium reserves, and billions of barrels of shale oil exist on reservation land. On the 15–million–acre Navajo Reservation, there are approximately 100 million barrels of oil, 25 trillion cubic feet of natural gas, 80 million pounds of uranium, and 50 billion tons of coal. The 440,000–acre Northern Cheyenne Reservation in Montana sits atop a 60–foot–thick layer of coal. In New Mexico, geologists estimate that the Jicarilla Apache Reservation possesses 2 trillion cubic feet of natural gas and as much as 154 million barrels of oil. [93]

This led directly to the second quirk. The more sophisticated federal officials, even then experiencing the results of opening up Oklahoma's lush oil fields to unrestrained corporate competition, realized the extent of the disequilibriums and inefficiencies involved in this line of action when weighed against the longer–term needs of U.S. industrial development.[94] Only by retaining its "trust authority" over reservation assets would the government be in a continuing position to dictate which resources would be exploited, in what quantities, by whom, at what cost, and for what purpose, allowing the North American political economy to evolve in ways preferred by the country's financial élite.[95] Consequently, it was quickly perceived as necessary that both Indians and Indian Country be preserved, at least to some extent, as a facade behind which the "socialistic" process of central economic planning might occur.

For the scenario to work in practice, it was vital that the reservations be made to appear "self–governing" enough for them to be exempt from the usual requirements of the U.S. "free market" system whenever this might be convenient to their federal "guardians." On the other hand, they could never become independent or autonomous enough to assume control over their own economic destinies, asserting demands that equitable royalty rates be paid for the extraction of their ores, for example, or that profiting corporations underwrite the expense of environmental clean–up once mining operations had been concluded.[96] In effect, the idea was that many indigenous nations should be maintained as outright internal colonies of the United States rather than being liquidated out–of–hand.[97] All that was needed to accomplish this was the creation of a mechanism through which the illusion of limited Indian self–rule might be extended.

The vehicle for this purpose materialized in 1934, with passage of the Indian Reorganization Act, or "IRA," as it is commonly known. Under provision of this statute, the traditional governing bodies of most indigenous nations were supplanted by "Tribal Councils," the structure of which was devised in Washington, DC, functioning within parameters of formal constitutions written by BIA officials.[98] A democratic veneer was maintained by staging a referendum on each reservation prior to its being reorganized, but federal authorities simply manipulated the outcomes to achieve the desired results.[99] The newly installed IRA councils were patterned much more closely upon the model of corporate boards than of governments, and possessed little power other than to sign off on business agreements. Even at that, they were completely and "voluntarily" subordinated to U.S. interests: "All decisions of any consequence (in thirty–three separate areas of consideration) rendered by these 'tribal councils' were made 'subject to the approval of the Secretary of Interior or his delegate,' the Commissioner of Indian Affairs."[100]

One entirely predictable result of this arrangement has been that an inordinate amount of mining, particularly that related to "energy development," has occurred on Indian reservations since the mid–to–late 1940s. *All* uranium mining and milling during the life of the U.S. Atomic Energy Commission's (AEC's) ore buying program (1954–1981) occurred on reservation land; Anaconda's Jackpile Mine, located at the Laguna Pueblo in New Mexico, was the largest open–pit uranium extraction operation in the world until it was phased out in 1979.[101] Every year, enough power is generated by Arizona's Four Corners Power Plant alone—every bit of it from coal mined at Black Mesa, on the Navajo Reservation—to light the lights of Tucson and Phoenix for two decades, and present plans include a fourfold expansion of Navajo coal production.[102] Throughout the West, the story is the same.

On the face of it, the sheer volume of resource "development" in Indian Country over the past half–century should—even under disadvantageous terms—have translated into *some* sort of "material improvement" in the lot of indigenous people. Yet the mining leases offered to selected corporations by the BIA "on behalf of" their native "wards"—and duly endorsed by the IRA councils—have consistently paid such a meager fraction of prevailing market royalty rates that no such advancement has been discernible. Probably the best terms were those obtained by the Navajo Nation in 1976, a contract paying a royalty of 55 cents per ton for coal; this amounted to 8 percent of market price at a time when Interior Secretary Cecil Andrus admitted the *minimum* rate paid for coal mined in off–reservation settings was 12.5 percent (more typically, it was upwards of 15 percent).[103] Simultaneously, a 17.5 cents per ton royalty was being paid for coal on the Crow Reservation in Montana, a figure which was raised to 40 cents—less than half the market rate—only after years of haggling.[104] What is at issue here is not profit, but the sort of "super–profits" usually associated with U.S. domination of economies elsewhere in the world.[105]

Nor has the federally coordinated corporate exploitation of the reservations translated into wage income for Indians. As of 1989, the government's own data indicated that reservation unemployment nationwide still hovered in the mid–sixtieth percentile, with some locales running persistently in the ninetieth.[106] Most steady jobs involved administering or enforcing the federal order, reservation by reservation. Such "business–related" employment as existed tended to be temporary, menial, and paid the minimum wage, a matter quite reflective of the sort of transient, extractive industry—which brings its cadre of permanent, skilled labor with it—the BIA had encouraged to set up shop in Indian Country.[107] Additionally, the impact of extensive mining and associated activities had done much to disrupt the basis for possible continuation of traditional self–sufficiency occupations, destroying considerable acreage which held potential as grazing or subsistence garden plots.[108] In this sense, U.S. governmental and corporate activities have "underdeveloped" Native North America in classic fashion.[109]

Overall, according to a federal study completed in 1988, reservation–based Indians experienced every indice of extreme impoverishment: by far the lowest annual and lifetime incomes of any North American population group, highest rate of infant mortality (7.5 times the national average), highest rates of death from plague, malnutrition, and exposure, highest rate of teen suicide, and so on. The average life expectancy of a reservation–based Native American male is 44.6 years, that of a female less than three years longer.[110] The situation is much more indicative of a Third World context than of rural areas in a country that claims to be the world's "most advanced industrial state." Indeed, the poignant observation of many Latinos regarding their relationship to the United States, that "your wealth is our poverty," is as appropriate to the archipelago of Indian reservations in North America itself as it is to the South American continent. By any estimation, the "open veins of Native America" created by the IRA have been an incalculable boon to the maturation of the U.S. economy, while Indians continue to pay the price by living in the most grinding sort of poverty.[111]

And there is worse. One of the means used by the government to maximize corporate profits in Indian Country over the years—again rubber–stamped by the IRA councils—has been to omit clauses requiring corporate reclamation of mined lands from leasing instruments. Similarly, the cost of doing business on reservations has been pared to the bone (and profitability driven up) by simply waiving environmental protection standards in most instances.[112] Such practices have spawned ecological catastrophe in many locales. As the impact of the Four Corners plant, one of a dozen coal–fired electrical generation facilities currently "on–line" on the Navajo reservation, has been described elsewhere:

> The five units of the 2,075 megawatt power plant have been churning out city–bound electricity and local pollution since 1969. The plant burns ten tons of coal per minute—five million tons per year—spewing three hundred tons of fly–ash and other waste particulates into the air each day. The black cloud hangs over ten thousand acres of the once–pristine San Juan River Valley. The deadly plume was the only visible evidence of human enterprise as seen from the Gemini–

12 satellite which photographed the earth from 150 miles in space. Less visible, but equally devastating is the fact that since 1968 the coal mining operations and power plant requirements have been extracting 2,700 gallons from the Black Mesa water table each minute—60 million gallons per year—causing extreme desertification of the area, and even the sinking of some ground by as much as twelve feet.[113]

Corporations engaged in uranium mining and milling on the Navajo Reservation and at the Laguna site were also absolved of responsibility by the BIA for cleaning up upon completion of their endeavors, with the result that hundreds of tailings piles were simply abandoned during the 1970s and 1980s.[114] A fine sand retaining about 75 percent of the radioactive content of the original ore, the tailings constitute a massive source of windblown carcinogenic/mutogenic contaminants affecting all persons and livestock residing within a wide radius of each pile.[115] Both ground and surface water have also been heavily contaminated with radioactive by–products throughout the Four Corners region.[116] In the Black Hills region, the situation is much the same.[117] At its Hanford Nuclear Weapons Facility, located on the Yakima Reservation in Washington State, the AEC itself secretly discharged some 440 billion gallons of plutonium, strontium, celsium, tritium, and other high level radioactive contaminants into the local aquifer between 1955 and 1989.[118]

Given that the half–life of the substances involved is as long as 125,000 years, the magnitude of the disaster inflicted upon Native North America by IRA colonialism should not be underestimated. The Los Alamos National Scientific Laboratory observed in its February 1978 *Mini–Report* that the only "solution" its staff could conceive of for the problems presented by wind–blown radioactive contaminants would be "to zone the land into uranium mining and milling districts so as to forbid human habitation." Similarly:

> A National Academy of Sciences (NAS) report states bluntly that [reclamation after any sort of mining] cannot be done in areas with less than 10 inches of rainfall a year; the rainfall over most of the Navajo Nation [and many other western reservations] ranges from six to ten inches a year. The NAS suggests that such areas be spared development or honestly labeled "national sacrifice areas."[119]

Tellingly, the two areas considered most appropriate by the NAS for designation as "national sacrifices"—the Four Corners and Black Hills regions—are those containing the Navajo and "Sioux Complex" of reservations, the largest remaining blocks of acknowledged Indian land and concentrations of land–based indigenous population in the United States. For this reason, many American Indian activists have denounced both the NAS scheme and the process of environmental destruction which led up to it as involving not only National Sacrifice Areas but "National Sacrifice Peoples" as well.[120] At the very least, having the last of their territory zoned "so as to forbid human habitation" would precipitate an ultimate dispersal of each impacted people, causing its disappearance as a "human group" per se.[121] As American Indian Movement leader Russell Means has put it, "It's genocide ... no more, no less."[122]

Regardless of whether a policy of national sacrifice is ever implemented in the manner envisioned by the NAS, it seems fair to observe that the conditions of dire poverty and environmental degradation fostered on Indian reservations by IRA colonialism have contributed heavily to the making of the contemporary native diaspora in the United States. In combination with the constriction of the indigenous land base brought about through earlier policies of removal, concentration, allotment, and assimilation, they have created a strong and ever–increasing pressure upon reservation residents to "cooperate" with other modern federal programs meant to facilitate the outflow and dispersal of Indians from their residual land base. Chief among these have been termination and relocation.

Termination and Relocation

As the IRA method of administering Indian Country took hold, the government returned to such tasks as "trimming the fat" from federal expenditures allocated to support Indians, largely through manipulation of the size and disposition of the recognized indigenous population.

> By 1940, the ... system of colonial governance on American Indian reservations was largely in place. Only the outbreak of World War II slowed the pace of corporate exploitation, a matter that retarded initiation of maximal "development" activities until the early 1950s. By then, the questions concerning federal and corporate planners had become somewhat technical: what to do with those indigenous nations which had refused reorganization? How to remove the portion of Indian population on even the reorganized reservations whose sheer physical presence served as a barrier to wholesale strip mining and other profitable enterprises anticipated by the U.S. business community?[123]

The first means to this end was found in a partial resumption of nineteenth–century assimilationist policies, focused this time on specific peoples, or parts of peoples, rather than upon Indians as a whole. On August 1, 1953, Congress approved House Resolution 108, a measure by which the federal legislature empowered itself to enact statutes "terminating" (that is, withdrawing recognition from, and thus unilaterally dissolving) selected native peoples, typically those which had rejected reorganization, or who lacked the kinds of resources necessitating their maintenance under the IRA.[124]

> Among the [nations] involved were the comparatively large and wealthy Menominee of Wisconsin and the Klamath of Oregon— both owners of extensive timber resources. Also passed were acts to terminate ... the Indians of western Oregon, small Paiute bands in Utah, and the mixed–bloods of the Uintah and Ouray Reservations. Approved, too, was legislation to transfer administrative responsibility for the Alabama and Coushatta Indians to the state of Texas.... Early in the first session of the Eighty–Fourth Congress, bills were submitted to [terminate the] Wyandotte, Ottawa, and Peoria [nations] of Oklahoma. These were enacted early in August of 1956, a month after passage of legislation directing the Colville Confederated Tribes of Washington to come up with a termination plan of their own.... During the second administration of President Dwight D. Eisenhower, Congress enacted three termination bills relating to ... the Choctaw of Oklahoma, for whom the termination process was never completed, the Catawba of South Carolina, and the Indians of the southern California *rancherias.*[125]

It is instructive that the man chosen to implement the policy was Dillon S. Myer, an Indian Commissioner whose only apparent "job qualification" was in having headed up the internment program targeting Japanese Americans during the Second World War.[126] In total, 109 indigenous nations encompassing more than 35,000 people were terminated before the liquidation process had run its course during the early 1960s.[127] Only a handful, like the Menominee and the Siletz of Oregon, were ever "reinstated."[128] Suddenly landless, mostly poor and largely unemployed, they were mostly scattered like sand in the wind.[129] Even as they went, they were joined by a rapidly swelling exodus of people from unterminated reservations, a circumstance fostered by yet another federal program.

Passed in 1956, the "Relocation Act" (P.L. 959) was extended in the face of a steady diminishment throughout the first half of the decade in federal allocations to provide assistance to people living on reservations. The statute provided funding to underwrite the expenses of any Indian agreeing to move to an urban area, establish a residence, and undergo a brief period of job training. The *quid pro quo* was that each person applying for such relocation was required to sign an agreement that s/he would never return to his or her reservation to live. It was also specified that all federal support would be withdrawn after relocatees had spent a short period—often no more than six weeks—"adjusting" to city life.[130] Under the conditions of near–starvation on many reservations, there were many takers; nearly 35,000 people signed up to move to places like Los Angeles, Minneapolis, San Francisco, Chicago, Denver, Phoenix, Seattle, and Boston during the period from 1957 to 1959 alone.[131]

Although there was ample early indication that relocation was bearing disastrous fruit for those who underwent it—all that was happening was that relocatees were exchanging the familiar squalor of reservation life for that of the alien Indian ghettos that shortly emerged in most major cities—the government accelerated the program during the 1960s. Under the impact of termination and relocation during the '50s, the proportion of native people who had been "urbanized" rose dramatically, from 13.5 percent at the beginning of the decade to 27.9 percent at the end. During the sixties, relocation alone drove the figure upwards to 44.5 percent. During the 1970s, the program began to be phased out, and the rate of Indian urbanization decreased sharply, with the result that the proportion had risen to "only" 49 percent by 1980.[132] Even without a formal federal relocation effort on a national scale, the momentum of what had been set in motion over an entire generation carried the number into the mid–fiftieth percentile by 1990, and there is no firm indication the trend is abating.[133]

Despite much protestation to the contrary, those who "migrated" to the cities under the auspices of termination and relocation have already begun to join the legions of others, no longer recognized as Indians even by other Indians, who were previously discarded and forgotten along the torturous route from 1776 to the present.[134] Cut off irrevocably from the centers of their socio–cultural existence, they have increasingly adopted arbitrary and abstract methods to signify their "Indianness." Federally sanctioned "Certificates of Tribal Enrollment" have come to replace tangible participation in the political life of their nations as emblems of membership. Federally issued "Certificates of Degree of Indian Blood" have replaced discernible commitment to Indian interests as the ultimate determinant of identity.[135] In the end, by embracing such "standards," Indians are left knowing no more of being Indian than do non–Indians. The process is a cultural form of what, in the physical arena, has been termed "autogenocide."[136]

Conclusion

The Indian policies undertaken by the United States during the two centuries since its inception appear on the surface to have been varied, even at times contradictory. Openly genocidal at times, they have more often been garbed, however thinly, in the attire of "humanitarianism." In fact, as the matter was put by Alexis de Tocqueville, the great French commentator on the early American experience, it would occasionally have been "impossible to destroy men with more respect to the laws of humanity."[137] Always, however, there was an underlying consistency in the sentiments which begat policy: to bring about the total dispossession and disappearance of North America's indigenous population. It was this fundamental coherence in U.S. aims, invariably denied by responsible scholars and officials alike, which caused Adolf Hitler to ground his own notions of *lebensraumpolitik* ("politics of living space") in the U.S. example.[138]

> Neither Spain nor Britain should be the models of German expansion, but the Nordics of North America, who had ruthlessly pushed aside an inferior race to win for themselves soil and territory for the future. To undertake this essential task, sometimes difficult, always cruel—this was Hitler's version of the White Man's Burden.[139]

As early as 1784, A British observer remarked that the intent of the fledgling United States with regard to American Indians was that of "extirpating them totally from the face of the earth, men, women and children."[140] In 1825, Secretary of State Henry Clay opined that U.S. Indian policy should be predicated on a presumption that the "Indian race" was "destined to extinction" in the face of persistent expansion by "superior" Anglo–Saxon "civilization."[141] During the 1870s, General of the Army Phil Sheridan is known to have called repeatedly for the "complete extermination" of targeted native groups as a means of making the West safe for repopulation by Euroamericans.[142] Subsequent assimilationists demanded the disappearance of any survivors through cultural and genetic absorption by their conquerors.[143] Well into the twentieth century, Euroamerica as a whole typically referred—often hopefully—to indigenous people as "the vanishing race," decimated and ultimately subsumed by the far greater number of invaders who had moved in upon their land.[144]

Many of the worst U.S. practices associated with these sensibilities have long since been suspended (arguably, because their goals were accomplished). Yet, large–scale and deliberate dislocation of native people from their land is anything but an historical relic. Probably the most prominent current example is that of the Big Mountain Diné, perhaps the largest remaining enclave of traditionally oriented Indians in the United States. Situated astride an estimated 24 billion tons of the most accessible low sulfur coal in North America, all 13,000 people in the Big Mountain area are even now being forcibly expelled to make way for the Peabody Corporation's massive shovels. There being no place left on the remainder of the Navajo Reservation in which to accommodate their sheep–herding way of life, the refugees, many of them elderly, are being "resettled" in off–reservation towns like Flagstaff, Arizona.[145] Some have been sent to Phoenix, Denver, and Los Angeles. All suffer extreme trauma and other maladies resulting from the destruction of their community and consequent "transition."[146]

Another salient illustration is that of the Western Shoshone. Mostly resident to a vast expanse of the Nevada Desert secured by their ancestors in the 1863 Treaty of Ruby Valley, the Shoshones have suffered the fate of becoming the "most bombed nation on earth" by virtue of the United States having located the majority of its nuclear weapons testing facilities in the southern portion of their homeland since 1950. During the late seventies, despite its being unable to demonstrate that it had ever acquired valid title to the territory the Shoshones call Newe Segobia, the government began to move into the northern area as well, stating an intent to construct the MX missile system there. While the MX plan has by now been dropped, the Shoshones are still being pushed off their land, "freeing" it for use in such endeavors as nuclear waste dumps like the one scheduled to be built at Yucca Mountain over the next few years.[147]

In Alaska, where nearly 200 indigenous peoples were instantly converted into "village corporations" by the 1971 Alaska Native Claims Settlement Act, there is a distinct possibility that the entire native population of about 22,000 will be displaced by the demands of tourism, North Slope oil development, and other "developmental" enterprises by some point early in the next century. Already, their land base has been constricted to a complex of tiny "townships" and their traditional economy mostly eradicated by the impacts of commercial fishing, whaling, and sealing, as well as the effects of increasing Arctic industrialization on regional caribou herds and other game animals.[148] Moreover, there is a plan—apparently conceived in all seriousness—to divert the waterflow of the Yukon River southward all the way to the Río Grande, an expedient to support continued non–Indian population growth in the arid regions of the "lower 48" states and create the agribusiness complex in the northern Mexican provinces of Sonora and Chihuahua envisioned in a "free trade agreement" proposed by the Bush administration.[149] It seems certain that no traditional indigenous society can be expected to stand up against such an environmental onslaught.

Eventually, if such processes are allowed to run their course, the probability is that a "Final Solution of the Indian Question" will be achieved. The key to this will rest, not in an official return to the pattern of nineteenth–century massacres or emergence of some Auschwitz–style extermination center, but in the erosion of socio–cultural integrity and confusion of identity afflicting any people subjected to conditions of diaspora. Like water flowing from a leaking bucket, the last self–consciously Indian people will pass into oblivion silently, unnoticed and unremarked. The deaths of cultures destroyed by such means usually occur in this fashion, with a faint whimper rather than resistance and screams of agony.

There are, perhaps, glimmers of hope flickering upon the horizon. One of the more promising is the incipient International Convention on the Rights of Indigenous Peoples. Drafted over the past decade by the United Nations Working Group on Indigenous Populations, the instrument was due for submission to the General Assembly during the summer of 1992. It was supposed to be ratified by the latter body in October—the 500th anniversary of the Columbian expedition which unleashed the forces discussed herein. The Convention would at last have extended to native peoples the essential international legal protections enjoyed by their colonizers the world over. Unfortunately, as of 1995, it was still pending.[150] Should it be adhered to by this "nation of laws," the instrument will effectively bar the United States from completing its quietly ongoing drive to obliterate the remains of Native North America. If not—and the United States has historically demonstrated a truly remarkable tendency to simply ignore those elements of international legality it finds inconvenient— the future of American Indians looks exceedingly grim.[151]

Notes

1. U.S. Bureau of the Census, *Report on Indians Taxed and Indians Not Taxed in the United States* [except Alaska] *at the Eleventh United States Census: 1890* (Washington, DC: U.S. Government Printing Office, 1894), pp. 637–38.

2. Texts of 371 ratified treaties may be found in Charles J. Kappler, comp., *Indian Treaties, 1778–1883* (New York: Interland Publishing [2d ed.], 1973).

3. U.S. Bureau of the Census, *1980 Census of the Population, Vol. I: Characteristics of the Population*, Table 69, "Persons by Race and Sex for Areas and Places: 1980" (Washington, DC: U.S. Government Printing Office, 1983), pp. 201–12.

4. National Congress of the American Indian (NCAI) Briefing Paper (Washington, DC: NCAI, Apr. 1991).

5. *See* Jack D. Forbes, "Undercounting Native Americans: The 1980 Census and Manipulation of Racial Identity in the United States," *Wicazo Sa Review*, Vol. VI, No. 1 (Spring 1990), pp. 2–26.

6. U.S. Bureau of the Census, *1980 Census of the Population, Supplementary Report: American Indian Areas and Alaska Native Villages, 1980* (Washington, DC: U.S. Government Printing Office, PC80–S1–13, 1984), p. 24.

7. Ibid., Table I, p. 14.

8. Henry F. Dobyns, *Their Numbers Become Thinned: Native American Population Dynamics in Eastern North America* (Knoxville: University of Tennessee Press, 1983), p. 41.

9. Francis Paul Prucha, *Atlas of American Indian Affairs* (Lincoln: University of Nebraska Press, 1990), pp. 151–57.

10. U.S. Bureau of the Census, *1980 Census of the Population, Supplementary Report*, Table I, op. cit. The American Indian population reported for Hawai'i in 1980 was 2,655.

11. Reginald Horsman, *Expansion and American Indian Policy, 1783–1812* (Ann Arbor: University of Michigan Press, 1967), pp. 6–7.

12. *See* Thomas Perkins Abernathy, *Western Lands and the American Revolution* (Albuquerque: University of New Mexico Press, 1979).

13. The complete text of the 1783 Treaty of Paris may be found in Hunter Miller, ed., *Treaties and Other International Acts of the United States of America* (Washington, DC: U.S. Government Printing Office, 1931), pp. 151–57.

14. This interpretation corresponds to conventional understandings of contemporaneous international law ("Discovery Doctrine"). *See* Robert A. Williams, Jr., *The American Indian in Western Legal Thought: The Discourses of Conquest* (London/New York: Oxford University Press, 1990).

15. Reflections on initial U.S. stature as a legal pariah are more fully developed in Vine Deloria, Jr., "Sovereignty," in *Economic Development in American Indian Reservations*, Roxanne Dunbar Ortiz and Larry Emerson, eds. (Albuquerque: Native American Studies Center, University of New Mexico, 1979).

16. On the Northwest Territory, *see* Randolph C. Downes, *Council Fires on the Upper Ohio: A Narrative of Indian Affairs on the Upper Ohio Until 1795* (Pittsburgh: University of Pittsburgh Press, 1940). On the situation further south, *see* R. S. Cotterill, *The Southern Indians: The Story of the Five Civilized Tribes Before Removal* (Norman: University of Oklahoma Press, 1954).

17. A. L. Burt, *The United States, Great Britain, and British North America, from the Revolution to the Establishment of Peace After the War of 1812* (New Haven, Connecticut: Yale University Press, 1940), pp. 82–105.

18. Arthur P. Whitaker, *The Spanish–American Frontier, 1783–1795* (Boston: self–published, 1927). *See* also John W. Caughey, *McGillivray of the Creeks* (Norman: University of Oklahoma Press, 1938).

19. David R. Edmunds, *Tecumseh and the Quest for Indian Leadership* (Boston: Little, Brown, & Co., 1984).

20. Reginald Horsman, op. cit., p. 7.

21. Letter from Schuyler to Congress, July 29, 1783, in *Papers of the Continental Congress, 1774–1789* (Washington, DC: National Archives, Item 153, III), pp. 601–07.

22. Letter from Washington to James Duane, September 7, 1783, in *The Writings of George Washington from Original Manuscript Sources, 1745–1799*, John C. Fitzpatrick, ed. (Washington, DC: U.S. Government Printing Office, 1931–1944, Vol. XXVII), pp. 133–40.

23. Northwest Ordinance (1 *Stat.* 50). In actuality, legitimate Conquest Rights never had bearing on the U.S. relationship to indigenous nations, exercise of such rights being restricted to the very confined parameters of what was at the time defined as being prosecution of a "Just War." For details, *see* Robert A. Williams, Jr., op. cit.

24. For analysis, *see* Bernard W. Sheehan, *Seeds of Extinction: Jeffersonian Philanthropy and the American Indian* (Chapel Hill: University of North Carolina Press, 1973).

25. Quoted from "Report and Resolutions of October 15, 1783," *Journals of the Continental Congress, Vol. XXV* (Washington, DC: U.S. Government Printing Office, n.d.), pp. 681–93.

26. The idea accords quite perfectly with George Washington's notion that all eastern Indians should be pushed into the "illimitable regions of the West," meaning what was then Spanish territory beyond the Mississippi (letter from Washington to Congress, June 17, 1783, in John C. Fitzpatrick, ed., op. cit., pp. 17–18). In reality, however, the United States understood that it possessed no lawful right to unilaterally dispose of the territory in question in this or any other fashion. In purchasing the rights of France (which had gained them from Spain in 1800) to "Louisiana" in 1803, the United States plainly acknowledged indigenous land title in its pledge to Napoleon Bonaparte that it would respect native "enjoyment of their liberty, property and religion they profess." Hence, the United States admitted it was not purchasing land from France, but rather a monopolistic French right within the region to acquire title over specific areas through the negotiated consent of individual Indian nations.

27. *Fletcher v. Peck* (10 U.S. 87). Further elaboration on the implications of the cases mentioned herein may be found in Ward Churchill, "Perversions of Justice: Examining the Doctrine of U.S. Rights to Occupancy in North America," in *Struggle for the Land: Indigenous Resistance to Genocide, Ecocide and Expropriation in Contemporary North America* (Monroe, Maine: Common Courage Press, 1992). It should be noted here, however, that Chief Justice Marshall was hardly a disinterested party in the issue he addressed in *Peck*. Both the Chief Justice and his father were holders of the deeds to 10,000–acre parcels in present–day West Virginia, awarded for services rendered during the revolution but falling within an area never ceded by its aboriginal owners. *See* L. Baker, *John Marshall: A Life in Law* (New York: Macmillan Publishing Co., 1963), p. 80.

28. On the War of 1812, *see* Sidney Lens, *The Forging of the American Empire* (New York: Thomas Y. Crowell Co., 1971), pp. 40–61. On Tecumseh, *see* John Sugden, *Tecumseh's Last Stand* (Norman: University of Oklahoma Press, 1985). On the Redsticks, *see* Joel W. Martin, *Sacred Revolt: The Muskogees' Struggle for a New World* (Boston: Beacon Press, 1991).

29. C. C. Griffin, *The United States and the Disruption of the Spanish Empire, 1810–1822* (New York: Columbia University Press, 1937).

30. Edwin C. McReynolds, *The Seminoles* (Norman: University of Oklahoma Press, 1957).

31. *Johnson v. McIntosh* (21 U.S. 98 Wheat. 543). For information on President Monroe's doctrine, *see* Frederick Merk, *The Monroe Doctrine and American Expansionism* (New York: Alfred A. Knopf Publishers, 1967). *See* also Albert K. Weinberg, *Manifest Destiny* (New York: Quadrangle Books, 1963), pp. 73–89.

32. *See* the Indian Removal Act (Ch. 148, 4 *Stat.* 411); *Cherokee v. Georgia* (30 U.S. [5 Pet.] 1 [1831]); and *Worcester v. Georgia* (31 U.S. [6 Pet.] 551 [1832]). This was the ultimate in playing both ends against the judicial middle. Thereafter, Indians could always be construed as sovereign for purposes of alienating their lands to the United States, thus validating U.S. title to territory it desired, but never sovereign enough to refuse federal demands. *See* generally, Vine Deloria, Jr., and Clifford M. Lytle, *American Indians, American Justice* (Austin: University of Texas Press, 1983).

33. *See* generally, Grant Foreman, *Advancing the Frontier, 1830–1860* (Norman: University of Oklahoma Press, 1933).

34. Gloria Jahoda, *The Trail of Tears: The Story of the American Indian Removals, 1813–1855* (New York: Holt, Rinehart & Winston, Inc., 1975). *See* also Grant Foreman, *Indian Removal: The Immigration of the Five Civilized Tribes* (Norman: University of Oklahoma Press, 1953).

35. Driven from Illinois, the main body of Sauks were trapped and massacred—men, women, and children alike—at the juncture of the Bad Axe and Mississippi Rivers in Wisconsin. *See* Cecil Eby, *"That Disgraceful Affair": The Black Hawk War* (New York: W. W. Norton, 1973), pp. 243–61.

36. In many ways, the Seminole "holdouts" were the best guerrilla fighters the United States ever faced. The commitment of 30,000 troops for several years was insufficient to subdue them. Ultimately, the United States broke off the conflict, which was stalemated, and which was costing several thousand dollars for each Indian killed. *See* Fairfax Downey, *Indian Wars of the United States Army, 1776–1865* (New York: Doubleday Publishers, 1963), pp. 116–17.

37. Wilcomb E. Washburn, *The Indian in America* (New York: Harper Torchbooks, 1975), p. 169.

38. Russell Thornton, "Cherokee Losses During the Trail of Tears: A New Perspective and a New Estimate," *Ethnohistory*, No. 31 (1984), pp. 289–300.

39. Ibid., p. 293.

40. U.S. Bureau of the Census, *1980 Census of the Population, Supplementary Report*, op. cit.

41. Duane H. King, *The Cherokee Nation: A Troubled History* (Knoxville: University of Tennessee Press, 1979), pp. 103–09.

42. Angie Debo, *A History of the Indians of the United States* (Norman: University of Oklahoma Press, 1977), p. 157.

43. Very little work has been done to document this proliferation of communities, although their existence has been increasingly admitted since the 1960s.

44. Marquis James, *Andrew Jackson: Border Ruffian* (New York: Grossett and Dunlap Publishers, 1933). Jackson's stated goal was not simply to defeat the Redsticks, but to "exterminate" them. At least 557 Indians, many of them noncombatants, were killed after being surrounded at the Horseshoe Bend of the Tallapoosa River, in northern Alabama.

45. The text of Jackson's talk of March 23, 1829, was originally published in *Documents and Proceedings Relating to the Formation and Progress of a Board in the City of New York, for the Emigration, Preservation, and Improvement of the Aborigines of America* (New York: Indian Board for the Emigration, Preservation, and Improvement of the Aborigines of America, 1829), p. 5.

46. Frederick Merk, *Manifest Destiny and Mission in American History* (New York: Alfred A. Knopf, 1963).

47. Quoted in Sidney Lens, op. cit., p. 100.

48. Actually, this transcontinental gallop represents a rather reserved script. As early as 1820, Luis de Onis, former Spanish governor of Florida, observed that, "The Americans ... believe that their dominion is destined to extend, now to the Isthmus of Panama, and hereafter over all the regions of the New World.... They consider themselves superior to the rest of mankind, and look upon their republic as the only establishment upon earth founded on a grand and solid basis, embellished by wisdom, and destined one day to become the sublime colossus of human power, and the wonder of the universe (quoted in Sidney Lens, op. cit., pp. 94–95). It is a matter of record that William Henry Seward, Secretary of State under Lincoln and Johnson in the 1860s, advanced a serious plan to annex all of Canada west of Ontario, but was ultimately forced to content himself with acquiring Alaska Territory. *See* R. W. Van Alstyne, The Rising American Empire (London/New York: Oxford University Press, 1960).

49. A map delineating the "permanent" territories assigned these peoples after removal is contained in Jack D. Forbes, *Atlas of Native History* (Davis, California: D–Q University Press, n.d.).

50. The federal government recognizes less than half (32) of these nations as still existing; *see* Map 76 in John W. Morris, Charles R. Goins, and Edward C. McReynolds, *Historical Atlas of Oklahoma* (Norman: University of Oklahoma Press [3d ed.], 1986).

51. According to the U.S. Bureau of the Census, *1980 Census of the Population, Supplementary Report* (Table I, op. cit.), Oklahoma's Indian population of 169,292 is second only to California's 198,275. The Osage Reservation evidences a population of 4,749 Indians, 12.1 percent of its 39,327 total inhabitants (ibid., p. 22).

52. On the war with Mexico, *see* George Pierce Garrison, *Westward Expansion, 1841–1850* (New York: Harper, 1937).

53. David Svaldi, *Sand Creek and the Rhetoric of Extermination: A Case–Study in Indian–White Relations* (Washington, DC: University Press of America, 1989).

54. Much of this is covered in Ralph K. Andrist, *The Long Death: The Last Days of the Plains Indians* (New York: Collier Books, 1964). *See* also Paul Andrew Hutton, *Phil Sheridan and His Army* (Lincoln: University of Nebraska Press, 1985).

55. L. R. Bailey, *The Long Walk: A History of the Navajo Wars, 1846–68* (Pasadena, California: Westernlore Publications, 1978).

56. This episode is covered adequately in Edward Lazarus, *Black Hills, White Justice: The Sioux Nation Versus the United States, 1775 to the Present* (New York: Harper Collins, 1991), pp. 71–95.

57. *See* Robert Clark, ed., *The Killing of Chief Crazy Horse* (Lincoln: University of Nebraska Press, 1976), and the concluding chapter of Stanley Vestal's *Sitting Bull: Champion of the Sioux* (Norman: University of Oklahoma Press, 1957).

58. The imprisonment program is described in some detail in the memoirs of the commandant of Marion Prison, later superintendent of the Carlisle Indian School. *See* Richard Henry Pratt, *Battlefield and Classroom: Four Decades with the American Indian, 1867–1904* (New Haven, Connecticut: Yale University Press [reprint], 1964).

59. U.S. Bureau of the Census, *Report on Indians Taxed and Indians Not Taxed*, op. cit., pp. 637–38.

60. Edward Lazarus, op. cit., p. 29. It should be noted that, contrary to myth, scalping was a practice introduced to the Americas by Europeans, not native people. It was imported by the British—who had previously used it against the Irish—during the seventeenth century. *See* Nicholis P. Canny, "The Ideology of English Colonialism: From Ireland to America," *William and Mary Quarterly*, 3d Series, Vol. 30 (1973), pp. 575–98.

61. Lenore A. Stiffarm and Phil Lane, Jr., "The Demography of Native North America: A Question of American Indian Survival," in *The State of Native America: Genocide, Colonization and Resistance*, M. Annette Jaimes, ed. (Boston: South End Press, 1992), p. 35. It is instructive that the Texas state legislature framed its Indian policy as follows: "We recognize no title in the Indian tribes resident within the limits of the state to any portion of the soil thereof; and ... we recognize no right of the Government of the United States to make any treaty of limits with the said Indian tribes without the consent of the Government of this state" (quoted in Wilcomb E. Washburn, op. cit., p. 174). In other words, the intention was extermination.

62. James M. Mooney, "Population," in *Handbook of the Indians North of Mexico, Vol. 2*, Frederick W. Dodge, ed. (Washington, DC: Bureau of American Ethnology, Bulletin No. 30, Smithsonian Institution, 1910), pp. 286–87.

63. Sherburn F. Cook, *The Conflict Between the California Indian and White Civilization* (Berkeley: University of California Press, 1976), pp. 282–84.

64. Russell Thornton, *American Indian Holocaust and Survival: A Population History Since 1492* (Norman: University of Oklahoma Press, 1987), p. 49.

65. Russell Thornton (ibid.) estimates the aboriginal North American population to have been about 12.5 million, most of it within what is now the continental United States. Henry F. Dobyns (op. cit.) estimates it as having been as high as 18.5 million. Kirkpatrick Sale, in his *The Conquest of Paradise: Christopher Columbus and the Columbian Legacy* (New York: Alfred A. Knopf, 1990), splits the difference, placing the figure at 15 million. Extreme attrition due to disease and colonial warfare had already occurred prior to the American War of Independence. Something on the order of 2 million survivors in 1776 therefore seems a

reasonable estimate. Whatever the exact number in that year, it had been reduced to 237,196 according to U.S. census data for 1900. *See* U.S. Bureau of the Census, *Fifteenth Census of the United States, 1930: The Indian Population of the United States and Alaska*, Table 2, "Indian Population by State, 1890–1930" (Washington, DC: U.S. Government Printing Office, Washington, 1937), p. 3.

66. Sherburn F. Cook, op. cit., p. 284.

67. Donald J. Berthrong, *The Cheyenne and Arapaho Ordeal: Reservation and Agency Life in the Indian Territory, 1875–1907* (Norman: University of Oklahoma Press, 1976). *See* also Mari Sandoz, *Cheyenne Autumn* (New York: Avon Books, 1964).

68. Dan L. Thrapp, *The Conquest of Apacheria* (Norman: University of Oklahoma Press, 1967).

69. Merril Beal, *I Will Fight No More Forever: Chief Joseph and the Nez Percé War* (Seattle: University of Washington Press, 1963).

70. Kenneth Carley, *The Sioux Uprising of 1862* (St. Paul: Minnesota Historical Society, 1961).

71. Edmund Wilson, *Apology to the Iroquois* (New York: Farrar, Strauss, and Cudahy, 1960).

72. As of 1980, a grand total of 582 members of these amalgamated peoples were reported as living on the Stockbridge Reservation. *See* U.S. Bureau of the Census, *1980 Census of the Population, Supplementary Report*, Table I, op. cit.

73. The rider to the annual congressional appropriations act can be found at Ch. 120, 16 *Stat.* 544, 566; *See* also the Major Crimes Act (Ch. 341, 24 *Stat.* 362, 385) and *U.S. v. Kagama* (118 U.S. 375 [1886]). The next major leap in this direction was passage of the Assimilative Crimes Act (30 *Stat.* 717) in 1898, applying state, territorial, and district criminal codes to "federal enclaves" such as Indian reservations. *See* generally, Robert N. Clinton, "Development of Criminal Jurisdiction on Reservations: A Journey Through a Jurisdictional Maze," *Arizona Law Review*, Vol. 18, No. 3 (1976), pp. 503–83.

74. General Allotment Act (Ch. 119, 24 *Stat.* 388). Overall, *see* Janet A. McDonnell, *The Dispossession of the American Indian, 1887–1934* (Bloomington/Indianapolis: Indiana University Press, 1991).

75. As is stated in the current procedures for enrollment provided by the Cherokee Nation of Oklahoma, "Many descendants of the Cherokee Indians can neither be certified nor qualify for tribal membership in the Cherokee Nation because their ancestors were not enrolled during the final enrollment [during allotment, 1899–1906]. Unfortunately, these ancestors did not meet the [federal] requirements for the final enrollment. The requirements at the time were ... having a permanent residence within the Cherokee Nation (now the 14 northeastern counties of Oklahoma). If the ancestors had ... settled in the states of Arkansas, Kansas, Missouri, or Texas, they lost their citizenship within the Cherokee Nation at that time."

76. D. S. Otis, *The Dawes Act and the Allotment of Indian Land* (Norman: University of Oklahoma Press, 1973).

77. James S. Olson and Raymond Wilson, *Native Americans in the Twentieth Century* (Urbana: University of Illinois Press, 1984), pp. 82–83.

78. Kirk Kicking Bird and Karen Ducheneaux, *One Hundred Million Acres* (New York: Macmillan Publishing Co., 1973).

79. The powers of individual agents in this regard accrued from an amendment (26 *Stat.* 794) made in 1891. The language describing these powers comes from Vine Deloria, Jr., and Clifford M. Lytle, op. cit., p. 10.

80. This is known as the "Heirship Problem," meaning that if a family head with four children began with a 160–acre parcel of marginal land in 1900, his/her heirs would each inherit 40 acres somewhere around 1920. If each of these heirs, in turn, had four children, then their heirs would inherit 10 acres, circa 1940. Following the same formula, their heirs would have inherited 2.5 acres each in 1960, and their heirs would have received about one–half an acre each in 1980. In actuality, many twentieth–century families have been much larger during the twentieth century—as is common among peoples recovering from genocide—and contemporary descendants of the original allottees often find themselves measuring their "holdings" in square inches. For a fuller discussion of the issue, and a description of the material circumstances otherwise confronting Indians during the early twentieth century, *see* the opening chapters of Vine Deloria, Jr., and Clifford M. Lytle, *The Nations Within: The Past and Future of American Indian Sovereignty* (New York: Pantheon Books, 1984).

81. Rebecca L. Robbins, "Self–Determination and Subordination: The Past, Present and Future of American Indian Governance," in *The State of Native America*, op. cit., p. 93. The quote from Leupp comes from his book, *The Indian and His Problem* (New York: Charles Scribner and Sons, Publishers, 1910), p. 93; that from Burke from a letter to William Williamson on September 16, 1921 (William Williamson Papers, Box 2, File—Indian Matters, Misc., I. D. Weeks Library, University of South Dakota).

82. *Lonewolf v. Hitchcock* (187 U.S. 553); among other things, the decision meant that the United States had decided it could unilaterally absolve itself of any obligation or responsibility it had incurred under provision of any treaty with any indigenous nation while simultaneously considering the Indians to still be bound by *their* treaty commitments. *See* Ann Laquer Estin, *"Lonewolf v. Hitchcock*: The Long Shadow," in *The Aggressions of Civilization: Federal Indian Policy Since the 1880s*, Sandra L. Cadwallader and Vine Deloria, Jr., eds. (Philadelphia: Temple University Press, 1984), pp. 215–45. This was an utterly illegitimate posture under international custom and convention at the time, a matter amply reflected in contemporary international black letter law. *See* Sir Ian Sinclair, *The Vienna Convention on the Law of Treaties* (Manchester: Manchester University Press [2d ed.], 1984).

83. *See* the Burke Act (34 *Stat.* 182) and the Indian Citizenship Act (Ch. 233, 43 *Stat.* 25), as well as Vine Deloria, Jr., and Clifford M. Lyte, *American Indians, American Justice* (Austin: University of Texas Press, 1983).

84. Much of this is covered—proudly—in Richard Henry Pratt, op. cit. *See* also Estelle Fuchs and Robert J. Havighurst, *To Live on This Earth: American Indian Education* (Garden City, New York: Anchor Books, 1973).

85. Evelyn C. Adams, *American Indian Education: Government Schools and Economic Progress* (Morningside Heights, New York: King's Crown Press, 1946), pp. 55–56, 70.

86. The phrase used was picked up by the author in a 1979 conversation with Floyd Red Crow Westerman, a Sisseton Dakota who was sent to a boarding school at age six. For a broader statement of the same theme, *see* Vine Deloria, Jr., "Education and Imperialism," *Integrateducation*, Vol. XIX, Nos. 1–2 (Jan. 1982), pp. 58–63. For ample citation of the federal view, *see* J. U. Ogbu, "Cultural Discontinuities and Schooling," *Anthropology and Education Quarterly*, Vol. 12, No. 4 (1982), pp. 1–10.

87. On adoption policies, including those pertaining to so–called blind adoptions (where children are prevented by law from ever learning their parents' or tribe's identities), *see* Tillie Blackbear Walker, "American Indian Children: Foster Care and Adoptions," in

Conference on Educational and Occupational Needs of American Indian Women, U.S. Office of Education, Office of Educational Research and Development, National Institute of Education (Washington, DC: U.S. Government Printing Office, 1980), pp. 185–210.

88. The entire program involving forced transfer of Indian children is contrary to Article II (d) of the United Nations 1948 Convention on Punishment and Prevention of the Crime of Genocide. *See* Ian Brownlie, *Basic Documents on Human Rights* (Oxford: Clarendon Press, 1982), p. 32.

89. Russell Thornton, *American Indian Holocaust*, op. cit., p. 227.

90. These estimates have been arrived at by deducting the reservation population totals from the overall census figures deployed in Francis Paul Prucha (op. cit.), and then subtracting the urban population totals used by Russell Thornton, op. cit., p. 227.

91. The United States, as is well known, undertook the Spanish–American War in 1898 primarily to acquire oversees colonies, notably the Philippines and Cuba (for which Puerto Rico was substituted at the last moment). It also took the opportunity to usurp the government of Hawai'i, about which it had been expressing ambitions since 1867, and to obtain a piece of Samoa in 1899. This opened the door to its assuming "protectorate" responsibility over Guam and other German colonies after World War I, and many of the Micronesian possessions of Japan after World War II. *See* Julius Pratt, *The Expansionists of 1898* (Baltimore: Johns Hopkins University Press, 1936). *See* also Richard O'Connor, *Pacific Destiny: An Informal History of the U.S. in the Far East, 1776–1968* (Boston: Little, Brown & Co., Inc., 1969).

92. Anita Parlow, *Cry, Sacred Ground: Big Mountain, USA* (Washington, DC: Christic Institute, 1988), p. 30.

93. James S. Olson and Raymond Wilson, op. cit., p. 181.

94. For a good overview, *see* Craig H. Miner, *The Corporation and the Indian: Tribal Sovereignty and Industrial Civilization in Indian Territory, 1865–1907* (Columbia: University of Missouri Press, 1976).

95. This is brought out in thinly veiled fashion in official studies commissioned at the time. *See*, for example, U.S. House of Representatives, Committee of One Hundred, *The Indian Problem: Resolution of the Committee of One Hundred Appointed by the Secretary of Interior and Review of the Indian Problem* (Washington, DC: H. Doc. 149, Ser. 8392, 68th Cong., 1st Sess., 1925). *See* also Lewis Meriam et al., *The Problem of Indian Administration* (Baltimore: Johns Hopkins University Press, 1928).

96. This was standard colonialist practice during the same period. *See* Mark Frank Lindsey, *The Acquisition and Government of Backward Territory in International Law* (London: Longmans Green, 1926).

97. For what may be the first application of the term "internal colonies" to analysis of the situation of American Indians in the United States, *see* Robert K. Thomas, "Colonialism: Classic and Internal," *New University Thought*, Vol. 4, No. 4 (Winter 1966–67).

98. Indian Reorganization Act (Ch. 576, 48 *Stat.* 948); for the best account of how the IRA "package" was assembled, *see* the relevant chapters of Vine Deloria, Jr., and Clifford M. Lytle, *The Nations Within*, op. cit.

99. The classic example of this occurred at the Hopi Reservation, where some 85 percent of all eligible voters actively boycotted the IRA referendum in 1936. Indian Commissioner John Collier then counted these abstentions as "aye" votes, making it appear as if the Hopis had been nearly unanimous in affirming reorganization rather than overwhelmingly rejecting it. *See* Oliver LaFarge, *Running Narrative of the Organization of the Hopi Tribe of Indians*

(unpublished manuscript in the LaFarge Collection, University of Texas at Austin). In general, the IRA referendum process was similar to—and served essentially the same purpose as—those more recently orchestrated abroad by the State Department and CIA; *see* Edward S. Herman and Frank Brodhead, *Demonstration Elections: U.S.–Staged Elections in the Dominican Republic, Vietnam, and El Salvador* (Boston: South End Press, 1984).

100. Rebecca L. Robbins, op. cit., p. 95.

101. *See* generally, Ward Churchill and Winona LaDuke, "Native America: The Political Economy of Radioactive Colonization," in *Critical Issurs in Native North America*, Vol. II (Copengagen: IWGIA Doc. 63, 1991), pp. 71–106. *See* also "The Earth Is Our Mother," included in this book.

102. Alvin Josephy, "Murder of the Southwest," *Audubon Magazine* (Sept. 1971), p. 42.

103. Bruce Johansen and Roberto Maestas, *Wasi'chu: The Continuing Indian Wars* (New York: Monthly Review Press, 1979), p. 162. The minimum rate was established by the Federal Coal Leasing Act of 1975, applicable everywhere in the United States except Indian reservations.

104. James S. Olson and Raymond Wilson, op. cit., p. 200.

105. The term "super–profits" is used in the manner defined by Richard J. Barnet and Ronald E. Müller in their *Global Reach: The Power of the Multinational Corporations* (New York: Touchstone Books, 1974).

106. U.S. Department of the Interior, Bureau of Indian Affairs, *Indian Service Population and Labor Force Estimates* (Washington, DC: U.S. Government Printing Office, 1989). The study shows one–third of the 635,000 reservation–based Indians surveyed had an annual income of less than $7,000.

107. U.S. Senate, Committee on Labor and Human Resources, *Guaranteed Job Opportunity Act: Hearing on S. 777* (Washington, DC: 100th Cong., 1st Sess., 23 Mar. 1987, Appendix A).

108. The classic image of this is that of Emma Yazzie, an elderly and very traditional Diné who subsists on her flock of sheep, standing forlornly before a gigantic Peabody coal shovel which is digging up her scrubby grazing land on Black Mesa. The coal is to produce electricity for Phoenix and Las Vegas, but Yazzie has never had electricity (or running water) in her home. She gains nothing from the enterprise. To the contrary, her very way of life is being destroyed before her eyes. *See* Bruce Johansen and Roberto Maestas, op. cit., p. 141.

109. The term "underdevelopment" is used in the sense defined by André Gunder Frank in his *Capitalism and Underdevelopment in Latin America* (New York: Monthly Review Press, 1967).

110. U.S. Bureau of the Census, *A Statistical Profile of the American Indian Population* (Washington, DC: U.S. Government Printing Office, 1984). *See* also U.S. Department of Health and Human Services, *Chart Series Book* (Washington, DC: Public Health Service HE20.9409.988, 1988).

111. The terminology accrues from Eduardo Galeano, *The Open Veins of Latin America: Five Centuries of the Pillage of a Continent* (New York: Monthly Review Press, 1973).

112. Thus far, the only people who have been able to turn this around have been the Northern Cheyenne, who won a 1976 lawsuit to have Class I environmental protection standards applied to their reservation, thereby halting construction of two coal–fired generating plants before it began. The BIA had already waived such protections on the Cheyennes' "behalf." *See* Bruce Johansen and Roberto Maestas, op. cit., p. 174.

113. Rex Weyler, *Blood of the Land: The U.S. Government and Corporate War Against the American Indian Movement* (New York: Everest House Publishers, 1982), pp. 154–55.

114. Tom Barry, "Bury My Lungs at Red Rock," *The Progressive* (Feb. 1979), pp. 197–99.

115. On tailings and associated problems such as radon gas emissions, *see* J. B. Sorenson, *Radiation Issues: Government Decision Making and Uranium Expansion in Northern New Mexico* (Albuquerque: San Juan Regional Study Group, Working Paper 14, 1978). On carcinogenic/mutogenic effects, *see* J. M. Samet et al., "Uranium Mining and Lung Cancer in Navajo Men," *New England Journal of Medicine*, No. 310 (1984), pp. 1481–484. *See* also Harold Tso and Laura Mangum Shields, "Navajo Mining Operations: Early Hazards and Recent Interventions," *New Mexico Journal of Science*, Vol. 20, No. 1 (June 1980).

116. Richard Hoppe, "A stretch of desert along Route 66—the Grants Belt—is chief locale for U.S. uranium," *Engineering and Mining Journal* (Nov. 1978). *See* also Nancy J. Owens, "Can Tribes Control Energy Development?" in *American Indians and Energy Development*, Joseph Jorgenson, ed. (Cambridge, Massachusetts: Anthropology Resource Center, 1978).

117. Amelia Irvin, "Energy Development and the Effects of Mining on the Lakota Nation," *Journal of Ethnic Studies*, Vol. 10, No. 2 (Spring 1982).

118. Elouise Schumacher, "440 Billion Gallons: Hanford Wastes Would Fill 900 King Domes," *Seattle Times* (13 Apr. 1991).

119. Bruce Johansen and Roberto Maestas, op. cit., p. 154. They are referring to Thadis Box et al., *Rehabilitation Potential for Western Coal Lands* (Cambridge, Massachusetts: Ballinger Publishing Co., 1974). The book is the published version of a study commissioned by the National Academy of Sciences and submitted to the Nixon administration in 1972.

120. Russell Means, "Fighting Words on the Future of Mother Earth," *Mother Jones* (Dec. 1980), p. 27.

121. Bringing about the destruction of an identifiable "human racial, ethnical or racial group" as such, is and always has been the defining criterion of genocide. As the matter was framed by Raphael Lemkin, who coined the term: "Generally speaking, genocide does not necessarily mean the immediate destruction of a nation, *except when* accomplished by mass killing of all the members of a nation. It is intended rather to signify a coordinated plan of different actions aimed at destruction of the essential foundations of the life of national groups, with the aim of annihilating the groups themselves. The objective of such a plan would be disintegration of the political and social institutions, of culture, language, national feelings, religion, and the economic existence of national groups, and the destruction of personal security, liberty, health, dignity, and the lives of individuals belonging to such groups. Genocide is the destruction of the national group as an entity, and the actions involved are directed against individuals, not in their individual capacity but as members of the national group" (emphasis added); *see* Raphael Lemkin, *Axis Rule in Occupied Europe* (Concord, New Hampshire: Carnegie Endowment for International Peace/Rumford Press, 1944), p. 79. The view is reflected in the 1948 Convention on Punishment and Prevention of the Crime of Genocide; *see* Ian Brownlie, op. cit.

122. Russell Means, op. cit.

123. Rebecca L. Robbins, op. cit., p. 97.

124. The complete text of House Resolution 108 appears in Part II of Edward H. Spicer's *A Short History of the United States* (New York: Van Nostrum Publishers, 1968).

125. James E. Officer, "Termination as Federal Policy: An Overview," in *Indian Self–Rule: First–Hand Accounts of Indian–White Relations from Roosevelt to Reagan*, Kenneth R. Philp, ed. (Salt Lake City: Howe Brothers, 1986), p. 125.

126. Richard Drinnon, *Keeper of Concentration Camps: Dillon S. Myer and American Racism* (Berkeley: University of California Press, 1987).

127. Raymond V. Butler, "The Bureau of Indian Affairs Activities Since 1945," *Annals of the American Academy of Political and Social Science*, No. 436 (1978), pp. 50–60. The last dissolution, that of the Oklahoma Ponca, was delayed in committee and was not consummated until 1966.

128. *See* generally, Nicholas Peroff, *Menominee DRUMS: Tribal Termination and Restoration, 1954–1974* (Norman: University of Oklahoma Press, 1982).

129. Oliver LaFarge, "Termination of Federal Supervision: Disintegration and the American Indian," *Annals of the American Academy of Political and Social Science*, No. 311 (May 1975), pp. 56–70.

130. *See* generally, Donald L. Fixico, *Termination and Relocation: Federal Indian Policy, 1945–1960* (Albuquerque: University of New Mexico Press, 1986).

131. Sharon O'Brien, *American Indian Tribal Governments* (Norman: University of Oklahoma Press, 1989), p. 86.

132. U.S. Bureau of the Census, *General Social and Economic Characteristics: United States Summary* (Washington, DC: U.S. Government Printing Office, 1983), p. 92. *See* also Russell Thornton, *American Indian Holocaust*, op. cit., p. 227.

133. NCAI Briefing Paper, op. cit.

134. For use of the term "migration" to describe the effects of termination and relocation, *see* James H. Gundlach, Nelson P. Reid, and Alden E. Roberts, "Native American Migration and Relocation," *Pacific Sociological Review*, No. 21 (1978), pp. 117–27. On the "discarded and forgotten," *see* American Indian Policy Review Commission, Task Force Ten, *Report on Terminated and Nonfederally Recognized Tribes* (Washington, DC: U.S. Government Printing Office, 1976).

135. Alan L. Sokin, *The Urban American Indian* (Lexington, Massachusetts: Lexington Books, 1978).

136. The term was coined in the mid–1970s to describe the self–destructive behavior exhibited by the Khmer Rouge regime in Kampuchea (Cambodia) in response to genocidal policies earlier extended against that country by the United States. For analysis, *see* Noam Chomsky and Edward S. Herman, *After the Cataclysm: Postwar Indochina and the Reconstruction of Imperial Ideology* (Boston: South End Press, 1979).

137. Alexis de Tocqueville, *Democracy in America* (New York: Harper and Row, 1966), p. 312.

138. "Hitler's concept of concentration camps as well as the practicality of genocide owed much, so he claimed, to his studies of British and United States history. He admired the camps for Boer prisoners in South Africa and for the Indians in the wild West; and often praised to his inner circle the efficiency of America's extermination—by starvation and uneven combat—of the red savages who could not be tamed by captivity." John Toland, *Adolf Hitler* (New York: Doubleday, 1976), p. 802.

139. Norman Rich, *Hitler's War Aims: Ideology, the Nazi State, and the Course of Expansion* (New York: W. W. Norton, 1973), p. 8. Rich is relying primarily on the secret but nonetheless official policy position articulated by Hitler during a meeting on November 5, 1937, and recorded by his adjutant, Freidrich Hossbach. The "Hossbach Memorandum" is contained in *Trial of the Major War Criminals Before the International Military Tribunal, Proceedings and Documents, Vol. 25* (Nuremberg: 1947–1949), pp. 402–06.

140. John F. D. Smyth, *A Tour of the United States of America* (London: Privately Published, 1784), p. 346.

141. Quoted in Reginald Horsman, *Race and Manifest Destiny: The Origins of Racial Anglo–Saxonism* (Cambridge, Massachusetts: Harvard University Press, 1981), p. 198.

142. *See* the various quotes in Paul Andrew Hutton, op. cit.

143. Henry E. Fritz, *The Movement for Indian Assimilation, 1860–1890* (Philadelphia: University of Pennsylvania Press, 1963).

144. The classic articulation, of course, is Joseph K. Dixon's 1913 *The Vanishing Race*, recently reprinted by Bonanza Books, New York. An excellent examination of the phenomenon may be found in Stan Steiner's *The Vanishing White Man* (Norman: University of Oklahoma Press, 1976).

145. Anita Parlow, op. cit. *See* also Jerry Kammer, *The Second Long Walk: The Navajo–Hopi Land Dispute* (Albuquerque: University of New Mexico Press, 1980).

146. Thayer Scudder et al., *No Place to Go: Effects of Compulsory Relocation on Navajos* (Philadelphia: Institute for the Study of Human Issues, 1982).

147. Dagmar Thorpe, *Newe Segobia: The Western Shoshone People and Land* (Battle Mountain, Nevada: Western Shoshone Sacred Lands Association, 1981). *See* also Glenn T. Morris, "The Battle for Newe Segobia: The Western Shoshone Land Rights Struggle," in *Critical Issues in Native North America, Vol. II*, Ward Churchill, ed. (Copenhagen: IWGIA Document 68, 1991), pp. 86–98.

148. Alaska Native Claims Settlement Act (85 *Stat.* 688). *See* generally M. C. Barry, *The Alaska Pipeline: The Politics of Oil and Native Land Claims* (Bloomington/Indianapolis: Indiana University Press, 1975); and Thomas R. Berger, *Village Journey: The Report of the Alaska Native Review Commission* (New York: Hill and Wang, 1985).

149. The plan is known by the title of its sponsoring organization, the North American Water and Power Association (NAWAPA). It is covered in Mark Reisner's *Cadillac Desert: The American West and Its Disappearing Water* (New York: Viking Press, 1986).

150. For analysis, *see* S. James Anaya, "The Rights of Indigenous Peoples and International Law in Historical and Contemporary Perspective," in *American Indian Law: Cases and Materials*, Robert N. Clinton, Nell Jessup Newton, and Monroe E. Price, eds. (Charlottesville, Virginia: Michie Co., 1991), pp. 1257–269. *See* also Glenn T. Morris, "International Law and Politics: Toward a Right to Self–Determination for Indigenous Peoples," in *The State of Native America*, op. cit., pp. 55–86.

151. This includes a rather large array of covenants and conventions pertaining to everything from the binding effect of treaties to the Laws of War. It also includes Ronald Reagan's postulation, advanced in October 1985, that the International Court of Justice holds no authority other than in matters of trade. A detailed examination of U.S. posturing in this regard may be found in Lawrence W. LeBlanc, *The United States and the Genocide Convention* (Durham, North Carolina: Duke University Press, 1991).

The Bloody Wake of Alcatraz

Political Repression of the American Indian Movement During the 1970s*

The reality is a continuum which connects Indian flesh sizzling over Puritan fires and Vietnamese flesh roasting under American napalm. The reality is the compulsion of a sick society to rid itself of men like Nat Turner and Crazy Horse, George Jackson and Richard Oaks, whose defiance uncovers the hypocrisy of a declaration affirming everyone's right to liberty and life. The reality is an overwhelming greed which began with the theft of a continent and continues with the merciless looting of every country on the face of the earth which lacks the strength to defend itself.

Richard Lundstrom

In combination with the fishing rights struggles of the Puyallup, Nisqually, Muckleshoot, and other nations in the Pacific Northwest from 1965 to 1970, the 1969–71 occupation of Alcatraz Island by the San Francisco Bay Area's Indians of All Tribes coalition ushered in a decade of uncompromising and intensely confrontational American Indian political activism.[1] Unprecedented in modern U.S. history, the phenomenon represented by Alcatraz also marked the inception of a process of official repression of indigenous activists without contemporary North American parallel in its virulence and lethal effects.[2]

The nature of the post–Alcatraz federal response to organized agitation for native rights was such that by 1979 researchers were describing it as a manifestation of the U.S. government's "continuing Indian Wars."[3] For its part, in internal documents intended to be secret, the Federal Bureau of Investigation (FBI)—the primary instrument by which the government's policy of anti–Indian repression was implemented—concurred with such assessments,

*This essay was first published in the *American Indian Culture and Research Journal,* Vol. 18, No. 4 (Winter 1994).

abandoning its customary counterintelligence vernacular in favor of the terminology of outright counterinsurgency warfare.[4] The result, as the U.S. Commission on Civil Rights officially conceded at the time, was the imposition of a virtual "reign of terror" upon certain of the less compliant sectors of indigenous society in the United States.[5]

In retrospect, it may be seen that the locus of both activism and repression in Indian Country throughout the 1970s centered squarely upon one group, the American Indian Movement (AIM). Moreover, the crux of AIM activism during the '70s, and thus of the FBI's campaign to "neutralize" it,[6] can be found in a single locality: the Pine Ridge (Oglala Lakota) Reservation, in South Dakota. The purpose of the present paper, then, is to provide an overview of the federal counterinsurgency program against AIM on and around Pine Ridge, using it as a lens through which to explore the broader motives and outcomes attending it. Finally, conclusions will be drawn as to its implications, not only with respect to American Indians, but concerning non–indigenous Americans as well.

Background

AIM was founded in 1968 in Minneapolis, by a group of urban Anishinabes (Chippewas) including Dennis Banks, Mary Jane Wilson, Pat Ballanger, Clyde Bellecourt, Eddie Benton Benai, and George Mitchell. Modeled loosely after the Black Panther Party for Self–Defense, established by Huey P. Newton and Bobby Seale in Oakland, California, two years previously, the group took as its first tasks the protection of the city's sizable native community from a pattern of rampant police abuse, and the creation of programs on jobs, housing, and education.[7] Within three years, the organization had grown to include chapters in several other cities, and had begun to shift its focus from civil rights issues to an agenda more specifically attuned to the conditions afflicting Native North America.

What AIM discerned as the basis of the latter was not so much a matter of socio–economic discrimination against Indians as it was their internal colonization by the United States.[8] This perception accrued from the fact that, by 1871, when federal treaty making with native peoples was permanently suspended, the rights of indigenous nations to distinct, self–governing territories had been recognized by the United States more than 370 times through treaties duly ratified by its Senate.[9] Yet, during the intervening century, more than 90 percent of treaty–reserved native land had been expropriated by the federal government, in defiance of both its own constitution and international custom and convention.[10] One consequence of this was the creation of the urban diaspora from which AIM itself emerged; by 1970, about half of all Indians in the United States had been pushed off their land altogether.[11]

Within the residual archipelago of reservations—an aggregation of about 50 million acres, or roughly 2.5 percent of the 48 contiguous states—indigenous forms of governance had been thoroughly usurped through the imposition of U.S. jurisdiction under the federal government's self–assigned prerogative of exercising "plenary [full and absolute] power over Indian affairs."[12] Correspondingly, Indian control over what had turned out to be rather vast mineral resources within reservation boundaries—an estimated two–thirds of all U.S. "domestic" uranium deposits, a quarter of the low sulphur coal, 20 percent of the oil and natural gas, and so on—was essentially nonexistent.[13]

It followed that royalty rates set by the U.S. Bureau of Indian Affairs (BIA), in its exercise of federal "trust" prerogatives vis–à–vis corporate extraction of Indian mineral assets, amounted to only a fraction of what the same corporations would have paid had they undertaken the same mining operations in non–reservation localities.[14] The same principle of underpayment to Indians, with resulting "super–profit" accrual to non–Indian business entities, prevailed with regard to other areas of economic activity handled by the Indian Bureau, from the leasing of reservation grazing land to various ranching interests to the harvesting of reservation timber by corporations such as Weyerhauser and Boise–Cascade.[15] Small wonder that, by the late 1960s, Indian radicals like Robert K. Thomas had begun to refer to the BIA as "the Colonial Office of the United States."[16]

In human terms, the consequence was that, as an aggregate, American Indians—who, on the basis of known resources, comprised what should have been the single wealthiest population group in North America—constituted by far the most impoverished sector of U.S. society. According to the federal government's own data, Indians suffered, by a decisive margin, the highest rate of unemployment in the country, a matter correlated to their receiving by far the lowest annual and lifetime incomes of any group in the country.[17] Their situation also corresponded well with virtually every other statistical indicator of extreme poverty: a truly catastrophic rate of infant mortality and the highest rates of death from malnutrition, exposure, plague disease, teen suicide, and accidents related to alcohol abuse. The average life–expectancy of a reservation–based Indian male in 1970 was less than 45 years; reservation–based Indian females could expect to live less than three years longer than their male counterparts; urban Indians of either gender were living only about five years longer on average than their relatives on the reservations.[18]

AIM's response to its growing apprehension of this squalid panorama was to initiate a campaign consciously intended to bring about the decolonization of Native North America: "Only by reestablishing our rights as sovereign nations, including our right to control our own territories and resources, and our right to genuine self–governance," as Dennis Banks put it in 1971, "can we hope to successfully address the conditions currently experienced by our people."[19]

Extrapolating largely from the example of Alcatraz, the Movement undertook a multifaceted political strategy combining a variety of tactics. On the one hand, it engaged in activities designed primarily to focus media attention, and thus the attention of the general public, on Indian rights issues, especially those pertaining to treaty rights. On the other hand, it pursued the sort of direct confrontation meant to affirm those rights in practice. It also began to systematically reassert native cultural/spiritual traditions.[20] Eventually, it added a component wherein the full range of indigenous rights to decolonization/self–determination were pursued through the United Nations venue of international law, custom, and convention.[21]

In mounting this comprehensive effort, AIM made itself a *bona fide* National Liberation Movement, at least for a while.[22] Its members consisted of "the shock troops of Indian sovereignty," to quote non–AIM Oglala Lakota activist Birgil Kills Straight.[23] They essentially reframed the paradigm by which U.S.–Indian relations are to be understood in the late twentieth century.[24] They also suffered the worst physical repression at the hands of the United States of any "domestic" group since the 1890 massacre of Big Foot's Minneconjous by the 7th Cavalry at Wounded Knee.[25]

Prelude

AIM's seizure of the public consciousness may in many ways be said to have begun at that point in 1969 when Dennis Banks recruited a young Oglala named Russell Means to join the Movement. Instinctively imbued with what one critic described as a "bizarre knack for staging demonstrations that attracted the sort of press coverage Indians had been looking for,"[26] Means was instrumental in AIM's achieving several of its earliest and most important media coups: painting Plymouth Rock red before capturing the Mayflower replica on Thanksgiving Day 1970, for example, and staging a "4th of July Counter–celebration" by occupying the Mt. Rushmore National Monument in 1971.[27]

Perhaps more importantly, Means proved to be the bridge which allowed the Movement to establish its credibility on a reservation for the first time. In part, this was because when he joined AIM he brought along virtually an entire generation of his family—brothers Ted, Bill, and Dale, cousin Madonna Gilbert, and others—each of whom possessed a web of friends and acquaintances on the Pine Ridge Reservation. It was therefore rather natural that AIM was called upon to "set things right" concerning the torture–murder of a middle–aged Oglala in the off–reservation town of Gordon, Nebraska, in late February 1972.[28] As Bill Means would later recall:

When Raymond Yellow Thunder was killed, his relatives went first
to the BIA, then to the FBI, and to the local police, but they got no

response. Severt Young Bear [Yellow Thunder's nephew and a friend of Ted Means] then ... asked AIM to come help clear up the case.[29]

Shortly thereafter, Russell Means led a caravan of some 1,300 Indians into the small town, announcing from the steps of the courthouse that, "We've come here today to put Gordon on the map ... and if justice is not immediately forthcoming, we're going to take Gordon *off* the map." The killers, brothers named Melvin and Leslie Hare, were quickly arrested, and a police officer who had covered up for them was suspended. The Hares soon became the first whites in Nebraska history sent to prison for killing an Indian and "AIM's reputation soared among reservation Indians. What tribal leaders had dared not do to protect their people, AIM had done."[30]

By fall, things had progressed to the point that AIM could collaborate with several other native rights organizations to stage the "Trail of Broken Treaties" caravan, bringing more than 2,000 Indians from reservations and urban areas across the country to Washington, DC, on the eve of the 1972 presidential election. The idea was to present the incumbent chief executive, Richard M. Nixon, with a 20–point program redefining the nature of U.S.–Indian relations. The publicity attending the critical timing and location of the action as well as the large number of Indians involved were calculated to force serious responses by the administration to each point.[31]

In the event, Interior Department officials who had earlier pledged logistical support to caravan participants once they arrived in the capitol reneged on their promises, apparently in the belief that this would cause the group to meekly disperse. Instead, angry Indians promptly took over the BIA headquarters building on November 2, evicted its staff, and held it for several days. Russell Means, in fine form, captured the front page of the nation's newspapers and the six o'clock news by conducting a press conference in front of the building while adorned with a makeshift "war club" and a "shield" fashioned from a portrait of Nixon himself.[32]

Desperate to end what had become a major media embarrassment, the administration publicly agreed to formally reply to the 20–point program within a month, and to immediately provide $66,000 in transportation money, in exchange for a peaceful end to the occupation.[33] AIM honored its part of the bargain, leaving the BIA building on November 9. But, explaining that "Indians have every right to know the details of what's being done to us and to our property," it took with it a vast number of "confidential" files concerning BIA leasing practices, operation of the Indian Health Service (IHS), and so forth. The originals were returned as rapidly as they could be xeroxed, a process that required nearly two years to complete.[34]

Technically speaking, the government also honored its end of the deal, providing official—and exclusively negative—responses to the 20 points within the specified time frame.[35] At the same time, however, it initiated a campaign utilizing federally subsidized Indian "leaders" in an effort to discredit AIM members as "irresponsible ... renegades, terrorists and self–styled revolutionaries."[36] There is also a strong indication that it was at this point that the Federal Bureau of Investigation was instructed to launch a secret program of its own, one in which AIM's capacity to engage in further political activities of the kind and effectiveness displayed in Washington was to be, in the vernacular of FBI counterintelligence specialists, "neutralized."[37]

Even as this was going on, AIM's focus had shifted back to the Pine Ridge area. At issue was the January 23, 1973, murder of a young Oglala named Wesley Bad Heart Bull by a white man, Darld Schmitz, in the off–reservation village of Buffalo Gap, South Dakota. As in the Yellow Thunder case, local authorities had made no move to press appropriate charges against the killer.[38] At the request of the victim's mother, Sarah, Russell Means called for a demonstration at the Custer County Courthouse, in the jurisdiction in which the scene of the crime fell. Terming western South Dakota "the Mississippi of the North,"[39] Dennis Banks simultaneously announced a longer–term effort to force the abandonment "of the anti–Indian attitudes which result in Indian–killing being treated as a sort of local sport."[40]

When the Custer demonstration occurred on February 6, it followed a very different course than that of the protest in Gordon a year earlier. An anonymous call had been placed to the main regional newspaper, the *Rapid City Journal*, on the evening of February 5. The caller, saying he was "with AIM," asked that a notice canceling the action "because of bad weather" be prominently displayed in the paper the following morning. Consequently, relatively few Indians turned out for the protest.[41] Those who did were met by an amalgamated force of police, sheriff's deputies, state troopers, and FBI personnel when they arrived in Custer.[42]

For a while, there was a tense standoff. Then, a sheriff's deputy manhandled Sarah Bad Heart Bull when she attempted to enter the courthouse. In the melee that followed, the courthouse was set ablaze—reportedly by a police tear gas canister—and the local Chamber of Commerce building burned to the ground. Banks, Means, and other AIM members, along with Mrs. Bad Heart Bull, were arrested and charged with riot. Banks was eventually convicted, sentenced to three years imprisonment, and became a fugitive; Sarah Bad Heart Bull served five months of a one–to–five–year sentence. Her son's killer never served a day in jail.[43]

Wounded Knee

Meanwhile, on Pine Ridge, tensions were running extraordinarily high. The point of contention was an escalating conflict between the tribal administration headed by Richard "Dickie" Wilson, installed on the reservation with federal support in 1972, and a large body of reservation traditionals who objected to Wilson's nepotism and other abuses of his position.[44] Initially, Wilson's opponents had sought redress of their grievances through the BIA. The BIA responded by providing a $62,000 grant to Wilson for purposes of establishing a "Tribal Ranger Group"—a paramilitary entity reporting exclusively to Wilson which soon began calling itself "Guardians of the Oglala Nation" (GOONs)—with which to physically intimidate the opposition.[45] The reason underlying this federal largesse appears to have been the government's desire that Wilson sign an instrument transferring title over a portion of the reservation known as the Sheep Mountain Gunnery Range—secretly known to be rich in uranium and molybdenum—to the U.S. Forest Service.[46]

In any event, forming what was called the Oglala Sioux Civil Rights Organization (OSCRO), the traditionals next attempted to obtain relief through the Justice Department and the FBI. When this too failed to bring results, they set out to impeach Wilson, obtaining more signatures from eligible voters on their petitions than had cast ballots for him in the first place. The BIA countered by naming Wilson himself to chair the impeachment proceedings, and the Justice Department dispatched a 65–member "Special Operations Group" (SOG: a large SWAT unit) of U.S. Marshals to ensure that "order" was maintained during the travesty. Then, on the eve of the hearing, Wilson ordered the arrest and jailing of several members of the tribal council he felt might vote for his removal. Predictably, when the impeachment tally was taken on February 23, 1973, the tribal president was retained in office. Immediately thereafter, he announced a reservation–wide ban on political meetings.[47]

Defying the ban, the traditionals convened a round–the–clock emergency meeting at Calico Hall, near the village of Oglala, in an effort to determine their next move. On February 26, a messenger was sent to the newly established AIM headquarters in nearby Rapid City to request that Russell Means meet with the Oglala elders. As one of them, Ellen Moves Camp, later put it:

> We decided we needed the American Indian Movement in here....
> All of our older people from the reservation helped make that
> decision.... This is what we needed, a little more push. Most of the
> reservation believes in AIM, and we're proud to have them with us.[48]

Means came on the morning of the 27th, then drove on to the village of Pine Ridge, seat of the reservation government, to try and negotiate some sort of resolution with Wilson. For his trouble, he was physically assaulted by GOONs in the parking lot of the tribal administration building.[49] By then, Dennis Banks and a number of other AIM members had arrived at Calico Hall. During subsequent meetings, it was decided by the elders that what was necessary was to draw public attention to the situation on the reservation. For this purpose, a 200–person AIM contingent was sent to the symbolic site of Wounded Knee to prepare for an early morning press conference; a much smaller group was sent back to Rapid City to notify the media and to guide reporters to Wounded Knee at the appropriate time.[50]

The intended press conference never occurred because, by dawn, Wilson's GOONs had established roadblocks on all four routes leading into (or out of) the tiny hamlet. During the morning, these positions were reinforced by uniformed BIA police, then by elements of the Marshals' SOG unit, and then by FBI "observers." As this was going on, the AIM members in Wounded Knee began the process of arming themselves from the stores of the local Gildersleeve Trading Post and building defensive positions.[51] By afternoon, General Alexander Haig, military liaison to the Nixon White House, had dispatched two special warfare experts—Colonel Volney Warner of the 82nd Airborne Division and Colonel Jack Potter of the Sixth Army—to the scene.[52]

> Documents later subpoenaed from the Pentagon revealed Colonel Potter directed the employment of 17 APCs [tank–like armored personnel carriers], 130,000 rounds of M–16 ammunition, 41,000 rounds of M–40 high explosive[s] [for the M–79 grenade launchers he also provided], as well as helicopters, Phantom jets, and personnel. Military officers, supply sergeants, maintenance technicians, chemical officers, and medical teams [were provided on site]. Three hundred miles to the south, at Fort Carson, Colorado, the Army had billeted a fully uniformed assault unit on twenty–four hour alert.[53]

Over the next 71 days, the AIM perimeter at Wounded Knee was placed under siege. The ground cover was burned away for roughly a quarter–mile around the AIM position as part of the federal attempt to staunch the flow of supplies—food, medicine, and ammunition—backpacked in to the Wounded Knee defenders at night; at one point such material had to be airdropped by a group of supporting pilots.[54] More than 500,000 rounds of military ammunition were fired into AIM's jerry–rigged "bunkers" by federal forces, killing two Indians—Frank Clearwater, an Apache, and Buddy Lamont, an Oglala—and wounding several others.[55] As many as 13 more people may have been killed by roving GOON patrols while they were trying to carry supplies through federal lines, and their bodies were secretly buried in remote locations around the reservation.[56]

At first, the authorities sought to justify what was happening by claiming that AIM had "occupied" Wounded Knee, and that the Movement had taken several hostages in the process.[57] When the latter allegation was proven to be false, a press ban was imposed, and official spokespersons argued that the use of massive force was needed to "quell insurrection." Much was made of two federal casualties who were supposed to have been seriously injured by AIM gunfire.[58] In the end, it was Dickie Wilson who perhaps expressed matters most candidly when he informed reporters that the purpose of the entire exercise was to see to it that "AIM dies at Wounded Knee."[59]

Despite Wilson's sentiments—and those of FBI senior counterintelligence specialist Richard G. Held, expressed in a secret report prepared at the request of his superiors early in the siege[60]—an end to the standoff was finally negotiated for May 7, 1973. AIM's major condition, entered on behalf of the Pine Ridge traditionals and agreed to by government representatives, was that a federal commission would meet with the chiefs to review U.S. compliance with the terms of the 1868 Fort Laramie Treaty with the Lakota, Cheyenne, and Arapaho Nations.[61] The idea was to generate policy recommendations as to how the United States might bring itself into line with its treaty obligations. A White House delegation did in fact meet with the elders at the home of Chief Frank Fools Crow, near the reservation town of Manderson, on May 17. The delegates' mission, however, was to stonewall all efforts at meaningful discussion.[62] They promised a follow–up meeting on May 30, but never returned.[63]

On other fronts, the authorities were demonstrating no comparable lack of vigor. Before the first meeting at Fools Crows', the FBI had made 562 arrests of those who had been involved in defending Wounded Knee.[64] Russell Means was in jail awaiting release on a $150,000 bond; OSCRO leader Pedro Bissonette was being held for $152,000; AIM leaders Stan Holder and Leonard Crow Dog for $32,000 and $35,000 respectively. Scores of others were being held pending the posting of lesser sums.[65] By the fall of 1973, agents had amassed some 316,000 separate investigative file classifications on those who had been inside Wounded Knee.[66]

This allowed federal prosecutors to obtain 185 indictments over the next several months (Means alone was charged with 37 felonies and three misdemeanors).[67] Although in 1974 AIM and the traditionals used the 1868 Treaty as a basis upon which to challenge in federal court the U.S. government's jurisdiction over Pine Ridge, the trials of the "Wounded Knee Leadership" went forward.[68] Even after the FBI's and the prosecution's willingness to subvert the judicial process became so blatantly obvious that U.S. District Judge Fred Nichol was compelled to dismiss all charges against Banks and Means, cases were still pressed against Crow Dog, Holder, Carter Camp, Madonna Gilbert, Lorelei DeCora, and Phyllis Young.[69]

Ultimately, the whole charade resulted in a paltry 15 convictions, all of them on such paltry offenses as trespass and "interference with postal inspectors in performance of their lawful duties."[70] Still, in the interim, the virtual entirety of AIM's leadership was tied up in a seemingly endless series of arrests, incarcerations, hearings, and trials. Similarly, the great bulk of the Movement's fundraising and organizing capacities was diverted into posting bonds and mounting legal defenses for those indicted.[71]

On balance, the record suggests a distinct probability that the post–Wounded Knee prosecutions were never seriously intended to result in convictions at all. Instead, they were designed mainly to serve the time–honored—and utterly illegal—expedient of "disrupting, misdirecting, destabilizing or otherwise neutralizing" a politically objectionable group.[72] There is official concurrence with this view: As army counterinsurgency specialist Volney Warner framed matters at the time, "AIM's best leaders and most militant members are under indictment, in jail or warrants are out for their arrest.... [Under these conditions] the government can win, even if nobody goes to [prison]."[73]

The Reign of Terror

While AIM's "notables" were being forced to slog their way through the courts, a very different form of repression was being visited upon the Movement's rank–and–file membership and grassroots traditionals of Pine Ridge. During the three–year period beginning with the Siege of Wounded Knee, at least 69 members and supporters of AIM died violently on the reservation.[74] During the same period, nearly 350 others suffered serious physical assaults. Overall, the situation on Pine Ridge was such that, by 1976, the U.S. Commission on Civil Rights was led to describe it as a "reign of terror."[75]

> Using only documented political deaths, the yearly murder rate on the Pine Ridge Reservation between March 1, 1973, and March 1, 1976, was 170 per 100,000. By comparison, Detroit, the reputed "murder capital of the United States," had a rate of 20.2 per 100,000 in 1974. The U.S. average was 9.7 per 100,000.... In a nation of 200 million persons, the murder rate comparable with that on Pine Ridge between 1973 and 1976 would have left 340,000 persons dead for political reasons alone in one year; 1.32 million in three.... The political murder rate at Pine Ridge was almost equivalent to that in Chile during the three years after a military coup supported by the United States killed President Salvador Allende.[76]

Despite the fact that eyewitnesses identified the assailants in 21 of these homicides, the FBI—which maintains preeminent jurisdiction over major crimes on all American Indian reservations—was responsible for not one of the killers ever being convicted.[77] In many cases, no active investigation of the murder of an AIM member or supporter was undertaken by the Bureau.[78] In others, those associated with the victims were falsely arrested as "perpetrators."[79]

When queried by reporters in 1975 as to the reason for his office's abysmal record in investigating murders on Pine Ridge, George O'Clock, the agent in charge of the FBI's Rapid City Resident Agency—under which the operational authority at the reservation falls most immediately—replied that he was "too short of manpower" to assign agents to such tasks.[80] O'Clock omitted to mention that, at the time, he had at his disposal the highest sustained ratio of agents to citizens enjoyed by any FBI office in the history of the Bureau.[81] He also neglected the fact that the same agents who were too busy to look into the murders of AIM people appear to have had unlimited time to undertake the investigative activities covered in the preceding section. Plainly, O'Clock's pat "explanation" was and remains implausible.

A far more likely scenario begins to take shape when it is considered that in each instance where there were eyewitness identifications of the individuals who had killed an AIM member or supporter, those identified were known GOONs.[82] The FBI's conspicuous inability to apprehend murderers on Pine Ridge may thus be located, not in the incompetence of its personnel, but in the nature of its relationship to the killers. In effect, the GOONs seem to have functioned under a more or less blanket immunity from prosecution provided by the FBI so long as they focused their lethal attentions upon targets selected by the Bureau. Put another way, the appearance is that the FBI used the GOONs as a surrogate force against AIM on Pine Ridge in precisely the same manner that Latin American death squads have been utilized by the CIA to destroy the opposition in countries like Guatemala, El Salvador, and Chile.[83]

The roots of the FBI/GOON connection can be traced back at least as far as April 23, 1973, when U.S. Marshals Service Director Wayne Colburn, driving from Pine Ridge village to Wounded Knee, was stopped at what the Wilsonites referred to as "The Residents' Roadblock." One of the GOONs manning the position, vocally disgruntled with what he called the "soft line" taken by the Justice Department in dealing with AIM, leveled a shotgun at the head of Colburn's passenger, Solicitor General Kent Frizzell. Colburn was forced to draw his own weapon before the man would desist. Angered, Colburn drove back to Pine Ridge and dispatched a group of his men to arrest everyone at the roadblock. When the marshals arrived at the Pennington County Jail in Rapid City with those arrested, however, they found an FBI man waiting with instructions to release the GOONs immediately.[84]

By this point, Dickie Wilson himself had reestablished the roadblock, using a fresh crew of GOONs. Thoroughly enraged at this defiance, Colburn assembled another group of marshals and prepared to make arrests. Things had progressed to the point of a "High Noon" style showdown when a helicopter appeared, quickly landing on the blacktop road near the would–be combatants. In it was FBI counterintelligence ace Richard G. Held, who informed Colburn that he had received instructions "from the highest level" to ensure that no arrests would be made and that "the roadblock stays where it is."[85]

Humiliated, and increasingly concerned for the safety of his own person-nel in a situation where the FBI was openly siding with a group hostile to them, Colburn ordered his men to disarm GOONs whenever possible.[86] Strikingly, as the marshals impounded the sort of weaponry the Wilsonites had up until then been using—conventional deer rifles, World War II surplus M–1s, shot-guns, and other firearms normally found in a rural locality—the same GOONs

Colburn's men had disarmed began to reappear, well–stocked with ammunition and sporting fully automatic, military–issue M–16s.[87]

The Brewer Revelations

It has always been the supposition of those aligned with AIM that the FBI provided such hardware to Wilson's GOONs. The Bureau and its apologists, meanwhile, pointing to the absence of concrete evidence with which to confirm the allegation, have consistently denied any such connection, charging those referring to its probability with journalistic or scholarly "irresponsibility."[88] It was not until the early 1990s, with the publication of extracts from an interview with former GOON commander Duane Brewer, that AIM's premise was borne out.[89]

Not only does the one–time death squad leader make it clear that the FBI provided him and his men with weaponry, but with ample supplies of armor–piercing ammunition, hand grenades, "det cord" and other explosives, communications gear, and additional paraphernalia.[90] Agents would drop by his house, Brewer maintains, to provide key bits of field intelligence which allowed the GOONs to function in a more efficient manner than might otherwise have been the case. And, perhaps most importantly, agents conveyed the plain message that members of the death squad would enjoy virtual immunity from federal prosecution for anything they did, so long as it fell within the realm of repressing dissidents on the reservation.[91]

Among the murders which Brewer clarifies in his interview is that of Jeanette Bissonette, a young woman shot to death in her car as she sat at a stop sign in Pine Ridge village at about one o'clock in the morning on March 27, 1975. The FBI has all along insisted, for reasons which remain mysterious, that it is "probable" Bissonette was assassinated by AIM members.[92] Brewer, on the other hand, explains on the basis of firsthand knowledge that the killing was "a mistake" on the part of his execution team, which mistook Bissonette's vehicle for that of area resistance leader Ellen Moves Camp.[93]

It is important to note, before moving ahead, that at the time he functioned as a GOON leader, Duane Brewer also served as second–in–command of the BIA police on Pine Ridge. His boss as a policeman, Delmar Eastman—primary liaison between the police and the FBI—was simultaneously in charge of all GOON operations on the reservation.[94] In total, it is reliably estimated that somewhere between one–third and one–half of all BIA police personnel on Pine Ridge between 1972 and 1976 moonlighted as GOONs. Those who didn't become directly involved actively covered for their colleagues who did, or at least kept their mouths shut about the situation.[95]

Obviously, whatever meager hope for relief AIM and the Oglala traditionals might have extended to the workings of local law enforcement quickly disappeared under such circumstances.[96] In effect, the police were the killers, their crimes not only condoned but, for all practical intents and purposes, commanded and controlled by the FBI. Other federal agencies did no more than issue largely uncirculated reports confirming that the bloodbath was in fact occurring.[97] "Due process" on Pine Ridge during this crucial period was effectively nonexistent.

The Oglala Firefight

By the spring of 1975, with more than 40 of their number already dead, it had become apparent to the Pine Ridge resisters that they had been handed a choice of either acquiescing to the federal agenda or being annihilated. All other alternatives, including a 1974 electoral effort to replace Dickie Wilson with AIM leader Russell Means, had been met by fraud, force, and unremitting violence.[98] Those who wished to continue the struggle and survive were therefore compelled to adopt a posture of armed self–defense. Given that many of the traditionals were elderly, and thus could not reasonably hope to accomplish the latter on their own, AIM was asked to provide physical security for them. Defensive encampments were quickly established at several key locations around the reservation.[99]

For its part, the FBI seems to have become increasingly frustrated at the capacity of the dissidents to absorb punishment, and at the consequent failure of the Bureau's counterinsurgency campaign to force submission. Internal FBI documents suggest that the coordinators of the Pine Ridge operation had come to greatly desire some sensational event which might serve to justify in the public mind a sudden introduction onto the reservation of the kind of overwhelming force that might break the back of the resistance once and for all.[100]

Apparently selected for the staging of such a shocking event was a security camp set up by the Northwest AIM Group at the request of traditional elders Harry and Cecilia Jumping Bull on their property, along Highway 18, a few miles south of the village of Oglala. During the early evening of June 25, 1975, two agents, Ron Williams and Jack Coler, escorted by a BIA policeman (and known GOON) named Robert Eccoffey, entered the Jumping Bull Compound. They claimed to be attempting to serve an arrest warrant on a 17–year–old Lakota and AIM supporter named Jimmy Eagle on spurious charges of kidnapping and aggravated assault.[101]

Told by residents that Eagle was not there and had not been seen for weeks, the agents and their escort left. On Highway 18, however, the agents accosted three young AIM members—Mike Anderson, Norman Charles, and Wilfred "Wish" Draper—who were walking back to camp after taking showers in Oglala, drove them to the police headquarters in Pine Ridge village, and interrogated them for more than two hours. As the young men reported when they finally returned to the Jumping Bulls', no questions had been asked about Jimmy Eagle. Instead, the agents had wanted to know how many men of fighting age were in the camp, what sort of weapons they possessed, and so on.

Thus alerted that something bad was about to happen, the Northwest AIM contingent put out an urgent call for support from the local AIM community.[102]

At about 11:00 a.m. the following morning, June 26, Williams and Coler returned to the Jumping Bull property. Driving past the compound of residences, they moved down into a shallow valley, stopped and exited their cars in an open area, and began to fire in the general direction of the AIM encampment in a treeline along White Clay Creek.[103] Shortly, they began to take a steadily growing return fire, not only from the treeline, but from the houses above. At about this point, agent J. Gary Adams and BIA police officer/GOON Glenn Two Birds attempted to come to Williams' and Coler's aid. Unexpectedly taking fire from the direction of the houses, they retreated to the ditch beside Highway 18.[104]

Some 150 SWAT–trained BIA police and FBI personnel were prepositioned in the immediate locale when the firefight began. This, especially when taken in combination with the fact that more than 200 additional FBI SWAT personnel were on alert awaiting word to proceed *post haste* to Pine Ridge from Minneapolis, Milwaukee, and Quantico, Virginia, raises the probability that Williams and Coler were actually assigned to provoke an exchange of gunfire with the AIM members on the Jumping Bull land.[105] The plan seems to have been that they would then be immediately supported by the introduction of overwhelming force, the Northwest AIM Group destroyed, and the FBI afforded the pretext necessary to launch an outright invasion of Pine Ridge.[106]

A number of local AIM members had rallied to the call to come to the Jumping Bulls'. Hence, instead of encountering the eight AIM "shooters" they anticipated, there were about 30, and the two agents were cut off from their erstwhile supporters.[107] While the BIA police, reinforced by GOONs, put up roadblocks to seal off the area, and the FBI agents on hand were deployed as snipers, no one made a serious effort to get to Williams and Coler until 5:50 p.m. By that point, they'd been dead for some time, along with a young Coeur D'Alene AIM member, Joe Stuntz Killsright, killed by FBI sniper Gerard Waring as he attempted to depart the compound.[108] Aside from Killsright, all AIM participants had escaped across country.

By nightfall, hundreds of agents equipped with everything from APCs to Vietnam–style Huey helicopters had begun arriving on the reservation.[109] The next morning, Tom Coll, an FBI "Public Information Specialist" imported for the purpose, convened a press conference in Oglala—the media was barred from the firefight site itself—in which he reported that the dead agents had been "lured into an ambush" by AIM, attacked with automatic weapons from a "sophisticated bunker complex," dragged wounded from their cars, stripped of their clothing, and then executed in cold blood while one of them pleaded with his killer(s) to spare him because he had a wife and children. Each agent, Coll asserted, had been "riddled with 15–20 bullets."[110]

Every word of this was false, as Coll well knew—the FBI had been in possession of both the agents' bodies and the ground on which they were killed for nearly 18 hours before he made his statements—and the report was retracted in full by FBI Director Clarence Kelley at a press conference conducted in Los Angeles a week later.[111] By then, however, a barrage of sensational media coverage had "sensitized" the public to the need for a virtually unrestricted application of force against the "mad dogs of AIM." Correspondingly, the Bureau was free to run air assaults and massive sweeping operations on Pine Ridge—complete with the wholesale use of no–knock searches and John Doe warrants—for the next three months.[112] By the end of that period, its mission had largely been accomplished.[113] In the interim, on July 27, 1975, it was finally felt, given the preoccupation of all concerned parties with the FBI's literal invasion of Pine Ridge, that the time was right for Dickie Wilson to sign a memorandum transferring the Gunnery Range to the federal government; on January 2, 1976, a more formal instrument was signed and, in the spring, Congress passed a Public Law assuming U.S. title over this portion of Oglala territory.[114]

The Case of Leonard Peltier

It is unlikely that the FBI intended its two agents be killed during the Oglala Firefight. Once Coler and Williams were dead, however, the Bureau capitalized on their fate, not only as the medium through which to pursue its anti–AIM campaign with full ferocity, but as a mechanism with which to block an incipient congressional probe into what the FBI had been doing on Pine Ridge. This took the form of a sympathy play: Bureau officials pleaded that the "natural" emotional volatility engendered among their agents by the deaths made it "inopportune" to proceed with the investigation "at the present time." Congress responded, on July 3, 1975, by postponing the scheduling of preliminary interviews, a delay which has become permanent.[115]

Still, with two dead agents, it was crucial for the Bureau's image that someone be brought directly to account. To fill this bill, four names were selected from the list of 30 "shooters" field investigators had concluded were participants in the exchange. Targeted were a pair of Anishinabe/Lakota cousins, Leonard Peltier and Bob Robideau, and Darrelle "Dino" Butler, a Tuni, the heads of Northwest AIM. Also included was Jimmy Eagle, whose name seems to have appeared out of expediency, since the Bureau claimed Williams and Coler were looking for him in the first place (all charges against him were later simply dropped, without investiture of discernible prosecutorial effort).[116]

Butler and Robideau, captured early on, were tried first, as co–defendants, separate from Peltier.[117] The latter, having managed to avoid arrest in a trap set for him in Oregon, had found sanctuary in the remote encampment of

Cree leader Robert Smallboy, in northern Alberta.[118] By the time he could be apprehended, extradited via a thoroughly fraudulent proceeding involving the presentation of an "eyewitness" affidavit from a psychotic Lakota woman named Myrtle Poor Bear to a Canadian court, and docketed in the United States, the proceedings against Peltier's cohorts were ready to begin.[119] He was thus scheduled to be tried later and alone.

During the Butler/Robideau trial, conducted in Cedar Rapids, Iowa, during the summer of 1976, the government's plan to turn the defendants—and AIM itself—into examples of the price of resistance began to unravel. Despite the calculated ostentation with which the FBI prepared to secure the judge and jurors from "AIM's potential for violence," and despite another media blitz designed to convince the public that Butler and Robideau were part of a vast "terrorist conspiracy," the carefully selected, all–white Midwestern panel of jurors was unconvinced.[120] After William Muldrow of the U.S. Commission on Civil Rights was called by the defense to testify regarding the FBI–fostered reign of terror on Pine Ridge, and Director Kelley himself was forced to admit under oath that he knew of nothing which might support many of the Bureau's harsher characterizations of AIM, the jury voted to acquit on July 16, 1976.[121]

The "not guilty" verdict was based on the panel members' assessment that—although both defendants acknowledged firing at the agents and Robideau that he had in fact hit them both[122]—they had acted in self–defense. Under the conditions described by credible witnesses, jury foreman Robert Bolin later recounted, "we felt that any reasonable person would have reacted the same way when the agents came in there shooting." Besides, Bolin continued, their personal observations of the behavior of governmental representatives during the trial had convinced most jury members that "it was the government, not the defendants or their movement, which was dangerous."[123]

Although the Cedar Rapids jury had essentially determined that Coler and Williams had not been murdered, the FBI and federal prosecutors opted to proceed against Peltier. In a pretrial conference they analyzed what had "gone wrong" in the Butler/Robideau case and, in a report dated July 20, 1976, concluded that among the problems encountered was the fact that the defendants had been allowed to present a self–defense argument and their lawyers allowed "to call and question witnesses" and subpoena government documents.[124] They then removed the Peltier trial from the docket of the judge at Cedar Rapids, Edward McManus, and reassigned it to another, Paul Bensen, whom they felt would be more amenable to their view.[125]

When Peltier was brought to trial in Fargo, North Dakota, on March 21, 1977, Benson ruled virtually everything presented by the defense at Cedar Rapids, including the Butler/Robideau trial transcript itself, inadmissible.[126] Prosecutors then presented a case against Peltier which was precisely the opposite of what they—and their FBI witnesses—professed to believe was true in the earlier trial.[127] A chain of circumstantial evidence was constructed, often through resort to fabricated physical evidence,[128] perjury,[129] and the use of demonstrably suborned testimony,[130] to create a plausible impression among jurors—again all–white Midwesterners—that the defendant was guilty.

Following a highly emotional closing presentation by Assistant Prosecutor Lynn Crooks, in which he waved color photos of the agents' bloody bodies under the jury's collective nose and graphically described the "cold–bloodedness" with which "Leonard Peltier executed these two wounded and helpless human beings," they voted on April 18, after only six hours of deliberation, to convict on both counts of first–degree murder.[131] Bensen then sentenced Peltier to serve two consecutive life–terms in prison, and he was transported straight-away to the federal "super–maximum" facility at Marion, Illinois.[132]

Almost immediately, an appeal was filed on the basis of FBI misconduct and multiple judicial errors on Bensen's part. The matter was considered by a three–member panel of the Eighth Circuit Court—composed of judges William Webster, Donald Ross, and Gerald Heaney—during the spring of 1978. Judge Webster wrote the opinion on behalf of his colleagues, finding that although the record revealed numerous reversible errors on the part of the trial judge, and many "unfortunate misjudgments" by the FBI, the conviction would be allowed to stand.[133] By the time the document was released, Webster was no longer there to answer for it. He had moved on to a new position as Director of the FBI. On February 12, 1979, the U.S. Supreme Court declined, without stating a reason, to review the lower court's decision.[134]

Undeterred, Peltier's attorneys had already filed a suit under the Freedom of Information Act (FOIA) to force disclosure of FBI documents withheld from the defense at trial. When the paperwork, more than 12,000 pages of investigative material, was finally produced in 1981, they began the tedious process of indexing and reviewing it.[135] Finding that the Bureau had suppressed ballistics reports which directly contradicted what had been presented at trial, they filed a second appeal in 1982.[136] This led to an evidentiary hearing and oral arguments in 1984 during which the FBI's chief ballistics expert, Evan Hodge, was caught in the act of perjuring himself,[137] and Lynn Crooks was forced to admit that the government "really has no idea who shot those agents."[138]

Crooks then attempted to argue that it didn't matter anyway, because Peltier had been convicted of "aiding and abetting in the murders rather than of the murders themselves."[139] This time, the circuit court panel—now composed of judges Heaney and Ross, as well as John Gibson—took nearly a year to deliberate. On October 11, 1986, they finally delivered an opinion holding that the content of Crooks' own closing argument to the jury, among many other factors, precluded the notion that Peltier had been tried for aiding and abetting. They also concluded that the circumstantial ballistics case presented by the prosecution at trial was hopelessly undermined by evidence available even then to the FBI.[140]

Still, they refused to reverse Peltier's conviction because "We recognize that there is evidence in this record of improper conduct on the part of some FBI agents, but we are reluctant to impute even further improprieties to them" by remanding the matter to trial.[141] On October 5, 1987, the Supreme Court once again refused to review the lower court's decision.[142] Most recently, a third appeal, argued on the basis of *habeas corpus*—if Peltier was never tried for aiding and abetting, and if the original case against him no longer really exists, then why is he in prison?—was filed. In November 1992, the Eighth Circuit, without ever really answering such questions, allowed his "conviction" to stand. The matter remains pending before the Supreme Court, but that august body is expected to once again decline to review the matter.

Aftermath

The government repression of AIM during the mid–70s had the intended effect of blunting the movement's cutting edge. After 1977, things occurred in fits and starts rather than within a sustained drive. AIM's core membership, those who were not dead or in prison, scattered to the winds, many, like Wounded Knee security head Stan Holder, seeking other avenues into which to channel their activism.[143] Others, exhausted and intimidated by the massive violence directed against them, "retired" altogether from active politics.[144] Among the remainder, personal, political, and intertribal antagonisms, often exacerbated by the rumors spread by federal *provocateurs*, instilled a deep and lasting factional fragmentation.[145]

In 1978, Dennis Banks, occupying the unique status in California of having been officially granted sanctuary by one state of the union against the extradition demands of another, sought to bring things back together by organizing what he called the "Longest Walk."[146] To some extent replicating on foot the Trail of Broken Treaties caravan of 1972, the Walk succeeded in its immediate objective; the walkers made it from Alcatraz Island—selected as a point of departure because of the importance of the 1969–71 occupation in forging AIM—to Washington, DC, presenting a powerful manifesto to the Carter Administration in July.[147] But there was no follow–up, and the momentum was quickly lost.

Much hope was placed in the formation of the Leonard Peltier Defense Committee (LPDC) the same year, and, for a time it seemed as though it might serve as a kind of spark plug reenergizing the movement as a whole.[148] However, with the February 12, 1979, murder of AIM Chair John Trudell's entire family on the Duck Valley Reservation in Nevada, apparently as a deterrent to the effectiveness of Trudell's fiery oratory, things took an opposite tack.[149] The result was the abolition of all national officer positions in AIM; "These titles do nothing but provide a ready–made list of priority targets for the feds," as Trudell put it at the time.[150] The gesture consummated a trend against centralization which began with the dissolution of AIM's national office at the time Banks had gone underground in 1975, a fugitive from sentencing after his conviction on charges stemming from the Custer Courthouse confrontation.[151]

In 1979 and 1980, large–scale "Survival Gatherings" were held outside Rapid City in an attempt to bring together Indian and non–Indian activists in collaborative opposition to uranium mining and other corporate "development" of the Black Hills.[152] An ensuing organization, the Black Hills Alliance (BHA), achieved momentary national prominence, but petered out after the demise of domestic uranium production in the early 1980s dissolved several of the more pressing issues it confronted.[153]

Meanwhile, Russell Means, fresh out of prison, launched a related effort in 1981, occupying an 880–acre site in the Black Hills to establish a "sustainable, alternative, demonstration community" and "to initiate the physical reoccupation of Paha Sapa by the Lakota people and our allies." The occupation of what was dubbed *Wincanyan Zi Tiospaye* (Yellow Thunder Camp) in memory of Raymond Yellow Thunder lasted until 1985.[154] By that point, its organizers had obtained what on its face was a landmark judicial opinion from a federal district judge; not only did the Yellow Thunder occupiers have every right to do what they were doing, the judge decreed, but the Lakota—and other Indians as well—are entitled to view entire geographic areas such as the Black Hills, rather than merely specific sites within them, to be of sacred significance.[155] The emergent victory was gutted, however, by the Supreme Court's controversial "G–O Road Decision" in 1988.[156]

Elsewhere, an AIM security camp was established on Navajo land near Big Mountain, Arizona, during the mid–80s, to support the traditional Diné elders of that area in their resistance to forced relocation.[157] It has been maintained, and, somewhat comparably, AIM contingents began to become involved in the early–90s in providing physical security to Western Shoshone resisters to forced removal from their land in Nevada.[158] Similar scenarios have been played out in places as diverse as northern Minnesota and Wisconsin, Oregon, California, Oklahoma, Illinois, Florida, Georgia, Nebraska, Alaska, and upstate New York. The issues confronted have been as wide–ranging as the localities in which they've been confronted.

Another potential bright spot which was ultimately eclipsed was the International Indian Treaty Council (IITC). Formed at the request of the Lakota elders in 1974 to "carry the message of indigenous people into the community of nations" and to serve more generally as "AIM's international arm," it had by August 1977 gotten off to a brilliant start, playing a key role in bringing representatives of 98 native peoples throughout the Americas together in an unprecedented convocation before the United Nations Commission on Human Rights. This led directly to the establishment of a formal Working Group on

Indigenous Populations—mandated to draft a Universal Declaration of the Rights of Indigenous Peoples for incorporation into international law by 1992—under the U.N. Economic and Social Council.[159]

Despite this remarkable early success, with the 1981 departure of its original director, Cherokee activist Jimmie Durham, IITC began to unravel.[160] By 1986, his successors were widely perceived as using the organization's reputation as a vehicle for personal profit and prestige, aligning themselves for a fee with various nation–state governments against indigenous interests. Allegations that they were also using their de facto diplomatic status as a medium through which to engage in drug trafficking also abounded. Whether or not such suspicions were well–founded, IITC today has reduced itself to the stature of a small sectarian corporation, completely divorced from AIM and the traditional milieu which legitimated it, subsisting mainly on donations from the very entities it was created to oppose.[161]

The early '90s, with the imminence of the Columbian Quincentennial Celebration, presented opportunities for the revitalization of AIM. Indeed, the period witnessed a more or less spontaneous regeneration of autonomous AIM chapters in at least 16 localities around the country.[162] In Colorado, an escalating series of confrontations with Columbus Day celebrants organized by the state AIM chapter which began in 1989 led to the galvanizing of a coalition of some 50 progressive organizations, Indian and non–Indian alike, by 1992.[163] In Denver, the city where Columbus Day was first proclaimed an official holiday, Quincentennial activities were stopped in their tracks. Much the same process was evident in San Francisco and, to a lesser extent, in other locations.

Perhaps ironically, the most vicious reaction to the prospect of a resurgent movement came, not from the government per se, but from a small group in Minneapolis professing itself to be AIM's "legitimate leadership." How exactly it imagined it had attained this exalted position was a bit murky, there not having been an AIM general membership conference to sanction the exercise of such authority since 1975. Nonetheless, in July 1993, the clique constituted itself under the laws of the State of Minnesota as "National–AIM, Inc.," announced formation of a "National Board" and "Central Committee," and provided the address to what it described as the "AIM National Office."[164] Among the very first acts of this interesting amalgam—which proudly reported it was receiving $4 million per year in federal funding, and more than $3 million annually from corporations like Honeywell—was the issuance of letters "expelling" most of the rest of the movement from itself.[165]

A Legacy

It may be, as John Trudell has said, that "AIM died years ago. It's just that some people don't know it yet."[166] Certainly, as a viable organization, the evidence exhibits every indication of bearing him out. And yet there is another level to this reality, one which has more to do with the spirit of resistance than with tangible form. Whatever else may be said about what AIM was (or is), it must be acknowledged that, as Russell Means contends:

> Before AIM, Indians were dispirited, defeated and culturally dissolving. People were *ashamed* to be Indian. You didn't see the young people wearing braids or chokers or ribbon shirts in those days. Hell, *I* didn't wear 'em. People didn't Sun Dance, they didn't Sweat, they were losing their languages. Then there was that spark at Alcatraz, and we took off. Man, we took a *ride* across this country. We put Indians and Indian rights smack dab in the middle of the public consciousness for the first time since the so–called Indian Wars. And, of course, we paid a heavy price for that. Some of us are still paying it. But now you see braids on our young people. There are dozens of Sun Dances every summer. You hear our languages spoken again in places they had almost died out. Most important, you find young Indians all over the place who understand that they don't have to accept whatever sort of bullshit the dominant society wants to hand them, that they have the right to fight, to struggle for their rights, that in fact they have an obligation to stand up on their hind legs and fight for their future generations, the way our ancestors did. Now, I don't know about you, but I call that pride in being Indian. And I think that's a very positive change. And I think—no, I *know*—AIM had a lot to do with bringing that change about. We laid the groundwork for the next stage in regaining our sovereignty and self–determination as nations, and I'm proud to have been a part of that.[167]

To the degree this is true, and much of it seems very accurate, AIM may be said to have succeeded in fulfilling its original agenda. The impulse behind Alcatraz was carried forward into dimensions its participants could not yet envision. And that legacy is even now being refashioned and extended by a new generation, as it will be by the next, and the next. The continuity of Native North America's traditional resistance to domination was reasserted by AIM in no uncertain terms.[168]

There are other aspects of the AIM legacy, to be sure. Perhaps the most crucial should be placed under the heading of "Lessons Learned." These go to defining the nature of the society we now inhabit, the lengths to which its government will go to maintain the kinds of domination AIM fought to cast off, and the techniques it uses in doing so. The experience of the American Indian Movement, especially in the mid–1970s, provides what amounts to a textbook exposition of these things. It teaches what to expect, and, if properly understood, how to overcome many of these methodologies of repression. The lessons are applicable, not simply to American Indians, but to anyone whose lot in life is to be oppressed within the American conception of business as usual.[169]

Ultimately, the gift bestowed by AIM is in part an apprehension of the fact that the Third World is not something "out there." It is everywhere, behind the facade of liberal democracy masking the substance of the United States as much as anywhere else.[170] It is there on every reservation in the country, in the teeming ghettos of Brownsville, Detroit, and Compton, in the barrios and migrant fields and sharecropping farms of the Deep South.[171] It is there in the desolation of the Appalachian coal regions. It is there in the burgeoning prison industry of America, warehousing by far the most incarcerated population on the planet.[172]

The Third World is there in the nation's ever more proliferate and militarized police apparatus. And it is there in the piles of corpses of those—not just AIM members, but Black Panthers, Brown Berets, Puerto Rican *independentistas*, labor organizers, civil rights workers, and many others—who tried to say "no" and make it stick.[173] It is there in the fate of Malcolm X and Fred Hampton, Mark Clark and Ché Payne, Geronimo ji Jaga Pratt and Alejandina Torres, Susan Rosenberg and Martin Luther King, George Jackson and Ray Luc Lavasseur, Tim Blunk and Reyes Tijerina, Mutulu Shakur and Marilyn Buck, and so many others.[174]

To win, it is said, one must know one's enemy. Winning the sorts of struggles engaged in by the individuals and organizations just mentioned is unequivocally necessary if we are to effect a constructive change in the conditions they faced, and that we continue to face. In this, there are still many lessons to be drawn from the crucible of the AIM experience. These must be learned by all of us. They must be learned well. And soon.

Notes

1. On the fishing rights struggles, *see* American Friends Service Committee, *Uncommon Controversy: Fishing Rights of the Muckleshoot, Puyallup and Nisqually Indians* (Seattle: University of Washington Press, 1970). On the Alcatraz occupation, *see* Peter Blue Cloud, ed., *Alcatraz Is Not an Island* (Berkeley: Wingbow Press, 1972). *See* also Adam Fortunate Eagle (Nordwall), *Alcatraz! Alcatraz! The Indian Occupation of 1969–1971* (Berkeley: Heyday Books, 1992).

2. This is not to say that others—notably, members of the Black Panther Party—have not suffered severely and often fatally at the hands of official specialists in the techniques of domestic political repression in the United States. The distinction drawn with regard to American Indian activists in this respect is purely proportional. For comprehensive background on the experiences of non–Indians, *see* Robert Justin Goldstein, *Political Repression in Modern America, 1870 to the Present* (Cambridge/New York: Schenkman Publishing/Two Continents Publishing Group, 1978).

3. Bruce Johansen and Roberto Maestas, *Wasi'chu: The Continuing Indian Wars* (New York: Monthly Review Press, 1979).

4. Counterinsurgency is *not* a part of law enforcement or intelligence–gathering missions. Rather, it is an integral aspect of low–intensity warfare doctrine and methodology, taught at the U.S. Army's Special Warfare School at Fort Bragg, North Carolina; *see* Major John S. Pustay, *Counterinsurgency Warfare* (New York: The Free Press, 1965); *see* also Michael T. Klare and Peter Kornbluh, eds., *Low Intensity Warfare: Counterinsurgency, Proinsurgency, and Antiterrorism in the Eighties* (New York: Pantheon Books, 1988). For an illustration of the FBI's use of explicit counterinsurgency terminology to define its anti–Indian operations in 1976, *see* Ward Churchill and Jim Vander Wall, *The COINTELPRO Papers: Documents from the FBI's Secret Wars Against Dissent in the United States* (Boston: South End Press, 1990), p. 264.

5. The U.S. Department of Justice, Commission on Civil Rights, *Events Surrounding Recent Murders on the Pine Ridge Reservation in South Dakota* (Denver: Rocky Mountain Regional Office, 31 Mar. 1976).

6. In his (at the time) definitive study of the Bureau, Sanford J. Ungar quotes a senior counterintelligence specialist to the effect that "success in this area is not measured in terms of arrests and prosecutions, but in our ability to neutralize our targets' ability to do what they're doing"; Sanford J. Ungar, *FBI: An Uncensored Look Behind the Walls* (Boston: Little, Brown & Co., Inc., 1975), p. 311.

7. On the early days of the Black Panther Party, *see* Gene Marine, *The Black Panthers* (New York: New American Library, 1969). On the beginnings of AIM, and its obvious reliance on the Panther model, *see* Peter Matthiessen, *In the Spirit of Crazy Horse* (New York: Viking Press [2d. ed.], 1991), pp. 34–37.

8. Although AIM was probably the first to begin attempting to put together a coherent program to challenge the internal colonization of American Indians, it was by no means the first to perceive the native situation in this light. That distinction probably belonged to the Cherokee anthropologist Robert K. Thomas, with his brief but influential essay "Colonialism: Internal and Classic," first published in the 1966–67 issue of *New University Thought*.

9. The United States is constitutionally prohibited, under Article 1 of its constitution, from entering into treaty relations with any entity other than another fully sovereign nation. Senate ratification of a treaty therefore confirms formal U.S. recognition of the unequivocal sovereignty of the other party or parties to the instrument. The texts of 371 ratified treaties between the United States and various indigenous nations appear in Charles J. Kappler, *Indian Treaties, 1778–1883* (New York: Interland Publishing, 1972). The United States suspended such treaty making by law in 1871 (Ch. 120, 16 *Stat.* 544, 566, now codified at 25 U.S.C. 71) with the provision that "nothing herein contained shall be construed to invalidate or impair the obligation of any treaty heretofore lawfully made with any Indian nation or tribe."

10. Following the findings of the Indian Claims Commission in its 1979 Final Report, an independent researcher summarized that, "about half the land area of the [United States] was purchased by treaty or agreement ... another third of a [billion] acres, mainly in the West, were [sic] confiscated without compensation; another two–thirds of a [billion] acres were claimed by the United States without pretense of a unilateral action extinguishing native title"; *see* Russel Barsh, "Indian Land Claims Policy in the United States," *North Dakota Law Review*, No. 58 (1982), pp. 1–82. The last category mentioned, to which native title is still plainly applicable, amounts to about 35 percent of the 48 contiguous states; it should be contrasted to the approximately 2.5 percent of the "lower 48" currently retaining reservation trust status.

11. The U.S. Bureau of the Census, *1970 Census of the Population, Subject Report: American Indians* (Washington, DC: U.S. Government Printing Office, 1972).

12. U.S. Plenary Power Doctrine is perhaps best articulated in the Supreme Court's 1903 *Lonewolf v. Hitchcock* opinion (187 U.S. 553). The most relevant statutes are the 1885 Major Crimes Act (Ch. 341, 24 *Stat.* 362, 385, now codified at U.S.C. 1153), the 1887 General Allotment Act (Ch. 119, 24 *Stat.* 388, now codified as amended at 25 U.S.C. 331 *et seq.*), and the Indian Reorganization Act (Ch. 576, 48 *Stat.* 948, now codified at 25 U.S.C. 461–279).

13. On resource distribution, see generally, Michael Garrity, "The U.S. Colonial Empire Is as Close as the Nearest Indian Reservation," in *Trilateralism: The Trilateral Commission and Elite Planning for World Government*, Holly Sklar, ed. (Boston: South End Press, 1980), pp. 238–68.

14. *See* generally, Joseph G. Jorgensen, ed., *Native Americans and Energy Development, II* (Cambridge, MA: Anthropology Resource Center/Seventh Generation Fund, 1984).

15. *See* generally, Roxanne Dunbar Ortiz, ed., *Economic Development in American Indian Reservations* (Albuquerque: Native American Studies Center, University of New Mexico, 1979).

16. Robert K. Thomas, "Colonialism: Classic and Internal," *New University Thought*, Vol. 4, No. 4 (Winter 1966–1967).

17. U.S. Department of Health, Education and Welfare (DHEW), *A Study of Selected Socio–Economic Characteristics of Ethnic Minorities Based on the 1970 Census, Vol. 3, American Indians* (Washington, DC: U.S. Government Printing Office, 1974). It should be noted that the economic and health data pertaining to certain sectors of other U.S. minority populations—inner–city blacks, for example, or Latino migrant workers—are very similar to those bearing on American Indians. Unlike these other examples, however, the data on American Indians encompass the condition of the population as a whole.

18. U.S. Bureau of the Census, Population Division, Racial Statistics Branch, *A Statistical Profile of the American Indian Population* (Washington, DC: U.S. Government Printing Office, 1974).

19. Dennis J. Banks, speech before the United Lutheran Board, Minneapolis, Minnesota, March 1971.

20. Notable in this respect was the resuscitation of the Lakota Sun Dance (forbidden by the BIA since 1881) when, in August of 1972, AIM members showed up *en masse* to participate in the ceremony at Crow Dog's Paradise, on the Rosebud Reservation. As the revered Oglala spiritual leader Frank Fools Crow put it in 1980, "Before that, there were only one, two Sun Dances each year. Just a few came, the real traditionals. And we had to hold 'em in secret. After the AIM boys showed up, now there are [Sun Dances] everywhere, right out in the open, too. Nobody hides anymore. Now, they're all proud to be Indian" (the author was present at the event). The same principle pertains to the resurgence of numerous other ceremonies among a variety of peoples.

21. The U.N. component was developed pursuant to the creation of the International Indian Treaty Council (IITC), "AIM's international diplomatic arm," in 1974. Under the director-ship of Cherokee activist Jimmie Durham, IITC was responsible for convening the first Assembly of Indigenous Nations of the Western Hemisphere at the U.N. Palace of Nations in Geneva, Switzerland, during the summer of 1977. IITC then became the world's first Non–Governing Organization (NGO; Type–II, Consultative) to the United Nations, and played a major role in bringing about the establishment of the Working Group on Indigenous Populations—charged with annual review of native grievances and the drafting of a

Universal Declaration of the Rights of Indigenous Peoples—under auspices of the U.N. Economic and Social Council (ECOSOC) in 1981. With Durham's departure from IITC the same year, the organization went into decline. The progressive dynamic it inaugurated, however, is ongoing. *See* generally, S. James Anaya, "The Rights of Indigenous Peoples and International Law in Historical and Contemporary Perspective," in *American Indian Law: Cases and Materials*, Robert N. Clinton, Nell Jessup Newton, and Monroe E. Price, eds. (Charlottesville, Virginia: Michie Co., 1991), pp. 1257–276.

22. The term "National Liberation Movement" is not rhetorical. Rather it bears a precise meaning under Article I, Paragraph 4 of Additional Protocol I of the 1949 Geneva Convention. *See* also United Nations Resolution 3103 (XXVIII), 12 Dec. 1973.

23. Birgil Kills Straight, mimeographed statement circulated by the Oglala Sioux Civil Rights Organization (Manderson, South Dakota) during the 1973 Siege of Wounded Knee.

24. By the mid–70s, even elements of the federal government had begun to adopt AIM's emphasis on colonialism to explain the relationship between the United States and American Indians. *See*, for example, the U.S. Commission on Civil Rights, *The Navajo Nation: An American Colony* (Washington, DC: U.S. Government Printing Office, Sept. 1975).

25. This remained true until the government's 1993 slaughter of 86 Branch Davidians in a single hour near Waco, Texas. The standard text on the 1890 massacre is, of course, Dee Brown's *Bury My Heart at Wounded Knee: An Indian History of the American West* (New York: Holt, Rinehart & Winston, Inc., 1970).

26. Robert Burnette and John Koster, *The Road to Wounded Knee* (New York: Bantam Books, 1974), p. 196.

27. Peter Matthiessen, *In the Spirit of Crazy Horse* (New York: Viking Press [end ed.], 1991), pp. 38, 110.

28. Yellow Thunder, burned with cigarettes, was forced to dance nude from the waist down for the entertainment of a crowd assembled in the Gordon American Legion Hall. He was then severely beaten and stuffed, unconscious, into the trunk of a car where he froze to death. *See* Rex Weyler, *Blood of the Land: The U.S. Government and Corporate War Against the American Indian Movement* (New York: Everest House, 1982), p. 48. *See* also Peter Matthiessen, op. cit. [end ed., 1991], pp. 59–60.

29. Quoted in Rex Weyler, op. cit., p. 49.

30. Alvin M. Josephy, Jr., *Now That the Buffalo's Gone: A Study of Today's American Indian* (New York: Alfred A. Knopf, 1982), p. 237.

31. The best overall handling of these events, including the complete text of the Twenty Point Program, is Vine Deloria, Jr.'s *Behind the Trail of Broken Treaties: An Indian Declaration of Independence* (New York: Delta Books, 1974).

32. *See* Editors, *BIA, I'm Not Your Indian Anymore* (Rooseveltown, New York: *Akwesasne Notes*, 1973).

33. The money, comprised of unmarked 20, 50, and 100 dollar bills, came from a slush fund administered by Nixon's notorious Committee to Reelect the President (CREEP), and was delivered in brown paper bags. The bagmen were administration aids Leonard Garment and Frank Carlucci (later National Security Council chief and CIA director under Ronald Reagan).

34. It was from these files that, among other things, the existence of a secret IHS program to perform involuntary sterilizations on American Indian women was first revealed. *See* Brint Dillingham, "Indian Women and IHS Sterilization Practices," *American Indian Journal*, Vol. 3, No. 1 (Jan. 1977).

35. The full text of the administration's response is included in *BIA, I'm Not Your Indian Anymore*, op. cit.

36. The language is that of Webster Two Hawk, then President of the Rosebud Sioux Tribe and the federally funded National Tribal Chairmen's Association. Two Hawk was shortly voted out of both positions by his constituents and replaced as Rosebud President by Robert Burnette, an organizer of the Trail of Broken Treaties. *See* Ward Churchill, "Renegades, Terrorists and Revolutionaries: The Government's Propaganda War Against the American Indian Movement," *Propaganda Review*, No. 4 (Apr. 1989).

37. One firm indication of this was the arrest by the FBI of Assiniboin/Lakota activist Hank Adams and Les Whitten, an associate of columnist Jack Anderson, shortly after the occupation. They were briefly charged with illegally possessing government property. The men, neither of whom was an AIM member, were merely acting as go–betweens in returning BIA documents to the federal authorities. The point seems to have been to isolate AIM from its more "moderate" associations. *See* Vine Deloria, Jr., op. cit., p. 59.

38. Although he had stabbed Bad Heart Bull repeatedly in the chest with a hunting knife, Schmitz was charged only with second–degree manslaughter and released on his own recognizance.

39. Don and Jan Stevens, *South Dakota: The Mississippi of the North, or Stories Jack Anderson Never Told You* (Custer, South Dakota: self–published pamphlet, 1977).

40. More broadly, AIM's posture was a response to what it perceived as a nationwide wave of murders of Indians by whites. These included not only those of Yellow Thunder and Bad Heart Bull, but of a 19–year–old Papago named Phillip Celay by a sheriff's deputy in Arizona, an Onondaga Special Forces veteran (and member of the honor guard during the funeral of John F. Kennedy) named Leroy Shenandoah in Philadelphia, and, on September 20, 1972, of Alcatraz leader Richard Oaks near San Francisco. *See* Ward Churchill and Jim Vander Wall, *Agents of Repression: The FBI's Secret Wars Against the Black Panther Party and the American Indian Movement* (Boston: South End Press, 1988), p. 123.

41. The individual receiving the call was reporter Lynn Gladstone. Such calls are a standard FBI counterintelligence tactic used to disrupt the political organizing of targeted groups. *See* Brian Glick, *War at Home: Covert Action Against U.S. Activists and What We Can Do About It* (Boston: South End Press, 1989).

42. A January 31, 1973, FBI teletype delineates the fact that the Bureau was already involved in planning the police response to the Custer demonstration. It is reproduced in Ward Churchill and Jim Vander Wall, *The COINTELPRO Papers: Documents from the FBI's Secret Wars Against Dissent in the United States* (Boston: South End Press, 1990), p. 241.

43. Rex Weyler, op. cit., pp. 68–69. It should also be noted that Banks was convicted in June 1975, and immediately went underground. Finally, in September 1984, Banks surrendered. He ultimately served 14 months. *See* Ward Churchill and Jim Vander Wall, *Agents of Repression*, op. cit., pp. 346–47.

44. The average annual income on Pine Ridge at this time was about $1,000; Cheryl McCall, "Life on Pine Ridge Bleak," *Colorado Daily* (16 May 1975). Wilson hired his brother, Jim, to head the tribal planning office at an annual salary of $25,000 plus $15,000 in "consulting fees"; *New York Times* (22 Apr. 1975). Another brother, George, was hired at a salary of $20,000 to help the Oglalas "manage their affairs"; Wilson's wife was named director of the Reservation Head Start program at a salary of $18,000; his son, "Manny" (Richard, Jr.) was placed on the GOON ("Guardians of the Oglala Nation") payroll, along with several cousins and nephews; Wilson also upped his own salary from $5,500 per year to $15,500 per year, plus lucrative consulting fees, within his first six months in office; Peter Matthi-

essen, op. cit. [end. ed. 1991], p. 62. When queried about the propriety of all this, Wilson replied, "There's no law against nepotism"; Editors, *Voices from Wounded Knee, 1973* (Rooseveltown, NY: *Akwesasne Notes*, 1974), p. 34.

45. In addition to this BIA "seed money," Wilson is suspected of having misappropriated some $347,000 in federal highway improvement funds to meet GOON payrolls between 1972 and 1975. A 1975 General Accounting Office report indicates that the funds had been expended without any appreciable road repair having been done, and that the Wilsonites had kept no books with which to account for this mysterious situation. Nonetheless, the FBI declined to undertake a further investigation of the matter.

46. The Gunnery Range, comprising the northwestern eighth of Pine Ridge, was an area "borrowed" from the Oglalas by the War Department in 1942 as a place to train aerial gunners. It was to be returned at the end of World War II, but never was. By the early '70s, the Oglala traditionals had begun to agitate heavily for its recovery. The deposits had been secretly discovered in 1971, however, through a technologically elaborate survey and mapping project undertaken jointly by the National Aeronautics and Space Administration (NASA) and a little-known entity called the National Uranium Resource Evaluation Institute (NURE). At that point, the government set out to obtain permanent title over the property; it's quid pro quo with Wilson seems to have been his willingness to provide it. *See* J. P. Gries, *Status of Mineral Resource Information on the Pine Ridge Indian Reservation, S.D.* (Washington, DC: BIA Bulletin No. 12, U.S. Department of the Interior, 1976). *See* also Jacqueline Huber et al., *The Gunnery Range Report* (Pine Ridge, South Dakota: Office of the Oglala Sioux Tribal President, 1981).

47. *Voices from Wounded Knee*, op. cit., pp. 17–26.

48. Quoted in Peter Matthiessen, op. cit. [end. ed., 1991], p. 66.

49. Robert Burnette and John Koster, op. cit., p. 74.

50. The action was proposed by OSCRO leader Pedro Bissonette and endorsed by traditional Oglala chiefs Frank Fools Crow, Pete Catches, Ellis Chips, Edgar Red Cloud, Jake Kills Enemy, Morris Wounded, Severt Young Bear, and Everette Catches. *See Voices from Wounded Knee, 1973*, op. cit., p. 36.

51. Rex Weyler, op. cit., pp. 76–78.

52. One of their first actions was to meet with Colonel Vic Jackson, a subordinate of future Federal Emergency Management Agency (FEMA) head Louis Giuffrida, brought in from California to "consult." Through an entity called the California Civil Disorder Management School, Jackson and Giuffrida had devised a pair of "multi–agency domestic counterinsurgency scenarios" code–named "Garden Plot" and "Cable Splicer" in which the government was interested. There is thus more than passing indication that what followed at Wounded Knee was, at least in part, a field test of these plans. *See* Rex Weyler, op. cit., pp. 80–81. *See* also Ken Lawrence, *The New State Repression* (Chicago: International Network Against the New State Repression, 1985).

53. Rex Weyler, op. cit., p. 83. The quantity of M–16 ammunition should actually read 1.3 million rounds. The military also provided state–of–the–art communications gear, M–14 sniper rifles and ammunition, "Starlight" night vision scopes and other optical technology, tear gas rounds and flares for M–79 grenade launchers, and field provisions to feed the assembled federal forces. All of this was in flat violation of the *Posse Comitatus* Act (18 USCS § 1385), which makes it illegal for the government to deploy its military against "civil disturbances." For this reason, Colonels Warner and Potter, and the other military personnel they brought in, wore civilian clothes at Wounded Knee in an effort to hide their involvement.

54. Bill Zimmerman, *Airlift to Wounded Knee* (Chicago: Swallow Press, 1976).

55. Clearwater was mortally wounded on April 17, 1973, and died on April 25; *Voices from Wounded Knee, 1973*, op. cit., p. 179. Lamont was hit on April 27, after being driven from his bunker by tear gas. Federal gunfire then prevented medics from reaching him until he died from loss of blood; ibid., p. 220.

56. Robert Burnette later recounted how, once the siege had ended, Justice Department Solicitor General Kent Frizzell asked his assistance in searching for such graves; Robert Burnette and John Koster, op. cit., p. 248. *See* also *Voices from Wounded Knee, 1973*, op. cit., p. 193.

57. The "hostages" were mostly elderly residents of Wounded Knee: Wilbert A. Reigert (age 86), Girlie Clark (75), Clive Gildersleeve (73), Agnes Gildersleeve (68), Bill Cole (82), Mary Pike (72), and Annie Hunts Horse (78). Others included Guy Fritz (age 49), Jeane Fritz (47), Adrienne Fritz (12), and Father Paul Manhart (46). When South Dakota Senators George McGovern and James Abourezk went to Wounded Knee on March 2 to "bring the hostages out," the supposed captives announced they had no intention of leaving. Instead, they stated they wished to stay to "protect [their] property from federal forces" and that they considered the AIM people to be the "real hostages in this situation." *See* Robert Burnette and John Koster, op. cit., pp. 227–28.

58. The first federal casualty was an FBI agent named Curtis Fitzpatrick, hit in the wrist by a spent round on March 11, 1973. Interestingly, with his head swathed in bandages, he was evacuated by helicopter before a crowd of reporters assembled to witness the event; Robert Burnette and John Koster, op. cit., pp. 237–38. The second, U.S. Marshal Lloyd Grimm, was struck in the back and permanently paralyzed on March 23. Grimm was, however, facing the AIM perimeter when he was hit. The probability is therefore that he was shot—perhaps unintentionally—by one of Wilson's GOONs, who were at the time firing from positions behind those of the marshals; *Voices from Wounded Knee, 1973*, op. cit., p. 128.

59. Quoted in ibid., p. 47.

60. Held was simultaneously serving as head of the FBI's Internal Security Section and as Special Agent in Charge (SAC) of the Bureau's Chicago Office. He had been assigned the latter position, in addition to his other duties, so that he might orchestrate a cover–up of the FBI's involvement in the 1969 murders of Illinois Black Panther leaders Fred Hampton and Mark Clark. At the outset of the Wounded Knee Siege, he was detached from his SAC position—a very atypical circumstance—and sent to Pine Ridge in order to prepare a study of how the Bureau should deal with AIM "insurgents." The result, entitled "FBI Paramilitary Operations in Indian Country"—in which the author argued, among other things, that "shoot to kill" orders should be made standard—is extremely significant in light of subsequent Bureau activities on the reservation and Held's own role in them.

61. The terms of the standdown agreement are covered in *Voices from Wounded Knee, 1973*, p. 231. The full text of the treaty may be found in Charles J. Kappler, op. cit., pp. 594–96.

62. Federal representatives plainly obfuscated, arguing that they were precluded from responding to questions of treaty compliance because of Congress's 1871 suspension of treaty making with Indians (Title 25 USC § 71). As Lakota elder Matthew King rejoined, however, the Indians were not asking that a new treaty be negotiated. Rather, they were demanding that U.S. commitments under an *existing* treaty be honored, a matter which was not only possible under the 1871 Act, but *required* by it. *See Voices from Wounded Knee, 1973*, op. cit., p. 252–54.

63. Instead, a single Marshal was dispatched to Fools Crow's home on the appointed date to deliver to those assembled there a note signed by White House Counsel Leonard Garment. The missive stated that "the days of treaty–making with Indians ended in 1871, 102 years ago"; quoted in *Voices from Wounded Knee, 1973*, op. cit., pp. 257–58.

64. U.S. House of Representatives, Committee on the Judiciary, Subcommittee on Civil and Constitutional Rights, *1st Session on FBI Authorization, March 19, 24, 25; April 2 and 8, 1981* (Washington, DC: 97th Cong., 2nd Sess., U.S. Government Printing Office, 1981).

65. Rex Weyler, op. cit., p. 95; Robert Burnette and John Koster, op. cit., p. 253.

66. *1st Session on FBI Authorization*, 1981, op. cit.

67. Ibid. Means was convicted on *none* of the 40 federal charges. Instead, he was finally found guilty in 1977 under South Dakota State Law of "Criminal Syndicalism" and served a year in the maximum security prison at Sioux Falls. Means was, and will remain, the only individual ever convicted under this statute; the South Dakota legislature repealed the law while he was imprisoned. Amnesty International was preparing to adopt him as a Prisoner of Conscience when he was released in 1979; Amnesty International, *Proposal for a Commission of Inquiry into the Effect of Domestic Intelligence Activities on Criminal Trials in the United States of America* (New York: Amnesty International, 1980).

68. For excerpts from the transcripts of the "Sioux Sovereignty Hearing" conducted in Lincoln, Nebraska, during the fall of 1974, *see* Roxanne Dunbar Ortiz, ed., *The Great Sioux Nation: Sitting in Judgement on America* (New York/San Francisco: International Indian Treaty Council/Moon Books, 1977).

69. Tried together in the second "Leadership Trial," Crow Dog, Holder, and Camp were convicted of minor offenses during the spring of 1975. Holder and Camp went underground to avoid sentencing. Crow Dog was granted probation (as were his co–defendants when they surfaced), and then placed under charges unrelated to Wounded Knee the following November. Convicted and sentenced to five years, he was imprisoned first in the federal maximum security facility at Lewisburg, Pennsylvania, and then at Leavenworth, Kansas. The National Council of Churches and Amnesty International were preparing to adopt him as a Prisoner of Conscience when he was released on parole in 1977. *See* Rex Weyler, op. cit., p. 189; *Amnesty International*, op. cit.

70. As a congressional study concluded, this was "a very low rate considering the usual rate of conviction in Federal Courts and the great input of resources in these cases"; *1st Session on FBI Authorization, 1981*, op. cit.

71. This is a classic among the counterintelligence methodologies utilized by the FBI. For example, according to a Bureau report declassified by a Senate Select Committee in 1975, agents in Philadelphia, Pennsylvania, offered as an "example of a successful counterintelligence technique" their use of "any excuse for arrest" as a means of "neutralizing" members of a targeted organization, the Revolutionary Action Movement (RAM) during the summer of 1967. "RAM people," the document went on, "were arrested and released on bail, but they were re–arrested several times until they could no longer make bail." The tactic was recommended for use by other FBI offices to "curtail the activities" of objectionable political groups in their areas. Complete text of this document will be found in Ward Churchill and Jim Vander Wall, *Agents of Repression*, op. cit., pp. 45–47. More broadly, *see* U.S. Senate, Select Committee to Study Government Operations with Respect to Intelligence Activities, *Final Report: Supplementary Detailed Staff Reports on Intelligence Activities and the Rights of Americans, Book III* (Washington, DC: 94th Cong., 2nd Sess., U.S. Government Printing Office, 1976).

72. This is the standard delineation of objectives attending the FBI's domestic counterintelligence programs (COINTELPROs); *see* the document reproduced in Ward Churchill and Jim Vander Wall, *The COINTELPRO Papers*, op. cit., pp. 92–93.

73. Quoted in Martin Garbus, "General Haig of Wounded Knee," *The Nation* (9 Nov. 1974).

74. A complete list of those killed and dates of death is contained in Ward Churchill and Jim Vander Wall, *The COINTELPRO Papers,* op. cit., pp. 393–94.

75. The U.S. Department of Justice, Commission on Civil Rights, *Events Surrounding Recent Murders on the Pine Ridge Reservation in South Dakota,* op. cit.

76. Bruce Johansen and Roberto Maestas, *Wasi'chu: The Continuing Indian Wars,* op. cit., pp. 83–84.

77. FBI jurisdiction on reservations accrues under the 1885 Major Crimes Act (Ch. 341, 24 *Stat.* 362, 385, now codified at 18 USC 1153).

78. As examples: Delphine Crow Dog, sister of AIM's spiritual leader, was beaten unconscious and left to freeze to death in a field on November 9, 1974; AIM member Joseph Stuntz Killsright was killed by a bullet to the head and apparently shot repeatedly in the torso after death on June 26, 1975.

79. Consider the case of the brothers Vernal and Clarence Cross, both AIM members, who were stopped along the road with car trouble outside Pine Ridge village on June 19, 1973. Individuals firing from a nearby field hit both men, killing Clarence and severely wounding Vernal. Another bullet struck nine–year–old Mary Ann Little Bear, who was riding in a car driven by her father and coming in the opposite direction, in the face, blinding her in one eye. Mr. Little Bear identified three individuals to police and FBI agents as being the shooters. None of the three were interrogated. Instead, authorities arrested Vernal Cross in the hospital, charging him with murdering Clarence (the charges were later dropped). No charges were ever filed in the shooting of Mary Ann Little Bear. *See* Rex Weyler, op. cit., p. 106.

80. Quoted in Bruce Johansen and Roberto Maestas, op. cit., p. 88. Actually, O'Clock's position fits into a broader Bureau policy. "When Indians complain about the lack of investigation and prosecution on reservation crime, they are usually told the Federal government does not have the resources to handle the work"; U.S. Department of Justice, *Report of the Task Force on Indian Matters* (Washington, DC: U.S. Government Printing Office, 1975), pp. 42–43.

81. In 1972, the Rapid City Resident Agency was staffed by three agents. This was expanded to 11 in March 1973, and augmented by a 10–member SWAT team shortly thereafter. By the spring of 1975, more than 30 agents were assigned to Rapid City on a long–term basis, and as many as two dozen others were steadily coming and going while performing "special tasks." *See* Bruce Johansen and Roberto Maestas, op. cit., p. 93; the U.S. Department of Justice, *Report of the Task Force on Indian Matters,* op. cit., pp. 42–43.

82. In the Clarence Cross murder, for example, the killers were identified as John Hussman, Woody Richards, and Francis Randall, all prominent members of the GOONs. Or again, in the January 30, 1976, murder of AIM supporter Byron DeSersa near the reservation hamlet of Wamblee, at least a dozen people identified GOONs Billy Wilson (Dickie Wilson's younger son), Charles David Winters, Dale Janis, and Chuck Richards as being among the killers. Indeed, the guilty parties were still on the scene when two FBI agents arrived. Yet the only person arrested was a witness, an elderly Cheyenne named Guy Dull Knife, because of the vociferousness with which he complained about the agents' inaction. The BIA police, for their part, simply ordered the GOONs to leave town. *See* U.S. Commission on Civil Rights, *American Indian Issues in South Dakota: Hearing Held in Rapid City, South Dakota, July 27–28, 1978* (Washington, DC: U.S. Government Printing Office, 1978), p. 33.

83. On the CIA's relationship to Latin American death squads, *see* Penny Lernoux, *Cry of the People: United States Involvement in the Rise of Fascism, Torture, and Murder, and the Persecution of the Catholic Church in Latin America* (New York: Doubleday, 1980).

84. *Voices from Wounded Knee, 1973*, op. cit., p. 189. Frizzell himself has confirmed the account.

85. *Voices from Wounded Knee, 1973*, op. cit., p. 190.

86. The directive was issued on April 24, 1973.

87. Ibid., p. 213; Rex Weyler, op. cit., pp. 92–93.

88. *See*, for example, Athan Theoharis, "Building a Case Against the FBI," *Washington Post* (30 Oct. 1988).

89. Ward Churchill, "Death Squads in America: Confessions of a Government Terrorist," *Yale Journal of Law and Liberation*, No. 3 (1992). The interview was conducted by independent film makers Kevin Barry McKiernan and Michelle DuBois several years earlier, but not released in transcript form until 1991.

90. "Det cord" is detonation cord, a rope–like explosive often used by the U.S. military to fashion booby traps. Brewer also makes mention of Bureau personnel introducing himself and other GOONs to civilian right–wingers who provided additional ordnance.

91. Another example of this sort of thing came in the wake of the February 27, 1975, beating and slashing of AIM defense attorney Roger Finzel, his client, Bernard Escamilla, and several associates at the Pine Ridge Airport by a group of GOONs headed by Duane Brewer and Dickie Wilson himself. The event being too visible to be simply ignored, Wilson was allowed to plead guilty to a petty offense carrying a $10 penalty in his own tribal court. Federal charges were then dropped on advice from the FBI—which had spent its investigative time polygraphing the victims rather than their assailants—because pressing them might constitute "double jeopardy"; Ward Churchill and Jim Vander Wall, *Agents of Repression*, op. cit., pp. 186, 428.

92. At one point, the Bureau attempted to implicate Northwest AIM leader Leonard Peltier in the killing. This ploy was abandoned only when it was conclusively demonstrated that Peltier was in another state when the murder occurred; interview with Peltier defense attorney Bruce Ellison (Oct. 1987) (tape on file).

93. Both Moves Camp and Bissonette drove white over dark blue Chevrolet sedans. It appears the killers simply mistook one for the other in the dark. The victim, who was not herself active in supporting AIM, was the sister of OSCRO leader Pedro Bissonette, shot to death under highly suspicious circumstances by BIA police officer–cum–GOON Joe Clifford on the night of October 17, 1973; Ward Churchill and Jim Vander Wall, *Agents of Repression*, op. cit., pp. 200–03.

94. Eastman, although a Crow, is directly related to the Dakota family of the same name, made famous by the writer Charles Eastman earlier in the century. Ironically, two of his relatives, the sisters Carole Standing Elk and Fern Matthias, purport to be AIM members in California.

95. Ward Churchill, "Death Squads in America," op. cit., p. 96.

96. Structurally, the appropriation of the formal apparatus of deploying force possessed by client states for purposes of composing death squads, long a hallmark of CIA covert operations in the Third World, corresponds quite well with the FBI's use of the BIA police on Pine Ridge; *see* A. J. Langguth, *Hidden Terrors: The Truth About U.S. Police Operations in Latin America* (New York: Pantheon Press, 1978); *see* also Edward S. Herman, *The Real Terror Network: Terrorism in Fact and Propaganda* (Boston: South End Press, 1982).

97. *See*, for example, the U.S. Department of Justice, Commission on Civil Rights, *Events Surrounding Recent Murders on the Pine Ridge Reservation in South Dakota*, op. cit.

98. In late 1973, Means took a majority of all votes cast in the tribal primaries. In the 1974 runoff, however, Wilson retained his presidency by a 200–vote margin. A subsequent investigation by the U.S. Commission on Civil Rights revealed that 154 cases of voter fraud—non–Oglalas being allowed to vote—had occurred. A further undetermined number of invalid votes had been cast by Oglalas who did not meet tribal residency requirements. No record had been kept of the number of ballots printed or how and in what numbers they had been distributed. No poll watchers were present in many locations, and those who were present at the others had been appointed by Wilson rather than an impartial third party. There was also significant evidence that pro–Means voters had been systematically intimidated, and in some cases roughed up, by Wilsonites stationed at each polling place; U.S. Commission on Civil Rights, *Report of Investigation: Oglala Sioux Tribe, General Election, 1974* (Denver: Rocky Mountain Regional Office, Oct. 1974). Despite these official findings, the FBI performed no substantive investigation, and the BIA allowed the results of the election to stand; Ward Churchill and Jim Vander Wall, *Agents of Repression*, op. cit., pp. 190–92.

99. As the Jumping Bulls' daughter, Roselyn, later put it, "We asked those AIM boys to come help us ... [defend ourselves against] Dickie Wilson and his goons"; quoted in an unpublished manuscript by researcher Candy Hamilton, p. 3 (copy on file).

100. *See*, for example, a memorandum from SAC Minneapolis (Joseph Trimbach) to the FBI Director, dated June 3, 1975, and captioned "Law Enforcement on the Pine Ridge Indian Reservation," in which it is recommended that armored personnel carriers be used to assault AIM defensive positions.

101. No such warrant existed. When an arrest order was finally issued for Eagle on July 9, 1975, it was for the petty theft of a pair of used cowboy boots from a white ranch hand. Eagle was acquitted even of this when the case was taken to trial in 1976. Meanwhile, George O'Clock's assignment of two agents to pursue an Indian teenager over so trivial an offense at a time when he professed to be too shorthanded to investigate the murders of AIM members speaks for itself; Peter Matthiessen, op. cit. [end. ed., 1991], p. 173.

102. Ibid., p. 156.

103. The agents followed a red pickup truck, which, unbeknownst to them, was full of dynamite, onto the property. In the valley, the truck stopped, and its occupants got out. Williams and Coler also stopped and got out of their cars. They then began firing toward the pickup, a direction which carried their rounds into the AIM camp, where a number of noncombatant women and children were situated. AIM security then began to fire back. It is a certainty that AIM did not initiate the firefight because, as Bob Robideau later put it, "Nobody in their right mind would start a gunfight, using a truckload of dynamite for cover." Once the agents were preoccupied, the pickup made its escape (Northwest AIM was toying with the idea of using the explosives to remove George Washington's face from the nearby Mt. Rushmore National Monument.); interview with Bob Robideau, May 1990 (notes on file).

104. Peter Matthiessen, op. cit. [end. ed., 1991], p. 158.

105. An additional indicator is that the inimitable William Janklow also seems to have been on alert, awaiting a call telling him things were under way. In any event, when called, Janklow was able to assemble a white vigilante force in Hot Springs, S.D., and drive about 50 miles to the Jumping Bull property, arriving there at about 1:30 p.m., an elapsed time of approximately two hours.

106. A further indication of preplanning by the Bureau is found in a June 27, 1975, memorandum from R. E. Gebhart to Mr. O'Donnell at FBI Headquarters. It states that Chicago SAC/Internal Security Chief Richard G. Held was contacted by headquarters about the firefight *at the Minneapolis field office* at 12:30 p.m. on June 26. It turns out that Held

had already been detached from his position in Chicago and was in Minneapolis—under which the authority of the Rapid City resident agency, and hence Pine Ridge, falls—awaiting word to temporarily take over from Minneapolis SAC Joseph Trimbach. The only ready explanation for this highly unorthodox circumstance, unprecedented in Bureau history, is that it was expected that Held's peculiar expertise in political repression would be needed for a major operation on Pine Ridge in the immediate future; Bruce Johansen and Roberto Maestas, op. cit., p. 95.

107. Peter Matthiessen, op. cit. [end. ed., 1991], pp. 483–85.

108. The FBI sought to "credit" BIA police officer Gerald Hill with the lethal long–range shot to the head, fired at Killsright at about 3 p.m., despite the fact that he was plainly running away and therefore presented no threat to law–enforcement personnel (it was also not yet known that Coler and Williams were dead). However, Waring, who was with Hill at the time, was the trained sniper of the pair, and equipped accordingly. In any event, several witnesses who viewed Killsright's corpse *in situ*—including Assistant South Dakota Attorney General William Delaney and reporter Kevin Barry McKiernan—subsequently stated that it appeared to them that someone had fired a burst from an automatic into the torso from close range and then tried to hide the fact by putting an FBI jacket over the *postmortem* wounds; ibid., p. 183.

109. The agents' standard attire was Vietnam–issue "boonie hats, jungle fatigues, and boots. Their weapons were standard army M–16s. The whole affair was deliberately staged to resemble a military operation in Southeast Asia"; *see* the selection of photographs in Ward Churchill and Jim Vander Wall, *Agents of Repression*, op. cit.

110. Williams and Coler had each been shot three times. The FBI knew, from the sound of the rifles during the firefight if nothing else, that AIM had used no automatic weapons. Neither agent was stripped. There were no bunkers, but rather only a couple of old root cellars and tumble–down corrals, common enough in rural areas and not used as firing positions in any event (the Bureau would have known this because of the absence of spent cartridge casings in such locations). Far from being "lured" to the Jumping Bull property, they had returned after being expressly told to leave (and, in any event, they were supposed to be serving a warrant). Instructively, no one in the nation's press corps thought to ask how, exactly, Coll might happen to know either agent's last words, since nobody from the FBI was present when they were killed; Joel D. Weisman, "About that 'Ambush' at Wounded Knee," *Columbia Journalism Review* (Sept.–Oct. 1975); *see* also Ward Churchill, "Renegades, Terrorists and Revolutionaries," op. cit.

111. The director's admission came during a press conference conducted at the Century Plaza Hotel on July 1, 1975, in conjunction with Coler's and Williams' funerals. It was accorded inside coverage by the press, unlike the page–one treatment given Coll's original disinformation; Tom Bates, "The Government's Secret War on the Indian," *Oregon Times* (Feb.–Mar. 1976).

112. Examples of the air assault technique include a 35–man raid on the property of AIM spiritual leader Selo Black Crow, near the village of Wamblee, on July 8, 1975. Crow Dog's Paradise, on the Rosebud Reservation, just across the line from Pine Ridge, was hit by 100 heliborne agents on September 5. Meanwhile, an elderly Oglala named James Brings Yellow had suffered a heart attack and died when agent J. Gary Adams suddenly kicked in his door during a no–knock search on July 12. By August, such abuse by the FBI was so pervasive that even some of Wilson's GOONs were demanding that the agents withdraw from the reservation; *see* Ward Churchill and Jim Vander Wall, *The COINTELPRO Papers*, op. cit., pp. 268–70.

113. By September, it had become obvious to everyone that AIM lacked the military capacity to protect the traditionals from the level of violence being imposed by the FBI by that point. Hence, it began a pointed disengagement in order to alleviate pressure on the traditionals. On October 16, 1975, Richard G. Held sent a memo to FBI Headquarters advising that his work in South Dakota was complete and that he anticipated returning to his position in Chicago by October 18; a portion of this document is reproduced in ibid., p. 273.

114. "Memorandum of Agreement Between the Oglala Sioux Tribe of South Dakota and the National Park Service of the Department of Interior to Facilitate Establishment, Development, Administration and Public Use of the Oglala Sioux Tribal Lands, Badlands National Monument" (Washington, DC: U.S. Department of the Interior, 2 Jan. 1976). The Act assuming title is P.L. 90–468 (1976). If there is any doubt as to whether the transfer was about uranium, consider that the law was amended in 1978—in the face of considerable protest by the traditionals—to allow the Oglalas to recover *surface* use rights any time they decided by referendum to do so. Subsurface (mineral) rights, however, were permanently retained by the government. Actually, the whole charade was illegal, insofar as the still-binding 1868 Fort Laramie Treaty requires three–fourths express consent of all adult male Lakotas to validate land transfers, not land recoveries. Such consent, obviously, was never obtained with respect to the Gunnery Range transfer; *see* Jacqueline Huber et al., *The Gunnery Range Report*, op. cit.

115. The congressional missive read: "Attached is a letter from the Senate Select Committee (SSC), dated 6–23–75, addressed to [U.S. Attorney General] Edward S. Levi. This letter announces the SSC's intent to conduct interviews relating ... to our investigation at 'Wounded Knee' and our investigation of the American Indian Movement.... On 6–27–75, Patrick Shae, staff member of the SSC, requested we hold in abeyance any action ... in view of the killing of the Agents at Pine Ridge, South Dakota."

116. The selection of those charged seems to have served a dual purpose: 1) to "decapitate" one of AIM's best and most cohesive security groups, and 2) in not charging participants from Pine Ridge, to divide the locals from their sources of outside support. The window-dressing charges against Jimmy Eagle were explicitly dropped in order to "place the full prosecutorial weight of the government on Leonard Peltier"; quoted in Jim Messerschmidt, *The Trial of Leonard Peltier* (Boston: South End Press, 1984), p. 47.

117. Butler was apprehended at Crow Dog's Paradise during the FBI's massive air assault there on September 5, 1975. Robideau was arrested in a hospital where he was being treated for injuries sustained when his car exploded on the Kansas Turnpike on September 10; Ward Churchill and Jim Vander Wall, *Agents of Repression*, op. cit., pp. 448–49.

118. Acting on an informant's tip, the Oregon State Police stopped a car and a motor home belonging to the actor Marlon Brando near the town of Ontario on the night of November 14, 1975. Arrested in the motor home were Kamook Banks and Anna Mae Pictou Aquash, who was a fugitive with minor charges against her in South Dakota; arrested in the automobile were AIM members Russell Redner and Kenneth Loudhawk. Two men—Dennis Banks, a fugitive from sentencing after being convicted of inciting the 1972 Custer Courthouse "riot" in South Dakota, and Leonard Peltier, a fugitive on several warrants, including one for murder in the deaths of Williams and Coler—escaped from the motor home. Peltier was wounded in the process. On February 6, 1976, acting on another informant's tip, the Royal Canadian Mounted Police arrested Peltier, Frank Black Horse (a.k.a., Frank DeLuca), and Ronald Blackman (a.k.a., Ron Janvier) at Smallboy's Camp, about 160 miles east of Edmunton, Alberta; Peter Matthiessen, op. cit. [end ed., 1991], pp. 249–51, 272–78. On the outcome for Dennis Banks and the others, *see* Ward Churchill, "Due Process Be Damned: The Case of the Portland Four," *Zeta* (Jan. 1988).

119. Poor Bear, a clinically unbalanced Oglala, was picked up for "routine questioning" by agents David Price and Ron Wood in February 1976 and then held incommunicado for nearly two months in the Hacienda Motel, in Gordon, Nebraska. During this time she was continuously threatened with dire consequences by the agents unless she "cooperated" with their "investigation" into the deaths of Coler and Williams. At some point, Price began to type up for her signature affidavits that incriminated Leonard Peltier. Ultimately, she signed three mutually exclusive "accounts"; one of them—in which Peltier is said to have been her boyfriend, and to have confessed to her one night in a Nebraska bar that he had killed the agents—was submitted in Canadian court to obtain Peltier's extradition on June 18, 1976. Meanwhile, on March 29, Price caused Poor Bear to be on the stand against Richard Marshall in Rapid City, during the OSCRO/AIM member's state trial for killing Martin Montileaux. She testified that she was Marshall's girlfriend and that he had confessed the murder to her one night in a Nebraska bar. Marshall was then convicted. Federal prosecutors declined to introduce Poor Bear as a witness at either the Butler/Robideau or Peltier trials, observing that her testimony was "worthless" due to her mental condition. She has publicly and repeatedly recanted her testimony against both Peltier and Marshall, saying she never met either of them in her life. For years, members of the Canadian parliament have been demanding Peltier's return to their jurisdiction due to the deliberate perpetration of fraud by U.S. authorities in his extradition proceeding, and to block renewal of the U.S.–Canadian Extradition Treaty in the event that the United States fails to comply. The Poor Bear affidavits are reproduced in Ward Churchill and Jim Vander Wall, *The COINTELPRO Papers*, op. cit., pp. 288–91. On her testimony against Marshall and recantations, *see* Ward Churchill and Jim Vander Wall, *Agents of Repression*, op. cit., pp. 339–42. On the position of the Canadian Parliament, *see*, for example, "External Affairs: Canada–U.S. Extradition Treaty—Case of Leonard Peltier, Statement of Mr. James Fulton," in *House of Commons Debate, Canada*, Vol. 128, No. 129 (Ottawa: 1st Sess., 33rd Par. Official Report, Thurs., 17 Apr. 1986).

120. The disinformation campaign centered on the Bureau's "leaks" of the so–called Dog Soldier Teletypes on June 21 and 22, 1976—in the midst of the Butler/Robideau trial—to "friendly media representatives." The documents, which were never in any way substantiated but were nonetheless sensationally reported across the country, asserted that 2,000 AIM "Dog Soldiers," acting in concert with SDS (a long–defunct white radical group) and the Crusade for Justice (a militant Chicano organization), had equipped themselves with illegal weapons and explosives and were preparing to embark on a campaign of terrorism which included "killing a cop a day ... sniping at tourists ... burning out farmers ... assassinating the Governor of South Dakota ... blowing up the Fort Randall Dam" and breaking people out of the maximum security prison at Sioux Falls. The second teletype is reproduced in Ward Churchill and Jim Vander Wall, *The COINTELPRO Papers*, op. cit. pp. 277–82.

121. Defense attorney William Kunstler queried Kelley as to whether there was "one shred, one scintilla of evidence" to support the allegations made by the FBI in the Dog Soldier Teletypes. Kelley replied, "I know of none." Nonetheless, the FBI continued to feature AIM prominently in its *Domestic Terrorist Digest*, distributed free of charge to state and local police departments nationally; ibid., p. 276.

122. The initial round striking both Coler and Williams was a .44 magnum. Bob Robideau testified that he was the only AIM member using a .44 magnum during the firefight; Bob Robideau interview (Nov. 1993), tape on file.

123. Videotaped NBC interview with Robert Bolin, 1990 (raw tape on file).

124. FBI personnel in attendance at this confab were Director Kelley and Richard G. Held, by then promoted to the rank of Assistant Director, James B. Adams, Richard J. Gallagher, John C. Gordon, and Herbert H. Hawkins, Jr. Representing the Justice Department were

prosecutor Evan Hultman and his boss, William B. Grey; memo from B. H. Cooke to Richard J. Gallagher, 10 Aug. 1976.

125. McManus professes to have been "astonished" when he was removed from the Peltier case; Peter Matthiessen, op. cit. [end. ed. 1991], p. 566.

126. *United States v. Leonard Peltier*, CR–75–5106–1, U.S. District Court for the District of North Dakota, 1977 (hereinafter referred to as *Peltier Trial Transcript*).

127. Butler and Robideau were tried on the premise that they were part of a conspiracy which led to a group slaying of Williams and Coler. Peltier was tried as the "lone gunman" who had caused their deaths. Similarly, at Cedar Rapids, agent J. Gary Adams had testified that the dead agents followed a red pickup onto the Jumping Bull property; during the Fargo trial, he testified they'd followed a "red and white van" belonging to Peltier. The defense was prevented by the judge's evidentiary ruling at the outset from impeaching such testimony on the basis of its contradiction to sworn testimony already entered against Butler and Robideau; *see Peltier Trial Transcript*, op. cit., and *United States v. Darrelle E. Butler and Robert E. Robideau*, CR76–11, U.S. District Court for the District of Iowa, 1976, for purposes of comparison; the matter is well analyzed in Jim Messerschmidt, op. cit.

128. No slugs were recovered from Williams' and Coler's bodies, and two separate autopsies were inconclusive in determining the exact type of weapon from which the fatal shots were fired. The key piece of evidence in this respect was a .223 caliber shell casing which the FBI said was ejected from the killer's AR–15 rifle into the open trunk of Coler's car at the moment he fired one of the lethal rounds. The Bureau also claimed its ballistics investigation proved only one such weapon was used by AIM during the firefight. Ipso facto, whichever AIM member could be shown to have used an AR–15 on June 26, 1975, would be the guilty party. The problem is that the cartridge casing was not found in Coler's trunk when agents initially went over the car with fine tooth combs. Instead, it was supposedly found later, on one of two different days, by one of two different agents, and turned over to someone whose identity neither could quite recall, somewhere on the reservation. How the casing got from whomever and wherever that was to the FBI crime lab in Washington, DC, is, of course, equally mysterious. This is what was used to establish the "murder weapon"; *Peltier Trial Transcript*, op. cit., pp. 2114, 3012–13, 3137–38, 3235, 3342, 3388.

129. Agent Frank Coward, who did not testify to this effect against Butler and Robideau, claimed at the Fargo trial that shortly after the estimated time of Coler's and Williams' deaths, he observed Leonard Peltier, who he conceded he'd never seen before, running away from their cars and carrying an AR–15 rifle. This sighting was supposedly made through a 7x rifle scope at a distance of 800 meters (one–half mile) through severe atmospheric heat shimmers while Peltier was moving at an oblique angle to the observer. Defense tests demonstrated that any such identification was impossible, even among friends standing full–face and under perfect weather conditions. In any event, this is what was used to tie Peltier to the "murder weapon"; ibid., p. 1305.

130. Seventeen–year–old Wish Draper, for instance, was strapped to a chair at the police station at Window Rock, Arizona, while being "interrogated" by FBI agents Charles Stapleton and James Doyle; he thereupon agreed to "cooperate" by testifying against Peltier; ibid., pp. 1087–098. Seventeen–year–old Norman Brown was told by agents J. Gary Adams and O. Victor Harvey during their interrogation of him that he'd "never walk this earth again" unless he testified in the manner they desired; ibid., pp. 4799–4804, 4842–843. Fifteen–year–old Mike Anderson was also interrogated by Adams and Harvey. In this case, they offered both the carrot and the stick: to get pending charges dismissed against him if he testified as instructed, and to "beat the living shit" out of him if he didn't; ibid., pp. 840–42.

All three young men acknowledged under defense cross–examination that they'd lied under oath at the request of the FBI and federal prosecutors.

131. Crooks' speech is worth quoting in part: "Apparently Special Agent Williams was killed first. He was shot in the face and hand by a bullet ... probably begging for his life, and he was shot. The back of his head was blown off by a high powered rifle.... Leonard Peltier then turned, as the evidence indicates, to Jack Coler lying on the ground helpless. He shoots him in the top of the head. Apparently feeling he hadn't done a good enough job, he shoots him again through the jaw, and his face explodes. No shell comes out, just explodes. The whole bottom of his chin is blow out by the force of the concussion. Blood splattered against the side of the car"; *Peltier Trial Transcript*, op. cit., p. 5011.

132. Peltier's being sent directly contravenes federal Bureau of Prisons regulations restricting placement in that facility to "incorrigibles" who have "a record of unmanageability in more normal penal settings." Leonard Peltier had no prior convictions and therefore no record, unmanageable or otherwise, of behavior in penal settings.

133. *United States v. Peltier*, 858 F.2d 314, 335 (8th Cir. 1978).

134. *United States v. Peltier*, 440 U.S. 945, *cert. denied* (1979).

135. Another 6,000–odd pages of FBI file material on Peltier are still being withheld on the basis of "National Security."

136. At trial, FBI ballistics expert Evan Hodge testified that the actual AR–15 had been recovered from Bob Robideau's burned–out car along the Wichita Turnpike in September 1975. The weapon was so badly damaged by the fire, Hodge said, that it had been impossible to perform a match–comparison of firing pin tool marks by which to link it to the cartridge casing supposedly found in the trunk of Coler's car. However, by removing the bolt mechanism from the damaged weapon and putting it in an undamaged rifle, he claimed, it had been possible to perform a rather less conclusive match–comparison of extractor tool marks, with which to tie the Wichita AR–15 to the Coler car casing. Among the documents released under provision of the FOIA in 1981 was an October 2, 1975, teletype written by Hodge stating that he had in fact performed a firing pin test using the Wichita AR–15, and that it failed to produce a match to the crucial casing; *United States v. Peltier*, Motion to Vacate Judgement and for a New Trial, Crim. No. CR–3003, U.S. District Court for the District of North Dakota, (filed 15 Dec. 1982). The Eighth Circuit Court's decision to allow the appeal to proceed, despite Judge Bensen's rejection of the preceding motion, is listed as *United States v. Peltier*, 731 F.2d 550, 555 (8th Cir. 1984).

137. During the evidentiary hearing on Peltier's second appeal, conducted in Bismark, North Dakota, during late October 1984, it began to emerge that AIM members had used—and the FBI had *known* they had used—not one but several AR–15s during the Oglala Firefight. This stood to destroy the "single AR–15" theory used to convict Peltier at trial. Moreover, the evidentiary chain concerning the Coler car casing was brought into question. In an effort to salvage the situation, Bureau ballistics chief Evan Hodge took the stand to testify that he, and he *alone*, had handled ballistics materials related to the Peltier case. Appeal attorney William Kunstler then queried him concerning margin notes on the ballistics reports which were not his own. At that point, he retracted, admitting that a lab assistant, Joseph Twardowski, had also handled the evidence and worked on the reports. Kunstler asked whether Hodge was sure that only Twardowski and himself had had access to the materials and conclusions adduced from them. Hodge responded emphatically in the affirmative. Kunstler then pointed to yet another handwriting in the report margins and demanded a formal inquiry by the court. Two hours later, a deflated Hodge was allowed by Judge Bensen to return to the stand and admit he'd "misspoken" once again; he really had no idea who had handled the evidence, adding or subtracting pieces at will.

138. *United States v. Peltier*, CR–3003, Transcript of Oral Arguments Before the U.S. Eighth Circuit Court of Appeals, St. Louis, Missouri (15 Oct. 1985), p. 19.

139. Ibid., p.18.

140. U.S. Eighth Circuit Court of Appeals, "Appeal from the United States District of North Dakota in the Matter of *United States v. Leonard Peltier*," Crim. No. 85–5192, St. Louis, Missouri (11 Oct. 1986).

141. Ibid., p. 16.

142. The high court declined review despite the fact that the Eighth Circuit decision had created a question—deriving from a Supreme Court opinion rendered in *U.S. v. Bagley* (U.S. 105 S. Ct. 3375 [1985])—of what standard of doubt must be met before an appeals court is bound to remand a case to trial. The Eighth Circuit had formally concluded that while the Peltier jury might "possibly" have reached a different verdict had the appeals evidence been presented to it, it was necessary under Bagley guidelines that the jury would "probably" have rendered a different verdict before remand was appropriate. Even this ludicrously labored reasoning collapses upon itself when it is considered that, in a slightly earlier case, the Ninth Circuit had remanded on the basis that the verdict might possibly have been different. It is in large part to resolve just such questions of equal treatment before the law that the Supreme Court theoretically exists. Yet it flatly refused to do its job when it came to being involved in the Peltier case; Ward Churchill, "Leonard Peltier: The Ordeal Continues," *Zeta* (March 1988).

143. Holder moved into secondary education and works for Indian control of their schools in Kansas and Oklahoma. Others, such as Wilma Mankiller, Ted Means, and Twila Martin, have moved into more mainstream venues of tribal politics. Still others, like Phyllis Young and Madonna (Gilbert) Thunderhawk, have gone in the direction of environmentalism.

144. Examples include Jimmie Durham and John Arbuckle, both of whom now pursue—in dramatically different ways—careers in the arts.

145. Actually, this began very early on, as when AIM National President Carter Camp shot founder Clyde Bellecourt in the stomach in 1974 over a factional dispute instigated by Bellecourt's brother, Vernon. In the ensuing turmoil, Russell Means openly resigned from AIM, but was quickly reinstated; *see* Peter Matthiessen, op. cit. [end. ed. 1991], pp. 85–86.

146. Banks was granted sanctuary by California Governor Jerry Brown in 1977, because of such campaign statements by South Dakota Attorney General William Janklow as "the way to deal with AIM leaders is a bullet in the head" and that, if elected, he would "put AIM leaders either in our jails or under them." An enraged Janklow responded by threatening to arrange early parole for a number of South Dakota's worst felons on condition they accept immediate deportation to California. During his time of "refugee status" Banks served as chancellor of the AIM–initiated D–Q University, near Sacramento; *Rapid City Journal* (7 Apr. 1981). When Georgia Deukmajian replaced Brown as Governor of California in 1982, he rescinded his predecessor's protection of Banks. The latter then fled to the Onondaga Reservation in upstate New York. Finally, in September 1984, Janklow signed a personal guarantee of his safety, and Banks surrendered. *See* Ward Churchill and Jim Vander Wall, *Agents of Repression*, op. cit., pp. 346–47.

147. Rebecca L. Robbins, "American Indian Self–Determination: Comparative Analysis and Rhetorical Criticism," *Issues in Radical Therapy/New Studies on the Left*, Vol. XIII, Nos. 3–4 (Summer–Fall 1988).

148. An intended offshoot of the Peltier Defense Committee, designed to expose the identity of whoever had murdered AIM activist Anna Mae Pictou Aquash in execution style on Pine Ridge sometime in February 1976 (at the onset, it was expected this would be members of

Wilson's GOONs), quickly collapsed when it became apparent that AIM itself might be involved. It turned out that self–proclaimed AIM National Officer Vernon Bellecourt had directed security personnel during the 1975 AIM General Membership Meeting to interrogate Aquash as a possible FBI informant. They were, he said, to "bury her where she stands" if unsatisfied with her answers. The security team, composed of Northwest AIM members, did not act upon this instruction, instead incorporating Aquash into their own group. The Northwest AIM Group was rapidly decimated after the Oglala Firefight, however, and Aquash was left unprotected. It is instructive that, once her body turned up near Wamblee, Bellecourt was the prime mover in quashing an internal investigation of her death. For general background, *see* Johanna Brand, *The Life and Death of Anna Mae Aquash* (Toronto: James Lorimer Publishers, 1978).

149. Killed were Trudell's wife, Tina Manning, their three children—Ricarda Star (age five), Sunshine Karma (age three), and Eli Changing Sun (age one)—and Tina's mother, Leah Hicks Manning. They were burned to death as they slept in the Trudell's trailer home; the blaze occurred less than 12 hours after Trudell delivered a speech in front of FBI headquarters during which he burned an American flag; although there was ample reason to suspect arson, no police or FBI investigation ensued; Ward Churchill and Jim Vander Wall, *Agents of Repression*, op. cit., pp. 361–64.

150. Personal conversation with the author, 1979.

151. None of this is to say that LPDC did not continue. It did, even while failing to fulfill many of the wider objectives set forth by its founders. In terms of service to Peltier himself, aside from maintaining an ongoing legal appeals effort, the LPDC is largely responsible for the generation of more than 14 million petition signatures worldwide, all of them calling for his retrial. It has also been instrumental in bringing about several television documentaries, official inquiries into his situation by several foreign governments, an investigation by Amnesty International, and Peltier's receipt of a 1986 human rights award from the government of Spain. the LPDC has also engaged in a campaign to convince President Bill Clinton to bestow clemency.

152. *Keystone to Survival* (Rapid City, South Dakota: Black Hills Alliance, 1981).

153. On the U.S. uranium industry and its impact on reservation and reservation–adjacent lands, *see* Ward Churchill, "Radioactive Colonization: Hidden Holocaust in Native North America," in *Struggle for the Land: Indigenous Resistance to Genocide, Ecocide and Expropriation in Contemporary North America* (Monroe, Maine: Common Courage Press, 1993), pp. 261–328.

154. On the occupation, *see* Ward Churchill, "Yellow Thunder *Tiospaye*: Misadventure or Watershed Action?" *Policy Perspectives*, Vol. 2, No. 2 (Spring 1982).

155. *United States v. Means* et al., Civ. No. 81–5131, U.S. District Court for the District of South Dakota (9 Dec. 1985).

156. *Lyng v. Northwest Indian Cemetery Protection Association*, 485 U.S. 439 (1988). For further information, *see* Vine Deloria, Jr., "Trouble in High Places: Erosion of American Indian Rights to Religious Freedom in the United States," in *The State of Native America*, op. cit.

157. Anita Parlow, *Cry, Sacred Ground: Big Mountain, USA* (Washington, DC: Christic Institute, 1988).

158. Ward Churchill, "The Struggle for Newe Segobia: The Western Shoshone Battle for Their Homeland," in *Struggle for the Land*, op. cit., pp. 197–216.

159. On the early days of IITC, *see* "Chapter 7: The Fourth World," in Rex Weyler, op. cit., pp. 212–50.

160. On Durham's recent activities, *see* Ward Churchill, "Nobody's Pet Poodle: Jimmie Durham, an Artist for Native North America," in Ward Churchill, *Indians Are Us? Culture and Genocide in Native North America* (Monroe, Maine: Common Courage Press, 1993), pp. 89–113.

161. *See* Glenn T. Morris and Ward Churchill, "Between a Rock and a Hard Place: Left–Wing Revolution, Right–Wing Reaction, and the Destruction of Indigenous Peoples," originally in *Cultural Survival Quarterly*, Vol. 11, No. 3 (Fall 1988). The essay is also included in this book.

162. The AIM Chapters—Colorado, Dakota, Eastern Oklahoma, Florida, Illinois, Maryland, Mid–Atlantic (LISN), Northern California, New Mexico (Albuquerque), Northwest, Ohio, Southeast (Atlanta), Southern California, Texas, Western Oklahoma, and Wraps His Tail (Crow)—organized themselves as the Confederation of Autonomous AIM Chapters at a national conference in Edgewood, New Mexico, on December 17, 1993.

163. M. Annette Jaimes, "Racism and Sexism in the Media: The Trial of the Columbus Day Four," *Lies Of Our Times* (Sept. 1992).

164. Incorporation documents and attachments on file. The documents of incorporation are signed by Vernon Bellecourt, who is listed as a Central Committee member; the address listed for annual membership meetings is Bellecourt's residence. Other officers listed in the documents are Clyde Bellecourt, Dennis Banks, Herb Powless, John Trudell, Bill Means, Carole Standing Elk, and Sam Dry Water. Trudell and Banks maintain that they were neither informed of the incorporation nor agreed to be officers.

165. Expulsion letter and associated documents on file. Bill Means states that he was asked, but refused to sign the letter.

166. Statement during a talk at the annual Medicine Ways Conference, University of California at Riverside, May 1991.

167. Statement during a talk at the University of Colorado at Denver (Feb. 1988) (tape on file).

168. This assessment, of course, runs entirely counter to those of pro–Wilson publicists such as syndicated columnist Tim Giago—supported as he is by a variety of powerful non–Indian interests—who has made it a mission in life to discredit and degrade the legacy of AIM through continuous doses of disinformation. Consider, as but one example, his eulogy to Dickie Wilson in the February 13, 1990, issue of the *Lakota Times* in which he denounced careful chroniclers of the Pine Ridge terror such as Peter Matthiessen, Onondaga Faithkeeper, Oren Lyons, and myself, described the victims of Wilson's GOONs as "violent" and "criminal," and then embraced Wilson as "our friend." In a more recent editorial, he announced that his research indicates that "only 10" people were killed by Wilson's gun thugs on Pine Ridge during the mid–70s (the FBI itself concedes more than 40). Rather than being horrified that his "friend" might have been responsible for any such deaths, he uses his faulty revelation to suggest that the Wilson régime really wasn't so bad after all, especially when compared with AIM's "violence" and irreverence for "law and order."

169. A good effort to render several of these lessons will be found in Brian Glick, *War at Home: Covert Action Against U.S. Activists and What We Can Do About It,* op. cit.

170. For superb analysis of this point, *see* Isaac Balbus, *The Dialectic of Legal Repression* (New York: Russell Sage Foundation, 1973).

171. A fine survey of the conditions prevailing in each of these sectors will be found in Teresa L. Amott and Julie A. Matthaei, *Race, Gender and Work: A Multicultural Economic History of the United States* (Boston: South End Press, 1991).

172. For details and analysis, *see* Ward Churchill and J. J. Vander Wall, eds., *Cages of Steel: The Politics of Imprisonment in the United States* (Washington, DC: Maisonneuve Press, 1992).

173. For a survey of the repression visited upon most of these groups, *see* Ward Churchill and Jim Vander Wall, *The COINTELPRO Papers*, op. cit.

174. For biographical information concerning those mentioned who are currently imprisoned by the United States, *see Can't Jail the Spirit: Political Prisoners in the United States (Chicago: Committee to End the Marion Lockdown, 1989).*

White Studies

The Intellectual Imperialism of U.S. Higher Education*

> Education should be adapted to the mentality, attitudes, occupation, and traditions of various peoples, conserving as far as possible all the sound and healthy elements in the fabric of their social life.
>
> *David Abernathy*, The Dilemma of Popular Education

> Since schooling was brought to non–Europeans as a part of empire ... it was integrated into the effort to bring indigenous peoples into imperial/colonial structures.... After all, did not the European teacher and the school built on the European capitalist model transmit European values and norms and begin to transform traditional societies into "modern" ones?
>
> *Martin Carnoy*, Education as Cultural Imperialism

Over the past decade, the nature and adequacy of educational content has been a matter of increasingly vociferous debate among everyone from academics to policy makers to lay preachers in the United States. The American educational system as a whole has been amply demonstrated to be locked firmly into a paradigm of eurocentrism, not only in terms of its focus, but also its discernible heritage, methodologies, and conceptual structure. Among people of non–European cultural derivation, the kind of "learning" inculcated through such a model is broadly seen as insulting, degrading, and functionally subordinative. More and more, these themes have found echoes among the more enlightened and progressive sectors of the dominant Euroamerican society itself.[1]

---

* An earlier version of this essay appeared in *Integrateducation*, Vol. XIX, Nos. 1–2 (Winter–Spring 1982).

Such sentiments are born of an ever–widening cognition that, within any multicultural setting, this sort of monolithic pedagogical reliance upon a single cultural tradition constitutes a rather transparent form of intellectual domination, achievable only within the context of parallel forms of domination. This is meant in precisely the sense intended by David Landes when he observed, "It seems to me that one has to look at imperialism as a multifarious response to a common opportunity that consists simply as a disparity of power."[2] In this connection, it is often pointed out that while education in America has existed for some time, by law, as a "common opportunity," its shape has all along been defined exclusively via the "disparity of power" exercised by members of the ruling Euroamerican élite.[3]

Responses to this circumstance have, to date, concentrated primarily upon what might be best described as a "contributionist" approach to remedy. This is to say they seek to bring about the inclusion of non–Europeans and/or non–European achievements in canonical subject matters, while leaving the methodological and conceptual parameters of the canon itself essentially in tact.[4] The present essay represents an attempt to go a bit further, sketching out to some degree the preliminary requisites in challenging methods and concepts as well. It should be noted before proceeding that while my own grounding in American Indian Studies leads me to anchor my various alternatives in that particular perspective, the principles postulated should prove readily adaptable to other "minority" venues.

White Studies

As currently established, the university system in the United States offers little more than the presentation of "White Studies" to students, the "general population," and minorities alike.[5] The curriculum is virtually totalizing in its emphasis, not simply upon an imagined superiority of Western endeavors and accomplishments, but upon the notion that the currents of European thinking comprise the only really "natural"—or at least truly useful—formation of knowledge/means of perceiving reality. In the vast bulk of curriculum content, Europe is not only the subject (i.e., in its conceptual mode, the very process of "learning to think"), but the object (subject matter) of investigation as well.

Consider a typical introductory level philosophy course. Students will in all probability explore the works of the ancient Greek philosophers;[6] the fundamentals of Cartesian logic and Spinoza; stop off for a visit with Hobbes, Hume, and John Locke; cover a chapter or two of Kant's aesthetics; dabble a bit in Hegelian dialectics; and review Nietzsche's assorted rantings. A good leftist professor may add a dash of Marx's famous "inversion" of Hegel and, on a good day, his commentaries on the frailties of Feuerbach. In an exemplary class, things will end up in the twentieth century with discussions of Schopenhauer, Heidegger and Husserl, Bertrand Russell and Alfred North Whitehead, and perhaps an "adventurous" summarization of the existentialism of Sartre and Camus.

Advanced undergraduate courses typically delve into the same topics, with additive instruction in matters such as "Late Medieval Philosophy," "Monism," "Rousseau and Revolution," "The Morality of John Stuart Mill," "Einstein and the Generations of Science," "The Phenomenology of Merleau–Ponty," "Popper's Philosophy of Science," "Benjamin, Adorno, and the Frankfurt School," "Meaning and Marcuse," "Structuralism/Post–Structuralism," or even "The Critical Theory of Jürgen Habermas."[7] Graduate work usually consists of effecting a coherent synthesis of some combination of these elements.

Thus, from first–semester surveys through the Ph.D., philosophy majors—and non–majors fulfilling elective requirements, for that matter—are fed a consistent stream of data defining and presumably reproducing Western thought at its highest level of refinement, as well as inculcating insight into what is packaged as its historical evolution and line(s) of probable future development. Note that this is construed, for all practical intents and purposes, as being representative of philosophy *in toto* rather than of western European thought per se.

It seems reasonable to pose the question as to what consideration is typically accorded the non–European remainder of the human species in such a format. The answer is often that course work does in fact exist, most usually in the form of upper–division undergraduate "broadening" curriculum: surveys of "Oriental Philosophy" are not unpopular;[8] "The Philosophy of Black Africa" exists as a catalogue entry at a number of institutions;[9] even "Native American Philosophical Traditions" (more casually titled "Black Elk Speaks," from time–to–time) makes its appearance here and there.[10] But nothing remotely approaching the depth and comprehensiveness with which Western thought is treated can be located in any quarter.

Clearly, the student who graduates, at whatever level, from a philosophy program constructed in this fashion—and all of them are—walks away with a concentrated knowledge of the European intellectual schema rather than any genuine appreciation of the philosophical attainments of humanity. Yet, equally clearly, a degree in "Philosophy" implies, or at least should imply, the latter.

Nor is the phenomenon in any way restricted to the study of philosophy. One may search the catalogues of every college and university in the country, and undoubtedly the search will be in vain, for the department of history which accords the elaborate oral/pictorial "prehistories" of American Indians anything approximating the weight given to the semiliterate efforts at self–justification scrawled by early European colonists in this hemisphere.[11] Even the rich codigraphic records of cultures like the Mayas, Incas, and Mexicanos (Aztecs) are uniformly ignored by the "historical mainstream." Such matters are more properly the purview of anthropology than of history, or so it is said by those representing "responsible" scholarship in the United States.[12]

As a result, most introductory courses on "American History" still begin for all practical intents and purposes in 1492, with only the most perfunctory acknowledgment that people existed in the Americas in precolumbian times. Predictably, any consideration accorded to precolumbian times typically revolves around anthropological rather than historical preoccupations such as the point at which people were supposed to have first migrated across the Beringian Land Bridge to populate the hemisphere,[13] or whether native horticulturists ever managed to discover fertilizer.[14] Another major classroom topic centers on the extent to which cannibalism may have prevailed among the proliferation of "nomadic Stone Age tribes" presumed to have wandered about America's endless reaches, perpetually hunting and gathering their way to the margin of raw subsistence.[15] Then again, there are the countless expositions on how few indigenous people there really were in North America prior to 1500,[16] and that genocide is an "inappropriate" term by which to explain why there were almost none by 1900.[17]

From there, many things begin to fall into place. Nowhere in the modern American academe will one find the math course acknowledging, along with the importance of Archimedes and Pythagoras, the truly marvelous qualities of precolumbian mathematics: that which allowed the Mayas to invent the concept of zero, for example, and, absent computers, to work with multi–digit prime numbers.[18] Nor is there mention of the Mexicano mathematics which allowed that culture to develop a calendrical system several decimal places more accurate than that commonly used today.[19] And again, the rich mathematical understandings which went into Mesoamerica's development of what may well have been the world's most advanced system of astronomy are typically ignored by mainstream mathematicians and astronomers alike.[20]

Similarly, departments of architecture and engineering do not teach that the Incas invented the suspension bridge, or that their 2,500 mile Royal Road—paved, leveled, graded, guttered, and complete with rest areas—was perhaps the world's first genuine superhighway, or that portions of it are still used for motorized transport in Peru.[21] No mention is made of the passive solar temperature control characteristics carefully designed by the Anasazi into the apartment complexes of their cities at Chaco Canyon, Mesa Verde, and elsewhere.[22] Nor are students drawn to examine the incorporation of thermal mass into Mandan and Hidatsa construction techniques,[23] the vast north Sonoran irrigation systems built by the Hohokam,[24] or the implications of the fact that, at the time of Cortéz's arrival, Tenochtitlán (now Mexico City) accommodated a population of 350,000, a number making it one of the largest cities on earth, at least five times the size of London or Seville.[25]

In political science, readers are invited—no, defied—to locate the course acknowledging, as John Adams, Benjamin Franklin, and others among the U.S.

"Founding Fathers" did, that the form of the American Republic and the framing of its constitution were heavily influenced by the preexisting model of the Haudenosaunee (Six Nations Iroquois Confederacy of present–day New York and Québec).[26] Nor is mention made of the influence exerted by the workings of the "Iroquois League" in shaping the thinking of theorists such as Karl Marx and Friedrich Engels.[27] Even less discussion can be found on the comparably sophisticated political systems conceived and established by other indigenous peoples—the Creek Confederation, for example, or the Cherokees or Yaquis—long before the first European invader ever set foot on American soil.[28]

Where agriculture or the botanical sciences are concerned, one will not find the conventional department which wishes to "make anything special" of the fact that fully two–thirds of the vegetal foodstuffs now commonly consumed by all of humanity were under cultivation in the Americas, and nowhere else, in 1492.[29] Also unmentioned is the hybridization by Incan scientists of more than 3,000 varieties of potato,[30] or the vast herbal cornucopia discovered and deployed by native pharmacologists long before that.[31] In biology, pre–med, and medicine, nothing is said of the American Indian invention of surgical tubing and the syringe, or the fact that the Incas were successfully practicing brain surgery at a time when European physicians were still seeking to cure their patients by applying leeches to "draw off bad blood."[32]

To the contrary, from matters of governance, where the Greek and Roman democracies are habitually cited as being the sole antecedents of "the American experiment,"[33] to agriculture, with its "Irish" potatoes, "Swiss" chocolate, "Italian" tomatoes, "French" vanilla, and "English" walnuts,[34] the accomplishments of American Indian cultures are quite simply expropriated, recast in the curriculum as if they had been European in origin.[35] Concomitantly, the native traditions which produced such things are themselves deculturated and negated, consigned to the status of being "people without history."[36]

Such grotesque distortion is, of course, fed to indigenous students right along with Euroamericans,[37] and by supposedly radical professors as readily as more conservative ones.[38] Moreover, as was noted above, essentially the same set of circumstances prevails with regard to the traditions and attainments of all non–Western cultures.[39] Overall, the situation virtually demands to be viewed from a perspective best articulated by Albert Memmi:

> In order for the colonizer to be a complete master, it is not enough for him to be so in actual fact, but he must also believe in [the colonial system's] legitimacy. In order for that legitimacy to be complete, it is not enough for the colonized to be a slave, he must also accept his role. The bond between colonizer and colonized is thus destructive and creative. It destroys and recreates the two partners in colonization into colonizer and colonized. One is disfigured into an oppressor, a partial, unpatriotic and treacherous being, worrying only about

his privileges and their defense; the other into an oppressed creature, whose development is broken and who compromises by his defeat.[40]

In effect, the intellectual sophistry which goes into arguing the "radical" and "conservative" content options available within the prevailing monocultural paradigm, a paradigm which predictably corresponds to the culture of the colonizer, amounts to little more than a diversionary mechanism through which power relations are reinforced, the status quo maintained.[41] The monolithic White Studies configuration of U.S. higher education—a content heading which, unlike American Indian, Afroamerican, Asian American, and Chicano Studies, has yet to find its way into a single college or university catalogue—thus serves to underpin the hegemony of white supremacism in its other, more literal manifestations: economic, political, military, and so on.[42]

Those of non–European background are integral to such a system. While consciousness of their own heritages is obliterated through falsehood and omission, they are indoctrinated to believe that legitimacy itself is something derived from European tradition, a tradition which can never be truly shared by non–Westerners despite—or perhaps because of—their assimilation into eurocentrism's doctrinal value structure. By and large, the "educated" American Indian or black thereby becomes the aspect of "broken development" who "compromises [through the] defeat" of his or her people, aspiring only to serve the interests of the order he or she has been trained to see as his or her "natural" master.[43]

As Frantz Fanon and others have observed long since, such psychological jujitsu can never be directly admitted, much less articulated, by its principle victims. Instead, they are compelled by illusions of sanity to deny their circumstances and the process which induced them. Their condition sublimated, they function as colonialism's covert hedge against the necessity of perpetual engagement in more overt and costly sorts of repression against its colonial subjects.[44] Put another way, the purpose of White Studies in this connection is to trick the colonized into materially supporting her/his colonization through the mechanisms of his/her own thought processes.[45]

There can be no reasonable or "value neutral" explanation for this situation. Those, regardless of race or ethnicity, who endeavor to apologize for or defend its prevalence in institutions of higher education on "scholarly" grounds do so without a shred of honesty or academic integrity.[46] Rather, whatever their intentions, they define themselves as accepting of the colonial order. In Memmi's terms, they accept the role of colonizer, which means "agreeing to be a ... usurper. To be sure, a usurper claims his place and, if need be, will defend it with every means at his disposal.... He endeavors to falsify history, he rewrites laws, he would extinguish memories—anything to succeed in transforming his usurpation into legitimacy."[47] They are, to borrow and slightly modify a term, "intellectual imperialists."[48]

An Indigenist Alternative

From the preceding observations as to what White Studies is, the extraordinary pervasiveness and corresponding secrecy of its practice, and the reasons underlying its existence, certain questions necessarily arise. For instance, the query might be posed as to whether a simple expansion of curriculum content to include material on non–Western contexts might be sufficient to redress matters. It follows that we should ask whether something beyond data or content is fundamentally at issue. Finally, there are structural considerations concerning how any genuinely corrective and liberatory curriculum or pedagogy might actually be inducted into academia. The first two questions dovetail rather nicely, and will be addressed in a single response. The third will be dealt with in the following section.

In response to the first question, the answer must be an unequivocal "no." Content is, of course, highly important, but, in and of itself, can never be sufficient to offset the cumulative effects of White Studies indoctrination. Non–Western content injected into the White Studies format can be—and, historically, has been—filtered through the lens of eurocentric conceptualization, taking on meanings entirely alien to itself along the way.[49] The result is inevitably the reinforcement rather than the diminishment of colonialist hegemony. As Vine Deloria, Jr., has noted relative to just one aspect of this process:

> Therein lies the meaning of the white's fantasy about Indians—the problem of the Indian image. Underneath all the conflicting images of the Indian one fundamental truth emerges—the white man knows that he is an alien and he knows that North America is Indian—and he will never let go of the Indian image because he thinks that by some clever manipulation he can achieve an authenticity that cannot ever be his.[50]

Plainly, more is needed than the simple introduction of raw data for handling within the parameters of eurocentric acceptability. The conceptual mode of intellectuality itself must be called into question. Perhaps a bit of "pictographic" communication will prove helpful in clarifying what is meant in this respect. The following schematic represents the manner in which two areas of inquiry, science and religion (spirituality), have been approached in the European tradition.

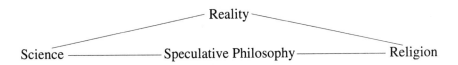

In this model, "knowledge" is divided into discrete content areas arranged in a linear structure. This division is permanent and culturally enforced; witness the Spanish Inquisition and "Scopes Monkey Trial" as but two historical illustrations.[51] In the cases of science and religion (as theology), the mutual opposition of their core assumptions has given rise to a third category, speculative philosophy, which is informed by both, and, in turn, informs them. Speculative philosophy, in this sense at least, serves to mediate and sometimes synthesize the linearly isolated components, science and religion, allowing them to communicate and "progress." Speculative philosophy is not, in itself, intended to apprehend reality, but rather to create an abstract reality in its place. Both religion and science, on the other hand, are, each according to its own internal dynamics, meant to effect a concrete understanding of and action upon "the real world."[52]

Such compartmentalization of knowledge is replicated in the departmentalization of the eurocentric education itself. Sociology, theology, psychology, physiology, kinesiology, biology, cartography, anthropology, archaeology, geology, pharmacology, astronomy, agronomy, historiography, geography, cartography, demography—the whole vast proliferation of Western "ologies," "onomies" and "ographies"—are necessarily viewed as separate or at least separable areas of inquiry within the university. Indeed, the Western social structure both echoes and is echoed by the same sort of linear fragmentation, dividing itself into discrete organizational spheres: church, state, business, family, education, art, and so forth.[53] The structure involved readily lends itself to—perhaps demands—the sort of hierarchical ordering of things, both intellectually and physically, which is most clearly manifested in racism, militarism, and colonial domination, class and gender oppression, and the systematic ravaging of the natural world.[54]

The obvious problems involved are greatly amplified when our schematic of the eurocentric intellectual paradigm is contrasted to one of non–Western, in this case Native American, origin.

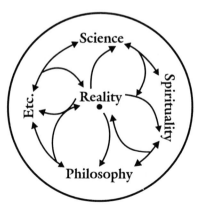

Within such a conceptual model, there is really no tangible delineation of compartmentalized "spheres of knowledge." All components or categories of intellectuality (by eurocentric definition) tend to be mutually and perpetually informing. All tend to constantly concretize the human experience of reality (nature) while all are simultaneously and continuously informed by that reality. This is the "Hoop" or "Wheel" or "Circle" of Life—an organic rather than synthesizing or synthetic view, holding that all things are equally and indispensably interrelated—which forms the core of the native worldview.[55] Here, reality is not something "above" the human mind or being, but an integral aspect of the living/knowing process itself. The mode through which native thought devolves is thus inherently anti–hierarchical, incapable of manifesting the extreme forms of domination so pervasively evident in eurocentric tradition.[56]

The crux of the White Studies problem, then, cannot be located amidst the mere omission or distortion of matters of fact, no matter how blatantly ignorant or culturally chauvinistic these omissions and distortions may be. Far more importantly, the system of Eurosupremacist domination depends for its continued maintenance and expansion, even its survival, upon the reproduction of its own intellectual paradigm—its approved way of thinking, seeing, understanding, and being—to the ultimate exclusion of all others. Consequently, White Studies simply cannot admit to the existence of viable conceptual structures other than its own.[57]

To introduce the facts of pre–colonial American Indian civilizations to the curriculum is to open the door to confronting the utterly different ways of knowing which caused such facts to be actualized in the first place.[58] It is thoroughly appreciated in ruling circles that any widespread and genuine understanding of such alternatives to the intrinsic oppressiveness of eurocentrism could well unleash a liberatory dynamic among the oppressed resulting in the evaporation of eurosupremacist hegemony and a corresponding collapse of the entire structure of domination and élite privilege which attends it.[59] The academic "battle lines" have therefore been drawn, not so much across the tactical terrain of fact and data as along the strategic high ground of Western versus non–Western conceptualization. It follows that if the latter is what proponents of the White Studies status quo find it most imperative to bar from academic inclusion, then it is precisely that area upon which those committed to liberatory education must place our greatest emphasis.

A Strategy to Win

Given the scope and depth of the formal problem outlined in the preceding section, the question of the means through which to address it takes on a crucial importance. If the objective in grappling with White Studies is to bring about conceptual—as opposed to merely contentual—inclusion of non–Western traditions in academia, then appropriate and effective methods must be employed. As was noted earlier, resort to inappropriate "remedies" leads only to co–optation and a reinforcement of White Studies as the prevailing educational norm.

One such false direction has concerned attempts to establish, essentially from scratch, whole new educational institutions, even systems, while leaving the institutional structure of the status quo very much in tact.[60] Although sometimes evidencing a strong showing at the outset, these perpetually under-funded, understaffed, and unaccredited, "community–based"—often actually separatist—schools have almost universally ended up drifting and floundering before going out of existence altogether.[61] Alternately, more than a few have abandoned their original reason for being, accommodating themselves to the "standards" and other requirements of the mainstream system as an expedient to survival.[62] Either way, the outcome has been a considerable bolstering of the carefully nurtured public impression that "the system works" while alternatives don't.

A variation on this theme has been to establish separatist centers or programs, even whole departments, within existing colleges and universities. While this approach has alleviated to some extent (though not entirely) difficulties in securing funding, faculty, and accreditation, it has accomplished little if anything in terms of altering the delivery of White Studies instruction in the broader institutional context.[63] Instead, intentionally self–contained "Ethnic Studies" efforts have ended up "ghetto–ized"—that is, marginalized to the point of isolation and left talking only to themselves and the few majors they are able to attract—bitter, frustrated, and stalemated.[64] Worse, they serve to reinforce the perception, so desired by the status quo, that White Studies is valid and important while non–Western subject matters are invalid and irrelevant.

To effect the sort of transformation of institutional realities envisioned in this essay, it is necessary *not* to seek to create parallel structures as such, but instead to penetrate and subvert the existing structures themselves, both peda-gogically and canonically. The strategy is one which was once described quite aptly by Rudi Deutschke, the German activist/theorist, as amounting to a "long march through the institutions."[65] In this, Ethnic Studies entities, rather than constituting ends in themselves, serve as "enclaves" or "staging areas" from which forays into the mainstream arena can be launched with ever increasing frequency and vitality, and to which non–Western academic guerrillas can withdraw when they need to rest and regroup among themselves.[66]

As with any campaign of guerrilla warfare, however metaphorical, it is important to concentrate initially upon the opponents' point(s) of greatest vulnerability. Here, three prospects for action come immediately to mind, the basis for each of which already exists within most university settings in a form readily lending itself to utilization in undermining the rigid curricular compart-mentalization and pedagogical constraints inhering in White Studies institutions. The key is to recognize and seize such tools, and then to apply them properly.

1) While tenure–track faculty must almost invariably be "credentialed"— i.e., hold a Ph.D. in a Western discipline, have a few publications in the "right" journals, etc.—to be hired into the academy, the same isn't necessarily true for guest professors, lecturers, and the like.[67] Every effort can and should be expended by the regular faculty— "cadre," if you will—of Ethnic Studies units to bring in guest instructors lacking in Western academic pedigree (the more conspicuously, the better), but who are in some way exemplary of non–Western intellectual traditions (especially oral forms). The initial purpose is to enhance cadre articulations with practical demonstrations of intellectual alternatives by consistently exposing students to "the real thing." Goals further on down the line should include incorporation of such individuals directly into the core faculty, and, eventually, challenging the current notion of academic credentialing in its entirety.[68]

2) There has been a good deal of interest over the past 20 years in what has come to be loosely termed "Interdisciplinary Studies." Insofar as there is a mainstream correspondent to the way in which American Indians and other non–Westerners conceive of and relate to the world, this is it. Ethnic Studies practitioners would do well to push hard in the Interdisciplinary Studies arena, expanding it whenever and wherever possible at the direct expense of customary Western disciplinary boundaries. The object, of course, is to steep students in the knowledge that nothing can be understood other than in its relationship to everything else; that economics, for example, can never really make sense if arbitrarily divorced from history, politics, sociology, and geography. Eventually, the goal should be to dissolve the orthodox parameters of disciplines altogether, replacing them with something more akin to "areas of interest, inclination and emphasis."[69]

3) For a variety of reasons, virtually all colleges and universities award tenure to certain faculty members in more than one discipline or department. Ethnic Studies cadres should insist that this be the case with them. Restricting their tenure and rostering exclusively to Ethnic Studies is not only a certain recipe for leaving them in a "last hired, first fired" situation during times of budget exigency, it is a standard institutional maneuver to preserve the sanctity of White Studies instruction elsewhere on campus. The fact is that an Ethnic Studies professor teaching American Indian or Afroamerican history is just as much an historian as a specialist in nineteenth–century British history; the Indian and the black should therefore be rostered to and tenured in History, *as well as* in Ethnic Studies. This "foot in the door" is important, not only in terms of cadre longevity and the institutional dignity such appointments signify vis–à–vis Ethnic Studies, but it also offers important advantages by way of allowing cadres to reach a greater breadth of students, participate in departmental policy formation and hiring decisions, claim additional resources, and so

forth. On balance, success in this area can only enhance efforts in the two above.[70]

The objective is to begin to develop a critical mass, first in given spheres of campuses where opportunities present themselves—later throughout the academy as a whole—which is eventually capable of discrediting and supplanting the hegemony of White Studies. In this, the process can be accelerated, perhaps greatly, by identifying and allying with sectors of the professorate with whom a genuine affinity and commonality of interest may be said to exist at some level. These might include those from the environmental sciences who have achieved, or begun to achieve, a degree of serious ecological understanding.[71] It might include occasional mavericks from other fields, various applied anthropologists,[72] for instance, and certain of the better and more engaged literary and artistic deconstructionists,[73] as well as the anarchists like Murray Bookchin who pop up more or less randomly in a number of disciplines.[74]

By and large, however, it may well be that the largest reservoir or pool of potential allies will be found among the relatively many faculty who profess to consider themselves, "philosophically" at least, to be marxian in their orientation. This is not said because marxists tend habitually to see themselves as being in opposition to the existing order (fascists express the same view of themselves, after all, and for equally valid reasons).[75] Nor is it because where it has succeeded in overthrowing capitalism marxism has amassed an especially sterling record where indigenous peoples are concerned.[76] In fact, it has been argued with some cogency that, in the latter connection, marxist practice has proven even more virulently eurocentric than has capitalism in many cases.[77]

Nonetheless, one is drawn to conclude that there may still be a basis for constructive alliance, given Marx's positing of dialectics—a truly nonlinear and relational mode of analysis and understanding—as his central methodology. That he himself consistently violated his professed method,[78] and that subsequent generations of his adherents have proven themselves increasingly unable to distinguish between dialectics and such strictly linear propositions as cause/effect progressions,[79] does not inherently invalidate the whole of his project or its premises. If some significant proportion of today's self–proclaimed marxian intelligentsia can be convinced to actually learn and apply dialectical method, it stands to reason that they will finally think their way in to a posture not unlike that elaborated herein (that they will in the process have transcended what has come be known as "marxism" is another story).[80]

Conclusion

This essay presents only the barest glimpse of its subject matter. It is plainly, its author hopes, not intended to be anything approximating an exhaustive or definitive exposition on its topics. To the contrary, it is meant only to act as, paraphrasing Marcuse, the archimedian point upon which false consciousness may be breached en route to "a more comprehensive emancipation."[81] By this, we mean not only a generalized change in perspective which leads to the abolition of eurocentrism's legacy of colonialist, racist, sexist, and classist domination, but the replacement of White Studies' eurosupremacism with an educational context in which we can all, jointly and with true parity, "seek to expand our knowledge of the world" in full realization that:

> The signposts point to a reconciliation of the two approaches to experience. Western science must reintegrate human emotions and intuitions into its interpretation of phenomena; [non–Western] peoples must confront ... the effects of [Western] technology.... [We must] come to an integrated conception of how our species came to be, what it has accomplished, and where it can expect to go in the millennia ahead.... [Then we will come to] understand as these traditionally opposing views seek a unity that the world of historical experience is far more mysterious and eventful than previously expected.... Our next immediate task is the unification of human knowledge.[82]

There is, to be sure, much work to be done, both practically and cerebrally. The struggle will be long and difficult, frustrating many times to the point of sheer exasperation. It will require stamina and perseverance, a preparedness to incur risk, often a willingness to absorb the consequences of revolt, whether overt or covert. Many will be required to give up or forego aspects of a comfort zone academic existence, both mentally and materially.[83] But the pay–off may be found in freedom of the intellect, the pursuit of knowledge in a manner more proximate to truth, unfettered by the threats and constraints of narrow vested interest and imperial ideology. The reward, in effect, is participation in the process of human liberation, including our own. One can only assume that this is worth the fight.

Notes

1. For an overview of the evolution of the current conflict, *see* Ira Shore, *Culture Wars: School and Society in the Conservative Restoration, 1969–1984* (Boston: Routledge & Kegan Paul, 1986); for reactionary analysis, *see* Roger Kimball, *Tenured Radicals: How Politics Has Corrupted Our Higher Education* (New York: Harper & Row, 1990).

2. David S. Landes, "The Nature of Economic Imperialism," *Journal of Economic History* 21 (Dec. 1961), as quoted in Harry Magdoff, *The Age of Imperialism* (New York: Monthly Review Press, 1969), p. 13.

3. Gerald Jayne and Robbin Williams, eds., *A Common Destiny: Blacks and American Society* (Washington, DC: National Academy Press, 1989).

4. One solid summary of the contributionist trend can be found in Troy Duster, *The Diversity Project: Final Report* (Berkeley: University of California Institute for Social Change, 1991); for complaints, *see* Robert Alter, "The Revolt Against Tradition," *Partisan Review*, Vol. 58, No. 2 (1991).

5. General population, or "G–Pop" as it is often put, is the standard institutional euphemism for white students.

6. A good case can be made that there is a great disjuncture between the Greek philosophers and the philosophies later arising in western Europe; *see* Martin Bernal, *Black Athena: The Afro–Asiatic Roots of Ancient Greece, Vol. 1* (Princeton, New Jersey: Princeton University Press, 1987).

7. Marxian academics make another appearance here, insofar as they do tend to teach courses, or parts of courses, based in the thinking of non–Europeans. It should be noted, however, that those selected for exposition—Mao, Ho Chi Minh, Vo Nguyen Giap, Kim El Sung, et al.—are uniformly those who have most thoroughly assimilated Western doctrines in displacement of their own intellectual traditions.

8. Probably the most stunning example of still giving superiority to western–based philosophy I've ever encountered came when Will Durant casually attributed the thought of the East Indian philosopher Shankara to a "preplagiarism" (!!!) of Kant: "To Shankara the existence of God is no problem, for he defines God as existence, and identifies all real being with God. But the existence of a personal God, creator or redeemer, there may, he thinks, be some question; such a deity, says this *pre–plagiarist* of Kant, cannot be proved by reason, he can only be postulated as a practical necessity [emphasis added]"; Will Durant, *The History of Civilization, Vol. 1: Our Oriental Heritage* (New York: Simon & Schuster, 1954), p. 549. It should be remarked that Durant was not a reactionary of the stripe conventionally associated with white supremacism, but rather an intellectual of the marxian progressive variety. Yet, in this single book on the philosophical tradition of Asia, he makes no less than ten references to Kant, all of them implying that the earlier philosophers of the East acted "precisely as if [they] were Immanual Kant" (p. 538), never that Kant might have predicated his own subsequent philosophical articulations on a reading of Asian texts. The point is raised to demonstrate the all but unbelievable lengths even the more dissident Western scholars have been prepared to go to in reinforcing the mythos of eurocentrism, and thus how such reinforcement transcends ideological divisions within the eurocentric paradigm.

9. It should be noted, however, that the recent emergence of an "Afrocentric" philosophy and pedagogy, natural counterbalances to the persistence of eurocentric orthodoxy, has met with fierce condemnation by defenders of the status quo; *see* David Nicholson, "Afrocentrism and the Tribalization of America," *Washington Post National Weekly Edition* (8–14 Oct. 1990).

10. A big question, frequently mentioned, is whether American Indians ever acquired the epistemological sensibilities necessary for their thought to be correctly understood as having amounted to "philosophical inquiry." Given that epistemology simply means "investigation of the limits of human comprehension," one can only wonder what the gate–keepers of philosophy departments make of the American Indian conception, prevalent in myriad traditions, of there being a "Great Mystery" into which the human mind is incapable of penetrating; *see*, e.g., John G. Neihardt, ed., *Black Elk Speaks* (New York: William Morrow Publisher, 1932); *see also* J. R. Walker, *Lakota Belief and Ritual* (Lincoln: University of Nebraska Press, 1980). For an unconsciously comparable Western articulation, *see* Noam Chomsky's discussions of accessible and inaccessible knowledge in the chapters entitled "A

Philosophy of Language?" and "Empiricism and Rationalism," in *Language and Responsibility: An Interview by Mitsou Ronat* (New York: Pantheon Books, 1977).

11. For an illustration, *see* Wilcomb E. Washburn, "Distinguishing History from Moral Philosophy and Public Advocacy," in *The American Indian and the Problem of History*, Calvin Martin, ed. (New York: Oxford University Press, 1987), pp. 91–97.

12. For a veritable case–study of this mentality, *see* James Axtell, *After Columbus: Essays in the Ethnohistory of Colonial North America* (New York: Oxford University Press, 1988).

13. For a solid critique of the Beringia Theory, *see* Jeffrey Goodman, *American Genesis: The American Indian and the Origins of Modern Man* (New York: Summit Books, 1981); *see* also Jonathan E. Ericson, R. E. Taylor, and Rainier Berger, eds., *The Peopling of the New World* (Los Altos, California: Ballena Press, 1982). For an overview of the issues involved, *see* "About That Bering Strait Land Bridge..." in this book.

14. For an exhaustive enunciation of the "fertilizer dilemma," *see* James C. Hurt, *American Indian Agriculture* (Lawrence: University Press of Kansas, 1991).

15. An excellent analysis of this standard description of indigenous American realities may be found in Jack Weatherford, *Indian Givers: How the Indians of the Americas Transformed the World* (New York: Crown, 1988). On cannibalism specifically, *see* W. Arens, *The Man–Eating Myth: Anthropology and Anthropophagy* (New York: Oxford University Press, 1979).

16. The manipulation of data undertaken by succeeding generations of Euroamerican historians and anthropologists in arriving at the official twentieth–century falsehood that there were "not more than one million Indians living north of the Rio Grande in 1492, including Greenland" is laid out very clearly by Francis Jennings in his *The Invasion of America: Indians, Colonialism and the Cant of Conquest* (Chapel Hill: University of North Carolina Press, 1975). For a far more honest estimate, deriving from the evidence rather than ideological preoccupations, *see* Henry F. Dobyns, *Their Numbers Become Thinned: Native American Population Dynamics in Eastern North America* (Knoxville: University of Tennessee Press, 1983); *see* also Russell Thornton, *American Indian Holocaust and Survival: A Population History Since 1492* (Norman: University of Oklahoma Press, 1987). Dobyns places the actual number as high as 18.5 million; Thornton, more conservative, places it at 12.5 million.

17. During a keynote presentation at the annual meeting of the American History Association in 1992, James Axtell, one of the emergent "deans" of the field, actually argued that genocide was an "inaccurate and highly polemical descriptor" for what had happened. His reasoning? That he could find only five instances in the history of colonial North America in which genocides "indisputably" occurred. Leaving aside the obvious—that this in itself makes genocide an appropriate term by which to describe the obliteration of American Indians—a vastly more accurate chronicle of the process of extermination will be found in David E. Stannard, *American Holocaust: Columbus and the Conquest of the New World* (New York: Oxford University Press, 1992).

18. Syvanus G. Morely and George W. Bainerd, *The Ancient Maya* (Stanford, California: Stanford University Press, 1983); Robert M. Carmack, *Quichean Civilization* (Berkeley: University of California Press, 1973).

19. Anthony Aveni, *Empires of Time: Calendars, Clocks and Cultures* (New York: Basic Books, 1989).

20. Mexicano astronomy is discussed in D. Durán, *Book of Gods and Rites and the Ancient Calendar* (Norman: University of Oklahoma Press, 1971); *see* also Paul Radin, *The Sources*

and Authenticity of the History of Ancient Mexico (Berkeley: University of California Publications in American Archaeology and Ethnology, Vol. 17, No. 1, 1920).

21. Victor Wolfgang Von Hagen, *The Royal Road of the Inca* (London: Gordon and Cremonesi, 1976).

22. Robert H. and Florence C. Lister, *Chaco Canyon: Archaeology and Archaeologists* (Albuquerque: University of New Mexico Press, 1981); *see* also Buddy Mays, *Ancient Cities of the Southwest* (San Francisco: Chronicle Books, 1962).

23. Peter Nabokov and Robert Easton, *American Indian Architecture* (New York: Oxford University Press, 1988); the "submerged" building principles developed by the Mandan and Hidatsa, ideal for the plains environment but long disparaged by the Euroamericans who displaced them, are now considered the "cutting edge" in some architectural circles. The Indians, of course, are not credited with having perfected such techniques more than a thousand years ago.

24. Emil W. Haury, *The Hohokam: Desert Farmers and Craftsmen* (Tucson: University of Arizona Press, 1976), pp. 120–51; the City of Phoenix and its suburbs still use portions of the several thousand miles of extraordinarily well–engineered Hohokam canals, constructed nearly a thousand years ago, to move their own water supplies around.

25. Cortéz was effusive in his descriptions of Tenochtitlán as being, in terms of its design and architecture, "the most beautiful city on earth"; Bernal Díaz del Castillo, *The Discovery and Conquest of Mexico, 1519–1810* (London: George Routledge & Sons, 1928), p. 268. On the size of Tenochtitlán, *see* Rudolph van Zantwijk, *The Aztec Arrangement: The Social History of Pre–Spanish Mexico* (Norman: University of Oklahoma Press, 1985), p. 281; on the size of London in 1500, *see* Lawrence Stone, *The Family, Sex and Marriage in England, 1500–1800* (New York: Harper & Row, 1977), p. 147; for Seville, *see* J. H. Elliott, *Imperial Spain, 1469–1716* (New York: St. Martin's Press, 1964), p. 177.

26. Donald A. Grinde, Jr., and Bruce E. Johansen, *Exemplar of Liberty: Native America and the Evolution of Democracy* (Los Angeles: UCLA American Indian Studies Center, 1992).

27. Between December 1880 and March 1881, Marx read anthropologist Lewis Henry Morgan's 1871 book, *Ancient Society*, based in large part on his 1851 classic *The League of the Hau–de–no–sau–nee or Iroquois*. Marx took at least 98 pages of dense notes during the reading, and, after his death, his collaborator, Friedrich Engels, expanded these into a short book entitled *The Origin of the Family, Private Property and the State: In Light of the Researches of Lewis Henry Morgan*. The latter, minus its subtitle, appears in *Marx and Engels: Selected Works* (New York: International Publishers, 1968).

28. Jack Weatherford, *Indian Givers*, op. cit.

29. Alfred W. Crosby, Jr., *The Columbian Exchange: Biological and Cultural Consequences of 1492* (Westport, Connecticut: Greenwood Press, 1972); Carol A. Bryant, Anita Courtney, Barbara A. Markesbery, and Kathleen M. DeWalt, *The Cultural Feast* (St. Paul, Minneapolis: West, 1985).

30. Redcliffe N. Salaman, *The History and Social Influence of the Potato* (Cambridge: Cambridge University Press, 1949).

31. Clark Wissler, Wilton M. Krogman, and Walter Krickerberg, *Medicine Among the American Indians* (Ramona, California: Acoma Press, 1939); Norman Taylor, *Plant Drugs That Changed the World* (New York: Dodd, Mead & Co., 1965).

32. Virgil Vogel, *American Indian Medicine* (Norman: University of Oklahoma Press, 1970); Peredo Guzmán, *Medical Practices in Ancient America* (Mexico City: Ediciones

Euroamericana, 1985). On contemporaneous European medical practices, *see* William H. McNeill, *Plagues and Peoples* (Garden City, New York: Anchor/Doubleday, 1976).

33. For good efforts at debunking such nonsense, *see* Germán Arciniegas, *America in Europe: A History of the New World in Reverse* (New York: Harcourt Brace Jovanovich, 1986); and William Brandon, *New Worlds for Old: Reports from the New World and Their Effect on Social Thought in Europe, 1500–1800* (Athens: Ohio University Press, 1986).

34. Carl O. Sauer, "The March of Agriculture Across the Western World," in his *Selected Essays, 1963–1975* (Berkeley: Turtle Island Foundation, 1981); *see* also Jack Weatherford, op. cit.

35. This is nothing new, or unique to the treatment of American Indians. Indeed, the West has comported itself in similar fashion vis–à–vis all non–Westerners since at least as early as the inception of "Europe"; *see* Philippe Wolf, *The Awakening of Europe: The Growth of European Culture from the Ninth Century to the Twelfth* (London: Cox & Wyman, 1968).

36. For a much broader excursus on this phenomenon, *see* Eric R. Wolf, *Europe and the People Without History* (Berkeley: University of California Press, 1982).

37. For surveys of the effects, *see* Thomas Thompson, ed., *The Schooling of Native America* (Washington, DC: American Association of Colleges for Teacher Education, 1978); James R. Young, ed., *Multicultural Education and the American Indian* (Los Angeles: UCLA American Indian Studies Center, 1979); and Charlotte Heath and Susan Guyette, *Issues for the Future of American Indian Studies* (Los Angeles: UCLA American Indian Studies Center, 1985).

38. Consider, e.g., the "Sixteen Theses" advanced by the non–marxist intellectual Alvin Gouldner as alternatives through which to transform the educational status quo. It will be noted that the result, if Gouldner's pedagogical plan were implemented, would be tucked as neatly into the paradigm of eurocentrism as the status quo itself. *See* Alvin W. Gouldner, *The Future of Intellectuals and the Rise of the New Class* (New York: Seabury Press, 1979). For marxian views falling in the same category, *see* Theodore Mills Norton and Bertell Ollman, eds., *Studies in Socialist Pedagogy* (New York: Monthly Review Press, 1978).

39. *See* generally, Edward W. Said, *Orientalism* (New York: Oxford University Press, 1987).

40. Albert Memmi, *Colonizer and Colonized* (Boston: Beacon Press, 1965), p. 89.

41. The procedure corresponds well in some ways to the kind of technique described by Herbert Marcuse as being applicable to broader social contexts in his essay "Repressive Tolerance," in *A Critique of Pure Tolerance* (Boston: Beacon Press, 1969).

42. The theme is handled well in Vine Deloria, Jr., "Education and Imperialism," *Integrateducation*, Vol. XIX, Nos. 1–2 (Jan. 1982). For structural analysis, *see* Giovanni Arrighi, *The Geometry of Imperialism* (London: Verso, 1978).

43. Memmi develops these ideas further in his *Dominated Man* (Boston: Beacon Press, 1969).

44. *See* especially, Frantz Fanon's *Wretched of the Earth* (New York: Grove Press, 1965), and *Black Skin/White Masks: The Experiences of a Black Man in a White World* (New York: Grove Press, 1967).

45. Probably the classic example of this, albeit in a somewhat different dimension, were the Gurkas, who forged a legendary reputation fighting on behalf of their British colonizers, usually against other colonized peoples; *see* Patrick McCrory, *The Fierce Pawns* (Philadelphia: J. B. Lippencott, 1966).

46. *See*, e.g., Allan Bloom, *The Closing of the American Mind* (New York: Simon & Schuster, 1988); Dinesh D'Sousa, *Illiberal Education: The Politics of Race and Sex on Campus* (New York: Free Press, 1991); Arthur Schlesinger, Jr., *The Disuniting of America* (New York: W. W. Norton, 1992).

47. Albert Memmi, op. cit., pp. 52–53.

48. Martin Carnoy, *Education as Cultural Imperialism* (New York: David McKay, 1974); *see* also Laurie Anne Whitt, "Cultural Imperialism and the Marketing of Native America," forthcoming in *Historical Reflections*, 1995.

49. A fascinating analysis of how this works, distorting the perspectives of perpetrator and victim alike, may be found in Richard James Blackburn, *The Vampire of Reason: An Essay in the Philosophy of History* (London: Verso Press, 1990).

50. Vine Deloria, Jr., "Forward: American Fantasy," in *The Pretend Indians: Images of Native Americans in the Movies*, Gretchen M. Bataille and Charles L. P. Silet, eds. (Ames: Iowa State University Press, 1980), p. xvi.

51. On the Inquisition, *see* Mary Elizabeth Perry and Anne J. Cruz, eds., *Cultural Encounters: The Impact of the Inquisition in Spain and the New World* (Berkeley: University of California Press, 1991). On the context of the Scopes trial, *see* Stephan Jay Gould, *The Mismeasure of Man* (New York: W. W. Norton, 1981).

52. For a sort of capstone rendering of this schema, *see* Karl Popper, *Objective Knowledge: An Evolutionary Approach* (New York: Oxford University Press, 1975).

53. Useful analysis of this dialectic will be found in David Reed, *Education for Building a People's Movement* (Boston: South End Press, 1981).

54. For an interesting analysis of many of these cause/effect relations, *see* Jerry Mander, *In the Absence of the Sacred: The Failure of Technology and the Survival of Indian Nations* (San Francisco: Sierra Club Books, 1991). *See* also William H. McNeill, ed., *Pursuit of Power: Technology, Armed Force and Society Since A.D. 1000* (Chicago: University of Chicago Press, 1982).

55. For elaboration, *see* Vine Deloria, Jr., *God Is Red* (New York: Grosset & Dunlap, 1973). *See* also John Mohawk, *A Basic Call to Consciousness* (Rooseveltown, New York: *Akwesasne Notes*, 1978).

56. A Westerner's solid apprehension of this point may be found in Stanley Diamond, *In Search of the Primitive: A Critique of Civilization* (New Brunswick, New Jersey: Transaction Books, 1974); *see* also Keith Thomas, *Man and the Natural World: A History of Modern Sensibility* (New York: Pantheon Books, 1983).

57. The matter has been explored tangentially, from a number of angles. Some of the best, for purposes of this essay, include Tala Asad, ed., *Anthropology and the Colonial Encounter* (New York: Humanities Press, 1973); Robert Berkhofer, *The White Man's Indian: Images of the American Indian from Columbus to the Present* (New York: Alfred A. Knopf, 1978); Tzvetan Todorov, *The Conquest of America: The Question of the Other* (New York: Harper & Row, 1984); and Robert Young, *White Mythologies: Writing History and the West* (London: Routledge, 1990).

58. More broadly, the thrust of this negation has always pertained in the interactions between European/Euroamerican colonists and native cultures; *see* Richard Drinnon, *Facing West: The Metaphysics of Indian Hating and Empire Building* (Minneapolis: University of Minnesota Press, 1980).

59. Aside from the paradigmatic shift, culturally speaking, imbedded in this observation, it shares much with the insights into the function of higher education achieved by New Left

theorists during the 1960s; *see* Carl Davidson, *The New Student Radicals in the Multiversity and Other Writings on Student Syndicalism* (Chicago: Charles Kerr, 1990).

60. In essence, this approach is the equivalent of Mao Tse Tung's having declared the Chinese revolution victorious at the point it liberated and secured the Caves of Hunan.

61. One salient example is the system of "survival schools" started by AIM during the mid–70s, only two of which still exist in any form; *see* Susan Braudy, "We Will Remember Survival School: The Women and Children of the American Indian Movement," *Ms. Magazine*, No. 5 (July 1976).

62. For a case study of one initially separatist effort turned accommodationist, *see* Maryls Duchene, "A Profile of American Indian Community Colleges"; more broadly, *see* Gerald Wilkenson, "Educational Problems in the Indian Community: A Comment on Learning as Colonialism"; both essays will be found in *Integrateducation*, Vol. XIX, Nos. 1–2 (Jan.–Apr. 1982).

63. Ward Churchill and Norbert S. Hill, Jr., "Indian Education at the University Level: An Historical Survey," *Journal of Ethnic Studies*, Vol. 7, No. 3 (1979).

64. Further elaboration of this theme will be found in Ward Churchill, "White Studies or Isolation: An Alternative Model for American Indian Studies Programs," in James R. Young, ed., *American Indian Issues in Higher Education* (Los Angeles: UCLA American Indian Studies Center, 1981).

65. So far as is known, Deutschke, head of the German SDS, first publicly issued a call for such a strategy during an address of a mass demonstration in Berlin during January 1968.

66. Mao Tse–Tung, *On Protracted War* (Peking: Foreign Language Press, 1967); Che Guevara, *Guerrilla Warfare* (New York: Vintage Books, 1961).

67. For an excellent and succinct examination of the implications of this point, *see* Jurgen Herget, *And Sadly Teach: Teacher Education and Professionalization in American Culture* (Madison: University of Wisconsin Press, 1991).

68. The concept is elaborated much more fully and eloquently in Paulo Freire's *Pedagogy of the Oppressed* (New York: Continuum Books, 1981).

69. Again, one can turn to Freire for development of the themes; *see* his *Education for Critical Consciousness* (New York: Continuum Books, 1982). For the results of a practical—and very successful—application of these principles in the United States, *see* M. Annette Jaimes, *TRIBES 1989: Final Report and Evaluation* (Boulder: University of Colorado University Learning Center, Aug. 1989).

70. For overall analysis, *see* Vine Deloria, Jr., "Indian Studies—The Orphan of Academia," *Wicazo Sa Review*, Vol. II, No. 2 (1986); *see* also José Barriero, "The Dilemma of American Indian Education," *Indian Studies Quarterly*, Vol. 1, No. 1 (1984).

71. As examples, Bill Devall and George Sessions; *see* their *Deep Ecology: Living as if Nature Mattered* (Salt Lake City, Utah: Peregrine Smith Books, 1985). *See* also André Gorz, *Ecology as Politics* (Boston: South End Press, 1981).

72. The matter is well–handled in Edward W. Said, "Representing the Colonized: Anthropology's Interlocutors," *Critical Inquiry*, No. 15 (1989).

73. *See*, for instance, Lucy Lippard, *Mixed Blessings: New Art in Multicultural America* (New York: Pantheon Books, 1990).

74. Murray Bookchin, *The Ecology of Freedom* (Palo Alto, California: Cheshire Books, 1982); see also Steve Chase, ed., *Defending the Earth: A Dialogue Between Murray Bookchin and Dave Foreman* (Boston: South End Press, 1991).

75. Fritz Stern, *The Politics of Cultural Despair: A Study in the Rise of Germanic Ideology* (Berkeley: University of California Press, 1961); *see* also Wilhelm Reich, *The Mass Psychology of Fascism* (New York: Farrar, Straus & Giroux, 1970).

76. *See* generally, Walker Connor, *The National Question in Marxist–Leninist Theory and Strategy* (Princeton, New Jersey: Princeton University Press, 1984).

77. Russell Means, "The Same Old Song," in *Marxism and Native Americans*, Ward Churchill, ed. (Boston: South End Press, 1983).

78. Ward Churchill and Elisabeth R. Lloyd, *Culture Versus Economism: Essays on Marxism in the Multicultural Arena* (Denver: University of Colorado Center for the Study of Indigenous Law and Politics, 1990).

79. Michael Albert and Robin Hahnel, *Unorthodox Marxism* (Boston: South End Press, 1978).

80. As illustration of one who made the transition, at least in substantial part, *see* Rudolph Bahro, *From Red to Green* (London: Verso, 1984).

81. Herbert Marcuse, op. cit.

82. Vine Deloria, Jr., *The Metaphysics of Modern Existence* (New York: Harper & Row, 1979, p. 213).

83. For insights, *see* Ellen Schrecker, *No Ivory Tower: McCarthyism and the Universities* (New York: Oxford University Press, 1986).

About That Bering Strait Land Bridge.... Let's Turn Those Footprints Around

> There is no argument among serious researchers that a mongoloid stock first colonized the New World from Asia. Nor is there controversy about the fact that these continental pioneers used the Bering Land Bridge that then connected the Asian Far East with Alaska.
>
> Gerald F. Shields et al., American Journal of Genetics, 1992

> The bigger the lie, the more likely it will be believed.
>
> Joseph Goebbels, nazi propaganda minister, 1937

Tailoring the facts to fit one's theory constitutes neither good science nor good journalism. Rather, it is intellectually dishonest and, when published for consumption by a mass audience, adds up to propaganda. Such is the case with Tim Friend's September 22, 1993, article in *USA Today*, "Genetic Detectives Trace the Origin of the First Americans," advancing the latest set of "proofs" that the Western Hemisphere was initially populated by people migrating across a Bering Strait land bridge from Asia. One problem with the version of this idea described by Friend, as with all its previous incarnations, is that it is politically rather than scientifically motivated. It ignores or contradicts much available evidence, and it is at least tacitly racist. Since this is such a sterling example of what is commonly referred to as "eurocentric bias" in academia and the media, it seems worth going into in some depth. To do this, we must first trace the history of the myth. We will then address defects in current iterations of Bering Strait migration orthodoxy, and draw conclusions accordingly.

Enforcement of a Myth

I prefer archaeological dates, when available, but the archaeology of America is more like a battlefield than a research topic. Given the circumstances, I suppose it is reasonable to be cautious. Only if I were forced to bet, I would prefer older dates.

Luca Cavalli–Sforza, 1992

Clearly, the maintenance of the "status quo" is a powerful force to be reckoned with. However, the World—and what we don't know about it—would be less than it is today if we did not allow ourselves to challenge traditional foundations, knowledge and assessments. The current resistance to ideas of change in many scientific fields ... parallels the difficulty faced by turn–of–the–century American avocational and professional anthropologists in [asserting] that American Indians had an autochthonous origin in the Americas.

Alvah M. Hicks, 1994

When Thomas Jefferson first used his *Notes of Virginia* to advance in 1781 what became the "Bering Strait Hypothesis" in the United States, he not only attributed a mysterious "origin in Asia" to American Indians, he used "Biblical Time" to frame the argument.[1] By this he meant that Indians could not have arrived in this hemisphere more than three millennia earlier.[2] His express purpose was to foster the misimpression that our coming was so recent that we were no more indigenous than the Europeans who were invading our territories. It followed, so said Jefferson, that we could therefore be no more possessed of "aboriginal" rights to our land than were he and the other invaders.[3] They themselves were thereby freed from moral constraint, in their own minds at least, to take whatever they wanted, whenever they wanted it.[4]

Although Jefferson's timetable never made the least scientific sense, mainstream anthropologists—for political, economic, and cultural reasons which are in hindsight easy enough to see—quickly queued up to defend it, and continued to do so for well over a century.[5] As late as the 1940s, the canonical "truth" insisted upon by anthropology's leading "experts"—men like Ales Hrdlicka, curator of the Smithsonian Institution's National Museum from 1909 to 1941—was that Indians could not have arrived in the Americas more than 3,000 years ago; in 1928, Hrdlicka even "had the boldness to decree at a meeting of the New York Academy ... that there could not have been a Paleo–Indian."[6]

[Hrdlicka's] authoritarian and negative stance on matters of early
man—that is, an American population earlier than historic Indian—
was so rigorous and ably defended that for decades American
scholars gave no serious thought to the possibility that the occupancy
of the Americas was anything but recent—no deeper than 2,000 to
3,000 years in time.[7]

Meanwhile, anyone suggesting that Indians might have been here for
some longer period was branded a crackpot or scholarly heretic, their evidence
automatically dismissed as being fabricated or at least too "controversial" to be
taken seriously.

The first skeleton discovered in North America from deposits from
the last glacial age, which lasted from 70,000 to 10,000 years ago,
was an apparent drowning victim (1931, Minnesota Man). The relic
had an appearance much like present Indians, and Hrdlicka quickly
attacked the conclusions of the excavator, Dr. A. E. Jenks of the
University of Minnesota, claiming Jenks had merely discovered the
recent burial of a modern Sioux Indian.[8]

Similarly, the pathbreaking discoveries in southern California made
during the 1930s by Dr. George F. Carter, then Curator of Anthropology at the
San Diego Museum of Man, later a geologist at Texas A&M University—
among them the pair of so-called San Diego Skulls—were laughingly
dismissed as "Carterfacts."[9] It was only when the cumulative weight of evidence from sites near Folsom, New Mexico, and Clovis, Texas, forced the issue
did the "truth" of "responsible" anthropological dating begin to be revised to
some extent.[10] Even as projectile points from these two locations were found
intermixed with, and even imbedded in, the bones of animals known to have
been extinct since the last Ice Age—thus proving that Indians *had* to have been
in North America for at least 10,000 years, Hrdlicka and his followers were still
"denying everything to maintain [their] position that man could be anything,
anything at all, but not ancient in America."[11]

Finally, in 1948, reigning dean of American anthropology Alfred L.
Kroeber "resolved" the dispute, offering a grudging admission that Indians had
unquestionably been present in North America for "as long as" 12–15,000
years, while, in the next breath, announcing that this was to be the new limit
for "responsible estimates" concerning the duration of human occupancy in
America.[12]

It may be said that in the opinion of most Americanists, ethnologists
as well as archaeologists, the first human immigrants arrived in the
Western Hemisphere in late Pleistocene times. The meagerly known
Clovis, Folsom and similar cultures ... represent this early level of

culture.... If anything earlier than Clovis and Folsom existed in America, it has not been found.[13]

Not only did Kroeber's canonical pronouncement conspicuously avoid mention of the anthropological establishment's earlier dating "errors," it was itself deliberately inaccurate and misleading. Logically, the notion that people might have first migrated across the Bering Strait into America 15 millennia ago, and have been simultaneously living in Texas and New Mexico, made no sense at all; in order to have been residing in these southerly locales, they would have necessarily had to have crossed over the fabled land bridge at some point *much* earlier.[14] Moreover, at the time of Kroeber's pontification, a number of finds—Carter's, for example—clearly pointed to southerly habitation by humans thousands of years before they supposedly first arrived in Alaska.[15]

Yet, more than two decades later, champions of orthodoxy like the University of Arizona's Vance C. Haynes were still parroting Kroeber's line, all evidence to the contrary notwithstanding: "After 40 years of searching, little positive evidence for earlier occupation of the New World has been found."[16] During the interim, of course, a number of discoveries had so thoroughly put the lie to Haynes' assertion as to render it absurd. From 1951 to 1955, for instance, a series of excavations by geologist Thomas E. Lee on the Sheguiandah Reserve, on Manitoulin Island in Lake Huron, yielded materials dated at "30,000 years minimum" by Dr. Ernst Antevs of Haynes' home institution.[17] Then, in 1956, Phil Orr, an anthropologist with the Santa Barbara Museum of Natural History, collected bone fragments from a site on southern California's Santa Rosa Island which were radiocarbon–dated at 30,000 years.[18]

In 1958, a bone sample found in conjunction with a Clovis projectile point near Lewisville, Texas, was radiocarbon–dated by scientists from the Humble Oil Company Laboratory at 37,000 years; a subsequent test at UCLA dated it at 38,000 years.[19] This was followed, in 1963, by the discovery by geologist A. MacStalker of remains near Taber, Alberta, which are at least 35,000—perhaps as much as 60,000—years old.[20] In 1967, the world–renowned Louis Leakey—the discoverer in 1959 of *Australopithecines*, the oldest known protohuman remains (9 million years), as well as those of *Homo hablis*, the second oldest (3 million years) during the 1960s—examined a skull found near Laguna Beach, California, by an amateur archaeologist named Howard Wilson; Leakey and Ranier Berger, a UCLA archaeologist and geophysicist, dated it at 17,000 years.[21]

And the evidence continued to pour in after Haynes' 1969 article. Although Orr's early reports on his Santa Rosa finds were, like Carter's on San Diego, ridiculed by the anthropological status quo, he was eventually born out. In 1977, Ranier Berger established conclusively through radiocarbon dating that remains taken from the same locality could be dated as at least 40,000 years old.[22] By that point, Carter's two San Diego Skulls had also been dated by Dr. Jeffrey Bada, using an even more sophisticated technique based on the racemization of aspartic acid, at 44,000 and 48,000 years respectively.[23] Meanwhile, another 1975 racemization test by Bada—this one of remains unearthed by Stanford University archaeologist Bert Garow near Sunnyvale, California, in 1972—had yielded a dating of 70,000 years.[24]

The response of mainstream anthropologists to all this was probably best articulated in 1976 by Robert Heizer, at the time nearing the end of his career as a Brahmin of the Anthropology Department at the University of California at Berkeley. The dates reported by Berger, Bada, and others were simply "too old," he stated unequivocally and without further investigation.[25] Plainly, as an ordained "expert" on indigenous "prehistory," Heizer rejected the idea that his convenient theories should be confused by the introduction of mere facts. Certainly, he was not alone in holding this profoundly anti–intellectual view, nor did it prove to be transient.

Even after another 15 years of revelations accruing from discoveries—including the Meadowcroft site in Pennsylvania (dated at 20,000 years),[26] the Alice Boer site in Brazil (20,000 years plus),[27] the Monte Verde site in Chile (30,000 years plus),[28] the Tlapacaya site near Mexico City (22–24,000 years),[29] Old Crow and Bluefish Lake sites in the Yukon (40,000 years plus),[30] the dating of skulls found much earlier near Los Angeles (23,600 years)[31] and Otavalo, Ecuador (30,000 years),[32] the dating of a skull found in California's Yuha Valley (22,000 years)[33] and the so–called Black Box Skull (52,000 years),[34] and others—in mid-1992, an exhibition on Aztec culture held in celebration of the Columbian Quincentennial at the Denver Museum of Natural History included a placard proclaiming categorically that American Indians first came to this hemisphere "across the Bering Strait ... some 15,000 years ago."[35]

At the same time, those who have challenged convention in this respect by finding and publicizing physical evidence contradictory to it—Berger and Bada, for instance, or the independent archaeologist Jeffrey Goodman, and even Richard "Scotty" MacNeish, former President of the Society for American Archaeology, Director of the R. S. Peabody Foundation for Archaeology, and winner of the A. V. Kidder Award for Archaeology in 1971—are consistently ridiculed and marginalized wherever possible.[36] Nor have figures like George Carter ever really been rehabilitated by their "colleagues" in the discipline of anthropology, even long after their "ridiculous" contentions have been proven correct.[37]

The fact that "The Great Man," Louis Leakey—because of his own discovery of what he thought might be a 100,000–year–old site in the Calico Hills in southern California during the 1960s—shared many of the opinions of dissidents like Carter and Bada towards the end of his life is a matter carefully excluded from polite academic conversation.[38] With the exception of a few arch–reactionary nay–sayers like the inimitable Vance Haynes,[39] the anthropological establishment has opted to turn a blind eye, essentially pretending the

Map I

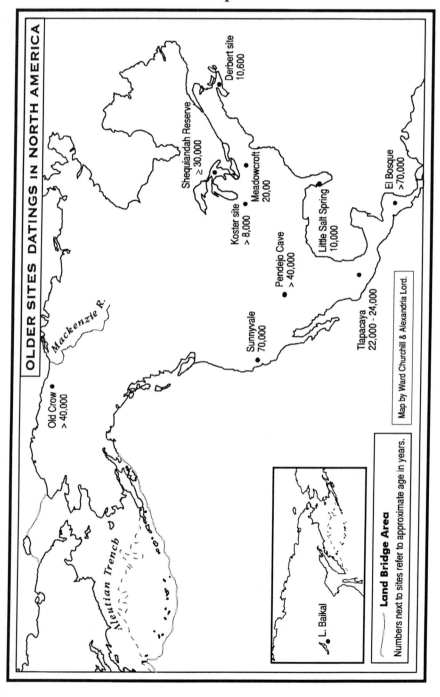

OLDER SITES DATINGS IN NORTH AMERICA

Derbert site
10,600

Shequiandah Reserve
≥ 30,000

Meadowcroft
20,00

El Bosque
>70,000

Koster site
> 8,000

Little Salt Spring
10,000

Pendejo Cave
> 40,000

Mackenzie R.

Sunnyvale
70,000

Tlapacaya
22,000 - 24,000

Old Crow ●
> 40,000

Neutian Trench

L. Baikal

Land Bridge Area

Numbers next to sites refer to approximate age in years.

Map by Ward Churchill & Alexandria Lord.

Map II

OLDER SITES DATINGS IN SOUTH AMERICA

Otavalo
30,000

Alice Boer
>20,000

Pedra Furada
40,000

Monte Verde
>30,000

Fells Cave
8,500

Map by Ward Churchill & Alexandria Lord.

Calico Hills phase of Leakey's work never occurred.[40] (For an overview of the most important sites in North and South America, *see* Maps I and II.)

The Land Bridge

Data have been presented on site after site with dates and geological context telling of occupations [in America] earlier than Clovis.

Herbert L. Alexander, 1978

I sense that most conservative thinkers, on the basis of the evidence reported from widely separated localities ... are now willing to concede that man probably entered America during a major interstadial of the last Glacial Period (at least 25,000 years ago).

Alan Bryan, 1978

> With rare exceptions, no general archaeological formulations attempt to weave the phenomenon presented as evidence to the Pre–Clovis contention into the generally acknowledged fabric of world prehistory.
>
> *Roger Owen, 1984*

Actually, aside from arrogance and obstinacy, there are some very solid reasons for anthropology's Brahmins to have been so adamant in their resistance to datings earlier than 13,000 B.C. in the Americas. One of these concerns the geological realities of the Bering land bridge itself. There have in fact been three, and perhaps four, appearances of this phenomenon within "Human Time." The most recent of these began about 23,000 years in the past, and ended 8,000 years ago. The one before that lasted from about 35,000 to 27,000 years ago. While there may have been another approximately 70,000 years back, the next occurrence which has definitely been established dates from a point ending some 170,000 years ago. Earlier than that, not enough is known to say.[41]

The problems with this are monumental. As was noted in the preceding section, there were irresolvable questions of chronology already imbedded in Alfred Kroeber's extremely limited acknowledgment of site datings. For his descendants now to admit to the accuracy of datings of even 20,000 years in locales like Texas or southern California—given the absolute minimum time required for humans to have dispersed from Beringia to these locales under *ideal* conditions[42]—would be to render orthodoxy untenable. This is to say that they would, as a concomitant, be forced to concede that passage over the most recent Bering Strait Bridge, even if they were to revise their estimates of the moment for its first usage backward all the way to 23,000 years, cannot possibly account for indigenous American populations *en toto*.

Noted Mexican anthropologist José Lorenzo has remarked upon such chronological difficulties with respect to the 8,500–year–old Fells Cave site near Tierra del Fuego, at the very tip of South America. Although the dating of Fells Cave falls within the conventional timeframe, strictly speaking, Lorenzo finds it bizarre to suggest that some sense of "manifest destiny [caused its inhabitants] to set track records for the course from the Bering steppes to Patagonia."[43]

On their face, these problems might be solved, and Bering Strait ideology sustained, simply by abandoning the most recent land bridge in favor of the next older, placing the date of first entry into the hemisphere at some point 30–35,000 years ago. Clearly, such a Kroeberesque maneuver would encompass a host of the datings which so flatly contradict convention in its present form. However, any such revision is blocked by meteorological considerations. Both of the most recent land bridges emerged during the so–called Wisconsin glacial period, which lasted from about 70,000 years ago to a point around 10,000 years ago.[44] During this Ice Age, access routes southward from Beringia were completely blocked by a glacial mass up to two miles thick.[45]

Most advocates of orthodoxy have attempted to address this dilemma by suggesting—based on no discernible evidence—the existence of an "ice–free central passage" or "corridor" through the glaciers, by which early migrants supposedly moved southward from Beringia, en route to dispersal across the continent.[46] There have, to be sure, always been more than a few issues attending this proposition. As Knute R. Fladmark, an anthropologist at Simon Frasier University, has pointed out:

> If the initial population moved southward through a mid–continental corridor, one would expect that the oldest sites would occur closest to the southern ice margin, there would be a perceptible temporal gradient from north to south, and that movement into peripheral areas such as ... the Pacific Coast would show a secondary temporal gradient with decreasing age from west to east. In fact, the available evidence reflects no such gradient.[47]

In addition, Reid Bryson, head of the Department of Meteorology at the University of Wisconsin and specialist in Arctic conditions, studied the matter intensively during the 1970s and found that—far from being the lush passage, laden with game, as proponents described it—any such corridor would have been even more frigid and barren than the glacial mass surrounding it: "Assuming the structure of Arctic air then was like Arctic air now, air moving into southern Alberta and the plains ... should have been about 20° colder after the corridor opened than before."[48] Worse, in many ways, Bryson also concluded that, if the corridor ever existed at all, it could not have come into being until the very end of the Wisconsin Period. Certainly, no such passage existed at a point 30–35,000 years ago, during the very peak of the Ice Age.[49] Consequently, no southward dispersal by land was possible during the time the second most recent Beringian land bridge existed.

Some of the more thoughtful proponents of the Beringian hypothesis have attempted to circumvent this dilemma by facing it squarely. Fladmark, for example, has proposed an alternative dispersal theory which has people crossing the Bering Strait and then moving southward, along both the west and east coasts, before turning inland at some point below the glaciers. This at least would certainly retire the "corridor controversy," and explain some of the otherwise chronologically inexplicable datings along the Atlantic Coast (the 10,600–year–old Debert site in Nova Scotia, for instance).[50] What it does not explain is why early migrants would have chosen to traverse the entire Arctic before turning southward along the eastern seaboard rather than following the lead of their relatives moving southward along the few more obvious routes down the Pacific coastline.

Fladmark's alternative dispersal theory also fails to address the question of how people living deep in the interior of North America at dates contemporaneous with the initial appearances of their coastal cousins managed to get there so quickly, much less why they evidenced a degree of refinement in material culture suggesting they'd been there a very long time; the Koster site in Illinois, to name but one illustration, is more than 8,000 years old, and is indicative of a long–settled agrarian civilization, living in a substantial town complete with plastered walls in its dwellings.[51] Still less does the concept explain how or why so many sites along the southern Atlantic Coast—the 10,000–year–old Little Salt Spring, near Sarasota, Florida, comes to mind—predate by a considerable margin those in New England and eastern Canada.[52] And then there are the many, many sites which are simply too old to be accounted for by any of these "adjustments."

For the Bering Strait idea to be salvaged through some revision which might withstand geological/meteorological scrutiny, it would be necessary to seek recourse in the next earlier appearance of the land bridge phenomenon, about 70–odd millennia in the past. Moreover, given the strong possibility that no such formation actually existed at that time—or at least not in any traversable form—what is really at issue is the *next* earlier verifiable Beringian Bridge, 170,000 or more years ago.[53]

Adoption of either of these alternatives would encompass virtually all of the older datings of sites and remains which are relatively well confirmed (e.g., the Sunnyvale and the Black Box Skull), and afford the kind of temporal latitude necessary for possible resolution of questions about how people had arrived in several parts of South America long before they seem to have resided in much of North America. Relying upon the crossing of the bridge 170,000 or so years ago also accommodates the oldest and most speculative of all datings of artifacts—those at Hueyatlaco and El Horno, Mexico (170,000 years plus),[54] for example, as well as those at Mission Valley, California (120,000 years plus),[55] Texas Street" in San Diego (70–170,000 years),[56] and at El Bosque, Nicaragua (70,000 years plus)[57]—currently on the table.

On the other hand, incorporation of such geological coherence and consistency with existing datings serves to slam Bering Strait adherents squarely up against another sort of chronology. Resort to even the more recent of the two older land bridges, while it might redeem the theory per se, would necessarily place *Homo sapiens sapiens* ("Modern Man") in the "New World" more than 20,000 years before "he" is supposed to have originated in the "Old World" of what is now western Europe.[58] To accept the older, but more certain, of the two available options would be to destroy anthropological orthodoxy concerning the "ascent of man" entirely.[59] Confronted with this quandary, even a few subscribers to convention have begun casting about for alternative sources of the population which supposedly composed the original "peopling of the Americas."[60]

> Chagrined by the major flaws in the Bering route scenario, a few
> establishment archaeologists put forth alternative entry routes. The
> first serious proposal came in 1963 from the late Dr. E. F. Greenman,

Map III

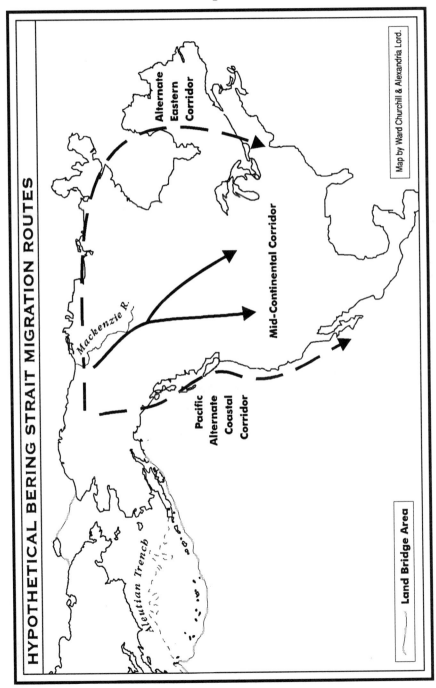

a highly respected anthropology professor at the University of Michigan and curator of the university's museum. A bit desperate for an explanation, Greenman argued that man reached the New World *from Europe* by canoe.... Greenman (who had a detailed knowledge of both Paleo–Indian artifacts and the artifacts of Europe) was startled by the many similarities he discovered between Paleo–Indian and European artifacts. This led him to postulate the theory that during Europe's Upper Paleolithic cultural period (35,000 to 12,000 years ago) men from France and Spain traveled to North America by crossing the Atlantic in "Beothuk," unique deep–water skin canoes.... He proposed Newfoundland as the point of entry, with subsequent migrations to the southwestern United States, including portions of Mexico.[61]

More recently, there have been straight–faced suggestions that initial migration occurred via water travel across the Pacific, with entry points posited in various localities along the North American coastline from British Columbia to southern California, and at points as far southward as Peru.[62] Ideas accruing from less "reputable" quarters have been that Indians are actually remnants of the populations of the so–called Lost Continents of Atlantis or Lemmuria (or both),[63] that American Indians are among the "Lost Tribes of Israel,"[64] that the migration came across the Atlantic from sub–Saharan Africa,[65] or that Indians are accounted for, at least in part, by the arrival of extraterrestrials on earth at some time a few thousand years ago.[66] In the end, one theory makes about as much sense as another since proponents of the alleged "Polynesian Route" cannot account for the fact that, while places like Australia and New Guinea were occupied by humans as long as 50,000 years ago, Hawai'i—the Pacific archipelago most proximate to the Americas—has been inhabited for only about 2,000 years.[67] (For an overview of the proposed migration routes, *see* Map III.)

Turning the Footprints Around

Evidence from a number of archaeological sites distributed in the western part of the hemisphere from the Yukon into South America now indicates a minimum possible date of 40,000 years for the earliest entry of man into the North American continent.

Ruth Gruhn, 1977

Given a theoretical vacuum left by the shaking of traditional archaeological ideas and conventions, we must seek new ideas, concepts, and their theoretical integration with reference to how the world works, why man behaves the way he does at different times and places, and how we may understand recognized patterns of changes and diversity in organized human behavior. Only to such theories may the scientific method be properly addressed. Thus, today's challenge is in theory building, and thus far little progress has been made, although many persons have seen the challenge and accepted it.

Lewis R. Binford, 1984

The fact of the matter is that none of this can be made to work out, nor will it ever. There is no evidence available to support the Bering Strait Hypothesis and related theories, nor has there ever been. Quite the opposite, when the late German anthropologist Werner Müller began to investigate Greenman's contentions during the mid–1960s, he quickly discovered that all evidence of shared transatlantic material cultural characteristics indicated that by far the oldest datings accrued from eastern Canada, not Europe.[68] Intrigued, he examined the evidence linking western Canada and Alaska to Siberia. The result was the same: the datings at Old Crow and Blue Fish Lake in particular predate the oldest site in Siberia, at Lake Baikal, by at least 17,000 years.[69] After two decades of exhaustive study, Müller concluded that there was solid evidence of very early migration *outward* from the North American Arctic region into both Asia and Europe.[70]

These findings would do much to explain things which are otherwise currently inexplicable. For instance, there is the sudden and mysterious appearance—it is usually likened to an "invasion"—of Cro–Magnons in Europe during the Upper Paleolithic.

> One of the most hotly debated topics of research in the past decade has been that surrounding the first appearance in Western Eurasia of hominids that can be considered anatomically and culturally modern. Between 50,000 and 30,000 years ago, the Neanderthals and Mousterian [Middle Paleolithic] industries were replaced, from the Near East to the Atlantic seaboard, by physically modern humans whose culture showed significant innovations, many of them never seen before on earth. These included graphic representations, true blade technology, personal ornaments, complex weapon and propulsion systems, long distance procurement of durable raw materials, subsistence systems based on strategically organized use of the landscape over the course of the year, rapid and continual technological change through time, and cultural systems that vary greatly from region to region.[71]

The problem with this formulation is that such things *had* been "seen before on earth." When one considers that the oldest known projectile points of the type used in Europe during this period have been consistently found in

North America, not in Spain or France, the likely source of the influx of modern humans to the "Old World" begins to clarify.[72]

> While the ancestral forms of the European projectile points have *not* been found on the Eurasian plains as prehistorians believed would be the case, ancestral forms for the American projectile points [dating from the same time] *have* been found. The Clovis point from Lewisville, Texas, which has been dated to over 38,000 years, shows that these projectile points were first invented in the Americas. The projectile points from geographically diverse sites such as Meadow-croft, Pennsylvania; McGee's Point, Nevada; and Tlapacoya, Mexico, support the validity of the Lewisville point. In fact, by the end of the Pleistocene epoch, there were a number of different point types and cultural traditions extant in the Americas, demonstrating that a great range of technological diversity had already been developed.[73]

The types of points involved here clearly indicate use of "complex weapons systems" such as spearthrowers and bows and arrows. With regard to graphic representations, there is a pictorially carved llama bone recovered from a site dated at 30,000 years or more at Tequixquiac, near Mexico City,[74] an engraved mastodon bone—also found in Mexico and directly comparable to the art of European Cro–Magnons—dating back at least 22,000 years,[75] and three massive stone carvings near Malakoff, Texas, dated at more than 30,000 years.[76] The remainder of the list, from personal ornamentation to cultural variation by region, is also plainly evidenced as having been present in the Americas at points as early as, and often much earlier than, was the case in Europe.

The idea that modern humans in the Americas predate those in other parts of the world also explains why agriculture seems to have emerged here rather than elsewhere. Although no wild form of corn has ever been discovered—meaning it is a plant type wholly dependent upon human hybridization for its very existence—fossilized grains of corn pollen were identified by Elsa Barghoorn, a Harvard botanist, in a drill sample taken from a depth of 200 feet below Mexico City in 1954. The interglacial date assigned to samples from that strata was 80,000 years.[77] Grinding technologies, associated with preparation of vegetal foodstuffs like corn, have been found in sites dating back 20,000 or more years on the Scripps campus,[78] at the Alice Boer site,[79] and elsewhere. By comparison, the Old World's Mesopotamian "Cradle of Civilization" in the Euphrates Valley—dating from the first known cultivation of wheat and rye, circa 7,000 B.C.—is quite recent.[80]

The same can be said for domestication of animals. While this "great leap towards civilization" supposedly occurred in Mesopotamia with the domesticating of dogs, pigs, sheep, goats, and finally cattle over a span running from 7,000 to 5,000 B.C.,[81] evidence from the Old Crow region indicates that

American Indians were keeping dogs many thousands of years earlier. As paleontologist Brenda Beebe remarked at the time of the find, "Our most surprising discovery is the jaws of several domesticated dogs, some of which appear to be 30,000 years old. This is almost 20,000 years older than any other known animals anywhere in the world."[82] Certainly, there have been no remotely comparable datings on the east Asian landmass.[83]

Even the invention of pottery, another aspect of civilization long thought to have occurred in Mesopotamia somewhere between 8,000 and 9,000 years ago—a premise more lately superseded by the discovery of 13,000–year–old pots in the Fukuki Cave and Senfukuji rock shelter, both on the island of Kyushu, Japan—may well have occurred in Peru much earlier, the concept then carried into the Old World by migrating Indians.[84] Be that as it may, it is true, as Alan Bryan observed in 1978, that "diffusion from America to Japan would be just as possible as diffusion in the opposite direction."[85]

Indeed, such a direction of diffusion might explain why the Ainu, an ancient "Caucasoid genetic isolate" in northern Japan, shows a far greater degree of cranial similarity to the equally isolated Yauyos Indians of Peru, than they do to the cranial characteristics of any of their "Mongoloid" neighbors.[86] For that matter, it would explain why both the Yauyos and the Ainu demonstrate a much greater similarity in cranial structure with the Norse of northern Scandinavia than they do with anyone else, or why, to quote physical anthropologist Janice Austin, "the [earliest] Paleo–Indians demonstrate population affinities with Caucasian [rather than Mongolian] groups."[87]

> It appears from [Austin's] statistical analysis that the traditional anthropological classification of American Indians as a branch of the Asian Mongolians is all wrong. The traditional interpretation was highly subjective, based on the lumping together of physically diverse American Indian groups; it is supported by little metric data and no chronology. Based on the new datings and the new statistical data, the Paleo–Indians should be classified as proto–Caucasoids who evolved into various American Indian peoples, giving the modern–day American Indians their own racial grouping as separate from the Mongoloids or Caucasoids. On the other hand, European Cro–Magnons should be classified as a branch of the proto–Caucasoid Paleo–Indians who evolved into what we now describe as modern Caucasoids. Similarly, based on the many analogies noted between ancient Mongolian skulls and some ancient American Indian skulls, the first Asians should also be classified as a branch of proto–Caucasoid Paleo–Indians who became Asiatic Mongolians.[88]

This conclusion corrects certain of the persistent and perplexing "anomalies" detected even by such hidebound racialist anthropologists as Carlton S.

Coon, who has been forced to admit—without abandoning his commitment to orthodoxy—that overall differences in fingerprints, blood types, earwax, and other "genetic indicators" have served to "drive a thick wedge between Asiatic Mongoloids and American Indians."[89] There is also the matter of the "shovel–shaped" incisors shared by American Indians, the Ainu, and a portion of the northern European population.[90]

Acceptance of the growing weight of evidence that American Indians didn't "come from somewhere else" would address a few other matters as well. These begin with confirmation that we are, and always have been, literally correct when we've insisted that we come from here, from this land, that we are truly *indigenous* to the hemisphere.[91] And, if our Origin Stories are thus verified as accurate, it follows that the rest of our "legends" are deserving of reconsideration for being exactly what we've always said they are: our Histories.[92] A revision of the chronology of human occupancy in the Americas backwards to, say, a quarter–million years would, to take a salient example, have the effect of making the "Four Worlds" chronicle of the Hopi—a saga in which the people's habitat is destroyed by volcanic fire at one point, by flooding at another, and by ice at still another—entirely plausible.[93]

> The destruction of the Hopi's third world by water may correspond to the inter–mountain basin damming and flooding that took place about 25,000 years ago in the [San Francisco Peaks area of Arizona]. The destruction of the second world by ice could represent the glacial activity that took place in the peaks approximately 100,000 years ago. And the destruction of the first world by fire could represent the volcanic activity that took place in the mountains approximately 250,000 years ago.[94]

It is their very plausibility, however, which precludes acceptance of such things by the anthropological establishment, bound up as it is in the construction supporting the imperatives of the broader eurocentric status quo. Theirs is not a preoccupation with truth, knowledge, or science. Rather, it is, as it must be, academic subterfuge: the careful orchestration of the illusion of such virtues in support of the prevailing hegemony of eurosupremacism. Ideologically, and therefore canonically, it *must* be held as true that the first modern human came into being on the soil of Europe and that s/he was of "Caucasoid stock."[95] From there, it can and *must* be held as true that all that has been humanly worth saying, doing, or thinking was first said, done, or thought by representatives of the Caucasian persuasion.[96] And, from there, all the classic arguments of European imperialism emerge, reducible for all their sophistry and variation to the basic proposition that being first signifies superiority and that superiority implies an intrinsic right to dominate the lives, lands, and resources of the "inferior."[97]

To discard or abandon the Bering Strait Hypothesis, absent some viable replacement serving the same purpose, would be to jerk a cornerstone from beneath the whole ideological edifice of white supremacy. Hence, the Brahmins of anthropology—and any who aspire to become such—have little choice but to continue their engagement in the theory's defense, nibbling importantly at their pipe stems as they pronounce their deeply "responsible" skepticism with regard to the valid, pontificate in their avid embrace of the ludicrous, reward those who toe their line while seeking to destroy the credibility and careers of those who deviate, striving all the while to indoctrinate yet another generation with their distortions while guarding their indefensible land bridge viciously and to the last gasp, even as it sags, buckles, and begins to sink beneath their feet.

On the Matter of mtDNA

Objectivity is not an unobtainable emptying of the mind but a willingness to abandon a set of preferences when the world seems to work in a contrary way.... Good theories invite a challenge but do not bias the outcome.... We say, in our mythology, that old theories die when new observations derail them. But too often, indeed I would say usually, theories act as straightjackets to channel observations toward their support and to forestall data that might refute them.

Stephen Jay Gould, 1992

Comes now geneticist Douglas Wallace and his colleagues, the subject of Tim Friend's story in *USA Today*, to resuscitate the dying doctrine of Bering Strait migration. Their technique is to rely upon the esotericism of their topic and the technical nomenclature they use to describe it to mystify those who might otherwise be critical, all the while peddling the same old bill of goods: by tracing "DNA Footprints," Wallace is quoted as saying, they are demonstrating "beyond reasonable doubt" that humans did indeed move into the New World from the Old "as long as" 40,000 years ago (i.e., across the second most recent Beringian land bridge).

Although Friend carefully casts the impression that this represents a sort of "revolution" in anthropological thinking, it is not. Wallace is merely engaging in a Kroeber–style revision of American anthropology's most bedrock tenets. A certain amount of chronological ground is given up in order to contain and absorb accumulated counter–evidence, with the result that the main premise of the status quo—the Bering Strait hypothesis itself, and the concept of Old World primacy over the New which comes with it—can be not only maintained, but reinforced in the public mind once again. As Wallace himself has elsewhere announced his intellectual alignment, "*Traditional anthropological analysis has confirmed that American Indians came from Asia ... across the Bering land* bridge when it was exposed during an episode of glaciation [emphasis added]."[98] His job is to prove it, or to create a popular appearance that he has.

In pursuing this objective, Wallace assembled a lab team at Emory University to conduct restriction analysis sequencing maternally inherited genetic material in samples taken from selected groups of Asians and American Indians. They then catalogued the diversity found in the mitochondrial DNA (mtDNA) genome of each group in order to chart transmission over time from one locality to the next. What the team expected to discover, according to its own published material, was evidence indicating a diffusion of genetic traits from southeast Asia northwards, across Beringia and into America.[99] What they found instead was precisely the opposite: four distinct mutations which are very rare in southern Asia, somewhat more common in northern and central Asia, and occurring at "surprisingly higher frequencies" among American Indians.[100]

To avert the obvious conclusion that the source of such genetic traits would be where they are most prevalent, a matter indicating diffusion from America *to* Asia, Wallace's team, in a performance worthy of such earlier exemplars of scientific racism as Morton, Coon, and Earnest Hooten, hurriedly cobbled up a whole new genetic theory which they dubbed "The Founder Effect."[101] In this odd concoction, put together on no more discernible evidentiary basis than the rest of the Bering Strait theory, those Asians who supposedly first came to America did so in such small groups and, unlike the relatives they left behind, stayed so completely isolated until so recently that they experienced a "genetic bottleneck" which preserved their peculiar mtDNA characteristics in ways which proved impossible in Asia itself.[102]

It is this blatant display of facts tortured into conformity with reactionary postulation that *USA Today* opted to trumpet as a "radical" breakthrough in anthropology. And what of the mass of countervailing evidence: dating, for instance? It is handled in kind: the Old Crow site is described as being "30,000 years old" instead of more than 40,000; Monte Verde is treated in the same manner, and so on. Newer finds, such as Scotty MacNeish's discovery of 40,000–plus–year–old human hair in the Pendejo Cave in New Mexico,[103] and the Pedra Furada site in Brazil, as old as 40,000 years,[104] suffer the same fate. Other, even more inconvenient data, such as that embodied in the existence of the San Diego and Black Box skulls, are left entirely unmentioned.

Still less does Friend acknowledge that the conclusions drawn by the Wallace team are flatly contradicted by the findings of the bulk of geneticists involved in comparable studies of mtDNA transmission. A team headed by University of Utah researcher Ryk Ward, for example, studied a single tribal population in the Pacific Northwest, the Nuu–Chal–Nulths, and arrived at some rather less theoretically strained positions in a 1991 study published by the National Academy of Science.[105]

> Ward's analysis shows that: 1) minimum estimates indicate that the sequence divergence (unshared lineages) in [a single] Amerindian

tribe is over 60% of the mitochondrial sequence diversity observed in major Old world groups such as Japanese or sub–Saharan Africans; 2) the magnitude of the sequence difference between this tribe's lineage clusters suggest that their origin must predate [the supposed] Pleistocene colonization of the Americas; and 3) "since a single Amerindian can maintain such intensive molecular diversity, it is unnecessary to presume that substantial genetic bottlenecks occurred during the formation of contemporary groups or, in particular 'Dramatic Founding Effect' resulted in the peopling of the Americas."[106]

Ward and his associates have also pointed out that "preliminary analysis of sequence data for the same mitochondrial segment from other Amerindian tribal groups indicates that a majority of tribes are as diverse as the Nuu–Chal–Nulths and that only a small subset of the lineages found in one tribe are shared with others."[107] In other words, there is substantial evidence that American Indians long ago achieved "mutational drift equilibrium" or "steady–state genetic distribution," a matter which militates strongly against Wallace's "founding effect thesis."[108] This is all the more true since, as the Wallace team's own data suggests, no such drift equilibrium has as yet been achieved in Eurasia.[109] The upshot is the so–called Eve Hypothesis in which it is argued that American Indians are responsible for their limited mtDNA commonalities with Asians, and not the other way around.[110] More broadly, it is easily arguable that such evidence bolsters archaeological data suggesting a rapid influx of humans from America into both Asia and Europe at some point around 50,000 years ago.[111]

All in all, then, the material produced by Douglas Wallace must be assigned its rightful place among the welter of anthropological/historical myths—for instance, that North American Indians numbered "not more than a million nomadic Stone Age hunters and gatherers" in 1492,[112] that most of us "inadvertently died of disease" after the arrival of Columbus,[113]—which have been so persistently fabricated and utilized in pseudo–scientific support of Euroamerica's overweening sense of its own intrinsic superiority and corresponding "manifest destiny" to dominate all it encounters.[114] His conclusions are not counter to those of the status quo, but rather synonymous with them. The extraordinarily cordial treatment extended to him by "McPaper" should, if nothing else, be proof enough of that.[115]

Toward a New Understanding

Certain errors are stations on the way to truth.

Robert Musil, 1972

Aside from the endemic condition of eurocentrism which presently afflicts both the public and academia, any notion that modern humans may have evolved in the Americas first, spreading eventually across Eurasia, is considered problematic because of an ostensible absence in this hemisphere of a place from which humans might have sprung. This presumption is, however, not necessarily true. To begin with, the exact nature of humanity's simian ancestors is not presently known.[116] Second, even if it were, the evolutionary progression culminating in *Homo sapiens sapiens* is anything but clear. For more than a century after the initial discovery of fossilized European hominids in 1856, canonical wisdom wrongly held that the Neanderthals were part of this chain.[117]

> There is now a near consensus among students of evolutionary biology that the origins of our own species, *Homo sapiens*, is somehow intimately linked with the first intercontinental ancient hominid, *Homo erectus*. However, neither the transformation of *erectus* to *sapiens* nor the transformation of ancient (archaic) populations of *Homo sapiens* to their anatomically modern successors (*H s sapiens*) are matters of agreement in this scientific fraternity.... In fact, there is no consensus.[118]

Louis Leakey, for one, believed that evolutionists were following the wrong line, and that *Homo erectus* represented an "evolutionary dead end" of the same sort as Neanderthal.[119] He also felt strongly that *Homo sapiens* might well have originated in the Americas, and he died with the expectation that modern human remains would eventually be discovered in this hemisphere dating back one–half million years or more.[120] Although Leakey, posthumously, has come to be the target of frequent criticism by the anthropological establishment, the record amply demonstrates that he was much more often right than wrong, and his critics just the reverse.[121]

Nor does he stand alone in his "eccentricity." In adopting his view of a possible "American Genesis" for humanity, Leakey joined a distinctively able minority of scholars running back to the sixteenth–century priest, Bartolomé de Las Casas, and later flowering amidst the scientism of the late nineteenth century.[122]

> One such apostate was Alfred Russell Wallace (1823–1913). In 1887, Wallace examined the evidence for early man in the New World, and like the German anatomist Julian Kollman (1834–1918), who three years earlier had made a similar survey, found not only considerable evidence of antiquity for available specimens, but also

a continuity of type through time. In an effort to explain this, Wallace suggested that once man had become morphologically differentiated from his apish kin (during the mid–Tertiary period), he remained physically stable.[123]

In the 1880s and 1890s, these pioneers were joined by Frederick Larkin, Charles C. Abbott, William Henry Holmes, and, after 1910, by both the eminent British naturalist Sir Arthur Keith and Florentino Ameghino, founder of Argentina's National Museum.[124] The 1920s saw the addition of Charles F. Lummis, founder of the Southwest Museum of Archaeology, and geologist/paleontologist H. J. Cook to the ranks.[125] More recently, there have been George Carter, Jeffrey Goodman, the late Bruce Raemsch, and Alvah Hicks.[126] Scotty MacNeish, Paul Mellars, Lewis Binford, Bruce MacFadden, Eric Delson, A. L. Rosenberger, Christopher B. Singer, Nelson Eldridge, Ian Tattersal, and a number of others have lately hinted that their thinking is, from various standpoints, moving in more or less the same direction.[127]

The work of the last six is particularly interesting insofar as they have been steadily chipping away at the alleged "primate barrier" preventing autochthonous emergence of *Homo sapiens* in the Western Hemisphere. As MacFadden has put it, there is "good reason to lament the fragmentary record that must be used to decipher the evolution of ... New World primates. It can truly be said that the paleontological record of New World platyrrhines [prehumans] is indeed the weakest of the lot. There are several reasons for this, but these mostly stem from the fact that, with the push to find human ancestors, emphasis has been outside South America."[128]

> Ongoing assessments of Platyrrhini (ancient New World) primates have depicted them as unmistakable members of the order "Haplorrhini," a monophyletic taxon encompassing both New and Old World anthropoids. The source for the Ecocene (55–32 million years ago) presence of both New and Old World primates must be an earlier common ancestral form. Perhaps the North American and European Adapidae, the earliest of the known pre–primates, is the progenitor of today's higher primate groups [including humans].[129]

The question hinges, according to Hicks, upon "what constitutes acceptable evolutionary terms for investigating the earliest archaeological remains of mid–Pleistocene man in the Americas. The present effort is to distinguish compatible analogies that might instigate a change in paradigm and allow us to reconsider the antiquity of the modern human anatomy and to bring in New World considerations as to whether today's humans were ever 'linked' to *Homo erectus*."[130] Or, to put it another way, "Could the Western Hemisphere have spawned its own distinct hominid form, the indigenous Native American and, in turn, his fully modern human contemporaries of the Old World Pleistocene epoch? Does the American genesis perspective offer a viable alternative for those hypothesizing a rapid replacement [of *Homo erectus* in Europe]?"[131]

The answers to such queries are surpassingly obscure at present. While an American genesis may someday be documented beyond all doubt, it is at least equally possible that the whole notion of human monogenesis will be proven wrong, and that some form of polygenesis occurred.[132] Such could be the interpretation of the recent finds of 90,000–year–old sites near the mouth of the Klasies River in southern Africa when taken in combination with the evidence accruing from America.[133] Alternately, it may be shown that there was monogenesis in some area of the earth other than the Western Hemisphere, but at some point much more remote in time than has heretofore been accepted.[134] Whatever the truth turns out to be, it is long past time for us to face the questions squarely and toss the dogmas of Beringia and the European origin of modern man in the historical slag heap where all such racist propaganda properly belongs.

Notes

1. *See* generally, David M. Hopkins, ed., *The Bering Land Bridge* (Stanford, California: Stanford University Press, 1967); *see* also Harold S. Gladwin, *Men Out of Asia* (New York: McGraw–Hill, 1947).

2. Jefferson was actually adapting ideas which had originated in Europe, for equally self–serving reasons, to his own purposes; *see* Lee H. Huddleston, *Origins of the American Indians, European Concepts, 1492–1729* (Austin: University of Texas Press, 1969); *see* also Margaret T. Hogden, *Early Anthropology in the Sixteenth and Seventeenth Centuries* (Philadelphia: University of Pennsylvania Press, 1964).

3. Bernard W. Sheehan, *Seeds of Extinction: Jeffersonian Philanthropy and the American Indian* (Chapel Hill: University of North Carolina Press, 1973).

4. The principle that the United States held a preemptive right to acquire native property more or less at its convenience was enshrined in U.S. juridical doctrine by Chief Justice John Marshall in his opinions in *Johnson v. McIntosh* (21 U.S. 98 Wheat. 543 [1823]), *Cherokee Nation v. Georgia* (30 U.S. [5 Pet.] 1 [1831]) and *Worchester v. Georgia* (31 U.S. [6 Pet.] 551 [1832]).

5. Overall, *see* Gordon R. Willey and Jeremy A. Sabloff, *A History of American Archaeology* (San Francisco: W. H. Freeman & Co., 1974).

6. Jeffrey Goodman, *American Genesis: The American Indian and the Origins of Modern Man* (New York: Summit Books, 1981), quote p. 43; additional information p. 47.

7. Jesse D. Jennings, *Prehistory of North America* (New York: McGraw–Hill, 1974), p. 39.

8. Jeffrey Goodman, op. cit., p. 44.

9. George F. Carter, "Evidence for Pleistocene Man in Southern California," *Geographical Review*, Vol. XL, No. 1 (1950), "Man in America: A Criticism of Scientific Thought," *Scientific Monthly*, Vol. XXIII, No. 5 (Nov. 1951).

10. On the implications of the Folsom and Clovis finds, *see* C. W. Ceram, *The First American* (New York: Mentor Books, 1972), p. 292.

11. Edwin Wilmsen, "An Outline of Early Man Studies," *American Antiquity*, quoted in C. W. Ceram, op. cit., p. 306.

12. Kroeber also played a major role in falsifying estimates of the size of the preinvasion indigenous population in North America; for analysis, *see* the chapter entitled "The Widowed Land" in Francis Jennings, *The Invasion of America: Indians, Colonialism and the Cant of Conquest* (Chapel Hill: University of North Carolina Press, 1975).

13. Alfred L. Kroeber, *Anthropology* (New York: Harcourt Brace, 1948), p. 777.

14. *See* José L. Lorenzo, "Early Man Research in the American Hemisphere," in *Early Man in America from a Circum–Pacific Perspective*, Alan Lyle Bryan, ed. (Edmonton: Archaeological Researches International, 1978), pp. 1–9; hereinafter cited as *Early Man in America*; *see* also K. R. Fladmark, "Routes: Alternative Migration Corridors for Early Man in North America," *American Antiquity*, Vol. 44, No. 1 (Jan. 1979); and Ruth Gruhn, "Linguistic Evidence in Support of the Coastal Route of Earliest Entry into the New World," *Man*, No. 23 (1988).

15. George F. Carter, "Evidence for Pleistocene Man at La Jolla, California," *Transactions of the New York Academy of Sciences*, Vol. 2, No. 7 (1949).

16. Vance C. Haynes, Jr., "The Earliest Americans," *Science*, Vol. 166, No. 7 (1969), p. 711. As concerns advanced technological dating of materials recovered from a number of sites by that point, Haynes simply dismissed it in favor of his "hunches"; *see* his "Carbon–14 Dates and Early Man in the New World," in *Pleistocene Extinctions: The Search for a Cause*, Paul S. Martin and H. E. Wright, eds. (New Haven: Yale University Press, 1967), pp. 267–68.

17. Thomas E. Lee, "Editorial Comments on Pebble Tools and Their Relatives in North America," *Anthropological Journal of Canada*, Vol. 4, No. 4 (1966).

18. Jeffrey Goodman, op. cit., p. 72.

19. H. M. Wormington, *Ancient Man in North America* (Denver: Denver Museum of Natural History, Pop. Ser. No. 4, 1967), p 58.

20. A. MacStalker, "Geology and Age of the Early Man Site at Taber, Alberta, *American Antiquity*, Vol. 32, No. 4 (1969).

21. Ranier Berger, "Advances and Results in Radiocarbon Dating: Early Man in America," *World Archaeology*, Vol. 7, No. 2 (1975). On the significance of Leakey's African discoveries, *see* LeGros W. E. Clark, *The First Evidence for Human Evolution* (Chicago: University of Chicago Press, 1969).

22. Rainer Berger used radiocarbon dating techniques, which can measure the age of organic material up to 40,000 years; the Santa Rosa material ran off the end of the scale, meaning it was more than 40 millennia in antiquity; *see* "Early Man Confirmed in America 40,000 Years Ago," *Science News* (26 Mar. 1977).

23. Jeffrey L. Bada, Patricia Masters Hilfman, R. A. Schroeder, and George F. Carter, "New Evidence for the Antiquity of Man in North America Deduced from Aspartic Acid Racemization," *Science*, No. 184 (17 May 1974).

24. Jeffrey L. Bada and Patricia Masters Hilfman, "Amino Acid Racemization Dating of Fossil Bones," *World Archaeology*, Vol. 7, No. 2 (1975).

25. Quoted in Boyce Rensberger, "Coast Dig Focuses on Man's Move to the New World," *New York Times* (16 Aug. 1976).

26. James M. Aldiviso, "Excavations at Meadowcroft Rock Shelter, 1973–75: A Progress Report," *Pennsylvania Archaeologist*, No. 45 (1975); "Meadowcroft Rockshelter, 1977: An Overview," *American Antiquity*, No. 43 (1978); "Meadowcroft Rock Shelter," in *Early Man in America*, op. cit., pp. 140–80, esp. p. 156. It should be noted that the University of Arizona's Vance Haynes weighed in on the matter with his usual incompetence; Vance Haynes, "Paleoindian Charcoal from Meadowcroft Rockshelter: Is Contamination a Problem?" *American Antiquity*, Vol. 45, No. 3 (1980).

27. W. J. von Puttamer, "Man in the Amazon: Stone Age Present Meets Stone Age Past," *National Geographic*, Vol. 155, No. 1 (Jan. 1979). More recently discovered sites in Brazil may date to 50,000 years; *see* Richard Wolkomir, "New Finds Could Rewrite the Start of American History," *Smithsonian*, No. 21 (Mar. 1991).

28. Tom D. Dillehay, *Monte Verde: A Late Pleistocene Settlement in Chile* (Washington, DC: Smithsonian Institution Press, 1989); *see* also N. Guidon and G. Delibrias, "Carbon–14 Dates Point to Man in the Americas 32,000 Years Ago," *Nature*, No. 321 (1986); and Tom Dillehay, "A Late Ice–Age Settlement in Southern Chile," *Scientific American*, No. 251 (1984).

29. Lorena Miriambell, "Tlapacoya: A Late Pleistocene Site in Central Mexico," in *Early Man in America*, op. cit., pp. 221–30.

30. William N. Irving and C. R. Harrington, "Upper Pleistocene Radiocarbon–Dater Artifacts from the Northern Yukon," *Science* (26 Jan. 1973); Robson Bonnichsen, "Critical Arguments for Pleistocene Artifacts from the Old Crow Basin, Yukon," in *Early Man in America*, op. cit., pp. 102–17; Richard E. Morlan, "Early Man in Northern Yukon Territory: Perspective as of 1977," in *Early Man in America*, op. cit., pp. 78–95; Jacques Cinq–Mars, "Bluefish Cave 1: A Late Pleistocene Eastern Beringian Cave Deposit in the Northern Yukon," *Canadian Journal of Archaeology*, Col. 3, 1979; William N. Irving, "New Dates from Old Bones: Twisted Fractures in Mammoth Bones and Some Flaked Bone Tools Suggest That Humans Occupied the Yukon More Than 40,000 Years Ago," *Natural History* (Feb. 1987); Dennis Stanford, "The Ginsberg Experiment: Archaeology Can Be Bone–breaking Work," *Natural History* (Sept. 1987).

31. Frederick Larkin, *Ancient Man in America* (New York: n. p. 1880), p. 231; Ranier Berger, "Advances and Results in Radiocarbon Dating," op. cit., p. 180.

32. David M. Davies, "Some Observations on the Otavalo Skeleton from Imbabara Province, Ecuador," in *Early Man in America*, op. cit., p. 273.

33. W. M. Childers, "Preliminary Report on the Yuha Burial, California," *Anthropological Journal of Canada*, Vol. 12, No. 1 (1974); S. L. Rogers, "An Early Human Fossil from the Yuha Desert of California—Physical Characteristics," *San Diego Museum Papers* (San Diego: San Diego Museum of Man, 1977).

34. Jeffrey Goodman, op. cit., pp. 97–98.

35. The "Aztec World" exhibition was mounted as a collaborative effort between Davíd Carrasco, then Professor of Religious Studies at the University of Colorado/Boulder, and Eduardo Matos Moctezuma, Director of the Museo del Templo Mayor in Mexico City and a direct lineal descendant of the last Aztec ruler, at the Denver Museum of Natural History, from September through November 1992; *see* Davíd Carrasco and Eduardo Matos Moctezuma, *Moctezuma's Mexico: Visions of the Aztec World* (Niwot: University Press of Colorado, 1992).

36. MacNeish went on record nearly 20 years ago as believing human occupancy in the Americas could be dated to a point 70,000 years in the past, "plus or minus 30,000 years";

Richard S. MacNeish, "Early Man in the New World," *American Scientist*, Vol. 64 (May–June 1976).

37. For a sample of the abuse Carter suffered through the end of his career, *see* the more or less indirect exchange between him and Vance Haynes on the topic of mastodon–hunting in Ice Age North America: Vance Haynes, "Elephant–hunting in North America, *Scientific American*, Vol. 214, No. 6 (1966); George F. Carter, "Uhle's Mastodon," *Anthropological Journal of Canada*, Vol. 16, No. 2 (1968). For two of Carter's better overall responses to his detractors, *see* his "Early Man in America," *Anthropological Journal of Canada*, Vol. 10, No. 3 (1972), and "On the Antiquity of Man in America," *Anthropological Journal of Canada*, Vol. 15, No. 1 (1977).

38. Louis S. B. Leakey, Ruth deEtte Simpson, Thomas Clements, Ranier Berger, and J. Whitthoft et al., "Archaeological Excavations in the Calico Mountains, California Preliminary Report," *Science*, Vol. 160 (1 Mar. 1968), "Man in America: The Calico Mountains Excavations," *Britannica Yearbook of Science and the Future* (Chicago: Encyclopedia Britannica, 1970), *Pleistocene Man at Calico* (San Bernardino, California: San Bernardino Museum Association, 1972).

39. Vance C. Haynes, "The Calico Site: Artifacts or Geofacts?" *Science*, Vol. 181 (27 July 1973); *see* also his "Geofacts and Fancy," *Natural History* (Feb. 1988).

40. For the classic example, *see* Sonia Cole, *Leakey's Luck* (New York: Harcourt Brace Jovanovich, 1975).

41. Jeffrey Goodman, op. cit., p. 50.

42. There are, of course, concrete examples by which minimum dispersal times can be estimated. The Athabascan (Dene) people are one of those relative handful who do seem to have migrated into the Beringian area of North America from Siberia approximately 15,000 years ago. A portion of them, now known as the Navajo (Diné), eventually broke off and moved southward, settling in the northern portion of Arizona and New Mexico around 1,000 A.D. This dispersal, all of it made at the end of or after the last Ice Age, required some 10,000 years to complete; *see* generally, Harold E. Driver, *Indians of the Americas* (Chicago: University of Chicago Press, 1975).

43. José L. Lorenzo, op. cit., p. 4.

44. Jeffrey Goodman, op. cit., p. 49.

45. Ibid., p. 63.

46. For a succinct elaboration of this thesis, made in the process of challenging it, *see* Froelich Rainey, "The Significance of Present Archaeological Discoveries in Inland Alaska," in *Asia and North America: Transpacific Contacts*, Marian W. Smith, ed. (Millwood, New York, Kraus Reprint, 1974), p. 46. The original edition was published by The Society for American Archaeology, Salt Lake City, in 1953.

47. K. R. Fladmark, op. cit., p. 60.

48. Reid Bryson, *Radiocarbon Isochrones of the Laurentian Tide Sheet* (Madison: University of Wisconsin Technical Report No. 35, 1967), p. 8.

49. The validity of Bryson's conclusion has been independently corroborated by Dr. Alan Bryan, an anthropologist at the University of Alberta, who observes that "there is a congruence of evidence from several lines of research which suggest the ice barrier did not disappear until 8,500 or 9,000 years ago"; Alan L. Bryan, "Early Man in America and the Late Pleistocene Chronology of Western Canada and Alaska," *Current Anthropology*, Vol. 10, No. 4 (19 Oct. 1969), p. 341.

50. K. R. Fladmark, op. cit.

51. Felicia A. Holton, "One of the Most Important Archaeological Digs in America," *New York Times* (15 July 1973).

52. "Florida Burial Site: Brains to Boomerangs," *Science News* (6 Aug. 1977).

53. Discussion of the probabilities that the "intermediate" land bridge did and did not exist will be found in David M. Hopkins, ed., *The Bering Land Bridge*, op. cit.

54. Barney J. Szabo, Harold E. Malde, and Cynthia Irwin–Williams, "Dilemma Posed by Uranium Series Dates on Archaeologically Significant Bones from Valsequillo, Puebla, Mexico," *Earth and Planetary Science Letters*, Vol. 6, No. 4 (July 1969); Jeffrey Goodman, op. cit., pp. 140–45.

55. Bryan O. Reeves, "Early Man at Mission Valley, California," unpublished paper presented at the Annual Meeting for the Society for American Archaeology, Tucson, Arizona, 1978.

56. "Texas Street Artifacts," *New World Antiquity*, Vol. 2, Nos. 9–12 (1955); "New World Archaeology: A 70,000 Year Old Site," *Science News*, No. 103 (26 May 1973); A. L. Bryan, "An Overview of Paleo–American Prehistory From a Circum–Pacific Perspective," in *Early Man in America*, op. cit., pp. 306–27, esp. p. 312; George F. Carter, "The American Paleolithic," in *Early Man in America*, op. cit., pp. 10–19.

57. William D. Page, "The Geology of the El Bosque Archaeological Site, Nicaragua," in *Early Man in America*, op. cit., pp. 231–60, esp. p. 254; Ruth Gruhn, "A Note on Excavations at El Bosque, Nicaragua in 1975," in *Early Man in America*, op. cit., pp. 261–62.

58. Orthodoxy holds that Modern Man, in the form of Cro–Magnons, first appeared in Europe about 35–40,000 years ago (lately revised to 50,000 years); J. B. Birdsell, *Human Evolution* (Chicago: Rand–McNally, 1972). A minority view, expressed by University of Arizona anthropologist Arthur Jelinek and others, has been that Cro–Magnons emerged a bit earlier in the Mideast; "Modern Man: Mid–East Origins?" *Science News* (3 Mar. 1979).

59. The conventional view is that *Homo sapiens sapiens* evolved from *Homo hablis* through *Homo erectus*; John Buettner–Janasch, *The Origins of Man* (New York: John Wiley & Sons, 1967); David Philbeam, *The Ascent of Man* (New York: Macmillan Publishing Co., 1972).

60. For the initial use of this expression, now prevalent, *see* J. B. Birdsell, "The Problem of the Early Peopling of the Americas as Viewed from Asia," in W. S. Laughlin and S. L. Washburn, eds., *Physical Anthropology of the American Indian* (New York: Viking Fund, 1951), pp. 1–68.

61. Jeffrey Goodman, op. cit., pp. 66–67; E. F. Greenman, "The Upper Paleolithic and the New World," *Current Anthropology*, Vol. 4 (Feb. 1963).

62. For a survey of these ideas, *see* Jesse D. Jennings, *The Prehistory of Polynesia* (Cambridge, Massachusetts: Harvard University Press, 1979); for a critique, *see* N. Alexander Easton, "Mal Del Mar Above Terra Incognita, or, 'What Ails the Coastal Migration Theory?'" *Arctic Anthropology*, Vol. 29, No. 2 (1992).

63. The literature is truly voluminous. On Atlantis, *see*, e.g., Ignatius Donnelly, *Atlantis: The Antidiluvian World* (New York: Harper & Row, 1949); Edgar Evans Cayce, *Edgar Cayce on Atlantis* (New York: Paperback Library, 1968); Charles Berlitz, *The Mystery of Atlantis* (New York: Grosset & Dunlap, 1969); Otto Muck, *The Secret of Atlantis* (New York: Pocket Books, 1979). On Lemmuria, *see* Wishar S. Cerve, *Lemmuria: Lost Continent of the Pacific* (San Jose, California: Rosicrucian Press, 1954); James Churchward, *The Lost Continent of Mu* (New York: Paperback Library, 1969).

64. In *The Book of Mormon* (Salt Lake City: Church of Jesus Christ of Later Day Saints, 1961), it is explained how the Tribe of Jared came to what is now Mexico in the third millennium B.C. and established the great Mesoamerican civilizations, as well, eventually, as the Incan civilization further south. After the Jaredites were destroyed by catastrophe somewhere around 2,000 B.C., they were replaced by a second Israelite group, the Tribe of Lehi. This bunch split itself in two, the progressive Nephites remaining in the south to become Olmecs, the degenerate Lamanites moving northward to become nomads. For a good overall analysis of these weird ideas in conjunction with those of the Atlantis/Mu school, *see* Robert Wauchope, *Lost Tribes and Sunken Continents* (Chicago: University of Chicago Press, 1970); *see* also Ronald Sanders, *Lost Tribes and Promised Lands* (Boston: Little, Brown & Co., Inc., 1978).

65. By and large, Afrocentrists usually attempt only to credit Africans with American Indian cultural attainments rather than with having established our populations per se; *see*, e.g., Nigel Davies, *Voyagers to the New World* (Albuquerque: University of New Mexico Press, 1979).

66. For a synthesis of just about every off–the–wall theory of American Indian origins imaginable, including extraterrestrial travel, *see* Rudolf Steiner, *Cosmic Memory: Atlantis and Lummeria* (Blaunett, New York: Rudolf Steiner Publications, 1959).

67. J. Peter White and J. F. O'Connell, *A Prehistory of Australia, New Guinea and Sahul* (Sidney: Academic Press, 1982); John R. H. Gibbons and Fergus G. A. U. Clunie, "Sea Level Changes and Pacific Prehistory: New Insight into Early Human Settlement of Oceania," *Journal of Pacific History*, No. 21 (1986).

68. Werner Müller, *America: The Old World or the New?* (New York: Peter Lang, 1989).

69. On the implications of certain of the dating problems involved here, *see* Fumiko Ikawa–Smith, "The Early Prehistory of America as Seen from Northeast Asia," in Jonathan E. Ericson, R. E. Taylor, and Ranier Berger, eds., *The Peopling of the New World* (Los Altos, California: Ballena Press, 1982), p. 23.

70. Werner Müller, op. cit.

71. Heidi Knecht, Anne Pike–Tay, and Randall White, eds., "Introduction," *Before Lascaux: The Complex Record of the Early Upper Paleolithic* (Boca Raton, Florida: CRC Press, 1993), p. 1.

72. For a comparison between points found in the Sandia Cave, New Mexico, with those take from the Laugerie–Haute Cave in France, *see* Francois Bordes, *A Tale of Two Caves* (New York: Harper & Row, 1972).

73. Jeffrey Goodman, op. cit., p. 162; *see* also Francois Bordes, *The Old Stone Age* (New York: McGraw–Hill, 1968), p. 214. On McGee's Point, *see* Richard S. MacNeish, op. cit., p. 318.

74. A. P. Kreiger, "Early Man in the New World," in *Prehistoric Man in the New World*, J. D. Jennings and E. Norbeck, eds. (Chicago: University of Chicago Press, 1964), p. 47.

75. Jesse D. Jennings, *Prehistory of North America*, op. cit., p. 57.

76. Ranier Berger, "Advances and Results in Radiocarbon Dating," op. cit., p. 178; José L. Lorenzo, op. cit., p. 6; Ruth Gruhn, "A Note on Excavations at El Bosque, Nicaragua in 1975," op. cit., p. 163.

77. P. Manglesdorf, R. MacNeish, and W. Galinat, "Domestication of Corn," in S. Struever, ed., *Prehistoric Agriculture* (New York: American Museum of Natural History, 1971), p. 474.

78. A. P. Kreiger, op. cit.; W. C. Galinat, "The Evolution of Corn and Culture in North America," in *Prehistoric Agriculture*, op. cit., p. 534.

79. Ruth Gruhn, "A Note on Excavations at El Bosque, Nicaragua in 1975," op. cit., p. 164.

80. A. P. Kreiger, op. cit., p. 33.

81. C. Reed, "Animal Domestication in the Prehistoric Near East," in *Prehistoric Agriculture*, op. cit., p. 436.

82. Quoted in T. Canby, "The Search for the First Americans," *National Geographic*, Vol. 156, No. 3 (Sept. 1979), p. 348.

83. Jean Aigner, "The Paleolithic in China," in *Early Man in America*, op. cit., pp. 25–41.

84. In 1928, Max Uhle, the "Father of Peruvian Archaeology," reported in a now–forgotten paper, presented to the Twenty–Third International Congress of the Americas but never published in English, that potsherds had been discovered in conjunction with mastodon bones dating back more than 15,000 years in the Andes; George F. Carter, "Uhle's Mastodon," op. cit., p. 21. On Fukuki and Senfukuji, *see* Fumiko Ikawa–Smith, op. cit.

85. A. L. Bryan, "An Overview of Paleo–American Prehistory," op. cit., pp. 309–10.

86. Janice Austin, "A Test of Birdsell's Hypothesis on New World Migrations" (unpublished paper presented at the annual meeting of the Society for California Archaeology, 1976, Abstract: pp. 3–5).

87. Ibid., p. 5.

88. Jeffrey Goodman, op. cit., p. 179.

89. Carlton S. Coon, *The Living Races of Man* (New York: Alfred A. Knopf, 1960), p. 255. For detailed examination of what Coon elected to describe as "anomalies," *see* Marshall T. Newman, "Geographic and Microgeographic Races," *Current Anthropology*, Vol. 45, No. 3 (1963); and Santiago T. Genoves, "Some Problems in the Physical Anthropological Study of the Peopling of America," *Current Anthropology*, Vol. 8 (Oct. 1967).

90. Santiago T. Genoves, op. cit., p. 298.

91. *See*, e.g., Frank Waters, *The Book of the Hopi* (New York: Viking Press, 1963).

92. One who took up this challenge was Jeffrey Goodman, who in 1973 initiated a dig at a site on the San Francisco Peaks, near Flagstaff, Arizona, where the Hopi elders told him their people had originated. In 1975, he was rewarded with the discovery of a chipped blade amidst organic deposits dated by Dr. Thor Karlstrom, a Senior Geologist with the U.S. Geological Survey, at 125,000 years; in 1979, he uncovered an inscribed stone dating from the same period; Jeffrey Goodman, op. cit., pp. 201–16.

93. *See*, e.g., Frank Waters, op. cit.; Harold Courlander, *The Fourth World of the Hopis* (New York: Fawcett, 1971).

94. Jeffrey Goodman, op. cit., p. 20.

95. For articulations of the standard line, *see* Carlton S. Coon, op. cit.; John Buettner–Janasch, op. cit.; O. Loring Brace, H. Nelson, and H. Korn, *Atlas of Fossil Man* (New York: Holt, Rinehart & Winston, Inc., 1971).

96. *See*, e.g., Alexander Marshack, *The Roots of Civilization* (New York: McGraw–Hill, 1972); and Will and Ariel Durant, *The Story of Civilization, Vols. 1–10* (New York: Simon & Schuster, 1953–1959).

97. The matter is extraordinarily well–handled by Martin Carnoy in his *Education as Cultural Imperialism* (New York: David McKay Publishers, 1974); *see* also Albert Memmi, *Colonizer and Colonized* (Boston: Beacon Press, 1965).

98. Douglas C. Wallace and Antonio Torrini, "American Indian Prehistory as Written in the Mitochondrial DNA: A Review," *Human Biology* (June 1992), p. 759.

99. D. C. Wallace, S. D. Ferris, M. C. Rattazi, and L. L. Cavalli–Sforza, "Radiation of Human Mitochondrial DNA Types Analyzed by Restriction Endonuclease Cleavage Patterns," *Journal of Molecular Evolution*, No. 19 (1983).

100. Theodore G. Schurr, Scott W. Ballenger, Yik–Tuen Gan, Judith A. Hodge, D. Andrew Merriweather, Dale N. Lawrence, William C. Knowler, Kenneth M. Weiss, and Douglas C. Wallace, "Amerindian Mitochondrial DNAs Have Rare Asian Mutations at High Frequencies, Suggesting They Derived from Four Primary Maternal Lineages," *American Journal of Human Genetics*, No. 46, 1990. The finding was quickly picked up by the more chauvinistic elements of Asia's scientific community; *see* Emoke J. E. Szathmary, "Peopling of North America: Clues from Genetic Studies," in *Out of Asia: The Peopling of the Americas and the Pacific*, R. L. Kirk and E. J. E. Szathmary, eds. (Canberra: Journal of Pacific History, 1985), pp. 79–104; Satoshi Horai, Rumi Kondo, Yuko Nakagawa–Hattori, Seiji Hayashi, Shundro Sonoda, and Kazua Tajima, "Peopling of the Americas: Founded by Four Major Lineages of Mitochondrial DNA," *Molecular Biology of Evolution*, Vol. 10, No. 1 (1993).

101. Douglas C. Wallace, Katherine Garrison, and William C. Knowler, "Dramatic Founder Effect in Amerindian Mitochondrial DNAs," *American Journal of Physical Anthropology*, No. 68 (1985). For comparison to the methods of the earlier racists mentioned, *see* Samual G. Morton, *Crania Americana, or a Comparative View of the Skulls of Various Aboriginal Nations of North and South America* (Philadelphia: John Pennington Publishers, 1839); Carlton S. Coon, op. cit.; and Earnest A. Hooten, *Up from the Ape* (New York: Macmillan Publishing Co., 1946).

102. Antonio Torrini, Theodore G. Schurr, Margaret F. Cabell, Michael D. Brown, James V. Neel, Merethe Larsen, David G. Smith, Carlos M. Vullo, and Douglas C. Wallace, "Asian Affinities and Continental Radiation of the Four Founding Native American Mitochondrial DNAs," *American Journal of Human Genetics* (Sept. 1993); Antonio Torrini, Rem I. Sukerik, Theodore G, Schurr, Yelena B. Starikovska, Margaret F. Cabell, Michael H. Crawford, Anthony G. Comizzie, and Douglas C. Wallace, "Mitochondrial DNA Variation of Aboriginal Siberians Reveals Distinct Genetic Affinities to American Indians," *American Journal of Human Genetics* (Sept. 1993). For the popularized replay, *see* John F. Hoffecker, W. Roger Powers, and Ted Goebel, "The Colonization of Beringia and the Peopling of the New World," *Science*, No. 259 (1993).

103. Richard S. MacNeish, "The 1992 Excavations of Pendejo Caves near Oro Grande, New Mexico" (Andover, New Hampshire: Andover Foundation for Archaeological Research, 1992).

104. N. Guidon and G. Delibrias, "Pedra Ferada: Carbon 14 Dates Point to Man in the Americas 32,000 Years Ago," *Nature*, No. 321 (1986); Neide Guidon, "Cliff Notes: Rock Artists May Have Left Their Mark in Brazil More Than 30,000 Years Ago," *Natural History* (Aug. 1987).

105. Ryk H. Ward, Barbara L. Frazier, and Kerry Dew–Jager, "Extensive Mitochondrial Diversity Within a Single Amerindian Tribe," *Proceedings of the National Academy of Science*, No. 88 (1991).

106. Alvah M. Hicks, "Rethinking *Homo Sapiens* in the Americas: A Working Hypothesis," unpublished paper currently under review, p. 14; he is quoting Ryk H. Ward et al., op. cit., p. 8720.

107. Ryk H. Ward et al., op. cit., p. 8723. The conclusion corresponds closely to that drawn by Gerald F. Shields, Kristen Hecker, Mikhail I. Voevoda, and Judy K. Reed in "Absence of Asian–specific Region V Mitochondrial Marker in Native Beringians," *American Journal of Human Genetics*, No. 50 (1992).

108. Ranjit Chakrabority and Kenneth M. Weiss, "Genetic Variation in the Mitochondrial DNA Genome in American Indians Is a Multi–Drift Equilibrium," *American Journal of Physical Anthropology*, No. 86 (1991). *See* also Rebecca L. Cahn, M. Stoneking, and A. C. Wilson, "Mitochondrial DNA and Human Evolution," *Nature*, No. 325 (1987).

109. D. Andrew Merriweather, "The Structure of Human Mitochondrial DNA Variation," *Journal of Molecular Evolution*, No. 33 (1991), esp. p. 552; Tom Dillehay, "Disease Ecology and Initial Human Migration," in Tom D. Dillehay and David J. Meltzer, eds., *The First Americans: Search and Research* (Boca Raton, Florida: CRC Press, 1991), pp. 231–64.

110. Alan R. Templeton, "The 'Eve Hypothesis': A Critique and Reanalysis," *American Anthropologist*, Vol. 93, No. 1 (1993), p. 59.

111. Randall White, "Rethinking the Middle/Upper Paleolithic Transition," *Current Anthropology*, No. 23 (1982); Christopher B. Stringer, "Towards a Solution of the Neanderthal Problem," *Journal of Human Evolution*, No. 11 (1982); Christopher B. Stringer, "Documenting the Origin of Modern Humans," in Eric Trinkhaus, ed., *The Emergence of Modern Humans* (Cambridge, Massachusetts: Cambridge University Press, 1989), pp. 67–96; Ian Tattersal, "Species Concepts and Species Identification in Human Evolution," *Journal of Human Evolution*, No. 22 (1992).

112. The estimate comes from James M. Mooney, *The Aboriginal Population of America North of Mexico* (Washington, DC: Smithsonian Misc. Coll. LXXX, No. 7, 1928), p. 3, as revised by Alfred Louis Kroeber in his *Cultural and Natural Areas of North America* (Berkeley: University of California Publications in American Archaeology and Ethnology, No. 38, 1939). Francis Jennings does a good job of laying out how successive generations of "responsible" historians and anthropologists essentially "cooked the books" on native demographic estimates in order to arrive at this absurdly low figure; Francis Jennings, *The Invasion of America: Indians, Colonialism and the Cant of Conquest* (New York: W. W. Norton, 1976), esp. the chapter entitled "The Widowed Land." For more recent and scientifically–based estimates, placing the 1492 indigenous population north of the Río Grande as high as 18.5 million, *see* Henry F. Dobyns, *Their Numbers Become Thinned: Native American Population Dynamics in Eastern North America* (Knoxville: University of Tennessee Press, 1983); Russell Thornton, *American Indian Holocaust and Survival: A Population History Since 1492* (Norman: University of Oklahoma Press, 1987). For a good survey on the realities, not mythologies, of indigenous material and intellectual life before Columbus, *see* Jack Weatherford, *Indian Givers: How the Indians of the Americas Transformed the World* (New York: Crown Publishers, 1987).

113. For an excellent overview of the magnitude of the outright physical genocide perpetrated against native populations by European/Euroamerican invaders and colonists, *see* David E. Stannard, *American Holocaust: Columbus and the Conquest of the New World* (New York: Oxford University Press, 1992).

114. Richard Drinnon, *Facing West: The Metaphysics of Indian Hating and Empire Building* (New York: Schocken Books [2d ed.], 1990); Reginald Horsman, *Race and Manifest Destiny: The Origins of Racial Anglo–Saxonism* (New York: Oxford University Press, 1983).

115. Insightful analysis of the interaction between mass media and approved sectors of academe will be found in Noam Chomsky, *Necessary Illusions: Thought Control in Democratic Societies* (Boston: South End Press, 1989).

116. For discussion of this and related issues, *see* Bernard Wood, Lawrence Martin and Peter Andrews, eds., *Major Topics in Primate and Human Evolution* (Cambridge, Massachusetts: Cambridge University Press, 1984).

117. *See*, e.g., F. Weidenreich, "The 'Neanderthal Man' and the Origins of Modern Humans," *American Anthropologist*, No. 42 (1943). For rebuttal, *see*, e.g., F. Spencer, "The Neanderthals and Their Evolutionary Significance: A Brief Historical Survey," in F. H. Smith and F. Spencer, eds., *The Origins of Modern Humans: A World Survey of the Fossil Evidence* (New York: Alan R. Liss, 1984); and M. H. Wolproff, "The Place of the Neanderthals in Human Evolution," in *The Emergence of Modern Humans*, op. cit., pp. 97–141.

118. Frederick C. Howell, "Preface," in *The Origins of Modern Humans*, op. cit., p. xiii.

119. Sally McBreaty, "The Origin of Modern Humans," *Man*, No. 25 (1990).

120. Jeffrey Goodman, op. cit., p. 128.

121. A classic example is Paul S. Martin, a colleague of Vance Haynes in the University of Arizona's Department of Anthropology, who has continued to assert that there have been no humans in America for more than twelve millennia; *see* his "Clovisia the Beautiful! If Humans Lived in the New World More Than 12,000 Years Ago, There'd Be No Secret About It," *Natural History* (Oct. 1987). Martin is mainly known for advancing the baseless notion that American Indian hunting methods such as "jumpkills" were responsible for the demise of most Ice Age mammals in this hemisphere; *Pleistocene Extinctions*, op. cit.; Paul S. Martin and J. E. Mosiman, "Simulating Overkill by Paleo–Indians," *American Scientist*, Vol. 63, No. 3 (May–June 1975).

122. Las Casas, based on his observations of the antiquity of hearths discovered in the process of silver mining in Mexico during the early– to mid–1500s, was among those who speculated that America might be the place of the Biblical Garden of Eden (birthplace of humanity), *see* his *Apologética Historia de las Indias* (Madrid: Bailliere, 1909).

123. F. Spencer, op cit., p. 7. *See* also Alfred R. Wallace, "The Antiquity of Man in America," *The Nineteenth Century* (Nov. 1889), and *Darwinism* (London: Macmillan Publishing Co., 1889).

124. Frederick Larkin, op. cit.; Charles C. Abbott, "Evidences of the Antiquity of Man in Eastern North America," *Proceedings of the American Association of Science*, No. 37 (1889); William Henry Holmes, "Auriferous Gravel Man," *American Anthropologist*, No. Ser. 1 (1899); Sir Arthur Keith, *Ancient Types of Man* (New York: Harper, 1911); Florentino Ameghino, "New Discoveries of Fossil Mamalia of Southern Patagonia," *American Naturalist* (1893); "La Antiguedad de los Hombres en El Plata, Obras Completas Correspondencia de Florentinio Ameghino," *La Plata*, Vol. 3 (1915).

125. Charles F. Lummis, *Mesa, Canyon and Pueblo* (New York/London: The Century Co., 1925); H. J. Cook, "New Geological and Paleontological Evidence Bearing on the Antiquity of Man in America," *Natural History*, No. 27 (1927).

126. George F. Carter, *Earlier Than You Think: A Personal View of Man in the Americas* (College Station: Texas A&M Press, 1980); Jeffrey Goodman, op. cit.; Alvah M. Hicks, op. cit.; Bruce Raemsch, *Native American Antecedents: An Encyclical* (unpublished manuscript in circulation at the time of his death in 1990).

127. Richard S. MacNeish, "1992 Excavations," op. cit.; Paul A. Mellars, ed., *The Emergence of Modern Humans: An Archaeological Perspective* (Ithaca, New York: Cornell University Press, 1991); Lewis R. Binford, *Working at Archaeology* (New York: Academic Press, 1983); Bruce MacFadden, "Chronology of Cenozoic Primate Localities in South America," *Journal of Human Evolution*, No. 19 (1990); Eric Delson and A. L. Rosenberger, "Phyletic Perspectives on Platyrrhine Origins and Anthropoid Relationships," in Russell L. Ciochon and A. Brunetto Chiarelli, eds., *Evolutionary Biology of the New World Monkeys and Continental Drift* (New York: Plenum Press, 1980); and Nelson Eldredge and Ian Tattersal, *The Myths of Human Evolution* (New York: Columbia University Press, 1982).

128. Bruce MacFadden, op. cit., p. 7.

129. Alvah M. Hicks, op. cit., p. 5; *see* also Eric Delson and A. L. Rosenberger, op. cit.; John G. Fleagle, *Primate Adaptation and Evolution* (London: Academic Press, 1988), pp. 316–17.

130. Alvah M. Hicks, op. cit., p. 6.

131. Ibid.

132. The possibility of polygenesis goes almost unmentioned in the literature. Probably the closest correspondent is the concept of "multiregional evolution" propounded by F. Weindenreich, op. cit., and M. H. Wolproff, op. cit.

133. Richard G. Klein, "The Stone Age Prehistory of Southern Africa," *Annual Review of Anthropology*, No. 12 (1983); Lewis R. Binford, *Faunal Remains at the Klasies River Mouth* (New York: Academic Press, 1984). For dissenting analyses of the dating, *see* R. Singer and J. Wymer, *The Middle Stone Age at the Klasies River Mouth in South Africa* (Chicago: University of Chicago Press, 1982); John Parkington, "A Critique of the Consensus View on the Age of Howieson's Poort Assemblages in South Africa," in *The Emergence of Modern Humans*, op. cit., pp. 34–55.

134. This position is advocated by Rebecca Cahn and her colleagues in "Mitochondrial DNA and Human Evolution," op. cit.; Alan R. Templeton, op. cit., splits the difference between "Africanists" and "Americanists" by holding that a rapid replacement of *Homo erectus* in Europe occurred about 50,000 years ago as the result of a sudden influx of Cro–Magnons from "somewhere ... not necessarily Africa."

On Gaining "Moral High Ground"

An Ode to George Bush and the "New World Order"*

Meet the new Boss, same as the old Boss

The Who, 1969

Since the onset of the Gulf War, we in the United States have been subjected to a relentless chorus of babble from George Bush and his colleagues concerning a supposed "moral imperative" for the United States to militarily enforce "international law, custom, and convention" because of "a dozen United Nations Security Council resolutions condemning Iraq's invasion, occupation, and annexation of Kuwait." Iraqi President Saddam (usually pronounced "Sodom" by U.S. officials) Hussein's "naked aggression cannot stand," Bush has solemnly and repeatedly intoned to wild applause. Kuwait's "territory must be liberated," its "legitimate government must be reinstated," its vast oil resources "returned to the rightful owners." Meanwhile, those Iraqi officials responsible for "the rape of Kuwait" should be tried for war crimes and/or crimes against humanity, says Bush, *en route* to gaining what he has taken to calling "the moral high ground." The net result of "the precedent we are now setting," according to the President, will be the ushering in of a "New World Order" predicated on "the rule of law" and, consequently, peace and civility among nations.[1]

---

*This essay originally appeared in *Collateral Damage*, Cynthia Peters, ed. (Boston: South End Press, 1992).

I know, I know, this is all basic Hitler–speak. But, forget for a moment that it's George Herbert Walker Bush talking. Forget that Kuwait was never a nation in its own right, that it was historically part of Iraq, an area stripped away and established as an administrative entity by British colonialists, an expedient to landlocking and thus controlling the much larger Iraqi territory and population to the north. Forget that the "legitimate government" under discussion is the harshly anti–democratic regime of an emir propped up for more than 50 years by external neocolonial forces rather than the internal consent of the governed. Forget also that the actual "owners" of the oil fields in question have always been a gaggle of transnational oil corporations rather than any Kuwaitis, even the emir. Forget all of this long enough to realize that intermingled with Bush's barrage of blatant untruths and self–serving rhetoric is the substance of some genuinely worthy ideas.[2]

Rather than pitching the baby out with the bath water simply because a figure as slimy as the President of the United States has articulated such principles, we might instead seize upon them, insisting that the U.S. government actually conform its behavior to the lofty posture described by its chief executive. To an extent which is startling, George Bush has unintentionally defined the contours of what should be the agenda for American progressivism. In a way, all that remains for us to do is demand consistency in the application of George's postulates. Well, that and to develop the muscle necessary to see to it that the government follows through. Even that, however, should be no overwhelming problem, given the sort of public sentiment Ol' George has whipped up while proving he's no wimp.

Unquestionably, we have a right to demand that all the millions of flag–waving little geeks who've recently turned out at George's request to "support our troops" in their quest for victory over evil in the Great Gulf Crusade join us in holding the United States strictly accountable to its newly proclaimed "standards of human decency." After all, as any ROTC cadet or Daughter of the American Revolution will tell you, "That's what America stands for." For once, we are in a position to insist that everyone, left and right, rich and poor, young and old, women and men, whites and "minorities," straights and gays, in the United States band together—on pain of otherwise being branded both a "reactionary asshole" *and* "un–american"—for a common glorious purpose articulated by "Our President." In such unity, we will find strength and righteousness. Together, we can help George and the boys put their performance where their mouths have been. You bet. Anyway, let's get on with it, proceeding to examine what will have to be done to mesh reality with recent official verbiage (set off herein by quotes).

International Law, Custom, and Convention

The President has said—"read my lips"—unequivocally that international laws "must be enforced. And they *will* be enforced. Period." This is certainly commendable, and something we should all be prepared to insist upon vociferously. Now that Iraq has been compelled to comply with "all relevant U.N. resolutions" by being battered into near oblivion through an unprecedented application of high–tech "defensive weaponry," we progressives should demand that everyone who supported the Gulf War join us in calling for redeployment of the "force levels" evident in "Operation Desert Storm" to insure that certain other, much longer standing, U.N. resolutions are honored. Let's start, say, with Israel's illegal occupation of Palestinian territories. This Israeli conduct has been, after all, the focus of more than a few U. N. condemnations over the years, as has Israel's occupation of the southern portion of Lebanon.[3] For that matter, there has long been a U.N. resolution equating zionism with racism, thereby rendering the ideology of the Israeli state illegal under the U. N. Convention on Elimination of All Forms of Racial Discrimination.[4]

For consistency's sake, there must be a U.S. ultimatum, comparable to that delivered to Iraq, ordering the Israelis to unassimilate the occupied territories immediately. If there is no compliance, it must be made plain, Tel Aviv will be flattened by massive air strikes, while every military installation in the country will be "surgically eliminated." In the event that Israel *does* begin an instantaneous withdrawal from Palestine and Lebanon, we should urge George to be somewhat more "magnanimous" in other respects. The people of Israel could, for instance, be given as long as six months to overthrow Yitzak Shamir and his colleagues, dissolve the totality of their state bureaucracy, and reconstitute their polity on the basis of a non–zionist model. In the event they fail to accomplish this latter U.N. requirement, a U.S. suspension of aid and orchestration of comprehensive international sanctions should probably be sufficient to bring them around in a couple of weeks.

Then there is the matter of South Africa.[5] Its apartheid socio–political organization has been condemned by a series of U.N. resolutions beginning as far back as the early '60s. So have its large and persistent military invasions of neighboring Namibia (one is a bit unclear as to whether these aggressions have been of the "naked" or "fully clad" varieties, but this is no time to be picky).[6] While it is true that previous U.S. administrations have sought to bring this "outlaw state" into line by "quiet diplomacy" (and the infusion of both military technology and tremendous quantities of economic support), there is still time for George Bush to "move things in the right direction."[7] "Diplomacy having failed," it's high time we played our "military card" to "set things right." U.S. martial prowess, when committed to such "appropriate objectives," obviously works much more quickly and leaves fewer loose ends dangling.

The Pretoria government could be given six weeks to dismantle its military and police apparatus, and a total of six months within which to conduct general elections under U.N. supervision. Should "responsible South African officials" refuse, the United States could stipulate that a major amphibious assault will occur at Capetown within "an unspecified but short interval," coupled to an airmobile invasion of the interior (spearheaded by "the redoubtable 82nd Airborne Division," and supported by "massive armored thrusts" from the coast). Given the relative size of the South African and Israeli military machines—as compared to "the world's fourth largest army,"[8] available to Iraq, but completely destroyed by the United States in just over 60 days—it is reasonable that we call upon President Bush to order Secretary of War (let's go back to calling this position by its right name) "Dick" Cheney to order middle–America's favorite house negro, Colin Powell, to plan and initiate operations against both countries simultaneously. Once we "have a schedule," we can "stick with our scenario," "fight on our terms," and clean up these offenders against international order most lickety–split.

Of course, there are a few other U.N. resolutions out there which might be a tad more difficult to handle. An example is the one which condemned U.S. mining of Nicaraguan harbors back in the mid–80s. Others condemned the U.S. invasion and occupation of, and installation of a puppet government in Grenada a bit earlier.[9] More recently, a resolution condemned the U.S. invasion and subordination of Panama.[10] Then there are quite a number of such items accruing from U.S. activities in Southeast Asia during the 1960s and 1970s.[11] These matters will undoubtedly prove most embarrassing to the multitudes who lately turned out wearing yellow ribbons in the belief that Saddam Hussein invented international aggression and was therefore subject to the first U.N. resolutions on record. What to do? What to do?

Short of calling in air strikes on Washington, D.C., and ordering liquidation of the residents of Kansas—an idea which might prove a bit unpopular with the congenitally red, white and blue–blooded populace of that state—it is difficult to see how the Bush administration and "American public" might visit the same sort of consequences upon the United States they so gleefully laid upon Iraq for an ugly but rather lesser aggregate of offenses. Perhaps the public's sense of propriety—redneck America having become obsessively concerned with international justice these days—could be satisfied that justice was being done if George were to deliver up some sizable assortment of perpetrators of the above–mentioned U.S. "excesses" to stand trial before an appropriate international body on charges of Crimes Against the Peace, Crimes Against Humanity, and War Crimes.[12] After all, the President has suggested that just such a body be convened in the wake of the Gulf War. We progressives might well take the lead in advising that it see more extensive use than Bush originally had in mind.

An International Tribunal

The President has said—"read my lips" again—that "Saddam Hussein and others" should be hauled in front of an "international tribunal" to stand trial for the "atrocities committed on their orders during the Iraqi occupation of Kuwait."[13] Fine. Carry on. Saddam and his compatriots have comported themselves for some time—with ample U.S. backing, it must be added—in the manner of the most brutal sort of thugs. The world would experience no loss were they to take a collective trip to the gallows. The problem is, to paraphrase no less an American patriot than U.S. Supreme Court Justice Robert Jackson (during similar proceedings against the nazis at Nuremberg in 1947; this should play well with all those beer–guzzling old World War II vets down at the VFW and American Legion halls in Peoria), such things have legal validity only when the prosecutors are held to the same standards of accountability as the defendants, the victors put to the same test as the vanquished.[14] Hence, it is necessary that a few other folks, from countries other than Iraq, take their rightful places alongside Saddam Hussein in the defendants' dock.

This leads us, unerringly, to the ranks of U.S. officialdom itself. No tribunal of the sort George Bush has proposed, concentrating on the sorts of matters he has raised for its consideration, could neglect to include individuals like Robert McNamara, architect of the U.S. "intervention" in Indochina. Or William Westmoreland, the U.S. general who conceived the "strategy of attrition" his troops ultimately directed in genocidal fashion against the Indochinese population.[15] Or Henry Kissinger, the diseased mind behind the "secret bombing" of neutral Cambodia during that war, a process which itself accounted for thousands of victims lumped in with the toll extracted by Khmer Rouge "autogenocide" thereafter. Or Richard M. Nixon, who ordered the bombing of civilian targets in North Vietnam in order to attain "peace with honor," and whose "madman theory of diplomacy" provided the conceptual umbrella under which Kissinger functioned.[16] How could the list of defendants facing the tribunal be complete without the presence of Ronald Wilson Reagan, the mighty "Conqueror of Grenada"?[17] Or George Schultz and Elliot Abrams, kingpins of the contra campaign against Nicaragua?[18]

For that matter, how could Bush's proposed tribunal be complete without George Bush himself numbering among the defendants, perhaps for his roles in supporting Roberto D'Aubison's death squads in El Salvador, or in the smuggling of drugs to the youth of his own country in order to finance the clandestine butchery of peasants and poets abroad?[19] One would hope—and people of conscience will demand—that justice might prevail with regard to his participation in the arming of and other murderous support to petty dictators the world over while "serving" as Director of the CIA, Vice President, and now President.[20] It is hard to conceive a performance more befitting the charges of Crimes Against the Peace and Crimes Against Humanity. At least he might be judged for that implausibly denied slit trench filled with at least some 4,000 slaughtered civilians his "Operation Just Cause" soldiers left behind in Panama.[21] Surely, the President will wish to continue to "do what's right" in his own case as well as the cases of his mentors, underlings, and opponents. And surely it is incumbent upon all Americans, particularly those who wave their flags so proudly, to ensure that he does. Justice Jackson, after all, required no less.

Liberating Territory, Reinstating Legitimate Governments

Truth be known, George Bush's recent speechifying has raised a range of issues much more fundamental than any mentioned thus far. If the swarm of supporters lately rallying to George's posture of ensuring the sovereignty of small nations against the designs of larger and more powerful predator states are in any way sincere, there is no shortage of action items to fill their agenda right here in North America. They can begin by insisting upon the honoring of all 400 treaties, duly ratified by the Senate and still legally binding, between the United States and various American Indian nations presently encapsulated within the United States.[22] This will mean, of course, that Bush will have to order "the immediate withdrawal" of all U.S. forces presently occupying each of the Native American national territories so clearly defined in the treaty texts, altogether totaling about a third of the land area the United States now claims as comprising the "lower 48" states.[23]

The President will also have to renounce the long–standing federal doctrine of exercising "trust" prerogatives ("annexation," by any other term) over all Indian acreage within the United States,[24] and forego the government's planned unilateral dissolution of native land title in Alaska (a move intended to open North Shelf oil to increased exploitation by U.S. energy corporations).[25] Accomplishing this will require repeal of numerous federal statutes, beginning with the "Major Crimes Act" of 1885 (through which the United States unilaterally extended its jurisdiction over Indian Country),[26] the "General Allotment Act" of 1887 (through which the United States unilaterally altered indigenous land tenure patterns and declared some two–thirds of the treaty–guaranteed native land base to be "surplus"),[27] and the "Indian Citizenship Act" of 1924 (through which the United States unilaterally imposed its citizenship upon native peoples, whether they liked it or not).[28]

Once American Indian national territories have been thus liberated—in conformity with what may come to be known as the "Bush Doctrine" of international affairs—it will be necessary that he engineer a repeal of the "Indian Reorganization Act" of 1934 (through which the United States unilaterally imposed a form of governance acceptable to itself upon most native peoples).[29] This will allow *legitimate* American Indian governments to at last be reinstated after more than a half–century's outright suppression at the hands of the United States. These newly reconstituted and revitalized native governments, functioning with *full* sovereign control over *all* the territory to which they are legally entitled by international treaty agreements, will finally be able to utilize the resources lying within and upon their land for the benefit of their own people rather than for the benefit of the occupiers. As the President has put it, "No benefits from naked aggression. Period."

This "restoration of resources to the rightful owners" means that about two–thirds of the uranium deposits the United States now considers as part of its own "domestic reserves" will pass from U.S. control. Along with the uranium will go approximately one–quarter of the readily accessible low sulfur coal, maybe 20 percent of the oil and natural gas, such bauxite as is to be found within present U.S. boundaries, all of the copper, most of the gold, a lot of the iron ore, the remaining stands of "virgin" timber, much prime grazing and farming acreage, the bulk of the water throughout the arid West, perhaps half the salmon and other available fish "harvests," hunting rights over vast areas, and a lot more.[30]

There is also a big question as to whether the United States shouldn't also pay substantial reparations for having unlawfully and immorally deprived native people of all these assets for so long, a matter which has induced incredible human suffering. Although the resources endowing American Indian treaty territories have always been sufficient to make native people by far the wealthiest sector of the North American population, they have instead existed for generations as the very poorest. According to the federal government's own statistics, Indians receive the lowest per capita income of any group on the continent. Their unemployment rate is far and away the highest, year in, year out Correspondingly, they suffer—by significant margins—the highest rates of malnutrition, infant mortality, death by exposure, tuberculosis, plague disease, and teen suicide. The average life expectancy of a reservation–based American Indian man is presently 44.6 years; a native woman may expect to live less than three years longer.[31]

Meanwhile, to select but one example among thousands, the Homestake Mining Corporation alone has taken more than $14 *billion* in gold from only one mine in the Black Hills of South Dakota, squarely in the middle of the treaty territory of the Lakota Nation.[32] It takes no Einstein to discern the relationship between this sort of wealth flowing into the economy of the U.S. occupiers on the one hand, and the abject poverty of the Lakota people on the other. The same situation prevails throughout Indian Country. This sort of thing has been going on for a long time now, and it hardly seems wild–eyed to suggest that some *very* serious pay–back is long overdue. We can hardly expect, given George Bush's continuous assertions that this is the world's leading "nation of

conscience" and the general adulation he has received because of such utter-
ances, that he and his admiring public will do less than "meet their just debts"
and "measure up to [their] moral obligations" in this regard.

Before moving on, it seems appropriate to observe that once the President
and his supporters have retired the United States' "Indian problem" in a manner
consistent with the "utmost good faith" pledged by Congress in 1789,[33] they
will wish to act with equal swiftness to resolve a couple of other issues involving
the outright U.S. occupation of land belonging to others, the theft of their
resources and/or usurpation of their governments. Undoubtedly, proponents of
Bushism will wish to see him "stand tall" and order an immediate withdrawal
of U.S. troops from their permanent bases in Puerto Rico, while the people of
that island are finally allowed to conduct whatever process they decide in order
to determine what politico–economic relationship (if any) they wish to maintain
with Washington, D.C.[34] The same principle will certainly apply to the "U.S."
Virgin Islands, "American" Samoa, Guam, the Marshall Islands, and several
other chunks of geography scattered around the globe.[35]

American super–patriots will no doubt also wish to see Bush and his
buddies ensure that the descendants of former Mexican nationals holding land
grants issued by the Crown of Spain and Republic of Mexico in what are now
the states of Texas, New Mexico, Colorado, Arizona, and California will finally
have their property restored. After all, the federal government promised "faith-
fully" to "honor and respect" these individual and group deeds under a provision
of the 1848 Treaty of Guadalupe Hidalgo, through which the United States
expropriated the northern half of Mexico and all the resources therein.[36]
Between the treaty rights of Indian nations to their own territorial integrity and
the extent of the acreage involved in the land grants, at least four of the states
affected will for all practical intents and purposes cease to exist. The "undeni-
able skills" of "Stormin' Norman" Schwartzkopf may well be needed if the
provincial governments seated in Santa Fe, Denver, Phoenix, and Sacramento
are to be convinced to "get with the program." But, of course, no price is too
high to pay while ensuring that "the Laws of Nations and common decency are
adhered to."

Advantages to Progressives

The advantages of all this to progressivism in the United States should
be obvious. Progressives having never been able to articulate a viable and
coherent agenda of their own—preferring instead to perpetually "bear moral
witness," combat cigarette smoke amidst the nation's smog belts, and bicker
with eternal meaninglessness among themselves about all manner of esoteric
and irrelevant topics—it is high time a visionary leader like George Bush has
come along to clarify our priorities and give shape to our programs. He has

completely crushed the false importance assigned to all those cutesy little carts most progressives have invariably attempted to place before their horses. Consequently, he has been able to energize and organize "the masses" in ways and to a degree we never have, and probably never could. All we need now is to tap into the dynamic he has unleashed and help him succeed in ways he and most of those parroting his rhetoric have yet to imagine.

In pursuing George's call for occupied national territories to be liberated, legitimate governments restored, expropriated resources returned, and transgressors punished, we can begin to dissolve the American Empire from within. Reasserting the territoriality and sovereignty of Native North America is not only "the right course of action" in itself; it inherently destroys the capacity of the United States to be what it is. Put simply, without the resources accruing from its ongoing occupation and "internal colonization" of Indian Country,[37] the United States would lack the material capacity to engage in the sort of military aggressiveness—both overt and covert—with which it has marked the second half of the twentieth century, most recently in the Persian Gulf. This has always been the case, a fact which should long since have established a leading prioritization of and emphasis upon American Indian rights within the progressive American consciousness. Unfortunately, progressivism has always managed to miss points so basic, and so it has been left to the President to point out, albeit in the most circuitous possible fashion, that "the First American must be our First Priority." For this, we owe him an immeasurable debt of gratitude.

Being a first priority does not, it must be noted, mean being the only agenda item, or the last. Certain things would stem inevitably from the liberation of Native North America. Consider that if the U.S. capacity to project military force were substantially diminished through erosion of its resource base, so too would its ability to exert corporate neocolonial control over the entirety of the Third World deteriorate. Similarly, the United States would rapidly lose the means by which it maintains literal colonial sway over external territories like Puerto Rico. And internal decolonization hardly ends with Native America. As the U.S. imperial potential recedes abroad, so too does its power to grasp the reigns of control over Afro–America, the internalized Latino population, recent Asian immigrants, even the Scotch–colony of Appalachia.[38]

Nor is this the end of it. As the physical reality of the U.S. status quo unravels, so too does its capability to impose continuation of the hegemonic socio–psychological structuration marking its existence, even among the "mainstream" population. The institutions of racism, sexism, classism, agism, homophobia, violence, and alienation which have defined American life are thereby opened at last to replacement by forms allowing for the actualization of "preferable alternatives." Now, how's *that* for a "New World Order"? How's that for "moral high ground"? The seeds of such things really *are* integral to the notions George Bush has been voicing, regardless of how much to the contrary he intended his remarks. All of it is possible, all of it follows, but it can only be approached on the basis of "first things first."

So, it's time we progressive types paid the President his due. It's time we got out there to show our support for the *real* meaning imbedded in his message, whether or not he knew or meant what he said. It's time we endorsed the valid principles underlying his script and pushed them along to their logical conclusions even though Ol' George may never have conceived the "end game moves." It's time we set out seriously to strangle this country full of conservative jackanapes with the tissue of their own contradictions. It's time we at long last brought things *home*, dealing with root causes rather than an unending series of grotesque symptoms. Let's not allow ourselves to become bogged down in some sort of "United States Out of the Middle East Campaign," just as we bogged ourselves down in "United States Out of Vietnam" a quarter–century ago, and "United States Out of Central America" during the '80s. The only meaningful thing we can pursue is getting the United States out of *North America*. Better yet, we should push it off the planet. And the hour is growing late.

Notes

1. For analysis of Bushian rhetoric and media handling of it before and during the Gulf War, *see* George Cheney, "'Talking War': Symbols, Strategies and Images," *New Studies on the Left*, Vol. XIV, No. 3 (Winter 1990–91). *See* also Denis F. Doyon, "Creating an 'Iraq Syndrome'," in *Mobilizing Democracy: Changing the U.S. Role in the Middle East*, Greg Bates, ed. (Monroe, Maine: Common Courage Press, 1991).

2. The lies were dissected to a considerable extent in *Z Magazine* and *Lies Of Our Times* during the entire prewar/wartime period.

3. For background, *see* Noam Chomsky, *The Fateful Triangle: Israel, the Palestinians, and the United States* (Boston: South End Press, 1983).

4. The text of the convention may be found in Ian Brownlie, ed., *Basic Documents on Human Rights* (London/New York: Oxford University Press, 1971).

5. For general context, *see* Ray Bunting, *The Rise of the South African Reich* (London: Penguin Books, 1964).

6. *See* John Ya–Otto, *Battle–Front Namibia* (Westport, Connecticut: Lawrence Hill Publishers, 1981). Also related, *see* David Martin and Phyllis Johnson, *The Struggle for Zimbabwe: The Chimurenga War* (New York: Monthly Review Press, 1981).

7. For details of U.S. support of the South African nazification process, *see* Western Massachusetts Association of Concerned African Scholars, *U.S. Military Involvement in Southern Africa* (Boston: South End Press, 1978).

8. The idea that Iraq's was the world's "fourth largest army"—never really substantiated to any extent, and grossly inaccurate in a number of ways—was dutifully parroted at least five times per day by CNN "military analyst" Wolf Blitzer from August 1990 through March 1991.

9. *See* Hugh O'Shaugnessy, *Grenada: Revolution, Invasion and Aftermath* (London: Zed Press, 1984).

10. This led to the famous Bushian retort that the United States was actually "enforcing the law" via its invasion of Panama by seeking to "serve a warrant" on the "international drug peddler" Manuel Noriega. As of this writing, however, federal prosecutors profess to "lack hard evidence" with which to bring Noriega to trial in U.S. courts, and even the DEA admits that drug trafficking through Panama has *increased* substantially since the defendant's ouster.

11. *See* Jay W. Baird, ed., *From Nuremberg to My Lai* (Lexington/Toronto/London: D.C. Heath and Co., Publishers, 1972) and Richard A. Falk, ed., *The Vietnam War and International Law* (Princeton: Princeton University Press, 1969).

12. Technically, a tribunal would not be required insofar as any nation is entitled to bring its own international criminals to justice. The mechanism is generally described in Richard B. Lillich, *International Claims: Their Adjudication by National Commission* (Syracuse: Syracuse University Press, 1962).

13. Bush is on firm legal ground in making the suggestion. For the mechanics of how such a tribunal should function, *see* John Alan Appleman, *Military Tribunals and International Crimes* (Westport, Connecticut: Greenwood Press, 1954).

14. On Justice Jackson, the "Nuremberg Principles," their application against the Germans in 1946–47, and the leading role the United States assumed in formulating them, *see* Bradley F. Smith, *The Road to Nuremberg* (New York: Basic Books, 1981), and *Reaching Judgement at Nuremberg* (New York: Basic Books, 1977). As concerns application of these principles against the Japanese during the same period, *see* Arnold C. Brackman, *The Other Nuremberg: The Untold Story of the Tokyo War Crimes Trials* (New York: William Morrow Publishers, 1987).

15. U.S. policy makers and military leaders were actually tried and convicted en absentia by a highly reputable tribunal convened to investigate events in Indochina during the American intervention there. The United States, of course, refused either to turn over its own international criminals for punishment or even to end the offending policies. *See* John Duffett, ed., *Against the Crime of Silence. Proceedings of the International War Crimes Tribunal* (New York: Simon and Schuster Publishers, 1968).

16. A detailed account of the "Nixinger" crimes in Cambodia may be found in William Shawcross, *Sideshow: Kissinger, Nixon and the Destruction of Cambodia* (New York: Simon and Schuster Publishers, 1979). For a broader assessment of U.S. conduct in Southeast Asia during the Nixon era and immediately thereafter, *see* Noam Chomsky and Edward S. Herman, *The Political Economy of Human Rights, Vol. II: After the Cataclysm, Postwar Indochina and the Reconstruction of Imperial Ideology* (Boston: South End Press, 1979).

17. On the Grenada adventure, *see* Chris Searle, *Grenada: The Struggle Against Destabilization* (London: Zed Press, 1983). *See* also William C. Gilmore, *The Grenada Intervention: Analysis and Documentation* (London: Bertrand Russell Foundation, 1984).

18. For a detailed summary of contra atrocities up to this point in time, *see* Reed Brody, *Contra Terror in Nicaragua* (Boston: South End Press, 1985). Ample documentation of the Reagan administration's crucial role in making this possible may be found in Holly Sklar, *Washington's War on Nicaragua* (Boston: South End Press, 1988).

19. *See* Michael McClintock, *The American Connection: State Terror and Popular Resistance in El Salvador* (2 Vols.) (London: Zed Press, 1985). More broadly, *see* Noam

Chomsky, *Turning the Tide: U.S. Intervention in Central America and the Struggle for Peace* (Boston: South End Press, 1985).

20. For a survey of the liaisons at issue, *see* Noam Chomsky and Edward S. Herman, *The Political Economy of Human Rights, Vol. I: The American Connection and Third World Fascism* (Boston: South End Press, 1978). *See* also Edward S. Herman, *The Real Terror Network* (Boston: South End Press, 1982).

21. Removal of a portion of these bodies, the existence of which had been steadfastly and officially denied by the Bush administration, from the slit trench into which they'd been dumped by U.S. troops was shown on a *60 Minutes* news program in April 1990.

22. The texts of 371 ratified treaties between the United States and various American Indian nations—formal and binding *international* instruments—may be found in Charles J. Kappler, *Indian Treaties, 1778–1883* (New York: Interland Publishers, 1972). The Lakota scholar Vine Deloria, Jr., has uncovered another two dozen ratified treaties which do not appear in conventional sources, as well as another 400–odd unratified treaties which the United States has elected to consider binding for purposes of vesting land title in itself, etc. This is aside from about 1,000 "agreements" of various sorts, engineered by the United States with indigenous nations, which even federal courts have acknowledged hold the same legal force and status as treaties. Plainly, even under U.S. law, "Indian affairs" are *not* merely an "internal concern" of the United States.

23. The federal government presently recognizes the existence of 515 "Indian tribes," although only about half retain some residue of their original land base. Altogether, these "reservations" add up to about 3 percent of the 48 coterminous states. Actually, indigenous entitlement to territory is, however, more than 10 times this amount. For a depiction of those portions of U.S. territoriality federal courts have admitted were never legally ceded by indigenous nations—and to which the United States therefore possesses no bona fide legal title—*see* the map ("Indian Lands Judicially Recognized as Unceded") on page 118 in "The Earth Is Our Mother" in this collection.

24. On U.S. "trust" prerogatives taken vis–à–vis Native America, a counterpart of what the federal government asserts is its rightful "plenary (full, absolute) power" over Indian Country, *see* Vine Deloria, Jr., and Clifford M. Lytle, *American Indians, American Justice* (Austin: University of Texas Press, 1983).

25. About 44 million acres are at issue. *See* the Alaska Native Claims Settlement Act of 1971, Public Law 92–203; 85 Stat. 688, codified at 43 U.S.C. § 1601 *et seq.*

26. Ch. 341, 24 Stat. 362, 385; now codified at 18 U.S.C. § 1153.

27. Ch. 119, 24 Stat. 388; now codified at 25 U.S.C. § 331 *et seq.*

28. Ch. 233, 43 Stat. 25.

29. Ch. 576, 48 Stat. 948; now codified at 25 U.S.C. §§ 461–279.

30. A summary of primary economic factors concerning Native North America may be found in Theresa L. Ammot and Julie A. Matthei, *Race, Gender and Work: A Multicultural Economic History of Women in the United States* (Boston: South End Press, 1991).

31. For official statistics on Native American health and related factors, *see* U.S. Department of Health and Human Services, *Chart Series Book* (Washington, D.C.: Public Health Service, 1988 [HE20.9409.988]).

32. On profits extracted by the Homestake Mine, *see* Rex Weyler, *Blood of the Land: The U.S. Government and Corporate War on the American Indian Movement* (Philadelphia: New Society Publishers [2nd ed.], 1992), pp. 262–63.

33. The language accrues from the Northwest Ordinance (1 Stat. 50), in which the United States formally renounced "rights of conquest" in North America.

34. *See* Alfredo López, *Doña Licha's Island: Modern Colonialism in Puerto Rico* (Boston: South End Press, 1987).

35. On the construction of this modern U.S. empire, *see* Howard Zinn, *Postwar America, 1945–1971* (Indianapolis: Bobbs–Merrill Publishers, 1973).

36. *See* Albert K. Weinberg, *Manifest Destiny: A Study of Nationalist Expansion in American History* (Baltimore: Johns Hopkins University Press, 1935).

37. The concept of internal colonization is of English origin, pertaining to the incorporation of the Scots, Welsh, and others into "Britain." *See* Michael Hecter, *Internal Colonialism: The Celtic Fringe in British National Development, 1536–1966* (Berkeley: University of California Press, 1975). For application to Native America, *see* Ward Churchill, "Indigenous Peoples of the U.S.: A Struggle Against Internal Colonialism," *Black Scholar*, Vol. 16, No. 1 (Jan.–Feb. 1985).

38. The Appalachian example is far too little studied. See Helen Lewis et al., eds., *Colonialism in Modern America: The Appalachian Case* (Boone, North Carolina: Appalachian Consortium Press, 1978). *See* also Rodger Cunningham, *Apples on the Flood: The Southern Mountain Experience* (Knoxville: University of Tennessee Press, 1987).

False Promises

An Indigenist Examination
of Marxist Theory and Practice*

Sure, I'm a Marxist. But I've never been able to decide which one of
them I like the best: Groucho, Harpo, Zeppo, or Karl.

American Indian Movement joke, circa 1975

H*au, Metakuyeayasi.* The greeting I have just given you is a Lakota phrase
meaning, "Hello, my relatives." Now, I'm not a Lakota, and I'm not particularly
fluent in the Lakota language, but I ask those of you who are to bear with me
for a moment while I explore the meaning of the greeting because I think it is
an important point of departure for our topic: the relationship, real and potential,
which exists between the marxist tradition on the one hand, and that of
indigenous peoples—such as American Indians—on the other.

Dialectics

The operant words here are "relatives," "relationship," and, by minor
extension, "relations." I have come to understand that when Lakota people use
the word *Metakuyeayasi,* they are not simply referring to their mothers and
fathers, grandparents, aunts and uncles, ancestors, nieces and nephews, children, grandchildren, cousins, future generations, and all the rest of humankind.
Oh, these relatives are certainly included, but things don't stop there. Also
involved is reference to the ground we stand on, the sky above us, the light from
the sun and water in the oceans, lakes, rivers, and streams. The plants that
populate our environment are included, as are the four–legged creatures around

---

* This essay originally appeared in *Society and Nature*, Vol. 1, No. 2 (1992).

us, those who hop and crawl, the birds who fly, the fish who swim, the insects, the worms. Everything. These are all understood in the Lakota way as being relatives. What is conveyed in this Lakota concept is the notion of the universe as a relational whole, a single interactive organism in which all things, all beings, are active and essential parts; the whole can never be understood without a knowledge of the function and meaning of each of the parts, while the parts cannot be understood other than in the context of the whole.

The formation of knowledge is, in such a construct, entirely dependent upon the active maintenance of a fully symbiotic, relational—or, more appropriately, *inter*relational—approach to understanding. This fundamental appreciation of things, the predicate upon which a worldview is established, is (I would argue) common not only to the Lakota but to all American Indian cultural systems. Further, it seems inherent to indigenous cultures the world over. At least I can say with certainty that I've looked in vain for a single concrete example to the contrary.

The ancient Greeks had a term, *dialitikus,* the idea of which was borrowed from an Egyptian concept, and which I'm told the civilization of the Nile had itself appropriated from the people of what is now called Ethiopia, describing such a way of viewing things. The Greeks held this to be the superior mode of thinking. In modern parlance, the word at issue has become "dialectics," popularized in this form by the German post–theological philosopher Friedrich Hegel. As has so often happened in the history of European intellectualism, Hegel's notable career spawned a bevy of philosophical groupies. Among the more illustrious, or at least more industrious, of these "Young Hegelians" was a doctoral student named Karl Marx.

Indeed, Marx was always clear in his student work—much of which can now be read in a volume titled *The Economic and Philosophic Manuscripts of 1844*—and forever after that it was the structure of "dialectical reasoning" he'd absorbed from Hegel that formed the foundation for his entire theoretical enterprise. He insisted to his dying day that this remained true despite his famous "inversion" of Hegel, that is: the reversal of Hegel's emphasis upon such "mystical" categories as "the spirit" in favor of more "pragmatic" categories like "substance" and "material."

Let us be clear at this point. The dialectical theoretical methodology adopted by Marx stands—at least in principle—in as stark an oppositional contrast, and for all the same reasons, to the predominate and predominating tradition of linear and non–relational European logic (exemplified by Locke, Hume, and Sir Isaac Newton) as do indigenous systems of knowledge. It follows from this that there should be a solid conceptual intersection between Marx, marxism, and indigenous peoples. Indeed, I myself have suggested such a possibility in a pair of 1982 essays, one published in the journal *Integratedu-cation,* and the other in an education reader produced by the American Indian Studies Center at UCLA.[1]

At an entirely abstract level, I remain convinced that this is in fact the case. There is, however, a quite substantial defect in such a thesis in any less rarified sense. The most lucid articulation of the problem at hand was perhaps offered by Michael Albert and Robin Hahnel in their book, *Unorthodox Marxism*:

> [Marxist] dialecticians have never been able to indicate exactly how they see dialectical relations as different from any of the more complicated combinations of simple cause/effect relations such as co–causation, cumulative causation, or simultaneous determination of a many variable system where no variables are identified as dependent or independent in advance.... [F]or orthodox practitioners [of marxian dialectics] there is only the word and a lot of "hand waving" about its importance.[2]

A substantial case can be made that this confusion within marxism began with Marx himself. Having philosophically accepted and described a conceptual framework which allowed for a holistic and fully relational apprehension of the universe, Marx promptly abandoned it at the level of his applied intellectual practice. His impetus in this regard appears to have been his desire to see his theoretical endeavors used, not simply as a tool of understanding, but as a proactive agent for societal transformation, a matter bound up in his famous dictum that "the purpose of philosophy is not merely to understand history, but to change it." Thus Marx, *a priori* and with no apparent questioning in the doing, proceeded to anchor the totality of his elaboration in the presumed primacy of a given relation—that sole entity which can be said to hold the capability of active and conscious pursuit of change, in other words, humanity—over any and all other relations. The marxian "dialectic" was thus unbalanced from the outset, skewed as a matter of *faith* in favor of humans. Such a disequilibrium is, of course, not dialectical at all. It *is*, however, quite specifically Eurocentric in its attributes, springing as it does from the late–Roman interpretation of the Judeo–Christian assertion of "man's" supposed responsibility to "exercise dominion over nature," a tradition which Marx (ironically) claimed oft and loudly to have "voided" in his rush to materialism.

All of this must be contrasted to the typical indigenous practice of dialectics, a worldview recognizing the human entity as being merely one relation among a myriad, each of which is *entirely* dependent upon all others for its continued existence. Far from engendering some sense of "natural" human dominion over other relations, the indigenous view virtually requires a human behavior geared to keeping humanity *within* nature, maintaining relational balance and integrity (often called "harmony") rather than attempting to harness and subordinate the universe. The crux of this distinction may be discovered in the Judeo–Christian assertion that "man was created in God's image," a notion which leads to the elevation of humans as a sort of surrogate deity, self–empowered to transform the universe at whim. Indigenous tradition, on the other hand, in keeping with its truly dialectical understandings, attributes the inherent ordering of things, not to any given relation, but to another force often described as constituting a "Great Mystery," far beyond the realm of mere human comprehension.

We may take this differentiation to a somewhat more tangible level for purposes of clarity. The culmination of European tradition has been a homing–in on rationality, the innate characteristic of the human mind lending humanity the capacity to disrupt the order and composition of the universe. Rationality is held by those of the European persuasion—marxist and anti–marxist alike—to be the most important ("superior") relation of all; humans, being the only entity possessing it, are thus held *ipso facto* to be *the* superior beings of the universe; manifestations of rationality, whether cerebral or physical, are therefore held to be the cardinal signifiers of virtue.

Within indigenous traditions, meanwhile, rationality is more often viewed as being something of a "curse," a facet of humanity which must be consistently leashed and controlled in order for it *not* to generate *precisely* this disruption. The dichotomy in outlooks could not be more pronounced. All of this is emphatically *not* to suggest that indigenous cultures are somehow "irrational" in their makeup (to borrow a pet epithet hurled against challengers by the Eurosupremacists of academia). Rather, it is to observe that, as consummate dialecticians, they long ago developed functional and functioning methods for keeping their own rationality meshed with the rest of the natural order. And this, in my view, is the most rational exercise of all.

Dialectical Materialism

In any event, having wholeheartedly accepted the European mainstream's anti–dialectical premise that the human relation is paramount beyond all others in what are termed "external relations," Marx inevitably set out to discover that which occupied the same preeminence among "internal relations" (that is, those relations comprising the nature of the human project itself). With perhaps equal inevitability, his inverted Hegelianism—which he dubbed "dialectical materialism"—led him to locate this in the need of humans to *consciously* transform one aspect of nature into another, a process he designated by the term "production." It is important to note in this regard that Marx focused upon what is arguably the most rationalized, and therefore most unique, characteristic of human behavior, thus establishing a mutually reinforcing interlock between that relation which he advanced as being most important externally, and that which he assigned the same importance to internally. So interwoven have these two relations become in the marxian mind that today we find marxists utilizing the terms "rationality" and "productivity" almost interchangeably, and with a virtually biblical circularity of reasoning. It goes like this: The ability to produce demonstrates human rationality, thereby distinguishing humans as superior to all other external relations, while rationality (left unchecked) leads unerringly to prolific productivity, thereby establishing the latter as more important than any other among humans (internally). The record, of course, can be played in reverse with equally satisfying results.

From here, Marx was in a position to launch his general theory, laid out in the thousands of pages of his major published works—*der Grundrisse, A Contribution to the Critique of Political Economy,* and the three volumes of *das Kapital*—in which he attempted to explain the full range of implications attendant to what he described as "the relations of production." Initially, he was preoccupied with applying his concepts temporally, a project he tagged as "historical materialism," in order to assess and articulate the nature of the development of society through time. Here, he theorized that the various relations of society—for example, ways of holding land, kinship structures, systems of governance, spiritual beliefs, and so on—represented not a unified whole, but a complex of "contradictions" (in varying degrees) to the central, productive relation. All history, for Marx, became a stream of conflict within which these contradictions were increasingly "reconciled with" (subordinated to) production. As such reconciliation occurred over time, various transformations in socio–cultural relations correspondingly took place. Hence, Marx sketched history as a grand "progression," beginning with the "pre–history" of the "Stone Age" (the most "primitive" level of truly human existence) and "advancing" to the emergent capitalism of his own day. "Productive relations," in such a schema, determine all and everything.

One of Marx's theoretical heirs, the twentieth–century French structuralist–marxist Louis Althusser, summed historical materialism up quite succinctly when he defined production as being the "overdetermined contradiction of all human history," and observed that from a marxian standpoint society would not, in fact *could not,* exist as a unified whole until the process had worked its way through to culmination, a point at which all other social relations stood properly reconciled to the "productive mission" of humanity. In a more critical vein, we might note another summation offered by Albert and Hahnel:

> [O]rthodox [marxism] doesn't stop at downgrading the importance of the creative aspect of human consciousness and the role it plays in historical development. According to the orthodox materialists, of all the different objective material conditions, those having to do with production are always the most critical. Production is the prerequisite to human existence. Productive activity is the basis for all other activity. Therefore, consciousness rests primarily on the nature of objective production relations. Cut to the bone, this is the essence of the orthodox materialist [marxist] argument.[3]

It is difficult to conceive of a more economistic or deterministic ideological construction than this. Indeed, the post–structuralist French philosopher Jean Baudrillard has pointed out in his book, *The Mirror of Production*, that Marx never so much as offered a critique or alternative to the capitalist mode of political economy he claimed to oppose as he *completed* it, plugging its theoretical loopholes. This, in turn, has caused indigenous spokespersons such as Russell Means to view marxism not as a potential revolutionary transformation of world capitalism, but as a *continuation* of all of capitalism's worst vices "in a more efficient form."[4]

But, to move forward, there are a number of aspects of the marxian general theory—concepts such as surplus value, alienation, and domination among them—which might be important to explore at this juncture. Within the limited space of this essay, however, it seems to me the most fruitful avenue of pursuit lies in what Marx termed "the labor theory of value." By this, he meant that value can be assigned to anything *only* by virtue of the quantity and quality of human labor—that is, productive, transformative effort—put into it. This idea carries with it several interesting sub–properties, most strikingly that the natural world holds no intrinsic value of its own. A mountain is worth nothing as a mountain; it only accrues value by being "developed" into its raw productive materials such as ores, or even gravel. It can hold a certain speculative value, and thus be bought and sold, but only with such developmental ends in view. Similarly, a forest holds value only in the sense that it can be converted into a product known as lumber; otherwise, it is merely an obstacle to valuable, productive use of land through agriculture or stock–raising, etcetera (an interesting commentary on the marxian view of the land itself). Again, other species hold value only in terms of their utility for productive processes (such as meat, fur, leather, various body oils, eggs, milk, transportation in some instances, even fertilizer); otherwise, they may, indeed *must,* be preempted and supplanted by the more productive use of the habitat by humans.

This, no doubt, is an extreme formulation. There have been a number of "mediations" of this particular trajectory by twentieth– century marxian theorists. Still, at base, the difference they offer lies more in the degree of virulence with which they express the thesis rather than any essential break with it. All self–professing marxists, in order to be marxists at all, must share in the fundamental premise involved. And this goes for sophisticated phenomenological marxists such as Merleau–Ponty, existential marxists such as Sartre, critical theorists such as Marcuse and Adorno, and semioticists such as Habermas, right along with "mechanistic vulgarians" of the leninist persuasion (a term I use to encompass all those who trace their theoretical foundations directly to Lenin: stalinists, maoists, castroites, althusserian structuralists, and others). To put a cap on this particular point, I would offer the observation that the labor theory of value is the underpinning of a perspective which is about as contrary to the indigenous worldview as it is possible to define.

It goes without saying that there are other implications in this connection, as concerns indigenous cultures and people. Marx's concept of value ties directly to his notion of history, wherein progress is defined in terms of the evolution of production. From this juxtaposition we may discern that agricultural society is viewed as an "advance" over hunting and gathering society, feudalism is an advance over simple agriculture, mercantilism is seen as an advance over feudalism, and capitalism over mercantilism. Marx's supposed "revolutionary" content comes from his projection that socialism will "inevitably" be the next advance over capitalism and that it, in turn, will give way to communism. Okay, the first key here is that each advance represents not only a quantitative/qualitative step "forward" in terms of productivity, but also a corresponding rearrangement of other social relations, both of which factors are assigned a greater degree of *value* than their "predecessors." In other words, agricultural society is seen by marxists as being more valuable than hunting and gathering society, feudalism as more valuable than mere agriculture, and so on. The picture should be becoming clear.

Now, there is a second facet. Marx was very straightforward in acknowledging that the sole cultural model upon which he was basing his theses on history and value was his own, that is to say European (or, more accurately, northwestern European) context. He even committed to paper several provisos stipulating that it would be inappropriate and misleading to attempt to apply the principles deriving from his examination of the dominant matrix in Europe to other, non–European contexts, each of which he (correctly) pointed out would have to be understood *in its own terms* before it could be properly understood vis-à-vis Europe. With this said, however, Marx promptly violated his own posited methodology in this regard, offering a number of non–European examples—of which he admittedly knew little or nothing—to illustrate various points he wished to make in his elaboration on the historical development of Europe. Chinese society, to name a prominent example of this, was cast (really *mis*cast) as "Oriental feudalism," thus supposedly shedding a certain light on this stage of European history. "Red Indians," about whom Marx knew even less than he did of the Chinese, became examples of "primitive society," illustrating what he wanted to say about Europe's stone age. In this fashion, Marx universalized what he claimed were the primary ingredients of Anglo–Saxon–Teutonic history, extending the de facto contention that *all* cultures are subject to the same essential dynamics and, therefore, follow essentially the same historical progression.

Insofar as all cultures were made to conform with the material correspondences of one or another moment in European history, and given that only Europe exhibited a "capitalist mode of production" and social organization—which Marx held to be the "highest form of social advancement" at the time he was writing—it follows that all non–European cultures could be seen as objectively lagging behind Europe. We are presented here with a sort of

"universal Euro yardstick" by which we can measure with considerable precision the relative ("dialectical") degree of retardation shown by each and every
culture on the planet, vis–à–vis Europe. Simultaneously, we are able to assign,
again with reasonable precision, a relatively ("dialectically") lesser value to
each of these cultures as compared to that of Europe. We are dealing here with
the internal relations of humanity, but in order to understand the import of such
thinking we must bear in mind the fate assigned "inferior" (less valuable)
external relations—mountains, trees, deer—within the marxian vision. In the
plainest terms, marxism holds as "an immutable law of history" that all
non–European cultures must be subsumed in what is now called "Europeani-
zation." It is their inevitable destiny, a matter to be accomplished in the name
of progress and "for their own good." Again, we may detect echoes of the Jesuits
within the "anti–spiritualist" marxian construct.

Those who would reject such an assessment should consider the matter
more carefully. Do not terms such as "pre–industrial" riddle the marxian
vernacular whenever analysis of non–European ("primitive") culture is at
hand? What possible purpose does the qualifier "pre" (as opposed to, say,
"non") serve in this connection other than to argue that such societies are *in the
process of becoming* capitalist? And is this not simply another way of stating
that they are lagging behind those societies which have *already become*
industrialized? Or, to take another example, to what end do marxists habitually
refer to those societies which have "failed" (refused) to even enter the productive progression as being "ahistorical" or "outside of history"? Is this to suggest
that such cultures have *no* history, or is it to say that they have the wrong *kind*
of history, that only a certain (marxian) sense of history is true? And again: Do
marxists not hold that the socialist revolution will be the outcome of history for
all humanity? Is there another sense in which we can understand the term
"*world* revolution"? Did Marx himself not proclaim—and in no uncertain
terms—that the attainment of the "capitalist stage of development" is an
absolute prerequirement for the social transformation *he* meant when he spoke
of the "socialist revolution"? I suggest that, given the only possible honest
answers to these questions, there really are no other conclusions to be drawn
from the corpus of marxist theory than those I am drawing here. The punch line
is that marxism as a worldview is not only diametrically opposed to that held
by indigenous peoples, it also quite literally precludes their right to a continued
existence as functioning socio–cultural entities. This, I submit, will remain true
despite the fact that we may legitimately disagree on the nuance and detail of
precisely how it happens to be true.

The National Question

Up to this point, our analysis has been restricted to the consideration of marxist theory. It is one thing to say that there are problems with a set of ideas, and that those ideas carry unacceptable implications *if* they were to be put into practice. The "proof," however, is *in* the practice, or "praxis" if you follow the marxian conception that theory and practice are a unified whole and must consequently be maintained in a dialectically reciprocal and interactive state at all times. Hence, it is quite another matter to assert that the negative implications of doctrine and ideology have in fact been actualized in "the real world" and are thereby subject to concrete examination. Yet Marxism offers us exactly this method of substantiating our theoretical conclusions.

To be fair, when we move into this area we are no longer concerned with the totality of marxism per se. Rather, we must focus upon that stream which owes a special allegiance to the legacy of Lenin. The reason for this is that *all* "marxist" revolutions, beginning with the one in the Soviet Union, have been carried out under the mantle of Lenin's interpretation, expansion, and revision of Marx. This is true for the revolutionary processes in China, Cuba, North Korea, Algeria, Kampuchea (Cambodia), Laos, Albania, Mozambique, Angola, and Nicaragua. Arguably, it is also true for Zimbabwe (Rhodesia), and it is certainly true for those countries brought into a marxian orbit by main force: Latvia, Lithuania, Estonia, Poland, East Germany, Czechoslovakia, Hungary, Rumania, Bulgaria, Mongolia, Tibet, and Afghanistan. Yugoslavia represents a special case, but its differentiation seems largely due to capitalist influences rather than that of other strains of marxism. One might go on to say that those self–proclaimed revolutionary marxist formations worldwide which seem likely to effect a seizure of state power at any point in the foreseeable future— for example, those in Namibia and El Salvador—are *all* leninist in orientation. They certainly have disagreements among themselves, but this does not change the nature of their foundations. There have been *no* non–leninist marxian revolutions to date, nor does it seem likely there will be in the coming decades.

Be this as it may, there are again a number of aspects of marxist–leninist post–revolutionary practice which we might consider, for example, the application of Lenin's concept of "the dictatorship of the proletariat," centralized state economic planning and the issue of forced labor, the imposition of rigid state parameters upon political discourse of all types, and so forth. Each of these holds obvious and direct consequences for the populations involved, including whatever indigenous peoples happen to become encapsulated within one or another (sometimes more than one) revolutionary state. But for the purposes of this essay, it is again necessary that we limit our scope. In this, it seems appropriate that we follow the lead of Albert and Hahnel in "cutting to the bone." We will therefore take up that aspect of marxist–leninist praxis which has led to indigenous peoples being encapsulated in revolutionary states at all.

In the vernacular, this centers upon what is called the "national question" (or "nationalities question").

The principle at issue here devolves from a concept which has come to be known as "the right to self–determination of all peoples," codified in international law by the United Nations during the 1960s, but originally espoused by Marx and his colleague, Friedrich Engels, during the London Conference of the First International in 1865.[5] In essence, the right to self–determination has come to mean that each people, identifiable as such (through the sharing of a common language and cultural understandings, system of governance and social regulation, and a definable territoriality within which to maintain a viable economy), is *inherently* entitled to decide for itself whether or not and to what extent it wishes to merge itself culturally, politically, territorially and economically with any other (usually larger) group. The right to self–determination thus accords to each identifiable people on the planet the prerogative of (re)establishing and/or continuing themselves as culturally distinct, territorially and economically autonomous, and politically sovereign entities (as *nations*, in other words). Correspondingly, no nation has the right to preempt such rights on the part of another. For these reasons, the right of self–determination has been linked closely with the movement toward global decolonization, and the resultant body of international law which has emerged in this regard. All this, to be sure, is very much in line with the stated aspirations of American Indians and other indigenous peoples around the world.

But marxism's handling of the right to self–determination has not followed the general development of the concept. Having opened the door in this regard, Marx and Engels adopted what seems (superficially, at least) to be a very curious posture. They argued that self–determining rights pertained only to *some* peoples. For instance, they were quite strong in their assertions that the Irish, who were even then waging a serious struggle to rid themselves of British colonization, must be supported in this effort. Similarly, Marx came out unequivocally in favor of the right (even the obligation) of the Poles to break free from Russian colonialism. On the other hand, Engels argued vociferously that "questions as to the right of independent national existence of those small relics of peoples" such as the Highland Scots (Gaels), Welsh, Manxmen, Serbs, Croats, Ruthenes, Slovaks, and Czechs constitute "an absurdity."[6] Marx concurred and proceeded to openly advocate the imposition of European colonialism upon the "backward peoples" of Africa, Asia, and elsewhere.[7]

Such positioning may initially seem confusing, even contradictory. A closer examination, however, reveals consistency with Marx's broader and more philosophical pronouncements. The Irish and Poles had been, over the course of several centuries of English and Russo–German colonization (respectively), sufficiently "advanced" by the experience (that is, reformed in the image of their conquerors) to be entitled to determine their own future in accordance with the "iron laws" of historical materialism. The other peoples in question, *especially* the tribal peoples of Africa and Asia (and one may assume American Indians were categorized along with these), were not seen as being comparably "developed." A continuing dose of colonization—subjugation by superior beings, from superior cultures—was thus prescribed to help them overcome their "problem."

A second level of consideration also entered Marx's and Engels' reasoning on these matters. This concerns the notion of "economies of scale." Marx held that the larger an "economic unit" became, the more rationalized and efficient it could be rendered. Conversely, smaller economic units were considered to be inefficient by virtue of being "irrationally" duplicative and redundant. The Irish and Poles were not only populous enough to be considered among Engels' "great peoples," but—viewed as economic units—large enough to justify support in their own right, at least during a transitional phase en route to the consolidation of "world communism." The other peoples in question were not only too backward, but too *small* to warrant support in their quest(s) for freedom and independence; their *only* real destiny, from the marxist perspective, was therefore to be consigned to what Leon Trotsky would later call "the dustbin of history," totally and irrevocably subsumed within larger and more efficient economic units.

The national question thus emerged for marxists as a problem in determining precisely which peoples were entitled to enjoy even a transient national existence along the way to the "true internationalism" of world communism, and which should have such rights foreclosed out–of–hand. This in itself became quite a controversial discussion when marxism faced the issue of adopting tactics with which to wage its own revolutionary struggles, rather than simply tendering or denying support to the struggles of others. At this point, things become truly cynical and mercenary.

While marxism is, as we have seen, hostile to the nationalistic aspirations of "marginal" peoples, it was simultaneously perceived by many marxists that a certain advantage might accrue to marxian revolutionaries if they were to *pretend* to feel otherwise. The struggles of even the smallest and least developed nationalities might be counted upon to sap the strength of the capitalist/colonialist status quo while marxist cadres went about the real business of overthrowing it; in certain instances, "national minorities" might even be counted upon to absorb the brunt of the fighting, thus sparing marxism the unnecessary loss of highly trained personnel. After the revolution, it was reasoned, the marxists could simply employ their political acumen to consolidate state power in their own hands and revoke as "unrealistic" (even "counterrevolutionary") the claims to national integrity for which those of the minority nationalities had fought and died. It was also calculated that, once in power, marxism could accomplish the desired abrogation of independent national minority existence either rapidly or more gradually, depending upon the dictates of "objective conditions." As Walker Connor has put it in his definitive study of the subject, "Grand strategy was ... to take precedence over ideological purity and consistency" where the national question was concerned.[8]

It is not that all this was agreed upon in anything resembling a harmonious or unanimous fashion by marxists. To the contrary, during the period leading up to the Russian Revolution, the national question was the topic of an extremely contentious debate within the Second International. On one side was Rosa Luxemburg and the bulk of all delegates arguing a "purist" line that the right to self–determination does not exist in–and–of itself and should thus be renounced by marxism. On the other side was a rather smaller group clustered around Lenin. They insisted not only that marxism should view with favor *any* struggle against the status quo prior to the revolution, but that the International should extend any and all sorts of guarantees which might serve to stir national minorities into action. Towards this end, Lenin wrote that from the bolshevik perspective all nations have an *absolute* right to self–determination, including the right to total secession and independence from any marxist revolutionary state. He also endorsed, as the party position on the national question, the formulation of Joseph Stalin that:

> The right to self–determination means that a nation can arrange its life according to its own will. It has the right to arrange its life on the basis of autonomy. It has the right to enter into federal relations with other nations. It has the right to complete secession. Nations are sovereign and all nations are equal.[9]

Of course, as Connor points out, "Lenin ... made a distinction between the abstract right of self–determination, which is enjoyed by all nations, and the right to exercise that right, which evidently is not," at least where small or "marginal" populations are concerned.[10] Thus, shortly after the bolshevik attainment of power came the pronouncement that, "The principle of self–determination must be subordinated to the principles of socialism."[11] The result, predictably, was that of the more than 300 distinct nationalities readily observable in what had been the czarist Russian empire, only 28—consisting almost entirely of substantial and relatively Europeanized population blocks such as the Ukranians, Armenians, Moldavians, Byelorussians, citizens of the Baltic states, etcetera—were accorded even the gesture of being designated as "republics," and this only after the matter of secession had been foreclosed. The supposed "right to enter into federal relations with other nations" was also immediately circumscribed to mean only with each other and with the central government which, of course, was seated in the former czarist citadel at Moscow. Those, such as the Ukranians, who persisted in pursuing a broader definition of self–determination were first branded as counter–revolutionary, and then radically undercut through liquidation of their socio–cultural and political leadership during the stalinist purges of the 1920s and 1930s. There is simply no other way in which to describe the Soviet marxist process of state consolidation other than as the ruthlessly forcible incorporation of all the various peoples conquered by the czars into a single, seamless economic polity. As Marx once completed the capitalist model of political–economy, so too did the bolsheviks complete the unification of the Great Russian empire.

In China, the practical experience was much the same. During the so–called Long March of the mid–1930s, Mao Tse Tung's army of marxist insurgents traversed nearly the whole country. In the midst of this undertaking, they "successfully communicated the party's public position [favoring] self–determination to the minorities they encountered," virtually all of whom were well known to be yearning for freedom from the domination of the Han empire.[12] The marxists gained considerable, perhaps decisive, support as a result of this tactic, but, to quote Connor:

> While thus engaged in parlaying its intermittent offers of national independence into necessary support for its cause, the party never fell prey to its own rhetoric but continued to differentiate between its propaganda and its more privately held commitment to maintaining the territorial integrity of the Chinese state.[13]

As had been the case in the USSR, the immediate wake of the Chinese revolution in 1949 saw marxist language suddenly shift, abandoning terms such as secession and self–determination altogether. Instead, the new Chinese constitution was written to decry "nationalism and national chauvinism," and "the peoples who, during the revolution, were promised the right of political independence were subsequently reincorporated by force and offered the diminished prospect of regional autonomy,"[14] Only Outer Mongolia was accorded the status of existing even in the truncated Soviet sense of being a republic.

In Vietnam and Laos, leaving aside the lowland ethnic Nungs (Chinese), the only peoples holding the requisites for national identity apart from the Vietnamese and Laotians themselves are the tribal mountain cultures—often referred to as "montagnards"—such as the Rhadé, Krak, Bru, Bahnar, and h'Mong. Insofar as they are neither populous nor "advanced" enough to comprise promising marxian–style economic units, they were never so much as offered the "courtesy" of being lied to before the revolution; national self–determination for the mountain peoples was never mentioned in Ho Chi Minh's agenda. Consequently, the "yards" (as they were dubbed by U.S. military personnel) formed their own political independence organization called the *Front Unife Pour la Liberation des Races Opprimees* (Unified Front for the Liberation of Oppressed Peoples) or, acronymically, FULRO during the early 1960s. The purpose of FULRO was/is to resist *any* Vietnamese encroachment upon montagnard national rights. Consequently, U.S. Special Forces troopers were able to utilize the FULRO consortium to good advantage as a highland mobile force interdicting the supply routes and attacking the staging areas of both the National Liberation Front (NLF) main force units and units of the regular North Vietnamese army (NVA) (both of which were viewed by the mountain people as threats). Much to the surprise of U.S. military advisers, however, beginning in 1964, FULRO *also* started using its military equipment to fight the troops of the American–backed Saigon regime, whenever *they* entered the mountains.[15]

The message was plain enough. The montagnards rejected incorporation into *any* Vietnamese state, whether "capitalist" or "communist." In post–revolutionary Vietnam, FULRO has continued to exist, and to conduct armed resistance against the imposition of Vietnamese hegemony. For its part, the Hanoi government refuses to acknowledge either the fact of the Resistance or its basis. The rather better known example of the h'Mong in Laos follows very much the same contours as the struggle in the south. Such a recounting could be continued at length, but the point should be made. In *no* marxist–leninist setting have the national rights of *any* small people been respected, most especially not those of land–based, indigenous ("tribal") peoples. Their very right to exist as national entities has instead been denied *as such*. Always and everywhere, marxism–leninism has assigned itself a practical priority leading directly to the incorporation, subordination, and dissolution of these peoples *as such*. This is quite revealing when one considers that the term "genocide" (as opposed to "mass murder") was coined to express the reality of policies which lead not simply to the physical liquidation of groups of individuals targeted as belonging to an identified "ethnic, racial, religious, or national" entity, but to bring about the destruction of the entity itself, *as such*, through any means. Marxism–leninism, viewed in this way, is a quite consciously and specifically *genocidal* doctrine, at least where indigenous cultures are concerned.

There has been no relaxation or deviation in this circumstance during the 1980s. Most notably, during the 1990s there has been the situation in Nicaragua where three Indian peoples—Miskitos, Sumus, and Ramas—are resisting their forced incorporation into yet another revolutionary state, tacitly acknowledged by two of its principle leaders (Daniel Ortéga and Tomas Borgé Martinez) to be guided by marxist–leninist principles. The Indian nations in question have historically maintained a high degree of insularity and autonomy vis–à–vis Nicaragua's dominant (latino) society, and they have also continued a viable economic life within their own territories on the Atlantic Coast.[16] The sole requirement of the Sandinista revolution has been that they be free to *continue* to do so, as an "autonomous zone"—by their own definition, and on their own terms—within revolutionary Nicaragua. The response of the "progressive" government in Managua has been that this would be impossible because such self–determination on the part of Indians would constitute a "state within a state" (*precisely* the sort of circumstance supposedly guaranteed in leninist doctrine), and because "there are no more Indians, Creoles or Latinos.... [W]e are *all* Nicaraguans now."[17] In other words, the Miskito, Sumu, and Rama are required by the revolution to cease to exist *as such.*

Conclusion

None of what has been said herein should be taken as an apology or defense, direct or indirect, of U.S. (or other capitalist) state policies. American Indians, first and foremost, know what the United States has done and what it's about. We've experienced the meaning of the United States since long before there were marxists around to "explain" it to us. And we've continued to experience it in ways which leave little room for confusion on the matter. That's *why* we seek change. That's *why* we demand sovereignty and self–determination. That's *why* we cast about for allies and alternatives of the sort marxists have often *claimed* to be.

The purpose of our endeavor here has thus been to examine the prospects for collaboration with marxism to the end that U.S. domination will be cast out of our lives once and for all. In doing so, we *must* ask—only fools would not—whether marxism offers an alternative vision to that which capitalism has imposed upon us. And from the answers to this we can discern whether marxists and marxism can really be the sort of allies which would, or even *could,* actually guarantee us a positive change "come the revolution." In this regard, we need to *know* exactly what is meant when a marxist "friend" such as David Muga assures us, as he recently did, that the solutions to our present problems lie in the models offered by the USSR, China, and revolutionary Nicaragua.[18] The answers (I would say) are rather painfully evident in what has been discussed above. Marxism, in its present form at least, offers us far worse than nothing. With friends such as these, we will be truly doomed.

So it is. But must it be? I think not. An increasing number of thoughtful marxists have broken with at least the worst of marxian economism, determinism, and human chauvinism. Salient examples such as Albert, Hahnel, and Baudrillard have been mentioned or quoted herein. The German Green Movement, involving a number of marxists or former marxists like Rudi Deutschke and Rudolph Bahro, is an extremely hopeful phenomenon (albeit, it has thus far failed spectacularly to congeal in this country). All in all, there is sufficient basis to suggest that at least some elements of the marxian tradition are capable of transcending dogma to the extent that they may possess the potential to forge mutually fruitful alliances with American Indians and other indigenous peoples (although, at the point where this becomes true, one has reason to ask whether they may be rightly viewed as marxists any longer).

The key for us, it would seem to me, is to remain firm in the values and insights of our own traditions. We must hold true to the dialectical understanding embodied in the expression *Metakuyeayasi* and reject anything less as an unbalanced and imperfect view, even a mutilation of reality. We must continue to pursue our traditional vision of a humanity *within* rather than *upon* the natural order. We must continue to insist, as an absolutely fundamental principle, upon the right of *all* peoples—each and every one, no matter how small and "primitive"—to freely select the fact and form of their ongoing national existence. Concomitantly, we must reject *all* contentions by *any* state that it has the right—for *any* reason—to subordinate or dissolve the inherent rights of *any* other nation. And, perhaps most important of all, we must choose our friends and allies accordingly. I submit that there's nothing in this game plan which contradicts any aspect of what we've come to describe as "the Indian way."

In conclusion, I must say that I believe such an agenda, which I call "indigenist," can and will attract real friends, real allies, and offer real alternatives to *both* marxism and capitalism. What will result, in my view, is the emergence of a movement predicated on the principles of what are termed "deep ecology," "soft–path technology," "anarchism" (or, probably more accurately, "minarchism"), and global "balkanization." But we are now entering into a topic of a whole different discussion. So, with that, allow me to close.

Notes

1. *See* "White Studies or Isolation: An Alternative Model for American Indian Studies Programs," *American Indian Issues in Higher Education* (Los Angeles: American Indian Studies Program, UCLA, 1982), and "White Studies: The Intellectual Imperialism of Contemporary U.S. Education," *Integrateducation*, Vol. XIX, Nos. 1–2.

2. Michael Albert and Robin Hahnel, *Unorthodox Marxism: An Essay on Capitalism, Socialism and Revolution* (Boston: South End Press, 1978), pp. 52–53.

3. Ibid., p. 58.

4. Russell Means, "The Same Old Song," in *Marxism and Native Americans*, Ward Churchill, ed. (Boston: South End Press, 1983). The essay was originally presented as a speech at the 1980 Black Hills International Survival Gathering (near Rapid City, South Dakota). It has been published in various forms, under various titles, in *Mother Jones*, *Lakota Eyapaha*, and *Akwesasne Notes*.

5. *See* G. Stekloff, *History of the First International* (New York: Russell and Russell Publishers, 1968).

6. Ibid; Engels is quoted here abundantly on the topic.

7. Shlomo Alvinari, in his book *Karl Marx on Colonization and Modernization* (New York: Doubleday, 1969), offers a truly remarkable selection of quotations from Marx on this subject.

8. Walker Connor, *The National Question in Marxist–Leninist Theory and Strategy* (Princeton, New Jersey: Princeton University Press, 1984), p. 14.

9. J. V. Stalin, *Marxism and the National Question: Selected Writings and Speeches* (New York: International Publishers, 1942), p. 23.

10. Walker Connor, op. cit., p. 35.

11. Quoted in Jesse Clarkson, *A History of Russia* (New York: Random House Publishers, 1961), p. 636.

12. Walker Connor, op. cit., p. 77.

13. Ibid., p. 79.

14. Ibid., p. 87.

15. For more information on U.S. involvement with the Saigon regime, *see* Frank Snepp, *Decent Interval* (New York: Random House, 1977); and Neil Sheehan, *A Bright and Shining Lie* (New York: Random House, 1988).

16. For further information on these issues, *see* "Between a Rock and a Hard Place: Left–Wing Revolution, Right–Wing Reactions, and the Destruction of Indigenous Peoples" in this book; *see* also Bernard Nietschmann, *The Unknown War: The Miskito Nation, Nicaragua and the United States* (New York: Freedom House, 1989).

17. Statements made to the author by Sandinista Interior Minister Tomas Borgé Martinez in Havana, Cuba, Dec. 1984.

18. David A. Muga, "Native Americans and the Nationalities Question: Premises for a Marxist Approach to Ethnicity and Self–Determination," *Nature, Society, Thought*, Vol. 1, No. 1 (1987).

Between a Rock and a Hard Place

Left–Wing Revolution, Right–Wing Reaction, and the Destruction of Indigenous Peoples*

Co–authored with Glenn T. Morris

> [To get a] picture of the Meo's situation in Laos, [there must be] discussion of the U.S. Program to organize them to fight for the United States, trapping them like desperate dogs and throwing away the leash when they [have] lost their usefulness.
>
> *Noam Chomsky and Edward S. Herman,*
> The Political Economy of Human Rights

As has been remarked elsewhere, it has become a hallmark of U.S. counter-insurgency/counterrevolutionary doctrine that indigenous peoples within Third World states can be manipulated to serve global anti–communist policies, providing a ready and on–site pool of combatants for deployment against progressive movements and governments.[1] Typically executed by Special Forces and/or Central Intelligence Agency (CIA) personnel, this cynical line of action has repeatedly resulted in the dislocation, dissolution, decimation, and, in some cases, virtual eradication of the native societies thus used. In this sense, the introductory observation offered by Chomsky and Herman, astute observers of America's imperial adventures abroad, is entirely accurate.[2]

For purposes of this essay, it will be accepted that the United States opts to enter into military alliances with indigenous peoples solely on the basis of

---

* This essay first appeared in *Cultural Survival Quarterly*, Vol. 11, No. 3 (Fall 1987).

its own geopolitical needs, and never for such altruistic motives as "saving them from genocide."[3] To the contrary, we accept the conclusion that it is primarily U.S. actions and firepower which have inflicted the bulk of all casualties upon America's erstwhile indigenous allies, consistently placing them in the position of "facing extinction as ... organized societies."[4] However, we seek to raise the deeper issues of why indigenous peoples seem susceptible to recruitment by U.S. low intensity warfare specialists, and whether there might not be principles imbedded in contemporary progressive theory and practice which contribute to such outcomes.

In considering these questions, two cases will be examined: the case of the "Meo" or h'Mong hill people within the context of the CIA's "secret war" in Laos during the 1960s and early 1970s, and the more recent case of the Miskito, Sumu, and Rama Indians of eastern Nicaragua and Honduras. Space limitations preclude more than the most general contours of each illustration, or more than the most rudimentary analysis. Nonetheless, the lack of literature on this topic demands that exploration begin. Because of the relative topicality of the situation in Miskitia, a greater emphasis will be placed on the details of that particular situation.

The Case of the h'Mong

According to Guy Morechand, "the Hmong consider the term Meo, used by the Lao, demeaning" (probably because they associate it with the Vietnamese word "Moi"—meaning "savage" or "subhuman"—used to describe tribal peoples generally), and "they have tended to avoid involvement with the lowlanders except for trade."[5] Richard S. D. Hawkins reinforces this latter point by observing that the h'Mong areas of Laos, centering upon the Plain of Jars, have historically been "the scene of frequent revolts against [i.e., resistance to] lowland control."[6] (For an overview of the h'Mong conflict area, *see* Map I.)

By all accounts, the h'Mong jealously guarded their cultural integrity, political autonomy, and the self–sufficiency provided by an economy based upon "the shifting cultivation of upland rice, maize, and opium as a cash crop."[7] Further, "the montagnards [the French word encompassing hill peoples such as the h'Mong] were neglected by the dominant Lao during the colonial period" (roughly 1880–1955), and were thereby able to maintain the full and relatively untrammeled range of characteristics marking the expression of de facto national sovereignty in the modern era. This situation was undoubtedly facilitated by the French colonists' lack of interest in the Annamese highland areas inhabited by the h'Mong, and their preference in viewing Laos as a potential lowland "river empire."[8]

It was not until military dynamics of World War II initiated a process of increasing encroachment on their territory that the h'Mong elected to enter into

Map I

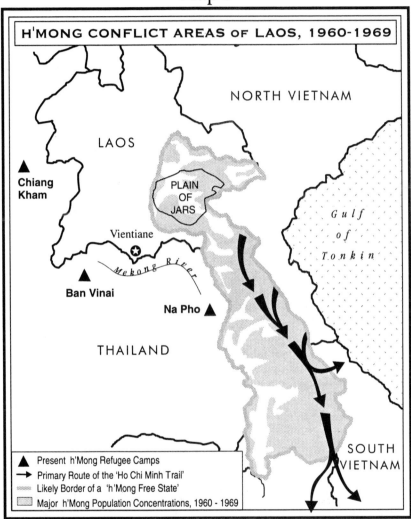

H'MONG CONFLICT AREAS OF LAOS, 1960-1969

NORTH VIETNAM

LAOS

▲
Chiang
Kham

PLAIN
OF
JARS

Gulf

of

Vientiane

T o n k i n

Mekong River

▲

Ban Vinai

Na Pho ▲

THAILAND

SOUTH
VIETNAM

▲ Present h'Mong Refugee Camps
→ Primary Route of the 'Ho Chi Minh Trail'
▨ Likely Border of a 'h'Mong Free State'
▨ Major h'Mong Population Concentrations, 1960 - 1969

alliances with outsiders. In 1946, this assumed the form of h'Mong leader Faydang's alliance with the anti–colonialist Lao Issara exile government headed by Prince Phetsarath and Phaya Khommao.[9] The objective of this particular union for the h'Mong appears to have been a hope for a return to the Lao "neglect" of highland internal affairs exhibited in earlier years. A "Free Laos" was perceived as corresponding nicely with a "h'Mong Free State." A significant snag in this arrangement can be detected in the fact that "all the Lao Issara exiles shared the belief that Laos was incapable of gaining freedom unassisted"; hence, an important "minority of the Lao Issara, grouped around Prince Souhpanouvong, were willing to use Vietnamese support to wage an armed struggle for total independence from France ... [and] came to share the Viet Minh view that the war for independence involved all of Indochina."[10] The question became one concerning the extent to which the Laotian nationalist movement would align itself with (or subordinate itself to) Ho Chi Minh's highly centrist Viet Minh organization.

This created a split within the Lao Issara, leading to the emergence of a "moderate" faction, finally headed by Prince Souvanna Phouma, and with which the h'Mong were allied. Souvanna Phouma assumed power through the 1954 Geneva Peace Accord in exchange for the "acceptance of anti–communist premises and forces including the French, the Thai, and lastly the Americans."[11] Considering the stipulations (accurately enough) to be a blatant manifestation of neocolonialism, the Souphanouvong faction, now identifying itself as the Pathet Lao, rejected the legitimacy of the new regime, aligned itself ever more closely with the nationalist/marxist Hanoi government, and prepared to refocus its armed struggle against its former colleagues in Vientiane (the capital city of Laos).[12]

For what may have been obvious tactical reasons, the Pathet Lao based themselves squarely in the midst of h'Mong territory, a matter which set off an inevitable spiral of friction between the two groups.[13] Worse, under a 1951 agreement granting reciprocal use of troops in "each other's territory," the Pathet Lao brought in Vietnamese cadres, representatives of a people whose traditional haughty disdain for all things "Moi" had hardly endeared them to the h'Mong.[14] Programs were quickly implemented in the "liberated" areas that included the strong–arm conscription of h'Mong youth into Pathet Lao guerrilla units, and the extraction of "taxes" from the villagers, usually in the form of food and opium crops.[15] Finally, the Pathet Lao promulgated as its vision of the future a program which had been formulated in Vietnam in 1950 and that openly called for the incorporation of "the people of all tribal groups" into the anticipated post–revolutionary progressive state and society.[16] Clearly, the h'Mong had little option but to see these developments as an outright denial of their right to national sovereignty, or even autonomy, in both theory and practice. Consequently, the h'Mong began to actively resist as soon as the Pathet Lao and Vietnamese arrived in their territory.[17]

Meanwhile, "America maneuvered to pull Laos away from neutrality" by integrating it into John Foster Dulles' collective security scheme (to "contain" countries such as North Vietnam), and having assisted Laos with the Southeast Asia Treaty Organization (SEATO), the next U.S. move was to strengthen the country in order to forestall a communist takeover: "Laos became the only foreign country in the world where the United States supported 100% of the military budget."[18] Under such conditions, the Vientiane government was prodded by the United States into mounting increasing operations against h'Mong territory in order to destroy the opposition's infrastructure, a policy which rapidly built h'Mong resentment of the Lao Issara no less than against the Pathet Lao, and for much the same reasons. The trend reached its head in 1957, when Vientiane entered into negotiations—from which the h'Mong were excluded—with the Pathet Lao concerning the "political disposition" of the highlands, and a possible coalition government.[19] Unsurprisingly, the h'Mong, led by Touby Ly Fong and rejecting the presumptions of both the Left and the Right, aligned themselves in 1960 with the neutralist revolt of Kong Le.[20]

For its part, the United States pursued its principle regional policy objective of walling North Vietnam in from the west and, proceeding from the assessment that the h'Mong were "the best fighting men in all of Laos," started, probably in 1958, to send in the first "Special Forces [which] began advising the scattered detachments of Meo which continued to hold mountain strongholds in Pathet Lao territory."[21] The CIA, quickly realizing the potential effectiveness of this program, increased the number of "Special Forces White Star Mobile Training Teams" by the end of 1960 and, with remarkable insight into the motives of the h'Mong, began selling its "package" with promises of "an autonomous 'Meo State' in return for [the h'Mong's] helping ... fight the [communists]."[22] h'Mong leader Vang Pao, with the agreement of Touby Le Fong, responded with a plan which "Special Forces advisors encouraged ... as the first step in building a substantial guerrilla army."[23] This "development process" was continued uninterrupted despite the 1962 Geneva Accord for a Laotian cease–fire, from which the h'Mong (as with all previous negotiations) had been excluded.[24]

As the Indochina war escalated throughout the 1960s, the h'Mong highlands area came to be of crucial importance to the North Vietnamese as the crux of its supply conduit (the so–called Ho Chi Minh Trail) to the south. Correspondingly, "the Meo outposts [were] seen as vital barriers to communist penetration" by U.S. strategists, and came to be "regarded as perhaps the single most important American program in Laos."[25] Guided by veteran CIA covert operative Edgar "Pops" Buell, Van Pao's ground forces were coupled to U.S. air power, which had shifted its emphasis "from tactical to strategic bombing" on the Plain of Jars at least as early as 1966.[26] The comparatively massive numbers of Vietnamese now operating within the highlands, and the extent of the devastation from the air, caused the h'Mong to fight with desperate ferocity for Vietnamese eviction. Caught in the cross fire between the United States, North Vietnam, and the Royal Laotian Army, the h'Mong were physically decimated. Buell wrote in March 1968:

> Vang Pao has lost at least a thousand men since Jan. 1, killed alone, and I don't know how many more wounded. He's lost all but one of his commanders.... A short time ago we rounded up three hundred fresh recruits. Thirty percent were fourteen years old or less, and ten of them were only ten years old. Another thirty percent were fifteen

and sixteen. The remaining forty percent were thirty–five or over. Where were the ones in between? I'll tell you, they're all dead ... and in a few weeks, 90 percent of [the new recruits] will be dead.[27]

Despite such sacrifices by the fighters, by 1970, Buell was estimating that 250,000 of the approximately 300,000 h'Mong had been displaced from their homeland.[28] Another source estimated that "of a quarter of a million Meos in 1962, only a pitiful remnant of ten thousand escaped to Thailand in 1975."[29] Vang Pao, with a forlorn absence of genuine alternatives available to him, continued the struggle, with his "ultimate motive ... to fight for a *de facto* autonomous Meo kingdom spreading through most of [eastern] Laos."[30] By 1975, with the final collapse of the U.S. military adventure in Indochina and consolidation of the Vietnamese statist agenda, even Vang Pao was gone, resettled on an upland ranch in Montana, his people largely dispersed into squalid refugee camps along the Lao–Thai border. The culture and society for which they had fought so hard and suffered so much was shattered.[31]

As Chomsky and Herman point out, at least as late as March of 1978, pockets of h'Mong were *still* in Laos and resisting subordination to lowland authority: "a major military campaign by Laotian and Vietnamese forces ... with long range artillery shelling, which was followed by aerial rocketing, bombing and strafing" was directed at them.[32] The h'Mong who continued to reside in Thai refugee camps—perhaps as many as 100,000 in 1987—continued to maintain a staunch loyalty to their traditional leaders, and the aspiration for a h'Mong Free State. Reports that Vang Pao had directed the h'Mong in these camps to regroup and carry on the struggle for their homeland indicated that their dream of sovereignty had not been extinguished.[33]

The Case of Miskitia

Essential to an understanding of current political conditions within Miskitia is a threshold recognition that the Miskito, Sumu, and Rama Indian Nations constitute the indigenous peoples of the eastern Nicaragua–Honduras region, having used and occupied their territories from time immemorial.[34] (*See* Map II.) Additionally, these native nations have staunchly and consistently defended their homelands from invasion and occupation, first by the Spanish, then by the British and Americans, and now by forces of both the left and the right from the contemporary Nicaraguan state. A significant population of Creoles has peacefully shared the area with the Indians since the seventeenth century and, more recently, latinos from western Nicaragua have begun migrating into the region.

Despite the efforts of European–rooted colonial regimes and settler states to assimilate and eradicate Indian identity in Miskitia, formidable and distinct

Map II

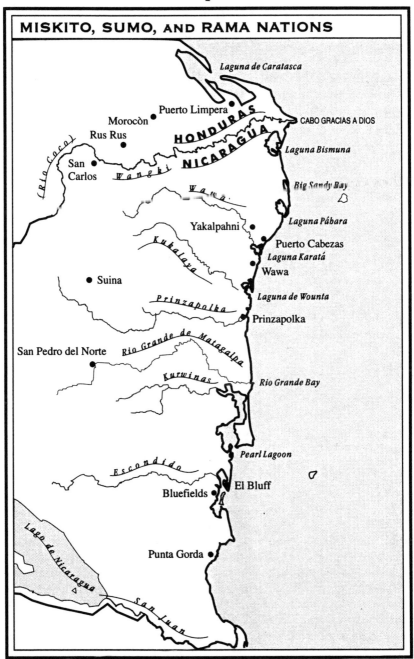

MISKITO, SUMO, AND RAMA NATIONS

Laguna de Caratasca

Puerto Limpera

Morocòn

Rus Rus

CABO GRACIAS A DIOS

HONDURAS

NICARAGUA

San Carlos

Wangki

Laguna Bismuna

Wawa

Big Sandy Bay

Yakalpahni

Laguna Pábara

Kukalaya

Puerto Cabezas

Laguna Karatá

Wawa

Suina

Laguna de Wounta

Prinzapolka

Prinzapolka

San Pedro del Norte

Rio Grande de Matagalpa

Kurwinas

Rio Grande Bay

Escondido

Pearl Lagoon

Bluefields

El Bluff

Lago de Nicaragua

Punta Gorda

San Juan

indigenous societies, characterized by separate languages, the perpetuation of traditional social, cultural, and political practices, and control of a substantial portion of their land base continue to be maintained.[35] Also significant is the strong animosity harbored by the Indians toward the modern descendants of the original Spanish invaders. Many Indians in Miskitia continue to refer derogatorily to Pacific–side Nicaraguans as "Spaniards," reflecting primary cultural and ideological rather than racial differences. A contributing factor is that condescension toward the Indians exists on the Pacific side, producing perceptions and policies which subordinate Indians as "backward" and "primitive," requiring "salvation" through application of "revolutionary principles."[36] The situation is thus similar to that which marks relations between h'Mongs and lowlanders in Laos.

Cultural divergence in Nicaragua is coupled with a geographic separation of the Pacific side from Miskitia. This separation facilitated Spanish/Catholic colonization of the Pacific area, leaving Miskitia more susceptible to the influence of Britain and the United States. Most of the sources of conflict in Miskitia today can be traced to attempts by both the Nicaraguans and the United States to extend hegemony over the sovereign Indian nations of the Atlantic Coast region. The ongoing Indian resistance is, at root, a response to those attempts, a circumstance which again corresponds rather well to the realities of Laos. (For a view of the Atlantic Coast conflict area, *see* Map III.)

The modern Indian movement in Miskitia was embodied initially in the organization ACARIC (Association of Agricultural Cooperatives of the Rio Coco), formed in 1967 to advance demands by Indians along the river for a recognized land base and freedom in agricultural production. In 1973, ACARIC was succeeded by ALPROMISU (**Al**liance **Pro**moting **Mi**skito and **Su**mu Development), which continued and expanded the drive for native self–determination. ALPROMISU joined the emergent international movement of indigenous peoples in an attempt to advance the aspirations of the Indians of Miskitia.[37] Although catalyzed by the Indian elders of the region, the organization was publicly led by a generation of Miskito students studying at the National University in Managua, among them Brooklyn Rivera and Steadman Fagoth Müller (typically referred to as Steadman Fagoth).

Although the Sandinista insurgency of the 1970s, which overthrew the despotic, U.S.–backed Somoza dynasty, was fought almost entirely in Pacific Nicaragua, Atlantic Coast Indian support and participation existed, including that of the ACARIC (and afterwards by ALPROMISU) leadership. After the triumph of the revolution in 1979, the Indian leadership was optimistic that conditions in Miskitia would improve, and that the Sandinistas would promote a truly revolutionary Indian policy which would respect aboriginal land rights, cultural and economic autonomy, and political self–determination.

Within three months of the Sandinista victory, however, the new government informed the ALPROMISU leaders that the Indian organization was

Map III

ATLANTIC COAST CONFLICT AREA OF NICARAGUA, 1980-1989

incongruent with advancement of the revolution. The government believed the Indians should be integrated into the national revolutionary mainstream through mass organizations designed to promote class consciousness, and to minimize the Indians' nationalist disposition.[38] Only after traveling to Miskitia personally in 1981 did Daniel Ortega, director of the revolutionary junta, concede that the effort to disband ALPROMISU was futile. Subsequently, a compromise was reached, whereby the organization would continue, but would be renamed (essentially merely a redesignation rather than an actual merger of the Sandinistas and ALPROMISU) MISURASATA, an acronym for Miskito, Sumu, Rama, and Sandinista Aslatakanka (United). Unfortunately, the enmity created within Miskitia as a consequence of the unilateral Sandinista policy that had been implemented, coupled with U.S. policy designed to destabilize the Managua government by any means available, led to a protracted warfare which continues to some extent even today.

Revolutionary Triumph/Indian Policy Failure

Initially, post–revolutionary relations between the Indians and the Sandinistas were relatively amicable and cooperative. The leadership of ALPROMISU endorsed the revolution and sought to advance indigenous aspirations through revolutionary channels. Within a short time, however, relations began to worsen, commencing a six–year period (1981–1987) which, as even the Sandinistas came to admit, was replete with "excesses and mistakes" on the part of the government. Many of Managua's policies during this time seem almost intended to provoke conflict with native peoples desiring self–determination. Among the more contentious were the following:

* Unilateral decisions to introduce cadres of government workers and foreign (primarily Cuban and Soviet Bloc) advisors and technicians into Miskitia in an effort to "integrate fully Indians into the Sandinista Front" (1979–89).[39]

* Implementation of literacy and medical programs which disregarded or ignored the needs and cultural traditions of the Indians. The regional literacy campaign was begun in Spanish, even though the predominant languages there are native and English (1980–81).

* Unilateral natural resource exploitation policies which denied Indians access to much of their traditional land base and severely restricted their subsistence activities (1979–89).

* The arrest and imprisonment of the entire MISURASATA leadership, and withdrawal of recognition of the organization, which was arguably the only representative indigenous political entity in Miskitia (1981).

* The military occupation, bombing, or deliberate destruction of over half of all Miskito and Sumu villages in the region, and the conscription of Indian youth into the Nicaraguan military (1980–89).

* Forced removal of at least 10,000 Indians from their traditional lands to "relocation centers" in the interior of the country, and destruction of their villages (1982–87).

* Embargoes and blockades against native villages known to support self–determination (1981–89).

* The death, disappearance, or imprisonment of hundreds of Indians attempting to secure an autonomous homeland for their nations (1981–89).

* Unilateral imposition of an "autonomy process" without adequate participation of all Indians affected, and without provisions sufficient to guarantee native self–determination (1985–89).

Each of these elements was present in Vietnamese/Pathet Lao policies vis–à–vis the h'Mong. Implementation of these subordinating "methods" led, directly or indirectly, to two circumstances: 1) escalation of antagonism in Miskitia toward the government, to the point of armed Indian opposition; and 2) a splintering of the Indian movement into at least three factions.

On the first point, animosity between the Indians and the government reached such a level in early 1981 that, on February 22, when the government arrested the MISURASATA leadership, young Indian men and women turned on Sandinista troops in the town of Prinzapolka, beginning the native armed struggle. Counter to the prevailing views of most of the Sandinistas' international supporters, Managua's repression and the consequent emergence of the armed conflict thus began nearly a year before the United States undertook its covert support of the Somocista–led counterrevolution from Honduras.[40]

On the second point, despite the release of most MISURASATA leaders within a few weeks of their arrest in 1981, the MISURASATA representative to the Nicaraguan Council of State, Steadman Fagoth, was detained longer, having been accused of serving as a government agent during the Somoza years. His release from incarceration was conditioned upon an agreement that he spend an extended period studying in Bulgaria. Although Fagoth initially accepted this condition, he fled instead to Honduras and joined the Somocista, lending credence to the Sandinista allegations against him. Brooklyn Rivera, general coordinator of MISURASATA, remained in Nicaragua after his own release, trying to mend the disintegrating relations between the government and the Indians. Rivera immediately condemned Fagoth, and urged international groups to ignore him.[41] Rivera's task of improving relations proved particularly difficult, however, as the Indian villages had become increasingly radicalized by the events of the preceding months. They were unwilling to make further compromises in their talks with Sandinista representatives.[42]

Subsequently, Managua withdrew recognition of MISURASATA, which had been formed with the consensus of 225 native villages throughout Miskitia. The government also made it clear to Rivera that if he did not renounce MISURASATA's self–determination perspective and "join the revolution," his "personal safety in Nicaragua could not be guaranteed." Taking this as a threat to his life, Rivera fled to Honduras. When he arrived there, he quickly discovered how well established Fagoth was with his CIA/Honduran hosts; the coordinator was arrested by the Hondurans, and spent several months in their jails or under house arrest. Finally, apparently by order of the CIA, he was deported to Costa Rica, and was allowed to return to Honduras for the first time in 1987.[43]

Immediately after arriving in Costa Rica, Rivera established a brief alliance with Eden Pastora, the former Sandinista commander and leader of the Alianza Revolucionaria Democrática (ARDE).[44] MISURASATA received a minimal amount of material support, presumably through the CIA's indirect conduits, but the alliance soon failed when Rivera refused to cooperate with the Agency. His consistent refusal to allow the CIA to dictate any of the terms of MISURASATA's resistance was to lead to serious and chronic material shortages for his movement throughout the period of armed struggle.[45]

With the primary leaders of MISURASATA, Rivera and Fagoth, out of the country, the Sandinistas changed their tactics and began to negotiate land agreements with individual Indian communities. Eventually, Managua realized the futility of such an approach when applied to fiercely communitarian peoples who informed the government that land agreements could be reached only by all villages acting together.[46] Therefore, in 1985, the Sandinistas resorted to creating their own sanctioned "Indian" organization, known as MISUTAN. For obvious reasons, this new entity was met with almost universal suspicion among Indians and ultimately established itself in only a few villages.

Despite the exodus of over 20,000 Miskitos, Sumus, and Ramas from Miskitia by 1987, Managua opted to move forward with its own design for "regional autonomy" in Miskitia. The Sandinista plan was touted by supporters of the government as "the most progressive Indian policy in the hemisphere."[47] It was also viewed as an indication that the Sandinistas had realized their past "errors" and were willing to make concessions to the Indians as proof. The plan, however, was all along wracked by non–cooperation and discord in the villages. A major reason for native skepticism was that, at base, the proposal simply advanced the Sandinista philosophy that all key decisions concerning Miskitia would "necessarily" fall under the purview of the central government in Managua. The powers left to Indian villages under the plan amounted to no more than administrative and consultative functions. According to the eventual "Autonomy Statute," unveiled on April 22, 1987, no original jurisdiction was vested in the Indians, other than with regard to the most rudimentary bureaucratic details.[48]

Issues such as territorial land rights remained unaddressed. Control of the military and police continued to be held exclusively by the central government. Decisions concerning natural resource exploitation within the "national economic strategy" were left entirely in the hands of Managua. Under the government's plan, autonomy remained explicitly "regional" (rather than national), leaving serious doubts as to whether the Indians would be able to retain control over their traditional lands if latino immigrants, who then outnumbered Indians on a regional basis, were allowed to exercise equal political participation. In sum, Managua's autonomy plan was little different in principle from Vietnamese centrist ideology, or the 1934 Indian Reorganization Act, used by the U.S. government to politically subordinate indigenous nations within its borders.

Indicative of the fact that this Sandinista posture was not the outcome of mere "confusion," in May of 1987, MISURASATA released its own autonomy proposal, in addition to a draft treaty of peace between the Indian nations and

Nicaragua. The MISURASATA plan called for significantly more control by native governments, and a cooperative system of decision making with the central government on issues such as military defense and resource development. The government refused even to respond to the MISURASATA initiative.[49]

Enter the CIA

The CIA is no stranger to Miskitia. In 1961, the town of Puerto Cabezas was used by the Agency to launch the ill–fated Bay of Pigs assault on Cuba. CIA policy in Latin America suggests that it is neither timid nor particularly secretive in its operations in the area, especially as regards Nicaragua.

In the case of the indigenous struggle in Miskitia, the CIA has been interested in manipulating Indian discontent, in much the same fashion as it used the h'Mong as surrogates against Hanoi, to serve its ends in countering and destroying *Sandinismo*. As Brooklyn Rivera has stated, "The CIA cowboys want us to be their little Indians."[50] The first motion in this direction came with the grooming of MISURASATA defector Steadman Fagoth in mid–1981. The conditions of support from the Agency to Fagoth were clear: his charisma as a Miskito leader, and as a member of the Nicaraguan Democratic Front (FDN, more commonly known as the "contras"), was to be utilized to open a military front in Miskitia with the ultimate goal of toppling the Sandinista government.

From 1982 through 1984, the CIA armed and maintained Fagoth as the sole Indian leader who was trusted to do the Agency's bidding. Correspondingly, he was the only indigenous leader with access to the CIA station in Honduras. During this period, military activity along the Rio Coco increased, as did reports of human rights abuses by both the Indian contras and Sandinista troops.[51] Accounts circulated about the egomaniacal Fagoth killing anyone who opposed him, and mistreating his own personnel. In late 1984, Fagoth showed two U.S. Senate investigators a "hit list" of 12 native leaders he planned to assassinate. He claimed to have killed five already, a matter he never recanted.[52] Fagoth also publicly condemned Rivera for negotiating with the Sandinistas in 1984, and threatened to kill him and anyone else who parlayed with Managua. By the end of the year, such bravado had led to his removal from leadership of the organization, MISURA (MISURASATA without the Sandinistas), that he had established. He was then exiled to Miami.

As a result, in September 1985, the CIA created a new Indian contra organization known as KISAN (an acronym derived from the Spanish for "Nicaraguan Coast Unity"), to be led by Wycliffe Diego, a protégé of Fagoth.[53] The CIA's control of KISAN was complete and deliberate. Diego was on the Agency payroll, and no leaders of MISURASATA—especially Brooklyn Rivera—were allowed into Honduras to challenge his authority. Nonetheless, KISAN showed signs of failure from the outset, a situation originating in the CIA's ethnocentric inability to perceive that native unity was/is predicated in consensus and internal cultural integrity. The inevitable disintegration of KISAN occurred in 1986, with an appreciable segment of its troops spontaneously resurrecting MISURA (without Fagoth), and other groups beginning individual cease–fire negotiations with the Sandinistas.[54]

With their organization deserting before their eyes, the remaining KISAN leaders resorted to strong–arm tactics to maintain themselves, invading refugee camps, kidnapping Indian teenagers, and forcing them into service.[55] Such methods caused some Indians to return to Nicaragua to take their chances with the Sandinista policy, rather than face the abuse of their brethren in the squalor of the camps.[56] There is an obvious irony in the fact that it was exactly the same approach by the Pathet Lao that so greatly exacerbated tensions between them and the h'Mong.

In 1987, with the looming demise of KISAN, the CIA's operatives in Honduras, in cooperation with Colonel Eric Sanchez of the Honduran Fifth Battalion Headquarters, near Morocón, invented yet a third Indian contra group, FAUCAN (derived from the Spanish for "United Armed Forces of the Atlantic Coast"). Their plan was again to bring the Indians under the unambiguous control of the CIA and Honduran military, and to insure they followed the Agency's strategy in Miskitia, subsuming their own nationalist aspirations to a "greater good."[57] Support for FAUCAN was even less than that evidenced for KISAN in its final days, with front–line troops refusing to fight for an organization without an Indian agenda. Even the former MISURA and KISAN leaders failed to support FAUCAN. One native fighter put it succinctly: "We left Nicaragua because the Sandinistas didn't want us. Now we see the gringos, who are supposed to be our allies, don't really care about us either ... [O]ur interests are small compared to theirs. It seems as though they just want to use us."[58] The CIA's failures in Miskitia, including that of FAUCAN, attracted international attention in mid–1987.[59] This resulted in the United States making two immediate changes with respect to the Indians: First, four of the five CIA agents working in Miskitia were reassigned to other stations, and, second, the State Department assumed control over policy in this connection. But it was by then too late to salvage the Indian contra effort.[60]

One upshot of the State Department's attempt to recoup the situation was a relaxation of the barriers preventing certain Indian leaders from entering Honduras for the first time in seven years. Consequently, from June 9–14, 1987, a regional gathering of all native factions (except MISUTAN) was convened in the village of Rus Rus.[61] The outcome was a new, unified, indigenous organization called YATAMA, committed to pursuit of native self–determination in its own right. Brooklyn Rivera emerged as de facto head of this reconfiguration, despite strong U.S. support for the idea of a return of Steadman Fagoth. Rivera still unequivocally rejected subordination to U.S. authority:

> Believe me that we have been and still spend much of our time, our
> energy, our resources, fighting against or defending ourselves

against the Contras and CIA actions against [our] organization. They have been using their influence, their funds, to divide the Indian people and to use our struggle for their own interests. They have been creating artificial organizations. They have been inventing leaders. They have even attempted to kill the MISURASATA leadership. The damage that the Contras and the CIA have effected against the Indian people, against the resistance of our people, is clear.[62]

On the other hand, he maintained his position of equally unequivocal rejection of subordination to the authority of the Sandinistas:

One thing is certain: Our people will continue their struggle, no matter the circumstances. We *will* continue. Many of our young people have given their lives for our people; they have sacrificed themselves. We will continue because that is the mandate of our elders, that the young people should continue to struggle until they have liberated our land, and we can live there peacefully. Our people have a long history of struggle and resistance, and we do not trust those who attack us. So, apparently we will be forced to continue our struggle for a very long time.[63]

Conclusion

Although the 1989 general election in Nicaragua averted such an outcome by unseating the Sandinista regime, it remained possible until that point that a prolonged war of attrition might have reduced the independent Indian fighters to a h'Mong–like dependence upon the CIA or other foreign agencies for their very survival. In that event, the contra war against Managua would have been bolstered substantially, and might have succeeded militarily. While it is not difficult to discern why the United States might have welcomed such an eventuality, the riddle of why the Sandinistas would allow themselves to follow the failed example of Vietnamese policy in this regard is much more elusive. The danger such a course posed to them seems plain enough, at least in retrospect.

The solution to this seeming paradox resides perhaps most squarely within the realm of theory. Although the Sandinista National Liberation Front (FSLN) purported to be "marxist–leninist" in orientation, as did the Vietnamese and Pathet Lao revolutionaries before them, the ideologies of all three groups diverged substantially from Lenin's own writings. Concerning the so–called national question—the marxian term encompassing the self–determining aspirations of all "marginal" peoples such as the h'Mong, Miskito, Sumu, and Rama Nations—both the Vietnamese and Sandinista prescriptions appear, in simplest form, to be that all "minorities" have not only the right, but indeed an *obligation* to pursue sovereignty so long as they are colonized by a "reactionary state." The best route to this end, it is claimed, is for indigenous nations to join forces with "progressive sectors" within the colonizing society itself, in order to destroy the existing order. Once encapsulated within a post–revolutionary "progressive state," however, such rights mysteriously disappear; indigenous people are then duty–bound to integrate themselves into the society of their "former" colonizers. The formulation at issue comes, not from Lenin, but from Joseph Stalin,[64] and finds its clearest reflection—albeit with reversed priorities—in the ideology of contemporary corporate capitalism. In either its capitalist or stalinist variants, when put into practice, such an outlook has been shown to yield an inevitably genocidal impact upon indigenous peoples.[65]

Confronted with the specter of their own extinction as peoples—a prospect patently bound up in their forced incorporation into some "broader" or "dominant" society—indigenous nations have no real alternative but to engage in the most desperate sorts of resistance, seeking succor and assistance (real, or only apparent) from whence it may come. The breadth and scale of this phenomenon today may be illustrated not only in the examples of the h'Mong, Sumu, Miskito, and Rama, but by the vast proliferation of similarly motivated conflicts described by Bernard Nietschmann in his article on the topic, published in *Cultural Survival Quarterly*.[66]

In contrast to the stalinist practice and perspective adopted by both the Sandinistas and Vietnamese communists, Lenin was *very* outspoken in his view that full rights of self–determination apply to peoples and nations in situations exactly like the h'Mong and the Indians of Miskitia (for example, the various "ethnicities" indigenous to the territory claimed by the Union of Soviet Socialist Republics). On this theme, Lenin wrote:

> Victorious socialism must necessarily establish a full democracy and consequently, not only introduce full equality of nations, but also realize the right of oppressed nations to self–determination, i.e., the right to free political separation. Socialist parties which did not show by all their activities, both now, during the revolution, and after its victory, that they would liberate the enslaved nations and build up relations with them on the basis of free union—and free union is false without the right to secede—these parties would be betraying socialism.[67]

He continues in this vein:

> The recognition of the right to secession for all; the appraisal of each concrete question of secession from the point of view of removing all inequality, all privileges, and all exclusiveness ... [L]et us consider the position of an oppressor nation. Can an oppressor nation be free if it oppresses other nations? It cannot.[68]

Until self–proclaimed marxist–leninist revolutionaries match their practice to such principles, their brand of "progressivism" will *not* be preferable to the capitalist order they seek to replace, at least insofar as the rights of indigenous peoples are concerned. To the contrary, their avowed "humane alternative" will simply represent a *continuation* of the process of destruction of indigenous societies ushered in by early capitalism, the "same old song" so aptly described by American Indian Movement leader Russell Means in a 1980 speech.[69] One need look no further than this to discover how it is that native peoples are presently trapped between the "rock" of right–wing reaction and the "hard place" of left–wing revolution.

In the interim, indigenous peoples have no choice but to continue to defend themselves, their sovereignty, and their cultural integrity, against the forces of both the right and the left. Toward that goal, they must continue to exercise the right of nations, forging alliances—including those which are temporary, desperate, or merely forced by expedience—in whatever way represents the least immediate threat to their existence.

Notes

1. This has been a guiding principle of the U.S. Army's John F. Kennedy Special Warfare School at Fort Bragg, North Carolina, since its inception.

2. Noam Chomsky and Edward S. Herman, *After the Cataclysm: Postwar Indochina and the Reconstruction of Imperial Ideology, The Political Economy of Human Rights, Vol. II* (Boston: South End Press 1979), p. 25.

3. Nina S. Adams, "Patrons, Clients, and Revolutionaries: The Laotian Search for Independence, 1945–1954," in *Laos: War and Revolution*, Nina S. Adams and Alfred W. McCoy, eds. (New York: Harper and Row, 1970), p. 363.

4. Noam Chomsky, "The Wider War," in his *For Reasons of State* (New York: Vintage Books, 1973), p. 180.

5. Guy Morechand, "The Many Languages and Cultures of Laos," in *Laos: War and Revolution*, op. cit., p. 32.

6. Richard S. D. Hawkins, "Contours, Cultures, and Conflict," in *Laos: War and Revolution*, op. cit., p. 6.

7. Guy Morechand, op. cit., p. 32.

8. Alfred W. McCoy, "French Colonialism in Laos: 1883–1945," in *Laos: War and Revolution*, op. cit., p. 77.

9. Ibid., p. 98.

10. Nina S. Adams, op. cit., p. 110.

11. Ibid., pp. 118–19.

12. Ibid., pp. 119–20.

13. *Laos: War and Revolution* (op. cit.) offer maps at pp. 210–11 which graphically demonstrate the correspondence of Pathet Lao basing areas and traditional h'Mong territories.

14. Nina S. Adams, op. cit., p. 117.

15. First Resistance Congress, "Statement of the First Resistance Congress: Tuyen Quang, Vietnam," in *Laos: War and Revolution*, op. cit., p. 116.

16. Walter Haney, "The Pentagon Papers and the United States' Involvement in Laos," in *The Pentagon Papers, Senator Gravel Edition: Vol. 5, Critical Essays*, Noam Chomsky and Howard Zinn, eds. (Boston: Beacon Press, 1972), p. 221.

17. D. Gareth Porter, "After Geneva: Subverting Laotian Neutrality," in *Laos: War and Revolution*, op. cit., p. 183.

18. Len P. Ackland, "No Place for Neutralism: The Eisenhower Administration and Laos," in *Laos: War and Revolution*, op. cit., pp. 142–43.

19. Ibid., pp. 146–47.

20. Jonathan Mirsky and Stephen E. Stoefield, "The Nam Crisis: Kennedy and the New Frontier on the Brink," in *Laos: War and Revolution*, op. cit., pp. 208–09.

21. D. Gareth Porter, op. cit., pp. 182–83.

22. Ibid., p. 183.

23. Ibid., pp. 183–84.

24. Bernard Fall, *Anatomy of a Crisis* (New York: Doubleday, 1967), p. 225.

25. Fred Branfman, "Presidential War in Laos," in *Laos: War and Revolution*, op. cit., p. 252.

26. Ibid., p. 232.

27. Ron Shaplen, *Time Out of Hand* (New York: Harper and Row Publishers, 1969), p. 348.

28. Fred Branfman, op. cit., p. 251; Guy Morechand, op. cit., p. 33.

29. Thomas Powers, *The Man Who Kept Secrets: Richard Helms and the CIA* (New York: Pocket Books, 1979), p. 226.

30. Fred Branfman, op. cit., p. 252.

31. Wendy Walker and David Moffat, "Hmong Children: A Changing World in Ban Vinai," *Cultural Survival Quarterly*, Vol. 10, No. 4 (Fall 1986).

32. Noam Chomsky and Edward S. Herman, op. cit., p. 125. The authors attribute the information to reactionary *New York Times* columnist Henry Kamm, but do not contest its accuracy. Strangely, for individuals holding well–deserved credentials as human rights advocates, the authors seem concerned in this instance only with whether the h'Mong might be receiving U.S. assistance, not with the legitimacy of people defending their own territories against external aggression. Indigenous peoples seem increasingly trapped between such left/right polarities, with scarcely a thought given to their needs, rights, or any agendas extending outside the parameters of the left/right paradigm.

33. Wendy Walker and David Moffat, op. cit., p. 54.

34. "Miskitia" is a generic term referring to the traditional territories of the Miskito, Sumu, and Rama Indian Nations in the Atlantic Coast region of contemporary Nicaragua and Honduras. Although the Wangki River (Rio Coco) was used by the World Court in 1960 to delineate the boundary between Nicaragua and Honduras, the Indians have consistently

ignored the boundary which bisects their traditional lands. The historical indigenous boundaries of Miskitia run roughly from just south of Puerto Limpera, Honduras, south to Punta Gorda, Nicaragua, and from the Continental Shelf in the Atlantic Ocean westward to the Nicaraguan communities of Siuna and Yakalpahni. Unless otherwise indicated, however, "Miskitia" (or referred by some as "Mosquitia") in this essay refers exclusively to the portion of Indian territory lying within Nicaragua.

35. K. Ohland and R. Schneider, *National Revolution and Indigenous Identity* (Copenhagen: IWGIA Document 47, 1983), p. 9.

36. Ibid., pp. 18, 160.

37. According to the *Draft Declaration of Principles for Indigenous Rights,* presented to the United Nations Working Group on Indigenous Populations, indigenous peoples have, among others, the following rights: A) The right to self–determination, including the right to whatever degree of autonomy or self–government they choose; B) Permanent control over their aboriginal, ancestral historical territories; C) Freedom from the imposition of jurisdiction over them by any State, except through their free, informed consent; and D) The right of self–defense against State actions which conflict with their right to self–determination. *See* K. Ohland and R. Schneider, op. cit., pp. 294–98.

38. *Trabil Nani (Many Troubles): Historical Background of the Current Situation on the Atlantic Coast of Nicaragua* (Managua: Center for Research and Documentation of the Atlantic Coast, 1984), pp. 16–18.

39. K. Ohland and R. Schneider, op. cit., p. 160.

40. Martin Diskin, Thomas Bossert, Salomon Nahmad, and Stefano Varese, "Peace and Autonomy on the Atlantic Coast of Nicaragua: A Report of the LASA Task Force on Human Rights and Academic Freedom, Part I," *Latin American Studies Association Forum,* Vol. 16, No. 14, p. 11.

41. Centro de Investigaciones y Documentacion de la Costa Atlantica, Managua (CIDCA), p. 24.

42. K. Ohland and R. Schneider, op. cit., p. 21.

43. Clem Chartier, *An Interview with Brooklyn Rivera* (Ottawa: World Council of Indigenous Peoples, 1987), p. xvi.

44. Theodore MacDonald, Jr., "Miskito Refugees in Costa Rica," *Cultural Survival Quarterly,* Vol. 8, No. 3 (Fall 1984), pp. 59–60.

45. Frederick Kempe and Clifford Krause, "U.S. Policy on Indians in Nicaragua Damages Anti–Sandinista Effort," *Wall Street Journal* (2 Mar. 1987), pp. 1, 13.

46. K. Ohland and R. Schneider, op. cit., p. 22.

47. For example: Vernon Bellecourt (representing the International Indian Treaty Council), interview on radio station KGNU, Boulder, Colorado, 4 Feb. 1986 (tape on file).

48. Government of National Reconstruction of the Republic of Nicaragua—Commission on Autonomy, *Preliminary Draft of the Law on the Autonomous Region of the Atlantic Coast,* Puerto Cabezas, Nicaragua (draft document circulated for review), 22 Apr. 1987.

49. MISURASATA, "Proposal of MISURASATA for Autonomy and a Treaty of Peace Between the Republic of Nicaragua and the Indian Nations of Yapti Tasba," *Akwesasne Notes,* Vol. 19, No. 3 (Late Spring 1987), pp. 18–19.

50. Quoted in Frederick Kempe and Clifford Krause, op. cit., p. 1.

51. Americas Watch, *The Miskitos in Nicaragua* (New York: Americas Watch Publications, 1984), and *With the Miskitos* (New York: Americas Watch Publications, 1986); Amnesty International, *Nicaragua: The Human Rights Record* (London: Amnesty International, 1986).

52. Ibid., p. 13.

53. S. James Anaya, *The CIA with the Honduran Army in Mosquitia: Taking Freedom out of the Fight in the Name of Accountability* (Albuquerque: Report of the National Indian Youth Council, 1987), p. 14.

54. Clifford Krause, "Sandinistas Promote Peace with the Indians on Rebel–Held Coast," *Wall Street Journal* (6 Mar. 1986), p. 1.

55. James LeMoyne, "U.S. Hopes Miskito Indian Parley Will Bolster Fight Against Sandinistas," *New York Times* (7 June 1987), p. 12.

56. Stephen Kinzer, "Nicaraguan Indians Are Back Home," *New York Times* (15 Apr. 1987), p. 3; S. James Anaya, op. cit., pp. 28–29.

57. S. James Anaya, Ibid.

58. S. James Anaya, Ibid., p. 20.

59. Editor, "Miskito Mistreatment," *Boston Globe* (15 June 1987); Frederick Kempe and Clifford Krause, op. cit.; S. James Anaya, op. cit.

60. Because of Rivera's adamant refusal to take orders from the CIA, MISURASATA had been denied any financial or military assistance in its resistance to Sandinista rule. Even after Congress specifically allocated $5 million for the organization in 1986, the funds were withheld because they were administered by the CIA, which sought to use them as a lever to bring Rivera "into the fold." By 1987, the degree of mistrust this had engendered among MISURASATA adherents as a whole was insurmountable.

61. James LeMoyne, op. cit.

62. Clem Chartier, op. cit., p. xxvii.

63. Glenn T. Morris, interview with Brooklyn Rivera, San Juan, Costa Rica, 5 Nov. 1985 (tape on file).

64. Joseph Stalin, "Marxism and the National Question," in *Selections from V. I. Lenin and J. V. Stalin on the National Question* (Calcutta: Calcutta House Books, 1975), pp. 66–106.

65. *See* Ward Churchill, "Genocide: Toward a Functional Definition," originally published in *Alternatives*, No. 11 (July 1986), pp. 418–26, and included in this book.

66. Bernard Nietschmann, "The Third World War: Militarization and Indigenous Peoples," *Cultural Survival Quarterly*, Vol. 11, No. 3 (Fall 1987), pp. 1–16. The author demonstrates that fully 85 percent of the more than 130 armed conflicts he catalogues as occurring in the world are between indigenous peoples seeking self–determination and assorted nation–states seeking to dominate them.

67. V. I. Lenin, *The Right of Nations to Self–Determination* (Moscow: Progress Publishers, 1974), p. 98.

68. Ibid.

69. Russell Means, "The Same Old Song," in *Marxism and Native Americans*, Ward Churchill, ed. (Boston: South End Press, 1983), p. 27.

On Support of the Indian Resistance in Nicaragua

A Statement of Position and Principle*

There appears of late to be considerable confusion in progressive circles concerning both the dynamics of the Atlantic Coast situation in Nicaragua and the nature, meaning, and implications of my own position on the matter of indigenous (American Indian) rights there vis-à-vis the interests of Nicaragua's revolutionary state. "Concern," some of it undoubtedly as sincere as it is misguided, has recently been expressed that I have "come out in support of Reagan's Central America policy," have "joined the Moonies," and/or "gone to work for the CIA." In less well–intentioned quarters, a veritable cottage industry has grown up in Colorado, busily "forgiving" me for having been a "Green Beret" (which I never was nor claimed to be), "a writer for *Soldier of Fortune* magazine" (ditto), and so on. Such clumsy attempts at discreditation would be laughable were it not that the larger issues involved are quite important.

In substantial part, it seems to me, such confusion is self–induced, resulting mainly from a staunch refusal of much of the left to seriously discuss, or even consider, circumstances on the Atlantic Coast. Rather, the measure of political correctitude on the left has increasingly come to be the extent of one's willingness to reduce the great complexity of the multilateral nationalist struggle occurring in Nicaragua to a simplistically convenient "us versus them" dichotomy. Hence, the Miskito, Sumu, and Rama Indian resistance organiza-

* This essay originally appeared in *Akwesasne Notes,* Vol. 18, No. 5 (Autumn 1986).

tions of the Atlantic Coast, such as MISURASATA, which reject the limitations to their self–determination offered by Managua are—without further ado, and despite the Sandinista government's own protestations to the contrary—consigned to the handy bracket of "Reagan–backed contras." Likewise, those like me, who have attempted to articulate the Indians' agenda in its own right, pointing out the fallacies of conventional left "wisdom" in this regard, and insisting that indigenous rights are more than a matter of situation ethics, have been automatically dubbed "counter–revolutionary."

One of the primary methods by which the latter impression has been created is through the "appointment," by the left, of a single "spokesman" in the person of Russell Means to "represent" all those advocating a radical alternative to the present Sandinista Atlantic Coast autonomy plan. In this way, each utterance or association undertaken by Means may be attributed to a whole range of individuals, myself included, who disagree—often quite strongly—with specific aspects of his overall posture. This remains true although many of us have publicly agreed, and continue to agree, with the major thrust of his that Atlantic Coast Indians have the inherent right to sovereignty.

An important point must be made with regard to Russell Means before I continue: In saying I sharply disagree with his view that "the enemies of my enemies are my friends" (e.g., his recent willingness to appear on Moonie platforms), I do *not* imply a severing of relations or denouncement of him. What I *do* mean is that he walks his road while I walk mine. And, while these roads often run parallel, they are different. I thus categorically reject the left's present polemical effort to make them synonymous. For me, the ability to disagree on particulars while working together towards a broader goal is the essence of alliance *and* the practice of the old adage about trusting your brother's vision.

Further, Means' record of standing for native rights—having been repeatedly shot, stabbed, beaten and jailed as a result, and *still* refusing to back down—is far too strong to be questioned by those whose interest in such matters has come lately and often from convenience. I will leave it to those whose service to Indians has been restricted to tongue–wagging to engage in silly games of denunciation. When they refer to Russell Means as a "defector," I can only reply that they themselves must be defec*tive*.

In any event, I appreciate the opportunity to clarify not only my own position regarding Indian rights in Nicaragua, but the basic principles underlying this position. To begin with the principles first:

- *I am indigenist.* Although the perspective of indigenism is considerably deeper and more complicated, it will suffice for the moment to note that I take as my analytical starting point in any consideration of the National Question the *absolute* right of indigenous peoples to exercise national sovereignty. In my view, no nation–state, whether capitalist or socialist, holds the intrinsic right to extend its sovereignty over an indigenous nationality. To exert such politico–economic hegemony is, by my definition, imperialist. I reject Marx' and Engels' notion that colonization is a positive development for "retarded" societies (e.g., German colonization of the Czechs being something "good" for the latter). Of course, this outlook leads me into immediate conflict with the Soviet (stalinist) conception of the rights of succession and the "progressive" resolution to the "Belgian Thesis" on decolonization which occurred via United Nation Resolution 1541 during the 1960s. I do not accept the idea that forced incorporation of an indigenous nation into a socialist state is particularly preferable to its forced incorporation into a capitalist state. Nor do I accept the socialist practice of attempting to define indigenous nations out of existence, any more than I accept such practices under capitalism.

* *I am anti–imperialist.* As I have stated repeatedly, I oppose assertions that the United States has a "right" to meddle in the affairs of Nicaragua. In the event of a U.S. invasion of Nicaragua, I would therefore be prepared to fight at the side of the Sandinistas in repelling such aggression. The North American shark has no right whatsoever to swallow the Nicaraguan fish. By the same token, the Nicaraguan fish has no valid prerogative to swallow the smaller Indian fish, and I will fight with the Indians against the Sandinistas in the event the latter persist in their contention that Atlantic Coast Indian territory is "theirs." Such a position is entirely consistent with my oft expressed belief that the indigenous nations of North America are entitled to a separate, autonomous, and sovereign existence apart from the United States and Canada.

* *I am socialist.* I offer this, not as a subscription to marxian principles of centralized government and planning, but as an affirmation of my belief in the viability of the "primitive communism"—I accept "primitive" here in its original meaning, "that which is first"—of indigenous peoples. By my estimation, the collectivism of traditional indigenous societies, the spiritual relationality (dialectics) of their worldviews, their accompanying ecologism and political egalitarianism are essential signposts necessary for the establishment of a new, just, and humane world order. I see indigenous nations, as discrete and ongoing entities, having a crucial role to play in informing the construction of revolutionary non–indigenous societies. Their compulsory dissolution in the name of a "progress" and "development" which has already proven itself worse than barren would be (and is) the height of contradiction.

From these three fundamental principles, certain pragmatic factors of my political stance should be evident. For instance, far from supporting Reagan's Central America policy or any other manifestation of U.S. imperialism, I heartily condemn it and continue to work against such things (as I have for 20 years now). This places among those I count as my enemies not only the CIA and its related functionaries both overt and covert, but the religious right of both the Moonie and "moral majority" persuasions, transnational corporations, and the U.S. military. I have no common ground with any of these. And, for the same reasons, I oppose those segments of the sectarian left which—maliciously or unthinkingly—adopt philosophies, outlooks, and policies which foreclose the rights and potentials of indigenous peoples.

This leads me directly to the example of Nicaragua and the question of why my critical energies have lately been expended in this connection rather than in opposition to Indian policies in, say, Guatemala. The query itself sets up a straw man, presuming as it does that preoccupation with native rights in one place implies unconcern about or even support of these rights being suppressed in another. The fact is that I've had a considerable amount to say in defense of the Maya of Guatemala over the years, and I will continue to support them, just as I support the indigenous in *any* conflict with *any* overweening state. The imagined distinction is therefore a false one.

It is also usually a ruse employed to divert attention from the real issue at hand. The issue is this: Within the entire Western Hemisphere, *only* Nicaragua presently offers the possibility of an acceptable resolution to the National Question for indigenous people. *Only* in Nicaragua is there a revolution in flux which can be made to formally recognize the fundamental national rights of native peoples encapsulated within colonially demarcated borders. *Only* in Nicaragua is it currently possible to establish the benchmark for indigenous rights which can serve to guide future revolutionary struggles the world over. *Only* in Nicaragua, right now, before things are "set in stone," can Indian people win their *real* fight, a struggle which is, after all, something more than an effort to achieve individual survival. No one in their right mind would contend that a comparable potential now exists in Guatemala or anywhere else in the Americas.

At base, it is my sincere belief that if the Indians of Nicaragua lose— whether by being finally subordinated to a marxian variation of colonialism's "greater good" or by being subverted by left–wing intransigence into the waiting arms of the CIA—the Sandinista revolution and the rest of us will have lost as well. My position on Indian rights in Nicaragua is thus one of hope and optimism, of perceiving that this revolution can succeed where all others have failed. I am doing my best—often in ways which perhaps seem utterly perverse to the more orthodox or doctrinaire–minded—to help this possibility become a reality. The outcome is too important to indigenous people and, I think, the world as a whole to accept positions which are polite, comfortable, and complacent.

Ironically, I see the left in North America, in its rush to trivialize, distort, and negate the legitimacy of the Indian autonomy issue in Nicaragua, as doing far more to destabilize and destroy the promise of the Sandinista revolution— and therefore to play into the hands of Ronald Reagan, George Schultz, and

Elliott Abrams—than anything I, Russell Means, or anyone else supporting MISURASATA could ever do. In foreclosing upon this genuine potential of Nicaragua, the left forecloses upon itself.

The Meaning of Chiapas

A North American Indigenist View*

> When the EZLN was only a shadow, creeping through the mist and
> darkness of the jungle, when the words "justice," "liberty," and
> "democracy" were only that: words; barely a dream that the elders of
> our communities, true guardians of the words of our dead ancestors, had
> given us in the moment when day gives way to night, when hate and
> fear began to grow in our hearts, when there was nothing but
> desperation; when the times repeated themselves, with no way out, with
> no door, no tomorrow, when all was injustice, as it was, the true
> [people] spoke, the faceless ones, the ones who go by night, the ones
> who are in the jungle.
>
> *EZLN Communiqué, February 26, 1994*

I have been asked to address a few remarks to the meaning of the recent armed
insurrection of the *Ejercito Zapatista Liberación Nacionale* (Zapatista National
Liberation Army: EZLN, or "Zapatistas," as they are popularly known) in
Chiapas Province, Mexico. I am happy to do so because the Chiapas revolt is
something I take to hold a genuinely profound significance. Before beginning,
however, I think it's important to note that I possess no special knowledge of
or relationship to the Zapatistas. The same holds true with regard to the
so–called Lancandon Maya communities—actually, five distinct groups which
are often erroneously lumped together under this rubric: Tzotzils in the highlands, Tzeltales and Tojolabales at lower elevations, and Chols and Choltis
down in the flatlands—from where the Zapatista fighters come.[1]

---

* This essay was first published in *Dark Night Field Notes*, Nos. 3–4 (Winter–Spring
1995).

My basis for speaking on the matter at all derives, I suppose, from my having spent the past dozen or so years involved in articulating essentially the same *indigenista* politics by which the EZLN professes itself to be guided; that, along with the fact that I have been a participant in the overall struggle, including some aspects of the armed struggle, to realize these politics on behalf of indigenous peoples the world over. So it's from a fairly general perspective of commonality, affinity, and solidarity, not from a position of directly shared experience or "insider" status, that I'll try to contextualize the situation in Chiapas to some extent. I think it's both appropriate and necessary to do this because what is happening in southern Mexico is by no means an isolated phenomenon. To the contrary, I see it as part of a far broader process which has in many ways come to redefine the socio–political and economic landscape over the years ahead.

With that said, maybe the place to start is with the observation that the Zapatistas have clearly endeavored to place themselves within the whole sweep of American Indian resistance to colonial domination which has been ongoing without real interruption since the first conquistador set foot in this hemisphere more than 500 years ago.[2] There are many ways of apprehending the intent of the EZLN to make this linkage, but, most obviously, it is signified in the organization's choice to identify itself with the name and spirit of Emiliano Zapata, undoubtedly the revolutionary figure in Mexico who is most closely associated with the historical assertion of native rights in that country. As the matter has been put elsewhere, "In the storehouse of Mexico's political heroes, Zapata becomes for [Indians] the nationalist hero of indigenous rights, a kind of post–revolutionary 'saint', a de Las Casas of this century, with a gun."[3]

For those who don't know, and I suspect there are some who don't, Zapata was himself an Indian—a Zapoteca, if I remember correctly—from Morelos Province west of Mexico City. During the Mexican Revolution of 1910–1917, he forged a powerful army composed mainly of other Indians and played a crucial role in bringing the rebels to power. All the while, his position, which he advanced quite strongly, was that in post–revolutionary Mexico the rights to land and political liberty of Indians should be accorded the same dignity and respect as those of any other social or economic sector of the population. For this, he was assassinated in the victorious aftermath of the Partido Revolucionario Institucional (PRI), the revolutionary front of which Zapata was a part, by his ostensible comrades–in–arms—the PRI's non–Indian leadership—because his notion that Indians possess such fundamental rights did not fit into their plans to "modernize" the Mexican state.[4]

Insofar as the PRI turned out to be just as bad a previous regimes, and in some ways even worse in terms of Indian interests, Zapata's unflinching stance on behalf of his people, and the fate he suffered as a result, converted him into something of an icon among those who feel that Indians have been and continue to be wronged by Mexico's post–revolutionary governments.[5] It is therefore both natural and appropriate that the EZLN seized upon the image of Zapata as its primary means of projecting itself to the broader public. One might even describe their usurpation of Zapata's legacy, whether real or imagined, as a media coup of the first order.

I would argue, however, that bound up in the insurgents' rhetoric of self–characterization is something which goes well beyond the embrace of a given moment, personality, or impulse of twentieth–century Mexican revolutionary politics, no matter how important these may have been—or continue to be—in their own right. It is centered first and foremost, I think, in the desire of the Zapatistas to reclaim their own tradition, that of the Maya—virtually the entire composition of the EZLN is Mayan, after all—from the systematic misrepresentation and negation it has suffered at the hands of eurocentric scholarship and other forms of colonialist propaganda. The point probably sounds much too abstract when framed this way, so let me break it down a bit.

As many are perhaps aware, the Maya are typically presented by "conventional" anthropology and historiography as being "naturally placid," even "docile."[6] If, by this, it means that they were/are simply a peaceful people, or an amalgam of peoples, the description would be rather stupid and derogatory, but nonetheless accurate to a considerable degree. What is meant to be conveyed in the depiction, however, is nothing so backhandedly positive. Instead, what is fostered is the idea that the Maya are basically unwilling or unable to defend themselves against whatever ravages the dominant society may wish to inflict upon them, that they are by individual temperament and cultural disposition malleable, abusable, exploitable, and ultimately expendable whenever their colonizers deem it expedient—usually for reasons of profitability—to liquidate them in whole or in part.[7]

There is of course a code imbedded in this supposedly "balanced, objective, and scientific" portrayal of the Maya, the crux of which is that being Mayan equates to being little more than a "natural victim" of the colonizers who have overrun or who are even now overrunning them, obliterating the Mayan way of life for their own purposes, appropriating all that rightly belongs to the Mayas for their own benefit, killing to suit their fancy. For the members of the colonizing culture itself, the message is one of authorization and validation: it is not only permissible but natural and inevitable to victimize the Maya, in more or less any way one sees fit, so long as "progress"—this is the euphemism used to encompass all forms of material gain accruing to the colonizing society—is served.[8]

For the Maya—and it is important to note that through such modes as missionarization/Christianization and, to some extent, the "public education system" and mass media, the Maya, like other indigenous peoples, have been increasingly indoctrinated with the same mythologies about themselves which have been inculcated among their colonizers. These are the messages: "Indianness" and victimization are synonymous; to be a victim of colonial oppression is therefore both your heritage and your destiny; to be truly consistent with yourself you must not only acquiesce in what is done to you by your oppressors, you must—at least if you are to be prideful of your tradition—comport yourself in ways which facilitate colonial activities at your expense.[9] The psychological matrix of conditioning inherent to advanced colonialism is thus seamless and complete: both colonizer and colonized are assigned their proper roles in perpetuating and perfecting the structure of colonial relations.[10]

What the Zapatistas have set out to do, at least in part, is to kick a very big hole in the imperial paradigm. First, they have organized themselves in a manner in which the Mayas have long been said to be incapable by colonialism's experts—that of an effective politico–military formation. And they have done it the hard way, creating a stable fighting force of about 8,000 before initiating hostilities (this is as compared to the 15–20,000 fielded by the Farabundo Marti Liberación National [FMLN] in El Salvador at its peak). As the Mexican analyst Arturo Santamaria Gomez has observed:

> The Zapatistas are not "foquistas" [in the manner of Che Guevara]; they do not advocate founding a small nucleus of armed fighters with the expectation of growing in the course of confrontations with the state. They appear to have followed a strategy of the "cold accumulation of forces (*'accumulation de fuerzas en frio'*)," which was previously used by the Revolutionary Organization of the People in Arms (ORPA) in Guatemala. ORPA, which is now part of the National Revolutionary Unity of Guatemala (URGN), was founded in 1972 ... and spent "seven long years of silent work" ... developing a guerrilla organization, one which was also made up largely of [Mayas].[11]

Second, they have successfully engaged that organization against the Mexican military in the provincial cities of San Cristobal and Ocosingo—another impossibility, according to "the experts." This separates the EZLN quite dramatically from other contemporary guerrilla efforts in Mexico, such as those undertaken by the non–Indians of the National Revolutionary Civic Association (ACNR) and the Party of the Poor (PP) between 1967 and 1974. As Santamaria Gomez has noted, the "Zapatistas constitute a novel type of armed political movement. They can be clearly distinguished from previous guerrillas in Mexico, as well as elsewhere in Latin America, in terms of their ideas and military practices."[12] The results tend to speak for themselves:

> The uprising led by the EZLN is much larger, better planned and more extensive geographically than any other in recent times. The ACNR and the PP [which could muster only 50 and 200 fighters, respectively] were never in a position to consider taking over cities the size of San Cristobal (population roughly 80,000) or Ocosingo (about 100,000).[13]

This directly leads to the point I'm trying to make: the Zapatistas have managed to do these things in such a way as to tie them into the *real* history and tradition of the Maya rather than the racist and self–serving falsification of that tradition contrived by academic minions of the colonial status quo.[14] The Zapatista method of organizing and fighting is consciously and unequivocally Mayan at every level:

> In another break with the traditional model of guerrilla insurgency, the EZLN has apparently rejected the idea of leadership by a single, charismatic "caudillo." In the early days of the insurrection, the government appeared intent on creating a principle leader by singling out the commander of the EZLN's military operation in San Cristobal de Las Casas, Commandante Marcos [one of the very few non–Maya fighters]. However, both Marcos and other representatives of the Zapatistas speak of [a] "committee" which makes decisions, rather than any individual.[15]

It turns out that this committee—"council" would probably be a better term—is composed of representatives selected for that purpose by the residents of the individual villages which have committed fighters to the struggle. It is this form of military administration and decision making, a form which plainly incorporates elements of the participatory manner of Mayan governance—a distinctly different proposition from other known revolutionary styles of command, Zapata's included—which allows the EZLN to maintain that "it is not a group of guerrillas but a regular army" representing a nation in its own right.[16] And this in turn is what most obviously connects the Zapatistas not to Zapata and the Mexican Revolution, but to Mayan tradition itself.

How and why? The answers lie squarely in those actualities of post–invasion Mayan history which the colonial intelligentsia has been most anxious to obfuscate or dissolve. To take an example from very early on, the Mayas of the northern Guatemalan highlands—the locale immediately south of Chiapas—organized themselves on the same village–by–village basis as the Zapatistas. When the army they put together went on the offensive during the 1630s, it possessed sufficient force to drive the recently arrived Spanish completely out of the area. It took nearly a half century before effective colonial rule could be reestablished in the area.[17] There are a number of other examples I could use to illustrate the theme—about 20, if memory serves. While none of them are on the scale of the seventeenth–century uprising, all of them have been effective in their own way. But the point is that the Mayan tradition is the exact opposite of what is taught in school or printed in the newspapers. Far from being passive in the face of colonial domination, the Mayas have been fighting back with every means at their disposal for the past 350 years.[18] And—witness the EZLN—their struggle is very much alive today.

Now, it may be that all this is a sort of "back–channel" communication of exemplary action being used by a certain group of Mayas to talk to other Mayas about the nature of Mayan culture and tradition. To some extent that must be true since such emic discourse (i.e., speaking from within a group's cultural context) is always an integral aspect of intellectual decolonization.[19] The advantage to non–Mayas in seeking to penetrate the veil of popularized Zapata imagery with which the EZLN has thus far shrouded its inner dynamics is that it allows for a much better apprehension of the magnitude of the alternative manifested in the Chiapas revolt. Like it or not, Emiliano Zapata was firmly wedded to the overall complex of goals, aspirations, and attitudes marking the Mexican revolution. Consequently, although he was martyred by it, his legacy can never be entirely divorced from the drive to consolidate the modern Mexican nation–state, an entity of the very sort which is most antithetical to native self–determination.[20]

The whole history of Mayan resistance, on the other hand, links itself to the exact opposite, to the native struggle against the emergence and eventual hegemony of such states in this hemisphere. Put another way, the Mayan tradition represents an undeviating and unextinguished refusal of indigenous peoples to abdicate their inherent rights, which include organizing themselves socially, culturally, and spiritually, developing and maintaining their own forms of economy, regulating and governing themselves, and controlling the resources within their own territories; in other words, asserting their national sovereignty.[21] Self–evidently, the motivations incorporated into this sort of "sovereigntist" or "ethnonationalist" outlook add up to something very different from those at play when the objective of insurgency is to achieve a transformation allowing a greater degree of socio–political and economic equity among groups *within* some overarching statist structure such as Mexico.[22]

At this level, I can only conclude that the Zapatista agenda must be sharply differentiated from that of the Mexican revolutionaries, including Zapata, just as it should be from the objectives espoused by marxian figures such as Che Guevara, Salvador Allende, Raul Sendic, and Fidel Castro, or the Sandinistas, Tupamaros, Sendero Luminoso, M–19, FMLN, and other leftist guerrilla organizations.[23] The EZLN should be viewed, through its deliberate internal alignment with the spirit of the 1630 Mayan revolt, as joining, conceptually and emotionally, the much broader stream of historical indigenous resistance in the Americas: that of the Manaus led by Ajuricaba in Brazil during the mid–1700s, for example,[24] or the Incan revolt headed by Túpac Amaru in the Andean highlands in 1780,[25] or the Araucaño fighters in Argentina and the Mapuche revolt in Chile during the 1870s and 1880s.[26] And then again there is the inspiration of the armed struggle of the Yaquis to maintain their Sonoran homeland free from Mexican domination, an effort that lasted well into the twentieth century, and which to this day has never been truly abandoned.[27]

Nor is there reason to stop at the Río Grande. The magic line dividing Ibero from Anglo America is something contrived for the convenience of Euroamerican colonizers, an arrangement among themselves; it has nothing at all to do with the interassociative traditions of American Indians. Hence, the Zapatista phenomenon is as much an extension of the resistance of Powhatan or Pontiac to British imperialism as is the example of Túpac Amaru or Ajuricaba.[28] It has as much to do with the 1680 Pueblo Revolt as with that of the Mayas a half–century before, as much to do with Tecumseh's confederation as with the Yaquis, as much to do with Roman Nose's Cheyenne Dog Soldiers as with the Araucaño resistance, as much to do with Sitting Bull, Gall, Crazy Horse, and the other Lakotas who destroyed Custer as with the Mapuches.[29] And, to be sure, there are many others who might be mentioned, both north and south of the river: Captain Jack, Seattle, Cochise and Geronimo, Satanta and Satank, Louis Riel, Almighty Voice, Quannah Parker, Hugo Blanco, Little Crow, the Redsticks, Osceola, John Ross and Nancy Ward; the list goes on and on.

I submit that *this* is the foundation upon which the EZLN is building its actions—actions which, when viewed through a Euroamerican perspective, are inexplicable. Theirs is a perspective developed and tempered in a worldview which is emphatically indigenous, not one that has been skewed into conformity with one or another variant of marxist or neomarxist doctrine. One suspects this will remain the case regardless of how many non–Indian university professors or students such as Commandante Marcos are incorporated into the ranks of the Zapatistas to act as liaisons to the "outer world," and why, as Salvador Castaneda, a former guerrilla and current director of the Center for Investigations of Armed Movements, has put it, the EZLN insurgents demonstrate "an original conception of popular warfare [and] great support for the [native] population."[30]

Obviously, there are many dimensions to this "Indianness" or, more accurately, *indigenismo*, discerned by Castaneda. I have touched upon only one aspect, that of resistance, in my commentary. In order to be thorough, it would be necessary to go into the nature of the spiritual grounding evident among Zapatista fighters,[31] the atypical—from the standpoint of most insurgent theory and practice—concern they manifest with regard to ecology,[32] the peculiar nature—again from the standpoint of more "classical" revolutionary ideologies—of their response to economic encroachment by the Mexican state and the threat posed by NAFTA.[33] Actually, quite a lot of cultural analysis having to do with the decentralization of Mayan governmental and social forms and the like would also be required to provide anything close to a comprehensive overview of the Zapatistas' indigenist content.[34] And of course there isn't space to cover all that, even if I were competent to deal with it adequately.

In any event, I wish to carry on with the theme I've been developing—that of native "cultures of resistance," if you will—and broaden it a little more. In this regard, let's just say that it would be a bit too facile and simplistic to merely announce that, at their core, the Zapatistas are a "Mayan thing" or an "Indian thing" and to let it go at that. This is certainly true insofar as they are Mayas and, thereby, Indians. But at another level still, and I think more importantly, they are conscious indigenists. This is the ingredient which not only completes the particular portion of their philosophical makeup I've been trying to reveal, but which makes them truly a force to be reckoned with, not only in Mexico, or Central America, or Latin America, or the Americas as a whole, but globally.

The significance of this point was perhaps best explained by Bernard Neitschmann, a cultural geographer at the University of California at Berkeley in an article published in *Cultural Survival Quarterly* in 1988.[35] Neitschmann did a survey of every armed conflict worthy of the name, which he could identify on the planet at the time, and he came up with some rather startling results: of the 125 or so "hot wars," he catalogued a full 85 percent as being waged by specific indigenous peoples, or amalgamations of indigenous peoples, against one or more nation–states—capitalist, socialist, and "nonaligned" alike—which claimed traditional native territories as their own. In each case, despite the vast range of cultural differentiation evident among the various indigenous peoples involved around the world, the crux of their agendas was precisely the same: the insurgents had taken up arms, usually against vastly superior forces, to assert their rights to sovereignty and self–determination within their own defined (or definable) homelands.[36]

It is vital to understand that in expressly identifying themselves as an indigenist movement, the Zapatistas have elected to link themselves not only with their own Mayan tradition of resistance, or the American Indian tradition of resistance more generally, but with the resistance of all indigenous peoples everywhere to nation–state colonization, exploitation, and domination. Hence, the outbreak of armed struggle in Chiapas—and the incipiently comparable situations emerging in its wake in the Mexican provinces of Oaxaca and Guerrerro[37]—should be read in terms of the protracted armed struggles waged by the Karins against the governments of Burma and India, the Euskadi (Basques) against Spain, the Tamils against Sri Lanka, the Irish against Great Britain, the Polisario Front against Morocco, the West Papuans against New Guinea, and so on.[38] Indeed, as two of Castaneda's colleagues, also ex–guerrillas, have noted, the situation in Chiapas already reflects this pattern: "The war is going to be much longer than we can imagine, it is going to be a war of attrition."[39]

So pervasive is this kind of conflict at the present historical juncture that, when he analyzed it, Neitschmann concluded that it constitutes a "Third World War."[40] From there, he went on to predict that, although the implications of the phenomenon had yet to be widely acknowledged, much less appreciated, armed struggle by indigenous nations against subordination to nation–states would likely redefine the geopolitical landscape during the next generation. This was especially true, he felt, given the collapse of the Western "socialist alternative" to capitalist or post–capitalist domination of the world. In "real world" terms, this is the essence of indigenism. And the Zapatista revolt is most definitely an important—I would say *critical*—part of it.

> Militant Indian struggles have already proven to be crucial in radical insurgencies throughout the hemisphere, including just across the border from Chiapas in Guatemala. The thought that these indigenous struggles might become the cutting edge of multiethnic resistance by the victims of neoliberalism must send chills down the backs of strategic planners in Washington and Mexico City [and many other places as well].[41]

A dozen years ago, at the onset of the major conflict between the Sandinista government of Nicaragua and the Sumu, Rama, and Miskito peoples of the country's Atlantic Coast region, some of us analyzed the situation as being one in which the Left demonstrated basically the same contempt for indigenous rights as the Right.[42] What we said at the time was that unless the Sandinistas fundamentally altered their posture vis-à-vis the national rights of the Sumus, Ramas, and Miskitos, they would not ultimately be preferable to the Right so far as the Indians were concerned. And, since it was plain that the Sandinistas needed the support of the Indians to survive, a failure to alter their posture in this respect would mean that their revolution would fail. Well, the fact is that the government in Managua never did reach an accommodation with the Indians, and the revolution failed.

By that point, having taken a hard look at the demographic realities of Latin America and the ideological tenets the Left was advancing as a basis for revolution in those localities, we had already concluded that the attitudes displayed by the Sandinistas were endemic. What we said in response was that there aren't going to be any more revolutions in this hemisphere until the Left addresses what it calls "the National Question" with reference to indigenous peoples, and in a manner which is satisfactory to those peoples themselves.[43] The Left has not done this—has in fact refused to acknowledge any real need to do it—with the result that there has been a dramatic ebbing of revolutionary potential in this hemisphere since 1980.

It's true that we could get into some kind of elaborate discussion of the effects of the Soviet dissolution on Left revolutionary potential in the Americas, but I want to head that one off right now. First, whatever anyone may have thought of it, the USSR is gone, and any revolutionary potential it may ever have generated in this hemisphere went along with it. Get used to it. Second, a major reason for its demise was the *way* it—just like the Sandinistas—suppressed the self–determining aspirations of its "minority nationalities." So, the seeds of self–destruction of these sorts of leninist states—and I want to lump China and Vietnam into this categorization—were all along contained within the supposedly revolutionary ideologies upon which they were founded.[44] The wisdom of trying to revive something of that sort as a revolutionary motivator, or as a working model for social transformation, utterly escapes me.

In short: Left revolution, here and elsewhere, is currently no more than a dead horse. It foundered on its own "internal contradictions," so to speak. There's no point in beating it any more. What's needed at this point is a whole new horse. Now, let me turn back to Santamaria Gomez, himself a leftist of the neomarxian persuasion, and in my judgment somewhat resultingly bewildered by the whole set of circumstances pertaining to Chiapas:

> At a time when the wave of revolutions in Central America has been receding, when few have believed in revolution at all, the Zapatistas have gone ahead and started one.... It is remarkable what a powerful impact the EZLN has had, seemingly against all odds. They have done it by defying the conventional wisdom, and they have apparently done it on their own.... They have found widespread sympathy in Mexico and abroad—not for the war, necessarily, but for the justice of their cause, and for their passionate demand to break with 500 years of oppression.[45]

In other words, the Zapatistas—and the *indigenismo* they incarnate—represent the revitalization of revolutionary potential in America. Given that they are part of a global struggle premised in the same indigenist principles they manifest, they can be said equally to represent the revitalization of world revolutionary potential. At each level, they make this representation in ways which are not so much distinct from but antithetical to not just the prevailing capitalist order, but the standard "oppositional" dogmas of marxism–leninism–maoism as well. They do so in ways that are corrective to the modes of oppression which are intrinsic to both capitalism and its Western alternatives: ways which finally and truly *do* lead toward self–determination for all peoples, no matter how small or "primitive"; ways which really *do* point toward the dissolution of colonial structures, both external and internal; directions which, if pursued to their logical terminus, would actually culminate in the dismantling of the crushing weight of statism which the past several centuries of eurosupremacism have imposed upon us all.

There is much more which really needs to be said; for those who are interested in pursuing such matters further, let me recommend the final chapter of my book, *Struggle for the Land*.[46] It should clear up a number of questions which the present discussion may have raised about what indigenism takes as its agenda, how settler populations fit into it, and other such issues.

To conclude, let me just observe that the characteristics of Zapatismo I've covered, in however hopscotched and cursory a fashion, are things to be applauded, to be supported, to be replicated whenever and wherever possible. In them I see a solid basis for getting beyond the theoretical/practical impasse in which we presently find ourselves, for eventually discovering a bona fide route to liberation. It was, I suspect, from this frame of mind that Che Guevara once called for "two, three, many Vietnams." For my part, from a very different perspective perhaps, but with absolute respect for what it was he tried to do, I would like to call for two, three, *many* Chiapas revolts.

Notes

1. On the indigenous ethnography of Chiapas, *see* James D. Nations, *Population Ecology of the Lancandon Maya* (Ann Arbor, Michigan: University Microfilms International, No. GAX79–20363, 1979).

2. For an excellent overview, *see* David E. Stannard, *American Holocaust: Columbus and the Conquest of the New World* (New York: Oxford University Press, 1992).

3. Duncan Earl, "Indigenous Identity at the Margin: Zapatismo and Nationalism," *Cultural Survival Quarterly*, Vol. 18, No. 1 (Spring 1994), p. 27.

4. For details on Zapata's life and politics, *see* John Womak, *Zapata and the Mexican Revolution* (New York: Random House, 1970).

5. For background on the PRI's performance in this respect, *see* George A. Collier, "Roots of the Rebellion in Chiapas," *Cultural Survival Quarterly*, Vol. 18, No. 1 (Spring 1994).

6. This perspective pertains even among most Euroamerican progressives; *see*, e.g., Ronald Wright, *Time Among the Maya: Travels in Belize, Guatemala and Mexico* (New York: Viking Press, 1990).

7. The sort of devaluation of the "Other" that this involves is analyzed well and thoroughly in Albert Memmi, *Colonizer and Colonized* (Boston: Beacon Press, 1967); *see* also Robert Jay Lifton and Eric Markuson, *The Genocidal Mentality: Nazi Holocaust and Nuclear Threat* (New York: Basic Books, 1990).

8. The psychology is well handled in David E. Stannard, op. cit.

9. Albert Memmi, op. cit., as well as his *Dominated Man* (Boston: Beacon Press, 1976).

10. For analysis and discussion, *see* Frantz Fanon, *The Wretched of the Earth* (New York: Grove Press, 1965).

11. Arturo Santamaria Gomez, "Zapatistas Deliver a Message from 'Deep Mexico'," *Z Magazine*, Vol. 7, No. 3 (March 1994), p. 33.

12. Ibid., p. 30.

13. Ibid., p. 33.

14. Interesting, if occasionally reactionary and misleading, observations on these dynamics will be found in Frank Cancian and Peter Brown, "Who Is Rebelling in Chiapas?" *Cultural Survival Quarterly*, Vol. 18, No. 1 (Spring 1994), pp. 22–25.

15. Arturo Santamaria Gomez, op. cit., p. 32.

16. Ibid.

17. Grant D. Jones, *Maya Resistance to Spanish Rule: Time and History on a Colonial Frontier* (Albuquerque: University of New Mexico Press, 1989).

18. George Lovell, *Conquest and Survival in Colonial Guatemala: A Historical Geography of the Chuchumatan Highlands, 1500–1821* (Montréal: McGill–Queen's University Press, 1985).

19. For elaboration on this point in a related setting, *see* Paulo Friere, *Pedagogy of the Oppressed* (New York: Herder and Herder, 1972).

20. *See* Hugh Seton–Watson, *Nations and States: An Inquiry into the Origins of Nations and the Politics of Nationalism* (Boulder, Colorado: Westview Press, 1977); and Greg Urban and Joel Sherzer, eds., *Nation–States and Indians in Latin America* (Austin: University of Texas Press, 1992).

21. For discussion of the principles of self–determination involved, *see* S. James Anaya, "The Rights of Indigenous People and International Law in Historical and Contemporary Perspective," in *American Indian Law: Cases and Materials*, Robert N. Clinton, Nell Jessup Newton, and Monroe E. Price, eds. (Charlottesville, Virginia: Michie Co., Law Publishers, 1991), pp. 1257–276.

22. For elaboration, *see* George Manuel and Michael Posluns, *The Fourth World: An Indian Reality* (New York: The Free Press, 1974).

23. On Guevara, *see The Bolivian Diaries of Che Guevara* (New York: Grove Press, 1968); on Allende, *see* James Petras and Morris Morely, *The United States and Chile: Imperialism and the Overthrow of the Allende Government* (New York: Monthly Review Press, 1975); on Sendic and the Tupamaros, *see* Maria Esther Gilio, *The Tupamaros Guerrillas: The Structure and Strategy of an Urban Guerrilla Movement* (New York: Saturday Review Press, 1970); on Castro, *see* Carlos Franqui, *Family Portrait with Fidel: A Memoir* (New York: Vintage Books, 1985); on the Sandinistas, *see* Henri Weber, *Nicaragua: The Sandinista Revolution* (London: Verso Press, 1981); on Sendero Luminoso, *see* Simon Strong, *Shining Path: Terror and Revolution in Peru* (London: HarperCollins Books, 1992); on the FMLN, *see* Robert Armstrong and Janet Shenk, *El Salvador: The Face of Revolution* (Boston: South End Press, 1982); overall, *see* Sheldon B. Bliss, *Marxist Thought in Latin America* (Berkeley: University of California, 1984).

24. David Hemming, *Red Gold: The Conquest of the Brazilian Indians, 1500–1760* (Cambridge, Massachusetts: Harvard University Press, 1978).

25. Editors, *Túpac Amaru II* (Lima: n.p., 1976).

26. Bernardo Berdichewsky, *The Araucanian Indian in Chile* (Copenhagen: IWGIA Doc. No. 20, 1975).

27. Evelyn Hu–DeHart, *Yaqui Resistance and Survival* (Madison: University of Wisconsin Press, 1984).

28. *See* Alvin Josephy, Jr., *The Patriot Chiefs* (New York: Viking Press, 1961).

29. On the Pueblo revolt, *see* Oakah L. Jones, Jr., *Pueblo Warriors and the Spanish Conquest* (Norman: University of Oklahoma Press, 1966); on Tecumseh, *see* David R. Edmunds, *Tecumseh and the Quest for Indian Leadership* (Boston: Little, Brown, & Co., Inc., 1984); on the rest, *see* Dee Brown, *Bury My Heart at Wounded Knee: An Indian History of the America West* (New York: Little, Brown, & Co., Inc., 1970).

30. Quoted in Arturo Santamaria Gomez, op. cit., p. 33.

31. For a succinct exploration, *see* Evon Z. Voght, "Possible Sacred Aspects of the Chiapas Rebellion," *Cultural Survival Quarterly*, Vol. 18, No. 1 (Spring 1994).

32. *See* James D. Nations, "The Ecology of the Zapatista Revolt," *Cultural Survival Quarterly*, Vol. 1, No. 1 (Spring 1994).

33. For a good examination of the likely impacts of the North American Free Trade Agreement on the Mayas of Chiapas, and hence the basis for the Zapatista response, *see* Gary C. Hufbauer and Jeffrey J. Schott, *NAFTA: An Assessment* (Washington, DC: Institute for International Economics, 1993).

34. Those interested in pursuing these matters further might be interested in Evon Z. Voght's *The Zincatecos of Mexico: A Modern Maya Way of Life* (New York: Holt, Rinehart & Winston, Inc., 1990).

35. Bernard Neitschmann, "World War III," *Cultural Survival Quarterly*, Vol. 11, No. 4 (Winter 1988).

36. For further background on the conditions precipitating these struggles, *see* Sadruddin Aga Khan and Hassan bin Talal, *Indigenous Peoples: A Global Quest for Justice* (London: Zed Books, 1987).

37. Arturo Santamaria Gomez (op. cit., p. 33) points out that there is also an indication of Zapatista–type activity in the provinces of Morelos, Chihuahua, Veracruz, Tabasco, and San Luis Potosí, and that there have been armed actions in Guadalajara and Mexico City. I know from personal experience that ferment among the people along the Yaqui River in Sonora Province is also leading in the same direction.

38. On the Karins and Tamils, *see* Sadruddin Aga Khan and Hassan bin Tabal, op. cit.; on the Euskadi, *see* Kenneth Medhurst, *The Basques and Catalans*, Minority Rights Support Group No. 9 (Sept. 1977); on the Irish, *see* J. Bowyer Bell, *The Irish Troubles: A Generation of Violence, 1967–1992* (New York: St. Martin's Press, 1993); on the Polisario, *see* Tony Hodges, *Western Sahara: The Roots of a Desert War* (Westport, Connecticut: Lawrence Hill & Co., 1983); on the Papuans, *see* David Robie, *Blood on Their Banner: Nationalist Struggles in the South Pacific* (London: Zed Books, 1989).

39. Quoted in Arturo Santamaria Gomez, op. cit., p. 33.

40. Bernard Neitschmann, op. cit.

41. Arturo Santamaria Gomez, op. cit., p. 31.

42. *See*, e.g., Glenn T. Morris and Ward Churchill, "Between a Rock and a Hard Place: Left–Wing Revolution, Right–Wing Reaction and the Destruction of Indigenous Peoples," originally published in *Cultural Survival Quarterly*, Vol. 11, No. 3 (Fall 1988), and included in this book.

43. *See*, e.g., Ward Churchill, "False Promises: An Indigenist Critique of Marxist Theory and Practice," originally published in *Society and Nature*, Vol. 1, No. 2 (1993), and included in this collection of essays. The issue is treated in greater detail, relying on exhaustive case histories, in Walker Connor, *The National Question in Marxist–Leninist Theory and Practice* (Princeton, New Jersey: Princeton University Press, 1983).

44. For discussion, *see* Walker Connor, op. cit.

45. Arturo Santamaria Gomez, op. cit., p. 33.

46. Ward Churchill, *Struggle for the Land: Indigenous Resistance to Genocide, Ecocide and Expropriation in Contemporary North America* (Monroe, Maine: Common Courage Press, 1993).

Generations of Resistance
American Indian Poetry and the Ghost Dance Spirit*

> I want my words to be as eloquent
> As the sound of a rattle snake.
>
> *Jimmie Durham*

In mid–1979, I transcribed and edited the statements of a middle–aged Oglala Lakota spiritual leader named Charles Fast Horse. One of the historical/anecdotal fragments of this process was a more or less autonomous piece I called simply "The Ghost Dance." The thematic concerns expressed therein, it seems to me, carry with them strong if unintended implications in terms of apprehending a central dynamic at play in the formation and generation of contemporary American Indian poetry, particularly those poetics overtly concerned with notions of resistance and identity. For this reason, it follows in its entirety.

> Always, since the beginning of time, the people considered themselves as a people by virtue of their relationship to the earth and the sky and to all living things. They were a part of life. To express this, there was the Hoop, the four directions, the wheel of life to which all things belong.

> When the wasíchus (whites) came, they wished to destroy all this. They wanted to take the earth and destroy it by digging it up and

---

* An earlier version of this essay appeared in the collection *Coyote Was Here: Essays on Contemporary Native American Literary and Political Mobilization*, Bo Schöler, ed. (Arrhus, Denmark: SEKLOS, University of Arrhus, 1984).

plowing away the grass. They wanted to destroy the beaver in order to make hats. They wanted to pen the people on little islands of land, cut off from the Hoop of life, made also to scratch and dig the earth. The black–robed preachers said that the old ways were false and that the people must become like the wasíchus in all things.

But the people knew that if this was done, all life would end. So, there were wars to drive this evil away. But there were many, many wasíchus while the people were few. The leaders were killed: Roman Nose of the Cheyenne, Little Thunder of the Brûlé, Black Kettle, Iron Shirt, Left Hand, Running Antelope. Many, far too many, of the people died with them, and so did the four–legged ones: the buffalo, the deer, the beaver, the antelope, even the horses.

Little by little, the people were pushed aside while the wasíchus dug away for gold in the Rockies, in Paha Sapa (the Black Hills), in Idaho and Montana. Finally, the people were everywhere defeated. Everywhere, there was death and hunger, from the Comanches of the south to the Blackfeet in Canada. Another great leader, Tesunke Witko (Crazy Horse), was killed—assassinated—and the people knew the wasíchus would never stop until all things lay dead. But it was too late for fighting. Even Sitting Bull came home to die.

Then arrived Wovoka, a prophet among the Paiute people far to the west. Young men were sent to learn the message he offered. It was this:

If the people would retain their belief in the old ways, if they would forego the food of the wasíchus, if they would dance for a vision and not destroy themselves in hopeless battles, they would see the wasíchus wither like the autumn leaves. Then all the dead of the many wars would return to life, and all the four–leggeds would return, as would all the other things destroyed by the wasíchus.

This was the Ghost Dance message of Wovoka. The people danced and prayed. They did not fight. But the troops came anyway. Sitting Bull was murdered and the followers of Big Foot were massacred at Wounded Knee. Then it was over. As Black Elk said, the Hoop was broken.

But now we see that what Wovoka said was true. The wasíchus are beginning to wither away, to choke on the gases their industry puts into the air, to gag on the waste they pour into the rivers and streams, to grow weak from the poisons they put into their food, to watch the very soil blow away beneath their plow.

When they are gone from power, the four–legged will return, and
the air will be fresh again, and pure. Crazy Horse and the other
leaders still walk among us. The Hoop will once more be the
container of life ... as it must be.

In my experience, this oral rendering of American Indian realities goes
directly to the heart of the matter. Rather than being a remote and curious
phenomenon of mere anthropological or historical interest, the Ghost Dance—a
vision born of the direst circumstances and most hopeful sentiments—is a
continuing tradition. In fact, it might be asserted that it is integral at some
important level to the outlook of any traditionalist Indian.

The message of the Ghost Dance has, to be sure, evolved and changed
since 1890, although there are still practitioners of the original form. In less
than a century, it has spread from the plains and basin regions of its birth to
encompass virtually all the tribal peoples of North America, and perhaps
portions of Central and South America as well.

Each indigenous nation which has absorbed the spirit of the Ghost Dance
has altered it to greater or lesser degrees to fit into its own context, its own
experience. In this way, each has made a distinct contribution to transforming
the seminal message of Wovoka into a multifaceted complex of related and
complimentary ideas perhaps best described in sum as a "worldview." And it
is this worldview which defines the continuing traditions of the indigenous
peoples of this hemisphere in the contemporary setting.

Many, perhaps most, of the peoples sharing in this perspective no longer
refer to their way of living as being of the Ghost Dance. And, by way of strict
definition, they are correct. Yet a certain strictness of definition goes beyond
relevance in describing the reality of America. It is a white man's game,
imported from Europe, long used to semantically removing continuing generations of native people from conscious existence. Besides, there is no need to
announce the vision by a given name. It is simply "the way," an objective fact
of life to its participants.

As forms change, so too do the roles of practitioners. Ghost Dancers, per
se, are now relatively few in number. But the dance itself was never more than
the medium through which to express the message, a means for the people to
communicate between one another, with the totality of relations comprising the
natural order which each proclaimed as the Great "Spirit" or "Mystery,"
and—perhaps most important in many ways—to communicate with themselves. Also, and not coincidentally, the dance served as a method through
which to sharply distinguish Indians from the dominate culture which was
acting to destroy life as it had been known, and, it is arguable, the basis for
viable life of any sort.

Today, there are other means of accomplishing this, poetry hardly least
among them. To the contrary, it is a medium which seems ideally suited to the
purpose. To appreciate this, it must be borne in mind that the Ghost Dance

vision, regardless of superficial alterations, contains several ingredients which rest at the core of its meaning and purpose. These are, first, the summing up of the past as a means of recognizing and perpetuating those values and beliefs critical to the maintenance of native culture. Second, the articulation of an assessment of the "state of things" in the present. From there, a concomitant mode of behavior is elaborated by which to offset or negate present dangers. And, finally, there is a projection of the participants' culture into the future, both immediate and long–term.

Clearly, poetry is an expressive vehicle capable of accommodating all four of these factors. Its interconnection with oral tradition is, moreover, the closest of all literate forms, a point not insignificant in view of the Ghost Dance imperative to retain tried and true and time–honored approaches to all things. In a sense, then, "the medium is the message" in terms of poetry's provision of structural communicative continuity between the American Indian past, present, and future.

From a Woman Warrior

Wendy Rose's *What Happened When the Hopi Hit New York**

A people is not defeated until the hearts of its women are on the ground.

Traditional Cheyenne saying

As I've observed elsewhere and often, women hold a crucial position within the context of contemporary American Indian poetry, an altogether unusual circumstance in a field of endeavor marked conventionally by a pronounced male domination. The field of endeavor which produced Homer, Shakespeare, Byron, and Emerson has, historically, rigidly denied anything approaching equal access to those of the female gender, a situation which cannot be said to have truly lapsed as of this writing.

The vitality of the female voice in modern Indian writing, especially poetry, cannot therefore be explained through customary modes of literary analysis. Both "literature" and "aesthetics" are, after all, definitional terms deriving from the European tradition. What is at issue in matters of American Indian poetry is the bringing to bear upon the world of letters an entirely different, and vibrantly ongoing, cultural heritage: that of Native America itself.

Although the various cultures indigenous to this hemisphere have always differed widely in things such as verbal and visual expression, there are a number of factors of fundamental importance which might be viewed as common denominators underlying what Vine Deloria, Jr., has called the "Indian Worldview." Central to these are conceptions of the balance existing between

---

* This essay originally appeared in *Akwesasne Notes*, Vol. 16, No. 1 (Mid–Winter 1984).

and ultimate unity of all the elements of any given situation, whether this be the forging of ingredients composing day–to–day community life, or the teaching of an understanding of the interactive nature of the universe.

A certain homage has been paid of late by non–Indians to this intrinsically Indian sense of balance and unity. For the most part, such recognition of the value and utility of native thought has been accorded by practitioners of religious studies, the environmental sciences, and, to a lesser extent, physics. While this limited acknowledgment is germane and long overdue, it ultimately accomplishes rather little in terms of addressing the totality of indigenous philosophical conceptualization, or the resulting actualization of the balance/unity principle in native life.

Within this latter consideration lies the nexus determining the "why" of the scope and magnitude of Indian women's participation in poetics. It is directly reflective of the core notion that sexual differentiation, like everything else in the indigenous worldview, must be balanced, unified, and rendered harmonious. The subordination of one sex to another—such as is represented in Europe's male domination of arts and letters—indicates an intersexual imbalance which is utterly untenable to anyone even marginally sharing in the traditional native perspective.

To Indians, a male–dominated form of social organization, a form in which the female vision is stifled, not only makes no sense, but must be seen as something unhealthy, repugnant, and as ultimately unworkable as the Euro-christian idea of a human–dominated cosmos. Indeed, one is quickly led to argue that any society which predicates its organization on a permanent—or perhaps even a temporary—subordination of one sex by the other must in the end prove itself incapable of achieving a balanced sort of relationship with the remainder of its environment.

Those who would sift out some portion of the American Indian worldview for conceptual integration into a "hard science" like biology while retaining the gender biases of Eurocentric outlooks and attitudes in their socio–political or economic lives are thus consigning themselves to failure before they begin. The indigenous worldview—in which the balancing of the masculine and the feminine is an integral and indispensable part—is itself an inherent unity; it cannot be effectively broken down into component parts for purposes of piecemeal (re)application elsewhere.

This Native American practice of maintaining equilibrium and harmony between the sexes has been concretized in myriad ways. Among the better known are the decisive political roles filled by women in the Iroquois Confederacy, in the arrangement of property relations among the Lakota, the kinship structure and lineage among the Cheyenne and Anishinabe, and the handling of spiritual matters among the Crow and Cherokee. The list could be extended to great length by citing lesser known illustrations. And, of course, Indians never required the rhetoric of affirmative action to achieve this social condition.

A traditional saying, variations of which are voiced within a host of native cultures, is that "the strength of a people rests among its women." Adherence to this worldview precludes the paying of mere lip service to this principle. Suffice it to say that women's voices are and always have been of importance in traditional societies, no less—and in some ways perhaps more—than those of men. Nowhere is this balance manifested more dramatically than in the poetry coming from the current generation of Indian writers. For every Maurice Kenny, there is a Joy Harjo; for every Peter Blue Cloud, a Paula Gunn Allen; for every Simon Ortiz, a Linda Hogan; for every Barney Bush or Carter Revard, a Leslie Silko or Mary TallMountain. Balance is quite tangibly achieved, a matter of stark contrast to the arrogance of the European tradition holding that thought and articulation are a more or less exclusive "male domain."

In the foremost ranks of native poets, male and female, is Wendy Rose. A Hopi, she has been a very active poetic voice for well over a decade, beginning her publication of book–length collections with the 1973 release of *Hopi Roadrunner Dancing*. There followed other books: *Long Division: A Tribal History* (1976; reprinted in 1981), *Academic Squaw* (1977), *Builder Kachina: A Home Going Cycle* (1979), and *Lost Copper* (1980). Over the years, she has attained a poetic stature which is virtually unassailable, simply obliterating "concerns," fashionable among white literary critics, that her material sees print only by virtue of her gender and ethnicity. Hers is a powerful voice in any language, any context.

Unquestionably, this is best evidenced in a tight little collection entitled *What Happened When the Hopi Hit New York*. Here, Rose displays, with the kind of mature virtuosity unmatched in her previous work, the true range of her ability to depict the subtlety of contemporary Indian experience in America, as well as the character of the intercultural conflict which shapes it. The sensitivity and gentleness with which she approaches many topics, and the skill and toughness with which she defends her identity while critiquing encroachments by the dominant society, combine to make *Hopi* a genuine tour d'force. In pieces such as "Stopover in Denver," "Indian in Iowa City," "Searching for Indians in New Orleans," "My Red Antennae Receiving: Vermont," and "Ghosts: Brooklyn," she may be said to have reached her full stride as a poet.

The release of *What Happened When the Hopi Hit New York* is thus an event which gives cause for rejoicing in all quarters of Indian Country. More than any writer in recent memory, Wendy Rose has reasserted the propriety of the proposition that not only the strength, but the vision and stamina of a people lie among its women. This is a book which must be read, a voice which must be read, for through the book and the voice we all gain fresh and necessary insights into how it is we must continue—for the sake of ourselves, and the sake of our future generations. To Wendy Rose: "Sister, thank you."

Another Vision of America

Simon J. Ortiz's *From Sand Creek**

Simon speaks in the tongue of time....

Joy Harjo

The field of contemporary American Indian poetry is studded with luminous writers, among them Wendy Rose, Paula Gunn Allen, Adrian C. Louis, Joy Harjo, James Welch, Chrystos, Peter Blue Cloud, Maurice Kenny, Linda Hogan, Duane Niatum, Elizabeth Woody, Dian Million, Barney Bush, Carter Revard, Mary TallMountain, Pam Colorado, Roberta Hill Whiteman, Geary Hobson, Bill Oandasan, Leslie Marmon Silko, John Trudell.... the list goes on and on. Without question, one of the very strongest voices to have emerged from this exceptionally strong showing over the past quarter–century has been that of Simon J. Ortiz, the Acoma poet.

Prior to his most recent effort, Ortiz has authored three collections of verse—*Going for the Rain* (1976), *A Good Journey* (1977), and *Fight Back: For the Sake of the Land, For the Sake of the People* (1980)—as well as a children's book entitled *The People Shall Continue* (1977). Aside from his compilations, his work has appeared over the years in numerous poetry journals and poetic anthologies in exclusively native venues as well as those of mixed ethnicity. In whatever context, his writing has always stood out in an extraordinary fashion.

Known primarily for his longer epic narratives, Ortiz has also excelled at short impactive statements. In either format, he has always opted to serve in

---

* This essay originally appeared in the journal *New Studies on the Left* (Spring–Summer, 1988).

the time–honored capacity of tribal storyteller/historian (a common motivating factor in much modern Indian poetic endeavors), and to incorporate overt political analysis into his material. Often, he draws direct connections between the historical experiences of his own and other native peoples on the one hand, and the current quandary in which most Indians find themselves on the other. He has also been wont to draw clear parallels between the situation of Indians and the conditions suffered by other disenfranchised groups, including poor whites, in North America.

Ortiz's political message is straightforward enough: colonialism, the predicate to emergence of European–style nation–states in this hemisphere, is not only alive and well today, its dynamic of domination has spread to societal proportions, becoming ever more prevalent, sublimated, and entrenched. In its most institutionalized form, colonialism, however unconsciously it may be received by those bent under its yoke, has become the normative expression of modern American life. It follows, according to Ortiz, that in order to be unburdened of colonialism—that is, to desublimate and decolonize—its victims must first be made aware of the true nature and dimension of their oppression. The best means to this end, he concludes, is to focus their attention upon their commonalties of circumstance with the most deeply oppressed and ignored of all social sectors: Native North America.

With the publication of *From Sand Creek* (Thunder's Mouth Press, 1981), Ortiz's most recent book, and his first full book–length poem, the author has accomplished two things aesthetically. First, he has transcended an earlier tension between his long and short narrative forms, revealing himself as an innovative and accomplished master of the epic. Second, in achieving this maturity, he has moved himself from his former status as a major talent among a welter of sometimes comparable indigenous writers to stand alone as the *poet laureate* of Native America. This description is not applied casually in any way at all; his is quite simply, and by a fair margin, the finest book of native verse ever produced.

From Sand Creek combines the various elements of its author's approach to poetic communication in a single continuous *tour de force* featuring a juxtaposing of biting prose passages on left–hand pages against bitterly brilliant segments of verse on the right. The emotive quality of the latter contrasts in eerily balanced harmony to the former, and the effect is devastating. At the outset, for instance, Ortiz employs a dry and matter–of–fact cadence to frame what will follow:

> November 29, 1864: On that cold dawn, about 600 Southern Cheyenne and Arapaho people, two–thirds of them women and children, were camped on a bend of Sand Creek in southeastern Colorado. The people were at peace.... The Reverend John Chivington and his Volunteers and Fort Lyons troops, numbering more than 700 heavily armed men, slaughtered 105 women and 28 men.... By mid–1865,

the Cheyenne and Arapaho had been driven out of Colorado Territory.

These facts have been recounted often enough, and come as no surprise to anyone acquainted with American history. To the contrary, their very redundancy has lead to a deadening of the reader to the intrinsic horror of their meaning; the information has long since lost whatever validity of general impact it may once have possessed. Hence, on the facing page Ortiz graphically depicts, not what has just been said, but its inference, the very *essence* of it:

> *This America*
> *has been a burden*
> *of steel and mad*
> *death*

The lines, at first glance, might well have been penned by, say, Allen Ginsberg as a passage to "Howl." But here, through an intentional shifting of context away from symptoms such as the urban *zeitgeist* Ginsberg assailed in the fifties to the causes of such symptoms, Ortiz acquires a power and vision unattainable for even the best of the more topical poets. In a word, his analysis is fundamentally more radical (from the Greek *radix*, meaning to go to the root, or source of things). With this position firmly established, he immediately proceeds to expose the overarching theme of his book, the basis laid in understanding the carnage of the past for achieving an altogether different sort of future:

> *but, look now,*
> *there are flowers*
> *and new grass*
> *and a spring wind*
> *rising*
> *from Sand Creek.*

Elsewhere, Ortiz posits with great lucidity what he takes to be the societal costs of a continuing default in coming to grips with the realities of Indian–white relations. On a left–hand page he notes that, "Repression works like a shadow, clouding memory and sometimes even to blind, and when it is on a national scale, it is just not good." Again, the reader might be prone to passing by the intensity of meaning imbedded in this sparse statement, were it not for the sudden jolt of implication Ortiz brings forth in the accompanying verse:

> *In 1969*
> *XXXX Coloradoans*
> *were killed in Vietnam.*

In 1978
XXX Coloradoans
were killed on the highways.

In 1864
there were no Indians killed.

Remember My Lai.

In fifty years,
nobody knew
what happened.

It wasn't only the Senators.

Remember Sand Creek.

The facts are portrayed as being related, interconnected. Failure to absorb the significance of the massacre at Sand Creek, to deal with the outlooks and attitudes which caused it to happen and which made it emblematic of Euroamerica's "Winning of the West," has led consequentially to endless repetition. My Lai, that hideous symbol of the American "effort" in Southeast Asia, can *only* be understood through comprehension that it had happened before, at Sand Creek. The reason for My Lai rests solidly in the forgetting of Sand Creek; the forgetting of My Lai leads inevitably to the bombing of a mental hospital in Grenada and the MOVE house in Philadelphia, a slit trench filled with at least 4,000 civilian corpses in Panama, and the "Highway of Death" in Iraq, even the gratuitous butchering of Branch Davidian children near Waco, Texas. Sand Creek, in the sense Simon Ortiz deploys the massacre, signifies the whole of an ongoing and very American process.

Had he ended his analysis at this point, the author's argument would have been primarily moral (albeit, correctly so). He is, however, much more far–reaching. As with any highly evolved system of colonization, the U.S. model long ago reached a point where the rank and file colonial victimizer began to become the victimized as well. Imperialism requires a continuously expanding pool of victims; it ultimately cares not a whit whether these be members of colonized nations like the Cheyenne and Vietnamese, or constituents of the colonizing state itself. Thus, Ortiz refers to the number of citizens of Colorado—the entity built most literally upon the blood and bones of Sand Creek—who died in Vietnam and the highways a century later, casualties of the same consumptive process which had claimed so many native non–combatants that morning in 1864.

Ultimately, the reader is called upon to engage, not in some metaphorical and altruistic crusade to render abstract justice to the long dead, but to recognize and respond to a very personal and immediate jeopardy. The burned and mutilated remains shipped home in body bags from places like Khe Sahn and Plei Me were, after all, not Vietnamese or Cambodians. They were "the boy next door." The bodies will continue to come home, and increasingly so, Ortiz asserts, until those clinging to the perspectives which now sanctify America's purported right to imperial intervention—and that, sadly, is most of the population—are forced to cease in their presumption. The price of their arrogance is tremendously expensive, prohibitively so in the long run. The chickens, to paraphrase Malcolm X, will just keep coming home to roost.

This is a harsh lesson, tough enough to cast sensibilities of domination and repression in sharp relief. So too, the haughty national chauvinism such mentality engenders:

> *no wonder*
> *they deny regret*
> *for the slaughter*
> *of their future.*
> *Denying eternity, it is no wonder*
> *they become so selflessly*
> *righteous.*

While comprehensible, the attitude is nonetheless untenable. While facts, both historical and contemporary, can be intellectually equivocated or denied, the costs attendant to the facts continue to accrue unabated. Here, Ortiz offers a timeless observation on the warfare which is the core of colonialist reality, once the glossy veneer of Manifest Destiny prevarication has been stripped away:

> *They were amazed*
> *at so much blood.*
> > *Spurting,*
> > *Sparkling,*
> *splashing, bubbling, steady*
> *hot arching streams.*
> > *Red*
> *and bright and vivid*
> *unto the grassed plains.*
> > *Steaming.*

In this passage, he could be referring equally to the agony of combat between the Cheyenne Dog Soldiers and the Colorado Volunteers during the summer of 1864, or between troopers of the 1st Air Cavalry Division and units of the People's Army of Vietnam in the Ia Drang Valley during the winter of 1965. Again, this very interchangeability of setting is precisely what Ortiz intended, and he succeeds admirably. The same synonymic deftness is then extended from Indian and Asian victims of Euroamerican "progress" to its white victims:

> Cold,
> *it is,*
> *the wind lurches*
> *blunt and sad.*
> *Below freezing in Colorado.*
> *Ghosts, Indian–like*
> *still driven*
> *towards Oklahoma.*

From these white settlers, displaced and forcibly relocated ("Indian–like") by the pressures and imperatives surrounding the consolidation of American capital, Ortiz turns to his ultimate signifier of the experience shared by all who have been ground under the nailed boots of the United States: those maimed military veterans of all colors—crippled residue of empire's cutting edge, used like toilet paper then cast aside—consigned to the dreary limbo–land reservations ("Indian–like," once again) of U.S. VA hospitals where he himself was forced to spend an over–abundance of his life:

> O
> *train and people and plains,*
> *look at me and the hospital*
> *where stricken men and broken boys*
> *are mortared and sealed*
> *into defensive walls.*   *O look*
> *now.*

In demonstrating finally and conclusively the commonality of pain and anguish wrought among colonial subjects, the author's insight is at last completely unveiled. He stares directly and unflinchingly into the depths of the pathos forming the duality of what has come to be known as "America": on the one hand, a lethal, screaming insanity which, like any cancer, destroys all it touches, including, eventually, itself; on the other, a wondrous physicality of earth, air, and water which gives, and has always given, promise of an infinitely different existence. His preoccupation with Indians and disabled veterans is, in this sense, merely the lensmatic tool with which he illuminates the nature of the transformative consciousness required to realize this second life–giving potentiality.

Given that the implied, if never quite stated, objective of *From Sand Creek* is to provide an expressive vehicle upon which the sheer necessity of human liberation can be articulated and understood, it is fair to say that Ortiz's project has been exceedingly ambitious. To the extent that the book attains this goal, it is equally fair to suggest that it transcends its prose/poetic medium. This, of course, is the acid test as to whether a given body of verse is only very good, or whether it can be legitimately said to have made the leap into the rarefied strata of poetry which is "great." *From Sand Creek* must, on balance, be accorded the latter distinction.

Even at that, however, the assessment seems insufficient. Such is the compelling quality of Ortiz's vision that we are all but helplessly drawn into a wholehearted pursuit of his essential dream:

> *That dream*
> *shall have a name*
> *after all,*
> *and it will not be vengeful*
> *but wealthy with love*
> *and compassion*
> *and knowledge.*
> *And it will rise*
> *in this heart*
> *which is our America.*

To Simon J. Ortiz, we are obliged, collectively, to offer our sincerest thanks for having written *From Sand Creek*. And, because of the magnitude and nature of his achievement, we must at the same time enter a demand for more of the same. We are all so desperately in need of it...

Bibliography

The following is an extensive but nonetheless selective bibliography of book–length materials, which readers may find useful in pursuing additional information and insights into American Indian subject matters.

Abernathy, Thomas Perkins. *Western Lands and the American Revolution*. New York: Russell and Russell, 1959.

Acuña, Rodolfo. *Occupied America: A History of the Chicanos*. 3d ed. New York: Harper and Row, 1988.

Adams, Evelyn C. *American Indian Education: Government Schools and Economic Programs*. New York: King's Crown Press, 1946.

Albers, Patricia, and Beatrice Medicine, eds. *The Hidden Half: Studies of Plains Indian Women*. Lanham, Maryland: University Press of America, 1983.

Alvord, Clarence Walworth. *The Mississippi Valley in English Politics: A Study of the Trade, Land Speculation and Experiments in Imperialism Culminating in the American Revolution*. 2 vols. New York: Russell and Russell, 1959.

Ambrose, Stephen E. *Crazy Horse and Custer: The Parallel Lives of Two American Warriors*. Garden City, New York: Doubleday, 1975.

American Friends Service Committee. *Uncommon Controversy: Fishing Rights of the Muckleshoot, Puyallup, and Nisqually Indians*. Seattle: University of Washington Press, 1970.

Ammot, Teresa L., and Julie A. Matthei. *Race, Gender and Work: A Multicultural Economic History of Women in the United States*. Boston: South End Press, 1991.

Amnesty International. *Proposal for a Commission of Inquiry into the Effects of Domestic Intelligence Activities on Criminal Trials in the United States of America*. New York: Amnesty International, 1980.

Andrews, Barbara T., and Marie Sansone. *Who Runs the Rivers? Dams and Decisions in the New West*. Palo Alto, California: Stanford Environmental Law Society, 1983.

Andrist, Ralph. *The Long Death: The Last Days of the Plains Indians*. New York: Collier Books, 1964.

Anonymous. *To Fish in Common: Fishing Rights in the Northwest*. Seattle: Native American Solidarity Committee (NASC), 1978; revised and reprinted, 1988.

Arens, W. *The Man–Eating Myth: Anthropology and Anthropophagy*. London/New York: Oxford University Press, 1979.

Armstrong, Virginia I. *I Have Spoken: American History Through the Voices of Indians*. New York: Pocket Books, 1975.

Asad, Tala, ed. *Anthropology and the Colonial Encounter*. New York: Humanities Press, 1973.

Ashburn, Percy M. *The Ranks of Death.* New York: Cowan and McCann, 1947.
Aten, Lawrence E. *Indians of the Upper Texas Coast.* New York: Academic Press, 1983.
Axtell, James. *The European and the Indian: Essays in the Ethnohistory of North America.* London/New York: Oxford University Press, 1981.
———. *The Invasion Within: The Contest of Cultures in Colonial North America.* London/New York: Oxford University Press, 1985.
———. *Beyond 1492: Encounters in Colonial North America.* London/New York: Oxford University Press, 1992.
Baily, L. R. *The Long Walk.* Los Angeles: Western Lore Press, 1964.
Balesi, Charles J. *The Time of the French in the Heart of North America, 1673–1818.* Chicago: Alliance Français, 1991.
Barriero, José, ed. *Indian Roots of American Democracy.* Ithaca, New York: American Indian Studies Program, Cornell University, 1989.
Barry, M. C. *The Alaska Pipeline: The Politics of Oil and Native Land Claims.* Bloomington/Indianapolis: Indiana University Press, 1975.
Barsh, Russel, and James Youngblood Henderson. *The Road: Indian Tribes and Political Liberty.* Berkeley: University of California Press, 1980.
Bataille, Gretchen, and Charles L. P. Silet, eds. *The Pretend Indians: Images of Native Americans in the Movies.* Ames: Iowa State University Press, 1980.
Baumhoff, Richard. *The Dammed Missouri Valley.* New York: Alfred A. Knopf, 1951.
Beal, Merril. *I Will Fight No More Forever: Chief Joseph and the Nez Percé War.* Seattle: University of Washington Press, 1963.
Beatty, William W. *Education for Culture Change.* Chilocco, Oklahoma: U.S. Department of Interior, Bureau of Indian Affairs (Chilocco Indian School), 1953.
Belch, Stanislaus F. *Paulus Vladamiri and His Doctrine Concerning International Law and Politics.* The Hague: Mouton, 1965.
Benedict, Ruth. *Race, Science, and Politics.* New York: Viking Press, 1945.
Bennett, Gordon. *Aboriginal Rights in International Law.* London: Royal Institute, 1978.
Berger, John. *Report from the Frontier: The State of the World's Indigenous Peoples.* London: Zed Press, 1987.
Berkhofer, Robert F., Jr. *Salvation and the Savage: An Analysis of Protestant Missions and American Indian Response, 1787–1862.* Knoxville: University of Kentucky Press, 1965.
———. *The White Man's Indian: Images of the American Indian from Columbus to the Present.* New York: Alfred A. Knopf, 1978.
Bernstein, Alison R. *American Indians and World War II.* Norman: University of Oklahoma Press, 1991.
Berry, Brewton. *Almost White: A Study of Certain Racial Hybrids in the Eastern United States.* New York: Macmillan Publishing Co., 1963.
Berthrong, Donald J. *The American Indian: From Pacifism to Activism.* St. Charles, Missouri: Forum Press, 1973.
Bledsoe, Anthony J. *Indian Wars of the Pacific Northwest.* San Francisco: Bacon and Co., 1885.
Blue Cloud, Peter. *Alcatraz Is Not an Island.* Berkeley: Wingbow Press, 1972.
Bodard, Lucien. *Green Hell: Massacre of the Brazilian Indians.* New York: Outerbridge and Dienstfrey, 1969.
Borah, Woodrow W., and Sherburn F. Cook. *The Aboriginal Population of Central Mexico on the Eve of the Spanish Conquest.* Ibero–Americana No. 43. Berkeley: University of California Press, 1963.
Bourne, Russell. *The Red King's Rebellion: Racial Politics in New England, 1675–1678.* New York: Atheneum Books, 1990.

Boxer, C. R. *Race Relations in the Portuguese Colonial Empire, 1415–1825.* Oxford: Clarendon Press, 1963.

Boyce, George A. *"When the Navajos Had Too Many Sheep": The 1940s.* San Francisco: Indian Historian Press, 1974.

Brand, Johanna. *The Life and Death of Anna Mae Aquash.* Toronto: James Lorimar, 1978.

Brandon, William. *The Last Americans: The Indian in American Culture.* New York: McGraw–Hill, 1974.

———. *New Worlds for Old: Reports from the New World and Their Effect on Social Thought in Europe, 1500–1800.* Athens: Ohio University Press, 1986.

Brod, Rodney L. *Choctaw Education.* Box Elder, Montana: LPS and Associates, 1979.

Brodeur, Paul. *Restitution: The Land Claims of the Mashpee, Passamaquoddy, and Penobscot Indians of New England.* Boston: Northeastern University Press, 1985.

Brody, J. J. *Indian Painters and White Patrons.* Albuquerque: University of New Mexico Press, 1971.

Brophy, William A., and Sophie E. Aberles. *The Indian, America's Unfinished Business: Report of the Commission on Rights, Liberties and Responsibilities of the American Indian.* Norman: University of Oklahoma Press, 1966.

Brown, Dee. *Bury My Heart at Wounded Knee: An Indian History of the American West.* New York: Holt, Rinehart & Winston, Inc., 1970.

———. *Fort Phil Kearny: An American Saga.* Lincoln: University of Nebraska Press, 1971.

Burke Leacock, Eleanor. *Myths of Male Dominance: Collected Articles on Women Cross–Culturally.* New York: Monthly Review Press, 1981.

Burnette, Robert, and John Koster. *The Road to Wounded Knee.* New York: Bantam Books, 1974.

Burt, Larry W. *Tribalism in Crisis: Federal Indian Policy, 1953–1961.* Albuquerque: University of New Mexico Press, 1982.

Burton, Lloyd. *American Indian Water Rights and the Limits of the Law.* Lawrence: University Press of Kansas, 1991.

Cadwalader, Sandra L., and Vine Deloria, Jr., eds. *The Aggressions of Civilization: Federal Indian Policy Since the 1880s.* Philadelphia: Temple University Press, 1984.

Cadwallader, Colden. *The History of the Five Indian Nations.* Ithaca, New York: Cornell University Press, 1958.

Carley, Kenneth. *The Sioux Uprising of 1862.* St. Paul: Minnesota Historical Society, 1961.

Carranco, Lynwood, and Estle Beard. *Genocide and Vendetta: The Round Valley Wars of Northern California.* Norman: University of Oklahoma Press, 1981.

Carter, George F. *Earlier Than You Think: A Personal View of Man in the Americas.* College Station: Texas A&M Press, 1980.

Castro, Michael. *Interpreting the Indian: Twentieth Century Poets and the Native American.* Albuquerque: University of New Mexico Press, 1983.

Catton, William, Jr. *Overshoot: The Ecological Basis for Revolutionary Change.* Urbana: University of Illinois Press, 1982.

Ceram, C. W. *The First American.* New York: Mentor Books, 1972.

Chapman, Abraham, ed. *Literature of the American Indians: Views and Interpretations.* New York: New American Library, 1978.

Churchill, Ward. *Fantasies of the Master Race: Literature, Cinema and the Colonization of American Indians.* Monroe, Maine: Common Courage Press, 1992.

———. *Struggle for the Land: Indigenous Resistance to Genocide, Ecocide and Expropriation in Contemporary North America.* Monroe, Maine: Common Courage Press, 1993.

————. *Indians Are Us?* Monroe, Maine: Common Courage Press, 1994.

————, ed. *Marxism and Native Americans.* Boston: South End Press, 1983.

————, ed. *Critical Issues in Native North America* (IWGIA Doc. 63). Copenhagen: International Work Group on Indigenous Affairs, 1989.

————, ed. *Critical Issues in Native North America, Vol. II* (IWGIA Doc. 68). Copenhagen: International Work Group on Indigenous Affairs, 1991.

Churchill, Ward, and Elisabeth R. Lloyd. *Culture versus Economism: Essays on Marxism in the Multicultural Arena.* 2d ed. Denver: Fourth World Center for the Study of Indigenous Law and Politics, University of Colorado at Denver, 1989.

Churchill, Ward, and Jim Vander Wall. *Agents of Repression: The FBI's Secret Wars Against the Black Panther Party and the American Indian Movement.* Boston: South End Press, 1988.

————. *The COINTELPRO Papers: Documents from the FBI's Secret Wars Against Dissent in the United States.* Boston: South End Press, 1990.

Clark, Robert, ed. *The Killing of Chief Crazy Horse.* Lincoln: University of Nebraska Press, 1976.

Clifton, James E., ed. *The Invented Indian: Cultural Fictions and Government Policies.* New Brunswick, New Jersey: Transaction Books, 1990.

Clinton, Robert N., Nell Jessup Newton, and Monroe E. Price. *American Indian Law: Cases and Material.* Charlottesville, Virginia: Michie Co., Law Publishers, 1991.

Cohen, Faye G. *Treaties on Trial: The Continuing Controversy over Northwest Indian Fishing Rights.* Seattle: University of Washington Press, 1986.

Cohen, Felix S. *Handbook on Federal Indian Law.* Albuquerque: University of New Mexico Press, n.d.; reprint of 1942 U.S. Government Printing Office edition.

————. *The Legal Conscience: Selected Papers.* New Haven, Connecticut: Yale University Press, 1960.

Cole, Douglas, and Ira Chaikan. *An Iron Hand upon the People: The Law Against Potlatch on the Northwest Coast.* Seattle: University of Washington Press, 1990.

Connell, Evan S. *Son of the Morning Star: Custer and the Little Big Horn.* San Francisco: North Point Press, 1984.

Cook, Sherburn F. *The Conflict Between the California Indians and White Civilization.* Berkeley: University of California Press, 1976.

Cook, Sherburn Friend, and Leslie B. Simpson. *The Population of Central Mexico in the Sixteenth Century.* Ibero–Americana No. 31. Berkeley: University of California Press, 1948.

Corkran, David H. *The Creek Frontier, 1540–1783.* Norman: University of Oklahoma Press, 1967.

Courlander, Harold. *The Fourth World of the Hopis.* New York: Fawcett, 1971.

Craig, Reginald S. *The Fighting Parson: The Biography of Colonel John M. Chivington.* Los Angeles: Westernlore Press, 1959.

Cronan, William. *Changes in the Land: Indians, Colonists and the Ecology of New England.* New York: Hill and Wang, 1983.

Crosby, Alfred W., Jr. *The Columbian Exchange: Biological and Cultural Consequences of 1492.* Westport, Connecticut: Greenwood Press, 1972.

Crow Dog, Mary, with Richard Erdoes. *Lakota Woman.* New York: Grove, Weidenfeld, 1990.

Danner, Mark. *The Massacre at El Mozote.* New York: Vintage Books, 1993.

Davis, Mark, and Robert Zannis. *The Genocide Machine in Canada: The Pacification of the North.* Montréal: Black Rose Books, 1973.

Deane, Herbert Andrew. *The Political and Social Ideas of St. Augustine.* New York: Columbia University Press, 1963.

Debo, Angie. *The Road to Disappearance: A History of the Creek Indians*. Norman: University of Oklahoma Press, 1941.
————. *A History of the Indians of the United States*. Norman: University of Oklahoma Press, 1970.
Deer, Ada, with R. E. Simon. *Speaking Out*. Chicago: Children's Press, 1970.
Deloria, Ella C. *Speaking of Indians*. New York: Friendship Press, 1944; reprinted in 1979 by Dakota Press, Vermillion, South Dakota.
Deloria, Vine, Jr. *Custer Died for Your Sins: An Indian Manifesto*. New York: Macmillan Publishing Co., 1969.
————. *We Talk, You Listen: New Tribes, New Turf*. New York: Macmillan Publishing Co., 1970.
————. *God Is Red*. New York: Grosset and Dunlap, 1973.
————. *A Better Day for Indians*. New York: Field Foundation, 1977.
————. *Indians of the Pacific Northwest: From the Coming of the White Man to the Present Day*. Garden City, New York: Doubleday, 1977.
————. *Metaphysics of Modern Existence*. New York: Harper and Row, 1979.
————. *Behind the Trail of Broken Treaties: An Indian Declaration of Independence*. New York: Delacourte, 1974. 2d ed. Austin: University of Texas Press, 1984.
————, ed. *American Indian Policy in the Twentieth Century*. Norman: University of Oklahoma Press, 1985.
Deloria, Vine, Jr., and Clifford M. Lytle. *American Indians, American Justice*. Austin: University of Texas Press, 1983.
————. *The Nations Within: The Past and Future of American Indian Sovereignty*. New York: Pantheon Press, 1984.
DeMallie, Raymond. *Lakota Society*. Lincoln: University of Nebraska Press, 1982.
DeMallie, Raymond, and Elaine Jahner, eds. *Lakota Belief and Ritual*. Lincoln: University of Nebraska Press, 1980.
DeMille, Richard B. *The Don Juan Papers: Further Castanéda Controversies*. Santa Barbara, California: Ross–Erikson, 1980.
Denevan, William H., ed. *The Native Population of the Americas in 1492*. Madison: University of Wisconsin Press, 1976.
Díaz del Castillo, Bernal. *The Discovery and Conquest of Mexico*. New York: Farrar, Strauss and Giroux, 1956.
————. *The Conquest of New Spain*. New York: Penguin Books, 1963.
Dillehay, Tom D., and David J. Meltzer, eds. *The First Americans: Search and Research*. Boca Raton, Florida: CRC Press, 1991.
Dobyns, Henry F. *Native American Historical Demography: A Critical Bibliography*. Bloomington: Indiana University Press, 1976.
————. *Their Numbers Become Thinned: Native American Population Dynamics in Eastern North America*. Knoxville: University of Tennessee Press, 1983.
Downes, Rudolph C. *Council Fires on the Upper Ohio*. Pittsburgh: University of Pittsburgh Press, 1940.
Dozier, Edward P. *The Pueblo Indians*. New York: Holt, Rinehart & Winston, Inc., 1970.
Dodge, Frederick W. *Handbook of the Indians North of Mexico*. 2 vols. Washington, DC: Bureau of American Ethnology, Bulletin No. 30, Smithsonian Institution, 1910.
Drinnon, Richard. *Keeper of Concentration Camps: Dillon S. Myer and American Racism*. Berkeley: University of California Press, 1987.
————. *Facing West: The Metaphysics of Indian Hating and Empire Building*. 2d ed. New York: Schocken Books, 1990.
Driver, Harold E. *The Indians of North America*. Chicago: University of Chicago Press, 1961.

Driver, Harold E., and William C. Massey. *Comparative Studies of American Indians.* American Philosophical Society, Transactions, Vol. XLVII, n.s., 1957.

Drucker, Philip. *Cultures of the Northwest Coast.* San Francisco: Chandler, 1965.

Dunbar Ortiz, Roxanne, ed. *The Great Sioux Nation: Sitting in Judgement on America.* New York/San Francisco: International Indian Treaty Council/Moon Books, 1977.

————. *Indians of the Americas: Human Rights and Self–Determination.* London: Zed Press, 1984.

Dunbar Ortiz, Roxanne, and Larry Emerson, eds. *Economic Development in American Indian Reservations.* Albuquerque: Native American Studies Program, University of New Mexico, 1979.

Dunlay, Thomas. *Wolves for the Blue Soldiers: Indian Scouts and Auxiliaries with the U.S. Army, 1860–90.* Lincoln: University of Nebraska Press, 1982.

Dunn, Lt. Col. William R. *"I Stand by Sand Creek": A Defense of Colonel John M. Chivington and the Third Colorado Cavalry.* Fort Collins, Colorado: The Old Army Press, 1985.

Durham, Jimmie. *Columbus Day.* Minneapolis: West End Press, 1983.

Eastman, Charles. *Old Indian Days.* New York: McClure, 1907.

————. *The Soul of the Indian: An Interpretation.* New York: Johnson Reprint Corp., 1971; originally published in 1911.

————. *From Deep Woods to Civilization: Chapters in the Autobiography of an American Indian.* Boston: Little, Brown, & Co., Inc., 1916.

————. *Indian Heroes and Great Chieftains.* Boston: Little, Brown, & Co., Inc., 1918.

Editors. *BIA, I'm Not Your Indian Anymore, Akwesasne Notes.* Mohawk Nation via Rooseveltown, New York, 1973.

————. *Voices from Wounded Knee, 1973, Akwesasne Notes.* Mohawk Nation via Rooseveltown, New York, 1974.

————. *A Basic Call to Consciousness, Akwesasne Notes.* Mohawk Nation via Rooseveltown, New York, 1978.

Edmunds, R. David. *Tecumseh and the Quest for Indian Leadership.* Boston: Little, Brown & Co., Inc. 1984.

Edwards, Paul D. *The Holland Company.* Buffalo, New York: Buffalo Historical Society, 1924.

Egerton, Hugh Edward. *A Short History of British Colonial Policy.* London: Methuen, 1897.

Eliot, John. *New England's First Fruits.* New York: Joseph Sabin, 1865.

Elliot, J. H. *The Old World and the New, 1492–1650.* Cambridge, Massachusetts: Cambridge University Press, 1970.

Englebert, Omer. *The Last of the Conquistadors: Junipero Serra.* New York: Harcourt, Brace and Co., 1956.

Englehart, Charles A. (Fr. Zephyrin). *The Missions and Missionaries of California.* 4 vols. San Francisco: James H. Barry, 1908–1916.

Ericson, Jonathan E., R. E. Taylor, and Rainier Berger, eds. *The Peopling of the New World.* Los Altos, California: Ballena Press, 1982.

Etienne, Mona, and Eleanor Burke Leacock, eds. *Women and Colonization: Anthropological Perspectives.* New York: Praeger, 1980.

Ewers, John C. *The Blackfeet: Raiders of the Northern Plains.* Norman: University of Oklahoma Press, 1958.

Falla, Ricardo. *Massacres in the Jungle: Ixcán, Guatemala, 1975–1982.* Boulder, Colorado: Westview Press, 1994.

Faulk, Obie B. *The Geronimo Campaign.* New York: Oxford University Press, 1969.

Fehrenbach, T. R. *Comanches: The Destruction of a People.* New York: Alfred A. Knopf, 1975.

Fey, Harold Edward, and D'Arcy McNickle. *Indians and Other Americans: Two Ways of Life Meet*. New York: Harper and Brothers (rev. ed.), 1959.

Fielder, Leslie. *The Return of the Vanishing American*. New York: Stein and Day, 1968.

Fisher, Robin. *Contact and Conflict: Indian–European Relations in British Columbia, 1774–1890*. Vancouver: University of British Columbia Press, 1977.

Fixico, Donald L. *Termination and Relocation: Federal Indian Policy, 1945–1960*. Albuquerque: University of New Mexico Press, 1986.

Flexner, James Thomas. *Lord of the Mohawks: A Biography of Sir William Johnson*. Boston: Little, Brown, & Co., Inc., 1979.

Floyd, Trof. *The Columbus Dynasty in the Caribbean, 1492–1526*. Albuquerque: University of New Mexico Press, 1973.

Folke–Williams, John. *What Indian Water Means to the West: A Sourcebook*. Santa Fe, New Mexico: Western Network, 1982.

Forbes, Jack D. *Native Americans and Nixon, Presidential Politics and Minority Self–Determination*. Los Angeles: UCLA American Indian Studies Center, UCLA, 1981.

———. *Black Africans and Native Americans: Race, Color and Caste in the Evolution of Red–Black Peoples*. London/New York: Oxford University Press, 1988.

Ford, Washington C., et al., eds. and comps. *Journals of the Continental Congress, 1774–1789*. 34 vols. Washington, DC: U.S. Government Printing Office, 1904–1937.

Foreman, Caroline. *American Indian Women Chiefs*. Muskogee, Oklahoma: Hoffman Printing Co., 1954.

Foreman, Grant. *Advancing the Frontier, 1830–1860*. Norman: University of Oklahoma Press, 1933.

———. *Indian Removal: The Immigration of the Five Civilized Tribes*. Norman: University of Oklahoma Press, 1953.

Franks, Kenny A. *Stand Watie and the Agony of the Cherokee Nation*. Memphis, Tennessee: Memphis State University Press, 1979.

Friar, Ralph, and Natasha Friar. *The Only Good Indian... The Hollywood Gospel*. New York: Drama Book Specialists/Publishers, 1972.

Fritz, Henry E. *The Movement for Indian Assimilation, 1860–1890*. Philadelphia: University of Pennsylvania Press, 1963.

Fuchs, Estelle, and Robert J. Havighurst. *To Live on This Earth: American Indian Education*. Garden City, New York: Anchor Books, 1973.

Galeano, Eduardo. *The Open Veins of Latin America: Five Centuries of the Pillage of a Continent*. New York: Monthly Review Press, 1973.

———. *Memory of Fire: Genesis*. New York: Pantheon Books, 1985.

———. *Memory of Fire: Faces & Masks*. New York: Pantheon Books, 1987.

———. *Memory of Fire: Century of the Wind*. New York: Pantheon Books, 1988.

Gates, Paul. *The History of Public Land Law Development*. Washington, DC: Zenger Publishing Co., 1968.

Gerbi, Antonello. *The Dispute over the New World: The History of a Polemic, 1750–1900*. Pittsburgh: University of Pittsburgh Press, 1955.

Getty, Ian L., and Donald B. Smith. *One Century Later: Western Canadian Reserve Indians Since Treaty 7*. Vancouver: University of British Columbia Press, 1978.

Giago, Tim. *Notes from Indian Country*. Vol. 1. Pierre, South Dakota: State Publishing Co., 1984.

Gibson, Arrell Morgan. *The American Indian: Prehistory to the Present*. Lexington, Massachusetts: DC Heath and Co., 1985.

Gibson, Charles, ed. *The Spanish Tradition in America*. New York: Harper and Row, 1968.

Gierke, Otto Friedrich von. *Natural Law and the Theory of Society, 1500–1800*. Cambridge, Massachusetts: Cambridge University Press, 1934.
————. *The Development of Political Theory*. New York: W. W. Norton, 1939.
Gist, Noel P., and Anthony J. Dworkin. *The Blending of Races: Marginality and Identity in World Perspective*. New York: Wiley–Interscience Books, 1972.
Glass, Mary Ellen. *Water for Nevada: The Reclamation Controversy, 1885–1902*. Reno: University of Nevada Press, 1964.
Goodman, James M. *The Navajo Atlas*. Norman: University of Oklahoma Press, 1982.
Goodman, Jeffrey. *American Genesis: The American Indian and the Origins of Modern Man*. New York: Summit Books, 1981.
Gordon–McCutchan, R. C. *The Taos Indians and the Battle for Blue Lake*. Sante Fe, New Mexico: Red Crane Books, 1991.
Gorz, Andre. *Ecology as Politics*. Boston: South End Press, 1981.
Gould, Steven Jay. *The Mismeasure of Man*. New York: W. W. Norton, 1981.
Graburn, Nelson H. H. *Ethnic and Tourist Arts: Cultural Expressions from the Fourth World*. Berkeley: University of California Press, 1976.
Gray, John E. *Centennial Campaign: The Sioux War of 1876*. Norman: University of Oklahoma Press, 1988.
Graymont, Barbara. *The Iroquois in the American Revolution*. Syracuse, New York: Syracuse University Press, 1972.
Great Lakes Indian Fish and Wildlife Commission. *Moving Beyond Argument: Racism and Treaty Rights*. Odanah, Wisconsin: Public Information Office, n.d.
Green, Donald E. *The Creek People*. Phoenix: Indian Tribal Series Books, 1973.
————. *The Politics of Indian Removal: Creek Government and Society in Crisis*. Lincoln: University of Nebraska Press, 1977.
Greene, Jerome. *Slim Buttes, 1877: An Episode in the Great Sioux War*. Norman: University of Oklahoma Press, 1982.
Grinde, Donald A. *The Iroquois in the Founding of the American Nation*. San Francisco: Indian Historian Press, 1977.
Grinde, Donald A., Jr., and Bruce Johansen. *Exemplar of Liberty: Native America and the Evolution of Democracy*. Los Angeles: UCLA American Indian Studies Program, 1991.
Guie, D. H. *Tribal Days of the Yakima*. North Yakima, Washington: Republic, 1937.
Gunder Frank, André. *Capitalism and Underdevelopment in Latin America*. New York: Monthly Review Press, 1969.
Gunn Allen, Paula. *The Sacred Hoop: Recovering the Feminine in American Indian Tradition*. Boston: Beacon Press, 1986.
————. *Spider Woman's Granddaughters: Traditional Tales and Contemporary Writing by American Indian Women*. Boston: Beacon Press, 1989.
Guzmán, Peredo. *Medical Practices in Ancient America*. Mexico City: Ediciones Euroamericana, 1985.
Haas, Theodore H., ed. *Felix S. Cohen: A Fighter for Justice*. Washington, DC: Alumni Association of the City College of New York, 1956.
Hafen, LeRoy R., and Francis Marion Young. *Fort Laramie and the Pageant of the West, 1834–1890*. Lincoln: University of Nebraska Press, 1938.
Hanke, Lewis. *The First Social Experiments in America: A Study of the Development of Spanish Indian Policy in the Sixteenth Century*. Cambridge, Massachusetts: Harvard University Press, 1934.
————. *The Spanish Struggle for Justice in the Conquest of America*. Philadelphia: University of Pennsylvania Press, 1949.
————. *Aristotle and the American Indians: A Study in Race Prejudice in the Modern World*. Bloomington/Indianapolis: Indiana University Press, 1959.

————. *All Mankind Is One: A Study in the Disputation Between Bartolomé de Las Casas and Juan Ginés de Sepúlveda in 1550 on the Intellectual and Religious Capacity of American Indians.* Dekalb: Northern Illinois University Press, 1974.

Harrison, David C. *Do We Need a National Water Policy?* Washington, DC: National Academy of Public Administration, 1981.

Hartigan, Francis, ed. *MX in Nevada: A Humanistic Perspective.* Reno: Nevada Humanities Press, 1980.

Harvey Pearce, Roy. *Savagism and Civilization: A Study of the American Indian in the American Mind.* Baltimore: Johns Hopkins University Press, 1953.

————. *The Savages of America: A Study of the Indian and the Idea of Civilization.* Baltimore: Johns Hopkins University Press, 1965.

Hassrick, Royal B. *The Sioux: Life and Customs of a Warrior Society.* Norman: University of Oklahoma Press, 1964.

Hauptman, Lawrence M. *The Iroquois Struggle for Survival: World War II to Red Power.* Syracuse, New York: Syracuse University Press, 1986.

Haury, Emil W. *The Hohokam: Desert Farmers and Craftsmen.* Tucson: University of Arizona Press, 1976.

Hay, Denys. *Europe: The Emergence of an Idea.* Edinburgh, Scotland: University of Edinburgh Press, 1968.

Hays, Samuel P. *Conservation and the Gospel of Efficiency.* Cambridge, Massachusetts: Harvard University Press, 1959.

Hebard, Grace, and E. A. Brindenstool. *The Bozeman Trail.* 2 vols. Cleveland: Arthur H. Clark, 1922.

Hechwelder, John G. E. *A Narrative of the Mission of the United Brethren Among the Delaware and Mohegan Indians from Its Commencement in 1740 to the Close of the Year 1808.* Philadelphia: McCartney and Davis, 1820.

Heizer, Robert F., ed. *The Destruction of the California Indians.* Salt Lake City/Santa Barbara: Peregrine Smith, Inc., 1974.

Hemming, John. *Red Gold: The Conquest of the Brazilian Indians.* London: Macmillan Publishing Co., 1978.

Hertzberg, Hazel W. *The Search for an Indian Identity: Modern Pan–Indian Movements.* Syracuse, New York: Syracuse University Press, 1971.

Heth, Charlotte, and Susan Guyette. *Issues for the Future of American Indian Studies.* Los Angeles: UCLA American Indian Studies Center, 1985.

Hickerson, Harold. *The Chippewa and Their Neighbors: A Study in Ethnohistory.* New York: Holt, Rinehart & Winston, Inc., 1970.

Hobson, Geary, ed. *The Remembered Earth.* Albuquerque, New Mexico: Red Earth Press, 1978.

Hoebel, E. Adamson. *The Law of Primitive Man: A Study in Comparative Legal Dynamics.* Cambridge, Massachusetts: Harvard University Press, 1964.

Hoig, Stan. *The Sand Creek Massacre.* Norman: University of Oklahoma Press, 1961.

————. *The Battle of the Washita: The Sheridan–Custer Campaign of 1867–69.* Lincoln: University of Nebraska Press, 1976.

Hoopes, Alban W. *Indian Affairs and Their Administration with Special Preference to the Far West, 1849–1860.* Philadelphia: University of Pennsylvania Press, 1932.

Hopkins, David M., ed. *The Bering Land Bridge.* Stanford, California: Stanford University Press, 1967.

Hornaday, William T. *Exterminating the American Bison.* Washington, DC: Smithsonian Institution, U.S. Government Printing Office, 1899.

Horsman, Reginald. *Expansion and American Policy, 1783–1812.* Lansing: Michigan State University Press, 1967.

————. *Race and Manifest Destiny: The Origins of Racial Anglo–Saxonism.* Cambridge, Massachusetts: Harvard University Press, 1981.

Hu–DeHart, Evelyn. *Yaqui Resistance and Survival.* Madison: University of Wisconsin Press, 1984.

Huddleston, Lee H. *Origins of the American Indians, European Concepts, 1492–1729.* Austin: University of Texas Press, 1969.

Hundley, Norris. *Water and the West.* Berkeley: University of California Press, 1975.

Hungry Wolf, Beverly. *The Ways of My Grandmothers.* New York: William Morrow, 1980.

Hunt, George T. *The Wars of the Iroquois.* Madison: University of Wisconsin Press, 1940.

Hunter Austin, Mary. *Path on the Rainbow: An Anthology of Songs and Chants from the Indians of North America.* New York: Liveright, 1918.

————. *The American Rhythm: Studies and Re–Expressions of Amerindian Songs.* Boston: Houghton–Mifflin Co., 1923.

Hurt, James C. *American Indian Agriculture.* Lawrence: University Press of Kansas, 1991.

Independent Commission on International Humanitarian Issues. *Indigenous Peoples: A Global Quest for Justice.* London: Zed Press, 1987.

Iverson, Peter. *The Navajo Nation.* Westport, Connecticut: Greenwood Press, 1981.

Jackson, Curtis E., and Marcia J. Galli. *A History of the Bureau of Indian Affairs and Its Activities Among Indians.* San Francisco: R&E Research Associates, 1977.

Jackson, Donald. *Custer's Gold: The United States Cavalry Expedition of 1874.* Lincoln: University of Nebraska Press, 1966.

Jackson, Helen Hunt. *A Century of Dishonor.* New York: Harper Torchbooks, 1965; reprint of the 1881 edition by A. F. Rolfe.

Jacobs, Paul, et al. *To Serve the Devil, Vol. I: Natives and Slaves.* New York: Random House, 1971.

Jacobs, Wilbur. *Dispossessing the American Indian: Indians and Whites on the Colonial Frontier.* New York: Charles Scribner, Publisher, 1972.

Jahoda, Gloria. *The Trail of Tears: The Story of the American Indian Removals, 1813–1855.* New York: Holt, Rinehart & Winston, Inc., 1975.

Jaimes, M. Annette, ed. *The State of Native America: Genocide, Colonization, and Resistance.* Boston: South End Press, 1992.

Jaimeson, Kathleen. *Indian Women and the Law in Canada: Citizens Minus.* Ottawa: Advisory Council on the Status of Women/Indian Rights for Indian Women, 1978.

James, Harry, ed. *Pages from Hopi History.* Tucson: University of Arizona Press, 1976.

Jennings, Francis. *The Invasion of America: Indians, Colonialism, and the Cant of Conquest.* New York: W. W. Norton and Co., 1976.

Jennings, Jesse D. *Prehistory of North America.* New York: McGraw–Hill, 1974.

Johansen, Bruce. *Forgotten Founders: How the American Indian Helped Shape Democracy.* Cambridge, Massachusetts: The Harvard Common Press, 1982.

Johansen, Bruce, and Roberto Maestas. *Wasi'chu: The Continuing Indian Wars.* New York: Monthly Review Press, 1979.

Johnson, Basil H. *Indian School Days.* Toronto: Key Porter Books, Ltd., 1988.

Johnson, Broderick R., ed. *Navajos and World War II.* Tsaile, Arizona: Navajo Community College Press, 1977.

Jones, David. *Sanapia: A Comanche Medicine Woman.* New York: Holt, Rinehart & Winston, Inc., 1968.

Jones, Dorothy V. *License for Empire: Colonialism by Treaty in Early America.* Chicago: University of Chicago Press, 1982.

Jones, Oakah L., Jr. *Pueblo Warriors and the Spanish Conquest.* Norman: University of Oklahoma Press, 1966.

Jordan, Winthrop D. *The White Man's Burden.* London/New York: Oxford University Press, 1974.

Jorgenson, Joseph, ed. *Native Americans and Energy Development.* Cambridge, Massachusetts: Anthropological Resource Center, 1978.

————, ed. *Native Americans and Energy Resource Development II.* Cambridge, Massachusetts: Anthropological Resource Center/Seventh Generation Fund, 1984.

Joseph, Gloria I., and Jill Lewis. *Common Differences: Conflicts in Black and White Feminist Perspectives.* Boston: South End Press, 1981.

Josephy, Alvin M., Jr. *Red Power: The American Indians' Fight for Freedom.* New York: McGraw–Hill, 1971.

————. *Now That the Buffalo's Gone: A Study of Today's American Indians.* 2d ed. Norman: University of Oklahoma Press, 1984.

Kahn, Herman, William Brown, and Leon Martle. *The Next 200 Years: A Scenario for America and the World.* New York: William Morrow, 1976.

Kammer, Jerry. *The Second Long Walk: The Navajo–Hopi Land Dispute.* Albuquerque: University of New Mexico Press, 1980.

Kappler, Charles J., ed. *Indian Treaties, 1778–1883.* New York: Interland Publishing Co., 1973.

Katz, Jane B. *I Am the Fire of Time: The Voices of Native American Women.* New York: E. P. Dutton Publisher, 1977.

Kelly, Lawrence C. *The Navajo Indians and Federal Policy, 1900–1935.* Tucson: University of Arizona Press, 1968.

————. *Navajo Roundup.* Boulder, Colorado: Pruett Publishing Co., 1970.

Kelly, William H., ed. *Indian Affairs and the Indian Reorganization Act: The Twenty Year Record.* Tucson: University of Arizona Press, 1954.

Kepner, Charles O., Jr., and Jay H. Soothill. *The Panama Empire.* New York: Vanguard Press, Inc., 1935.

Kicking Bird, Kirk, and Karen Ducheneaux. *One Hundred Million Acres.* New York: Macmillan Publishing Co., 1973.

King, Duane H. *The Cherokee Nation: A Troubled History.* Knoxville: University of Tennessee Press, 1979.

Kinney, Jay P. *A Continent Lost—A Civilization Won: Indian Land Tenure in America.* Baltimore: Johns Hopkins University Press, 1937.

Knorr, K. *British Colonial Theories, 1570–1850.* Toronto: University of Toronto Press, 1944.

Konig, Hans. *Columbus: His Enterprise.* New York: Monthly Review Press, 1976.

————. *The Conquest of America: How the Indian Nations of America Lost Their Continent.* New York: Monthly Review Press, 1993.

Kroeber, Alfred Louis. *Cultural and Natural Areas of Native North America.* University of California Publications in Archaeology and Ethnology, No. 38. Berkeley: University of California Press, 1939.

————. *Anthropology.* New York: Macmillan Publishing Co., 1948.

Kroeber, Theodora, ed. *A. L. Kroeber: An Anthropologist Looks at History.* Berkeley/Los Angeles: University of California Press, 1966.

Kvasnicka, Robert M., and Herman J. Viola, eds. *The Commissioners of Indian Affairs, 1824–1977.* Lincoln: University of Nebraska Press, 1979.

LaFarge, Oliver. *The Changing Indian.* Norman: University of Oklahoma Press, 1942.

Lanning, John T. *The Spanish Missions of Georgia.* Chapel Hill: University of North Carolina Press, 1935.

Larson, Charles R. *American Indian Fiction*. Albuquerque: University of New Mexico Press, 1978.

Lawson, Michael L. *Dammed Indians: The Pick–Sloan Plan and the Missouri River Sioux, 1944–1980*. Norman: University of Oklahoma Press, 1982.

Leach, Douglas Edward. *Flintlocks and Tomahawks: New England in King Philip's War*. New York: W. W. Norton, 1958.

Lee, Bobbi. *Bobbi Lee: Indian Rebel*. Richmond, British Columbia: LSM Information Center, 1975.

Leland, Joy. *Firewater Myths: North American Indian Drinking and Drug Addiction*. New Brunswick, New Jersey: Rutgers Center for Alcohol Studies, Rutgers University, 1976.

Leupp, Francis E. *The Indian and His Problem*. New York: Charles Scribner's Sons, 1910.

Levin, Stuart, and Nancy O. Lurie. *The American Indian Today*. Deland, Florida: Everett and Edwards, 1965.

Lewis, Gordon. *The Indiana Company, 1763–1798*. Glendale, California: Clark, 1941.

Limerick, Patricia Nelson. *The Legacy of Conquest: The Unbroken Past of the American West*. New York: W. W. Norton and Co., 1987.

Linderman, Frank. *Pretty Shield: Medicine Woman of the Crows*. New York: John Day, 1932; reprinted in 1974.

Lindsey, Mark Frank. *The Acquisition and Government of Backward Territory in International Law*. London: Longmans, Green, 1926.

Lummis, Charles. *Bullying the Hopi*. Prescott, Arizona: Prescott College Press, 1968.

MacLauchlin, Colin M. *Spain's Empire in the New World: The Role of Ideas in Institutional and Social Change*. Berkeley: University of California Press, 1988.

MacLeod, Murdo J. *Spanish Central America: A Socioeconomic History, 1520–1720*. Berkeley: University of California Press, 1973.

McCallum, James D., ed. *The Letters of Eleazer Wheelock's Indians*. Hanover, New Hampshire: Dartmouth College Publications, 1932.

McCleod, William C. *The American Indian Frontier*. New York: Alfred A. Knopf, 1928.

McCool, Daniel. *Command of the Waters: Federal Water Development, Iron Triangles, and Indian Water*. Berkeley: University of California Press, 1987.

McDonnell, Janet A. *The Dispossession of the American Indian, 1887–1934*. Bloomington/Indianapolis: Indiana University Press, 1991.

McGinnis, Anthony. *Counting Coup and Cutting Horses: Intertribal Warfare on the Northern Plains, 1738–1889*. Evergreen, Colorado: Cordillera Press, 1990.

McKinley, Francis, Steven Bayne, and Glen Nimnicht. *Who Should Control Indian Education?* Berkeley, California: Far West Laboratory for Educational Research and Development, 1970.

McNickle, D'Arcy. *Native American Tribalism: Indian Survivals and Renewals*. London/New York: Oxford University Press, 1973.

———. *The Surrounded*. 2d ed. Albuquerque: University of New Mexico Press, 1978.

McWhorter, Lucius. *Crime Against the Yakimas*. North Yakima, Washington: Republic, WA, 1913.

Maestas, John, ed. *Contemporary Native American Address*. Salt Lake City: Brigham Young University Press, 1976.

Madsen, Brigham D. *The Shoshone Frontier and the Bear River Massacre*. Salt Lake City: University of Utah Press, 1985.

Magdoff, Harry. *The Age of Imperialism*. New York: Monthly Review Press, 1969.

Manley, Henry M. *The Treaty of Fort Stanwix, 1784*. Rome, New York: Rome Sentinal Publications, 1932.

Martin, Calvin, ed. *The American Indian and the Problem of History.* London/New York: Oxford University Press, 1987.

Martin, Joel W. *Sacred Revolt: The Muskogees' Struggle for a New World.* Boston: Beacon Press, 1991.

Matthiessen, Peter. *Indian Country.* New York: Viking Press, 1984.

————. *In the Spirit of Crazy Horse.* 2d ed. New York: Viking Press, 1991.

Mays, Buddy. *Ancient Cities of the Southwest.* San Francisco: Chronicle Books, 1962.

Merk, Frederick. *Manifest Destiny and Mission in American Life.* New York: Vintage Books, 1966.

Merriam, Lewis, et al. *The Problem of Indian Administration.* Baltimore: Johns Hopkins University Press, 1928.

Messerschmidt, Jim. *The Trial of Leonard Peltier.* Boston: South End Press, 1983.

Meyer, William. *Native Americans: The New Indian Resistence.* New York: International, 1971.

Miner, H. Craig. *The Corporation and the Indian: Tribal Sovereignty and Industrial Civilization in Indian Territory, 1865–1907.* Columbia: University of Missouri Press, 1976.

Minugh, Carol J., Glenn T. Morris, and Rudolph C. Ryser, eds. *Indian Self–Governance: Perspectives on the Political Status of Indian Nations in the United States of America.* Kenmore, Washington: Center for World Indigenous Studies, 1989.

Mohawk, John. *A Basic Call to Consciousness, Akwesasne Notes.* Mohawk Nation via Rooseveltown, New York, 1978.

Mohr, Walter Harrison. *Federal Indian Relations, 1774–1788.* Philadelphia: University of Pennsylvania Press, 1933.

Mooney, James M. *The Ghost–Dance Religion and the Sioux Outbreak of 1890.* Washington, DC: Smithsonian Institution, Bureau of American Ethnology, U.S. Government Printing Office, 1896.

————. *The Aboriginal Population of America North of Mexico.* Washington, DC: Smithsonian Miscellaneous Collections, XXX, No. 7, 1928.

————. *Historical Sketch of the Cherokee.* Chicago: Aldine Publishing Co., Chicago, 1975; reprinted from the 1900 edition.

Morgan, Ted. *The Wilderness at Dawn: The Settling of the North American Continent.* New York: Simon & Schuster, 1993.

Morison, Samuel Eliot, ed. and trans. *Journals and Other Documents on the Life and Voyages of Christopher Columbus.* New York: Heritage, 1963.

Müller, Werner. *America: The Old World or the New?* New York: Peter Lang, 1989.

Mulvey, Sister Mary Doris. *French Catholic Missionaries in the Present United States, 1604–1791.* Washington, DC: Catholic University of America Press, 1936.

Murray, Keith A. *The Modocs and Their War.* Norman: University of Oklahoma Press, 1959.

Nammack, Georgiana C. *Fraud, Politics, and the Dispossession of the Indian: The Iroquois Land Frontier in the Colonial Period.* Norman: University of Oklahoma Press, 1969.

Nadeau, Remi. *Fort Laramie and the Sioux.* Lincoln: University of Nebraska Press, 1967.

Nash, Gerald D. *The American West Transformed: The Impact of the Second World War.* Bloomington/Indianapolis: Indiana University Press, 1988.

Nash, J. Brian. *The New Deal for Indians: A Survey of the Workings of the Indian Reorganization Act of 1934.* New York: Academy Press, 1938.

Neithammer, Carolyn. *Daughters of the Earth: The Lives and Legends of Native American Women.* New York: Macmillan Publishing Co., 1977.

Neihardt, John G., ed. *Black Elk Speaks.* New York: William Morrow, 1932.

Newcome, W. W., Jr. *The Indians of Texas.* Austin: University of Texas Press, 1961.

Nichols, Claude A. *Moral Education Among the North American Indians*. New York: Columbia University Teachers College Bureau of Publications, 1930.

Nabokov, Peter, and Robert Easton. *American Indian Architecture*. London/New York: Oxford University Press, 1988.

O'Brien, Sharon. *American Indian Tribal Governments*. Norman: University of Oklahoma Press, 1989.

O'Daniel, Victor F. *Dominicans in Early Florida*. New York: United States Catholic Historical Society, 1930.

Olsen, James C. *Red Cloud and the Sioux Problem*. Lincoln: University of Nebraska Press, 1965.

Otis, D. S. *The Dawes Act and the Allotment of Indian Land*. Norman: University of Oklahoma Press, 1973.

Orata, Pedro T. *Democracy and Indian Education*. Washington, DC: U.S. Department of Interior, Office of Indian Affairs, 1938.

Ortiz, Alfonso, ed. *New Perspectives on the Pueblos*. Albuquerque: School of American Research, University of New Mexico, 1972.

Ortiz, Simon J. *From Sand Creek*. New York: Thunder's Mouth Press, 1981.

Osgood, Herbert L. *The American Colonies in the Seventeenth Century*. 3 vols. New York: Macmillan Publishing Co., 1904.

Owsley, Frank Lawrence, Jr. *The Struggle for the Gulf Borderlands: The Creek War and the Battle of New Orleans, 1812–1815*. Gainesville: University Presses of Florida, 1981.

Paiewonsky, Michael. *The Conquest of Eden, 1493–1515*. St. Thomas, Virgin Islands: Mapes Monde Editore, 1991.

Parrins, James W. *John Rollin Ridge: His Life and Works*. Lincoln: University of Nebraska Press, 1991.

Parlow, Anita. *Cry, Sacred Ground: Big Mountain, USA*. Washington, DC: Christic Institute, 1988.

Parry, John Horace. *The Spanish Theory of Empire in the Sixteenth Century*. Cambridge, Massachusetts: Cambridge University Press, 1940.

―――. *The Establishment of European Hegemony, 1415–1713*. New York: Harper and Row, 1966.

Paul, Doris. *They Talked Navajo: The United States Marine Corps Code Talkers of World War II*. Window Rock, Arizona: Navajo Tribal Museum, 1972.

Peckman, Howard, and Charles Gibson, eds. *Attitudes of the Colonial Powers Toward the American Indian*. Salt Lake City: University of Utah Press, 1969.

Peckman, Howard Henry. *Pontiac and the Indian Uprising*. New York: Russell and Russell, 1970.

Perdue, Theda. *Slavery and the Evolution of Cherokee Society, 1540–1866*. Knoxville: University of Tennessee Press, 1979.

Peroff, Nicholis. *Menominee DRUMS: Tribal Termination and Restoration, 1954–1974*. Norman: University of Oklahoma Press, 1982.

Phelps Kellogg, Louise. *The French Régime in Wisconsin and the Northwest*. Vol. 15. Madison: State Historical Society of Wisconsin, 1925.

Philp, Kenneth R. *John Collier's Crusade for Indian Reform, 1920–1954*. Tucson: University of Arizona Press, 1977.

―――, ed. *Indian Self–Rule: First–Hand Accounts of Indian–White Relations from Roosevelt to Reagan*. Salt Lake City: Howe Brothers, 1986.

Pirtle, Caleb, III. *The Trail of Broken Promises: Removal of the Five Civilized Tribes to Oklahoma*. Austin, Texas: Eakin Press, 1987.

Porter, Harry Culverwell. *The Inconsistent Savage: England and the American Indian, 1500–1600*. London: Duckworth, 1979.

Powers, Marla N. *Oglala Women: Myth, Ritual and Reality.* Chicago: University of Chicago Press, 1986.

Pratt, Richard H. *Battlefield and Classroom: Four Decades with the American Indian.* New Haven, Connecticut: Yale University Press, 1964.

Prescott, William H. *History of the Conquest of Mexico & History of the Conquest of Peru.* New York: Modern Library, n.d.

Price, Monroe, and Gary Weatherford. *American Indians and the Law.* New Brunswick, New Jersey: Transaction Books, 1976.

Prucha, Francis Paul. *American Indian Policy in the Formative Years: The Indian Trade and Intercourse Acts, 1790–1834.* Lincoln: University of Nebraska Press, 1970.

———. *Americanizing the American Indian: Writings of the "Friends of the Indian," 1800–1900.* Lincoln: University of Nebraska Press, 1973.

———. *Documents of United States Indian Policy.* Lincoln: University of Nebraska Press, 1975.

———. *American Indian Policy in Crisis: Christian Reformers and the Indian, 1865–1900.* Norman: University of Oklahoma Press, 1976.

———. *Atlas of American Indian Affairs.* Lincoln: University of Nebraska Press, 1990.

Quinn, David Beers, ed. *The Two Roanoak Voyages, 1584–1590.* 2d series, vols. 104–05. London: Haklyt Society Publications, 1955.

———. *England and the Discovery of America, 1481–1620.* New York: Alfred A. Knopf, 1974.

Rabasa, José. *Inventing A–M–E–R–I–C–A: Spanish Historiography and the Formation of Eurocentrism.* Norman: University of Oklahoma Press, 1993.

Rawls, James H. *The Indians of California: The Changing Image.* Norman: University of Oklahoma Press, 1984.

Reisner, Mark. *Cadillac Desert: The American West and Its Disappearing Water.* New York: Viking Press, 1986.

Richardson, Leon B. *The History of Dartmouth College.* 2 vols. Hanover, New Hampshire: Dartmouth College Publications, 1932.

Riddell, Jeff C. *The Indian History of the Modoc War and the Causes That Led to It.* Medford, Oregon: Pine Cone, 1973.

Robinson, Walter Stilt. *The Southern Colonial Frontier, 1607–1763.* Albuquerque: University of New Mexico Press, 1979.

Roe, Frank Gilbert. *The Indian and His Horse.* Norman: University of Oklahoma Press, 1955.

Ross, John. *Rebellion from the Roots: Indian Uprising in Chiapas.* Monroe, Maine: Common Courage Press, 1995.

Royce, Charles C. *Indian Land Cessions in the United States: 18th Annual Report, 1896–97.* 2 vols. Washington, DC: Smithsonian Institution, Bureau of American Ethnography, 1899.

Rushmore, Elsie M. *The Indian Policy During Grant's Administration.* New York: Marion Press, 1914.

Russell Tribunal. *The Rights of the Indians of the Americas.* Rotterdam, Netherlands: Fourth Russell Tribunal, 1980.

Ryser, Rudolph C. *Tribes and States in Conflict: A Tribal Proposal, Intertribal Study Group on Tribal/State Relations.* Seattle: Rational Island Press, 1981.

Salaman, Redcliffe N. *The History and Social Influence of the Potato.* Cambridge, Massachusetts: Cambridge University Press, 1949.

Sale, Kirkpatrick. *The Conquest of Paradise: Christopher Columbus and the Columbian Legacy.* New York: Alfred A. Knopf, 1990.

Sando, Joe. *The Pueblo Indians.* San Francisco: Indian Historian Press, 1976.

Sandoz, Mari. *Crazy Horse: Strange Man of the Oglalas*. Lincoln: University of Nebraska Press, 1961.
————. *The Beaver Men*. Lincoln: University of Nebraska Press, 1962.
————. *Cheyenne Autumn*. New York: Avon Books, 1964.
————. *The Battle of the Little Big Horn*. New York: Curtis Books, 1966.
Sargent, Daniel. *Christopher Columbus*. Milwaukee: Bruce Publishing, 1941.
Sauer, Carl O. *Sixteenth Century North America*. Berkeley: University of California Press, 1971.
Schaaf, Gregory. *Wampum Belts and Peace Trees: George Morgan, Native Americans and Revolutionary Diplomacy*. Golden, Colorado: Fulcrum, 1990.
Schmeckebier, Laurence. *The Office of Indian Affairs: Its History, Activities and Organization*. Baltimore: Johns Hopkins University Press, 1927.
Scholder, Fritz. *Indian Kitsch*. Flagstaff, Arizona: Northland Press, 1979.
Schöler, Bo, ed. *Coyote Was Here: Essays on Contemporary Native American Literary and Political Mobilization*. Arrhus, Denmark: SEKLOS, University of Arrhus, 1984.
Schusky, Ernest, ed. *Political Organization of Native North Americans*. Washington, DC: University Press of America, 1970.
Scott, James Brown. *The Spanish Origin of International Law*. London/New York: Oxford University Press, 1934.
Secoy, Frank Raymond. *Changing Military Patterns on the Great Plains, 17th Century–Early 19th Century*. New York: J. J. Augustin, 1953.
Shames, Deborah, ed. *Freedom with Reservation: The Menominee Struggle to Save Their Land and People*. Madison, Wisconsin: National Committee to Save the Menominee Land and People, 1972.
Sheehan, Bernard W. *Seeds of Extinction: Jeffersonian Philanthropy and the American Indian*. Chapel Hill: University of North Carolina Press, 1973.
Shipeck, Florence Conolly. *Pushed into the Rocks: Southern California Indian Land Tenure, 1769–1986*. Lincoln: University of Nebraska Press, 1988.
Silman, Janet. *Enough Is Enough: Aboriginal Women Speak Out*. Toronto: The Women's Press, 1987.
Simmons, Marc. *The Last Conquistador: Juan de Oñoate and Settling of the Far Southwest*. Norman: University of Oklahoma Press, 1991.
Sorkin, Alan L. *The Urban American Indian*. Lexington, Massachusetts: Lexington Books, 1978.
Stannard, David E. *American Holocaust: Columbus and the Conquest of the New World*. New York: Oxford University Press, 1992.
Stearn, E. Wagner, and Allen E. Stearn. *The Effects of Smallpox on the Destiny of the Amerindian*. Boston: Bruce Humphries, Inc., 1945.
Stedman, William Raymond. *Shadows of the Indian: Stereotypes in American Culture*. Norman: University of Oklahoma Press, 1982.
Steiner, Stan. *The New Indians*. New York: Harper and Row, 1968.
Stith, William. *The History of the First Discovery and Settlement of Virginia*. Williamsburg, Virginia: William Parks Publisher, 1747.
Stone, William L., Jr. *The Life and Times of Sir William Johnson*. 2 vols. Albany, New York: J. Munsell Publisher, 1865.
Strickland, Rennard. *The Indians in Oklahoma*. Norman: University of Oklahoma Press, 1980.
Sugden, John. *Tecumseh's Last Stand*. Norman: University of Oklahoma Press, 1985.
Sutton, Imre, ed. *Irredeemable America: The Indians' Estate and Land Tenure*. Albuquerque: University of New Mexico Press, 1985.
Svaldi, David. *Sand Creek and the Rhetoric of Extermination: A Case–Study in Indian–White Relations*. Washington, DC: University Press of America, 1989.

Swann, Brian, and Arnold Krupat, eds. *Recovering the World: Essays on Native American Literature.* Berkeley: University of California Press, 1987.

Swanton, John R. *Early History of the Creek Indians and Their Neighbors.* Washington, DC: Bureau of American Ethnology, Bulletin No. 73, U.S. Government Printing Office, 1922.

————. *The Indian Tribes of North America.* Washington, DC: Smithsonian Institution, Bureau of American Ethnography, Bulletin 145, U.S. Government Printing Office, 1952.

Talbot, Steve. *The Roots of Oppression: The American Indian Question.* New York: International, 1981.

Taylor, Graham D. *The New Deal and American Indian Tribalism: The Administration of the Indian Reorganization Act, 1934–45.* Lincoln: University of Nebraska Press, 1980.

Taylor, John. *Spanish Law Concerning Discoveries, Pacifications, and Settlements Among the Indians.* Salt Lake City: University of Utah Press, 1980.

Terrell, John Upton, and Donna M. Terrell. *Indian Women of the Western Morning.* Garden City, New York: Anchor Books, 1974.

Thompson, Laura. *A Culture in Crisis: A Study of the Hopi Indians.* New York: Harper and Brothers, 1950.

Thompson, Laura, and Alice Joseph. *The Hopi Way.* Ann Arbor: University of Michigan Press, 1944.

Thompson, Thomas, ed. *The Schooling of Native America.* Washington, DC: American Association of Colleges for Teacher Education, 1978.

Thornton, Russell. *American Indian Holocaust and Survival: A Population History Since 1492.* Norman: University of Oklahoma Press, 1987.

Thornton, Russell, and Mary K. Grasmick. *Sociology of American Indians: A Critical Bibliography.* Bloomington/Indianapolis: Indiana University Press, 1980.

Thornton, Russell, Gary D. Sandefur, and Harold Grasmick. *The Urbanization of American Indians: A Critical Bibliography.* Bloomington/Indianapolis: Indiana University Press, 1982.

Todorov, Tzetan. *The Conquest of America.* New York: Harper and Row, 1984.

Tucker, M. Belinda, Waddell M. Herron, Dan Nakasi, Luis Ortia–Franco, and Lenore Stiffarm. *Ethnic Groups in Los Angeles: Quality of Life Indicators.* Los Angeles: UCLA Ethnic Studies Centers, 1987.

Turner, Frederick. *Beyond Geography: The Western Spirit Against the Wilderness.* New Brunswick, New Jersey: Rutgers University Press, 1983.

Turney–High, Harry Holbert. *Primitive War: Its Practices and Concepts.* 2d ed. Columbia: University of South Carolina Press, 1934.

Twaites, Rubin G., ed. *The Jesuit Relations and Allied Documents.* 73 vols. Cleveland: Burrows Brothers, 1919.

Upton, Helen M. *The Everett Report in Historical Perspective: The Indians of New York.* Albany: New York State Bicentennial Commission, 1980.

Van Kirk, Sylvia. *Many Tender Ties: Women in Fur–Trade Society, 1670–1870.* Norman: University of Oklahoma Press, 1980.

Vaughan, Alden T. *The New England Frontier: Puritans and Indians, 1620–1675.* Boston: Little, Brown, & Co., Inc., 1965.

————. *Early American Indian Documents: Treaties and Laws, 1607–1789.* Washington, DC: University Publications of America, 1979.

Vaughn, J. W. *With Crook at the Rosebud.* Lincoln: University of Nebraska Press, 1956.

Vennum, Thomas, Jr. *Wild Rice and the Ojibway People.* St. Paul: Minnesota Historical Society Press, 1988.

Vescey, Christopher, and William A. Starna, eds. *Iroquois Land Claims*. Syracuse, New York: Syracuse University Press, 1988.

Vestal, Stanley. *New Sources of Indian History, 1850–1891*. Norman: University of Oklahoma Press, 1934.

———. *Warpath and Council Fire: The Plains Indians' Struggle for Survival in War and Diplomacy, 1851–1891*. New York: Random House, 1948.

———. *Sitting Bull: Champion of the Sioux*. Norman: University of Oklahoma Press, 1957.

Vogel, Virgil J. *American Indian Medicine*. Norman: University of Oklahoma Press, 1970.

———. *This Country Was Ours: A Documentary History of the American Indian*. New York: Harper and Row, 1972.

Von Hagen, Victor Wolfgang. *The Royal Road of the Inca*. London: Gordon and Cremonesi, 1976.

Walker, Deward E., Jr., ed. *The Emergent Native Americans: A Reader in Cultural Contact*. Boston: Little, Brown, & Co., Inc., 1977.

Walker, J. R. *Lakota Belief and Ritual*. Lincoln: University of Nebraska Press, 1980.

Wallace, Anthony F. C. *The Death and Rebirth of the Seneca*. New York: Alfred A. Knopf, 1969.

Wanamaker, Rodman. *The Vanishing Race: A Record in Picture and Story of the Last Great Indian Council, Including the Indians' Story of the Custer Fight*. New York: Crown Publisher, MCMXIII; New York: Eagle Books (reprint), 1972.

Wardell, Morris L. *A Political History of the Cherokee Nation, 1838–1907*. Norman: University of Oklahoma Press, 1977.

Washburn, Wilcomb E., ed. *The Indian and the White Man*. Garden City, New York: Anchor Books, 1964.

———. *Red Man's Land, White Man's Law*. New York: Charles Scribner's Sons, 1971.

———. *The Indian in America*. New York: Harper and Row, 1975.

Waters, Frank. *The Book of the Hopi*. New York: Viking Press, 1963.

Weatherford, Jack. *Indian Givers: How the Indians of the Americas Transformed the World*. New York: Fawcett Columbine, 1988.

Weems, John Edward. *Death Song: The Last of the Indian Wars*. Garden City, New York: Doubleday, 1976.

Weyler, Rex. *Blood of the Land: The U.S. Government and Corporate War Against the American Indian Movement*. New York: Everest House, 1983.

Whitney Canfield, Gae. *Sarah Winnemucca of the Northern Paiutes*. Norman: University of Oklahoma Press, 1983.

Wilkins, Thurman. *Cherokee Tragedy: The Story of the Ridge Family and the Decimation of a People*. New York: Macmillan Publishing Co., 1970.

Wilkinson, Charles F. *Indians, Time and Law*. New Haven, Connecticut: Yale University Press, 1987.

Williams, Francis F. *The Blending of Cultures*. Port Moresby, New York: Walter Alfred Bock, Government Printer, 1935.

Williams, Robert A., Jr. *The American Indian in Western Legal Thought: The Discourses of Conquest*. London/New York: Oxford University Press, 1990.

Williams, Walter, ed. *Southeastern Indians Since the Removal Era*. Athens: University of Georgia Press, 1979.

———. *The Spirit and the Flesh: Sexual Diversity in American Indian Culture*. Boston: Beacon Press, 1986.

Wilson, Edmund. *Apology to the Iroquois*. New York: Farrar, Strauss, and Cudahy, 1960.

Wilson, Raymond. *Ohiyesa: Charles Eastman, Santee Sioux*. Urbana: University of Illinois Press, 1983.

Winnemucca Hopkins, Sarah. *Life Among the Piutes: Their Wrongs and Claims.* Boston: privately published, 1883; reprinted by Chalfant Press, Bishop, California, 1969.

Wissler, Clark. *Indians of the United States: Four Centuries of Their History and Culture.* New York: Doubleday, Dornan, and Co., 1940.

Wissler, Clark, Wilton M. Krogman, and Walter Krickerberg. *Medicine Among the American Indians.* Ramona, California: Acoma Press, 1939.

Wood, Gordon. *The Creation of the American Republic, 1776–1787.* Chapel Hill: University of North Carolina Press, 1969.

Worcester, Donald, ed. *Forked Tongues and Broken Treaties.* Caldwell, Idaho: Caxton, 1975.

———. *Rivers of Empire.* New York: Pantheon Books, 1985.

Wright, Ismalliello, and Robin Wright, eds. *Native Peoples in Struggle: Cases from the Fourth Russell Tribunal and Other Forums.* Bombay, New York: Anthropology Resource Center and ERIN Publications, 1982.

Wrong, George M. *The Rise and Fall of New France.* 2 vols. New York: Macmillan Publishing Co., 1928.

Young, James R., ed. *Multicultural Education and the American Indian.* Los Angeles: UCLA American Indian Studies Center, 1979.

———, ed. *American Indian Issues in Higher Education.* Los Angeles: UCLA American Indian Studies Center, 1981.

Young, Robert. *A Political History of the Navajo Nation.* Taile, Arizona: Navajo Community College Press, 1978.

———. *White Mythologies: Writing History and the West.* London: Routledge, 1990.

Young, Warren L. *Minorities in the Military.* Westport, Connecticut: Greenwood Press, 1982.

Young Bear, Ray. *Winter of the Salamander: The Keeper of Importance.* New York: Harper and Row, 1979.

Index

– X –

– Y –

– Z –

About the Author

Ward Churchill is associate professor of American Indian Studies and associate director of the Center for Studies in Ethnicity and Race in America, University of Colorado at Boulder. A member of the governing council of the American Indian Movement of Colorado, he has served as national spokesperson for the Leonard Peltier Defense Committee, as Vice Chairperson of the American Indian Anti–Defamation Council, and as a delegate of the International Indian Treaty Council. A prolific author, Churchill's books include *Agents of Repression, Fantasies of the Master Race, Struggle for the Land*, and *Indians Are Us?* Of Creek and Cherokee descent, he is an enrolled associate member of the United Keetoowah Band of Cherokees.

About Aigis Publications

Aigis Publications is a publishing house founded with a commitment to radical perspectives on democracy, ecology, and society and a strong emphasis on international, feminist, indigenous, and multicultural perspectives. It is our belief that to create a movement towards a free and ecological society we must infuse the popular debate with the knowledge of alternatives that can help us conceive of and create the future in which we want to live. We publish *Society and Nature: The International Journal of Political Ecology*, books, and monographs. In our publications, we strive to present a solid historical and cross–cultural understanding of the past, a radical and incisive analysis of the present, and a reconstructive vision for the future, while addressing the issues in ways that make clear the connections to larger and broader struggles. We publish both new and established authors that will appeal to activists, academics, and concerned citizens. If you are interested in a list of our publications or a copy of our writers guidelines, please write:

Aigis Publications
1449 West Littleton Boulevard, Suite 200
Littleton, CO 80120-2127 USA
books@aigis.com